THE JOURNAL OF INDUSTRIAL ECONOMICS

SYMPOSIUM ON SPATIAL COMPETITION AND THE THEORY OF DIFFERENTIATED MARKETS

Edited by LOUIS PHLIPS and JACQUES-FRANÇOIS THISSE

ISSN 0022-1821
BASIL BLACKWELL OXFORD ENGLAND

CONTENTS

Volume XXXI September/December 1982 Nos. 1/2

LOUIS PHLIPS and JACQUES-FRANÇOIS THISSE
Spatial Competition and the Theory of Differentiated Markets: An Introduction 1

I. UNIFORM F.O.B. PRICING: THE HOTELLING-LÖSCH APPROACH
List of Abstracts 11

DOMINIQUE GRAITSON
Spatial Competition *à la* Hotelling: A Selective Survey 13

DENNIS R. CAPOZZA and ROBERT VAN ORDER
Product Differentiation and the Consistency of Monopolistic Competition: A Spatial Perspective 27

KELVIN LANCASTER
Innovative Entry: Profit Hidden Beneath the Zero 41

R. ROTHSCHILD
Competitive Behaviour in Chain-Linked Markets 57

R. W. SHAW
Product Proliferation in Characteristics Space: The UK Fertiliser Industry 69

A. SHAKED
Existence and Computation of Mixed Strategy Nash Equilibrium for 3-Firms Location Problem 93

KONRAD STAHL
Differentiated Products, Consumer Search, and Locational Oligopoly 97

J. JASKOLD GABSZEWICZ and J.-F. THISSE
Product Differentiation with Income Disparities: An Illustrative Model 115

II. DISCRIMINATORY PRICING: THE GREENHUT–OHTA APPROACH
List of Abstracts 131

NEIL DORWARD
Recent Developments in the Analysis of Spatial Competition and Their Implications for Industrial Economics 133

GEORGE NORMAN and NANCY K. NICHOLS
Dynamic Market Strategy under Threat of Competitive Entry: An Analysis of the Pricing and Production Policies Open to the Multinational Company 153

RICHARD E. SCHULER and BENJAMIN F. HOBBS
Spatial Price Duopoly Under Uniform Delivered Pricing 175

MENAHEM SPIEGEL
Pricing Policies Under Conditions of Spatial Competition 189

P. W. S. ANDREWS MEMORIAL ESSAY PRIZE.—£300

The P. W. S. Andrews memorial prize is awarded annually for an essay by a young scholar (under the age of 30 or within eight years of taking his first degree) in the general field of Industrial Economics and the Theory of the Firm, broadly interpreted. The prize is £300 (or the equivalent in other currency) and the winning essay will normally be published in *The Journal of Industrial Economics*. An essay submitted should be a work of original research by the candidate only, not previously published and not previously awarded any other prize. It should be submitted in English and should not normally exceed 10,000 words in length.

The closing date for entries is 31 December in each year. Intending candidates for the prize should obtain details of the conditions of entry from Miss B. Cox, University House, The University of Lancaster, Lancaster LA1 4YW, England.

THE JOURNAL OF INDUSTRIAL ECONOMICS
Volume XXXI September/December 1982 Nos. 1/2

SPATIAL COMPETITION AND THE THEORY OF DIFFERENTIATED MARKETS: AN INTRODUCTION

Louis Phlips and Jacques-François Thisse

Spatial economics has been both in the very center of microeconomic theory and at its periphery. It has been at the center, to the extent that it has followed a tradition taking its roots in Hotelling's classic "Stability in Competition" paper [15] and has used spatial concepts to explain, by analogy, the pricing of differentiated commodities. It has been at the periphery, to the extent that it has considered spatial pricing as observed in real life situations, and tried to rationalize and evaluate observed spatial pricing techniques. The former approach focuses on f.o.b. pricing, which is apparently taken for granted. The latter focuses on discriminatory pricing, which appears as the most frequently used technique in the industrial world.

The purposes of this special issue are to bring those two approaches together and to explore some of their analytical possibilities and limitations. The philosophy of this introductory paper is to show the need for an integration of both avenues in an analysis of differentiated markets.

We begin by discussing the assumptions of what we will call the Hotelling-Lösch approach and their implications in terms of the problems they allow us to tackle. Several papers in this issue contribute new insights in this respect. We then undertake a similar exercise for what may be called the Greenhut-Ohta approach focusing on spatial price discrimination, to discover the possibilities it may provide for an analysis of quality choice.

At the outset, we note that its *spatial approach typically implies partition of the buyers in sales areas which do not overlap*, with the implication that each buyer buys one product only, i.e. gets his supplies from one seller only (for example, the seller charging the lowest delivered price in his location). While a seller may of course sell in different sub-markets scattered over the plane, a buyer never has two suppliers simultaneously. His choice between products (suppliers) cannot, therefore, be modelled using indifference curves that are convex to the origin.[1]

This raises a problem of semantics which should be clarified right away. Following a well-established tradition we think of a 'differentiated commodity' as a set of products located at different places, made available at different moments or combining different levels of characteristics.[2] Products

[1] For a study of a differentiated industry when consumers have convex preferences see Dixit and Stiglitz [6].

[2] This tradition is rooted in different theories including the Arrow–Debreu model, the market area theory and intertemporal discounting.

therefore take different positions. Their relative position, i.e. the degree of differentiation, can be expressed in two different ways. (i) Differentiation is said to be *horizontal* when the commodity comprises products that are differentiated in space or quality in the following manner: between two products the level of some characteristics is augmented while it is lowered for some others, as in the case of different versions—called varieties—of a car. Here a consumer is supposed to take a less preferred variety (to move from his location to some seller's location) if his most preferred variety is not on the market (if the two locations do not coincide). He will buy the "closest" product in terms of a certain *distance* function. (ii) Differentiation is called *vertical* when the commodity refers to products that are differentiated in time or quality in the following manner: between two products the level of all characteristics is augmented or lowered, as in the case of cars of different series. Now any consumer is supposed to desire the top quality products more than the standard quality ones (to prefer a consumption today to a similar consumption in the future). There is unanimity to rank the products according to a certain *order*.[3]

The non-overlapping nature of sales areas then implies that demands appear as *chain-linked*: demand for a product is a function of its price and of the price of the neighbouring products in case of horizontal as well as vertical differentiation. The possibility of transferring one's demand to a neighbouring product is at the heart of the pricing problem. The discrimination techniques have the particular feature that they make such transfers unprofitable for the buyer, thus effectively separating market segments, and increase the seller's profit as compared with a non-discriminatory (f.o.b.) pricing technique.

F.o.b.-mill pricing: the Hotelling-Lösch approach

Hotelling [15] wanted to show that horizontal product differentiation can lead to a stable solution in the competitive struggle between a small number of competitors, and to characterize this solution.[4] His basic idea is that product differentiation implies that customers prefer certain varieties over others, so that a price reduction for one variety by its producer will not necessarily induce all customers to switch[5] to this variety. The purpose of his analysis is obviously to get away from the assumption of homogeneous products which underlies the perfect competition and the Cournot–Bertrand models. It will become clear, in a moment, that Hotelling did not depart far enough from the

[3] Those two structures, i.e. distance and order, are discussed and compared within the context of space and time in Beguin and Thisse [2]. It is shown that, in some circumstances, one structure is amenable to the other in which case we face a single form of differentiation.

[4] The problem of the existence of an equilibrium in price (and location) is not discussed here but the reader must be aware that it is a troublesome one; see, e.g. Novshek [23].

[5] A natural way to model switches from one product to another is to assume that indifference curves between products are linear, as argued in Phlips [25]. For a general framework see Novshek and Sonnenschein [24].

other assumptions that underpin these models, to come to grips with the phenomenon of price discrimination.

To make the presentation simple, Hotelling exploits the analogy between the space domain and the quality domain and treats differences among varieties as if they were differences in the location of sellers along a straight line. Differences in the preferences of the buyers for particular varieties are then treated as transport costs from the buyer's place to the seller's location. A particular distance thus represents the extent to which a variety is different from what the buyer would like it to be. More specifically, Hotelling uses the following assumptions:

1. Each consumer buys a single unit of the commodity and has only one reservation price, which means that his demand function is rectangular.[6] The consumers possess identical demand functions.
2. Marginal costs of production are constant (possibly zero). There are no fixed costs but there are a fixed number of sellers. Without this restriction entry could take place up to the point where there are as many products (firms) as consumers, exactly one variety being designed (one plant being established) for one consumer. In Lösch [21] fixed costs are positive and associated with the marketing of a product (the set up of a plant). They determine the number of products (the space between firms) at the long-run zero-profit equilibrium. A variety (a plant) is now designed (established) for a group of customers who define its sale share. Furthermore, under some assumptions of homogeneity, *the number of products (firms) varies inversely with the degree of increasing returns.*[7]
3. Change in the locations is costless. This is a curious assumption indeed. It is essential to the convergence of the entry process. When existing locations are immobile (positive moving costs), *entry does not necessarily take place when profits in the industry are positive.* Although the incumbent firms earn a positive profit (possibly large), new entrants can only expect losses when the market between existing firms is not sufficiently large to sustain a new production place.[8] On the other hand, if firms accept to relocate (no moving costs), then a long-run zero-profit equilibrium can be reached. Needless to say, during this process, profits are decreasing.
4. The customers are located uniformly along a straight line (or a circle). To each unit of distance corresponds a one unit element of differentiation. Thus the space (of locations or of characteristics) is endowed with a distance verifying the usual assumptions of symmetry. This assumption is fundamental to the spatial theory of horizontal product differentiation.

[6] Lösch [21] takes a local demand function which is linear in the delivered price. This assumption, together with that of Hotelling, is now commonplace in spatial competition theory. It is somewhat disturbing that certain results prove to be very sensitive to the shape of the local demand function; see, e.g. Benson [3].

[7] See e.g. Lancaster [19].

[8] See Eaton and Lipsey [8].

Furthermore the choice of a particular framework (the straight line or the circle) is not neutral. It is well known that the geometry of the straight line is different from the geometry of the circle. Developing the circle onto a line indeed destroys the neighbouring relations between some points (compare a map of the world on a sphere with a map of the world printed on a page). As a result, the implicit structure of preferences assumed in both cases is different.[9]

5. The cost of transporting one unit of the commodity over one unit of distance is constant. This transport cost represents the degree of disutility which results from the fact that a consumer does not obtain, given the varieties offered (the locations of the producers), the variety he prefers.
6. Assumption 5 is crucial and implies that producers adopt f.o.b.-mill prices: it is the buyer who takes care of the transportation problem. Producers somehow ignore that they could sell at delivered prices and absorb freight or charge phantom freight (sell different varieties at discriminatory prices).
7. Assumptions 5 and 6 in turn are quite naturally accompanied by the assumption that each producer has only one location (sells one variety only).

Given the above framework *spatial competition* refers to the simple mechanism according to which firms try to capture the largest number of customers from their neighboring competitors, by choosing a certain position in the geographical space.[10] It was Hotelling's belief that the outcome of spatial competition was some kind of minimal differentiation among producers, i.e. a clustering of firms. In fact, d'Aspremont *et al.* [5] have shown that the model rather leads to some dispersion of production over space. Each firm wants *to avoid the damaging effects on profit of competition with a too close rival* and to this end selects a separate location.[11] In the Lösch framework, the presence of increasing returns makes it profitable to concentrate production in some plants. A firm can indeed cover its fixed costs only if the volume of its demand is sufficiently large. Nevertheless, the geographical extension of the market, and the resulting transportation costs, imply that the entire production is generally not concentrated in one place. As a result we face *some dispersion in production.*

[9] See Horstmann and Slivinski [14].

[10] The reader will be aware of the different behavioral assumptions made on the competitors' reactions to a firm's price change. Denoting respectively by m_f and m_c the mill prices set by a representative firm and by its competitors, we have: (i) each firm takes its market areas as fixed so that $dm_c/dm_f = 1$ (Lösch [21]); (ii) each firm takes the mill price of its competitor as fixed so that $dm_c/dm_f = 0$ (Hotelling [15]); (iii) each firm takes the delivered price at the edge of its market area (before and after a price change) as fixed so that $dm_c/dm_f = -1$ (Greenhut *et al.* [10]). Within the second family, it must also be distinguished between the unrestricted mill pricing (the Cournot–Nash equilibrium) and the no-mill-price-undercutting restriction (as advocated by Eaton and Lipsey [7]). Not surprisingly, in view of Laitner's [18] analysis on equilibria with conjectural variations, the results derived are *very sensitive* to the assumption made (see, e.g. Capozza and Van Order [4]).

[11] Spatial competition *à la* Hotelling is therefore not able to account for the agglomeration of firms over space. In this respect, the approach in terms of spatial search seems much more promising; see, e.g. Stuart [34].

Furthermore, as each consumer in any market segment is served by only one firm, firms look like local monopolists. But the fact that a finite number of firms only supply the whole market after entry shows that *the differentiation, though positive, is bounded.*

Assumptions five to seven allow us to get away from perfect competition or homogeneous duopoly into a very simple form of monopolistic competition, in which consumers move around while producers care only about finding *the* optimal location (variety), but never consider more refined forms of pricing and locating, involving multiple-product profit maximization. Nevertheless, these assumptions do not seem to have been questioned in the voluminous standard literature on product selection and monopolistic competition.

Vertical differentiation can be handled to some extent in the above framework, replacing assumptions five and six by that of a unanimous ranking of the different qualities. Instead of a distance function, an order is defined on the set of possible qualities. If the reservation price of a product is the same for all the consumers as in the Hotelling model, then a single product is ultimately on the market. In the present context, product differentiation arises because consumers are differentiated by their income. In other words, the position of a consumer is now expressed by his location in the income domain. The market is segmented according to the willingness to pay of the customers: high quality products are purchased by rich consumers, standard quality products by middle class consumers and low quality products by poor consumers. Finally, each quality is still associated with a single firm as in assumption seven.[12]

Unlike the model with horizontal differentiation, there is no need for fixed costs to determine the number of qualities on the market. It is required only that the (constant) marginal costs of the different firms do not increase "too much" with quality.[13] Under this condition, the disparities in income distribution bound the number of qualities which can coexist on the market: *the higher the income dispersion, the larger the number of qualities with a positive market share.* Even when the maximal number of qualities is reached, profits are positive. Here entry is still possible. The entry of new products (of given qualities) is accompanied by the exit of some existing products. During this process, individual profits are driven down to zero but profits in the industry remain positive. This story is very different from that of the model with horizontal differentiation. If firms are now allowed to vary their product specification, again *they have some incentive to differentiate their qualities.*[14] This differentiation takes place up to a point which reflects the shape of the income distribution.

[12] See Jaskold Gabszewicz and Thisse [16], [17].
[13] See Shaked and Sutton [33].
[14] See Jaskold Gabszewicz and Thisse [16] and Shaked and Sutton [32].

Discriminatory pricing: the Greenhut–Ohta approach

Readers who are familiar with the abstract theory of the "discriminating monopolist" know that Robinson [30] has shown that if a single price monopoly selling in two markets under constant marginal costs is allowed to discriminate between them, total output is unchanged when both markets have linear demand curves. However, Robinson is careful to point out that this depends crucially on the assumption that both markets are served under *both* regimes. This is a most unrealistic assumption, since price discrimination typically serves to open *new* markets and thus to increase sales.

Greenhut and Ohta [11], [12] confirm this observation when they show that spatial price discrimination leads—under fairly general conditions—to larger market areas, more production and larger profits than f.o.b.-mill pricing. To put it crudely, the message is then: *if you can discriminate, it is profitable to do so.* The recent literature on nonlinear pricing in the income domain[15] or on intertemporal discrimination[16] confirms that the presence of income and time differences as well as of transport costs suffices to make discrimination possible and the most profitable policy to follow for the monopolist. This is not totally surprising, as discrimination enlarges the choice set of the firm. Perhaps more surprising are the results concerning the social optimality of discriminatory pricing. Indeed, nonuniform discriminatory spatial prices correspond, in the space domain, to nonlinear prices in the quantity domain. The Willig [35] theorem, showing that nonlinear prices are, in the aggregate, socially superior to uniform prices when these prices are above marginal cost, thus also applies here. In other words, profit maximizing discriminatory pricing leads to a higher social benefit than f.o.b. pricing in the case of the spatial monopolist.[17] The extent to which these conclusions remain valid when one leaves the realm of the spatial monopolist to consider oligopolists competing over space is an important subject for further research.[18]

Recognizing the opportunities for further profit created by an enlarged choice set leads one to question Hotelling's assumption seven. According to this assumption each firm has a single plant (or product). There is no reason why a firm should not open several plants (sell several products) in order to extract more of the consumer surplus. The firm is now concerned with the location but also with the number of plants (products) to establish. Again, in the case of horizontal product differentiation, this number is bounded from above because of increasing returns to scale. Without fixed costs, the firm could open a plant (offer a product) close to each consumer and extract the totality of his surplus.[19] The same holds with vertical differentiation, but here

[15] See Leland and Meyer [20].
[16] See Phlips [26], Phlips and Phlips [29] and Phlips and Thisse [28].
[17] See also Holahan [13].
[18] A first exploration in this direction has been undertaken recently by Norman [22].
[19] Interestingly enough, the trade-off between transportation costs and fixed costs of production is at the heart of several operational models of location; see, e.g. Erlenkotter [9].

the income distribution comes into play.[20] Typically, *the supply of several products by the same firm appears to be a surplus extracting device.*[21] The practice of "commodity bundling" belongs to this family.[22] We refer here to firms selling their products in packages: concert halls offer subscriptions to concert series (while simultaneously maintaining the possibility of buying a ticket for a particular performance right on the spot a couple of hours before the concert starts); restaurants offer complete meals with several courses at a bargain price (while simultaneously giving you the possibility of ordering your preferred dishes at the regular price printed on the menu). This bundling gives greater sales and profits to the extent that it allows the capture of new customers.

In addition, freight absorption—which is at the heart of the Greenhut–Ohta approach—also allows one to penetrate new markets in space and can be combined with multiplant operation. The analogy with changing price-quality ratios as quality increases is an unduly neglected topic in the product selection literature.

LOUIS PHLIPS,
C.O.R.E.,
34 Voie du Roman Pays,
1348 Louvain-la-Neuve,
Belgium.
and
JACQUES-FRANÇOIS THISSE,
S.P.U.R.,
Bâtiment Vinci,
Place du Levant 1,
1348 Louvain-la-Neuve,
Belgium.

REFERENCES

[1] Adams W. J. and J. Yellen, "Commodity Bundling and the Burden of Monopoly", *The Quarterly Journal of Economics*, **90** (1976), pp. 475–98.
[2] Beguin, H. and J.-F. Thisse, "Space and Time in Geography: An Axiomatic Approach", in *Dynamic Spatial Models*, D. A. Griffith and R. McKinnon (eds). (Sijthoff & Noordhoof, Alphen aan den Rijn, 1981).
[3] Benson, B. L., "Löschian Competition under Alternative Demand Conditions", *The American Economic Review*, **70** (1980), pp. 1098–105.
[4] Capozza, D. R. and R. Van Order, "A Generalized Model of Spatial Competition", *The American Economic Review*, **68** (1978), pp. 896–908.

[20] See Phlips and Schuler [27].
[21] Note also that a multiproduct strategy allows one to preempt entry of new firms; see Schmalensee [31].
[22] See Adams and Yellen [1].

[5] d'Aspremont, C., Jaskold Gabszewicz, J. and J.-F. Thisse, "Price and Product Difference", *Economics Letters*, forthcoming.
[6] Dixit, A. and J. Stiglitz, "Monopolistic Competition and Optimum Product Diversity", *The American Economic Review*, **67** (1977), pp. 297–308.
[7] Eaton, B. C. and R. G. Lipsey, "The Introduction of Space into the Neoclassical Model of Value Theory", in *Studies in Modern Economics* Artis, M. J. and A. P. Nobay (eds). (Oxford, Basil Blackwell, 1977).
[8] Eaton, B. C. and R. G. Lipsey, "Freedom of Entry and the Existence of Pure Profit", *The Economic Journal*, **88** (1978), pp. 455–69.
[9] Erlenkotter, D., "A Dual Based Procedure for Uncapacitated Facility Location", *Operations Research*, **26** (1978), pp. 992–1009.
[10] Greenhut, M. L., Hwang, M. and H. Ohta, "Observations on the Shape and Relevance of thc Spatial Demand Function", *Econometrica*, **43** (1975), pp. 669–82.
[11] Greenhut, M. L. and H. Ohta, "Monopoly Output Under Alternative Spatial Pricing Techniques", *The American Economic Review*, **62** (1972), pp. 705–13.
[12] Greenhut, M. L. and H. Otha, *Theory of Spatial Pricing and Market Areas*. (Duke University Press, Durham, 1975).
[13] Holahan, W. L., "The Welfare Effects of Spatial Price Discrimination", *The American Economic Review*, **65** (1975), pp. 498–503.
[14] Horstmann, I. and A. Slivinski, "The Foundations of Location Models of Product Differentiation", University of Western Ontario, Department of Economics, 1982.
[15] Hotelling, H., "Stability in Competition", *The Economic Journal*, **39** (1929), pp. 41–57.
[16] Jaskold Gabszewicz, J. and J.-F. Thisse, "Price Competition, Quality and Income Disparities", *Journal of Economic Theory*, **20** (1979), pp. 340–59.
[17] Jaskold Gabszewicz, J. and J.-F. Thisse, "Entry (and Exit) in a Differentiated Industry", *Journal of Economic Theory*, **22** (1980), pp. 327–38.
[18] Laitner, J., "Rational Duopoly Equilibria", *The Quarterly Journal of Economics*, **94** (1980), pp. 641–62.
[19] Lancaster, K., *Variety, Equity and Efficiency*. (Columbia University Press, New York, 1979).
[20] Leland, H. E. and R. Meyer, "Monopoly Pricing Structures with Imperfect Information", *The Bell Journal of Economics*, **7** (1976), pp. 449–62.
[21] Lösch, A., *Die raumliche Ordnung der Wirtschaft*. (G. Fisher, Iena, 1944) second edition.
[22] Norman, G., "Spatial Competition and Spatial Price Discrimination", *Review of Economic Studies*, **48** (1981), pp. 97–111.
[23] Novshek, W., "Equilibrium in Simple Spatial (or Differentiated Product) Models", *Journal of Economic Theory*, **22** (1980), pp. 313–26.
[24] Novshek, W. and H. Sonnenschein, "Marginal Consumers and Neo-Classical Demand Theory", *The Journal of Political Economy*, **87** (1979), pp. 1368–76.
[25] Phlips, L., "Demand Curves and Product Differentiation", *Kyklos*, **17** (1964), pp. 408–18.
[26] Phlips, L., "Intertemporal Price Discrimination and Sticky Prices", *The Quarterly Journal of Economics*, **94** (1980), pp. 525–42.
[27] Phlips, L. and R. E. Schuler, "Product Selection and Price Discrimination", CORE Discussion Paper no. 8126, Université Catholique de Louvain, 1981.
[28] Phlips, L. and J.-F. Thisse, "Pricing, Distribution and the Supply of Storage", *European Economic Review*, **15** (1981), pp. 225–43.
[29] Phlips, P. J. and L. Phlips, "Price Variability, Changes in Demand and the Rate of Interest", *Economics Letters*, **7** (1981), pp. 7–10.

[30] ROBINSON, J., *The Economics of Imperfect Competition.* (Macmillan, London, 1933).
[31] SCHMALENSEE, R., "Entry Deterrence in the Ready-to-eat Breakfast Cereal Industry", *The Bell Journal of Economics*, **9** (1981), pp. 305–27.
[32] SHAKED, A. and J. SUTTON, "Relaxing Price Competition Through Product Differentiation", *Review of Economic Studies*, **44** (1982), pp. 3–13.
[33] SHAKED, A. and J. SUTTON, "Natural Oligopolies", ICERD Discussion Paper no. 27, London School of Economics.
[34] STUART, C., "Search and the Spatial Organization of Trading", in *Studies in the Economics of Search*, Lippmans and J. J. McCall (eds). (North Holland, Amsterdam, 1979).
[35] WILLIG, R., "Pareto-Superior Nonlinear Outlay Schedules", *The Bell Journal of Economics*, **9** (1978), pp. 56–69.

THE JOURNAL OF INDUSTRIAL ECONOMICS
Volume XXXI September/December 1982 Nos. 1/2

UNIFORM FOB PRICING: THE HOTELLING—LÖSCH APPROACH

DOMINIQUE GRAITSON, *Spatial Competition à la Hotelling: A Selective Survey*

THIS paper surveys the Hotelling spatial competition model and its main extensions. It examines how Hotelling's result is modified by the relaxation of some of his assumptions relative to (i) the number of firms, (ii) the shape of the demand curve, and (iii) the type of space. First pure locational models are considered. Then models with price determination as well are discussed. The analysis shows that, in many cases, the so-called "Principle of Minimum Differentiation" as based on the Hotelling paper does not hold.

DENNIS R. CAPOZZA and ROBERT VAN ORDER, *Product Differentiation and the Consistency of Monopolistic Competition: A Spatial Perspective*

This paper addresses a controversy initiated by Demsetz concerning the consistency of the assumptions underlying monopolistic competition. Placing the issues in spatial context confirms Demsetz' argument that free entry does not necessarily imply zero profit but refutes the argument that free entry leads to perfect competition. Some monopoly power is retained by firms as long as consumers have different tastes and there are fixed costs to developing new products.

KELVIN LANCASTER, *Innovative Entry: Profit Hidden Beneath the Zero*

It is shown in this paper that firms may achieve a zero-profit local Nash equilibrium in a multi-characteristics product-differentiated market even though there exists another Nash equilibrium for the same number of firms in which profits are positive, as can happen in a locational model. This gives rise to the possibility of *innovative*-entry, in which entry occurs although all profits in the industry are zero, because an entrepreneur perceives the profit possibilities in an alternative structure. It is argued that innovative entry situations are more likely in characteristics space than in real locational space because the industry configuration is more difficult to observe in the former case.

R. ROTHSCHILD, *Competitive Behaviour in Chain-linked Markets*

This paper deals with price competition in a "chain-linked" market, in which a change in the price of one variety of a differentiated product affects its "proximate" competitors more than it does others. We consider alternative formulations of the problem, possible outcomes and the effect of changes in both the number of varieties and the level of advertising expenditure.

R. W. SHAW, *Product Proliferation in Characteristics Space: the UK Fertilizer Industry*

The paper analyses the development of product competition from 1958 until 1978 using an adaptation of Lancaster's "goods characteristics" framework together with the spatial competition analogy. Four conclusions emerged. Firstly, competition for market share resulted mainly in product proliferation rather than competitive leapfrogging. Secondly, a significant proportion of products remained unchanged for long periods perhaps indicating that products, like physical plant, are not freely relocated. Thirdly, the leapfrogging that did occur reflected largely the introduction of technically improved products displacing existing products. Finally there was some weak support for the hypothesis that clusters of minimally differentiated products develop in the competitive process.

A. SHAKED, *Existence and Computation of Mixed Strategy Nash Equilibrium for 3-Firms Location Problem*

It is shown that the 3-firms location problem, for which there exists no equilibrium in pure strategies, has a unique equilibrium in mixed strategies when the possible strategies are such that all firms choose the same mixed strategy and that this strategy is symmetric around the market center.

KONRAD STAHL, *Differentiated Products, Consumer Search, and Locational Oligopoly*

A simple noncooperative equilibrium model is developed in which firms react, by choice of location, to consumers' search for their most preferred among several substitutable alternatives. Conditions are given under which the noncooperative behavior of firms in equilibrium always leads to some spatial concentration, if not an agglomeration of all firms in one marketplace. The latter is shown to be excessive from the firms', if not from a general welfare, point of view. Thus a spatial decentralization of retailing activities may not only lead to an increase in the firms' profits, but also to a welfare improvement.

J. JASKOLD GABSZEWICZ and J.-F. THISSE, *Product Differentiation with Income Disparities: An Illustrative Model*

In a simple model comprising a high and low income class of consumers, we analyze competition between two merchants selling, respectively, a high and low quality product, which are substitutes to each other. The noncooperative solution is compared with the collusive solution, and the welfare implications of these market arrangements are clarified. Finally this simple framework is used to shed some light on issues related to product selection and sequential entry.

THE JOURNAL OF INDUSTRIAL ECONOMICS
Volume XXXI September/December 1982 Nos. 1/2

SPATIAL COMPETITION *A LA* HOTELLING: A SELECTIVE SURVEY

Dominique Graitson*

I. INTRODUCTION

In his celebrated paper on duopolistic location, Hotelling [18] analysed the behaviour of two sellers of an homogeneous product locating a single plant on a finite one-dimensional geographical market. He asserted that successive location moves will lead the duopolists to an equilibrium in which both firms are located at the center of the market and set identical prices.

This spatial competition process has been extended by Hotelling and his successors to the general problem of product selection in a Lancasterian space of characteristics in which consumers' locations correspond to their most preferred combination of characteristics (their "ideal" product). Thus would emerge the "Principle of Minimum Differentiation" according to which there would be a tendency to reduce product variety (see e.g. Boulding [4]).[1]

Subsequent researchers, however, have shown that this result is very sensitive to the assumptions made by Hotelling and that the relaxation of some of them can lead to an equilibrium with firms being scattered over the market.

This paper aims at setting forth the Hotelling model and its main extensions. They refer to the number of firms, the shape of the demand curve and the type of space. It is divided into two main sections. In the first one, prices are exogeneously fixed, that is, firms compete on location only. The other one focuses on the interaction between price and location, which corresponds to the original Hotelling model. Some remarks conclude the paper.

* * *

The problem to which our analysis relates is defined by the following set of assumptions:

H1. In the economy there is one commodity together with money.

H2. The market, denoted by X_d, is either a line segment or a circle, both of length L.[2]

* I am grateful to Jacques Thisse for his comments. Financial support of the F.N.R.S. is also acknowledged.

[1] Spatial competition models have also been used in political science to deal with the selection of electoral platforms by political parties; see, e.g. Davis, Hinich and Ordeshook [6], Downs [8] and Kramer [19].

[2] The model has been extended to the plane by Eaton and Lipsey [11] and Shaked [26] and to the network by Wendell and McKelvey [31]. See also Demange [7] for some developments in the n-dimensional space.

H3. Consumers are evenly spread along X_d. Without loss of generality, density is taken as unity.
H4. Consumers have identical demand curves for the commodity.
H5. The commodity is sold by n firms.
H6. Each firm sells the commodity at a uniform mill price. Transportation cost is paid by the customers; this cost is assumed to be a linear function of distance.
H7. Average cost is constant and identical for all sellers. Without loss of generality, we take this cost to be zero.
H8. Each customer purchases the commodity from the seller who quotes the lowest delivered price.

II. THE PURE SPATIAL COMPETITION MODEL

In this section, the mill price is taken as fixed and identical for all sellers, that is, firms compete on location only.

First, the problem of existence of a Nash equilibrium in location is examined. Then some dynamic models of entry and/or location are discussed.

II.1 *Existence of locational equilibria*

Consider a non cooperative n-persons game, with each player having a set of strategies and a payoff function denoted respectively by S_i and $P_i(s_1, \ldots s_n)$ with $s_i \in S_i$. A *Nash equilibrium* is a n-uple $(s_1^*, \ldots, s_n^*)$ such that, for every player i:

$$P_i(s_1^*, \ldots, s_{i-1}^*, s_i^*, s_{i+1}^*, \ldots, s_n^*) \geq P_i(s_1^*, \ldots, s_{i-1}^*, s_i, s_{i+1}^*, \ldots s_n^*)$$

for any $s_i \in S_i$

(1) *Spatial competition on a linear market*

Hotelling analyses the duopoly problem with firms competing on a linear bounded market. Each customer buys one unit of the product per unit of time, irrespective of its price. Then each firm maximizes its profit by locating as close as possible to its rival so as to obtain the greatest hinterland. In equilibrium, the duopolists are both located at the center of the market.

Eaton and Lipsey [11] have extended Hotelling's model to the case where more than two sellers supply the commodity. They assume that no more than one firm can occupy a given location; two firms must be separated from each other by a distance at least equal to ε, where ε is arbitrarily small. When such a distance lies between two firms, they are said to be *paired*. This implies that if a seller is paired with one of his rivals, he does not capture any of the consumers who are situated beyond that one.

The above-mentioned authors state the following necessary conditions for an equilibrium, where a half-market is defined as one of the two sides of each firm's market share:

(a) Each peripheral firm is paired. Otherwise it would increase its market share by moving towards its neighbor.
(b) No firm's whole market is smaller than any other firm's half market. Indeed, any seller can obtain a market equal to either half market of any other seller by pairing with him.

It can be shown that these conditions are also sufficient (see Graitson [14]). As a consequence, they allow one to characterize and to check the existence of the equilibrium. Moreover the results remain true even though more than one firm can occupy a given location (see Graitson [14]. They are stated in the next proposition.

PROPOSITION 1. *In the pure spatial competition model:*

(i) *when the number of firms is two, a Nash equilibrium exists for which the duopolists are located at the center of the market;*
(ii) *if three sellers supply the commodity, no equilibrium exists;*
(iii) *with four firms, there exists an equilibrium for which two firms are located at the first quartile and the two others at the third one;*
(iv) *if $n = 5$, at the equilibrium, two firms are located at the first sextile, two others at the fifth one and one firm is isolated at the center of the market;*
(v) *when more than five sellers compete on the market, there exists an infinite number of equilibrium configurations, characterized as follows: peripheral firms occupy the same location as their neighbor and have identical hinterlands. Each peripheral pair is separated from the closest seller by a distance twice as long as the hinterland. The interior firms are paired or alone.*

In the last case the number of isolated firms can vary from 0 to $n - 4$ with n even and from 1 to $n - 4$ with n odd. For example, when six firms supply the commodity, Eaton and Lipsey [11] show that, at the equilibrium, the hinterland of peripheral firms can vary from $L/8$ to $L/6$. Peripheral firms are paired with their neighbor while the two others are separated from their neighboring peripheral pair by a distance equal to twice the hinterland. Consequently, these firms can be separated from each other by any distance between ε and $L/4$.

(2) *Spatial competition on a circular market*

Eaton and Lipsey [11] have transferred their model to a circle, which may be regarded as an unbounded, finite, one-dimensional market. In this case there are only interior firms so that the only necessary and sufficient condition for an equilibrium is that no seller's whole market is smaller than any other seller's half market.

It follows that, with two firms, any pair of locations is an equilibrium. As a result, the duopolists may be clustered or separated. Similarly, when more than two sellers compete along the market, there is an infinite number of equilibria, with firms being paired or alone. The number of isolated firms can thus vary from 0 to n with n even and from 1 to n with n odd.

PROPOSITION 2. *Consider a circular market. The results of Proposition 1 are then modified in the following way:*
(i) *there exists an infinite number of equilibria, whatever the number of firms may be;*
(ii) *at the equilibrium, all firms may be isolated.*

(3) *Rectangular demand function*

One of the aspects on which subsequent work about Hotelling's model has concentrated is the relaxation of the assumption of inelastic demand. This problem was first treated by Smithies [27]. This author asserted that, with a price elastic demand curve, the duopolists are no longer necessarily clustered at the center of the market because the gains resulting from moving towards the rival can be offset by the loss incurred in the hinterland. This conclusion was confirmed by Hartwick and Hartwick [16], Eaton [9] and Webber [30].

Another type of demand curve attracted the attention of Lerner and Singer [20] and Beckmann [3]: a consumer purchases one, and only one, unit of the commodity if the delivered price is lower than a given upper limit and none in the opposite case. Such a demand function is called "rectangular".

The upper limit to the delivered price is taken as equal to p_0 for every customer. The maximum distance, denoted by d, for which the firm faces a positive demand, may be defined as follows:

$$\bar{p} + rd = p_0$$

where $\bar{p}$ and r respectively denote the mill price and the transport rate.
Thus:

$$d = \frac{p_0 - \bar{p}}{r}.$$

The potential market area, denoted by m, is equal to twice this distance.

Suppose first that $m \leq L/n$. In this case, the market is sufficiently long to allow n firms to supply their whole potential market area. Thus there exists at least one equilibrium point, for which the distance between two sellers is greater than or equal to m and the hinterland of each peripheral firm is greater than or equal to $m/2$.

When m is greater than L/n, there must necessarily be some firms which do not capture all consumers living in their potential market area, because it overlaps the neighbor's one. In this case, the necessary and sufficient conditions for an equilibrium are the following[3]:

(a) A peripheral firm holding an hinterland smaller than $m/2$ is paired with its neighbor. Otherwise it can increase its market share by moving towards that one.
(b) A peripheral firm holding an hinterland longer than $m/2$ is separated from its neighbor by a distance greater than or equal to m. If not, it can raise its profit by locating nearer to the end of the market.
(c) If a peripheral firm's hinterland is smaller than or equal to $m/2$, no seller's whole market is smaller than it. Indeed, any seller can capture a market equal to this hinterland by pairing with the peripheral firm.
(d) If a peripheral firm's hinterland is equal to $m/2 + x$, $x \in [0, m[$ no seller's whole market is smaller than $m/2 + x/2$. Indeed a seller could obtain a market share equal to $m/2 + x/2$ by locating at a distance x from the firm in question.
(e) No peripheral firm's hinterland is greater than or equal to $3/2\ m$. Otherwise every seller must have a market share equal to m, which is inconsistent with $m > L/n$.
(f) If the distance between two firms is smaller than $2m$, no seller's whole market is smaller than half this space. Indeed, any seller can obtain a market share equal to half this interval by locating between the two firms in question.
(g) The distance between two firms is smaller than $2m$. Otherwise, each seller must have a market share equal to m, which is inconsistent with $m > L/n$.
(h) When a firm is located at a distance greater than m from one of its neighbors, it is separated from the other by a distance at least equal to m. Otherwise it can increase its market share by moving to the first one.

That those conditions are also sufficient is proved in Graitson [14]. Now it remains to obtain, for $n \geq 2$, the sets of locations satisfying these conditions. The conclusions achieved in [14] are summarized in Proposition 3.

PROPOSITION 3. *In the pure spatial competition model with rectangular demand:*

(i) *so long as the potential market area is smaller than or equal to L/n, there exists at least an equilibrium for which the distance between any two sellers is greater than or equal to m and the hinterland of each peripheral firm is greater than or equal to $m/2$;*
(ii) *When the potential market area is greater than L/n:*
  (a) *with two firms, an equilibrium exists, whatever the potential market area may be. If m is smaller than L, the duopolists are symmetrically located around the*

[3] It is supposed here that the distance between any two firms must be at least equal to ε.

center of the market and are separated by a distance equal to $L - m$. *If* $m \geq L$, *the sellers are clustered at the middle;*

(b) *when the number of firms is three, there exists an infinity of equilibria for any* $m \leq L/2$. *If* $m > L/2$, *no equilibrium exists;*

(c) *for* $n > 3$, *there exists an equilibrium, whatever the length of* m *may be. If* m *is lower than* $L/(n - 1)$, *all sellers are isolated. If* m *is greater than or equal to* $2L/n$, *the equilibrium location sets are identical to the ones which prevail with an inelastic demand. Between these two values, several equilibrium configurations may occur.*

II.2. *Entry and locational process*

So far attention has been concentrated upon the problem of existence of a Nash equilibrium. Nothing has been said about the dynamic process of entry and location. In particular, it would be interesting to examine if the decision rules that the competitors are likely to follow will lead to an equilibrium.

Prescott and Visscher [23] have constructed a model of dynamic locational adjustment in which firms locate in sequence, with each firm correctly anticipating the location rules that subsequent entrants will follow. The number of firms is endogeneous in this model. Its equilibrium value is achieved when there are no gaps left where a new entrant could obtain a positive profit. Indeed, there are economies of scale in production: average costs decrease with output. Consequently, below a given threshold, market share is no longer sufficient to ensure a positive profit. Relocation costs are supposed to be prohibitive so that firms, once located, cannot be moved to new locations. A consequence of the immobility of located plants is that each firm, in making its location decision, will try to maximize its own present value of profit. Thus it will adopt an entry-preventing strategy, that is, it will attempt to ensure a market area that is free from the danger of new entry in the long run. The other hypotheses of the model are the same as in Hotelling [18] and Eaton and Lipsey [11].

The authors show that the result of the dynamic locational process will be *a regular spacing of firms at about twice the minimum required for an entrant plant to realize a positive profit*. This configuration is not a Nash equilibrium since, in this case, peripheral firms should be paired with their neighbor. This difference is due to the entry-deterring strategy followed here by the firms.

Rothschild [24] has extended the analysis of Prescott and Visscher for a given number of firms, denoted by n, which each firm perfectly anticipating the number of entrants. Moreover, the author supposes that demand is price elastic. He shows that if $n = 2^m - 1$, for any $m > 1$, the firms will locate equidistant. If the number of entrants differs from $2^m - 1$, they will not be evenly spaced, *early entrants obtaining larger markets than those who enter later.*

In [14] we have studied the dynamic locational adjustment in the duopoly problem[4]. Each seller is supposed to locate without expecting any further entrant. Once both firms are located, so long as relocation costs are not prohibitive, each one maximizes its profit by relocating as close as possible to its rival in order to obtain the greatest hinterland. But it must not occupy the same location, otherwise its market share falls to $L/2$. For the sake of simplicity, we then suppose that the interval lying between the duopolists cannot be smaller than ε.

We first assume that relocation costs are zero so that firms can easily move and do it taking their rival's location as fixed. The result of the dynamic locational adjustment differs according to whether the duopolists enter in sequence or simultaneously. In the first case, an equilibrium is achieved, whatever initial locations may be. In the second case, it is possible that, at a given time, firms wish to occupy locations too close to each other so that an equilibrium may not be attained. When relocation costs are positive, it can happen that the duopolists never reach the center of the market because the gain resulting from shifting to a new position is offset by the cost of moving.

III. THE HOTELLING SPATIAL COMPETITION PROBLEM

We first deal with the spatial duopoly problem when firms compete on both price and location. Some works extending this model to more than two firms are then presented. Equilibrium prices and locations are determined in the following manner: taking locations as fixed, Nash equilibrium prices are first sought; then profit can be expressed as a function of locations alone and Nash equilibrium locations are sought.

III.1. *Equilibrium locations and prices in the duopoly model*

(1) *The Hotelling model*

Locations being fixed, both sellers have a set of strategies $p_1 \in S_1 = [0, \infty[$ and $p_2 \in S_2 = S_1$ respectively. D'Aspremont *et al.* [2] show that the pair (p_1^*, p_2^*) is an equilibrium point only if:

$$(1) \qquad |p_1^* - p_2^*| < r(L - h_1 - h_2)$$

where h_1 and h_2 denote the hinterland of sellers 1 and 2 respectively.

[4] An illustration of this process is contained in Freeman and Dungey [13]. These authors deal with the geography of the western Canadian fur trade during the period 1770–1835, which was an era of intense competition between the Hudson's Bay Company and the North West Company. They show that this rivalry resulted in leapfrogging of competitors to more advantageous locations along interior waterways, leading to tight clustering of rival posts. This period of hard competition came to an end in 1821 with the merger of the two companies, after which closely neighboring posts were removed, yet an increase in the total number of posts, in order to rationalize the trading system. The western Canadian fur companies therefore anticipated the spatial competition process described by Hotelling one hundred years later on!

Under this condition, profit functions are given by:

$$P_1(p_1^*, p_2^*) = \frac{p_1^*}{2}(L + h_1 - h_2) - \frac{p_1^{*2}}{2r} + \frac{p_1^* p_2^*}{2r} \tag{2}$$

$$P_2(p_1^*, p_2^*) = \frac{p_2^*}{2}(L - h_1 + h_2) - \frac{p_2^{*2}}{2r} + \frac{p_1^* p_2^*}{2r} \tag{3}$$

Taking first-order conditions, we obtain:

$$p_1^* = r\left(L + \frac{h_1 - h_2}{3}\right) \tag{4}$$

$$p_2^* = r\left(L - \frac{h_1 - h_2}{3}\right) \tag{5}$$

Recall that for the pair of prices given by (4) and (5) to be an equilibrium point, p_1^* must maximize $P_1(p_1, p_2^*)$ on the whole domain S_1 and similarly for p_2^*. Thus, for any equilibrium, no seller can increase his profit by undercutting the other. D'Aspremont *et al.* [2] show that this condition is satisfied only if:

$$\left(L + \frac{h_1 - h_2}{3}\right)^2 \geq \frac{4}{3} L(h_1 + 2h_2) \tag{6}$$

$$\left(L - \frac{h_1 - h_2}{3}\right)^2 \geq \frac{4}{3} L(h_2 + 2h_1) \tag{7}$$

As conditions (6) and (7) imply (1), they are also sufficient for (p_1^*, p_2^*) to be an equilibrium.

If these conditions are strictly verified, then both $\partial P_1(p_1^*, p_2^*)/\partial h_1$ and $\partial P_2(p_1^*, p_2^*)/\partial h_2$ are strictly positive, so that, as Hotelling points out, both sellers will tend towards the center. But once the firms are located relatively close to each other, conditions (6) and (7) are violated which implies that Nash equilibrium prices do not exist and therefore *nothing can be said about the central tendency*.

A similar conclusion is achieved for a circular market. For given locations, Nash equilibrium prices exist, such that $p_1^* = p_2^* = rL/2$, if and only if the distance between the duopolists is greater than or equal to $L/4$. But when firms compete on location as well, no equilibrium price solution exists.

PROPOSITION 4 *In the Hotelling model, whether the market is a line segment or a circle:*

- *—for given locations, a Nash equilibrium in prices exists if and only if the duopolists are sufficiently far from each other;*
- *—when firms compete on both price and location, no Nash equilibrium exists.*

(2) *Maximin equilibrium*

To circumvent the difficulty raised by the non-existence of equilibrium prices when firms are too close to each other, we assume that the seller adopts a different strategy according to whether or not, when charging the profit-maximizing price against his rival's price, he is likely to be undercut. In the first case, we suppose that, to avoid the worst, he plays a maximin strategy, i.e. he quotes the price which maximizes his profit taking the other's price as equal to zero. In the second case, he charges the Nash equilibrium price, expecting that his opponent will do the same. Taking his competitor's location as fixed, he will then settle so as to obtain the largest profit. As it appears, the duopolist will maximize his profit by locating at a distant point such that Nash equilibrium prices may exist. It can be demonstrated that this behavior will lead to what we call a *maximin equilibrium,* in which the firms are located respectively at the first and third quartiles and charge the Nash prices (see Graitson [15]).

PROPOSITION 5. *In the Hotelling duopoly problem, a maximin equilibrium exists for which sellers charge Nash equilibrium prices and are located respectively at the first and third quartiles. This equilibrium is unique.*

(3) *Rectangular demand function*

The problem of existence of a Nash equilibrium in the case where the duopolists face a rectangular demand on a circular market has been treated in Graitson [14]. The reasoning used is rather long and to develop it in this paper would be quite tedious. Thus only the conclusions are set forth in Proposition 6. Let us recall that p_0 and r are respectively the upper limit imposed to the delivered price and the transport rate and let denote by z the smaller interval between the sellers.[5]

PROPOSITION 6. *In the spatial duopoly problem, suppose that firms compete along a circular market and face a rectangular demand.*

(i) *Locations being fixed, three equilibrium pairs of prices may exist according to the relative values of* p_0, r *and* z. *But for given values of these parameters, the equilibrium, if it exists, is unique.*
(ii) *When firms jointly choose price and location, a Nash equilibrium exists if and only if* $p_0 \leq rL/2$. *In this case, a pair of locations is an equilibrium point if and only if it is such that* $p_0 \leq rz$. *In equilibrium, sellers quote the monopolist profit-maximizing price and potential market areas are disjointed.*

[5] The case where two firms face a rectangular demand on a finite linear market has been recently studied by Economides [12]. Taking locations as fixed, this author shows that equilibrium prices exist if p_0 is not too high relative to the distance between the duopolists. But his analysis is limited to the case where p_0 and the locations of firms are such that for any $p_1, p_2 \geq 0$, each seller's hinterland is larger than the maximum distance for which he faces a positive demand. He then states that if there are locations which satisfy this last assumption, they correspond to a Nash equilibrium point if they are such that a "local monopolist" equilibrium in prices exists i.e. potential market areas are disjoint.

III.2. *Equilibrium in the oligopolistic case*

The extension of the Hotelling problem to more than two sellers is quite complex and has received relatively little attention in the literature.

Eaton [9] examines the case of three firms on a linear bounded market with a price elastic demand curve. He demonstrates that when the market is sufficiently long, a Nash equilibrium exists for which one firm is located at the center and the two others are symmetrically located around it.

Carruthers [5] applies the Hotelling model to n firms facing an inelastic demand. The behavioral assumptions a firm makes about its rivals are slightly different here: each seller assumes that his competitors will not move but will adapt their price to his own price and location choices. This implies that no firm will try to undercut one of its rivals because it knows that it will immediately react by diminishing its price.[6]

The author finds that the n firms equilibria derived by Eaton and Lipsey [11] characterize the n interior firms in a $n + 2$ firms model with price determination as well. That is, in equilibrium, peripheral firms are isolated while the second firms from the market boundary are paired with their inside neighbor. The other interior firms may or may not be paired. This result only applies to a bounded linear market. On a circular market, the equilibrium patterns are the same as in the fixed price model developed by Eaton and Lipsey.

Hay [17] has constructed a free entry model with price being also a decision variable. He assumes that firms locate in sequence on a linear unbounded market, with each firm having a perfect foresight of further competitors' location pattern. The entrant supposes that, when entry occurs, existing firms will adjust their price in order to maximize their profit. But once located, plants are immobile so that each seller, when locating, will adopt an entry-deterring strategy. Indeed, technology is characterized by decreasing average costs so that a minimum market share is required for profit to be positive. The author shows that the result to be expected is a regular spacing of firms at about twice the minimum required for an entrant plant, with each firm charging the same profit-maximizing price. As Hay points out, one interesting conclusion of this model is that the *firms deter new entry by locating in such a way as to leave an insufficient gap for a new entrant rather than by a limit-pricing policy.*

Salop [25] analyses the case where, whenever entry occurs, existing firms costlessly relocate to adapt themselves to the new situation. He shows that free

[6] Ali and Greenbaum [1] retain an identical hypothesis in a free entry model dealing with spatial competition in the banking industry. Firms are supposed to locate in sequence on an infinite line and face a linear total cost function with decreasing average cost. The model assumes a normal distribution of consumers over the market, with the modal point of the distribution being thought of as the origin, and a price elastic demand. Relocation costs are prohibitive i.e. existing banks cannot move. Using a simulation approach, the authors show that in equilibrium, firms are clustered at multiple locations, with the spatial density of banks following the spatial density of population, while prices are lowest at the center and increase with distance from the origin.

entry leads to a symmetric zero-profit Nash equilibrium defined as follows: (a) the firms are equally spaced and charge identical profit-maximizing price (b) each firm earns zero profit. A similar result is achieved by Novshek [22], who supposes that each firm, when choosing its price and location, views the strategies of its rivals as fixed, unless its own strategy undercuts some other firm in which case it knows that this seller will react by diminishing his price. In other words, price wars are ruled out in this model. The author demonstrates that when fixed costs are sufficiently small relative to the other market parameters, a free entry equilibrium exists, is symmetric and approximately competitive (i.e. prices are approximately equal to marginal cost). Eaton [10] points out that, because the technology is characterized by an indivisible fixed cost, *free entry need not lead to a zero-profit equilibrium* (see also Salop [25]).

IV. CONCLUSION

In view of the above analysis, it appears that the *spatial competition process does not generally lead to minimum differentiation.* On the contrary, in several cases, *firms locate apart from each other,* in order to enjoy some local monopoly.

Yet, in the real world, firms selling an identical product often establish themselves at a same place. In particular, this is the case in retail trade, as discussed by Lewis [21]. To explain this phenomenon, some other factors must therefore be introduced into the model. In this respect, Stahl and Varaiya [28] suggest that the clustering of sellers of an homogeneous product could result from their imperfect information about spatial distribution of demand. As uncertainty is reduced at points where some firms are already established, a new entrant will decide to settle close to them in order to benefit from the corresponding *information externalities.* The perspective is reversed by Stuart [29] who focuses on uncertainty on the consumer side. According to this author, agglomeration of firms could be explained by the wishes of customers to visit places with many sellers in order to minimize *search costs* for best prices and/or qualities. It may be expected that such ingredients will bring some more realism into the theory.

Université de Liège,
Faculté de Droit, d'Economie et de Sciences Sociales,
Boulevard du Rectorat, 4000 Liège, Belgium.

REFERENCES

[1] Ali, M. M. and Greenbaum, S. I., "A Spatial Model of the Banking Industry", *The Journal of Finance,* **32** (1977), pp. 1283–1303.

[2] D'Aspremont, C., Gabszewicz, J. Jaskold, and Thisse, J.-F., "On Hotelling Stability in Competition", *Econometrica,* **47** (1979), pp. 1145–50.

[3] Beckmann, M., "Spatial Cournot Oligopoly", *Papers of the Regional Science Association,* **21** (1972), pp. 37–47.

[4] BOULDING, K., *Economic Analysis;* Vol. **1**, Microeconomics (Harpers, New York, 1966).

[5] CARRUTHERS, N., "Location Choice when Price is also a Decision Variable", *The Annals of Regional Science,* **14** (1981), pp. 29–42.

[6] DAVIS, O. A., HINICH, M. J. and ORDESHOOK, P. C., "An Expository Development of a Mathematical Model of the Electoral Process", *American Political Science Review,* **44** (1970), pp. 426–48.

[7] DEMANGE, G., "Spatial Models of Collective Choice", THISSE, J.-F. and ZOLLER, H. G. (eds.) in *Locational Analysis of Public Facilities,* (North Holland, Amsterdam, 1982).

[8] DOWNS, A., *An Economic Theory of Democracy* (Harper and Row, New York, 1957).

[9] EATON, B. C., "Spatial Competition Revisited", *Canadian Journal of Economics,* **5** (1972), pp. 268–77.

[10] EATON, B. C., "Free Entry in One Dimensional Models: Pure Profits and Multiple Equilibria", *Journal of Regional Science,* **16** (1976), pp. 21–33.

[11] EATON, B. C. and LIPSEY, R. G., "The Principle of Minimum Differentiation Reconsidered: Some New Developments in the Theory of Spatial Competition", *Review of Economic Studies,* **42** (1975), pp. 27–49.

[12] ECONOMIDES, N., "The Principle of Minimum Differentiation Revisited", Columbia University, Department of Economics (Discussion Paper Series **134**, 1982).

[13] FREEMAN, D. B. and DUNGEY, F. L., "A Spatial Duopoly: Competition in the Western Canadian Fur Trade, 1770–1835", *Journal of Historical Geography,* **7** (1981), pp. 252–70.

[14] GRAITSON, D., "On Spatial Competition Process", Unpublished Paper, Université de Liège, (1979).

[15] GRAITSON, D., "On Hotelling's 'Stability in Competition' Again", *Economics Letters,* **6** (1980), pp. 1–6.

[16] HARTWICK, J. and HARTWICK P., "Duopoly in Space", *Canadian Journal of Economics,* **4** (1971), pp. 485–505.

[17] HAY, D. A., "Sequential Entry and Entry-Deterring Strategies", *Oxford Economic Papers,* **28** (1976), pp. 240–57.

[18] HOTELLING, H., "Stability in Competition", *Economic Journal,* **39** (1929), pp. 41–57.

[19] KRAMER, G. H., "A Dynamical Model of Political Equilibrium", *Journal of Economic Theory,* **16** (1977), pp. 310–34.

[20] LERNER, A. and SINGER, H., "Some Notes on Duopoly and Spatial Competition", *Journal of Political Economy,* **45** (1937), pp. 145–86.

[21] LEWIS, W. A., "Competition in Retail Trade", *Economica,* **12** (1945), pp. 202–34.

[22] NOVSHEK, W., "Equilibrium in Simple Spatial (or Differentiated Product) Models", *Journal of Economic Theory,* **22** (1980), pp. 313–26.

[23] PRESCOTT, E. C. and VISSCHER, M., "Sequential Location among Firms with Foresight", *The Bell Journal of Economics,* **8** (1977), pp. 378–93.

[24] ROTHSCHILD, R., "The Effect of Sequential Entry on Choice of Location", *European Economic Review,* **12** (1979), pp. 227–41.

[25] SALOP, S. C., "Monopolistic Competition with Outside Goods", *The Bell Journal of Economics,* **10** (1979), pp. 141–56.

[26] SHAKED, A., "Non-Existence of Equilibrium for the Two-Dimensional Three Firms Location Problem", *Review of Economic Studies,* **42** (1975), pp. 51–56.

[27] SMITHIES, A., "Optimum Location in Spatial Competition", *Journal of Political Economy,* **44** (1941), pp. 423–39.

[28] STAHL, K. and VARAIYA, P., "Economics of Information: Examples in Location and Land-Use Theory", *Regional Science and Urban Economics,* **8** (1978), pp. 43–56.

[29] STUART, CH., "Search and the spatial organization of trading", in Lippman, S. A. and McCall, J. J. (eds.), *Studies in the Economics of Search* (North Holland, Amsterdam, 1979).

[30] WEBBER, M., *Impact of Uncertainty on Location* (The M.I.T. Press Cambridge, Massachusetts and London, England, 1972).

[31] WENDELL, R. E. and MCKELVEY, R. D., "New Perspectives in Competitive Location Theory", *European Journal of Operational Research*, **6** (1981), pp. 174–82.

THE JOURNAL OF INDUSTRIAL ECONOMICS
Volume XXXI September/December 1982 Nos. 1/2

PRODUCT DIFFERENTIATION AND THE CONSISTENCY OF MONOPOLISTIC COMPETITION: A SPATIAL PERSPECTIVE

Dennis R. Capozza and Robert Van Order

INTRODUCTION

In recent years researchers have increasingly recognized the similarities between problems in spatial economics and problems of product differentiation in monopolistic competition. Authors working from the spatial side have tried to outline some of the implications of spatial economics for traditional micro-theory. At the same time, other writers such as Lancaster [17] have developed models of product differentiation which have a spatial flavor.

It has become apparent that spatial economics can provide considerable insight into monopolistic competition. In this paper we address a long smoldering debate in the theory of the firm concerning whether or not monopolistic competition is a distinctly different case from perfect competition and monopoly. The issue was ignited by Demsetz [8], [9], [10] who questioned both the "excess capacity theorem" of monopolistic competition and the consistency of the underlying assumptions. Later Barzel [1] and Schmalensee [22] presented analyses that appeared to have successfully doused Demsetz' criticism of the excess capacity theorem. Recently, however, the debate has been rekindled by Greenhut [14], Ohta [21] and Murphy [20]. Most of the disagreement has been encamped around the excess capacity/efficiency question.

A separate but related series of papers in the spatial competition literature (e.g. Eaton and Lipsey [11], [12], [13], and Capozza and Van Order [7]) has challenged the consistency of the free entry and zero profits assumptions. The link between the Demsetz inconsistency arguments and similar reasoning in the spatial competition literature is most apparent if one views product differentiation, a basis of monopolistic competition, as a locational concept (see for example Lovell [18], Eaton and Lipsey [13]). Indeed product differentiation in many large firms is a marketing problem where modern methods call for "positioning" products in the consumers' n-dimensional characteristics space.

We try to demonstrate that monopolistic competition is indeed a distinct structure. We use a spatial model where monopolistic competition is the typical intermediate case while monopoly and perfect competition are extreme cases. We then argue that product differentiation, which has been the usual rationale for monopolistic competition, can be modelled in a manner analogous to the spatial model, implying a large degree of generality than our model.

The next section reviews some of Demsetz' criticisms and the closely related criticisms of Kaldor. The second section discusses the nature of product differentiation in the context of modern marketing strategy. The third section evaluates the Demsetz critique. The fourth section presents the model and interprets its marketing implications.

I. CONSISTENCY

Demsetz [8] argues that the three basic assumptions of monopolistic competition are:

1. a large number of firms;
2. free entry (presumably with perfect knowledge);
3. product differentiation.

Demsetz [9, p. 639], writes

> Product differentiation which is used to confront firms with negatively sloped demand curves, and free entry, basically are inconsistent assumptions. The most plausible source of product differentiation is to be found in the laws of trademark, copyright, and patent. The laws clearly are barriers to imitative entry; they may be socially justified by the incentive that they give to new product production or by the reduction in information cost that they help to bring about, benefits which should, of course, be taken account of in judging the overall efficiency of markets in which products are differentiated. Nonetheless, these barriers provide neither more nor less than the prerequisites for simple monopoly. In the presence of such barriers it is difficult to apply or interpret the assumption of free entry. If a firm produces a profitable brand, 'entry' need not eliminate profits because there is not free entry into the production of that brand. Product differentiation undermines the logic of using 'free entry' to deduce the familiar zero profit Chamberlin equilibrium. As a result, the equilibrium rate of output for a firm to the left of the low point of its average cost curve is no more necessary than for simple monopoly. Entry via a different brand or product variety analytically is no different than entry into the electricity market to compete with natural gas. Such indirect entry need never succeed in reducing profits to zero because the electricity output, or in the case at hand, the output of rival brands, that is required to reduce profits to zero may be so large that 'entering' firms, in order to accomplish this, would need to accept losses. The zero-profit equilibrium is not a correct deduction of the monopolistic competition model; it is a hidden assumption, and one that is difficult to reconcile with product differentiation.

A related argument appears in Kaldor [15] where it is asserted that indivisibilities are the problem rather than patent laws. Kaldor writes:

> Let us now introduce indivisibilities and economies of scale. The movement of new firms into the field will then not continue until the elasticities of demand for the individual producers become infinite; it will be stopped long before that by the increase in costs as the output of producers is reduced. But there is no reason to assume that it will stop precisely at the point where the demand and cost curves are tangential. For, on account of the very reasons of economics of scale, the potential producer cannot hope to enter the field profitably with less than a certain magnitude of output; and that additional output may reduce demand, both to his nearest neighbours and to him, to such an extent that the demand curves will lie below the cost curves and will be involved in losses. The interpolation of a third producer in between any two producers may thus transform profits into losses. The same reason therefore which prevents competition from becoming perfect—i.e. indivisibility—will also prevent the complete elimination of "profits". It will secure a monopolistic advantage to anybody who is first in the field and merely by virtue of priority. The ultimate reason for this is that it is not the original resources themselves, but the various uses to which they are put that are indivisible—you can divide "free capital", but you cannot invest less than a certain amount of it in a machine—and consequently the investment of resources cannot be so finely distributed as to equalize the level of marginal productivities.

Thus there are two lines of argument that question the free entry assumption of monopolistic competition—Demsetz', based on the laws of trademark and patent and Kaldor's indivisibility argument. Both are valid in some circumstances but not in general.

The indivisibilities of Kaldor can be dismissed if capital is mobile and the market is large relative to the indivisible unit of capital (see Capozza and Van Order [7]). In the limit for large numbers of firms in an industry, the profit that firms gain before the market is large enough to support the next firm is insignificant in general. However, if the lumpiness involves fixed locations, the positive profits problem cannot be dismissed easily. Indeed, Eaton and Lipsey [12], [13] have formalized Kaldor's argument and shown that equilibrium returns can be as much as twice the normal rate in some cases.

A simple example of the Kaldor/Eaton-Lipsey issue can be constructed. Suppose firms are arrayed along a linear market where the density of customers is uniform. Each firm requires market length R to break even. If firms enter only if expected profits after entry are positive, then no new firm will enter unless the existing firms have markets of length $2R$ or more. This occurs because a new firm will capture a market half the size of existing firms upon entry. At twice the breakeven market size firms presumably earn substantial economic profits. Thus indivisibilities can be quite important if capital is immobile.

While this sort of barrier to zero profit equilibrium may be important in practice, it does not invalidate other elements of monopolistic competition such as the excess capacity/inefficiency theorem. We will ignore this barrier by focussing on what might be called ice cream vender models where firms are able to move easily (in either physical space or characteristics space) even in the short run and where the market is 'large'. Hence, while the number of firms may be fixed, their ability to shift location removes discontinuities like those in Kaldor or Eaton and Lipsey. We concentrate instead on the Demsetz legal arguments.

II. PRODUCT DIFFERENTIATION AND MARKETING STRATEGY

The strategy of product differentiation for firms with national markets and advertising is analogous to the location and spacing problem of local firms. Recent developments in marketing make the similarity more obvious. Marketing strategy for a firm selling a differentiated product is heavily dependent on advertising. Market research is an essential preface to a successful promotional campaign. In the typical marketing research effort a firm will try to determine where consumers are located in a hypothetical "characteristics space". The density of consumers along various dimensions will then be compared with consumer perceptions of the locations of existing products along these same dimensions. An optimal strategy then consists of creating a new product or moving consumer perceptions of an existing brand to a point in the characteristics space that is heavily populated by consumers but sparsely settled by existing brands.[1]

Economists are familiar with this kind of argument, which is closely related to the theory of consumer demand developed by Lancaster [16], [17] and others. Economists are less aware of the extent to which the characteristics approach dominates modern marketing strategy. Quite independent of the literature in economics, researchers in marketing have developed both the theory and the necessary algorithms for implementation (see Schocker and Srinivasan [23]).

The marketing literature is implicitly locational. Advertising is used to "position" products or "move" them to new locations in characteristics space. Commonly used statistical techniques such as multidimensional scaling are essentially locational. Thus, the locational approach to product differentiation is not just implicit in the marketing strategies of firms; it is the underlying basis for most modern advertising campaigns.

Some examples may be illuminating. A study of the breakfast food market some years ago found that consumers were primarily concerned with nutrition and convenience in breakfast foods. Existing products were perceived to be

[1] This assumes that consumers have different preferences but the same perceptions of products.

either convenient (coffee and donuts) or nutritious (ham and eggs) but not both. The obvious strategy was to create new products that satisfied both consumer desires. Products such as Breakfast Squares were created and advertised to be convenient yet "as nutritious as a bacon and egg breakfast" in order to draw from both groups of consumers. The attempt to fill the gap in consumer characteristics space was clear.

More recently a similar sequence of events has transpired in the beer industry with devastating impact on some competitors. The marketing battle between Miller and Anheuser-Busch has been widely reported by the financial press. The structural changes in the industry can easily be given a locational interpretation. The rapid growth of light or low calorie beers is the result of manufacturers discovering a heavily populated but commercially unsatisfied segment of the market. The first firms to discover the market (e.g. Coors and later Miller) earned excess returns and/or increased market share.

III. DEMSETZ AND PRODUCT DIFFERENTIATION

If we accept the locational nature of product differentiation, Demsetz' arguments can be dissected. First, trademark, copyright, etc. of themselves need not be significant barriers to entry. The fact that "Coors" is trademarked does not prevent other firms from entering the same market. The relevant market is not the market for a specific brand but rather the market for products with similar characteristics (e.g. low calorie, natural, etc.). Characteristics are difficult or impossible to patent. Clearly a trademark does not make a firm a monopoly.

Secondly, the issue may not be so much whether monopolistic competition is a distinct case but rather whether pure monopoly is an observable form. Monopoly has a simple definition in a spatial context that is rarely if ever met within the product differentiation context. Spatial monopoly is the case where a firm has no competitors serving customers just beyond its market area. Consumers buy from the spatial monopolist or don't buy any of the product at all. In product space firms almost always have competition in terms of the relevant characteristics. In the Demsetz gas and electric example, the electricity monopoly must compete in the home heating and cooking markets with natural gas. Since gas and electricity share some characteristics neither utility is a monopolist in the spatial sense. It is difficult to conceive of a product that does not have competition along some characteristic. Thus pure monopoly may be the implausible and inconsistent case rather than monopolistic competition.

There is a third issue. If the electricity monopoly does have competitors, is there any difference between entry into that industry and entry into the typical differentiated consumer product industry? Contrary to Demsetz, we believe there is a difference. While the gas or electric monopolies do have competition in characteristics, they are nevertheless afforded a greater degree of entry protection than most firms. The protection arises from natural barriers rather than legal proscription. There is a discontinuity in the gas and electric characteristics. A firm can compete with electricity by supplying gas or home heating oil but there are no intermediate cases. There is no economically viable product half way between gas and electricity, therefore there can be no entry between the two. The typical firm deals in a space with continuous characteristics. "Nutrition" or "calorie content" are continuous variables. It is possible for a firm to create a slightly less caloric or somewhat more nutritious food. The protection that discontinuities in characteristics space afford electric utilities is similar to the protection that an ocean or other natural barrier provides to local firms in their competition with distant rivals. Therefore, there is a distinction between cases like the electric utility and monopolistic firms. Entry is inherently "freer" for the monopolistic firm.

A fourth issue concerns the import of positive profits when there is free entry. Do positive profits invalidate the concept of monopolistic competition? Clearly some modification of textbook accounts on the subject is needed given the recent work of Eaton and Lipsey [13] and others. Free entry does not necessarily imply zero profits. However, as we have argued in Capozza and Van Order [7], zero profits are a deducible result in a spatial context if capital is costlessly transportable.

The remaining principal conclusions of monopolistic competition are, however, for the most part intact. In particular the excess capacity inefficiency theorems are replicated even if profits are not completely vitiated by entry. The inefficiency of monopolistic competition arises from two sources in a spatial framework: (1) there are too many firms, and (2) consumers buy too little output at too high a price (see Mills and Lav [19], or Capozza and Van Order [5]. Assuming that entry continues only until entering firms expect zero profits while existing firms still earn positive profits mitigates the first source of inefficiency. Since fewer firms exist in equilibrium, the average cost of production and distribution is reduced.

The second source of inefficiency is retained and in general will be exacerbated. The typical case is one where entry reduces prices, although the opposite case cannot be ruled out (See Capozza and Van Order [5]). Placing the restriction on entry causes prices to rise further above marginal cost and increases inefficiency in consumption.

The crucial aspect of the captious remarks of Demsetz and others is the attempt to eliminate monopolistic competition as a distinct case between perfect competition and oligopoly or monopoly. It is not clear what purpose the original writers on the subject had in mind when making the three assumptions of monopolistic competition. One possibility might have been a desire to eliminate the need for a detailed analysis of reaction functions while retaining the downward sloping demand curves. A logical line of argument in discussions of monopolistic competition asserts that free entry implies large numbers of firms. A large number of competitors suggests that a change in price by any one competitor would be ignored by other firms. Product differentiation then provides the monopoly power needed to prevent each firm's demand curve from becoming horizontal. That line of reasoning has been accepted with few exceptions for decades, but Demsetz *et al.* have shown that it is not an airtight argument. The spatial analogy provides an opportunity for a more rigorous foundation and at the same time highlights the weaknesses in the theory.

IV. AN EQUILIBRIUM MODEL

This section has two purposes: First, we develop a simple locational approach to monopolistic competition. The model is adapted from Capozza and Van Order [5] and serves to counter Demsetz, by showing that monopolistic competition is a distinct and interesting structure. The model is one of equilibrium, perfect information, and portable firms. The monopolistic elements derive from locational aspects (transportation costs and U shaped cost curves). The second purpose is to demonstrate that product differentiation can be modelled in a manner analogous to the location models. This is intended both to help in understanding marketing problems and to imply that the location approach to monopolistic competition is quite general.

The locational interpretation is presented first. Assume the following:

1. Individuals are evenly dispersed on an infinite plane and buy one unit of the good in question. Their only choice is from whom to buy, which is resolved by buying from the seller with the lowest delivered price.[2]
2. Firms produce one good with the U shaped cost curve

   (1) $$C = f + cX + dX^2$$

   where X is output and C is cost. Firms maximize profit while following the usual assumption in monopolistic competition that their actions do not affect competitors' prices or locations.[3]
3. The cost of the consumer of transporting one unit of the good one mile is fixed and given by t. It is assumed that firms cannot distinguish customers by their location so that they charge all of them the same mill price. The delivered price to an individual at distance R from the store is $p + tR$, where p is the price of the good. The consumer tries to minimize this delivered price in choosing the store from which to buy.
4. There is perfect information and firms enter and move freely if there are profits, so that the long run is characterized by zero profits.
5. Short run equilibrium occurs when existing firms have no desire to change either price or location. Since firms are identical, they will be evenly spaced and charge the same price.

[2] In Capozza and Van Order [5] we discuss a model with downward sloping demand. The analysis is more complicated but does not affect any of the results of this paper.
[3] Other variational assumptions will be discussed later. See also Capozza and Van Order [5].

As yet no market structure has been imposed on the model. We intend, instead, to derive it. To do so, it is first necessary to consider the individual firm's optimization.

If all individuals buy one unit and all firms are identical, then the market areas will be hexagons, and the amount demanded will be given by the market area, or

$$X = kDR^2 \tag{2}$$

where D is the population density and k is a constant, and R is market radius.

The firm uses equation (2) in maximizing profit; but the inside radius of the hexagon will depend on its price relative to other firm's prices. The firm's delivered price at the edge of its border is $p^d = p + tR$. All firms are identical and are assumed initially to be evenly distributed over the plain. Assume that the distance between firms is given by $2U$. Then, taking the location of the firm in question as the origin, the delivered price of other firms is given by

$$p_0^d = p_0 + t(2U - R)\,. \tag{3}$$

where p_0 is the (constant to the firm) competing firms' mill price.

The firm's market area ends where its delivered price equals the delivered price of competitors.

$$p + tR = p_0 + t(2U - R)$$

so that

$$R = U - (p - p_0)/2t \equiv R(p) \tag{4}$$

which when substituted into (2) gives the demand curve faced by the individual firm.

Hence, the firm's problem is to maximize profits given by:

$$Y = pkDR(p)^2 - [f + ckDR(p)^2 + dk^2D^2R(p)^4] \tag{5}$$

It can be shown that this maximization yields the optimal price.

$$\begin{aligned} p &= c + 2dkDR^2 + tR \\ &= MC + tR \end{aligned} \tag{6}$$

where MC is marginal cost.

Since firms are identical, $R = U$ in equilibrium. The profit maximizing price is a mark-up over marginal cost. Perfect competition ($p = MC$) occurs when transportation costs are zero.

Long run equilibrium is given by eq. (6) and a zero profit condition, which jointly determines R (or U) and p. The zero profit condition is

$$p = \frac{f}{kdR^2} + c + dkDR^2 \tag{7}$$

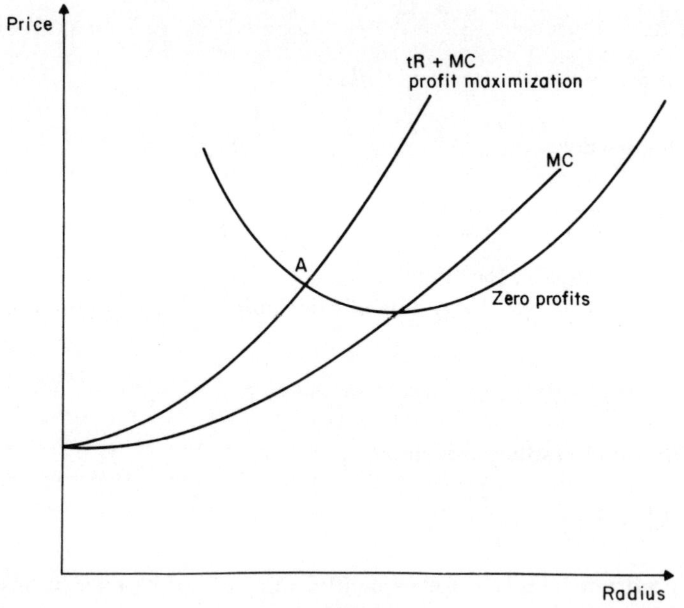

FIGURE 1
Long Run Equilibrium

The solution is depicted in figure 1. Curve MC gives marginal cost as a function of R, and the "zero profits" curve gives average cost as a function of R. The two must, of course, intersect at the minimum average cost. The "$MC + tR$" curve is equation (7) and the intersection at A gives long run equilibrium. The figure reveals that (with $t > 0$) the long run must involve excess capacity and that a monopolistic competition solution is derived from the model.

A question that naturally arises is whether or not this monopolistic competition equilibrium is efficient. Since consumption is fixed, the welfare question is simply whether or not average total costs (transportation + production) are minimized.[4]

Total transportation costs are given by

$$(8) \qquad TTC = \int_0^R 2tU \cdot 2kUdU = \tfrac{2}{3}ktDR^3$$

Total production costs are given by

$$(9) \qquad TPC = f + ckDR^2 + dk^2D^2R^4$$

[4] See Capozza and Van Order [4] for a closely related discussion.

and average total costs are given by

$$ATC = \tfrac{2}{3}tR + \frac{f}{dDR^2} + c + dkDR^2 \tag{11}$$

Minimizing this gives

$$R_0^4 = \frac{f}{dkD^2} - \frac{t}{3dkD}R_0^3 \tag{12}$$

which is difficult to solve for directly.

It can be shown that the radius of minimum average production cost is given by

$$R_c^4 = \frac{f}{dk^2D^2} \tag{13}$$

and that the actual radius is given by

$$R_a^4 = \frac{f}{dk^2D^2} - \frac{t}{dkD}R_a^3 \tag{14}$$

These need not be solved for explicitly, since it can be seen by inspection that

$$R_c \geq R_0 \geq R_a \tag{15}$$

That is, the optimal radius is greater than the actual but less than the zero excess capacity radius. Hence, the system is suboptimal; but forcing price to minimum average cost would be suboptimal as well. This result arises when fixed costs, f, and transport costs, t are positive. If either is zero, the competitive solution is obtained.

Of some interest is the role of fixed costs. We interpret it as representing the lumpiness of capital, (e.g., minimum plant size or setup costs). Without it location would not be a factor, and all goods would be produced everywhere. But given that plants are located at discrete points, monopoly power is inevitable, since a customer a block away is much less likely to switch stores than a customer a mile away. This difference is what generates the downward sloping demand curve faced by the individual firm. The curve does not become flat as entry drives profits to zero. Hence, our basic result is that *free entry and perfect information do not lead to perfect competition as long as fixed costs and transportation costs are positive.*

Our second purpose here is to interpret the model in a marketing context. Instead of spatial locations, the two dimensional plane will now depict quantities of characteristics of the good in question. The problem is more complicated because characteristics space is more complicated than physical space. For instance, characteristics are generally such that people always want more of all of them, so that the analogy with buyers being evenly spaced on a plane is not straightforward. However, as Lancaster [17] shows, we can obtain the analogy by assuming that there is a technology that limits the amounts of characteristics that can be obtained in a single unit of a "good." For instance, if "nutrition" and "convenience" are characteristics of a breakfast food and there is a transformation curve giving the maximum amount of convenience for various levels of nutrition in a unit of the breakfast food, then we can define the "good" in terms of nutrition. Consumers' positions on the nutrition line are defined by where an indifference curve is tangent to the above-mentioned transformation curve. This gives the preferred amount of nutrition (and convenience); and the analogy with our model would be to assume that consumers have different tastes, and these tangencies are evenly distributed as seen from the nutrition line. We then interpret transport costs, tR, as the amount needed to bribe consumers to move R units from their preferred position, and consumers buy from the firm with the lowest $p + tR$.

For n characteristics we can use the transformation curve to reduce the characteristics to $n - 1$ independent choices, so that our two dimension example above involves three characteristics. Issues involved in defining units of goods in models like this are discussed in Lancaster [17].

If the above transformation curve is defined as the locus of characteristics associated with a given level of cost, and if the transformation curves are homothetic expansions of one another, then we can define cost curves in the usual way. Fixed costs are the set up or advertising costs involved in supplying a good with a new bundle of characteristics. As in the location version, these fixed costs insure that only discrete bundles will be produced and that individual firms will have monopoly power.

The point is that a marketing model with properties similar to the location-monopolistic competition model can be developed. Of course, it was necessary to make some strong assumptions to make the analogy perfect. Most of these can be weakened considerably. For instance, we doubt that uneven distribution of consumers over characteristic space or non linear representations of the loss from consuming a less preferred bundle will make much difference. We suspect that, as long as there are fixed costs and preferences for particular bundles of characteristics, the results will be broadly similar.

CONCLUSIONS

In this paper we have tried to elaborate on the spatial analogy to product differentiation in order to clarify some issues in monopolistic competition. The excess capacity theorem was reaffirmed. Consistency of the assumptions was shown to be somewhat uncertain. Demsetz argued that free entry does not necessarily imply zero profits. Recent papers in location theory confirm his result and specify the necessary conditions for zero profit equilibrium.

One highly relevant aspect of consistency not explored by Demesetz is the economic foundations for the zero price reaction assumption of monopolitic competition. If firms compete in characteristics space and the number of characteristics (dimensions) is small, each firm may actually have binding competition from only a few of the firms in the industry. (Do Cadillacs compete with Hondas?) Our analysis elsewhere shows that there is likely to be a small price reaction (about 1/3) in one dimensional space (2 competitors) (see Capozza and Van Order [6]). As the number of directions increases the price reaction declines. Since product characteristics are typically numerous, the reaction is probably close to zero in most cases as assumed in monopolistic competition.

Finally and of greatest significance is the demonstration that even in the absence of patents and information imperfections, free entry does not lead to perfect competition. Firms retain some monopoly power as long as (1) tastes differ among consumers and (2) there are fixed costs to developing new products. These elements are comparable to the spatial assumptions of costly transportation and location specific capital.

DENNIS R. CAPOZZA,
University of British Columbia,
Faculty of Commerce and Business Administration,
2075 Westbrook Hall,
Vancouver, B.C., V6T 1W5, Canada

and

ROBERT VAN ORDER,
Department of Housing and Urban Development,
Washington, D.C., 20410, U.S.A.

REFERENCES

[1] BARZEL, V., "Excess Capacity in Monopolistic Competition", *Journal of Political Economy*, **78** (September/October 1972), pp. 1142–49.
[2] BAUMOL, W., "Calculation of Optimal Product and Retailer Characteristics: The Abstract Product Approach", *Journal of Political Economy*, **75** (August 1975), pp. 674–85.
[3] BECKMANN, M., "Spatial Price Policies Revisited", *Bell Journal of Economics*, **7** (Fall, 1976), pp. 619–30.
[4] CAPOZZA, D. and VAN ORDER, R., "A Simple Model of Spatial Competition", *Southern Economic Journal*, **44** (October 1977), pp. 361–67.
[5] CAPOZZA, D. and VAN ORDER, R., "A Generalized Model of Spatial Competition", *American Economic Review*, **68** (December 1978), pp. 896–908.
[6] CAPOZZA, D. and VAN ORDER, R., "Competitive Reactions in Spatial Monopolistic Competition", mimeo, (University of British Columbia, 1979).
[7] CAPOZZA, D. and VAN ORDER, R., "Unique Equilibria, Pure Profits, and Efficiency in Location Models", *American Economic Review*, **70**, 5, (December 1980), pp. 1046–53.
[8] DEMSETZ, H., "The Nature of Equilibrium in Monopolistic Competition" *Journal of Political Economy*, **67** (February 1959), pp. 21–30.
[9] DEMSETZ, H., "The Welfare Implications of Monopolistic Competition", *Economic Journal*, **74** (September 1964), pp. 623–41.

[10] Demsetz, H., "Do Competition and Monopolistic Competition Differ?", *Journal of Political Economy*, **76** (January/February 1968), pp. 146–48.

[11] Eaton, B. C. and Lipsey, R., "The Principle of Minimum Differentiation Reconsidered", *Review of Economic Studies*, **42** (1975), pp. 27–49.

[12] Eaton, B. C. and Lipsey, R., "The non-Uniqueness of Equilibrium in the Löschian Model", *American Economic Review*, **66** (March 1976), pp. 77–93.

[13] Eaton, B. C. and Lipsey, R., "Freedom of Entry and the Existence of Pure Profit", *Economic Journal*, **88** (1978), pp. 455–69.

[14] Greenhut, M. L., "A Theoretical Mapping from Perfect Competition to Imperfect Competition", *Southern Economic Journal*, **42** (October 1975), pp. 177–92.

[15] Kaldor, N., "Market Imperfections and Excess Capacity", *Economica*, **2** (February 1935), pp. 33–50.

[16] Lancaster, K., *Consumer Demand: A New Approach*, (Columbia University Press, New York, 1971).

[17] Lancaster, K., "Socially Optimal Product Differentiation", *American Economic Review*, **65** (September 1975), pp. 567–86.

[18] Lovell, M., "Product Differentiation and Market Structure", *Western Economic Journal*, **8** (January 1970), pp. 120–143.

[19] Mills, E. S. and Lav, M., "A Model of Market Areas with Free Entry", *Journal of Political Economy*, **72** (June 1964), pp. 278–88.

[20] Murphy, M. M., "The Consistency of Perfect and Monopolistic Competition", *Economic Inquiry*, **16** (January 1978), pp. 108–12.

[21] Ohta, H., "On the Excess Capacity Controversy", *Economic Inquiry*, **15** (April 1977), pp. 153–65.

[22] Schmalensee, R., "A Note on Monopolistic Competition and Excess Capacity", *Journal of Political Economy*, **80** (May/June 1972), pp. 586–91.

[23] Schocker, A. and Srinavasan, V., "Multiattribute Approaches for Product Concept Evaluation and Generation: A Critical Review", *Journal of Marketing Research*, **16** (May 1979), pp. 159–80.

[24] Schuster, H., "Further Remarks on the Theory of Product Differentiation", *Journal of Political Economy*, **77** (October 1969), pp. 827–33.

THE JOURNAL OF INDUSTRIAL ECONOMICS
Volume XXXI September/December 1982 Nos. 1/2

INNOVATIVE ENTRY: PROFIT HIDDEN BENEATH THE ZERO*

KELVIN LANCASTER

THE traditional models of free entry, zero profit monopolistic competition equilibrium do not, of course, exclude the possibility that positive profits might still be made by intra-marginal firms if the market is non-uniform, or that collusive actions plus barriers to further entry can almost always be used to convert a zero-profit non-cooperative equilibrium into a structure which is profitable for all existing firms.

This paper is concerned with situations giving rise to a local Nash equilibrium (no firm can improve by a marginal move), which are zero profit across all firms, but yet in which it is possible for a new firm to enter and make profits (at least in the short run) without collusive action. Entry in such situations will be referred to as *innovative entry*, since it involves potential entrants looking behind the zero-profit situation actually existing to a possible different structure in which profits are possible, or in which a larger number of firms can be accommodated without losses. This can be contrasted with *passive entry*, in which firms simply enter industries where actual profits are positive and do not enter those in which actual profits are nonpositive. We shall restrict ourselves to discussion of uniform cases in which all firms make identical profits at equilibrium so as to avoid any difficulty associated with the term "zero profit".

The general context will be that of monopolistic competition in which product differentiation takes place by variation in the specifications (combinations of characteristics) of the goods produced. The potential variations are considered as points in a space of characteristics, with dimensionality determined by the number of characteristics actually relevant to consumer choice among the products. The market structure arising within this context when there is free entry, no collusive behavior, frictionless change and complete information, has been termed "perfect monopolistic competition" by the author, and discussed fully (at least for the case of two characteristics) in Lancaster [5].

Within this structure, it will be shown that innovative entry is possible, even when there is passive entry equilibrium (because actual profits of all firms are zero), in at least two cases:

(1) The "ignored characteristics" case, in which there is a zero profit equilibrium when firms take note of k characteristics, but that there is a relevant

* The research on which this paper is based was supported by the National Science Foundation, Grant SES 8025048.

$(k + 1)$th characteristic which has been ignored. By differentiating the product in an additional dimension, a greater number of firms can be sustained at a non-negative profit level.

(2) The multiple equilibrium case (possible only if there are more than three characteristics) in which there is more than one configuration of firms over the goods spectrum, each giving a zero-profit Nash equilibrium but with more firms covering the spectrum in one configuration than in others.

I. OUTLINE OF THE BASIC MODEL

For a product group defined over $n + 1$ characteristics, it is assumed that suitable normalization for equivalent quality permits all potential products to be represented by points in a linear subspace of dimension n. It is further assumed that the set of all products that could actually be produced is a convex subset of L^n, so that continuous product differentiation is possible. The convex subset is the product spectrum, and any point within it is a potential product specification.

Consumers are assumed to have separable utility functions, so that there is a two-stage decision process in which intra-group choices are independent of the events occurring in the market for outside goods. The consumption technology for the group is taken to be of the non-combinable kind so that the consumer must choose one product from the group—a Volkswagon or a Toyota, not half a Volkswagon plus half a Toyota. Non-combinability is not essential to the analysis, but makes it somewhat simpler and seems the most relevant for typical differentiated product markets.[1] Each consumer has a point in the product spectrum which is his most-preferred specification, and is the product he would choose if all were available to him on the same terms. The utility of any other product, relative to the same quantity of his most preferred product, is taken to be a concave decreasing function of some measure of the difference between the specifications of the available and most-preferred goods.

The choice of which product to buy within the group will depend on both price and specification. If the prices of all available products are the same, the consumer will obviously choose the one which is closest to his most preferred specification, otherwise he will make the choice which gives the most utility per dollar—perhaps choosing one further from his most preferred specification, but cheaper. The quantity he will purchase, which is separable from his choice of the product, depends on its price relative to the price of the outside good, the elasticity of substitution between group and outside goods,

[1] Note that emphasis on non-combinability makes the analysis of demand somewhat different from that in the author's original statement of the characteristics approach, Lancaster [3], but non-combinability was discussed in the more extended analysis in Lancaster [4].

and also on the specification of the good relative to his most preferred specification.

It can be shown that the quantity, $q(u)$, that will be purchased by a consumer whose most preferred specification is at a distance u (in the characteristics space) from the good actually available to him, has properties which depend on the elasticity of substitution between outside goods and goods within the group. If this elasticity be denoted by σ, then, in particular,

$$(1) \qquad \frac{\partial q}{\partial u} \lesseqgtr 0 \text{ according as } \sigma \gtrless 1$$

The function $q(u)$ is decreasing in u if and only if $\sigma > 1$. Since $q'(u) < 0$ is necessary for satisfaction of the second order conditions for equilibrium, as well as a sufficient condition to guarantee that no two firms will produce the identical product, it will be assumed that $\sigma > 1$ throughout.

Now consider the market for a particular product. The market consists of two elements, the market area or set of consumers (identified by the specifications of their most preferred goods) who choose to buy that product, and the market density at each point or the quantity that will be purchased by consumers at that point in the market area. The quantity per consumer is determined by an individual demand function $q^i(p, u)$ the number of persons being given by the assumed distribution of consumer preferences over the spectrum. The following two simplifying assumptions are made:

(1) *Uniformity of preferences*. That is, every consumer has a utility function of the same form, with the same parameters so that the only variation over consumers is in the specification of each one's most preferred good.
(2) *Uniform density*. There is a continuous distribution of consumers (that is, of most preferred specifications) over the spectrum, with a uniform density and equal incomes. The density will be taken to be unity.

Due to these two simplifying assumptions, the quantity demanded from consumers in some element, dv, of the market "area" (actually a set in R^n) which is at a distance u from the point representing the specification of the good, is given by $q(u)\ dv$

$$(2) \qquad Q = \int_V q(u)\, dv$$

where the integral is taken over the whole market area V.

Since we shall be confining our attention to equilibrium configurations involving firms with identical cost functions under conditions of demand uniformity, equilibrium prices will be the same for all goods. Thus each consumer will buy the good which is closest to his preferred specification and the boundaries between market areas of firms adjacent on the spectrum will consist of points equidistant from those representing the specifications of the two goods.

These boundaries will thus be subsets of hyperplanes (dimension R^{n-1}) which are orthogonal to, and bisect, the line joining the two specification points. The market areas will necessarily be convex polytopes.

Although we shall be concerned with shapes in R^n, it is often convenient to use traditional terminology associated with R^3, such as polyhedra for the total shapes, facets for their bounding hypersurfaces in R^{n-1}. Furthermore we shall also use the conventional term "market areas" for what are actually the hypervolumes of shapes in R^n. In all cases, the terms really refer to the equivalents in R^n, and it is believed that no confusion will occur.

If the price of a good is raised slightly above the prices of the adjacent goods (which are all equal and constant), a consumer who was formerly on the boundary will now shift his purchasing from the good in question to the relevant adjacent good, so that the market area will shrink. Under the conditions specified, this shrinking can be taken to be uniform in all directions for a sufficiently small change in price. Similarly, a sufficiently small price reduction will lead to a uniform expansion of the market area.

We are thus interested in how the quantity changes for a small uniform expansion or contraction of the market area. Let r be any suitable linear measure of the market size, such as the radius of the smallest hypersphere enclosing the market. Then we can write $Q(r)$ as

$$Q(r) = \int_0^r f(\rho)\, d\rho \tag{3}$$

where $f(\rho)$ is the demand originating from the boundary layer of a market area of size ρ when the shape of the market area remains unchanged. It is the integral of $q(u)$ over the outer shell of the market area. If ρ increases, then the distance u of every point in the shell from the point representing the specification must increase, so that $q(u)$ increases everywhere if $\sigma < 1$, and decreases everywhere if $\sigma > 1$. Thus $Q'(r) = f'(r) \gtrless 0$ according as $\sigma \lesseqgtr 1$, and Q is a concave (convex) function of r if σ is greater than (less than) unity.

The effect of a small change in price on the demand for a given product is made up of three components:

(1) The market area expands or contracts slightly (according as the price falls or rises), the extent of this change being determined by the substitutability between price and specification at the market boundary.
(2) Expansion or contraction of the market area will, of itself, change the quantity demanded because of the change in the number of consumers covered.
(3) The value of $q(u)$ for every u will change as a result of the price change, less being purchased by every consumer if the price rises.

The elasticity of demand is the product of effects (1) and (2), which form the intragroup substitution effect, plus effect (3) which accounts for the substitution of outside goods and the income effect.[2] The resulting demand elasticity is not constant in this model, but varies with the distance between adjacent goods because the factors determining it depend on the size of the market (r). It can be shown that the elasticity increases as goods move closer to each other on the spectrum, implying that adjacent goods are better substitutes if they are closer in specification. (Substitution becomes perfect as the specifications coincide, with $E = \infty$). Note also that the elasticity relations change if the *shape* of the market changes.

The uniformity and uniform density assumptions give an isotropic demand spectrum, so that the demand for any good (given all prices) depends only on the specifications of other goods relative to its specifications, and not on the absolute specifications. Thus the demand for a good is unchanged if the whole constellation of goods is translated or rotated in the spectrum, provided the relative positions remain fixed.

Given the demand structure outlined above, each firm's sales, and thus its profits, are a function of its specification and its price. The firm will be in equilibrium, given the behavior of other firms, when its profit is stationary for first order changes in either specification or price and declining for second order changes in either separately or both together. We are interested here only in the free entry Nash equilibrium, in which every firm takes the specification and price of other firms as given and in which the number of firms is such as to give zero profits for all firms. All firms have identical cost functions.

It will be assumed that the reader is willing to accept the following properties of any equilibrium configuration as either obvious or following directly from the two-characteristics analysis set out in Lancaster [5]:[3]

(1) The market areas of all firms will be convex sets of the same size and shape.
(2) These market areas will form a proper partitioning of the spectrum.
(3) The prices of all goods will be the same, as will be the marginal revenues, marginal and average costs, and elasticities associated with them.
(4) For every firm, marginal revenue will equal marginal cost, and price will equal average cost.

These properties follow from the isotropic nature of demand, identity of the cost functions, and dependence of the quantity functions Q on both the shape and size of the market areas.

[2] The elasticity of demand can be shown to be given by the expression

$$E = Se_Q + (1 - m)\sigma + m$$

where S is the elasticity of market size with respect to price, e_Q the elasticity of quantity with respect to market size, m the expenditure on the group as a proportion of total consumer expenditure, and σ as already defined.

[3] It is assumed that boundary conditions on the spectrum can be ignored, by treating the spectrum as infinite in length or otherwise. It is now common to do this for the one dimensional location model by assuming everything is distributed on the circumference of a circle, but it is difficult to make sense of this in characteristics space.

II. PASSIVE-ENTRY EQUILIBRIUM CONFIGURATIONS

If the goods produced by the various firms are each represented by their appropriate specification points in characteristics space, what configurations are possible for zero profit equilibria which satisfy the conditions given in the last section (convex and space-filling) and which can be shown to be profit maximizing for each firm, given the prices and specifications of the other firms?

The dimensionality of the spectrum (number of characteristics) is clearly of very great importance. If there are only two characteristics, so that the spectrum is one-dimensional, there will be a unique configuration with the goods spread evenly along the linear spectrum at a spacing which depends on the parameters of demand and of cost, but is unique. Since much of the study of product differentiation when product characteristics are variable has been based on the linear model, itself derived from the Hotelling linear spatial competition model, the problem of non-uniqueness of equilibrium has received less attention than it deserves.

Just as the two-characteristic line spectrum analysis can be related to Hotelling's linear location model, it would seem that a first step towards analyzing the multi-characteristic model would be to examine the work on location in a plane, corresponding to the specification space for three characteristics. For a uniform distribution of consumers over an infinite plane (so that there are no boundary problems), the classic argument of Lösch [9] was that free entry by firms having identical cost functions and in which existing firms can relocate costlessly as new firms enter, would lead to market configurations in which firms equally spaced in such a manner as to give identical market areas, each of which was a regular hexagon. More recently, other authors, especially Eaton and Lipsey [2] have shown that the market solution is not confined to hexagonal markets but may include a great variety of shapes, so that the market equilibrium is not unique. The optimum (planning solution) is a unique hexagonal arrangement, but this not necessarily the only market equilibrium.

Since the demand and cost functions in the characteristics analysis are more general and more complex than the simplified functions typical of location theory, the relationship between the two analyses is not exact. Nevertheless, the non-uniqueness result that will be proved is similar to, and directly inspired by, the work of Eaton and Lipsey.

Locational theory is confined to two dimensions at most and thus is directly analogous only to the two of three characteristics case. For an n-dimensional spectrum ($n + 1$ characteristics) there is no analog in physical location, and the geometry of potential market shapes is complex. For example, contrary to what might perhaps be expected, there is no simple progression in the number of space-filling regular polyhedra as the dimensionality of the space increases. In R^2, for example, there are three such figures, equilateral triangles, squares, and hexagons. In R^3, there is only one figure, the cube, but in R^4 there are again three—the hypercube, a 16-facet figure, and a 24-facet figure.

The requirements that all market areas should be convex sets of the same size and shape form a partition (that is, exactly fill the space) clearly reduces the field, but still leaves many potential candidates for equilibrium configurations. In R^2, for example, the requirement is satisfied by equilateral triangles, squares, and hexagons, but it is also satisfied by right-angled triangles, rectangles, parallelograms, and hexagons elongated or shrunk along the principal axis. In R^3, it is satisfied by cubes, but also by hexagonal prisms, certain pyramids, and arbitrary rectangular boxes, but not by tetrahedra (which are not space-filling).

We will show that equilibrium conditions for zero profit monopolistic competition, namely the convexity and space-filling properties already given, plus first and second order conditions for profit maximization with respect to specification, together with conditions guaranteeing that no two firms will produce the same product and that profits of all firms converge uniformly to zero as the number of firms increases, are satisfied by all convex space-filling market shapes possessing the following symmetry property:

Basic Symmetry Property. A market area in R^n (that is, with $n + 1$ characteristics) possesses the basic symmetry property if there exist an orthogonal set of n hyperplanes (dimension $n - 1$) such that the market area is symmetric across every hyperplane, perhaps after rotation of one half-area about the normal to the hyperplane.

The basic symmetry property does *not* confine the equilibrium market areas to regular polyhedra. In fact, a wide variety of shapes satisfy it—in R^2, for example, these include arbitrary rectangles, parallelograms and stretched and skewed hexagons. Equilateral triangles, however, do not satisfy it, even though they are regular polyhedra, nor do any figures with an odd number of faces.

Consider a market area which satisfied the Basic Symmetry Condition, and consider an arbitrary small change in specification. Such a change can be measured with respect to the normals to the hyperplanes of symmetry, since these normals form an acceptable set of coordinate axes, so we shall consider a small movement along one of these normals. Since we are concerned only with equilibrium configurations, prices of all goods will be the same, so that all market boundaries will be equidistant from the two goods between which it forms the boundary.

To set the basis for the argument, consider the simple case of a hypercube, illustrated as a square in R^2 in Figure 1, and choose the normal to any face as our primary reference axis. In the Figure, this axis is $OA_{1'}$, with S as the hyperplane of symmetry. Since the facet must be normal to the line joining the specification points for the good and the relevant adjacent good, the point representing the specification of the latter lies on the primary axis, at the point

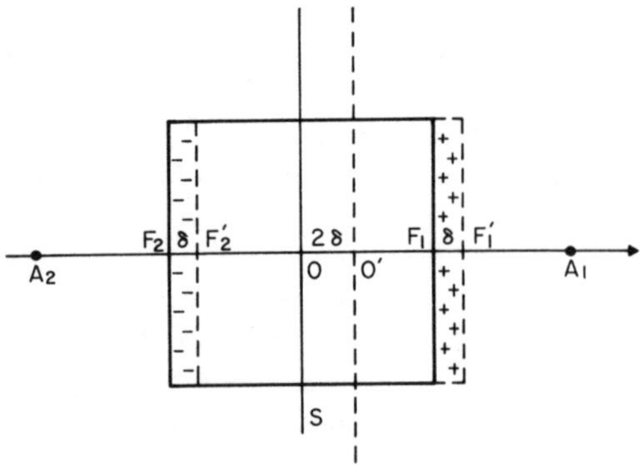

FIGURE 1

A_1. Since the line OA_1 must be bisected by the facet (since prices are equal), $OF_1 = \frac{1}{2}OA_1$.

Now consider a small change in the specification of the good, represented by a movement of 2δ along the primary axis so that the new specification is represented by point O'. The boundary between O and A_1 will now shift so that it is normal to, and bisecting, the segment $O'A_1$. That is, the boundary will remain vertical and intersect OA_1 at F'_1 where $F_1F'_1 = \delta$. Since $OO' = 2d$, the distance $O'F'_1$ is less than the distance OF_1 by an amount δ. The total demand for the product from consumers whose relevant choice is between goods O and A_1 has thus shrunk by an amount equal to the integral of $q(u)$ over the facet F_1, and multiplied by δ.

On the other side of the origin, OA_2 must equal OA_1 because of the assumed symmetry, and the shift from O to O' will shift the facet F_2 rightward to F'_2 by an amount δ, so that the distance $O'F'_2$ is larger than OF_2 by δ. Demand from consumers choosing between O and A_2 has increased by δ times the integral of $q(u)$ over the facet F_2.

For the first order condition, we ignore the slight change in the average distances of the two facets from the center which results from the small change in specification. Since the facets F_1 and F_2 are the same size and shape, from the symmetry condition, the integral of $q(u)$ is the same over both facets so that the gain of new consumers in direction A_1 is balanced by an equal loss of consumers in direction A_2 and thus demand is stationary for a first order change.

For the second order condition, we do not ignore changes in distances for the consumers. In the original situation, the market area extended from the symmetry plane S to F'_1 (a distance $r - \delta$ from O') in one direction, and to F'_2 (a distance $r + \delta$ from O') in the other. The difference resulting from the specification shift is a loss of consumers situated between two hyperplanes at distances r and $r - \delta$ from the origin, and a gain of consumers between two hyperplanes at distances r and $r + \delta$. The average distance from the origin of the consumers lost is less than that of the consumers gained. If the elasticity of substitution is greater than unity, $q(u)$ is a decreasing function of u, so that the demand associated with the lost consumers is greater than that associated with the consumers gained, and total demand falls. Since price is constant and average cost does not increase with output, the second order specification change results in lower profits. Thus the first and second order conditions are satisfied in this case if the symmetry and elasticity of substitution conditions are satisfied.

For market areas having shapes such that there are facets which are neither perpendicular nor parallel to the primary reference axis, the argument follows similar lines. Slight changes in the angles of the facets can be ignored and the effect of small changes along the primary axis treated as pure translations in that direction. The loss on a facet in one direction will be the integral of $q(u)$ over the facet times the amount of translation, and this will be balanced by a gain from a facet of the same size, shape, and relative position in the other direction, if the symmetry condition is satisfied. The second order condition will be satisfied if $q(u)$ is a decreasing function of u, and thus if the elasticity of substitution is greater than unity.

Note that the first order condition will not, in general, be satisfied by a market area which does not satisfy the symmetry condition, such as the triangle in Figure 2. For a movement in the direction of the arrow, the net gain or loss in demand involves comparing the integral of $q(u)$ over facets F_1 and F_2 with the integral over Facet F_3. Since the values of u, and thus of $q(u)$, follow quite a different pattern in traversing the facet F_3 from what they do over facets F_1 and F_2, the balance necessary to give stationarity in demand for a small change in specification could occur, if at all, only for some very special form of the function $q(u)$ and thus would be destroyed by a small arbitrary variation in $q(u)$.

It is now necessary to show that no two firms will produce the same product under the conditions already given. To prove this, we shall show that, if a given product were being produced by more than one firm, at least one firm would always gain by changing the specification of its good to differ from that of the other. In particular, if there is more than one firm producing a product

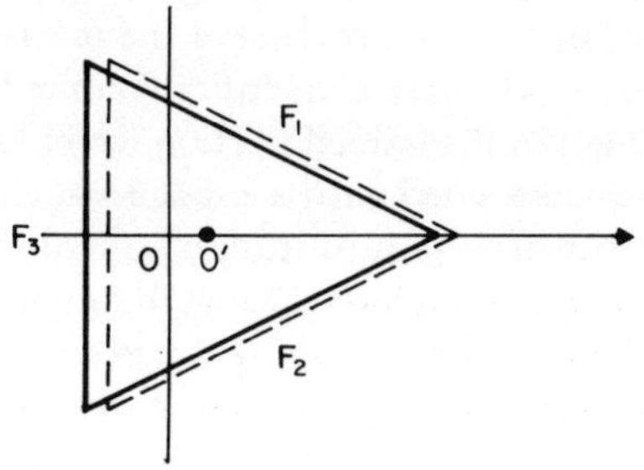

FIGURE 2

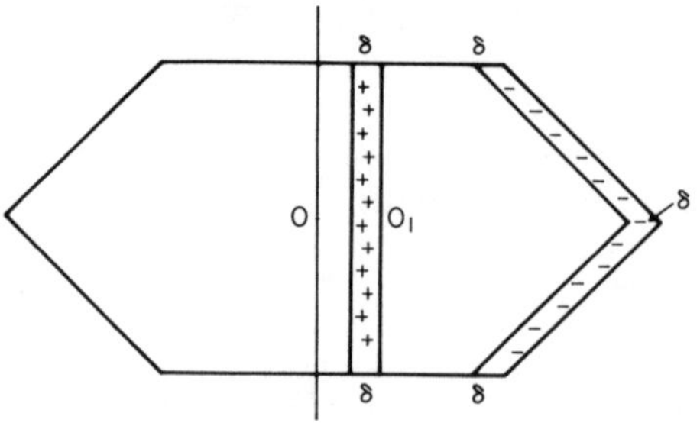

FIGURE 3

there is always a firm with sales no greater than half the total sales of the good. This firm can always gain by producing a product of its own.

Consider a change by this firm to the production of a new product with specification differing from that of the original good by an amount of 2δ in a direction normal to any of the hyperplanes of symmetry in the original market area, as shown in Figure 3 for R^2 space, where the new product is sold at the same price as the old. The new product's market area will have boundaries in the direction of movement but are translated in the direction of movement by an amount of δ, since the new good is closer to the adjacent goods in that direction by 2δ. Thus this boundary is closer to the specification point of the new good than the original boundary was to that of the original good by an amount δ. In the other direction, the original and new goods will divide the part of the market between their two specifications exactly in half, so that the boundary between them will be parallel to the hyperplane of symmetry and at distance δ from the new specification. Thus the market area for the new good is equivalent to the part of the original market area on one side of the symmetry plane (exactly half the original area because of symmetry) *less* a volume equal to that lost when the boundary in the direction of change is moved laterally inward by δ (marked $(-)$ in the figure), *plus* a volume equal to the cross-section of the original area at the center times δ (marked $(+)$ in the figure). Since the outer face consists of parallelopipeds having aggregate "heights" (projections on the vertical hyperplane) equal to the central cross section and bases of width δ, so the volume of the market area lost is equal to the volume gained. But every small element of volume in the lost portion can be paired with an element in the gained portion which is closer to the product specification and is thus associated with a smaller value of u and thus a larger value of $q(u)$, since the elasticity of substitution is greater than unity. The total demand for the new good is therefore greater than half the total demand for the original good, and thus greater than the firm's sales in the original position. Since price is unchanged and average cost nonincreasing, the firm's profits are increased by moving out of the original cluster to produce a product unique to itself.

Finally, we need to show that the maximum profit $\pi^*(r)$ associated with a market area of given shape (satisfying the conditions) and size r is a continuous increasing function of r, so that profits decline uniformly to zero as the number of firms increase (ignoring the integer problem) for all shapes having basic symmetry. This follows from the property that the elasticity of demand increases as r shrinks, so that the ratio of price to marginal cost falls as the market area gets smaller. The quantity sold obviously declines with r, and the ratio of average to marginal cost will not fall as quantity falls. Thus a decline in r implies a lower ratio of price to average cost and a smaller quantity, hence necessarily a smaller profit.

III THE SCOPE FOR INNOVATIVE ENTRY

A passive-entry equilibrium is a configuration such that no firm can increase its profit by price changes or small variations in specification, and all firms make zero profits. Innovative entry is still potentially profitable if there is another arrangement of the *same number* of firms which is also a Nash equilibrium but in which all firms make positive profits. Whether innovative entry would be actually profitable depends on whether new entry in an appropriate position on the spectrum would, of itself, induce such a rearrangement. The analysis here will be confined to the question of potential profitability, leaving the dynamics of rearrangement and actual profitability open except for one or two pointers from location theory.

The basic proposition to be established is the following:

There is scope for innovative entry in any passive-entry equilibrium in which the market areas are not regular polyhedra.

A sketch of a proof proceeds as follows. Any market area which is space-filling and satisfies the symmetry conditions of Section II can be related to some regular polygon by a process of uniform stretching or shrinking along one or more principal axes and/or skewing the principal axes so that they are no longer at the angles appropriate for regularity. In R^2, the four-facet market areas which give a passive-entry equilibrium but are not regular are the rectangle (stretching of the square along one axis) and the parallelogram (skewing of the rectangle, thus skewing plus stretching of the square). We shall show that since $q(u)$ is a decreasing function of u because the passive-entry equilibrium conditions are satisfied, the square market area gives higher total demand for a given coverage of the spectrum than does a rectangle or parallelogram.

Figure 4 shows a rectangle (in (a)) and a rhombus (in (b)), superimposed on a square with the same center and of the same area. The portions marked with plus signs (+) represent consumers gained in moving from the original figure to the square, while the portions marked with minus signs (−) represent consumers lost. Since the area remains the same, the number of consumers lost is equal to the number gained, but the consumers gained are all

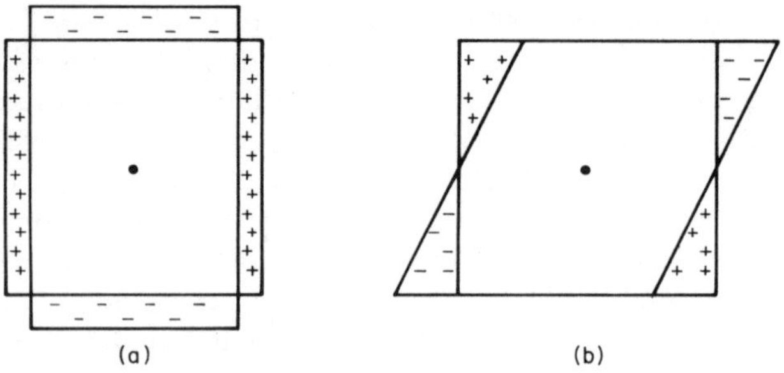

FIGURE 4

closer to the center (the specification of the good) than those lost. Since $q(u)$ is a decreasing function of u, total demand is greater for the square than for the non-regular figure.

A similar argument can be given for stretched and skewed hexagons in R^2 and for equivalent deformations of regular figures in R^n. The regular figure gives greater total demand for a given coverage of the spectrum than the equivalent non-regular figure. Thus any configuration in which the market areas are deformations of some specified regular figure can be rearranged so that the spectrum is covered by the same number of firms, but each firm has larger sales at the original prices. Since average cost is non-increasing, firms will make positive profits at the new configuration if they made zero profits at the old, which will be the case if the old configuration was a passive-entry equilibrium. Note that the rearrangement will, in general, change the elasticity of demand and thus the old prices will no longer be optimal, but the subsequent adjustment of prices can only increase profits further.

The above result relates demand in a specific regular polyhedra to demand in deformations of that polyhedron which have the same area. It does not compare configurations which consist of different regular polyhedra—a configuration of squares with a configuration of hexagons in R^2, for example, since these cannot be deformed into each other in any simple fashion. Can it be shown that a hexagonal market area of the same coverage (area) as a square will generate a larger demand, given only that the quantity function $q(u)$ is a declining function of u? The answer seems to be, no, although it is easy to generate acceptable functions $q(u)$ that do give this result, and the author has not yet been able to generate a counterexample. It does not seem impossible that each of some subset of the space-filling regular polyhedra associated with R^n may be found to give the greatest demand per unit coverage of the spectrum, for a specific choice of $q(u)$. Given $q(u)$ and the system parameters, however, there can be presumed to be a unique member of the set of space-filling regular polyhedra which gives a full innovative-entry equilibrium, at least in general.

We have shown the potential for innovative entry, but actual attainment of a full innovative-entry equilibrium is another matter. Location theorists[4] have studied the problems of entry and the dynamics of rearrangement for patterns in R^2 under simpler demand conditions than those of the present model, and the results are complex and somewhat uncertain. A general study is that of Eaton and Lipsey [2], using numerical methods, the overall tenor of which is that entry into a rectangular system is likely to generate other rectangles, perhaps squares, but not hexagons, while entry into a hexagonal configuration is likely to break up the hexagons. Nothing is known of the entry dynamics of systems in R^n with $n > 2$, but it can be presumed to be more complex, if anything, than that for R^2. There seems to be some evidence that passive-entry equilibria in which the market shapes are far from regular could result in innovative entry which moves the system closer to regularity, but that a smooth transition to the full innovative-entry equilibrium would be a rare event. The difficulties associated with innovative entry are, of course, much greater in an abstract space of characteristics than in location theory—maps of the market areas can at least be drawn in the latter case on the basis of fairly simple information. It is obvious that the point at which entry stops, even if that is not the full innovative-entry equilibrium, is likely to depend on the configuration which develops (perhaps due mainly to random factors) at early stages of the industry growth.

IV. THE "IGNORED CHARACTERISTICS" CASE

Although this case could be analysed separately, it is convenient to treat it as a special case of the multiple equilibrium phenomenon in passive entry equilibrium. Consider a market in which a passive entry equilibrium has been achieved on the mis-perception by all present firms that there are only two relevant characteristics, whereas there are really three. The existing industry can be considered to be organized along a line spectrum like AB in Figure 5. Each firm, such as that producing the good of specification X_i, perceives its potential customers' most preferred specifications as distributed along the line AB and its actual customers as distributed along the market segment $y_{i-1}y_i$. If this were the true situation, the passive entry equilibrium would be a partitioning of the spectrum into line segments of equal length, the length being determined by the parameters of the system and thus the equilibrium being unique. Since the true spectrum is in R^2, however, the firm's potential customers are not confined to the line AB but may have preferred specifications all over the plane. The true market areas for the ith firm is not the line segment $y_{i-1}y_i$, but the *rectangle* (shaded in Figure 5) having sides perpendicular to AB and which pass through y_{i-1}, y_i, respectively. The distance of the ends of the rectangles from the line AB depends on how fast $q(u)$ declines as u increases—if $q(u)$ approaches zero asymptotically, the rectangles are infinite

[4] See, for example, Mills and Lav [11], Beckmann [1], Eaton and Lipsey [2].

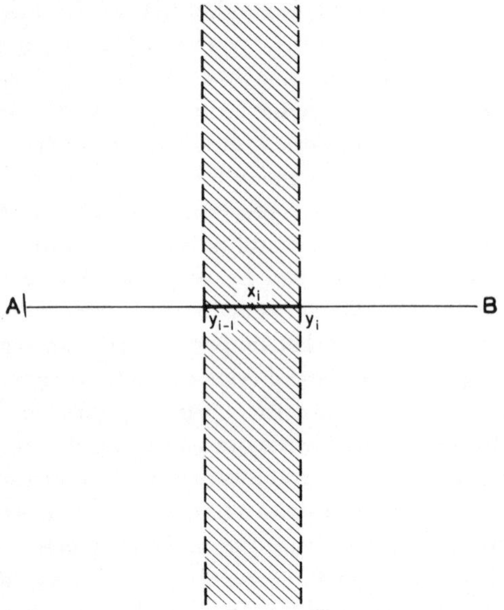

FIGURE 5

in length. In any case, it is necessarily true that the heights of the rectangles are always greater (much greater in general) than the widths $y_{-1}y_i$. Thus the true market areas generated by the false supposition that there are only two characteristics will be elongated rectangles, and the previous proof has shown that innovative entry is possible because the passive entry equilibrium configurations are not regular figures.

Note that the "ignored characteristics" case brings out the difference between perceptions in location theory and those in the theory of product differentiation in characteristics space perhaps more sharply than the question of multiple equilibria itself. To assume population was distributed along a line when it was actually distributed over a plane would be gross ignorance of reality in location theory. In characteristics space, however, it is not at all obvious which properties of goods are relevant characteristics for choice, nor are the goods clearly displayed with respect to their characteristics. From an operational point of view, all that could be observed for multiple equilibria under passive entry would be two zero-profit equilibria for identical industries in identical markets, or the same industry at two different periods, but with different numbers of firms and a different array of goods actually produced.

CONCLUSION

The main result that has been shown here is that it is quite possible for a product-differentiated industry to be in a stable local Nash equilibrium, with zero profits for all firms, and yet in which it is possible for the same number of firms to form a different configuration, also a stable local Nash equilibrium, in which all firms make positive profits. Looked at from another point of view, an industry may be in a passive entry equilibrium in which there may seem no room for any new firms, yet in which the re-structuring induced by new entry may result in greater profits for all even though the number of firms has increased. The analysis has been confined to examining the potential for innovative entry of this kind (essentially a multiple equilibrium phenomenon) rather than mechanisms by which new entry may set up movements appropriate to attaining the alternative equilibrium configuration.

The possibility that an industry may settle down to a passive entry equilibrium in which profits per firm are less than they might otherwise be, is very real in an industry in which products are differentiated by variations in their characteristics rather than by observable physical location. Multiple equilibria are then different configurations in an abstract space of characteristics, and the possibility of being in a less profitable configuration, but no firm in the industry being aware of it, is considerable.

The importance of innovative entry may be less in a closed economy than in an open one, where the impact of import competition may bring about major restructuring. The author has shown in Lancaster [7], [8], that intra-industry trade implies considerable such re-structuring in monopolistic competition industries, and innovative entry effects would increase these structural strains—but perhaps profitably.

KELVIN J. LANCASTER,
Columbia University,
Department of Economics,
International Affaires Building,
New York, N.Y., 10027, U.S.A.

REFERENCES

[1] Beckmann, M., *Location Theory.* (New York, 1968).
[2] Eaton, B. C., and Lipsey, R. G., "The Non-Uniqueness of Equilibrium in the Löschian Location Model", *American Economic Review,* **66** (1976), pp. 77–93.
[3] Lancaster, K., "A New Approach to Consumer Theory", *Journal of Political Economy,* **74** (1966), pp. 132–57.
[4] ———, *Consumer Demand: A New Approach.* (New York, Columbia Univ. Press, 1971).
[5] ———, *Variety, Equity, and Efficiency.* (New York, Columbia Univ. Press, and Oxford, Basil Blackwell, 1979).
[6] ———, "Product Uniqueness under Perfect Monopolistic Competition". The Economics Workshops, Columbia Univerity, June 1979.
[7] ———, "Intra-Industry Trade under Perfect Monopolistic Competition", *Journal of International Economics,* **10** (1980), pp. 151–76.
[8] ———, "Trade in Differentiated Products: Comment". In Bhagwati, J. (ed.) *Import Competition and Response.* (University of Chicago Press, 1982), pp. 208–16.

[9] Lösch, A., *The Economics of Location.* (New Haven, Yale University Press, 1954).

[10] Manning, H. P., *Geometry of Four Dimensions.* Macmillan, 1914. (Dover reprint, 1956).

[11] Mills, E. S. and Lav., M., "A Model of Market Areas with Free Entry", *Journal of Political Economy,* **72** (1964), pp. 278–88.

THE JOURNAL OF INDUSTRIAL ECONOMICS
Volume XXXI September/December 1982 Nos. 1/2

COMPETITIVE BEHAVIOUR IN CHAIN-LINKED MARKETS*

R. Rothschild

I. INTRODUCTION

This paper investigates an important but neglected aspect of price competition in a market for varieties of a differentiated product. We shall consider in particular the case where a change in the price of one variety affects only its more 'proximate'[1] competitors in the characteristics space.

The model to be analysed here is based on an idea discussed in Chamberlin [2]. Chamberlin's view that large group monopolistically competitive markets might be thought of as comprising numerous 'chain-linked' submarkets is reflected in the following extract:

> "Retail establishments scattered throughout an urban area are an instance of . . . a 'chain' linking of markets. Gasoline filling stations are another. In either of these cases the market of each seller is most closely linked (having regard only to the spatial factor) to the one nearest him, and the degree of connection lessens quickly with distance until it becomes zero . . . Where this is the case, considerations relative to small numbers hold even though the 'group' be large.
>
> Two new possibilities are suggested by the chain relationship. A cut by one seller may lead to a smaller reduction by the one next to him and soon dissipate itself without spreading far. Or . . . it might force those nearest him to meet it in full, this in turn forcing others, and so on indefinitely . . ."
>
> [2, pp. 103/104]

Chamberlin's treatment of the chain market phenomenon has not, generally speaking, been taken much further. Although, as Friedman [3] has observed,

> "Chamberlin's chain market appears . . . as the sensible way to model monopolistic competition because it does correspond to something recognizable in actual markets—quite unlike the customary version of monopolistic competition"
>
> [3, p. 60]

* I would like to thank K. Lancaster, S. Salop, R. Schmalensee and A. Wolinsky for helpful discussions. Responsibility for any shortcomings is entirely my own.

[1] In keeping with the traditions of this branch of analysis, the notion of 'proximity' may be interpreted here in terms either of physical distance (as, for example, in the case of gasoline filling stations) or of 'quality' or 'specification' (as, for example, in the case of types of cider).

theorists have in the main continued to regard monopolistically competitive markets as being made up of varieties of a differentiated product which are, in some sense, equally substitutable for one another. Where writers such as Kaldor [5], Henderson [4], Archibald and Rosenbluth [1], Lancaster [6] and Salop [7] have given some attention to the chain market concept, none of these has analysed its behavioural implications.

One of the reasons for this gap in an otherwise extensive literature on monopolistic competition must be the problem of identifying a tractable expectations structure for the model. An obvious difficulty lies in the fact that the reactions of competitors depend not only on the action of the initiator of a price reduction, but also on their expectations of how their *other* rivals will act, and these, in turn, are influenced by expectations of *their* rivals. And so on. A plausible expectations structure must somehow accommodate this phenomenon.

In this paper we consider the problem in the context of a particular expectations structure. The assumption on rival behaviour upon which the analysis rests is in many ways the most natural one which individuals can be expected to make: agents are assumed to believe that their rivals will react as they would to given opportunities. However, difficulties arise even when the assumption is so simple and apparently straightforward as this one. The powers of reasoning which must be attributed to agents in the model are quite substantial, and it should be said at the outset that the analysis is intended to reveal the ultimate consequences of behaviour based on our assumptions, rather than to prescribe to these agents a set of ostensibly feasible rules. Nevertheless, as we shall show, a number of useful insights can be generated by our approach.

The remainder of this paper is set out in four sections and organised in the following manner: Section II sets out the assumptions of the model. Section III deals with the *second* of Chamberlin's two conjectures in the passage cited above. We shall establish conditions necessary for matching price reductions to be profitable, and consider the implications of changes in the number of firms and the level of advertising expenditure. Section IV deals in similar fashion with the *first* of Chamberlin's conjectures. Section V offers a summary and conclusions.

II. ASSUMPTIONS

A.1. The characteristics space is represented by an arbitrarily long but finite line, L;

A.2. The product is available in an exogenously determined number of varieties (also called 'firms') k, indexed i, $i = 0, 1, 2, \ldots, N$, each identified by the point k_i on L.[2] The points k_i are equidistant;[3]

[2] The implicit assumption throughout this analysis is that the number of varieties on either side of a prospective price cutter is 'large'. This eliminates the corner solution problems associated with end-points.

[3] We assume that the adjustment in locations has already occurred. This enables us to isolate the price component of competition.

A.3. All k_i are subject to identical, constant average production and selling costs which, without excessive loss of generality, may be set at zero. Each k_i sells at a price denoted p_i, distinguished where necessary by the use of a superscript.

A.4. Consumers' most preferred variety specifications k^* are uniformly distributed over L. The correspondence between consumers and most preferred varieties is one-to-one. The 'distance' between k^* and any given k_i is $|k_i - k^*|$, and the 'cost' or 'disutility' implied by this distance is $\theta|k_i - k^*|$, where θ is a positive constant. Each consumer buys *one*[4] unit of the variety for which $p_i + \theta|k_i - k^*|$ is a minimum.

A.5. Firms behave non-cooperatively. Price changes, where they occur, are made in sequence according to the proximity of the individual firm to the initiator of the change. The choice of initiator is arbitrary. Each firm conjectures that all others entertain the same expectations on rival behaviour as it does, and that on the basis of these expectations any other firm will respond as it does to a given opportunity. Firms change price only if the consequence is an immediate and 'sustainable' increase in profit, given the expected responses of rivals.

Definition:

D.1. Given A.1. to A.5., an equilibrium in prices exists when no firm has an incentive to change its price unilaterally.

The question to which we turn now is: given A.1.–A.5., D.1., both N and θ, and an initial price (identical for all firms), (i) do there exist conditions on the elasticity of demand for individual varieties which enable some firms to enjoy sustained increases in profits through reduced prices, and (ii) what is the pattern of prices which characterises an equilibrium?

III. CASE A (MATCHING PRICE CHANGES)

Suppose that there exists for this market a price, p^1, which is joint profit maximising in the sense that at p^1 no individual would wish to *raise* his price unilaterally, whereas a price *reduction* by one firm alone would increase its profits. Suppose further that all firms initially sell at p^1. Then each firm sells the quantity L/N. Set $L/N = q^*$.

Consider Figure 1. Let p_i be reduced while all other prices in the market remain unchanged. Then the change in p_i will affect competitors according to their proximity to k_i. For instance, between p_i^1 and p_i^3 the sales of only firms $k_j, j = i-1, i+1$, decrease, while below p_i^3 the sales of firms adjacent to k_j are also affected. It is readily apparent that a continuous fall in p_i does not result in a corresponding continuous fall in the sales of all other firms; rather, there may be significant ranges of price in which only a subset of the N firms are affected, and there may be no choice of $p_i > 0$ which has an impact upon the sales of all firms.

[4] This assumption is similar to that made by Salop [7].

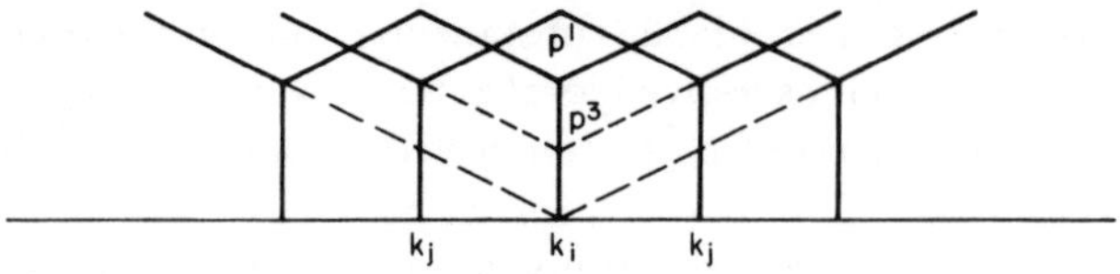

FIGURE 1

The quantity sold by k_i in the interval $|k_i - k_j|$ is a function of both p_i and p_j. Given $p_j = p^1$ and $p_i^0, p^1 \geq p_i^0 \geq p^3$, the corresponding sales of k_i are

(1) $$q^* - (p_i^0 - p^1)/\theta$$

If $p_j = p^1$ and k_i chooses $p_i^0 < p^1$, then the increase in k_i's sales is

(2) $$\Delta q_i = |p_i^0 - p^1|/\theta$$

or

(3) $$\Delta q_i = |\Delta p_i|/\theta$$

An increase in profit for k_i requires

(4) $$p_i^0(q^* + \Delta q_i) > p^1 q^*,$$

where $\Delta q_i > 0$.

Since our concern here must be with *discrete* price and output changes, and in order later to highlight the crucial roles of N and θ in determining outcomes, it will be convenient to take (4) as implying the following elasticity condition:[5]

(5) $$|\varepsilon_i| \geq 1 + (\Delta q_i/q^*)$$

Since (from (3)), $\theta = |\Delta p_i|/\Delta q_i$, (5) can be rewritten as

(6) $$p^1/\theta \geq q_i^\Delta$$

where $q_i^\Delta = q^* + \Delta q_i$.

If none of the other firms were permitted to change price, k_i would maximise his profits by choosing $q_i^\Delta = p^1/\theta$.

Suppose, however, that both k_j are free to match k_i's reduction if they so choose. Then there exist two possibilities:

(a) If k_j's neighbours in turn keep *their* prices unchanged, then k_j will always gain from a reduction which matches that of k_i. To show this, we denote by $q_j^{-\Delta}$ the sales of each of the two k_j after k_i has reduced price. Then $q_j^{-\Delta} = q^* - (\Delta q_i/2)$. If k_j matches k_i's price, then he regains the amount $\Delta q_i/2$ from k_i

[5] This condition is derived in the following way: From (4) $p_i^0(q^* + \Delta q_i) > p^1 q^*$, so $p_i^0 \Delta q_i > (p^1 - p_i^0)q^*$ which implies $p_i^0 \Delta q_i/q^* |\Delta p_i| > 1$. Writing $(p^1 - |\Delta p_i|)\Delta q_i/q^* |\Delta p_i| > 1$ yields $|\varepsilon_i| > 1 + \Delta q_i/q^*$, where $|\varepsilon_i| = p^1 \Delta q_i/q^* |\Delta p_i|$.

and an equal amount from his other neighbour. Hence, $\Delta q_j = \Delta q_i$. Then, if (6) holds for $q^* + \Delta q_i$, it must also hold for $q_j^{-\Delta} + \Delta q_j$.

In the event of a matching response by both k_j, k_i will clearly be worse off than at p^1, and therefore no price reduction will be initiated.

(b) If k_j's neighbours match k_j's reduction, then Δq_j is simply the sales originally lost by k_j to k_i i.e. $\Delta q_i/2$. If k_j is to find a matching reduction profitable in these circumstances, we require

(7) $$|\varepsilon_j| \geq 1 + (\Delta q_j / q_j^{-\Delta})$$

Since $\Delta q_j = \Delta q_i/2$, $\Delta q_j = |\Delta p_j|/2\theta$, and (7) can be rewritten as

(8) $$p^1/2\theta \geq q_j^{-\Delta} + \Delta q_j$$

Recall that $q_j^{-\Delta} + \Delta q_j = q^* = L/N$.

The first possibility discussed above is of limited interest as we can make no such *a priori* statement about the behaviour of k_j's neighbours. We therefore restrict our attention to the implications of the second possibility. We note first that if (6) and (8) *both* hold, then a price reduction by k_i will be matched by both neighbours k_j *irrespective* of the reactions of their own adjacent rivals. In this event k_i is clearly worse off than at p^1 and no price reduction will be initiated.

But suppose that (6) holds while (8) does not. Then there exist two further possibilities. Either

(9) $$p^1/2\theta \leq q_j^{-\Delta}$$

or

(10) $$q_j^{-\Delta} < p^1/2\theta < L/N$$

We defer discussion of (10) until Section IV. For the present we consider the implications of (9):

Given $p^1 > p_i^0 \geq p^3$, and the certainty of a matching price reduction by k_j's adjacent neighbours, then if (9) holds there is no profit increasing price change open to either of the firms k_j.

Proposition 1: Given A.1.–A.5. and D.1., if N and θ are such that (6) and (9) both hold for some q_i^{Δ} and $q_j^{-\Delta}$ then the equilibrium price configuration will be as follows. A firm k_i which reduces price will have two adjacent neighbours k_j whose price is p^1. Each of these will have a neighbour k_m, $m = i-2, i+2$, whose price is p^1. Each of k_m's neighbours k_n, $n = i-3, i+3$, will behave in the same manner as k_i.

Proof: Consider Figure 2. Let k_0 be the first to reduce his price. Then, since (9) holds by assumption, k_{-1} will find it profitable to follow the price reduction only if p_{-2} remains unchanged. But consider k_{-2}. Given a reduction by k_{-1}, k_{-2} would be forced to reduce price if k_{-3} reduced his. Now consider k_{-3}. If k_{-3} were to reduce price and k_{-2} were to follow, k_{-3} would encounter a

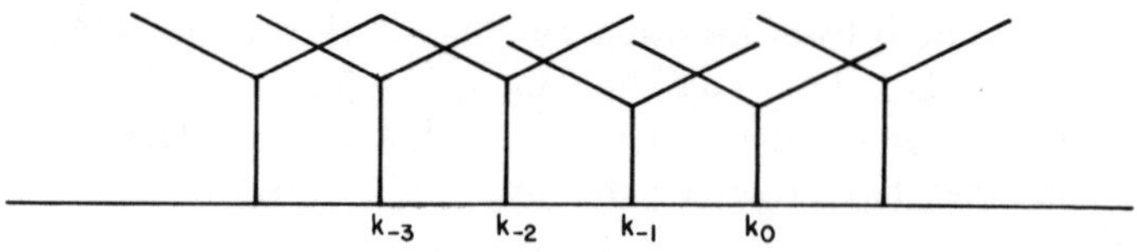

(a) k_{-1}'s 'ideal' outcome

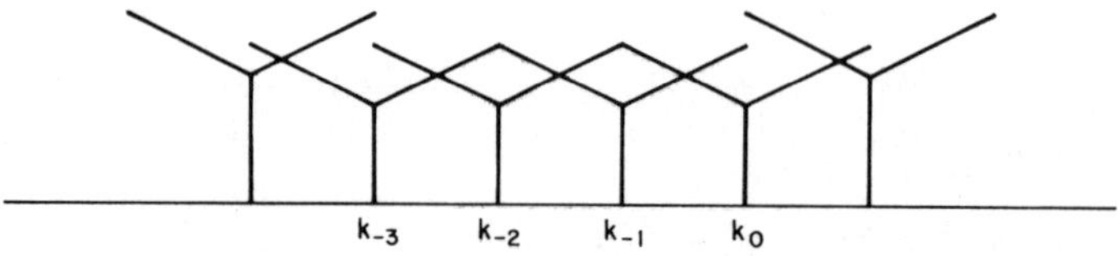

(b) k_{-1}'s 'actual' outcome

FIGURE 2

configuration of prices on either side of him which is identical to the most favourable outcome to k_{-1} after *his* reduction (i.e. p_0 reduced, p_{-2} unchanged). Hence, if k_{-1} were to reduce price, he would expect k_{-3} to do the same. But since this will force a reduction in k_{-2}, k_{-1} will then emerge worse off than at p^1. Consequently, k_{-1} will not follow k_0's price reduction.

Now consider Figure 3. We may suppose that k_{-1} will follow k_0's price reduction if k_{-2} reduces his price. Consider k_{-2}. A reduction in p_{-2} and a

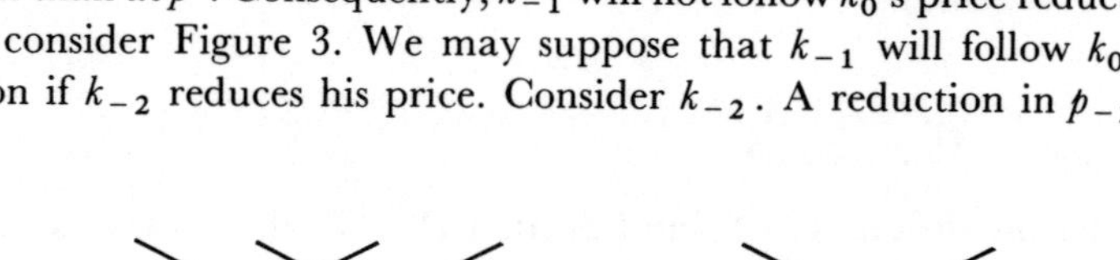

(a) k_{-2}'s 'ideal' outcome

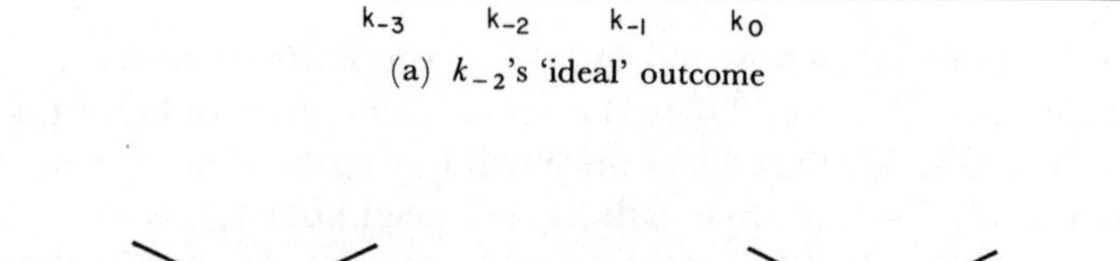

(b) k_{-2}'s 'actual' outcome

FIGURE 3

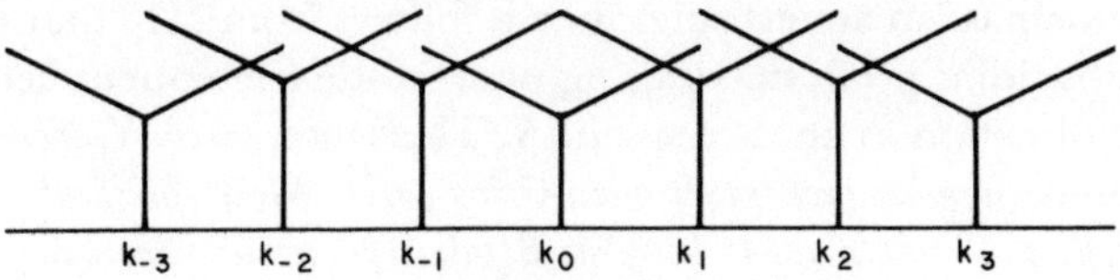

FIGURE 4

consequent reduction in p_{-1} would yield to k_{-2} an outcome identical to that open to k_{-3} if he were in turn to reduce *his* price. k_{-3} can therefore be expected to reduce price if k_{-2} does so. But if this happens, both of k_{-2}'s adjacent neighbours will have reduced their prices, and k_{-2} will clearly be worse off. Hence, k_{-2} will not reduce price and, consequently, neither will k_{-1}.

Finally, suppose that, given a reduction in p_0, k_{-3} were to be the next to reduce price. Then the foregoing arguments would apply, *mutatis mutandis*, to firms to the left of k_{-3}, and analogously to all other firms in the market. Q.E.D.

The outcome is depicted in Figure 4.

The characteristics of the equilibrium price set associated with this outcome can be easily identified. We need only recall that for this result to occur, both (6) and (9) must be satisfied. Since q_i^{Δ} and $q_j^{-\Delta}$ are inversely related, it follows straightforwardly that every firm which reduces price maximises its profits by choosing the lowest price consistent with the simultaneous satisfaction of (6) and (9).

It is apparent from (6), (8) and (9) that the roles of N and θ are quite crucial to the analysis. Given a price reduction by any k_i we can find an N sufficiently large for (8) to hold. Given this N, the response of k_j would clearly be the matching price reduction postulated earlier, and k_i would then be worse off than he is at p^1. Hence, we obtain the surprising result that *for given* p^1, θ *and* N *sufficiently large, no price reductions will be initiated.*

A result somewhat more in accord with intuition concerns the magnitude of the sustainable joint profit maximising price. Given θ, it is clear from (6) that no reduction will be initiated by any firm k_i if

(11) $$p^1 \leq \theta q^*$$

Recalling that $q^* = L/N$ when all firms sell at the same price, we observe that *the larger is* N, *the lower is the sustainable joint-profit maximising price.*

We now consider θ. We suppose that θ is defined for any given level of advertising expenditure. The justification for this is that the greater the amount of advertising expenditure, *ceteris paribus*, the lower is the disutility implied by the 'distance' $|k_i - k^*|$.[6] In this case, if all firms undertake the

[6] We suppose that one of the objects of advertising is to persuade buyers that the utility derived from a particular variety is in fact close to that which would be derived from the buyer's most preferred variety.

same given increase in advertising, then it follows from (11) that the effect on the sustainable joint profit maximising price of the consequent decrease in θ is in the same direction as an increase in N. Therefore, *given N, increased advertising lowers the sustainable joint profit-maximising price. More specifically, given N, p^1 and provided that (9) continues to hold, as θ falls (advertising increases) beyond some level, price reductions will be undertaken in the manner specified in Proposition 1.*

IV. CASE B (NON-MATCHING PRICE CHANGES)

We turn now to consideration of the implications of (10). Recall that in this case

$$p^1/2\theta > q_j^{-\Delta}$$

It follows that if k_i reduces price k_j will increase his profits by reducing his, irrespective of the response by k_m, $m = i - 2$, $i + 2$. Suppose that k_m will always match k_j's reduction. Then, given $p_i^0 < p^1$, k_j maximises his profits by increasing his sales to the point where

$$(12) \qquad p^1/2\theta = q_j^{-\Delta} + t, \; t > 0$$

Clearly (from our earlier argument), since $p^1/2\theta < L/N$, t must be smaller than $\Delta q_i/2$, and so $|\Delta p_j| < |\Delta p_i|$. In this sense, k_j's price reduction can be thought of as a 'non-matching' adjustment to k_i's price change. Given such an outcome, the natural question is then whether the first of Chamberlin's two conjectures can be shown to be valid.

In order to analyse this case, we suppose, as before, that all firms sell initially at the joint-profit maximising price, p^1. Hence, each sells q^*. Without loss of generality, set $q^* = 1$. We retain for the present the assumption that any reduction in the price of k_j will be *matched* by k_m. Whilst this is not an obviously justifiable assumption in the present context, it will simplify matters somewhat and we shall be in a position to validate it more easily at a later stage.

Now let p_i be reduced while all other prices in the market remain unchanged. Set the resulting $\Delta q_i = 2\beta$. Without loss of generality, we may suppose that $p^1 > p_i^0 > p^3$, so that $0.5 > \beta > 0$. From (5) we require

$$(13) \qquad |\varepsilon_i| \geq 1 + 2\beta$$

We now prove the following:

Proposition 2: Given A.1.–A.5. and D.1. (i) if $|\varepsilon_i| \leq 1.5$ $(0 < \beta \leq 0.25)$, then (9) holds, and *there is no reduction in p_j* which will be profitable; (ii) if $|\varepsilon_i| > 1.584$ $(\beta > 0.292)$, then k_j *will match the reduction* in p_i; and (iii) if $1.5 < |\varepsilon_i| \leq 1.584$ $(0.25 < \beta \leq 0.292)$, then *there exists a $|\Delta p_j| \leq |\Delta p_i|$ which is profit increasing for both k_j and k_i.*

Proof: As a first step, we prove the following Lemma.

Lemma: Given any β, $0.5 > \beta > 0$, let $|\varepsilon_i| = 1 + 2\beta$. Then

$$(14) \qquad |\varepsilon_j| = (1 + 2\beta)/2(1 - \beta)$$

Proof: Given p^1, $q^* = 1$, $|\Delta p_i| \geqslant |\Delta p_j|$, and β, $|\varepsilon_i| \equiv (2\beta/|\Delta p_i|)p^1$, and $|\varepsilon_j| \equiv (\beta/|\Delta p_j|)(p^1/(1 - \beta))$. Therefore, $|\varepsilon_j|/|\varepsilon_i| = 1/2(1 - \beta)$.
This completes the proof of the Lemma.

Now, given p^1, if

(i) $0 < \beta \leq 0.25$, then, from (14), $|\varepsilon_j| \leq 1$, and no $|\Delta p_j|$ is profit increasing for k_j;
(ii) $0.25 < \beta < 0.5$, then, from (14), $|\varepsilon_j| > 1$ and there is some increase t, $0 < t < \beta$, in k_j's sales, such that

$$(15) \qquad |\varepsilon_j| \geq 1 + t/(1 - \beta)$$

where $t/(1 - \beta) = \Delta q_j/q_j^{-\Delta}$.

Recalling (12), we may suppose that k_j will choose the largest t satisfying (15). It then follows from (14) that

$$(16) \qquad 1 + t/(1 - \beta) = (1 + 2\beta)/2(1 - \beta)$$

or

$$(17) \qquad t = 2\beta - 0.5$$

If both k_j increase their sales by t, then k_i obtains

$$\Delta q_i = 2(\beta - t)$$

If, in this new situation,

$$(18) \qquad |\varepsilon_i| \geq 1 + 2(\beta - t)$$

then k_i will find his price reduction profitable despite the reaction of k_j.
Now suppose that

$$1 + 2(\beta - t) \leq 1 + \beta/(1 - \beta)$$

or

$$(19) \qquad t > \beta - \beta/2(1 - \beta)$$

If both (18) and (19) hold, we have a contradiction of our assumption that $p^1/2\theta < L/N$. (18) and (19) together imply $|\varepsilon_j| \geq 1 + \beta/(1 - \beta)$, so that (8) holds and $t = \beta$ is also a feasible increase for k_j. Hence $|\Delta p_j| = |\Delta p_i|$ is the profit maximising response for k_j, and k_i is then clearly worse off.

For this result to occur, both (17) and (19) must hold for given t. The range of values for which this is the case is $0.292 < \beta < 0.5$. Hence, (ii) of Proposition 2 is proved.
(iii) $0.25 < \beta \leq 0.292$, then both (15) and (18) hold for some $t > 0$. However, while (17) holds by definition (19) does not. Hence, given $|\Delta p_i|$, the largest $|\Delta p_j|$ satisfying (15) is smaller than $|\Delta p_i|$. Thus, whilst profitable price

reductions are open to both k_j and k_i, $|\Delta p_j|$ is a *non-matching* adjustment to $|\Delta p_i|$. In this restricted sense, Chamberlin's first conjecture is valid. Q.E.D.

This completes the proof of Proposition 2.

The foregoing proof, as already indicated, is based on the assumption that k_j's neighbour k_m will always match k_j's price reduction. We now prove the following proposition.

Proposition 3: Given A.1.–A.5. and D.1., if $0.5 > \beta > 0$, then, given $|\Delta p_i|$ and $0 \leq |\Delta p_j| \leq |\Delta p_i|$, k_m will choose $|\Delta p_m| = |\Delta p_j|$.

Proof: Recall the Lemma. Then:

(i) If $0 < \beta \leq 0.25$, (9) holds. The proof of Proposition 1 now applies. Since $|\Delta p_j| = 0$, $|\Delta p_m| = 0$;

(ii) if $\beta > 0.292$, the proof of (ii) of Proposition 2 applies and k_j will find it profitable to *match* k_i's price reduction irrespective of the response of k_m. But since $|\Delta p_j| = |\Delta p_i|$ leaves k_i worse off than at p^1, no price reduction will be initiated. Hence $|\Delta p_m| = |\Delta p_j| = |\Delta p_i| = 0$;

(iii) if $0.25 < \beta \leq 0.292$, then the outcome is analogous to that in the proof of Proposition 1. To see this, we refer again to Figure 4. We note from the proof of Proposition 2 that when $0.25 < \beta \leq 0.292$, k_{-1} will find it profitable to make a non-matching adjustment in price irrespective of the response of k_{-2}. By analogous argument, k_{-2}, in turn, will be able to match k_{-1}'s reduction. If k_{-3} now reduces price by the same amount as k_0, then k_{-2} is placed in the same position vis-a-vis k_{-3} and k_{-1}, as k_{-1} is vis-a-vis k_{-2} and k_0. Since, by the proof of Proposition 1, this outcome is the best that k_{-1} can expect to obtain, it must also be best for k_{-2}. Q.E.D.

This completes the proof of Proposition 3.

The implications of this investigation of Case B are quite straightforward. The extent to which the adjacent neighbours of a price reducing firm will be able to adjust their prices depends upon the precise magnitude of β. Where full adjustment is possible (Prop. 2 (ii)), no price reduction will be initiated. Where non-matching adjustment is possible (Prop. 2 (iii)), the final equilibrium configuration resembles that described in Case A, except that in the present case *all* firms sell at a price less than p^1. In this sense, the outcome is rather different than that conjectured by Chamberlin. Of course, where no profitable adjustment in response to a price reduction is possible (Prop. 2(i)), the outcome is as described in Case A.

V. SUMMARY AND CONCLUSIONS

The analysis of interactions amongst firms in chain-linked markets is complex. The outcome to rivalrous behaviour in such markets depends crucially upon the expectations structures of the agents involved. This paper has analysed the phenomenon on the basis of a structure which is both simple and plausible. Yet even here the task is complicated by subtle spatial relationships.

Nevertheless, our approach has made it possible to derive a number of interesting results. As a first step, we showed that the expectations of the agents can yield different, determinate price equilibria according to the number of firms in the market and the level of advertising expenditure. Two results of particular interest here are (i) that the likelihood of price reductions may be positively related to the level of advertising, and (ii) that the larger is the number of firms, the less likely are such price reductions. These counter-intuitive results might usefully be compared with those of, for example, Chamberlin [2] and Sweezy [8], amongst the many who have addressed these questions.

Comparison of the outcomes in Cases A and B is interesting in itself: on our assumptions, both cases yield equilibrium price configurations. Moreover, the general pattern of prices in Case B is similar to that in Case A even though the *magnitude* of the price responses may be different. An interesting question, of course, is whether this will continue to be the case even if the assumption of zero-elastic individual demands is relaxed. It will be apparent that in some of the circumstances considered the answer is in the affirmative. Whether this will always be so, and what the further implications of the model might be, must remain as subjects for future research.

R. ROTHSCHILD,
Department of Economics,
University of Lancaster,
Gillow House,
Lancaster, LA1 4YX, England.

REFERENCES

[1] Archibald, G. C. and Rosenbluth, G., "The 'New' Theory of Consumer Demand and Monopolistic Competition", *Quarterly Journal of Economics*, Vol. 89 (1975), pp. 569–90.

[2] Chamberlin, E. H., *The Theory of Monopolistic Competition*, (Cambridge, Mass.: Harvard University Press, 1956).

[3] Friedman, J. W., *Oligopoly and the Theory of Games*, (Amsterdam: North-Holland Publishing Company, 1977).

[4] Henderson, A. M., "The Theory of Duopoly", *Quarterly Journal of Economics*, Vol. 68 (1954), pp. 565–84.

[5] Kaldor, N., "Market Imperfection and Excess Capacity", *Economica* NS. 2 (1935), pp. 33–50.

[6] Lancaster, K. J., "A New Approach to Demand Theory", *Journal of Political Economy*, Vol. 74 (1966), pp. 132–57.

[7] Salop, S. C., "Monopolistic Competition with Outside Goods", *The Bell Journal of Economics*, Vol. 10, (1979), pp. 141–56.

[8] Sweezy, P. M., "Demand under Conditions of Oligopoly", *Journal of Political Economy*, Vol. 47 (1939), pp. 568–73.

THE JOURNAL OF INDUSTRIAL ECONOMICS
Volume XXXI September/December 1982 Nos. 1/2

PRODUCT PROLIFERATION IN CHARACTERISTICS SPACE: THE UK FERTILISER INDUSTRY

R. W. SHAW

IN RECENT years a number of theoretical papers have addressed both the positive and normative aspects of the problem of how competitive products may be located in characteristics space. The major theoretical antecedents have been Hotelling's analysis of spatial competition [6], Chamberlin's analysis of product differentiation [1], [2], and Lancaster's "goods characteristics" theory of demand [7]. Unfortunately there has been little corresponding empirical analysis.[1] Two approaches in the theoretical analysis seem to have predominated: firstly, the examination of the welfare implications of product variety offered in equilibrium conditions,[2] and secondly, the dynamics of product competition using the spatial competition analogy.[3] This paper which adopts the second approach uses an adaptation of Lancaster's "goods characteristics" framework. It examines the process of product competition in the UK agricultural fertiliser market.

The first and second sections briefly outline the main features of the goods characteristics and spatial competition theories, and the UK fertiliser market respectively. The third section contains the empirical analysis.

I. THE SPATIAL COMPETITION ANALOGY AND THE GOODS CHARACTERISTICS FRAMEWORK

The simplest starting point to the theory of product competition is Hotelling's analogy of spatial competition. Consider a linear market (e.g. a road) along which consumers are evenly distributed. Each consumer is assumed, initially, to have a completely inelastic demand for the good, but has to pay the transport costs of obtaining it, and so he minimises this expenditure by going to the nearest supplier. Hotelling argued that a single firm, A, could locate its plant (shop) anywhere in the market and still obtain the total market. However, when a second firm, B, entered the market the two firms would, in equilibrium, be 'back-to-back' at the centre of the market in order to maximise their market shares.

[1] Exceptions are F. M. Scherer's [11] and R. Schmalensee's [12] analyses of product variety in the breakfast cereals industry.

[2] e.g. A. M. Spence "Product Differentiation and Welfare" [14], A. K. Dixit and J. E. Stiglitz, "Monopolistic Competition and Optimal Product Variety" [3] and K. Lancaster "Socially Optimal Product Differentiation" [8].

[3] e.g. B. C. Eaton and R. G. Lipsey "The Principle of Minimum Differentiation Reconsidered: Some New Developments in the Theory of Spatial Competition [4].

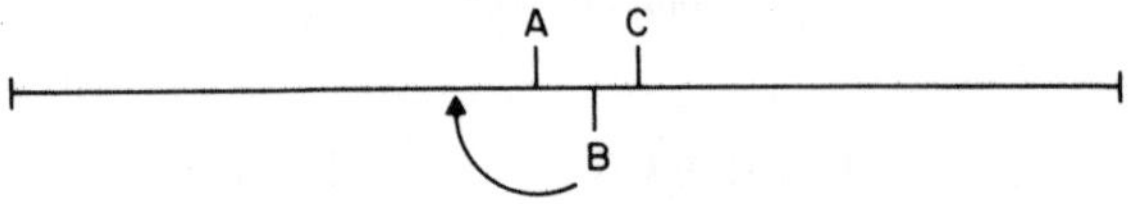

FIGURE 1
Product Location in a Linear Market.

According to Hay [5] extensions to Hotelling's work have concentrated on three aspects: the effect of increasing the number of competing firms; the relaxation of the inelastic demand assumption; and the analysis of spatial competition in a geographic plane. The effect of increasing the number of firms is considered first.

Chamberlin [1] and Lerner and Singer [9] showed that when a third firm, C, entered the market it would locate itself close to the other two but in an open segment of the market. A continuing process of leapfrogging would then ensue as the firm caught in the middle tried to expand its market share by relocating on the outer edge of the group in the largest open segment of the market. See Figure 1. In this case no equilibrium would be reached. Recently, Eaton and Lipsey [4] have extended the analysis both by further increasing the number of firms and by using more general forms of market space than Hotelling's linear market. They conclude that there can be no generalisations about the location of firms as each result depends on the number of firms, the detailed specification of their behaviour, the nature of the market space and the distribution of customers. However as Hay [5] points out they tentatively "suggest that a wide range of equilibrium and disequilibrium situations involve pairs (in one-dimensional models) or clusters (in two-dimensional models) of firms scattered over the market".

The relaxation of the inelastic demand assumption in Hotelling's model provides for the possibility of a trade-off between the desire to capture the maximum market share and the potential loss of custom as some consumers located at a distance from the firm stop buying. Thus elasticity of demand could lead to some dispersion of firms. The analysis of spatial competition in a geographic plane similarly reveals an incentive for dispersion as clustering tends to leave profitable opportunities for entry in the wide spaces with no firm. In the context of product competition in two dimensional market space it provides an incentive for established firms to increase the number and range of their products both to maintain or expand their market share and/or to deter entry, (see Scherer [11], Schmalensee [12]).

Hay's extension of the analysis was to examine the location decision of firms when the costs of relocating, or leapfrogging, were so high as to make such activity uneconomic. His model, involving sequential entry of new firms, resulted in firms being evenly scattered through the market, and hence rejected Eaton and Lipsey's outcome of clusters of firms at least in cases where demand is evenly distributed over the market. However, where demand is

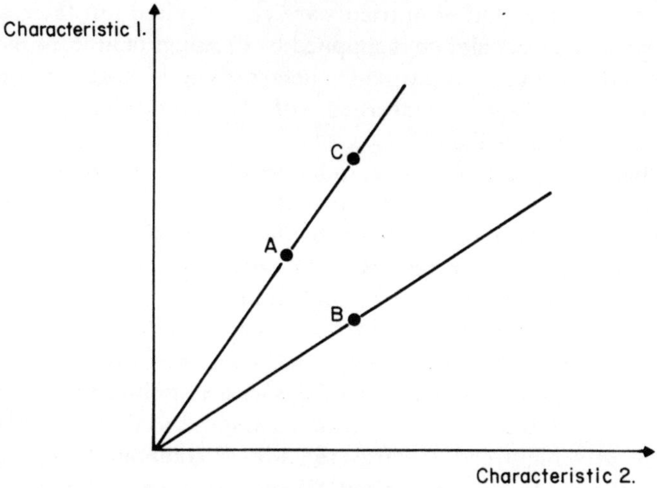

FIGURE 2
Product Location in Characteristics Space.

unevenly distributed Hay would expect a closer packing of firms in areas of high density demand with the spacing between firms increased in areas of low density. A limitation of Hay's model for the analysis of product competition is that he assumes given distributions of demand. This ignores the ability of firms to influence this distribution by advertising and other marketing techniques.

When considering product differentiation and variety it is possible to conceive of products as possessing characteristics and it is from these bundles of characteristics that consumers derive their actual utility (Lancaster [7]). Given this approach products may be located in goods characteristics space. This is illustrated in Figure 2. According to Lancaster each product is assumed to possess a given mixture of characteristics. Thus products located at A and B are clearly different since they possess the two characteristics in different proportions. However, points A and C merely represent different quantities of the same product.

The purpose of this paper is to examine two main aspects of product competition in the UK fertiliser industry. Firstly, the location of products in characteristics space will be related to the density of consumer demand in this space. Secondly, the process of competition from 1958 until 1978 will be analysed in terms of the introduction, relocation and proliferation of products using the goods characteristics framework.

II. THE UK FERTILISER INDUSTRY AND THE DEMAND FOR FERTILISERS

Agricultural fertilisers contain one or more of the following three main plant foods: nitrogen, phosphorus and potash. Individual products which contain only one of these foods are called straights, and those containing two or more are called compounds. Other nutrients are also required but these are either applied separately, e.g. calcium is supplied by dressings of lime, or included in the compounds to combat a particular deficiency, e.g. magnesium or boron. The analysis in this paper is concerned with the markets for both compound and straight nitrogen fertilisers.

At the beginning of the period under review in the late 1950s the UK compound fertiliser market was dominated by Fisons with a 40–45 per cent market share. It sold a range of compound fertilisers designed for various crops and conditions. In contrast, ICI, the other major competitor, produced only a single compound though it held approximately 20 per cent of the market (Monopolies Commission [10]). A large number of other firms also sold compound fertilisers based on materials purchased from Fisons, ICI and imports. However, there were no other firms with a significant market share.

About 1960 ICI began to expand its compound fertiliser interests partly reflecting a growing trend towards the use of compounds as opposed to straight fertilisers. In addition Shell Chemicals, which already produced straight nitrogen fertilisers, began importing compound fertilisers for the first time. In 1965 the Shell operation, now called Shellstar, became committed to manufacturing in the United Kingdom and announced that the firm intended to obtain a 20–25 per cent share of the UK fertiliser market. In 1973 Shellstar's fertiliser interests were sold to Unie van Kunstmestfabrieken (UKF) a major Dutch fertiliser firm. (The Shell-Shellstar-UKF firm will be referred to as UKF/Shellstar throughout this paper.) As a result of the latter firm's entry and ICI's expansion the compound fertiliser market was transformed from an apparently accepted (if somewhat uneasily) spheres of influence duopoly, with a large fringe of small firms, into an actively competitive oligopoly still with a fringe of small firms (Shaw [13]). By the mid 1970s the combined market share of Fisons, ICI and UKF/Shellstar was around 80 per cent.

The straight nitrogen sector of the market was dominated by ICI in the late 1950s (Shaw [13]). However UKF/Shellstar had entered the market in 1956 and by 1960 had gained approximately a 20 per cent market share. Fisons did not produce a straight nitrogen fertiliser in the 1950s and only entered the market in 1963. Although a few other firms such as Albright and Wilson also produce straight nitrogen fertilisers the market has been dominated throughout the 1960s and 1970s by the three major firms—ICI, Fisons and UKF/Shellstar. Their combined market share in the late 1970s was over 90 per cent.

This paper will concentrate on the development of competition between the three main producers.

The demand for agricultural fertilisers is based on their effects in protecting the health and stimulating the growth of crops. The particular fertiliser product required depends on the crop being grown, previous cropping history of the land, soil type and weather conditions. In the UK cereals, grass and to a lesser degree potatoes and sugar beet dominate the demand for fertilisers these crops together accounting for almost 90 per cent of the market.

As already indicated fertilisers may be classified as either straights (single plant food) or compounds (two or more plant foods). The compounds sector accounted for 73 per cent of the overall market at the beginning of the 1960s falling to 65 per cent by the late 1970s. In the straights sector nitrogen fertilisers were increasingly dominant with an 11 per cent share of the overall market at the beginning of the 1960s rising to 32 per cent by the late 1970s. Apart from some growth in the early 1960s the compound sector was virtually stagnant for most of the period while the straight nitrogen sector continued to grow at an average of over 7 per cent per year throughout the 1960s and 1970s.

III. THE LOCATION OF PRODUCTS IN CHARACTERISTICS SPACE

(i) *Identification of Product Characteristics and the Location of Products Relative to the Distribution of Demand*

In adopting the product characteristics approach it is necessary to recognise four main characteristics: a fertiliser product's percentage contents of each of the three major plant foods—nitrogen (N), phosphoric acid (P_2O_5), and potash (K_2O)—and the residual element.[4] Thus products are identified by both their plant food ratios and by the total plant food contents. For example, product A containing 16 per cent N, 8 per cent P_2O_5, 8 per cent K_2O is a 2 : 1 : 1 compound with a total of 32 per cent plant food and a 68 per cent residual; product B, containing 22 per cent N, 11 per cent P_2O_5, 11 per cent K_2O is also a 2 : 1 : 1 compound but with a total of 44 per cent plant food and a 56 per cent residual. Finally, product C, containing 10 per cent N, 10 per cent P_2O_5, 10 per cent K_2O is a 1 : 1 : 1 compound with a total of 30 per cent plant food and a 70 per cent residual.[5] Products A and C are clearly different in that they contain the three main plant foods in different proportions. Products A and B, however, share the same plant food ratios—2 : 1 : 1, the only difference being in the level of concentration of plant food. This difference is significant in that farmers can obtain the same total application of plant food from a smaller tonnage of product B than of product A. The farmer using the more concentrated compound may consequently benefit from savings in his storage, transport and application costs.[6]

Although there is an infinite number of possible combinations of the four characteristics some order can be imposed using the Fertiliser Manufacturers

[4] This is a simplification which ignores such factors as the hardness and the regularity in size and surface qualities of the fertiliser granules. These factors may affect the storage and spreading characteristics of the product.

[5] Hereafter it should be understood that plant food contents are expressed as percentages. Hence product A will be identified as 16N, $8P_2O_5$, $8K_2O$.

[6] Up to 1974 fertiliser subsidies were paid to farmers based on the plant food contents of the fertilisers. This lowered the effective price per tonne of product of more concentrated fertilisers by more than less concentrated fertilisers. No subsidy was paid on the potash content.

Association (FMA) classification of compounds. This classifies products according to whether there are two plant foods, the binary products, or three plant foods. In the latter case the classification is based on the distinctive characteristic of the product. Thus product A with 16N, $8P_2O_5$, $8K_2O$ and a plant food ratio of 2 : 1 : 1 is classified as a "high N" product. Conversely, another product with 10N, $20P_2O_5$, $20K_2O$ and a plant food ratio of 1 : 2 : 2 is classified as a "low N" product. In the same way other products are classified as high and low phosphoric acid, or "high P" and "low P" respectively. Similarly there are high and low potash products, or "high K" and "low K" respectively. Table I shows the changing number of compound fertiliser products from 1962/63 to 1977/78 using the FMA classification. It should be noted that from the mid 1970s the high N group was split into two categories "high N" and "extra high N". Table I also shows the changing distribution of

TABLE I

DISTRIBUTION OF COMPOUND FERTILISER PRODUCTS OF THE THREE MAJOR FIRMS BY PLANT FOOD CHARACTERISTICS AND UK DISTRIBUTION OF SALES.[1]

	1962/1963		*1966/1967*		*1970/1971*		*1974/1975*		*1977/1978*	
Product Group[2]	*Number of products*	*Percentage of total sales*	*Number of products*	*Percentage of total sales*	*Number of products*	*Percentage of total sales*	*Number of products*	*Percentage of total sales*	*Number of products*	*Percentage of total sales*
Extra High Nitrogen	1 }	27.6 (both groups)	3 }	44.3 (both groups)	3 }	48.4 (both groups)	7	11.0	9	17.4
High Nitrogen	5 }		7 }		12 }		12	46.0	11	37.8
Low Nitrogen	3	12.1	4	9.7	7	11.0	6	9.1	6	11.5
1 : 1 : 1	1	5.1	3	7.0	4	6.7	4	5.7	3	5.2
High Phosphoric Acid	1	7.9	3	4.8	4	4.5	4	3.5	5	3.5
Low Phosphoric Acid	4	3.5	5	2.9	7	2.6	9	4.7	13	5.6
High Potash	10	37.9	14	26.1	14	21.0	11	13.2	11	11.1
Low Potash	–	0.4	–	0.3	1	0.2	1	0.2	1	0.1
Binary	4	5.5	6	4.9	7	5.6	7	6.6	10	7.8
Total	29	100.0	45	100.0	59	100.0	61	100.0	69	100.0
Total products by Company[3,4]										
Fisons	22		30		37		39		43	
ICI	5		10		15		12		13	
UKF/Shellstar	2		5		7		10		13	

Sources: Fertiliser Statistics; Company Product Lists; Trade Press.

[1] The 1974/75 and 1977/78 sales distribution percentages relate to the United Kingdom. Earlier sales percentages relate to Great Britain.

[2] Product groups are based on contents of nitrogen, phosphoric acid and potash.

[3] The product list is confined to granular fertilisers and excludes powder and liquid fertilisers. Powder fertilisers were being phased out in the 1950s in the main agricultural fertiliser market. Liquid fertilisers were unimportant in the 1960s and accounted for under 5 per cent of the compound fertiliser market in the mid 1970s. Granular compounds, with additives such as aldrin or boron are counted as separate products. Only products included in the parent firm's product list are included. Products offered by subsidiaries such as Scottish Agricultural Industries and Hadfields are excluded. The specialist fruit and vegetable granular fertilisers originally produced by Fisons Horticultural but subsequently included in Fisons Agricultural Division main product list have been included throughout the period.

[4] The practice of introducing products in restricted geographical areas prior to their inclusion in the main product list is a potential source of ambiguity in dating the introduction of new products. In general the dating adopted is based on advertisements in the trade press.

compound fertiliser sales and finally the total number of compounds marketed by each of the three main companies. (See Table I footnotes).

Even before any detailed analysis of the competitive behaviour of the main firms it is apparent that the 1960s and to a lesser extent the 1970s have been periods of product proliferation. However, it should be noted that the growth in the number of products far outstripped the growth in total sales of compound fertilisers. The number of products doubled between 1962/63 and 1970/71, and increased by 17 per cent between 1970/71 and 1977/78. Based on the average sales of compound fertilisers (in tonnes of plant food) over the three years around each product census date sales increased in the two periods by only 18.5 per cent and 3.6 per cent respectively.

Table I also shows that although the distribution of products has broadly reflected the distribution of sales between product groups ("high N", "low N" etc.) the degree of correspondence between the market share of a product group and the number of products has been far from complete. In general the product groups with the largest market shares such as high potash and high (plus extra high) nitrogen have had the highest number of products. Conversely, product groups with low market shares such as low potash and high phosphoric acid have had only a small number of products. However the number of products did not increase proportionately as market share grew. For instance in 1977/78, considering only the products of the three major companies, the average market share of each compound in the "high N" product group as 3.4 per cent. For the low phosphoric acid and high potash groups it was 0.4 and 1.0 per cent respectively. The conclusion that the number of products is related only very roughly to the distribution of sales is unaltered if two other smaller "national" fertiliser firms are included in the analysis.[7]

The product groups identified in Table I provide the basis for much of the detailed analysis. Product space can be reduced to two dimensions for the important product groups because of a fortunate tendency of compound fertilisers to contain two of the three main plant foods in identical (or at least similar) proportions. Thus "high N" products often have plant food ratios of the 2 : 1 : 1 or 1.5 : 1 : 1 types where nitrogen is the major plant food with phosphoric acid and potash contributing smaller but identical food contents. Figure 3 illustrates the method for the "high N", "1 : 1 : 1", and "low N" product groups. The nitrogen content expressed as a percentage is shown on the vertical axis. The phosphoric acid and potash contents, again expressed as percentages, are shown on the horizontal axis. Increasing total food content (i.e. the sum of the percentage contents of the three main plant foods) is shown by moving northeasterly away from the origin. Such a movement necessarily denotes a decrease in the residual content of the fertiliser so that each point on the diagram simultaneously captures a particular plant food ratio and the

[7] Albright and Wilson, and Lindsey and Kesteven.

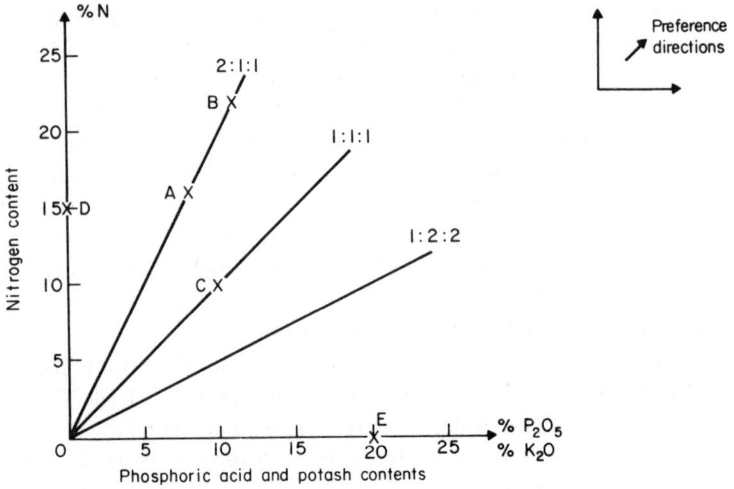

FIGURE 3
Location of Fertiliser Products in Characteristics Space.

residual content of the product. It should be noted that the theoretically feasible set is bounded at 100 per cent total plant food content. In practice technical and economic problems bounded the feasible set at between 40 and 60 per cent total plant food content in the 1960s and 1970s.

Products A, B and C previously referred to are shown in the diagram. Product A is a high N 2 : 1 : 1 product with 16N, $8P_2O_5$, $8K_2O$. Product B is also a high N 2 : 1 : 1 product but is more concentrated having 22N, $11P_2O_5$, $11K_2O$. Since products A and B have the same plant food ratio they lie on the same ray through the origin. Product C is a 1 : 1 : 1 product containing 10N, $10P_2O_5$, $10K_2O$. Since higher concentration products, if offered to farmers at the same price per unit of each plant food as a similar less concentrated product, as in practice they generally were,[8] enable the farmer to enjoy savings in storage, transport and application costs the preference directions are northeasterly. For completeness product D in figure 3 is a straight nitrogen fertiliser (i.e. zero phosphoric acid and potash contents) containing 15N, and product E is a binary compound fertiliser containing $20P_2O_5$, $20K_2O$ and zero nitrogen.

Aside from the questions of product proliferation and of how closely the distributions of products and sales are related there are four further questions that require attention. Firstly, are products "relocated" as firms engage in leapfrogging in an attempt to secure market share (Eaton and Lipsey [4]) or are products essentially fixed in location as assumed by Hay [5] in his analysis

[8] An exception occurred in the straight nitrogen sector where high concentration fertilisers (e.g. 34N) were offered at a lower price per unit of nitrogen than the less concentrated fertilisers (e.g. 26N).

of spatial competition? Secondly, is there a tendency for products to cluster together in characteristics space as suggested by the principle of minimum differentiation (Eaton and Lipsey [4])? Thirdly, are new products normally located in the largest open space? Finally, to what extent are product competition and technical progress related?

(ii) *Fixed versus "Relocated Products", Product Proliferation, and Technical Change*

The problem of fixed versus relocated products may be approached both by observing the number of years over which compound fertiliser products are retained, and by examining the relative number of products that firms keep unchanged compared with products that are replaced or relocated. In addition the extent of product proliferation can be identified by comparing the number of completely new products with the other two categories. Table II presents the relevant data on unchanged, relocated, and additional or new products. Four dates were chosen to allow three sets of product changes with each time period being sufficiently long to provide considerable scope for product changes if firms so desired. The starting year, 1958/59 was the first year in which ICI began to expand its compound fertiliser product range and was just before UKF/Shellstar entered the compound fertiliser market. The closing year, 1977/78, was the final year for which data were collected. The

TABLE II
COMPOUND FERTILISER PRODUCT CHANGES BY THE THREE MAJOR FIRMS 1958/59–1977/78.[1]

	Product List Comparisons: Number and Percentages of Products					
Change category	*1964/65 with 1958/59 number of products*	*Percentage of total products in 1964/65*	*1970/71 with 1964/65 number of products*	*Percentage of total products in 1970/71*	*1977/78 with 1970/71 number of products*	*Percentage of total products in 1977/78*
Unchanged products	6	17.1	21	35.6	33	47.8
Replacement products	11	31.5	13	22.0	14	20.3
(i) higher concentration unchanged plant food ratio	3		5		1	
(ii) higher concentration changed plant food ratio	7		7		2	
(iii) unchanged (roughly) concentration, changed plant food ratio	1		1		11	
New products	18	51.4	25	42.4	22	31.9
Total number of products at later date	35	100	59	100	69	100

See footnotes 3 and 4 table I for details of products included in the analysis.

two intermediate years, 1964/65 and 1970/71 were chosen largely to give approximately equal intervals for the product list comparisons.

Table II, which identifies the product changes made by the three main firms over the three subperiods, indicates clearly that unchanged products together with completely new products (proliferation) dominated any tendency for firms to relocate products by replacing existing with other products. For instance in 1964/65 only 31 per cent of products were replacement products relocated in characteristics space compared with the 1958/59 base year. However, 51 per cent of products were completely new indicating the extent of product proliferation in the early 1960s.

The second major feature of this period was the technical progress represented by the development of new products containing higher total plant food contents (i.e. a lower residual). Ten of the eleven replacement products had a higher total plant food content than their predecessors. Further the eighteen new products had an average total plant food concentration of 42.7 per cent compared with the average total plant food concentration of all products in 1958/59 of only 33.2 per cent. Indeed, only one of the new products had a lower total plant food concentration—30 per cent—than the 1958/59 average.

The relative importance of product relocation declined in the two subsequent subperiods with replacement products accounting for only about 20 per cent of all products in both 1970/71 and 1977/78. While new, or additional, products continued to be more important than replacement products the main change was in the growing importance of unchanged products. Over a third of all products in 1970/71 were unchanged compared with the 1964/65 list, and nearly a half of the 1977/78 products were unchanged compared with the 1970/71 list. Indeed, of the sixty-nine compound fertilisers available in 1977/78 approximately a third had remained unchanged for ten years and eight for fifteen years. Once a new product became established firms tended to retain it. It thus appears that either the "fixed" product location model suggested by Hay is more descriptive of the compound fertiliser market than the "free" relocation model or if the latter model is correct firms were often able to choose the optimal long term location of products immediately.

Technical progress, represented by the increased total plant food concentration of compound fertilisers, continued in the second sub-period between 1964/65 and 1970/71. Twelve of the thirteen replacement products had a higher total plant food concentration than their predecessors. The average total plant food concentration of the twenty-five new products listed in 1970/71 was 44.3 per cent compared with the average of all products in 1964/65 of 40.3 per cent.

In the final sub-period between 1970/71 and 1977/78 the movement towards higher total plant food concentration was not maintained. Of the fourteen replacement products eleven showed little or no change in the total plant food concentration compared with their predecessors. Further, the average total plant food concentration of the new, or additional products listed in

1977/78 was only 42.5 per cent compared with the average total plant food concentration for all products of 44.8 per cent already achieved in 1970/71. Thus, in the 1970s product competition has involved a continued proliferation of compound fertilisers together with some adjustment in plant food ratios but no overall movement towards increasing the plant food concentration of fertilisers. This change partly reflected technical limitations imposed by the basic raw materials and partly a growing emphasis on trimming plant food content in order to keep the price per tonne of product down.

(iii) *Product Clustering and the Location of New and Replacement Products*

The examination of Eaton and Lipsey's hypothesis that products will tend to cluster in groups and the related hypothesis that products will tend to be located in the largest open space is carried out in two ways. Firstly, there is a detailed analysis of product competition within the extra high nitrogen; high nitrogen; 1 : 1 : 1; and low nitrogen product groups identified in Table I. These groups together accounted for over 40 per cent of compound fertiliser sales in the early 1960s and over 70 per cent of sales in 1977/78. The analysis follows the approach outlined in Figure 3. As in Figure 3, for completeness, the very important straight nitrogen products and binary phosphoric acid and potash compounds are included. The second part of the analysis is devoted to a less detailed examination of the product clustering hypothesis for all compound and straight nitrogen fertilisers.

Figure 4 shows the proliferation of products in the product groups for detailed consideration at two yearly intervals from 1958/59 until 1976/77. Figure 5, on a larger scale shows the product distribution in 1970/71 and in 1977/78. The movement of products outwards from the origin as more concentrated fertilisers were developed is readily apparent. Similarly, there is the development of a clear frontier with total plant food concentration ranging from about 40 per cent for extra high nitrogen compounds to about 60 per cent for low nitrogen products. The examination of the dynamics of product competition requires at least initially a step by step approach as the pattern of product location in characteristics space emerged. The text should be read in conjunction with the sequence of diagrams in Figure 4. Attention is focussed initially on product developments in the "high N" sector above the 1 : 1 : 1 product ray.

In 1958/59 Fisons was the only one of the three major firms offering compounds in the groups under discussion. UKF/Shellstar had not entered the compound fertiliser market though it did offer a straight nitrogen product. ICI merely offered 12N, $12P_2O_5$, $18K_2O$ (high potash) and 16N, $0P_2O_5$, $16K_2O$ (binary-nitrogen and potash) compounds. Either of these compounds could be combined with ICI's straight nitrogen fertiliser to satisfy farmers requiring a high application of nitrogen along with other plant foods. While this might be satisfactory for some crops and soil conditions where it was

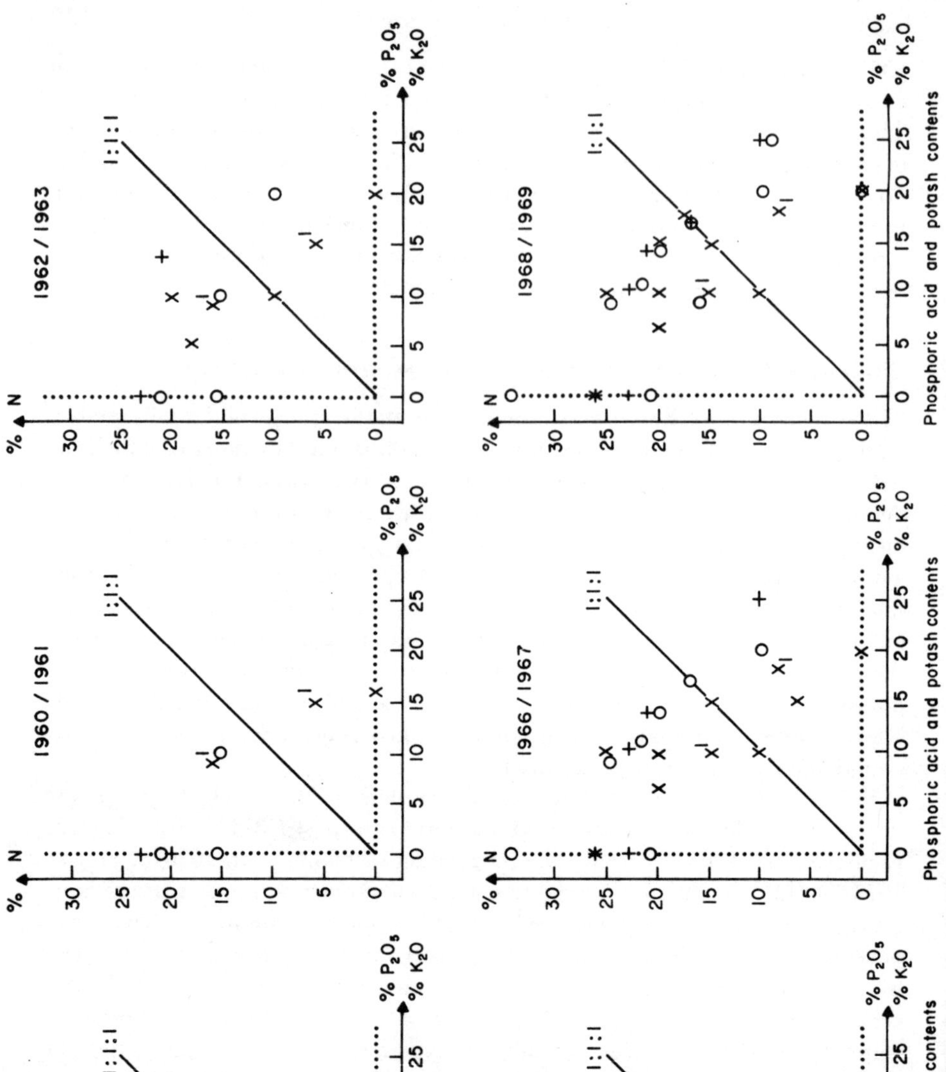

1958 / 1959
1960 / 1961
1962 / 1963
1964 / 1965
1966 / 1967
1968 / 1969
1:1:1
1.5:1:1
2:1:1
% N
Nitrogen content
% P2O5
% K2O
Phosphoric acid and potash contents

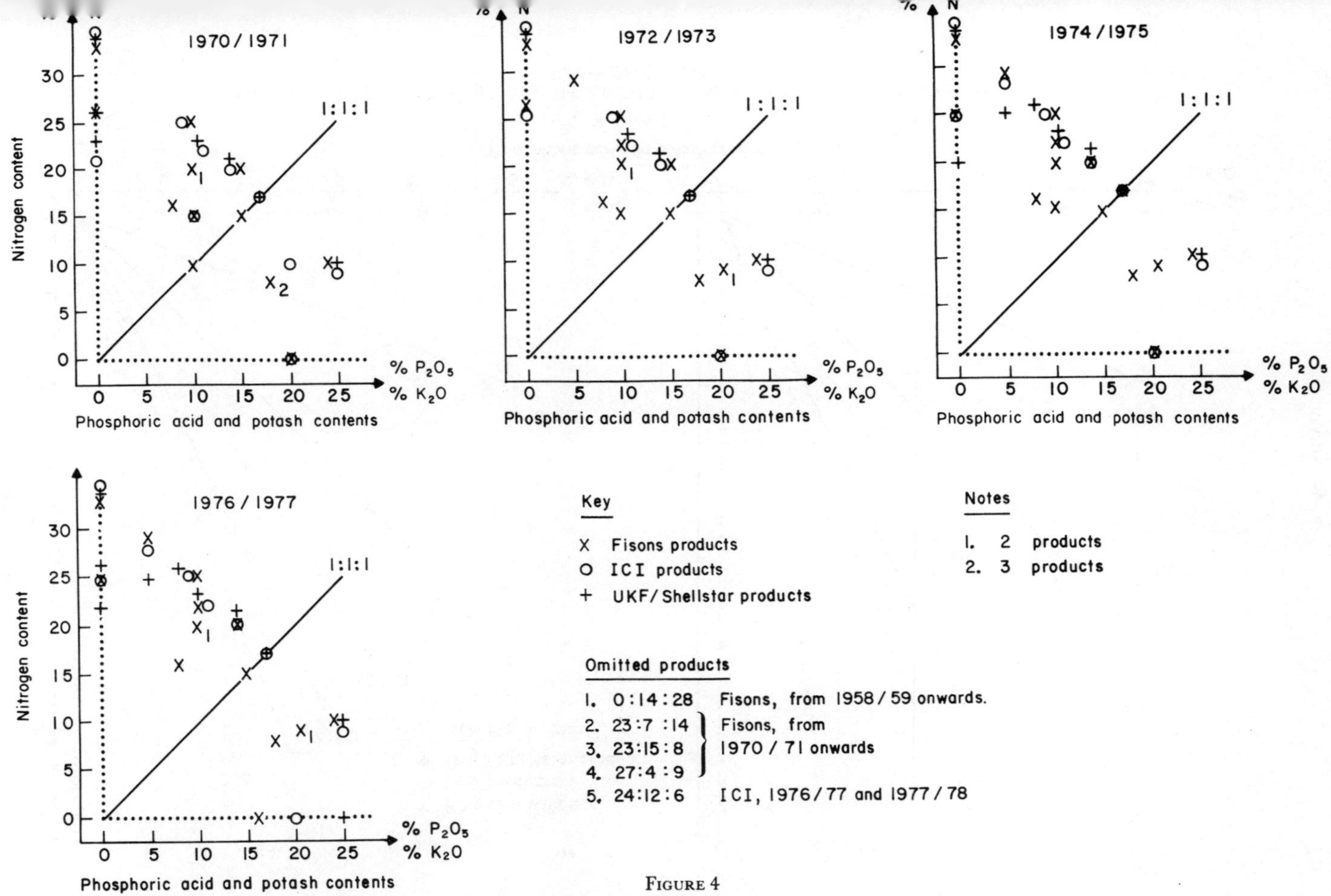

FIGURE 4

Distribution of Fertiliser Products in the Straight Nitrogen; High N; 1 : 1 : 1; Low N; and Binary PK Groups.

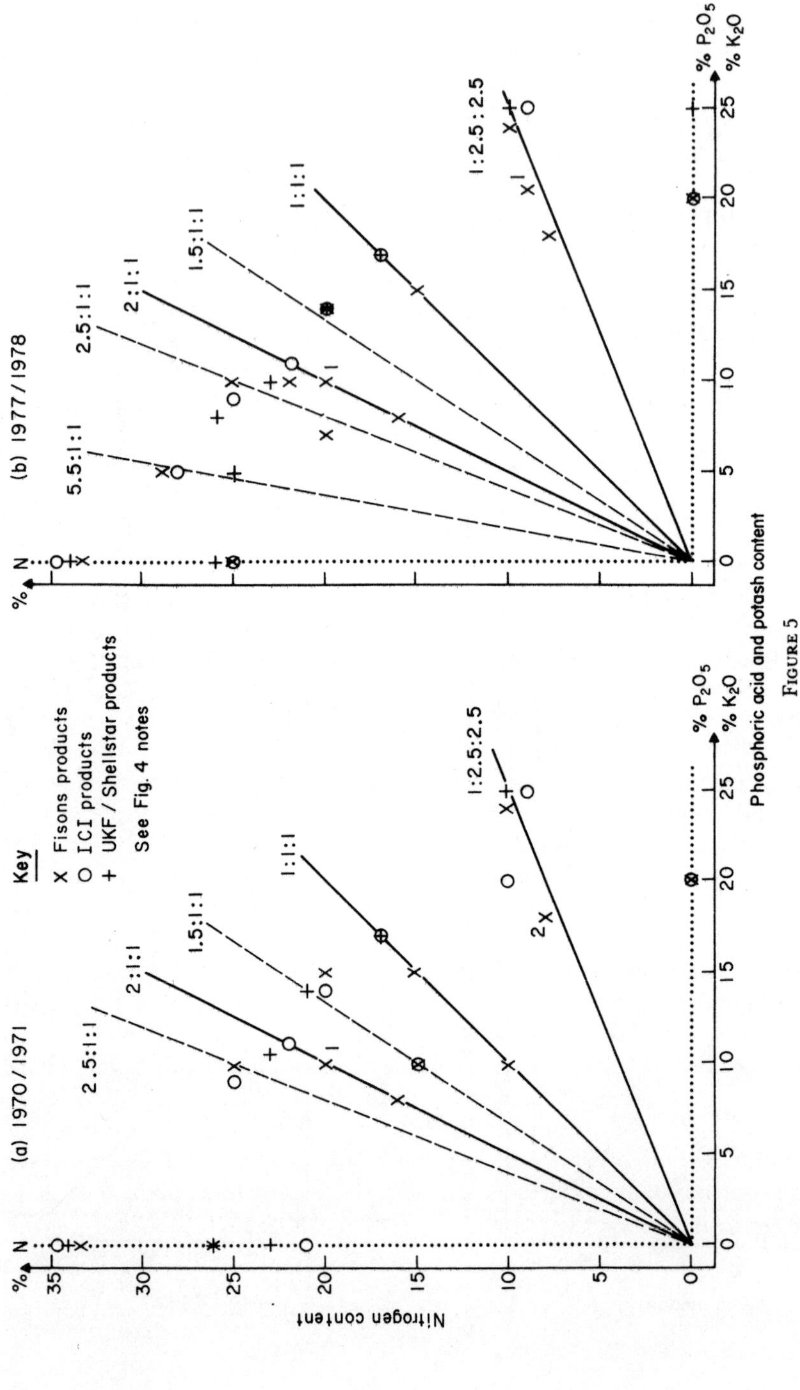

FIGURE 5

Distribution of Fertiliser Products in the Straight Nitrogen; High N; 1 : 1 : 1; Low N; and Binary PK Groups.

sensible to provide plant foods in two or more fertiliser applications (e.g. winter wheat) it was more costly, because of additional application costs, than providing all the required plant food in a single dressing where this was technically efficient, (e.g. spring wheat and barley). In the latter case ICI was at a competitive disadvantage compared to Fisons with its "high N" 12N, $9P_2O_5$, $9K_2O$ product.[9] This problem was exacerbated in 1959/60 when Fisons introduced its "high N" 16 : 9 : 9 compound which was explicitly advertised as enabling the farmer to provide "spring corn" with all its plant food requirements in a single application.

In 1960/61 ICI introduced its first "high N" compound with 15 : 10 : 10 plant food content. In conformity with the principle of minimum differentiation it seems to have been located both close to Fisons 16 : 9 : 9 product and perhaps in an open segment of the market bearing in mind that ICI already had a straight nitrogen fertiliser for farmers requiring particularly high applications of nitrogen.

By 1962/63 Fisons appear to have replied to the ICI challenge by adding two new products, 20 : 10 : 10 and 10 : 10 : 10 which neatly bracketed ICI's "high N" 15 : 10 : 10 so limiting the market space available to the latter product. Fisons also retained its 16 : 9 : 9 product. Finally, Fisons Horticulture introduced a range of specialist fertilisers for vegetable crops in May 1962 designed mainly for market gardeners. The range included a "high N" 18 : 5 : 6. However, since the market gardening and main agricultural markets were largely separate, and indeed served by separate parts of Fisons organisation, this last product did not figure significantly in the main product competition discussed in this section.

Meanwhile in 1961/62 UKF/Shellstar had entered the high nitrogen sector with its first product—21 : 14 : 14. This retained the 1.5 : 1 : 1 plant food ratio of ICI's 15 : 10 : 10 and Fisons roughly comparable 16 : 9 : 9 products but offered a higher total plant food concentration. In so far as farmers' requirements are defined partly in terms of particular plant food ratios the UKF/Shellstar product was minimally differentiated from the Fisons and ICI products but significantly differentiated by total plant food concentration in the preferred direction. In the latter sense it was located in the largest open space available.

The next move in 1963/64 was by ICI which countered, firstly, its having been squeezed by Fisons emerging range of products. This was done by offering an equivalent "high N" 2 : 1 : 1 product to Fisons 20 : 10 : 10, but with a marginally higher total plant food concentration, 22 : 11 : 11. This appears to be a case of minimum differentiation with the higher total plant food concentration providing open space in the preferred direction. Secondly, ICI's

[9] The contents of compounds are further abbreviated by omitting the chemical formulae. Thus the 12N, $9P_2O_5$, $9K_2O$ product is abbreviated to 12 : 9 : 9. The plant food contents are always shown in the same order—NPK.

product also partially countered UKF/Shellstar's 21 : 14 : 14 by limiting the product space available to the latter product.

Finally, for the "high N" compounds up to 1964/65 UKF/Shellstar responded in that year with its 23 : 10 : 11 compound. This product seems to satisfy two of the predictions in location theory: it was minimally differentiated from ICI's 22 : 11 : 11 and Fisons 20 : 10 : 10, and it was located in the largest open segment for the "high N" group.

As is apparent from the sequence of diagrams up to 1964/65 there were relatively few product developments outside the "high N" group. However, for the straight nitrogen products (on the vertical axis) there were two significant developments. Firstly, ICI introduced a substantially more concentrated product with 34.5N in 1964/65 than any of its rivals. Secondly, Fisons entered the straight nitrogen market for the first time in the same year. Finally, in the "low N" sector (below the 1 : 1 : 1 product ray) ICI introduced its first product in 1962/63, a 10 : 20 : 20 compound. As may be seen from the diagram for that year it was aimed at the same market as Fisons existing 6 : 15 : 15 products but it could hardly be described as minimally differentiated. Fisons responded by offering an additional product with 8N, $20P_2O_5$, $16K_2O$, (averaged as 8 : 18 : 18 in Figure 4). None of these products had plant food ratios or total plant food concentrations that were particularly close to each other.

By 1964/65 a clear pattern is apparent in the distribution of products in characteristics space. Firstly there were the rival straight nitrogen products on the vertical axis. Secondly there were two sub groupings of high nitrogen compounds on the 2 : 1 : 1 and 1.5 : 1 : 1 product rays. Thirdly, there were Fisons 1 : 1 : 1 products. Fourthly, there was the group of "low N" compounds referred to above, and finally Fisons had a binary phosphate and potash compound on the horizontal axis. The subsequent developments up to 1970/71 may be summarized in terms of these groupings with the addition of a new "high N" subgrouping along the 2.5 : 1 : 1 product ray.

On the vertical axis, or straight nitrogen ray, UKF/Shellstar precisely matched Fisons 26N product in 1966/67. This was the first time that two of the major firms had "identical" products in the groups being considered in Figure 4. The other development was that first Fisons with its 33.5N straight nitrogen product introduced in 1969/70 and then UKF/Shellstar with its 34N product introduced in 1970/71 combined to form a tight group of minimally differentiated products with ICI's 34.5N introduced in 1964/65. The long delay in these responses reflected ICI's technological lead in switching to a concentrated ammonium nitrate product. Neither UKF/Shellstar nor Fisons had the capacity or the technology to mount a swift response. This example suggests a possible weakness in the minimum differentiation hypothesis: firms may only offer minimally differentiated products if they have matching technological capabilities. In industries experiencing technological progress gaps in capability may emerge with resulting significant gaps between products.

On the extra high nitrogen 2.5 : 1 : 1 ray ICI and Fisons simultaneously introduced very similar products, 25 : 10 : 10, and 25 : 9 : 9 in 1966/67 in a segment which had previously been an open space. On the neighbouring 2 : 1 : 1 ray the only new products introduced after 1964/65 were Fisons 20 : 10 : 10 plus 0.32 per cent boron and its 16 : 8 : 8 plus 4 per cent magnesium. However these products were joining an existing group of compounds in which all three firms were already represented.

On the 1.5 : 1 : 1 ray UKF/Shellstars 21 : 14 : 14 compound was joined first by ICI's 20 : 14 : 14 compound in 1965/66 and then by Fisons 20 : 15 : 15 compound in 1967/68 to form a tight cluster of minimally differentiated products. At a lower level of plant food concentration ICI's 15 : 10 : 10 was first abandoned and later reinstated as a 15 : 10 : 10 plus a boron additive while Fisons filled the gap vacated by ICI. As a result of these moves the two firms again had minimally differentiated rival products.

On the 1 : 1 : 1 ray where only Fisons was represented in 1964/65 ICI introduced a more concentrated product in 1966/67. UKF/Shellstar responded with an identical 17 : 17 : 17 product in 1967/68 and Fisons added a 17.6 : 17.6 : 17.6 product a year later. The latter product seemed to be splitting hairs as far as increased concentration and minimum differentiation was concerned. Fisons later dropped this product.

In the "low N" sector beneath the 1 : 1 : 1 ray there were few developments. However, one further cluster of minimally differentiated products emerged. UKF/Shellstar introduced a 10 : 25 : 25 compound in 1966/67. Although intended for the same winter cereals market as the existing products in the "low N" segment it was clearly differentiated from its rivals (see 1966/67 diagram). However, ICI responded only a year later with its 9 : 25 : 25 compound and Fisons followed in 1969/70 with its 10 : 24 : 24 compound. These three products were clearly minimally differentiated. Finally, on the horizontal axis ICI introduced a binary phosphate and potash product identical to that of Fisons.

The step by step approach can now be abandoned since a clear pattern of product location had emerged by the beginning of the 1970s. This is illustrated in Figure 5 with its enlarged diagram for 1970/71. Firstly, despite the sharply increased number of products only rarely did any of the three major firms offer a product identical to that of another major firm. In the groupings being considered in Figures 4 and 5 there were only three pairs of identical products in 1970/71. Both Fisons and ICI had a binary 0 : 20 : 20 product; both ICI and UKF/Shellstar had a 17 : 17 : 17 product; and finally both Fisons and UKF/Shellstar had a 26N straight nitrogen product. The only other instance of apparently identical products is that both Fisons and ICI had a 15 : 10 : 10 compound. However, in this case ICI's 15 : 10 : 10 also had a boron additive thus differentiating it from Fisons product.

Secondly, as indicated by the rays drawn in the 1970/71 diagram nearly all the products at that stage conformed to seven main plant food ratios. All three firms offered straight nitrogen products and both ICI and Fisons had binary PK products. In the interior of the diagram in the "extra high N" and "high N" groups three main plant food ratios had emerged: 2.5 : 1 : 1; 2 : 1 : 1; and 1.5 : 1 : 1. On the 1.5 : 1 : 1 plant food ratio ray there were two clusters of products: firstly Fisons' 20 : 15 : 15, ICI's 20 : 14 : 14 and UKF/Shellstar's 21 : 14 : 14, and secondly the two 15 : 10 : 10 products, one with boron and one without. On the 2 : 1 : 1 ray there were Fisons' 20 : 10 : 10 and 20 : 10 : 10 plus boron, ICI's 22 : 11 : 11 and UKF/Shellstar's 23 : 10 : 11. In addition Fisons also had a less concentrated product containing 16 : 8 : 8 plus magnesium. Between these two groupings around the 1.5 : 1 : 1 and 2 : 1 : 1 rays no products were offered. The "extra high N" ray had two closely competitive products: Fisons' 25 : 10 : 10 and ICI's 25 : 9 : 9. Only three extra, and high nitrogen products are omitted from the diagram because their plant food contents cannot be reduced to two dimensions: Fisons 27 : 4 : 9; 23 : 7 : 14 and 23 : 15 : 8. These vegetable and fruit fertilisers were clearly isolated products with no close substitutes offered by ICI or UKF/Shellstar.

On the 1 : 1 : 1 plant food ratio ray ICI and UKF/Shellstar both offered 17 : 17 : 17 compounds and Fisons offered 10 : 10 : 10 and 15 : 15 : 15 compounds. Again, there were no products offered with plant food ratios between the "high N" 1.5 : 1 : 1 grouping and the 1 : 1 : 1 products. Another large gap then occurred before the first "low N" product with a 1 : 2 : 2 ratio—ICI's 10 : 20 : 20. Fisons offered three broadly competitive but obviously distinct products which have been given an averaged location on the diagram: 8 : 20 : 16; 8 : 20 : 16 plus boron; and 8 : 16 : 20. Finally there was a tight cluster on the 1 : 2.5 : 2.5 ray: Fisons' 10 : 24 : 24; ICI's 9 : 25 : 25; and UKF/Shellstar's 10 : 25 : 25. Another large gap existed with no products being offered until the two binary PK products are reached.

Although identical competitive products were rare there was a clear tendency for product clusters to emerge. In order to allow some quantification of the visual impression obtained from the diagram product clusters have been given an arbitrary, but hopefully reasonable, definition consistent with the concept of minimum differentiation. For three or more competitive products a cluster is a group of products offered by rival firms in which the total plant food content (nitrogen + phosphoric acid + potash)[10] of each product is within 10 per cent of the median percentage for the group, *and* each individual plant food percentage (e.g. nitrogen 20 per cent) is within 10 per cent of the median percentage for the group, or an individual plant food percentage content is only a single percentage point from a competitive product. An example is given in the appendix. For two competitive products a cluster exists where the products total plant food contents and the individual plant food percentages are within 10 per cent of each other. Once again if an

[10] Plus magnesium in the few cases it was added.

individual plant food content is within a single percentage point of the rival product a cluster may still exist despite the breaking of the 10 per cent rule.

According to these criteria the 1970/71 diagram in Figure 5 contains seven clusters of competitive products. In addition there were the three groups of identical products previously referred to. A further three products possessed the same, or very similar plant food ratios as other products but had significantly different total plant food content (e.g. Fisons 10 : 10 : 10 and 15 : 15 : 15 products were less concentrated than ICI and UKF/Shellstar's 17 : 17 : 17 products). Finally, the remaining eight products, including the three vegetable and fruit fertilisers, were isolated in the sense that they did not satisfy any of the above criteria for similarity to other firms products. Thus of the 36 products involved only 6 had an identical rival but 19 were minimally differentiated from rival products.

By 1977/78, the final year examined, two new clusters had formed and there was some suggestion of an increase in the number of identical products within clusters or groupings; see Figure 5. In the "straight N" group the cluster around 34N still existed but the low concentration cluster of 21 and 23N had regrouped with three products (two identical) around 25 per cent N. In the "extra High N" group the 2.5 : 1 : 1 cluster now had all three firms represented and a new cluster of three products with an even higher nitrogen concentration had emerged. In the "high N" groups the two earlier clusters on the 2 : 1 : 1 and 1.5 : 1 : 1 product rays remained.

The 2 : 1 : 1 cluster now consisted of five products (three Fisons and one each of ICI and UKF/Shellstar). By this stage the gaps between products on and between the 2 : 1 : 1 and 2.5 : 1 : 1 rays had become minimal. On the 1.5 : 1 : 1 ray all three firms now had identical products—20 : 14 : 14. The lower concentration cluster of 15 : 10 : 10 and 15 : 10 : 10 plus boron had disappeared. In the 1 : 1 : 1 group the only change was the disappearance of the lowest concentration product. ICI and UKF/Shellstar still offered identical 17 : 17 : 17 products with Fisons offering a less concentrated compound. In the "low N" group the 1 : 2.5 : 2.5 cluster of three products was unchanged. Finally, Fisons and ICI still offered identical binary 0 : 20 : 20 PK products with UKF/Shellstar now offering a more concentrated 0 : 25 : 25 PK compound. As in 1970/71 there were clear gaps between clusters of products. No products were offered between the 2 : 1 : 1 and 1.5 : 1 : 1 groupings, nor between the 1.5 : 1 : 1 and 1 : 1 : 1 groups. Even larger gaps existed between the 1 : 1 : 1 and 1 : 2.5 : 2.5, and finally the 1 : 2.5 : 2.5 and binary PK groupings. The four products with plant food ratios that cannot be shown in the diagram (see omitted products list in Figure 4) do not affect these gaps.

Despite some changes the general pattern apparent in 1970/71 still remained in 1977/78. Of the 39 products involved 9 were identical whereas 18 were minimally differentiated in clusters. A further 3 products shared the same plant food ratio as other products but were clearly differentiated by total plant food concentration. Finally, the 9 remaining products were isolated.

TABLE III
SELECTED EXAMPLES OF FERTILISER RECOMMENDATIONS (ICI, 1974/75)

Product group	Approximate plant food ratio	Spring cereals			Sugar beet			Grassland		
		N	P_2O_5	K_2O	N	P_2O_5	K_2O	N	P_2O_5	K_2O
"Extra High N"	5.6 : 1 : 1							28	5	5
	2.8 : 1 : 1	25	9	9				25	9	9
"High N"	2 : 1 : 1	22	11	11	22	11	11	22	11	11
	1.5 : 1 : 1	20	14	14	20	14	14	20	14	14
	2.5 : 1 : 1.75	20	8	14				20	8	14
"Low N"	1 : 2.5 : 2.5	9	25	25						
"High K"	1 : 1 : 1.5	15	15	21				15	15	21
	2 : 1 : 3				15	7	23			
Binary	1.5 : 0 : 1							20	0	16
"Straight N"		25	0	0				25	0	0
		34.5	0	0				34.5	0	0

Products were, on the whole differentiated, but in many cases the degree of differentiation was minimal.

One explanation for the clustering of products around such ratios as 2 : 1 : 1; 1.5 : 1 : 1 and 1 : 1 : 1 with few intermediate products would be based on the scientific evidence that crops required fertilisers close to these particular plant food ratios with the result that there would be no demand for fertilisers with ratios of 1.75 : 1 : 1 or 1.25 : 1 : 1. While it is possible that nature requires such tidy plant food combinations as 2 : 1 : 1 and 1 : 1 : 1 it is to say the least intuitively implausible. The evidence that farmers only ask for such ratios explains nothing; farmers ask for products that have been recommended—and these are, of course, the existing products. However, both the Ministry of Agriculture and the firms' own recommendations suggest that the agricultural science requirement is for a variety of fertiliser products. This may be illustrated by summarising ICI's range of recommended fertilisers for 1974/75 for three major crops. (See Table III.) It seems clear both that a wide range of recommended plant food ratios exists for individual crops and that there is some discretion as to the particular ratios firms choose to offer. It is suggested that the tendency for products to cluster tightly around such ratios as 2 : 1 : 1 and 1.5 : 1 : 1 is partly the result of the dynamics of competitive behaviour. Thus firms partly create the demand for products with particular plant food ratios and then deliberately offer minimally differentiated products close to those ratios.[11]

The pattern of product competition which has been examined in some detail for selected product groups is to a large extent paralleled in the remaining groups once allowance is made for the rather lower demand for fertilisers in these groups. For the two years previously discussed, 1970/71 and 1977/78, there were totals of 66 and 75 compound and straight nitrogen fertilisers produced by the three major firms. The numbers of identical products were

[11] The product chosen also depended on such factors as the type of raw materials available and the production processes used by the firm concerned.

only 8 and 11 in 1970/71 and 1977/78 respectively. The numbers of clustered or minimally differentiated products were 27 and 30 while products differentiated only by total plant food concentration were 8 in both years. Finally there were 23 and 26 isolated products in 1970/71 and 1977/78 with Fisons being responsible for 19 and 22 of them in the two years respectively. The reason for the relatively large numbers of isolated Fisons products was its policy of offering a much wider product range than either ICI or UKF/Shellstar (see Table I above). In many cases this meant offering a product to meet specialist crop requirements with very limited demand (e.g. Fisons specialist fruit and vegetable crop fertilisers). In these areas product clusters did not emerge as ICI and UKF/Shellstar felt that demand did not justify the introduction of a product.

Overall the evidence shows that the three major firms generally avoided offering identical products. Instead they chose to offer minimally differentiated products in market segments where demand was sufficient to justify competition. By and large, only in market segments with very low demand were isolated products offered.

IV. SUMMARY AND CONCLUSIONS

The preceding analysis of product competition in the UK fertiliser industry has been based on an adaptation of Lancaster's product characteristics approach and the location theory analogy. Several conclusions emerged.

Firstly, competition for market share resulted in product proliferation rather than in the competitive leapfrogging behaviour suggested in the location models which restrict the number of firms or products. For the three major firms the number of granular compound fertilisers offered in 1962/63 was 29, by 1977/1978 it was 69.

Secondly, a very significant proportion of products remained unchanged over long periods of time. For example the 1977/78 total of 69 compounds included 25 that had been available for ten or more years. This suggests either that many products were optimally located when first introduced irrespective of the subsequent product additions and/or that products, like physical plant, are not freely relocated. In practice some combination of the two reasons may have been operating, but at least it does indicate the need for some relocation costs to be introduced into models of product competition.

Thirdly, at least in the 1960s the leapfrogging that did occur, as well as the new product proliferation, reflected almost entirely technically improved products in the sense that the total plant food concentration of fertilisers was increased. In this respect leapfrogging is seen mainly as offering more technically advanced products rather than just changing the ratios between different product characteristics. However, there is some evidence particularly in the 1970s of plant food concentrations being trimmed back as firms attempted to keep prices down and their products competitive.

Fourthly, the choice of product locations provides some weak support for Eaton and Lipsey's [4] conclusion that clusters of minimally differentiated products will tend to develop in the process of competition. Further, the Eaton and Lipsey model which prevented firms from occupying the same location does not seem unduly restrictive. It appears that, even without such a restriction, the three major fertiliser firms generally chose not to offer identical products. In 1977/78 there were only 11 straight nitrogen and compound fertiliser products with an identical rival out of the total of 75 products. There were 30 clustered, or minimally differentiated products; 8 product differentiated only by the degree of plant food concentration; and 26 isolated products. However, a detailed examination of these groupings suggests that many of the isolated products were designed for very small segments of market demand and hence were unlikely to attract competitive products. In market segments where demand was larger, such as the "Extra High N", "High N" and to a lesser extent "Low N" and "High K" segments the firms chose to offer clusters of minimally differentiated products.

RICHARD SHAW
Department of Economics,
University of Stirling,
Stirling, FK9 4LA, Scotland.

APPENDIX

IDENTIFICATION OF PRODUCT CLUSTERS

The criteria for determining product clusters are intended to identify minimally differentiated products. The two requirements are that clustered products should have approximately the same total plant food concentration, and that the plant food ratios should also be very similar.

EXAMPLE OF A 3 PRODUCT CLUSTER

Firm	*Plant food contents (percentages)* N	P_2O_5	K_2O	*Total plant food content*	*Individual plant food (percentages)*[1] N	P_2O_5	K_2O
Fisons	10	24	24	58	17.24	41.38	41.38
ICI	9	25	25	<u>59</u>	15.25	42.37	42.37
UKF/Shellstar	10	25	25	60	<u>16.67</u>	<u>41.67</u>	<u>41.67</u>

[1] Median percentages are underlined.

Criterion 1

Since all products have a total plant food content within 10 per cent of the median percentage they satisfy the first criterion.

Criterion 2

Since all products have individual plant food percentages within 10 per cent of the median percentage they satisfy the second criterion. They would also satisfy the second criterion by the rule that individual plant food contents (e.g. 9 per cent N and 10 per cent N) are only a single percentage point apart (i.e. the minimum difference).

REFERENCES

[1] CHAMBERLIN, E. H., *Theory of Monopolistic Competition,* (Cambridge, Harvard University Press, 1933).

[2] CHAMBERLIN, E. H., "The Product as an Economic Variable", *Quarterly Journal of Economics,* Vol. **67**, No. 1, (February 1953), pp. 1–29.

[3] DIXIT, A. K. and STIGLITZ, J. E., "Monopolistic Competition and Optimum Product Diversity", *American Economic Review,* Vol. **67**, No. 3, (June 1977), pp. 297–308.

[4] EATON, B. C. and LIPSEY, R. G., "The Principle of Minimum Differentiation Reconsidered: Some New Developments in the Theory of Spatial Competition", *Review of Economic Studies,* Vol. **42**, (1), No. 129, (January 1975), pp. 27–49.

[5] HAY, D. A., "Sequential Entry and Entry-Deterring Strategies in Spatial Competition", *Oxford Economic Papers,* Vol. **28**, No. 2, (July 1976), pp. 240–57.

[6] HOTELLING, H., "Stability in Competition", *Economic Journal,* Vol. **39**, (March 1929), pp. 41–57.

[7] LANCASTER, K., "A New Approach to Consumer Theory", *Journal of Political Economy,* Vol. **74**, (April 1966), pp. 132–57.

[8] LANCASTER, K., "Socially Optimal Product Differentiation", *American Economic Review,* Vol. **65**, No. 4, (September 1975), pp. 567–85.

[9] LERNER, A. P. and SINGER, H. W., "Some Notes on Duopoly and Spatial Competition", *Journal of Political Economy,* Vol. **45**, No. 2, (April 1937), pp. 145–86.

[10] MONOPOLIES COMMISSION, *Report on the Supply of Chemical Fertilisers,* 1959, H.M.S.O.

[11] SCHERER, F. M., "The Welfare Economics of Product Variety: An Application to the Ready-to-Eat Cereals Industry", *Journal of Industrial Economics,* Vol. **28**, No. 2, (December 1979), pp. 113–34.

[12] SCHMALENSEE, R., "Entry deterrence in the ready-to-eat breakfast cereal industry", *Bell Journal of Economics,* Vol. **9**, No. 2, (Autumn 1978), pp. 305–27.

[13] SHAW, R. W., "New Entry and the Competitive Process in the UK Fertiliser Industry", *Scottish Journal of Political Economy,* Vol. **27**, No. 1, (February 1980), pp. 1–16.

[14] SPENCE, A. M., "Product Differentiation and Welfare", *American Economic Review,* Vol. **66**, No. 3, (May 1976), pp. 407–14.

THE JOURNAL OF INDUSTRIAL ECONOMICS
Volume XXXI September/December 1982 Nos. 1/2

EXISTENCE AND COMPUTATION OF MIXED STRATEGY NASH EQUILIBRIUM FOR 3-FIRMS LOCATION PROBLEM

A. SHAKED

Location problems of firms on a closed interval were introduced by Hotelling [3] and later investigated by Eaton & Lipsey [2]. Firms sell a homogeneous product at a fixed price, customers distributed along the interval buy one unit each from the firm nearest to them and firms aim to maximize the number of their customers. It is well known that where the customers are evenly distributed along the interval and the number of firms is other than 3 the location problem has a pure strategy Nash equilibrium (see [2]).

The case of 3 firms is peculiar in that no pure strategy Nash equilibrium exists, for in any situation one of the extreme firms (not located between the other two) can increase its revenue by either moving towards or away from the other two firms. The existence of mixed strategies is not obvious because the payoff functions are discontinuous whenever two or more firms are located at the same point.

In a recent paper Dasgupta and Maskin [1] investigate a class of games, all derived from economic problems and all with some discontinuities in their payoff functions. They demonstrate that the discontinuities in the payoff functions do not prevent the existence of mixed strategies Nash equilibria in the games investigated. In particular, location problems of the type described earlier have such "weak" discontinuities and hence possess a mixed strategy Nash equilibrium. Although their proof is constructive, offering a method of approaching these equilibria as a limit of equilibria of finite games, the equations involved very quickly become unmanageable. In this note we compute a mixed strategy Nash equilibrium for the 3 firms location problem.

Let the customers be evenly distributed along [0, 1] then a mixed strategy is a probability measure over [0, 1]. The symmetry of the problem suggests that the solution will be doubly symmetric in that all firms choose the same mixed strategy and that this strategy is symmetric around $\frac{1}{2}$ (symmetric locations are given the same probabilities). Dasgupta and Maskin confine their analysis to doubly symmetric solutions and prove that the strategies in any doubly symmetric equilibrium are atomless.

Given the symmetric nature of the game and following the analysis of Dasgupta and Maskin we shall confine ourselves here to such doubly symmetric equilibria. We demonstrate here that *the 3 firms location problem has a unique doubly symmetric mixed strategy equilibrium*, given by:

$$(*) \qquad g(x) = \begin{cases} 2 & \frac{1}{4} \le x \le \frac{3}{4} \\ 0 & \text{otherwise} \end{cases}$$

This implies that firms in equilibrium avoid the extreme quartiles and choose locations in the remaining half with equal probability.

Let two firms choose their location according to a symmetric (atomless) density probability function $f(x)$; we compute the payoff function for the third firm. For an equilibrium $f(x)$ the payoff function of the third firm assumes a single value over the support of f and a lower value outside the support. We assume without loss of generality that the support of f is a subset of $[\alpha, 1-\alpha]$ for $0 \le \alpha < \frac{1}{2}$.

Define:

$$Q(x) = \int_\alpha^x f(t)\,dt$$

$$R(x) = \int_x^{1-\alpha} f(t)\,dt = 1 - Q(x)$$

Then:

$$Q'(x) = f(x) = -R'(x)$$

Let the third firm locate itself at z, its payoff there is given by:

$$(1) \qquad A(z) = 2\int_\alpha^z f(x)Q(x)\left(1 - \frac{z+x}{2}\right) dx + 2\int_\alpha^z \int_z^{1-\alpha} f(x)f(y)\frac{y-x}{2}\,dy\,dx + 2\int_z^{1-\alpha} f(x)R(x)\frac{x+z}{2}\,dx.$$

The first integral represents payoff when the two firms are located to the left of z, and the last integral when both firms are to the right of z, the second integral corresponds to the case of one firm on each side of z.

Differentiating w.r.t. z:

$$(2) \qquad A'(z) = 2f(z)Q(z)(1-z) - \int_\alpha^z f(x)Q(x)\,dx + f(z)\int_z^{1-\alpha} f(y)(y-z)\,dy - f(z)\int_\alpha^z f(x)(z-x)\,dx - 2f(z)R(z)z + \int_z^{1-\alpha} f(x)R(x)\,dx.$$

Since:

$$R + Q \equiv 1, \int f(x)Q(x)\,dx = \tfrac{1}{2}Q^2(x), \int_{\alpha}^{1-\alpha} xf(x)\,dx = \tfrac{1}{2},$$

equation (2) becomes:

(3) $$A'(z) = (\tfrac{1}{2} - Q(z)) + f(z)[3(\tfrac{1}{2} - z) - 2(\tfrac{1}{2} - Q(z))].$$

We are looking for a function $Q(z)$ (with $Q'(z) = f(z)$) such that $A'(z) = 0$ whenever $f(z) \neq 0$. Under the transformation

$$h(z) = \frac{\tfrac{1}{2} - Q(z)}{\tfrac{1}{2} - z}$$

the differential equation $A'(z) = 0$ becomes:

(4) $$h'(2h - z)(\tfrac{1}{2} - z) = 2h(h - 2)$$

This is a simple separable equation whose solution is implicitly given by:

(5) $$h^3(h - 2) = K(\tfrac{1}{2} - z)^{-4},$$

where K is a constant.

Let $K = 0$, this defines one acceptable solution for h: $h \equiv 2$ (the other solution, $h \equiv 0$ implies $Q \equiv \frac{1}{2}$ and is therefore ruled out).

Hence

$$Q(z) = 2(z - \tfrac{1}{2}) + \tfrac{1}{2} = 2(z - \tfrac{1}{4})$$

which is the $Q(z)$ derived from the distribution $g(x)$ defined in (*). To show that this is an equilibrium we need to demonstrate that the payoff outside the support is lower than in it. For $z \leq \frac{1}{4}, f(z) \equiv 0$ and the payoff at z is:

$$A(z) = 2\int_{1/4}^{3/4} f(x)R(x)\left(\frac{x + z}{2}\right)dx$$

This is an increasing function of z and since $A(z)$ is continuous and symmetric in z, the payoff is highest in the support.

We now demonstrate that no other solution of the differential equation is suitable as an equilibrium. Let $Q(z)$ and $h(z)$ be the solutions of (4) for $K \neq 0$. Let z be the first point for which $Q(z) = \frac{1}{2}$, then z is the limit of points in the support. If $z < \frac{1}{2}$ (or $z > \frac{1}{2}$) then by the definition of h: $h(z) = 0$ but since (5) holds at that point, $h(z)$ cannot be zero, hence $z = \frac{1}{2}$. Rearranging the terms in (5):

$$[h(z)(\tfrac{1}{2} - z)]^3(h(z) - 2)(\tfrac{1}{2} - z) = K.$$

By the definition of $h(z)$ this becomes:

$$(\tfrac{1}{2} - Q(z))^3(2z - Q(z) - \tfrac{1}{2}) = K.$$

Taking the limit as $z \to \frac{1}{2}$, the left hand side converges to 0, i.e. $K = 0$. Hence (5) represents a solution to (4) only for $K = 0$.

AVNER SHAKED,
London School of Economics,
Houghton Street,
London WC2A 2AE, England.

REFERENCES

[1] DASGUPTA, P. and MASKIN, E., 'The Existence of Equilibrium in Discontinuous Economic Games', ICERD, LSE, London.
[2] EATON, B. C. and LIPSEY, R. G., 'The Principle of Minimum Differentiation Reconsidered: Some New Developments in the Theory of Spatial Competition', *Review of Economic Studies*, Vol. 42(1), No. 129, (January 1975), pp. 27–49.
[3] HOTELLING, H., 'Stability in Competition', *Economic Journal*, Vol. 39, (March 1929), pp. 41–57.

THE JOURNAL OF INDUSTRIAL ECONOMICS
Volume XXXI September/December 1982 Nos. 1/2

DIFFERENTIATED PRODUCTS, CONSUMER SEARCH, AND LOCATIONAL OLIGOPOLY

KONRAD STAHL*

I. INTRODUCTION

THE model presented in this paper deals with sellers' reactions, by choice of location, to consumers' search for their preferred product from a variety of imperfect substitutes. It differs in two aspects from models in the Stigler [8] tradition. First, search for optimal product characteristics, rather than minimal prices, is emphasized. For many nonstandardized commodities,[1] the former aspect of search appears more important: for such commodities, prices may convey less information than (true) signals about commodity characteristics. It is furthermore straightforward to sample prices from advertisements or by making telephone calls, whereas sampling product characteristics in many cases requires personal inspection.

Second, the consumers' search costs are not exogenous, but sellers influence these costs by their choice of location: they are the lower, the more closely sellers associate spatially. This reduction in search costs may, in turn, lead to such a spatial concentration of demand that sellers, despite being competitors, find it profitable to locate close to each other. While confirmed by empirical observations, this result is contradicting the inference one tends to draw from conventional one product search models, namely that sellers attempt to secure maximum monopolistic advantage by increasing search costs as much as possible and therefore choose locations distant from each other.[2]

One might thus tend to infer that the spatial concentration of sellers in a few marketplaces represents an efficient state of the world: not only consumers' search cost advantages are duly accounted for; but spatial proximity, so one

* This is a revised version of [6]. First ideas to that research were developed jointly with Luis Guasch during a stay at CORE, Louvain, Belgium. An earlier version of the paper was presented in seminars at Harvard, Queen's, and Chicago Universities, as well as at the University of Michigan, Ann Arbor, and MIT. Thanks are to the seminar participants, as well as to John Roberts, Norbert Schulz, Urs Schweizer, Jacques Thisse, and Pravin Varaiya for helpful comments. Financial supports from CORE, the Deutsche Forschungsgemeinschaft and NSF (grants SOC 76-8033 and 21905) are gratefully acknowledged.

[1] Examples are fashion clothes, antiques, or used cars. More generally, classes of commodities of interest here are handcrafted, and durable second hand goods.

[2] The spatial concentration of retailing resulting from consumers' search has been observed by Nelson [4], *cf.* the empirical evidence reported therein. Another empirical analysis is conducted by Rogers [5]. The phenomenon is also analyzed in a paper by Stuart [9] which was brought to my attention only after this paper had been written. However, he does not analyze the sellers' equilibrium location patterns resulting from consumers' search behavior, which is the emphasis of the present paper.

might conclude, increases the "intensity of competition" and thus drives prices down towards competitive levels. It turns out, however, that *the spatial concentration of sellers may be excessive*, and that *prices are not necessarily driven down to competitive levels*. In fact, the equilibrium prices charged by noncooperative one-product sellers in such a marketplace may be higher than those charged by a monopolist selling all the products at that location!

While these latter pricing aspects for a fixed spatial distribution of marketeers are dealt with in a companion paper (Stahl [7]), it is the objective of the present paper to characterize, and to some extent, to evaluate, the equilibrium locational choices of sellers. The separate treatment of pricing, and location decisions is largely motivated by the fundamental equilibrium existence problems arising whenever they are jointly incorporated.[3] To be more precise, the simple model analyzed below involves the locational choice of N firms that sell, at constant identical prices, one each of N differentiated commodities. Consumers, located in uniform density along a long line, are differentiated by their tastes for these commodities. The typical consumer knows which commodities in principle are available, but does not know which one of the commodities is offered where. In order to find out, he has to visit a marketplace, defined as an assembly of one or more firms. If he does so and he finds commodities suiting his preferences, he purchases one unit of the most preferred commodity offered thereat. The typical firm, knowing of consumers' preferences and behavior, chooses the location maximizing its sales under the Cournot assumption.

It follows quite naturally from the model specification, that the aggregate demand observed at a marketplace increases with its size, as defined by the number of commodities offered there. Therefore a seller, upon choosing a profit maximizing location, is confronted with the alternative either to establish a local monopoly with a small market area and a larger share of consumers purchasing, by lack of alternatives, his variety; or to join other firms in a competitive marketplace with a large market area in which he fetches the demand from only the small subset of consumers not substituting away towards the other alternatives available there. More precisely, the change in our seller's market demand when joining the latter marketplace may be decomposed into two effects: a negative *substitution effect* generated from competition about consumers' demand, and a positive *market area effect* generated from the joint location of sellers. Despite a fiercer competition, our seller will join the larger marketplace if the reduction in the demand due to the substitution effect will be more than outweighed by the increase in demand due to the market area effect. Furthermore, if joining the large market that seller will, by increasing its demand drawing power, confer an *external benefit* to the sellers already there. This external benefit is exclusively

[3] These are demonstrated, for example, in d'Aspremont, Gabsziewicz and Thisse [1].

due to consumers' imperfect information as to which products are offered where. It may be directly internalized by the typical seller in offering several varieties, or indirectly by a developer in providing an institutional framework for sellers' collusion. Armchair empiricism suggests, however, that there are limitations to both forms of internalization.

In the formal model developed here, we concentrate on a characterization of the noncooperative equilibria involving the $\mathcal{N}$ one product firms. After establishing the straightforward result that the drawing power of a marketplace varies with its size, we first give conditions under which there is no equilibrium involving locational monopolies for all firms, and second, that whenever consumers are choosey enough to consider acceptable only one variety of the commodities, the only equilibrium solution involves the joint location of all sellers at one marketplace. We then give sufficient conditions for a joint location at one marketplace to be in the set of equilibria, even if consumers consider several varieties acceptable. Furthermore, a threshold size for a larger marketplace is determined so that no single firm will ever spatially monopolize, but in joining the large marketplace will further increase its demand drawing power. After thus having established that a concentration of all firms in one marketplace is an equilibrium configuration very likely to arise, we show by a counterexample that it is *not* in the core of the location game discussed here. Thus, it would be profitable for *all* sellers to decentralize spatially, provided that the market is large enough. Furthermore, such a decentralization may lead to increases in both equity and Pareto-efficiency. One might wonder whether all these results also hold under less stringent conditions, such as sellers' endogenous choice of varieties and prices. This matter will be addressed in the last section of this paper (Section IV). Before that, we discuss the model and comment on the relevant assumptions (Section II). The results are demonstrated in Section III.

II. THE MODEL

Consider an economy involving $\mathcal{N}$ differentiated commodities i, $i \in \mathcal{N}$, $\mathcal{N} = \{1, \ldots, N\}$, and a numeraire good whose quantities are denoted by x. There are *N types of consumers making indivisible and mutually exclusive purchases of one of the N commodities*—a pattern certainly typical of the class of commodities discussed here. The consumers are distinguished by preferences and endowments. The latter consist of positive amounts of the numeraire and shares θ_{ij} in some firms j, $j = 1, \ldots, N$. Each consumer has positive shares from at least one firm, and all firms' proceeds are distributed over the consumers. The sum of endowments is denoted in R_i units of the numeraire. As to the consumers' preferences, we assume that at fixed unit prices, consumer type i derives positive utility from some subset a_i of the differentiated commodities. The typical element of a_i is called j_i. The size of consumer i's subset of acceptable alternatives is denoted by m_i, $1 \leq m_i \leq N$. The consumer's preferences are characterized by a utility function $u_i(j_i, x_i)$ satisfying the following properties:

$$\text{(i)} \qquad u_i(j_i, x_i) = u_i(j_i) + x_i, j_i \in a_i, x_i \geq 0$$

$$\text{(ii)} \qquad \max_{j_i \in a_i} u_i(j_i) = u_i(i_i) < +\infty$$

$$\text{(iii)} \qquad u_i(j_i) \begin{cases} > u_i((j+1)_i) & j = 1, \ldots, m_i - 1, j_i \in a_i \\ = 0 & j_i \neq a_i \end{cases}$$

Thus, *the consumer's utility function is additive and linear in the numeraire*, an assumption commonly used in the literature on differentiated commodities. Alternative i is the consumer's most preferred one, and preferences over the other acceptable alternatives are strictly transitive, with j_i denoting consumer i's jth preferred alternative.

In addition to these assumptions on the individual consumer's preferences, we will several times assume that up to the choice of i, all consumer's preferences are identical in the following sense:

$$\text{(iv)} \qquad j_i = i + k \bmod N \Rightarrow j_n = n + k \bmod N, \ k = 1, \ldots, m$$

$$\text{and} \qquad u_i(j_i) = u_n(j_n). \ i = 1, \ldots, N, j = 1, \ldots, N.$$

Thus, if the alternative labelled $i + k \bmod N$ is consumer type i's jth preferred alternative, then $n + k \bmod N$ is consumer type n's jth preferred alternative, and consumers' valuations of their respective jth preferred alternative are identical.[4] This, of course, is a fairly strong but again commonly used assumption.

The geographical space considered in the model is a nonempty interval $[\underline{y}, \bar{y}]$ on the nonnegative part of the real line, with y denoting a consumer's location. Using a line rather than a two dimensional geography is a convenient and, in the present case, unrestrictive assumption. All consumer types are distributed in uniform shares along $[\underline{y}, \bar{y}]$. Thus if $\phi_i(y)$ denotes the share of consumers type i located at y, we assume that

$$\text{(v)} \qquad \phi_i(y) = \frac{\alpha_i}{\bar{y} - \underline{y}}, y \in [\underline{y}, \bar{y}], \ i = 1, \ldots, N,$$

where $\alpha_i \in (0, 1)$ and $\sum_{i=1}^{N} \alpha_i = 1$. In line with, and with the same rationale as for assumption (iv), we will sometimes use a stronger alternative to (v), which is

$$\text{(vi)} \qquad \phi_i(y) = \frac{1/N}{\bar{y} - \underline{y}}, y \in [\underline{y}, \bar{y}], \ i = 1, \ldots, N$$

[4] As an example, let $N = 4$, and suppose that e.g. consumer type 2 orders the alternatives such that $u_2(2) > u_2(1) > u_2(3) > u_2(4) > 0$. Then the assumption implies that e.g. consumer type 4 orders the alternatives such that $u_4(4) > u_4(3) > u_4(1) > u_4(2) > 0$ with $u_4(j) = u_2(j), j = 1, \ldots, 4$.

implying that all consumers are distributed at equal densities.[5]

Turning now to the supply side of our simple economy, we consider $\mathcal{N}$ one product firms with firm i selling commodity i at location l_i at constant cost (below unity) and unit price. Commodity i is uniquely offered at l_i, whereas the numeraire good is produced at constant unit cost, and available everywhere along the line. That firms sell at constant cost and price seems a very rigid assumption indeed. In particular, standardizing costs contradicts the observation that rents vary considerably across space; furthermore, assuming away price competition interferes with standard hypotheses of microeconomic theory. In the present paper, both assumptions are made for analytical convenience. There is a straightforward rationalization for the first assumption, however: if rents to fixed factors (such as land at given locations) are determined as residuals, then we first have to concentrate on the forces generating the surpluses which, in turn, may be absorbed in land rent. This is done here. Furthermore, assuming away set up costs of location is justified by our consideration of a fixed number of firms. Thus, entry decisions, where such set up costs become important, are not modelled here. As to the second assumption, it is not at all clear, as mentioned before, that its relaxation will lead to prices being driven down in competitive marketplaces. In fact, would they go down, then the land rents generated at such marketplaces would also have to go down, contradicting all empirical evidence. A further comment on this point is in Section IV.

We define a marketplace k to consist of a location v_k with an assembly of one or more firms. There are K marketplaces, $1 \leq K \leq \mathcal{N}$. The size of marketplace k, s_k, is defined as the number of firms assembled at that marketplace. Thus $1 \leq s_k \leq \mathcal{N}$, $\sum_k s_k = \mathcal{N}$. The composition of marketplace k, e_k is the set of firms assembled in that marketplace. Thus, if firms $i \in e_k, j \in e_k$, then $l_i = l_j = v_k$.

Let us now turn to a description of the consumers' and the firms' decision making behavior. *The consumers are assumed to know the locations and the sizes of the marketplaces, but not their composition.* In order to find out about any e_k, they must visit k. In doing so they incur transportation costs to the marketplace linear in distance, at rate c. *Each consumer visits, at most, one marketplace.* If he does so, he samples all stores at no additional cost and decides either to purchase the commodity suiting his preferences best, or none if no acceptable commodity is available. His choice of a marketplace is based on *expected utility maximization, in which he assigns equal probability to finding therein any alternative.* He decides not to visit any marketplace, however, if the maximal expected utility from visiting a marketplace falls short of the utility derived from staying put and spending all

[5] Both assumptions (v) and (vi) may more realistically be reinterpreted in a situation in which sellers are uncertain about the spatial distribution of buyers according to tastes. Then either version specifies the typical seller's subjective prior to that distribution. The results generated below will follow directly under the provision that the sellers are risk neutral.

of his income on the numeraire good. Let sizes and locations of marketplaces be given. Let furthermore

$$\pi_j(s_k) = \text{Prob}\{1, 2, \ldots, j-1 \notin e_k, j \in e_k\} = \frac{N_{s_k} - j_{-1}}{N_{s_k}}$$

denote the probability that the first $(j-1)$ preferred commodities are not, but the jth preferred commodity indeed is offered in marketplace k of size s_k. Then the first step in the consumer's maximization process is given by

$$\max_k \left[\sum_{j=1}^{m_i} \pi_j(s_k) u_i(j, R_i - c\, d(v_k, y)) + \left(1 - \sum_{j=1}^{m_i} \pi_j(s_k)\right) \cdot u_i(0, R_i - c\, d(v_k, y)) \right]$$

where $d(v_k, y)$ is the Euclidian distance function.[6] Denoting by k^* his optimal choice, he does (not) visit marketplace k^* if

$$\text{(1)} \qquad \sum_{j=1}^{m_i} \pi_j(s_{k*}) u_i(j, R_i - c\, d(v_{k*}, y)) + \left[1 - \sum_{j=1}^{m_i} \pi_j(s_{k*})\right] \cdot u_i(0, R_i - c\, d(v_{k*}, y)) \gtrless u_i(0, R_i),$$

or, given (i),

$$\sum_{j=1}^{m_i} \pi_j(s_{k*})[u_i(j) - u_i(0)] \gtrless c\, d(v_{k*}, y).$$

These assumptions on consumers' behavior are quite restrictive. Probably the most bothersome ones to the theorist concerned with search models are first that search is restricted to one marketplace only; second that a special, namely a uniform prior probability distribution is used and prior beliefs are considered identical; and third, that intramarketplace search and recall costs are assumed zero.[7] While it is easy to relax any one of these assumptions, they in conjunction provide a useful framework for the analysis to be carried out: they allow us to computationally determine conditions for the (excessive) equilibrium concentration of marketeers.

[6] Since prices do not play any further role in the analysis, we assume them to be absorbed in the utility function.

[7] An additional implicit assumption is that consumers have perfect prior information as to the prices at which the varieties are offered. This asymmetry between price and quality information may be defended by the arguments discussed in section I.

Turning now to the firms' behavior, we assume them to have perfect knowledge about both sides of the market; in particular, about the varieties offered by the other firms and their locations, and about consumers' preferences, endowments and behavior. Let l_{-i} denote the collection of locations of all firms but i. Given l_{-i}, firm i selects at no cost the location $l_i^* \in [\underline{y}, \bar{y}]$ maximizing its sales. Thus, letting $\Pi_i\ (l_i, l_{-i})$ be the payoff (sales) i obtains at l_i, given l_{-i}, then $\Pi_i\ (l_i^*, l_{-i}) \geq \Pi_i\ (l_i, l_{-i})\ \forall l_i$.

An equilibrium of this game is a set of firms' locations $L^* = \{l_1^*, \ldots, l_i^*, \ldots, l_N^*\}$ such that, given consumers choose the marketplaces and varieties maximizing their expected utilities, no firm considers it profitable to relocate on its own. Thus, L^* is an equilibrium if

$$\Pi_i\ (l_i^*, l_{-i}^*) \geq \Pi_i\ (l_i, l_{-i}^*) \qquad \forall i,\ i = 1, \ldots, N.$$

The corresponding collection $\{e_1^*, \ldots, e_K^*\}$ is called an equilibrium configuration of marketplaces. The core of the game consists of the set of equilibria which are unblocked by any coalition of firms. Thus, if an equilibrium L^* is in the core, then there is no coalition of firms such that, resulting from a joint relocation, each firm in the coalition would maintain and some firms would increase their sales. Finally, an equilibrium is called Pareto-efficient if no relocation of firms will sustain the utility allocations to all, and improve those to some consumers.

The simple game considered here has the property that the typical seller i's payoff is discontinuous in his own strategy l_i at all $l_j = l_i, j \neq i$. This is implied by the assumption that consumers visit, at most, one marketplace. It follows that the existence of equilibria cannot be shown in general. However, since any location is feasible for any seller, existence follows from showing that in equilibrium each seller's location decision dominates all of the alternative choices open to him, given the other sellers' choices. The discontinuity of the payoff functions also implies that equilibrium configurations are influenced by the presumed initial locations of firms and the sequence in which firms are allowed to choose their optimal strategies.[8] It follows that a characterization of equilibria is not straightforward.

III. RESULTS

The conditions under which the following equilibrium characterizations are given involve the parameters m_i, $i = 1, \ldots, N$; s_k, $k = 1, \ldots, K$; and N. The number of alternatives m_i acceptable to consumers is critical in determining the *share of consumers* to which a firm sells its commodity when locating in marketplaces of alternative *structure*. The sizes of marketplaces s_k are important because they determine the *number of consumers* of each type a firm sells its

[8] This has interesting implications on the entry decisions of firms, which will be discussed in a later paper.

commodity to when locating in marketplaces of alternative *size*. All these parameters are related to N, the total number of commodities, consumers, and firms.

The first proposition, however, establishes the principal feature bringing about the spatial concentration of firms, namely that *the aggregate demand observed at a marketplace increases with its size*. In order to show this, let us define by $\tilde{z}_i(s)$ the maximal distance a consumer type i is willing to travel to a marketplace of size s. Thus,

$$\tilde{z}_i(s) = \left\{ z \mid \sum_{j=1}^{m_i} \pi_j(s)[u_i(j, R_i - cz) - u_i(0, R_i - cz)] + u_i(0, R_i - cz) = u_i(0, R_i) \right\}. \tag{2}$$

Proposition (1) : Suppose (i), (ii), (iii) *and* (iv) *hold. Then* $\tilde{z}_i(s)$ *is strictly increasing in* s, $i = 1, \ldots, N$.

Proof: Using (2), it suffices to show that for given z, $s' > s$ implies

$$\sum_{j=1}^{m_i} (\pi_j(s') - \pi_j(s))[u_i(j) - u_i(0)] > 0,$$

which is equivalent to showing that

$$\begin{aligned}&[\pi_1(s') - \pi_1(s)][u_i(1) - u_i(2)] \\ &\quad + [\pi_1(s') + \pi_2(s') - (\pi_1(s) + \pi_2(s))][u_i(2) - u_i(3)] + \cdots \\ &\quad + [\pi_1(s') + \cdots + \pi_{m_i}(s') - (\pi_1(s) + \cdots + \pi_{m_i}(s))] \\ &\quad \times [u_i(m_i) - u_i(0)] > 0.\end{aligned}$$

Using (iii) this inequality is satisfied if for $1 \leq \hat{m} \leq m_i$,

$$\sum_{j=1}^{\hat{m}} [\pi_j(s') - \pi_j(s)] > 0.$$

Observe that for any k

$$\begin{aligned}\sum_{j=1}^{\hat{m}} \pi_j(s_k) &= \text{Prob}\{1 \in e_k\} + \text{Prob}\{1 \notin e_k, 2 \in e_k\} + \cdots \\ &\quad + \text{Prob}\{1, 2, \ldots, \hat{m} - 1 \notin e_k, \hat{m} \in e_k\} \\ &= \text{Prob}\{(1 \in e_k) \vee \cdots \vee (\hat{m} \in e_k)\} \\ &= 1 - \text{Prob}(1 \notin e_k, 2 \notin e_k, \ldots, \hat{m} \notin e_k) \\ &= 1 - \frac{\binom{N - \hat{m}}{s}}{\binom{N}{s}}.\end{aligned}$$

But $s' > s$ implies

$$1 - \frac{\binom{N - \hat{m}}{s'}}{\binom{N}{s'}} > 1 - \frac{\binom{N - m}{s}}{\binom{N}{s}}. \qquad \blacksquare$$

We now turn to characterizations of locational equilibria. For this, we assume the market size, that is the length of the interval $[\underline{y}, \bar{y}]$ to be so large, relative to the number of sellers, that each seller may establish a locational monopoly unrestricted by "spatial competition" in the sense of Hotelling [3]. Formally, we assume that $[\underline{y}, \bar{y}] < \sum_{i=1}^{N} 2\tilde{z}_i(1)$. Since we are mainly interested in characterizing spatial concentration phenomena, this assumption is not restrictive. As will become obvious, conditions under which a spatial concentration of sellers will take place under this assumption will imply such a concentration once the market size is effectively restricted. The assumption finally implies that for any equilibrium configuration of marketplaces $\{e_1^*, \ldots, e_k^*\}$, there can never be a unique set L^* of equilibrium locations. Since the interest is in a characterization of equilibrium sizes and compositions, rather than locations of marketplaces, we henceforth identify all equilibria with identical equilibrium configurations. We now determine conditions under which *an equilibrium cannot involve spatial monopolies*, despite the fact that firms compete with each other about consumers' demand.

Proposition (2) *: Let* (i)–(iv) *and* (vi) *hold. Let N be even. Then there is an $\tilde{m}(N)$ such that for all $m < \tilde{m}(N)$, if l_i^* is an equilibrium location for firm i, there is at least one firm j choosing $l_j^* = l_i^*$. Furthermore, $\tilde{m}(N) > N/2$ if $N > 4$, and $N' > N$ implies $\tilde{m}(N') - \tilde{m}(N) > N' - N$.*

Proof: This follows from the construction of $\tilde{m}(N)$. Let $m > N/2$. Consider any pair of firms selling varieties (i, j) such that if locating jointly they will obtain equal sales. (All firms can be paired that way, by assumptions (iv) and (vi) and evenness of N.) Then a sufficient condition for $l_i^* = l_j^*$ is that

$$\Pi_k\ (l_k;\ l_i = l_j) > \Pi_k\ (l_k;\ l_i \neq l_j),\ k = i, j.$$

This condition is satisfied whenever

$$\frac{N}{2}\,\tilde{z}(2) - m\tilde{z}(1) > 0$$

or

$$\sum_{j=1}^{m} \left[\frac{N}{2}\,\pi_j(2) - m\pi_j(1)\right] u(j) > 0,$$

which in turn holds whenever

$$\frac{N}{2}\left[1-\frac{\binom{N-2}{m}}{\binom{N}{m}}\right]-m\left[1-\frac{\binom{N-2}{m}}{\binom{N}{m}}\right]>0.$$

Simplification yields

$$m < N\frac{2N-1}{3N-2}.$$

Let $\tilde{m}(N)$ be the maximal integer satisfying this inequality. This shows the first assertion. The others follow trivially. ■

Thus, under the conditions of this proposition, all firms will, despite competition, at least pairwise form marketplaces. That *all* firms do so is a consequence of assumptions (iv) and (vi). Without these a similar bound on the maximum number of acceptable alternatives would lead us to the statement that there cannot be an equilibrium involving N marketplaces. Observe that the upper bound on m becomes less stringent as N increases. For large N, $\tilde{m}(N)$ approaches $\frac{2}{3}N$, meaning that the desire to pair is upheld if in this case firms do loose, via the substitution effect, up to $\frac{1}{6}$ of the share of patrons they would otherwise sell to. This is quite a stringent condition. However, it is derived with the proviso that each firm may establish a spatial monopoly if so desired. Effective bounds on the space of locations will definitely weaken this condition. In fact, it will disappear (that is $\tilde{m}(N) = N$) for a sufficiently small size of the market. One might be tempted to ask at this point whether by contrast there are conditions guaranteeing an N marketplace equilibrium. Given that consumers are imperfectly informed, *the only sufficient condition for a spatial concentration of firms never to take place is that*, contrary to assumption (iii), *all commodities are considered perfect substitutes by all consumers*. For, if this does not hold for all consumers and for all commodities, some firms may gain from a spatial association.

Turning now to conditions under which all firms will concentrate at one marketplace we show first a formally trivial, but nevertheless educative result that if all consumers are choosey enough to desire, at current prices, one and only one commodity type, then concentration of all firms at one marketplace will be the only noncooperative (and cooperative) equilibrium possible.

Proposition (3) : Suppose that (i), (ii), (iii) and (v) *hold and in addition that* $m_i = 1$, $i = 1, \ldots, N$. *Then the only equilibrium configuration possible involves one marketplace.*

The proof of this proposition follows readily from proposition (1). This result should not be surprising by now: Firms stand only to gain from spatial association, since by assumption, there is no competition between them. Observe, however, that firms would locate arbitrarily, were the consumers fully informed about the varieties offered at any marketplace. Now the condition that $m_i = 1$ for all i is sufficient but obviously not at all necessary. For the reasons outlined in the exposition of the model a straightforward generalization of proposition (3) to the case where $m_i > 1$ is difficult. The following example therefore should support the intuition that $m_i = 1$ is far too restrictive.

Example: Let the set $\mathcal{N}$ of consumer types be partitioned into two mutually exclusive subsets $\mathcal{N}_1$, $\mathcal{N}_2$ of size n and $N - n$ respectively. Suppose that for consumers $i \in \mathcal{N}_1$, $m_i = 1$ whereas for consumers $i \in \mathcal{N}_2$, $m_i = 2$. Let (i)–(iv) and (vi) hold for all consumers $i \in \mathcal{N}$. We will show that there is an $\hat{n} < N$ such that $n \geq \hat{n}$ implies a spatial concentration of all firms. Let firms $i \in \mathcal{N}_2$ be selected such that they don't compete about consumers' demands; more precisely such that firm i, $i \in \mathcal{N}_2$ will realize the demand from all consumer types q_i, $q_i \equiv \{k \mid u_k(i, \cdot) > u_k(0, \cdot)\}$. Recall from proposition (3) that all firms $i \in \mathcal{N}_1$ will locate jointly—at $l_i = v_1$, $i \in \mathcal{N}_1$, say. The desired result will hold if for $i \in \mathcal{N}_2$

$$\Pi_i\,(v_1, l_{-i}) > \Pi_i\,(v_2, l_{-i})$$

where v_2 is the (worst case) location of all firms $i \in \mathcal{N}_2$. Using (2) this will hold if for $n > \hat{n}$

$$\sum_{j=1}^{2} \pi_j(n+1)u(j) > \sum_{j=1}^{2} \pi_j(N-n)u(j), j \in \mathcal{N}_2.$$

Observe that

$$\pi_j(s) = \frac{\binom{N-j}{s-1}}{\binom{N}{s}}, j \leq N - s + 1.$$

Hence the inequality is satisfied if

$$\frac{n+1}{N}\,u(1) + \frac{(n+1)(N-n-1)}{N(N-1)}\,u(2)$$

$$> 2\,\frac{N-n}{N}\,u(1) + 2\,\frac{(N-n)n}{N(N-1)}\,u(2).$$

Taking account of (iii) it is easily checked that the inequality holds if

$$n \geq \frac{3N^2 - 5N + 2}{4N - 6}.$$

Let $\hat{n}$ be the smallest integer satisfying the latter inequality. ■

The example demonstrates that even in the extreme case that by chance all firms in $\mathcal{N}_2$ would be selected and located jointly in a marketplace so that they would face no competition with each other, they would prefer to join the larger competitive marketplace, provided it is sizeable enough.

The following two propositions show first that *for m_i not too large, a concentration of all firms in one marketplace is in the set of noncooperative equilibria*; and second, that under the same provision there is a critical size of some marketplace such that no firm therein will want to leave it, and all firms not in it will prefer joining it to establishing a locational monopoly. Thus, *given* such *a "large" marketplace, no "small" marketplaces will be upheld in equilibrium.*

Proposition (4): Suppose (i)–(iv) *and* (vi) *hold. Then there is an $\hat{m}(\mathcal{N})$ such that whenever $m < \hat{m}(\mathcal{N})$, the location of all firms in one marketplace is an equilibrium.*

Proof: This again follows from the construction of $\hat{m}$. We need to determine $\hat{m}$ such that whenever $m < \hat{m}$,

$$\prod_i (l_i, l_i = l_j, j \in \mathcal{N}) > \prod_i (l_i \neq l_j, j \in \mathcal{N}).$$

The inequality holds if $\tilde{z}(\mathcal{N}) > m\tilde{z}(1)$. Simplifying (2) according to (i) and (iv), this is implied by

$$u(1) > m\left[\frac{1}{\mathcal{N}}\sum_{j=1}^{m} u(j)\right]$$

or

$$\frac{\mathcal{N}}{m} > \frac{\sum_{j=1}^{m} u(j)}{u(1)}.$$

Using (iii) we obtain as a sufficient condition

$$\frac{\mathcal{N}}{m} > \frac{mu(1)}{u(1)}.$$

Let $\hat{m} = \max\{k \in \mathcal{N} \mid k < \sqrt{\mathcal{N}}\}$. ■

Thus, *despite a large substitution effect* ($\mathcal{N} - \sqrt{\mathcal{N}} - 1$ consumer types substituting away from the typical seller), *an equilibrium involving all firms at one location may be upheld.* It should again be borne in mind that this condition is derived in the unrealistic situation that any firm may spatially monopolize. It is easy to check that for a sufficiently small market size, this condition again disappears. Finally, the condition can without problem be generalized to not involving assumptions (iv) and (vi). The only cost incurred is a messier notation.

Proposition (5): Suppose that (i)–(iv) *and* (vi) *hold. Consider a marketplace k at location v_k that is of size s_k. Then for each m, $m = 2, \ldots, \hat{m}$, $\hat{m} = \max\{k \in \mathcal{N} \mid k < \sqrt{\mathcal{N}}\}$ there is an $\hat{s}(m)$ such that $s_k > \hat{s}(m)$ implies*

$$\prod_i (v_k, l_{-i}) > \prod_i (l_i, l_{-i}),\ l_i \neq l_j,\ i \neq j.$$

Furthermore, $\hat{s}(m)$ is increasing in m.

Proof: This follows again from the construction of $\hat{s}$. Simplifying (2) according to the assumptions made and solving explicitly for $\tilde{z}(s)$, it follows that for $s > \hat{s}$ the following inequality must be satisfied:

$$\sum_{j=1}^{m} [\pi_j(s) - m\pi_j(1)]u(j) > 0.$$

Since $u(j) > 0, j = 1, \ldots, m$, this inequality holds if

$$\sum_{j=1}^{m} \pi_j(s) - m \sum_{j=1}^{m} \pi_j(1) > 0.$$

Observe that

$$\begin{aligned}\sum_{j=1}^{m} \pi_j(s) &= \text{Prob}\{1 \in e_k \vee 2 \in e_k \vee \cdots \vee m \in e_k\} \\ &= 1 - \text{Prob}\{1 \notin e_k, 2 \notin e_k, \ldots, m \notin e_k\} \\ &= 1 - \frac{\binom{N-m}{s}}{\binom{N}{s}} = 1 - \frac{\binom{N-s}{m}}{\binom{N}{m}}.\end{aligned}$$

Hence the inequality is satisfied if for $s > \hat{s}$

$$\frac{(N-s)!}{(N-s-m)!} < \frac{N-m^2}{N} \frac{N!}{(N-m)!},$$

or

$$\begin{aligned}&(N-s)(N-s-1) \cdots (N-m-s+1) \\ &\quad < (N-m^2)(N-1)(N-2) \cdots (N-m-1).\end{aligned}$$

This inequality holds always for $s \geq m^2$. Let $\hat{s}(m) = m^2, m = 2, \ldots, \hat{m}$. ■

Thus, *a sufficient condition for no firm establishing a marketplace on its own is that there is a marketplace large enough worth joining.* $\hat{s}(m)$ is the threshold size of this marketplace that, if surmounted, will lead all firms to join it.[9] This drawing power may not come into force only if the remaining firms cooperate or cooperation is induced by a developer. In that case, they may form a new marketplace. However, it is easily seen that the formation of a coalition is not a sufficient condition for the large marketplace not to attract all remaining sellers.[10]

[9] This is but one specification of the notion of "agglomeration economies", that is: increasing returns to scale from spatial concentration so frequently found in the urban economics literature.

[10] A reinterpretation of the above example, with $\mathcal{N}_2$ comprising the set of remaining sellers, may aid the intuition.

All of these results should give sufficient support to the conjecture that noncooperative equilibria tend to involve the location of firms in a few marketplaces only, and in the extreme in one marketplace.[11] The last result now will demonstrate that for $m \geq 2$ the latter equilibrium configuration is not in the core. Thus, *there are always coalitions among firms under which it would be profitable to establish several marketplaces.*

Proposition (6): Suppose that (i)–(iv) *and* (vi) *hold. Let $\mathcal{N}$ be even. Let finally $m \geq 2$. Then a noncooperative equilibrium involving one marketplace is not in the core.*[12]

Proof: It is sufficient to show that there is a coalition of firms blocking the one marketplace equilibrium. Let the payoffs in that equilibrium be denoted by Π_j^*, $j = 1, \ldots, \mathcal{N}$. Consider a coalition $\mathscr{C}$ consisting of $\mathcal{N}/2$ firms offering varieties such that each firm will sell to exactly two consumer types. Such a coalition exists, by assumption (iv). Let $j \in \mathscr{C}$ and $j \in \mathscr{N}\backslash\mathscr{C}$ be located in two separate marketplaces, respectively, and denote the resulting payoffs by Π'_j, $j = 1, \ldots, \mathcal{N}$. But $\Pi'_j > \Pi_j^*$ if and only if, using (i)–(iv), and employing (2),

$$u(1) < 2\sum_{i=1}^{m} \pi_i\left(\frac{\mathcal{N}}{2}\right)u(i).$$

Since

$$\pi_1\left(\frac{\mathcal{N}}{2}\right) = \frac{\mathcal{N}/2}{\mathcal{N}} = \frac{1}{2},$$

we can rewrite this inequality as

$$u(1) < u(1) + s\sum_{i=2}^{m} \pi_i\left(\frac{\mathcal{N}}{2}\right)u(i).$$

But

$$2\sum_{i=2}^{m} \pi_i\left(\frac{\mathcal{N}}{2}\right)u(i) > 0 \qquad \forall m = 2, \ldots, \mathcal{N}. \qquad \blacksquare$$

The example used in the proof of proposition (6) is quite intuitive: from proposition (1) we know that a separation of firms into two marketplaces of size $\mathcal{N}/2$ each will reduce the market area for each one firm. However, the structure of the coalitions suggested here induces the spatial separation of "close competitors". It thus guarantees that the loss in market demand due to

[11] If we consider a sequential entry of the $\mathcal{N}$ firms, the case for a spatial concentration of all firms will be even stronger: let the order in which firms enter be determined by the maximal profit obtained from selling some good, given the location decisions of inframarginal entrants. Then initially a marketplace will form in which firms don't compete. When competitors will enter, the marketplace will be sufficiently large to let entry be profitable even under competition. All this follows if firms act myopically, or if firms upon entry realistically anticipate further growth of the (large) marketplace.

[12] It is not easy to determine whether the core of this game is empty or not. However, this is immaterial for the interpretation of the present result.

the reduction in the market area is more than offset by the gain in sales due to restricted competition.

While the formal derivation of this result is trivial, its economic consequences are not: *individual sellers' interest in partaking in the "externalities" of the large marketplace is too strong despite the fiercer competition generated from spatial association.* This behavior leads definitely to an inefficient outcome from the sellers' point of view. Whether it is also inefficient relative to the Pareto-criterion depends on consumers' preferences. However, there is a straightforward condition under which relocation corresponding to the counterexample leads to a Pareto-improvement, namely that the loss in utility of those consumers who after relocation obtain only their second preferred alternative is more than outweighed by the income gain they obtain in shares from the firms' increased profits. Formally, the condition is

$$u(1) = u(2) < \sum_{j=1}^{N} \theta_{ij}[\Pi'_j - \Pi^*_j] \qquad \forall i = 1, \ldots, N.$$

In valuing the stringency of this condition it is useful to keep in mind that the notion of Pareto-efficiency used here involves an extremely restricted social choice set, namely only firms' locations. Would the social choice set involve, for instance, income transfers between consumers, a single marketplace equilibrium configuration would *never* be Pareto efficient under the conditions of proposition (6).[13] It should go without further explication that such a concentration is *inequitable* no matter what equity criterion is applied. Within the confines of this model, we therefore are confronted with the interesting situation that a *policy designed to remove an inefficiency conforms with, rather than contradicts, a policy directed towards an equity objective.* These last results should be regarded with caution, however, when it comes to an effective restriction in the geographical size of the market. It is quite intuitive that for a sufficiently small market size the resulting spatial concentration may cease to be excessive.

IV. CONCLUDING REMARKS

As usual, the model presented here leaves much to be desired. On the demand side, we have specified consumers' search behavior only in a crude form. On the supply side, we have restricted ourselves to model only the locational choices of a fixed number of firms selling given product varieties at given prices, rather than considering entry endogenously and modelling the choice of location jointly with the choice of product varieties supplied and prices charged. However, especially in the presence of the fundamental modelling

[13] The point that noncooperative behavior presents additional marketplaces from coming into existence and therefore leads to Pareto-inefficient outcomes is nicely related to a result by Hart [2], according to which market equilibria may be suboptimal if (differentiated) products not being produced are highly complementary in consumption. Here, the complementarity is between sellers of substitutes.

problems already mentioned, this is a well justified procedure as a first step. We plan to come back on a number of generalizations.

For the time being, it appears useful to reflect on two questions: One, if the forces towards spatial concentration are so strong, aren't there market forces leading to an internalization of that "demand externality" and thereby to a removal of the inefficiencies? Two, does not price competition substantially weaken the strength of these agglomerative forces? As to the first question, we expect decentralization to be fostered by both, intrafirm internalization by offering several varieties, and internalization by a developer providing an institutional framework for coalition formation. This is a straightforward outcome of proposition (6). Armchair observations suggests that many decisions to decentralize are made by "internalizers". Still, we observe, particularly in European cities, an extreme central city concentration of retailing activities especially for the classes of commodities under scrutiny here. Given the forces working against an internalization, such as capital market imperfections, sellers' risk aversion, or cost of land assembly to developers, one might conclude that this concentration is indeed inefficient.

Now to the second question. It was already mentioned that one-product sellers may end up absorbing the consumers' surplus generated from spatial concentration even more than a "spatial monopolist" selling all those products (*cf* Stahl [7]). This result holds with the proviso that the own price elasticity of the market share obtained by any one seller is sufficiently small. However, as the size of the marketplace—and therefore competition—increase, that elasticity also increases, leading one-product sellers' prices to be driven down towards, and eventually below the price they would charge under a spatial one-product monopoly. The consequences of this for our results are obvious: Noncooperative firms' freedom to set prices may reinforce a spatial concentration at some small scale, and may exercise a decentralizing force when it comes to larger agglomerations of firms. To conclude from this that price competition would after all lead to an efficient state of affairs would be dangerous, however. If the fixed costs of locating and merchandising products (which we so far disregarded) are sufficiently large, relative to the demand at the marketplace, then noncooperative equilibrium prices may permanently stay high. After all, a competitive downward adjustment of prices would lead firms' profits to shrink towards zero, thus generating a quite limited rent paying ability to then inpoverished central city landlords.

KONRAD STAHL,
Lehrstuhl Wirtschaftstheorie,
Universität Dortmund,
Postfach 500500,
4600 Dortmund 50, W. Germany

REFERENCES

[1] D'Aspremont, C., Gabsziewicz, J., and Thisse, J.-F., "On Hotelling's 'Stability in Competition'," *Econometrica*, **47** (1979), pp. 1145–50.

[2] Hart, O. D., "Perfect Competition and Optimal Product Differentiation", *Journal of Economic Theory*, **22** (1980), pp. 279–312.

[3] Hotelling, H., "Stability in Competition", *Economic Journal*, **29** (1929), pp. 41–57.

[4] Nelson, P., Information and Consumer Behavior, *Journal of Political Economy*, **78** (1970), pp. 311–29.

[5] Rogers, A., Quadrat Analysis of Urban Dispersions 2: Case Studies of Urban Retail Systems, Environment and Planning, **1**, 1969, pp. 155–171.

[6] Stahl, K., Oligopolistic Location under Imperfect Consumer Information, Working Papers in Economic Theory and Urban Economics, Dortmund, March 1980.

[7] ——, Consumer Search and Spatial Pricing Under Alternative Market Arrangements, Berkeley: Centre for Research in Management, Institute of Business and Economic Research, IP-306, September 1981.

[8] Stigler, G., "The Economics of Information", *Journal of Political Economy*, **69** (1961), pp. 213–25.

[9] Stuart, Ch., "Search and the Spatial Organization of Trading", in: Lippman, S.; McCall, J. J.: *Studies in the Economics of Search* (Amsterdam: North Holland, 1979)

THE JOURNAL OF INDUSTRIAL ECONOMICS
Volume XXXI September/December 1982 Nos. 1/2

PRODUCT DIFFERENTIATION WITH INCOME DISPARITIES: AN ILLUSTRATIVE MODEL

J. JASKOLD GABSZEWICZ AND J.-F. THISSE

I

MARKETING practitioners often define partitions over the set of households according to "socio-economic" criteria, like variety in individual tastes, locational dispersion, income differences, etc. Such divisions serve for instance in differentiating, between these classes, the impact of an advertising campaign, or in designing the products in accordance with particular "class" requirements. The existence of such classes gives rise in each industry to a wide spectrum of different brands which, in spite of their similitudes, are specialized to the "satisfecit" of a particular "niche" in the set of households. This "brand proliferation" organizes the industry into a number of submarkets, with an intricate network of competition between the firms operating inside each submarket, and between the firms in each submarket and those operating in its "neighboring" submarkets. The automobile industry is a good example of this organization, essentially based on income dispersion. Rolls-Royce, Daimler, Cadillac, a.s.o. are brands competing to capture customers from the high income class; at the intermediate level, numerous brands are designed to meet requirements from the middle income class, a.s.o. Competition takes place inside each level, and between the different levels. The present paper analyzes the simplest configuration of this type of competition, with the idea of providing a pattern for analyzing more complex structures at later stages. Here we focus on income disparities between the consumers, and we neglect other forms of socio-economic differences.

II

Let us imagine a population of consumers identical in all respects, except income: the population is subdivided into a "low income class", comprising $\mathcal{N}_1$ consumers (consumers of type 1) with income level R_1, and a "high income class", comprising $\mathcal{N}_2$ consumers (consumers of type 2) with income level R_2, $R_2 > R_1$.

The industry under consideration involves two different products which are substitutes for each other: product A, a "high-quality" product, and product B, a "standard" one. Furthermore we assume that consumers do indivisible and mutually exclusive purchases. Thus if a consumer decides to buy one out of products A or B, he buys that product only, and a single unit of it. Finally we suppose that all consumers have identical tastes and that their common preferences are defined by the utility function

$$u(0, R) = u_0 \cdot R$$

$$u(A, R - p_A) = u_A \cdot (R - p_A)$$

$$u(B, R - p_B) = u_B \cdot (R - p_B), \qquad u_A > u_B > u_0 > 0;$$

where $u(0, R)$ denotes the utility of having an income level R and neither unit of A or B, and $u(A, R - p_A)$ (resp. $u(B, R - p_B)$) denotes the utility of having an income R and a single unit of A (resp. B) obtained at a price p_A (resp. p_B).

With an income R_1, a consumer of type 1 will never buy a unit of A (resp. B) if

$$p_A > \frac{u_A - u_0}{u_A} \cdot R_1 \left(\text{resp. } p_B > \frac{u_B - u_0}{u_B} \cdot R_1\right):$$

Indeed, this inequality implies

$$u(0, R_1) = u_0 \cdot R_1 > u(A, R_1 - p_A) = u_A(R_1 - p_A)$$

$$(\text{resp. } u(0, R_1) = u_0 \cdot R_1 > u(B, R_1 - p_B) = u_B \cdot (R_1 - p_B)),$$

and the consumer would prefer to keep his income unchanged rather than spending as much as p_A (resp. p_B) for a unit of A (resp. B). Consequently, a necessary condition for a consumer of type 1 to buy a unit of product A (resp. B) is

$$(1) \qquad p_A \leq \frac{u_A - u_0}{u_A} \cdot R_1$$

(resp.

$$(2) \qquad p_B \leq \frac{u_B - u_0}{u_B} \cdot R_1\Big).$$

Assume that (2) holds. Then the inequality

$$(3) \qquad u_A p_A - u_B p_B > (u_A - u_B) \cdot R_1$$

must also hold for a consumer of type 1 to buy a single unit of B rather than a single unit of A. Indeed, suppose on the contrary that

$$u_A p_A - u_B p_B \leq (u_A - u_B) \cdot R_1,$$

then

$$u_A \cdot (R_1 - p_A) \geq u_B \cdot (R_1 - p_B),$$

so that A, rather than B, would be bought by the consumer.

Similar arguments show that necessary and sufficient conditions for a consumer of type 2 to buy A (resp. B) are

$$(4) \qquad p_A \leq \frac{u_A - u_0}{u_A} \cdot R_2$$

$\Bigg($resp.

$$(5) \qquad p_B \leq \frac{u_B - u_0}{u_B} \cdot R_2\Bigg)$$

and

$$(6) \qquad u_A p_A - u_B p_B \leq (u_A - u_B) \cdot R_2 .$$

Taking into account these inequalities, we obtain the following "rectangular" demand functions $D_A(p_A, p_B)$ and $D_B(p_A, p_B)$:

(7)

$$\begin{aligned} D_A(p_A, p_B) &= 0 && \text{iff } p_A > \frac{(u_A - u_B)R_2 + u_B p_B}{u_A}; \\ &= N_2 && \text{iff } \frac{(u_A - u_B)R_1 + u_B p_B}{u_A} < p_A \leq \frac{(u_A - u_B)R_2 + u_B p_B}{u_A}; \\ &= N_1 + N_2 && \text{iff } p_A \leq \frac{(u_A - u_B)R_1 + u_B p_B}{u_A}. \end{aligned}$$

(8)

$$\begin{aligned} D_B(p_A, p_B) &= 0 && \text{iff } p_B \geq \min \left\{ \frac{u_A p_A - (u_A - u_B)R_1}{u_B}, \frac{u_B - u_0}{u_B} R_1 \right\}; \\ &= N_1 && \text{iff } \min \left\{ \frac{u_A p_A - (u_A - u_B)R_2}{u_B}, \frac{u_B - u_0}{u_B} R_2 \right\} \leq p_B \\ & && < \min \left\{ \frac{u_A p_A - (u_A - u_B)R_1}{u_B}, \frac{u_B - u_0}{u_B} R_1 \right\}; \\ &= N_1 + N_2 && \text{iff } p_B < \min \left\{ \frac{u_B - u_0}{u_B} R_1, \frac{u_A p_A - (u_A - u_B)R_2}{u_B} \right\}. \end{aligned}$$

III

Some basic questions can be formulated and answered within this very simple framework. First, how will competition act if the industry consists of two firms—a firm selling product A and a firm selling product B—and prices are taken as strategic variables? One feels intuitively that the nature of the solution hinges crucially on both the differences in qualities u_A and u_B between the products, and the difference between the income "masses" $N_1 R_1$ and $N_2 R_2$ corresponding to the two types of consumers. Indeed firm A enjoys the privilege of selling a higher quality product and the solution should reflect this advantage. In fact, we shall show that whenever a non cooperative price equilibrium exists, only firm A obtains a positive market share at this equilibrium. On the other hand, a small difference between the income masses $N_1 R_1$ and $N_2 R_2$ must entail a stronger price competition in the effort for attracting the whole market to either product A or B. By contrast, a large difference between $N_1 R_1$ and $N_2 R_2$ must facilitate a price solution where each seller acts as a "local monopolist" on his own submarket. We shall show that, although no price equilibrium exists in the latter case, some alternative plausible solution (called hereafter "entry equilibrium") owns the property that both sellers act as local monopolists, seller A serving the rich income class and seller B the poor one. Second, imagine that firms A and B decide to merge so that the whole industry is now controlled by a single firm. One must expect that the resulting monopoly should, in some cases, take advantage of the income difference between the consumers, and practise a kind of price discrimination between them: then both products remain in the industry. In other cases, however, the monopolist should be able to exploit the possibility of withdrawing product B from the market in view of reinforcing his monopolistic power on the other one and selling it at a higher price. We find hereafter the precise conditions under which the first solution is more profitable than the second one or vice-versa. In other circumstances, firms A and B would prefer to organize into a cartel, and restrict cooperation to price arrangements only: then by assumption both products remain in the market. We examine also when this solution prevails, and which prices will then be quoted by the cartel.

Another important issue deals with welfare implications of the preceding market arrangements. The basic question consists here in identifying when private and social profitability do coincide, or diverge from each other. For instance, at the same price, a market solution where the whole market is served with the high quality product is certainly better than a solution where the high income class only enjoys this privilege. Here also one feels that income dispersion and quality differences should matter. Propositions 5 and 6 below define necessary and sufficient conditions for both the cooperative and non cooperative solutions to agree with the social optimum.

Finally, the simple framework proposed above allows to shed some light on issues related to product selection and sequential entry. To illustrate, assume for instance that seller A first occupies the market, and seller B is contemplating to enter the market with a product of lower quality. Is there a "limit pricing" policy for the existing seller so as to deter entry of seller B? When this policy is inoperant, which quality is the entrant expected to choose? If he chooses a quality close to the existing product, he may expect to attract the customers of product A, and thereby increase his profit; but then he runs the risk of price-war. If he differentiates from product A, he may avoid price-war, but loses his chance to capture the whole market. Thus *a priori* it seems that some intermediate solution should prevail. Surprisingly enough, we shall show, however, that a kind of "principle of minimal differentiation" here holds, at least as long as entry takes place with a lower quality product than the existing one. By contrast, entry with higher quality always leads to maximal differentiation.

The reader is probably surprised that we have not introduced costs in our model. Why not confess it? It is only for simplifying our life and his! In a short conclusion, we indicate how our results should be amended if simple cost structures are taken into account.

IV

Let us first study when a non-cooperative price solution exists for the situation described in section II. The prices

$$p_A \in \left[0, \frac{u_A - u_0}{u_A} \cdot R_2\right] \quad \text{and} \quad p_B \in \left[0, \frac{u_B - u_0}{u_B} \cdot R_2\right]$$

are the *strategies* of the two sellers. The profit functions $\Pi_A(p_A, p_B)$ and $\Pi_B(p_A, p_B)$ are defined, respectively, by

$$\Pi_A(p_A, p_B) = p_A \cdot D_A(p_A, p_B) \quad \text{and} \quad \Pi_B(p_A, p_B) = p_B \cdot D_B(p_A, p_B).$$

By definition, a *non cooperative price equilibrium* is a pair of prices (p_A^*, p_B^*) such that no seller can increase his profit by any unilateral deviation from (p_A^*, p_B^*).

Proposition (1): There exists no price equilibrium (p_A^*, p_B^*) such that $D_A(p_A^*, p_B^*) > 0$ and $D_B(p_A^*, p_B^*) > 0$.

Proof: Assume on the contrary that such an equilibrium exists. First take $p_B^* = 0$; then $\Pi_B(p_A^*, 0) = 0$. As $D_A(p_A^*, p_B^*) > 0$, we must have, by (7)

$$(u_A - u_B) \cdot R_1 < u_A p_A^* < (u_A - u_B) \cdot R_2.$$

Given that

$$p_A^* > \frac{u_A - u_B}{u_A} \cdot R_1,$$

seller B may then guarantee himself a strictly positive profit by slightly increasing his price; a contradiction. Accordingly $p_B^* > 0$ and $\Pi_B(p_A^*, p_B^*) = p_B^* \cdot N_1$. Since $D_A(p_A^*, p_B^*) > 0$, it follows from (7) that

$$u_A p_A^* - u_B p_B^* < (u_A - u_B) \cdot R_2. \tag{1.1}$$

Furthermore $D_A(p_A^*, p_B^*) > 0$ also implies

$$p_A^* \leq \frac{u_A - u_0}{u_A} \cdot R_2 .$$

Assume that this inequality would be strict; then there exists $\varepsilon > 0$ such that, for

$$\tilde{p}_A \underset{\text{def}}{=} p_A^* + \varepsilon,$$

the inequality (1.1) still holds, and that

$$\tilde{p}_A < \frac{u_A - u_0}{u_A} \cdot R_2 ,$$

yields a higher profit than $\Pi_A(p_A^*, p_B^*)$; a contradiction. Hence we must have

$$(1.2) \qquad p_A^* = \frac{u_A - u_0}{u_A} \cdot R_2$$

Substituting (1.2) into (1.1) leads to

$$(u_A - u_0) \cdot R_2 - u_B p_B^* < (u_A - u_B) \cdot R_2 ,$$

which amounts to

$$p_B^* > \frac{u_B - u_0}{u_B} \cdot R_2 > \frac{u_B - u_0}{u_B} \cdot R_1 .$$

But then we would have $D_B(p_A^*, p_B^*) = 0$; a contradiction. ■

Proposition (2): There exists a non-cooperative price equilibrium (p_A^*, p_B^*) *such that* $D_A(p_A^*, p_B^*) > 0$ *and* $D_B(p_A^*, p_B^*) = 0$ *if, and only if,*

$$(*) \qquad \frac{R_1}{R_2} \geq \frac{N_2}{N_1 + N_2}$$

Furthermore

$$p_A^* = \frac{u_A - u_B}{u_A} \cdot R_1 \quad \textit{and} \quad p_B^* = 0.$$

Proof: First, if an equilibrium exists with $D_A(p_A^*, p_B^*) > 0$ and $D_B(p_A^*, p_B^*) = 0$, it must be that $p_B^* = 0$. Assume indeed $p_B^* > 0$. Then $D_A(p_A^*, p_B^*) = N_1 + N_2$; in the opposite case, it would be sufficient for seller B to quote a price p_B smaller than

$$\frac{u_B - u_0}{u_B} \cdot R_1$$

to get a positive profit; a contradiction. Knowing that $D_A(p_A^*, p_B^*) = \mathcal{N}_1 + \mathcal{N}_2$, it follows from (7) that

$$p_A^* = \frac{(u_A - u_B)R_1 + u_B p_B^*}{u_A}$$

since this value of p_A maximizes $p_A D_A(p_A, p_B^*)$ under the constraint $D_A(p_A, p_B^*) = \mathcal{N}_1 + \mathcal{N}_2$, as required by the definition of an equilibrium. But then seller B could lower his price to

$$\tilde{p}_B \underset{\text{def}}{=} p_B^* - \varepsilon > 0,$$

and capture a positive market share. In this case, we would have $\Pi_B(p_A^*, \tilde{p}_B) > \Pi_B(p_A^*, p_B^*) = 0$, a contradiction. Consequently, if an equilibrium exists such that $D_A(p_A^*, p_B^*) > 0$ and $D_B(p_A^*, p_B^*) = 0$, it must be that $p_B^* = 0$.

Now we prove that such an equilibrium exists, if, and only if, (*) is satisfied, and that

$$p_A^* \text{ must be equal to } \frac{u_A - u_B}{u_A} \cdot R_1 .$$

Clearly, the price

$$p_A^* = \frac{u_A - u_B}{u_A} \cdot R_1 \quad \text{is such that} \quad \Pi_A(p_A^*, 0) \geq \Pi_A(p_A, 0)$$

for any

$$p_A \in \left[0, \frac{u_A - u_B}{u_A} \cdot R_1\right].$$

To show that p_A^* is an equilibrium strategy we must also have $\Pi_A(p_A^*, 0) \geq \Pi_A(p_A, 0)$ for any

$$p_A \in \left[\frac{u_A - u_B}{u_A} \cdot R_1, \frac{u_A - u_0}{u_A} \cdot R_2\right].$$

In

$$\left[\frac{u_A - u_B}{u_A} \cdot R_2, \frac{u_A - u_0}{u_A} \cdot R_2\right],$$

we have $D_A(p_A, 0) = 0$, so that $\Pi_A(p_A, 0) = 0 < \Pi_A(p_A^*, 0)$. In

$$\left[\frac{u_A - u_B}{u_A} \cdot R_1, \frac{u_A - u_B}{u_A} \cdot R_2\right],$$

the best reply against $p_B^* = 0$ is given by

$$\tilde{p}_A = \frac{u_A - u_B}{u_A} \cdot R_2 . \quad \text{For} \quad p_A^* = \frac{u_A - u_B}{u_A} \cdot R_1$$

to be an equilibrium price, it is then necessary and sufficient that

$$\Pi_A(p_A^*, 0) = \frac{u_A - u_B}{u_A} \cdot R_1(\mathcal{N}_1 + \mathcal{N}_2) \geq \Pi_A(p_A, 0)$$

$$= \mathcal{N}_2 \cdot \frac{u_A - u_B}{u_A} \cdot R_2,$$

which is satisfied if, and only if (*) holds. ■

Since it is evident that no equilibrium can exist where seller A would be thrown out of the market, we conclude from propositions 1 and 2 that a price equilibrium exists if, and only if, condition (*) is satisfied. Furthermore, in that case, only the high quality product is sold to both types of consumers. Does it mean that seller A behaves as a monopolist? From direct observation of the market, one may think, indeed, that seller A acts as a monopolist since no other product is sold to the consumers. *Notice however that p_A^* is lower than the price that a monopolist selling A would have quoted in a similar situation* (*i.e. if* (*) *is verified*) *without the potential presence of seller B* (see below propositions 3 and 4). Seller A is thus a "pseudo-monopolist": he is enforced to lower his price at the level p_A^* to prevent B's entry. Hereafter we call accordingly the price p_A^* the *limit price* of seller A.

It is difficult to speculate about the kind of price arrangement which should arise if condition (*) is violated. Certainly it would create incentives to price cooperation since price war is at the prejudice of both sellers. Another possibility, close to cooperation, will be considered in section VII, where sequential entry in the market is analyzed.

V

If we are now interested in the cooperative duopoly, we have first to define the nature of the collusion between the two sellers. If sellers A and B decide to merge, they face various possibilities. In particular they may decide to withdraw product B from the market if it is advantageous for them. This possibility can arise since products A and B are substitutes, and consumers do mutually exclusive purchase decisions. On the contrary, if the sellers restrict collusion and form only a cartel, the joint profit maximization must be calculated assuming that *both* products A and B have a positive market share.

If sellers A and B decide to merge, then the resulting merger becomes a monopolist, and has to decide whether he should sell product A only, or products A and B simultaneously. In the first alternative, he may choose to sell product A to consumers of type 2 only (let Π_1 denote the corresponding profit level), or to types 1 and 2 (let Π_2 denote the corresponding profit level). If he retains the second alternative, then of course he sells product A to type 2 and product B to type 1 (denote by Π_3 the corresponding profit level). Proposition 3 below determines, for each of these cases, the optimal price solution; proposition 4 orders the corresponding profit levels according to the parametric values N_1, N_2, R_1, R_2, u_A and u_B.

Proposition (3): If a monopolist sells product A to type 2 consumers only (resp. to types 1 and 2), then the optimal price is

$$p_A^M = \frac{(u_A - u_0)}{u_A} \cdot R_2 \left(\text{resp. } p_A^m = \frac{u_A - u_0}{u_A} \cdot R_1 \right).$$

If product A is sold to type 2 consumers and product B to type 1, then the optimal pair of prices $(\tilde{p}_A, \tilde{p}_B)$ *is given by*

$$\tilde{p}_A = \frac{(u_A - u_B)R_2 + (u_B - u_0)R_1}{u_A};$$

$$\tilde{p}_B = \frac{(u_B - u_0)}{u_B} \cdot R_1.$$

Proof: The first part of the proposition is obvious. As for the second part, we notice that the joint profit writes as

$$(3.1) \qquad N_2 p_A + N_1 p_B$$

subject to conditions that $(u_A - u_B) \cdot R_1 < u_A p_A - u_B p_B \leq (u_A - u_B) \cdot R_2$,

$$p_A \leq \frac{u_A - u_0}{u_A} \cdot R_2 \quad \text{and} \quad p_B \leq \frac{u_B - u_0}{u_B} \cdot R_1.$$

Since (3.1) is linear in p_A and p_B, one of the two following possibilities must arise:

$$\tilde{p}_A = \frac{u_A - u_0}{u_A} \cdot R_2 \quad \text{or} \quad \tilde{p}_B = \frac{u_B - u_0}{u_B} \cdot R_1.$$

Assume that

$$\tilde{p}_A = \frac{u_A - u_0}{u_A} \cdot R_2.$$

We then easily verify that $u_A \tilde{p}_A - u_B p_B > (u_A - u_B) \cdot R_2$ for any

$$p_B \in \left[0, \frac{u_B - u_0}{u_B} \cdot R_1\right],$$

so that condition $D_A(\tilde{p}_A, \tilde{p}_B) > 0$ is violated. Consequently,

$$\tilde{p}_B = \frac{u_B - u_0}{u_B} \cdot R_1.$$

Now $\tilde{p}_A$ must be chosen as high as possible under the constraint $D_A(\tilde{p}_A, \tilde{p}_B) > 0$. This condition is satisfied if, and only if, $\tilde{p}_A$ verifies

$$u_A \tilde{p}_A - u_B \tilde{p}_B = u_A \tilde{p}_A - (u_B - u_0) \cdot R_1 = (u_A - u_B) \cdot R_2,$$

i.e. iff

$$\tilde{p}_A = \frac{(u_A - u_B)R_2 + (u_B - u_0)R_1}{u_A}.$$

To conclude, it is easy to check that

$$\tilde{p}_A \leq \frac{(u_A - u_0)}{u_A} \cdot R_2$$

■

Proposition (4): The cooperative solution under merger involves both products A and B if, and only if

$$\frac{N_2 u_B}{N_2 u_B + N_1 u_0} > \frac{R_1}{R_2} > \frac{N_2 u_B}{N_2 u_B + N_1 u_A};$$

otherwise, only product A is sold at the cooperative solution: to types 1 and 2 of consumers, if

$$\frac{R_1}{R_2} > \frac{N_2 u_B}{N_2 u_B + N_1 u_0}$$

and to type 2 only if

$$\frac{N_2 u_B}{N_2 u_B + N_1 u_A} > \frac{R_1}{R_2}.$$

Proof: The proof follows from direct computation and comparisons of the profits Π_1, Π_2 and Π_3, which leads to the following orderings:

(i) $$\Pi_2 > \Pi_3 > \Pi_1 \Leftrightarrow \frac{R_1}{R_2} > \frac{N_2 u_B}{N_2 u_B + N_1 u_0};$$

(ii) $$\Pi_3 > \Pi_2 > \Pi_1 \Leftrightarrow \frac{N_2 u_B}{N_2 u_B + N_1 u_0} > \frac{R_1}{R_2} > \frac{N_2}{N_1 + N_2};$$

(iii) $$\Pi_3 > \Pi_1 > \Pi_2 \Leftrightarrow \frac{N_2}{N_1 + N_2} > \frac{R_1}{R_2} > \frac{N_2 u_B}{N_2 u_B + N_1 u_A};$$

(iv) $$\Pi_1 > \Pi_3 > \Pi_2 \Leftrightarrow \frac{N_2 u_B}{N_2 u_B + N_1 u_A} > \frac{R_1}{R_2} > 0.$$

■

As a corollary of propositions 2, 3 and 4, it is interesting to notice that *whenever a non cooperative price equilibrium exists, the price of product A*

$$\left(p_A^M = \frac{u_A - u_0}{u_A} \cdot R_2\right)$$

quoted at the cooperative solution under merger, always exceeds the price

$$p_A^* = \frac{u_A - u_B}{u_A} \cdot R_1$$

at the non cooperative solution.

If the sellers restrict collusion and form a cartel only, then the cooperative solution coincides with the optimal price structure $(\tilde{p}_A, \tilde{p}_B)$ which obtains under merging when product A is sold to type 2 and product B to type 1. Accordingly, if

$$\frac{N_2 u_B}{N_2 u_B + N_1 u_0} > \frac{R_1}{R_2} > \frac{N_2 u_B}{N_2 u_B + N_1 u_A},$$

the profit Π_3 realized through merging coincides with the profit that would realize a simple cartel so that, in that case, no incentive for merging exists. By contrast, if

$$\frac{N_2 u_B}{N_2 u_B + N_1 u_A} > \frac{R_1}{R_2}, \quad \text{or if} \quad \frac{R_1}{R_2} > \frac{N_2 u_B}{N_2 u_B + N_1 u_0},$$

the corresponding profits of merging Π_2, or Π_1, exceed in both cases, the profit Π_3 that the cartel would realize.

It may appear surprising that it is sometimes advantageous for a single firm to sell in the same market two products competing with each other. In fact, income dispersion allows price discrimination between the rich and the poor income class. Of course the high quality product has to be sold at a lower price than it would be if product B had been withdrawn from the market ($\tilde{p}_A < p_A^M$); but the profit increase obtained when serving the whole market at prices $(\tilde{p}_A, \tilde{p}_B)$ could be higher than the loss incurred by the price reduction of product A.

VI

If a welfare viewpoint is adopted, three dimensions must *a priori* be considered when comparing the social profitability of the various market solutions studied above, namely: prices, products and market shares.

If prices are not taken into account, but only products and market shares, the best welfare solution is undoubtedly when product A is sold to the whole market (denote this solution by w_1). The solution w_2 defined by "product A sold to type 2, and product B sold to type 1" follows in the ordering. The worst solution is clearly w_3 defined by "product A sold to type 2 only". Now, let us integrate price comparisons. Since by proposition 3, p_A^M in w_1 is smaller than p_A^m in w_2 and $\tilde{p}_A$ in w_3, w_1 dominates w_2 and w_3 in all respects. Indeed, consumers of type 1 are indifferent between buying product B at price

$$\tilde{p}_B = \frac{u_B - u_0}{u_B} \cdot R_1 \quad \text{(i.e. in } w_2\text{)},$$

and buying product A at

$$p_A^m = \frac{u_A - u_0}{u_A} \cdot R_1 \quad \text{(i.e. in } w_1\text{)}.$$

By contrast, consumers of type 2 are better off in w_1 than in w_2, since $\bar{p}_A > p_A^m$. Furthermore, comparing w_2 and w_3, we obtain a similar conclusion: consumers of type 2 prefer w_2 to w_3, while consumers of type 1 are again indifferent between the two situations. Accordingly, when prices, products and market shares are simultaneously integrated, we obtain the following unambiguous welfare classification: w_1 dominates w_2, which, in turn, dominates w_3. Using proposition 4 we deduce immediately:

Proposition (5): The cooperative solution under merger coincides with the optimal welfare solution w_1 if, and only if

$$\frac{R_1}{R_2} > \frac{N_2 u_B}{N_2 u_B + N_1 u_0}.$$

As for the non cooperative solution, when it exists, we know that it leads only to the solution w_1. Consequently, for the sake of completeness, we state

Proposition (6): The non cooperative solution coincides with the optimal welfare solution w_1 whenever it exists, i.e. if, and only if,

$$\frac{R_1}{R_2} \geq \frac{N_2}{N_1 + N_2}.$$

VII

The above approach implicitly assumes that when taking their decisions on prices, duopolists have already selected their products. Very often however, the sellers enter the market sequentially, and it introduces a kind of asymmetry between the strategic possibilities of the seller entered at the first date, and the new entrant. Since his product quality is already fixed, the first seller can only modulate his price, though the new entrant can still choose both the quality of his product *and* his price. If there exists a non cooperative equilibrium, i.e. if (*) holds, the sequential entry process reduces to a very simple scheme: no entry by inferior quality is allowed, while entry by higher quality leads to the exit of the existing firm. More significant is the process of entry when no non cooperative solution exists. Two different cases must be considered. In the first one, the product of the existing firm A embodies all the amount of current technological knowledge so that entry cannot occur with a higher quality product. On the contrary, in the second case, a more attractive substitute can be sold on the market due to some technological progress.

To start with, let us consider the first case. Then firm A is settled on the market and a firm B contemplates the entry possibilities with a lower quality index u_B as representing its product selection variable. For simplicity we assume that the quality set is defined by the interval $[u_0, u_A]$. Since by assumption there exists no non cooperative equilibrium, condition (*) does not hold, which implies that $\Pi_1 > \Pi_2$, with Π_1 and Π_2 as defined on p. 122 [see (iii) in the proof of proposition 4]. Consequently, firm A as a monopolist sells his product to the high income class only. Firm B has thus an incentive to capture the market segment corresponding to the low income class, which is not yet served. Of course, if seller B tries to enter, seller A could retaliate by using his limit price policy. Nevertheless, since there exists no non cooperative price equilibrium, whatever B's reaction to this retaliation may be, seller A will have afterwards an incentive to charge a higher price than his limit price, thus leaving room for the entry of seller B at a lower price. This instability, which does not exist when a non cooperative price solution exists, should favour in this case a kind of tacit agreement between the sellers. A possible solution could be as follows. Since using limit price entails a substantial profit loss for seller A, seller B could suggest to him some intermediate arrangement, implying of course some profit loss relative to the initial solution, but perhaps smaller than the loss incurred under the limit pricing policy. This agreement would lead to a pair of prices in which seller A keeps his customers at the highest price compatible with the presence of seller B on the market's segment corresponding to the low income class, and conversely for seller B. Formally we call the resulting price pattern an *Entry Equilibrium*, and we define it by a pair of prices $(\hat{p}_A, \hat{p}_B)$ such that $\Pi_A(\hat{p}_A, \hat{p}_B) \geq \Pi_A(p_A, \hat{p}_B)$ for all p_A such that $D_B(p_A, \hat{p}_B) > 0$, and $\Pi_B(\hat{p}_A, \hat{p}_B) \geq \Pi_B(\hat{p}_A, p_B)$ for all p_B such that $D_A(\hat{p}_A, p_B) > 0$.

Proposition (7): There exists a unique entry equilibrium[1] *given by*

$$\hat{p}_A = \frac{(u_A - u_B)R_2 + (u_B - u_0)R_1}{u_A}$$

$$\hat{p}_B = \frac{u_B - u_0}{u_B} \cdot R_1$$

Furthermore, if condition (*) *does not hold,* $\Pi_A(\hat{p}_A, \hat{p}_B) > \Pi_A(p_L, 0)$, *where* p_L *denotes the highest price which firm A can charge, guaranteeing* $D_B(p_A, 0) = 0$.

Proof: First, it is clear that if there exists an entry equilibrium, p_B is necessarily smaller or equal to $\hat{p}_B$. On the other hand, reducing p_B from $\hat{p}_B$ would lead either to a decrease in profit, or to the exit of seller A, which is not allowed by

[1] Incidentally notice that the values of prices at the entry equilibrium coincide with the optimal price pattern for a cartel who would sell simultaneously products A and B (see proposition 3). This may be surprising at first glance: the entry equilibrium has a non cooperative flavour since each seller is only concerned with his own profit. Probably this property is due to the inelasticity of demands in the restricted domain in which each seller chooses his strategy.

definition of an entry equilibrium. Accordingly, if there exists an entry equilibrium, $\hat{p}_B$ must be equal to

$$\frac{u_B - u_0}{u_B} \cdot R_1 .$$

Second, a simple calculation shows that the highest value of $\Pi_A(p_A, \hat{p}_B)$ compatible with $D_A(p_A, \hat{p}_B) > 0$ and $D_B(p_A, \hat{p}_B) > 0$ is given by $\hat{p}_A$. Accordingly $(\hat{p}_A, \hat{p}_B)$ is the unique entry equilibrium. Third, the last part of proposition 7 follows from a direct comparison of $\Pi_A(\hat{p}_A, \hat{p}_B)$ and $\Pi_A(p_L, 0)$ taking into account the fact that (*) does not hold, i.e.

$$\frac{R_1}{R_2} < \frac{N_2}{N_1 + N_2}. \qquad \blacksquare$$

If seller B is convinced that an entry equilibrium will be reached after his entry on the market, he will choose his quality index u_B in the interval $[u_0, u_A]$ so as to maximize his profit at the entry equilibrium. Since $\Pi_B(\hat{p}_A, \hat{p}_B)$ is an increasing function of u_B, we obtain immediately:

Proposition (8) : If entry takes place with an inferior quality product, then the maximal profit of the entrant at the entry equilibrium obtains when $u_B = u_A$, i.e. both products are perfect substitutes.

If entry can take place with a superior quality product, then firm B is settled on the market while firm A is the entrant. Formally, identify the choice set for u_A by $[u_0, u_{max}]$ where u_{max} corresponds to the highest quality available $(u_{max} > u_B)$. Again we assume that both sellers choose prices at the entry equilibrium. Then using proposition 7 and the fact that $\Pi_A(\hat{p}_A, \hat{p}_B)$ is increasing w.r.t. u_A on $[u_0, u_{max}]$, we have the following:

Proposition (9) : If entry can take place with a superior quality product, then the maximal profit of the entrant at the entry equilibrium obtains when $u_A = u_{max}$.

If some credibility is paid to the concept of entry equilibrium, propositions 8 and 9 reveal that two different situations may be observed in terms of product variety. When entry takes place with inferior quality, we observe afterwards a tendency to minimal differentiation between the products while prices tend also to be equal. On the contrary, when entry can occur by superior quality, product differentiation tends to be maximal, while now prices tend to deviate from each other. In any case, product selection by the entrant leads him to choose the highest quality available. This property could be viewed as a kind of "principle of maximal quality selection".

VIII

Our analysis does not supply more than an extremely simplified overview of the intricate geography of a differentiated industry. Even with this *caveat*, it does not provide us with any insight into basic problems of industrial reality, like cost structures (in particular the presence of economies of scale), the linkage between costs and product quality, and the dependence of product selection on taste dispersion. Among the multiple facets of the problem which have been skipped for facility, the incidence of the cost structures on the equilibrium market solution is probably the most urgent to be analyzed. Indeed, it is expected that the presence of costs should generate additional phenomena. For instance, if production costs of the high quality product A are large relative to those of the standard product B, it is evident that the advantage of product A over B can be weakened and at the limit cancelled, both from the viewpoints of private and social profitability. In that case, a non cooperative equilibrium may be observed at which product B is sold to the whole market, and product A is out of business. Again it can be shown that both products cannot "cohabit" at the non cooperative equilibrium. With respect to entry, the "principle of maximal quality selection" can be dampened by the corresponding increase in the production costs with quality. However, as long as the marginal increase in revenue exceeds the marginal cost of increasing quality, the principle remains valid.

JEAN JASKOLD GABSZEWICZ,
C.O.R.E.,
34 Voie du Roman Pays,
1348 Louvain-la-Neuve,
Belgium

and

JACQUES-FRANÇOIS THISSE,
S.P.U.R.,
Bâtiment Vinci,
Place du Levant 1,
1348 Louvain-la-Neuve, Belgium.

THE JOURNAL OF INDUSTRIAL ECONOMICS
Volume XXXI September/December 1982 Nos. 1/2

II. DISCRIMINATORY PRICING: THE GREENHUT–OHTA APPROACH

NEIL DORWARD, *Recent Developments in the Analysis of Spatial Competition and Their Implications for Industrial Economics*

Recent research into spatial competition suggests that the long-standing methodological convention of abstracting from space when constructing neo-classical models of competition is unsatisfactory as it materially affects the properties of such models. This paper reviews recent developments in the analysis of price discrimination and entry-deterrence within a spatial dimension. Both areas have been the scene of active research which has provided results very different from those given by neoclassical models without a spatial dimension. The implications of these developments for industrial economic analysis are discussed, particularly from the perspectives of economic welfare and public policy towards price regulation and monopoly.

GEORGE NORMAN and NANCY K. NICHOLS, *Dynamic Market Strategy Under Threat of Competitive Entry: An Analysis of the Pricing and Production Policies Open to the Multinational Company*

The strategy a firm adopts in supplying particular markets over time is determined by to which of four distinct sets these markets are allocated. Market allocation, and so market control, is determined by the relationship between marginal costs to the firm of supply from its plant and entry constraints—price and technology diffusion rate—facing potential rivals. Entry constraints have product-specific characteristics—brand image, technology—and market specific characteristics—market size, development, sophistication of competitors. There need, therefore, be no simple relationship between distance of a market from the firm and control of the market by the firm. Alternative supply modes are considered and factors influencing their choice shown to be consistent with recent analysis of the multinational enterprise.

RICHARD E. SCHULER and BENJAMIN F. HOBBS, *Spatial Price Duopoly Under Uniform Delivered Pricing*

In this short run analysis, the location and number of competitors is fixed, and the profit maximizing behavior of the producers is explored under a variety of inter-firm spacings and initial prices. Assuming zero-price-conjectural-variation (the only consistent myopic assumption), profit levels are computed under three pricing strategies: 1) incremental under-cutting of the neighbor's price, 2) moving directly to the spatial monopoly price, 3) or conceding the neighbor his existing service territory and moving to the optimal monopoly price for the remaining area.

The analysis shows that regardless of initial conditions, the dynamic paths will always converge to a cycle between the undercut strategy, somewhere above marginal cost, and the concession strategy, below the collusive price. Thus, in a spatial economy, the swings under price competition are less than Edgeworth suggested for spaceless duopoly.

MENAHEM SPIEGEL, *Pricing Policies Under Conditions of Spatial Competition*

The optimal pricing policy is that policy which is, from the single seller's point of view, the preferred one. To identify the optimal pricing policy, the profit performance of the representative firm is being compared under the following pricing policies: 1. Uniform F.O.B. price; 2. Uniform delivered price; 3. "Meet the competition" pricing policy.

Using some simple standard assumptions concerning the market, the comparison of the profit performance implies that, for any given market area the individual firm would prefer to choose its pricing policy in the reverse order of the one listed above, i.e., its first choice would be: "Meet the competition" pricing policy.

THE JOURNAL OF INDUSTRIAL ECONOMICS
Volume XXXI September/December 1982 Nos. 1/2

RECENT DEVELOPMENTS IN THE ANALYSIS OF SPATIAL COMPETITION AND THEIR IMPLICATIONS FOR INDUSTRIAL ECONOMICS

NEIL DORWARD*

THE methodological convention of excluding space from the neoclassical model of perfect competition has for long been regarded as an acceptable theoretical abstraction within microeconomic theory. Although the real economy is characterised by customers and producers being dispersed over geographic space with trade between them always incurring transport costs, the abstraction from space has not been thought materially to affect the results given by models based on the theory of perfect competition. In addition, the abstraction has made the theory of perfect competition that much simpler so assisting its long-standing pervasiveness throughout the economics literature. Consequently, the development of spatial theory had until the 1970s been largely isolated from mainstream economics and confined to a number of areas of special interest such as location theory, the oligopolistic structure of market areas, urban and regional economics. This historic neglect of spatial variables, or distance costs, in the analysis of economic relationships starkly contrasts with the considerable investment made in developing the neoclassical model within a time dimension.

Recently, a number of papers reporting research into spatial microeconomics, particularly those concerning partial equilibrium models of the theory of the firm in economic space, have claimed equilibrium solutions and predictions different from those resulting from the spaceless model of perfect competition (for example, see Greenhut [19], Greenhut *et al.* [28], Capozza and Van Order [7], [8], and Eaton and Lipsey [10], [11]). Indeed, given certain assumptions regarding competitors' reaction functions (Greenhut *et al.* [28] and Capozza and Van Order [6], [7]) and given certain specifications regarding the shape of the demand curve (Greenhut *et al.* [15], Ohta [39], [40] and Benson [3]) the results from models incorporating a spatial dimension can be the reverse of those suggested by the neoclassical model. This suggests that the conventional abstraction from space may be unsatisfactory as many neoclassical properties seem to be dependent upon the exclusion of space. For example, the incorporation of space permits the analysis of competition to overcome several theoretical drawbacks featured in the model of perfect competition. Firms no longer incorrectly perceive themselves facing horizontal demand curves as the spatially dispersed distribution of customers automati-

* The author wishes to thank Melvin Greenhut for his helpful critique and suggestions.

cally gives some monopoly power to firms scattered over the spatial market. Also, unlike the spaceless neoclassical model which assumes constant returns to scale, the very existence of firms in the spatial economy necessitates increasing returns to scale. And further, these increasing returns to scale need not preclude an equilibrium. Eaton and Lipsey [11] and Capozza and Van Order [8] have shown that with immobile firms this equilibrium is likely to be associated with pure profits and that it need not be unique. It thus appears that the incorporation of space into the analysis of competition has major indications for mainstream microeconomic theory in general and industrial economics in particular.

The purpose of this paper is to review recent developments in two areas of spatial economic theory which are likely to have considerable impacts on industrial economic analysis, namely: spatial price discrimination and entry-deterring strategies. Both areas have been the scene of active research in recent years providing results contrary to those expected from the use of neoclassical models of price theory.

In the next section the paper examines those characteristics inherent in the spatial economy as well as their importance in respect of the contrasts between spatial and non-spatial microeconomic theory. The following two sections review the implications for industrial economics of the distortions arising from incorporating space into the analyses of price discrimination and entry-deterrence, and assess these developments from the perspective of economic welfare. The final section examines the public policy issues.

I. THE CHARACTERISTICS OF SPATIAL COMPETITION

The neoclassical model of perfect competition contrasts with any spatial competitive model in that it has all economic activity taking place at one point in space and it assumes constant returns to scale. While either of these assumptions can be relaxed to include space or "minor" increasing returns to scale (Starr [48]), without substantially altering the properties of the model, the inclusion of both space and unrestricted increasing returns to scale make it impossible to prove equilibrium under general equilibrium theory. The existence of the perfectly competitive equilibrium can only be proved with existing techniques when the production technology is convex, having either constant or decreasing returns to scale. As such, the spatial models of competition have properties different from the neoclassical model of perfect competition.

The first essential characteristic of spatial competition is the dispersal of buyers over the market (generally assumed to be uniformly distributed) causing exchange to incur costly transport. So long as factors of production are scattered over the market, firms have an incentive to choose dispersed plant locations. As a result, transport costs give each dispersed firm a monopoly over its local customers. With firms always being monopolists or oligopolists they will be able to charge a higher ex-works price than their distant competitors without losing all their customers. So long as customers at any point in the market demand a finite quantity and always buy from the firm with the lowest delivered price, each firm will face a downward sloping demand curve. However, the incorporation of space does not seriously affect the neo-classical model assuming constant returns to scale and free-entry. All that happens is that firms keep entering the market until transport costs are minimised, eventually leaving a self-sufficient economy with all production occurring at the point of consumption. Unfortunately, the net result is as many firms as there are consumers with the effective elimination of spatial competition. Thus, if space alone is added to the neoclassical model there is no need to consider spatial models for the original properties remain unchanged.

Spatial competitive models take on different properties when their second essential characteristic of increasing returns to scale is incorporated. These increasing returns result from the indivisibilities of capital equipment and economies of scale in the process of production. This non-convexity of production technology acts as a restriction on the continued entry of new firms. As entry proceeds into the spatial market the scale of output of the new entrant is progressively reduced causing an increase in his average unit costs. The reduction in transport costs caused by the increasing density of new firms is eventually outweighed by the higher costs of smaller scale output. Thus, in a spatial market indivisibilities ensure both the existence of firms and the exchange economy in equilibrium.[1] Together with transport costs they explain the geographical concentration of production and the survival of oligopolistic competition with free-entry. Thus the monopolistic power of firms and their control over price are no longer trivial. Consequently, the neoclassical model of perfect competition ceases to be useful in the analysis of spatial competition wherever indivisibilities are other than "minor".

Empirical evidence suggests that whenever capital equipment is used physical indivisibilities are present. The effect is to cause the average total cost curve to decline over some initial range. This decline is generally of a non-trivial order of magnitude. Thus as transport is costly and most markets are characterised by a geographical dispersal of production and consumption, the spatial competitive model and not the neoclassical model of perfect competition, would appear to be the general analytical case.

II. SPATIAL COMPETITION AND PRICE DISCRIMINATION

The work of Singer [47] and Hoover [33] which was subsequently followed up and extended by Greenhut [17] and Beckman [2], suggests that a profit

[1] Eaton and Lipsey [11] develop a model which can be used to show that as the fixed cost associated with a minimum indivisible unit of capital decreases relative to its maximum value (that value of fixed costs at which the total market can be profitably served by one firm) the density of firms in that market increases. In the limit either fixed costs or the minimum indivisible unit will become so small that perfect competition will be approximated making the spatial model redundant.

maximising spatial monopolist should adopt a policy of spatial price discrimination by which he charges some variable proportion of the costs of transporting to buyers. This follows from the spatial market being naturally separable into a large number of demand curves each having different price and quantity intercepts as a result of transport costs rising with increasing distance from the plant. While buyers evenly distributed over a plane can be assumed to have identical gross demand curves, where the price charged is delivered price, the effect of deducting transport costs is to give different net demands, the intercepts successively decreasing with greater distance. Thus given positive transport costs, the spatial monopolist will gain from pricing in accordance with marginal revenue in each separable spatial market being equal to the marginal cost of the firm. Furthermore, Greenhut and Ohta [24] and [25] show that not only does spatial price discrimination lead to global profit maximisation but that it also results in a larger output than does free-on-board (f.o.b.) pricing (where the buyer meets the full cost of transport).

Until the work of Greenhut and Greenhut [14] and Phlips [41] the analysis of spatially competitive markets assumed that competitive firms, whether locationally concentrated or dispersed, would use an f.o.b. pricing policy. However, this and the later work of Norman [36], [37] have completely overturned the generality of this assumption by showing that where competitive firms are free of institutional constraints preventing any form of price discrimination, the pressures of profit maximisation will force them to price discriminate spatially. Further, under certain behavioural assumptions, spatially differentiated firms will progressively increase the degree of price discrimination as competition from distant firms intensifies until, in the limit, uniform pricing results. Thus as Greenhut stated:

> "(the) cost of distance . . . changes the theoretical perspective of what may be monopolistic and *what may be competitive pricing.*" (Greenhut [21, p. 24]).

Assuming that firms adopt Cournot type behaviour, Greenhut and Greenhut [14] derive the market equilibrium condition for spatial competitors who discriminate in price as

$$(1) \qquad P_d\left(1 - \frac{1}{er}\right) = \bar{K} + \bar{T}$$

where P_d is delivered price, e is the elasticity of market demand at price, P_d, r is the number of competitors in a given spatial market, $\bar{K}$ is the average of the r firms marginal costs, and T is the average transport cost of selling to the given market.

The Greenhuts assume the spaceless market demand to be of the power form

$$(2) \qquad P_d = \alpha - \beta_q^x$$

where the elasticity of demand e becomes

$$e = \frac{1}{x}\left(\frac{p}{\alpha - p}\right) \tag{3}$$

which when substituted into equation (1) and solving for the competitive discriminatory delivered price gives

$$P_d = \frac{1}{r + x}(x\alpha + r\bar{K}) + \left(\frac{r}{r + x}\bar{T}\right), \tag{4}$$

The ex-works price is given by the first term in (4) and the second term makes the slope of the delivered price schedule (DPS), a function of $\bar{T}$.

In order to examine the effect of changes in the level of competition upon the degree of spatial price discrimination, Greenhut and Greenhut [14] used two contrasting locational patterns: i) all sellers localised at one production centre, and ii) sellers located at two spatially separated centres linked by a one-dimensional market along which buyers are evenly distributed.

In the first case, all sellers have identical transport costs T so that T replaces $\bar{T}$ in equation (4). Assuming that x, α and r are constant over space, then differentiating (4) with respect to T gives the slope of the DPS as $r/r + x$. This is illustrated in Figure 1. The effect of increasing competition with free-entry to the one location of production is for the ex-works price to fall progressively towards $\bar{K}$ and for $r/r + x \rightarrow 1.0$. Obviously, in the limit the delivered price at a point z equals average marginal cost plus the full cost of transport to z which is analogous to the result under neoclassical perfect competition. In other words perfect "spatial" competition gives free-on-board pricing. Thus concentrated production centres and centralised markets are two special cases in spatial economics where the neoclassical pricing model forms an acceptable abstract from space. However, the limiting case of f.o.b. pricing implies very

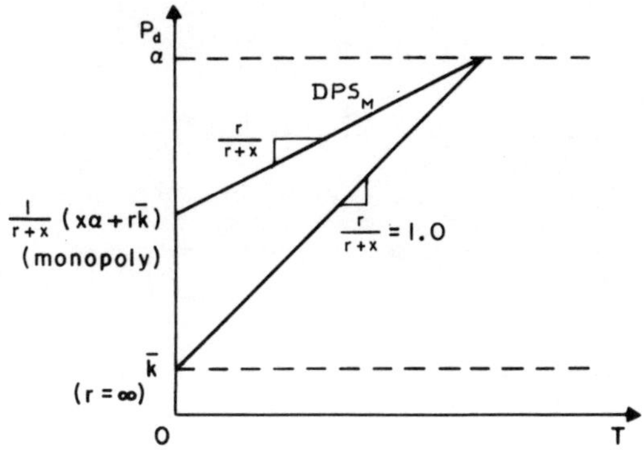

FIGURE 1
The DPS Given One Production Centre. (After Greenhut and Greenhut [14])

low fixed costs giving only "minor scale advantages and a very large number of competitors. It also implies that marginal costs rise as distance increases from the established production centre. Otherwise it would always pay a new entrant to locate away from the established production centre and gain some of the monopolistic protection of space. However, the point remains that other than where $r \rightarrow \infty$ firms competing for a market surrounding a concentrated production centre find it necessary to spatially price discriminate in order to maintain normal profits. If r fell to 1.0 the ex-works price would rise and the slope of the DPS would fall to that of the spatial monopolist. This is illustrated by DPS_M in Figure 1.

In the second case of two production centres at either end (A and B) of a linear market of length L, where the firms at A and B (r_A and r_B, respectively) can supply the whole of L, the delivered price schedule for a buyer at a transport cost T from A is given by

$$(5) \qquad P_d = \frac{1}{r+x}(x\alpha + r\bar{K}) + \frac{1}{r+x}(r_A T + r_A(L-T))$$

In this case the slope of the DPS is $r_A - r_B/r + x$ where $r = r_A + r_B$. An increase in the number of firms at either A or B will lower ex-work prices at A or B towards $\bar{K}$. However, in terms of production centre A, the DPS for each of the r_A firms will be influenced by the number of firms at B. As the number of firms at B rises to equal those at A, the DPS takes on a zero slope and uniform pricing results (all buyers pay the same delivered price wherever they are located between A and B). If $r_A < r_B$ then the DPS will take on a negative slope. These results are illustrated in Figure 2. As the Greenhuts stated

> ". . . the more competitive the distant location . . . the greater will be the freight absorption rate of firms located at site (A)." (Greenhut and Greenhut [14, p. 410]).

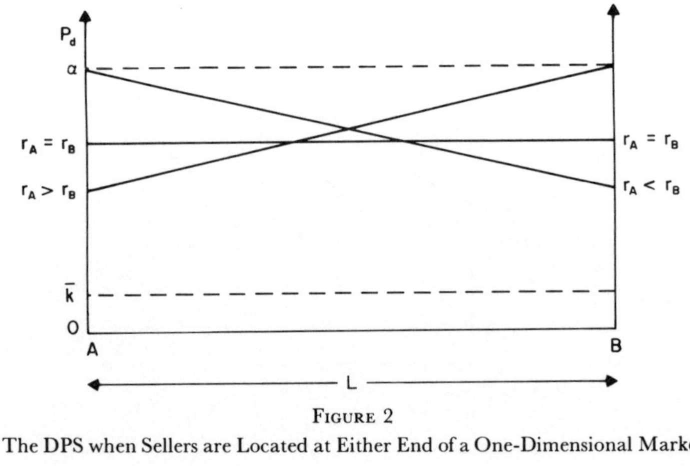

FIGURE 2
The DPS when Sellers are Located at Either End of a One-Dimensional Market

Greenhut and Greenhut [14] extended these results[2] to include heterogeneous demand where the convexity (the x parameter) of the demand function as well as the intensity of competition is permitted to vary over space. The resultant delivered price schedules would become curvilinear or kinked linear schedules depending upon the nature of the heterogeneities. For example, a firm meeting rapidly intensifying competition with increasing distance from its plant would tend to have a "sharply concave downward DPS" as it was increasingly forced to absorb the cost of transport to maintain sales.

The Greenhuts have shown that, subject to firms adopting a Cournot behavioural reaction function, any competitive entry at a distance from an existing production location will lower delivered prices (in those areas of the market where the new entrant competes) through an increase in the degree of spatial price discrimination. Also their work suggests that apart from where $r = \infty$ at concentrated production centres, price discrimination is to be expected so long as firms are profit maximisers. Thus, that body of research into free-entry spatial competition based on the assumption of f.o.b. pricing (see Lösch [35], Beckman [2], Capozza and Van Order [7], Eaton and Lipsey [11], and Holahan [32]) can no longer be accepted as the general theoretical framework for the analysis of Cournot type spatial markets. This is particularly so where sellers are able to charge a delivered price. In such cases, price discriminatory models are more likely to be analytically relevant.

Doubts as to the importance of models based on f.o.b. pricing have been strengthened by research recently reported by Norman [36] when investigating the properties of models based on the Löschian and Greenhut–Ohta price reaction functions. Under the Löschian price conjectural variation each firm assumes its market area to have a fixed boundary in the short-run implying that competitors price match, $dp_i/dp_j = 1$. However, free-entry has the effect of reducing market areas causing profits to be driven down to a zero-profit equilibrium. Under these competitive conditions Norman [36] finds that the Löschian competitor will be forced to price discriminate and absorb up to 50 per cent of the transport costs as price discrimination will always give higher profits than f.o.b. pricing for a given market area. In other words, if the Löschian competitor adopts an f.o.b. pricing policy as previous research suggested, new entry will force profits to zero, yet at that supposed equilibrium the firm will not be profit maximising. By spatially price discriminating the firm can raise its sales and recoup some of the profit lost due to previous new entry. Unfortunately for the firm, the success of this action will attract in yet more new entrants causing the market area to shrink further until profits are again zero. Obviously, under price discrimination the zero-profit equilibrium will result in more firms with smaller market areas than that given by f.o.b.

[2] Phlips [41] used the Greenhuts' model as the basis for his analysis of intertemporal price discrimination. Given differences between sales and production, in some periods, intertemporal price discrimination becomes an optimal policy with the absorption of inventory costs being analogous to that of transport costs.

pricing. Under free-entry the Löschian firm may only survive in the long-run by adopting a price discriminatory policy. Again, in this oligopolistic setting, it is the force of competition that causes the abandonment of any attempt at f.o.b. pricing.

The Greenhut–Ohta [25] price conjectural variation assumes that each firm selects a pricing policy to maximise profits subject to a given limit price constraint, p', at the edge of its market area. This means that with a limit price ceiling there is a maximum delivered price at the market boundary which, for the constraint to be effective, is less than the price intercept, α. Consequently, the optimal DPS becomes a function of the limit price ceiling. If the limit price is lowered the firm would suffer a reduction in its market radius, R, given by $dR/dp' > 0$. Its former pricing policy would no longer be optimal causing it to move to a new optimal DPS by absorbing a higher proportion of the transport costs of more distant buyers, thus lowering its maximum delivered price. Also, the firm will raise the ex-works price, m, to proximate buyers, as given by $dm/dp' < 0$. As a result the slope of the DPS will have become flatter[3] and the firm will have partially offset some of the loss of its market area.

Now as Norman points out, a lower limit price is indicative of greater competition so that "there is a direct, monotonic relationship between the level of (Greenhut–Ohta) competition and the degree of spatial price discrimination" [36, p. 103]. In fact, as competition intensifies Norman finds a greater likelihood of the firm being driven to adopt the limiting case of uniform pricing.[4] Thus low entry costs and high consumer densities will result in $r \rightarrow \infty$. This gives a zero profit equilibrium and a uniform price equal to limit price.

Therefore, it appears that *spatially competitive forms based on the Cournot, Löschian and Greenhut–Ohta conjectural variations can be added to spatial monopoly as market forms requiring spatial price discrimination for profit maximisation.*[5] *Other than in the special case of sellers being concentrated at one location, greater competition in spatial markets results in more, not less, spatial price discrimination.* Indeed, with increasing competition from distant sellers the DPS will tend towards uniform pricing.[6] This is in complete contrast to what might be expected from a spatial adaptation of the neoclassical pricing model where increasing competition

[3] Norman applies a non-negativity constraint to the degree of freight absorption so that the firm cannot absorb more than 100 per cent of the transport costs.

[4] Unlike Greenhut and Ohta's [25], [26] use of their model, Norman allowed the firm a relatively free choice of pricing policy, between the limits of f.o.b. and uniform pricing. Greenhut and Ohta restricted the choice of pricing policy to the alternatives of either f.o.b. or that of the price discriminating spatial monopolist. Thus, the firm could only absorb an upper limit of 50 per cent of the costs of transport.

[5] Of course, this is subject to an absence of institutional constraints on price discrimination. Where such constraints apply f.o.b. spatial pricing models will be more appropriate (for recent examples see Greenhut *et al.* [15] and Benson [4] where the analysis is applied to banking).

[6] As uniform delivered pricing is an optimal policy for profit maximisation only when spatial competition is intense, it will not be appropriate for a monopolist or a collusive oligopolist. Norman [37] has shown that such market forms would adopt uniform pricing only when operating as sales maximisers, and then only when the profit constraint is ineffective.

would result in a delivered price equal to marginal cost plus the full cost of transport to the buyer's site (f.o.b. pricing).

Welfare Implications

As already stated, Greenhut and Ohta [24], [25] showed that for a spatial monopolist "spatial price discrimination . . . yields larger outputs than does simple f.o.b. mill pricing, regardless of the shape of the gross demand curve" [24, p. 712]. Similar output results have been reported for spatial competitive market forms by Holahan [31] in respect of the Löschian behavioural assumption and by Greenhut and Ohta [25] for their limit price ceiling model when fixed costs were relatively high. However, Norman [36] provides evidence that the plant output for his version of the price discriminating Greenhut–Ohta firm exceeds that of the Löschian and the multi-plant monopolist whatever the level of fixed costs. The greater degree of possible price discrimination under his Greenhut–Ohta model gave higher output and lower average prices per consumer than the price discriminating Löschian model, with both models performing better than the multi-plant monopolist. Thus, the increased spatial competition that results from moving from multi-plant monopoly, through Löschian competition, to Greenhut–Ohta competition (Norman's version) gives price-output solutions consistent with spaceless neoclassical micro-economic expectations. However, it does so through greater, not lesser, spatial price discrimination.

When comparing the consumer and producer surplus arising from f.o.b. and spatial price discrimination, the welfare indices must be normalised in terms of welfare per unit area. Under conditions of free-entry and exit Greenhut [21] claimed a ". . . greater welfare (per unit area) typically existing under the price ceiling type of competition (Greenhut–Ohta) when firms price discriminatorily" (p. 29). While Beckman [2] found that f.o.b. pricing gave higher welfare than price discrimination when firms have market areas of a fixed size (Löschian type), Greenhut and Ohta [27] showed that if Beckman's model was modified to permit free-entry, the market areas would be smaller in size and greater in number at a zero-profit equilibrium under price discrimination. The resulting transport cost savings would give a lower DPS and greater welfare (consumers surplus) than in the Beckman "collusive" type model.

Although Norman [36] found the welfare benefits of f.o.b. pricing to be greater than those of discriminatory pricing in the cases of multi-plant monopoly and Löschian competition, the differences were slight and became trivial with low fixed costs and/or high consumer density. However, in the case of his version of the Greenhut-Ohta model, intense competition leading to uniform pricing (with low fixed costs or high consumer density) resulted in greater welfare than f.o.b. pricing.

The above welfare comparisons assume profit maximisation. Given the monopoly power that is a natural feature of spatial competition, the above results do not accord with the neoclassical definition of welfare maximisation. Norman [36] and Holahan [32] have shown that neoclassical welfare maximisation requires the spatial equivalent of marginal cost pricing

$$(6) \qquad P_d = K + tl$$

where t is the unit distance cost of transport and l the distance of the consumer from the supplier. With increasing returns to scale being an essential characteristic of spatial competition, Holahan [32] has pointed out that welfare maximisation will not allow firms to cover their fixed costs.[7] Thus, while the neoclassical spaceless concept of welfare maximisation requires spatial f.o.b. pricing, such a policy appears to be incompatible with the essential characteristics of spatial competition.[8]

In the spatial economy, whenever the behavioural assumptions do not restrict the firm to viewing its market as a fixed area within which it attempts monopoly pricing, as with multi-plant monopoly or Löschian competition, the increased price discrimination consequent upon increased competition will give progressively higher levels of welfare per unit area than f.o.b. pricing. *Thus uniform pricing, the limiting case with intense competition at a distance, can give the greatest level of welfare per unit area.*

III. ENTRY-DETERRENCE AND PURE PROFIT EQUILIBRIUM

Although spatial competition requires price discrimination for profit maximisation, spatial models examining the effect of free-entry on long-run equilibrium have generally assumed that transport costs are paid in full by the consumer. As pointed out by Eaton and Lipsey [11], the vast majority of these models also assume zero profits as an equilibrium condition. However, Hay [30] and Eaton and Lipsey [10], [11], [12] have developed models in which the long-run equilibrium is not unique and the zero profit condition is rejected. In this section the paper will review their work in the context of the condition of entry into spatially competitive markets. In line with current convention, f.o.b. pricing is assumed throughout.

As noted in Section I, spatial competition is characterised by economies of scale which effectively impede entry. In spaceless economics, the theory of impeded entry is dominated by the "Sylos postulate" which assumes that potential entrants expect already established firms to maintain their output at existing levels whenever new entry occurs.[9] As a result, only that part of the

[7] Benson [3], [5] seems to come to a similar conclusion in the case of the optimum Löschian ex-works price when he argues that it should equal plant marginal production cost only when both fixed and transport costs are zero.

[8] Counter arguments have been cited by Greenhut [19], Greenhut and Ohta [25], [27] and Ohta [38]. However, these arguments derive from models where all costs are covered in full (including fixed costs) at a zero-profit (or zero-surplus where uncertainty is included as a cost) equilibrium giving the equivalent of a non-negative profit constraint applied to the neoclassical welfare maximisation model (see Norman [36]).

[9] This assumption was named after its originator, Sylos-Labini [49].

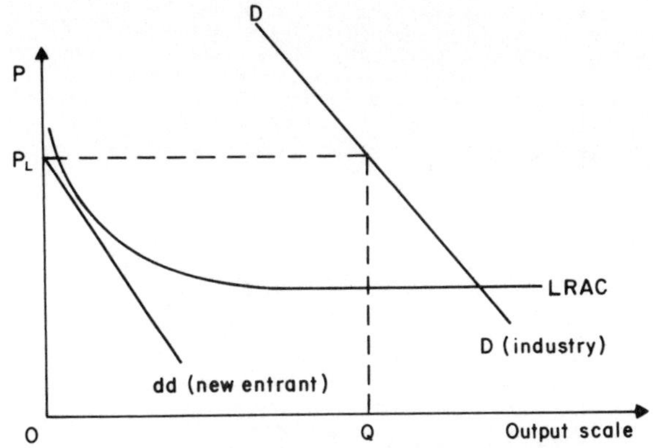

FIGURE 3
Limit Pricing and Economies of Scale

market demand curve to the right of the pre-entry quantity produced is available to the new entrant, as shown by curve *dd* in Figure 3. The entry-preventing price is given as P_L (limit price) and is the highest price that the existing firms can charge without inducing entry. At prices $\leq P_L$ the new entrant is unable to cover his costs. Thus, given economies of scale, firms in spaceless competition may deter entry by reducing price from the profit maximising level to the limit price.

Hay [30] and Eaton and Lipsey [12] have shown such a limit price strategy to be ineffective in deterring potential entrants to a spatial market. Their argument can be illustrated by considering entry into a one-dimensional market having an even distribution of consumers, each with an identical downward-sloping demand curve. Demand at each point in the market is assumed to be price elastic. Each customer purchases from the firm having the lowest delivered price. The cost of transporting one unit of the good a unit distance is unity.

Assume that all firms have identical cost curves with total costs equal to $X + Kq$, where X is the cost of an indivisible unit of capital and K is a constant marginal cost. Consequently, there are production economies of scale. Once installed, all capital is immobile. This forms a fairly realistic assumption as most industrial plant can only be moved by incurring heavy adjustment costs, often equal to the initial investment. Following Hay, it is also assumed that new entrants locate in sequence and not simultaneously.

Following Hay, the demand for firm A located at a in Figure 4, with its market extending a distance z both east and west is given by

$$(7) \qquad q = 2y \int_0^z [\alpha - \beta(P + l)]dl$$

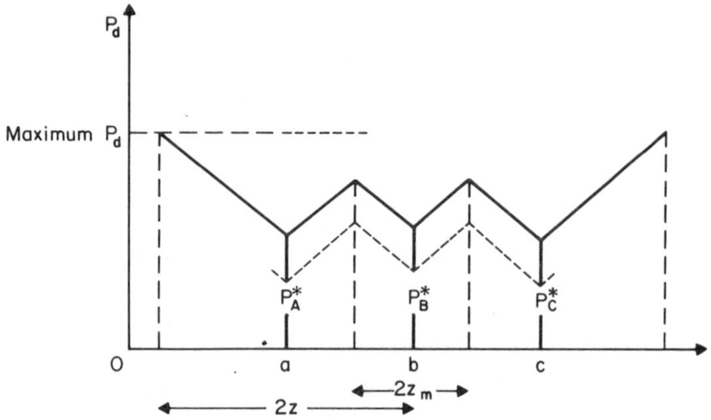

FIGURE 4
The Spacing of Existing Firms and the Minimum Market Area. (After Hay [30])

where y is consumer density at distance l from the firm, α and β are constants, P is ex-works price. The profits of the firm are given as

$$\pi = (P - k)yz(2\alpha - 2\beta P - \beta z) - X \tag{8}$$

Maximum profits are given by setting $\partial\pi/\partial P = 0$ from which the optimum price, P^*, can be derived.

$$P^* = \frac{\alpha}{2\beta} + \frac{k}{2} - \frac{z}{4}, \tag{9}$$

This gives the optimum ex-works price as inversely related to the size of the market area. When this value is substituted into equation (8) Hay derives the profits for markets of varying sizes as

$$\pi = \tfrac{1}{2}\beta zy\left(\frac{\alpha}{\beta} - k - \frac{z}{2}\right)^2 - X \tag{10}$$

Thus a potential entrant will only consider entering if it expects π to be positive. Given values for the parameters α, β, k, X, the profitability of entry depends upon the size of the market. Thus the minimum market ($2z_m$ in Figure 4) necessary to encourage entry is where

$$\tfrac{1}{2}\beta zy\left(\frac{\alpha}{\beta} - k - \frac{z}{2}\right)^2 = X$$

However, in spatial economies the market size conditions affecting potential entrants and existing firms are very different. Some new firm B considering locating between firms A and C in Figure 4 can expect less than half the market area held by each of the existing firms A and C prior to its entry. It could only have half the pre-entry market of the existing firms, i.e. a market of length z, if it charged the same ex-works price P.

Equation (9) gave the profit maximising ex-works price as being inversely related to the length of the market. By locating at point b firm B can only challenge for half the market between A and C giving it a higher ex-works price, P_B^*, and a resultant market area of $<z$ as seen in Figure 4. Given the immobile locations of firms A and C, firm B will enter only if the location at b, the mid-point between locations a and c,[10] gives it a market area at least equal to $2z_m$. This minimum market area would give firm B zero profits.

Consequently, *the existing firms can deter potential entrants by adopting a location strategy which leaves inadequate demand for profitable entry at intervening locations* such as b. This is achieved by locating at distances apart which leave the new entrant with a market area of just less than $2z_m$. Hay [30, p. 256] has calculated this as a distance apart of up to 2.215 times the minimum market area, $2z_m$.

If existing firms do not succeed in adopting this entry-deterring locational strategy, they will leave gaps in the market sufficient for profitable new entry. The adoption of the alternative strategy of limit pricing would not close the gap and so deter the potential entrant. From equations (9) and (10) we know that both demand at any point in the market and costs are the same for all firms, so that the profit maximising price and profit depend on the market size alone. Thus, if a gap $\geq 2z_m$ exists, then firm B will enter the market at location b knowing that as long as existing firms are profit maximisers its spatial demand curve will be either to the right or tangential to its long-run average cost curve. Obviously, existing firms will find their market areas and resultant profits reduced in consequence. However, their new profit maximising price will be determined by the new size of market area (equation 10) and as this will be smaller the optimum price will rise, not fall.

If existing firms did attempt to deter entry by limit pricing it would still pay a potential new entrant to come in and price match. As seen from the dotted delivered price lines of Figure 4, price matching would leave the new entrant with the same sized market area as that resulting from profit maximising pricing. While "limit pricing" would force the new entrant into a loss making situation, the existing firms, by virtue of their larger market areas, would suffer the greater absolute loss of profits. The existing firms would realise the complete ineffectiveness of limit pricing in closing the gap and revert back to profit maximizing pricing. The more effective, and costless, entry-deterring strategy is for existing firms to pre-empt the potential market[11] for the new

[10] Given that demand is elastic a firm locating between two other firms charging the same ex-works price will maximise its profits by locating mid-way between them. (See Eaton & Lipsey; [11] for a proof).

[11] Eaton and Lipsey [12] have developed a model which demonstrates that, subject to market growth being foreseen, it will always pay a monopolist to pre-empt the market by establishing branch plants earlier than it would pay a new firm to enter. Archibald and Rosenbluth [1], by extending Lancaster's [34] characteristics approach to demand theory, also show limit pricing to be ineffective at entry-deterrence in product differentiated markets.

entrant by initially locating apart by a distance less than 2.215 times the minimum market area. This will ensure larger market areas and from equation (10) larger profits in the long run than could ever be achieved by a more distant spacing of plants and an entry-deterring strategy of limit pricing. The inapplicability of limit pricing to spatial competition derives essentially from the fact that the monopoly power given by economic distance allows existing firms to continue to earn super-normal profits even after new entry. As stated by Eaton and Lipsey, "In spatial models the problem of natural monopoly is undiminished when the market is served by a large number of plants" [12, p. 155]. Thus limit pricing is contrary to profit maximising behaviour in spatial competition.

It follows from equations (7) and (10) that by virtue of their market areas being more than twice that of the new entrant, existing firms will have demand curves substantially to the right of that of a new entrant. Since all firms have the same long-run average costs, which are declining over some range, it is possible for existing firms to be earning positive pure profits from a market area of $2z$, while a potential new entrant could only expect losses (i.e. where the market gap is $< 2z_m$).

The resultant equilibrium would be consistent with positive pure-profits and not zero profits. This is a straightforward consequence of the indivisibilities of spatial competition and immobile plants.[12] The pure profit equilibrium condition means that both price and size of market areas are indeterminate unless the initial spatially competitive conditions are specified. This gives rise to multiple equilibria with the solution depending upon the initial plant locations and consumer densities. As stated by Eaton and Lipsey, "different markets that are today identical in customer distributions and demands will have different equilibrium patterns of firms depending on their past histories" (which give the current locational pattern of existing firms) [10, p. 79]. Eaton and Lipsey [11] also show that when assuming an individual exponential demand function and a price matching conjectural variation the rate of return for existing firms could be up to twice the normal rate of return on capital. However, as this maximum rate of return is possible only where economies of scale are trivial—the density of packing of firms per unit of market length approaches infinity—the expected divergence of the pure-profit rate of return from the normal would be considerably less than double under non-trivial spatial competition. Even so, with the new entrant expecting less than half the customers of any existing firm the super normal rate of return is still likely to be a significant quantity.

Capozza and Van Order [8] extended the Eaton–Lipsey [11] model by incorporating inelastic demand and a zero price conjectural variation and

[12] Although Eaton and Lipsey [11] attribute this result to capital indivisibilities, Capozza and Van Order [8] have proved that while indivisibilities are necessary the pure profit equilibrium primarily depends on the immobility of capital whenever markets are large relative to the size of firm.

compared the equilibrium conditions for mobile and immobile firms, respectively. The former gave a zero-profit unique equilibrium solution with smaller market areas (more firms) than the latter's pure profit multiple equilibria result. (In the former, existing firms can relocate to accommodate the new entrants with the result that new and existing firms will have equal sized market areas at the end of the first period). In terms of economic welfare both the mobile and immobile firm equilibrium solutions were found to be inefficient in that firms were producing at points to the left of their minimum average total costs (production cost plus transport cost). As average transport costs decline the market areas contract, the inefficiency is caused by new entrants forcing existing firms to reduce output and incur higher average production costs. With entrants continuing to come into the market the rise in production costs exceed the fall in transport costs as an equilibrium is reached. Thus, free-entry equilibrium in both models tends to result in "too many" firms,[13] each producing to the left of the minimum efficient scale. However, the relatively larger market areas of the immobile firms existing under the positive pure-profit equilibrium must necessitate them producing a larger output nearer the minimum efficient scale and charging lower ex-works prices (Equation (9)). Capozza and Van Order conclude that as a result, "the pure-profit equilibrium may entail higher welfare levels than zero-profit equilibrium" [8, p. 1053]. This would appear to be a case of impediments to resource mobility in the form of capital immobility leading to greater efficiency through cutting down on the excess number of firms that tends to result from free-entry spatial competition.[14] This is clearly the opposite of what would be expected from the application of spaceless economic theory.

IV. SPATIAL COMPETITION AND PUBLIC POLICY

This review of recent developments in spatial economic theory clearly suggests that the properties of the neoclassical model of perfect competition are dependent on its abstraction from economic space. While the incorporation of economic space into microeconomic theory generally leads to price and output solutions consistent with those of neoclassical theory, the conditions for their achievement are different. The Norman version of the Greenhut–Ohta model of spatial competition gives higher output and lower average prices than the more monopolistic Lösch model. However, it does so through a greater degree of spatial price discrimination. Unlike spaceless price theory, increased spatial

[13] By way of contrast, Gee [13] using a computer simulation model in which the only costs borne by firms were the transport costs of delivering to consumers (new entry was limited by a minimum profit constraint rather than by economies of scale) found that spatial competitive inefficiency largely resulted from too few firms ending up in the market.

[14] Greenhut [18], [19] (see also Ohta [38]) developed a determinate model of spatial oligopoly which by incorporating a fixed cost for investing capital under conditions of behavioural uncertainty gave a long-run equilibrium at the minimum optimum scale of production. However, the model's efficient solution depends upon behavioural uncertainty deterring excessive new entry. (See Gripsrud [29] and Dorward [9] for critiques and also Greenhut's replies [20], [23]).

price discrimination does not necessarily have harmful welfare effects. Although Capozza and Van Order found the Eaton–Lipsey model to result in sub-optimal resource allocation when compared with the perfectly competitive ideal, the divergence was considerably lessened (and in certain conditions disappeared) when capital was indivisible and spatially immobile (as expected in real life spatial competition).

It follows that the application of space to microeconomic theory has considerable implications for the formulation and implementation of public policy towards competition. The Robinson–Patman Act in the United States has imposed tight constraints on the ability of business to absorb transport costs, while in the United Kingdom the Price Commission [43], [44], [45] was very critical of any significant deviations from f.o.b. pricing. Such policies are based upon spaceless neoclassical theory which emphasises the monopolistic associations of price discrimination. The application of spatial economic theory would, on the contrary, suggest that any increased absorption of transport costs was more likely to be associated with increased, rather than decreased, spatial competition. Empirical work by Greenhut *et al.* [16] on the spatial pricing structure of firms in the United States strongly supports the proposition that greater transport cost absorption occurs at those points in the market where competition is more intense. The differences in competition over selected states gave rise to both non-linear and "dip-bump" delivered price schedules as predicted by Greenhut and Greenhut [14]. When comparing spatial pricing in the United States, West Germany and Japan, Greenhut [22] found that while two-thirds of the firms sampled in the United States tended to price discriminatorily, around four-fifths did so in the other two countries. Further, the delivered prices of firms in West Germany and Japan did not always increase with distance, some delivered price schedules taking on a negative slope. While the Robinson–Patman Act no doubt substantially contributed to the relatively smaller extent of spatial price discrimination in the United States as well as to the differences in application, the pressure of competitive forces was such that it remained as a dominant competitive pricing policy. Although reasonably effective, the Act has merely moderated rather than removed the practice.

Inadvertently, the post-War policy in the United Kingdom of encouraging a dispersal of manufacturing industry outwards from the West Midlands and the South-East to regions of relatively high unemployment, may have contributed to an increase in spatial price discrimination by increasing the number of competing sources of supply. If so, the policies on industrial location and price regulation were in conflict. By basing economic policy on a set of concepts which abstracted from space, policymakers would tend to overlook any interdependences between patterns of industrial location and the structure of spatial prices.

In the light of these findings, public policy on price discrimination needs to be reformulated in a spatial context. While f.o.b. pricing still tends to give greater consumer surplus in monopoly or quasi-monopoly (Löschian) market structures, spatial price discrimination gives the greatest consumer benefits when competition between locations is intense. This implies the need for a rather complex form of price regulation. Indeed, it could be the case that the costs of implementation would exceed the benefits.

Hay [30] has demonstrated that existing firms can effectively deter new entry by locating near enough to each other so as to leave less than profitable market areas for potential new entrants. Eaton and Lipsey [11] have also shown that capital indivisibilities and spatially immobile plant provide effective entry barriers. However, barriers to entry while being natural to spatial competition do not have the same welfare damaging effects as predicted by spaceless neoclassical theory. Capozzo and Van Order [8] have suggested that without those entry barriers spatial competition can result in excessive entry, far too many firms, excess capacity and a loss of welfare. This is analogous to the situation frequently found in product differentiated industries where product proliferation leads to the number of products being in excess of that necessary for welfare maximisation. (See Scherer [46], for an application of a type of Lösch–Hotelling spatial model to the analysis of the excessive product variety found in breakfast cereals). Thus, *given substantial economies of scale, sequential entry and immobile plant, competition policies aimed at breaking down entry barriers to encourage a greater number of competitors will neither tend to eliminate profits in excess of the normal rate of return, nor necessarily improve economic efficiency within the spatial economy.* Consequently, we need to look again at the criteria for monitoring the effectiveness of monopolies and restrictive practices legislation in the United Kingdom.

NEIL DORWARD,
The Polytechnic of North London,
Department of Accounting and Administrative Studies,
Holloway,
London N7 8DB, England

REFERENCES

[1] Archibald, G. C. and Rosenbluth, G., "The 'New' Theory of Consumer Demand and Monopolistic Competition", *Quarterly Journal of Economics*, **89**, 4 (November 1975), pp. 569–90.

[2] Beckman, M., "Spatial Price Policies Revisited", *Bell Journal of Economics*, **7**, 2 (Autumn 1976), pp. 619–30.

[3] Benson, B. L., "Löschian Competition Under Alternative Demand Conditions", *American Economic Review*, **70**, 5 (December 1980), pp. 1098–1105.

[4] Benson, B. L., "An Examination of U.S. v. Philadelphia National Bank in the Context of Spatial Economics", *Industrial Organisation Review*, **8**, 1 (1980), pp. 27–65.

[5] Benson, B. L., "The Optimal Size and Number of Market Areas", *Southern Economic Journal*, **47**, 4 (April 1981), pp. 1080–85.

[6] Capozza, D. R. and Van Order, R., "Pricing Under Spatial Competition and Spatial Monopoly", *Econometrica*, **45**, 6 (September 1977), pp. 1329–38.

[7] Capozza, D. R. and Van Order, R., "A Generalised Model of Spatial Competition", *American Economic Review*, **68**, 5 (December 1978), pp. 896–908.
[8] Capozza, D. R. and Van Order, R., "Unique Equilibria, Pure Profits, and Efficiency in Location Models", *American Economic Review*, **70**, 5 (December 1980), pp. 1046–53.
[9] Dorward, N., '"Impacts of Distance on Microeconomic Theory': A Critique", *Manchester School*, **49**, 3 (September 1981), pp. 245–58.
[10] Eaton, B. C. and Lipsey, R. G., "The Introduction of Space into the Neoclassical Model of Value Theory", in Artis, M. J. and Nobay, A. R. (eds), *Studies in Modern Economic Analysis*, (Blackwells, Oxford, 1977), pp. 59–96.
[11] Eaton, B. C. and Lipsey, R. G., "Freedom of Entry and the Existence of Pure Profit", *Economic Journal*, **88**, 351 (September 1978), pp. 455–69.
[12] Eaton, B. C. and Lipsey, R. G., "The Theory of Market Pre-emption: The Persistence of Excess Capacity and Monopoly in Growing Spatial Markets", *Economica*, **46**, 182 (May 1979), pp. 149–58.
[13] Gee, J. M. A., "A Model of Location and Industrial Efficiency with Free Entry", *Quarterly Journal of Economics*, **90**, 4 (November 1976), pp. 557–74.
[14] Greenhut, J. and Greenhut, M. L., "Spatial Price Discrimination, Competition, and Locational Effects", *Economica*, **42**, 168 (November 1975), pp. 401–19.
[15] Greenhut, J., Greenhut, M. L. and Kelly, W. H., "A Spatial-Theoretical Perspective for Bank Merger Regulations", *Federal Reserve Bank of Chicago Proceedings on Bank Structure and Competition*, 1977 pp. 210–54.
[16] Greenhut, J., Greenhut, M. L. and Li, S., "Spatial Pricing Patterns in the United States", *Quarterly Journal of Economics*, **94**, 2 (March 1980), pp. 329–50.
[17] Greenhut, M. L., *Plant Location in Theory and Practice*, (University of North Carolina Press, Chapel Hill, 1956).
[18] Greenhut, M. L., "The Theory of the Spatial and Nonspatial Firm", *Weltwirtschaftliches Archiv.*, **105**, 1 (September 1970), pp. 87–113.
[19] Greenhut, M. L., *A Theory of the Firm in Economic Space*, (Lone Star Publishing Co., Austin, 1974).
[20] Greenhut, M. L., "Mr Gripsrud and a Theory of Oligopoly", *Weltwirtschaftliches Archiv.*, **110**, 3 (September 1974), pp. 518–24.
[21] Greenhut, M. L., "Impacts of Distance on Microeconomic Theory", *Manchester School*, **46**, 1 (March 1978), pp. 17–40.
[22] Greenhut, M. L., "Spatial Pricing in the United States, West Germany and Japan", *Economica*, **48**, 189 (February 1981), 79–86.
[23] Greenhut, M. L., "Mr Dorward and the Impacts of Distance on Microeconomic Theory", *Manchester School*, **49**, 3 (September 1981), pp. 259–65.
[24] Greenhut, M. L. and Ohta, H., "Monopoly Output Under Alternative Spatial Pricing Techniques", *American Economic Review*, **62**, 4 (September 1972), pp. 705–13.
[25] Greenhut, M. L., and Ohta, H., *Theory of Spatial Pricing and Market Areas*, (Duke University Press, Durham, 1975).
[26] Greenhut, M. L. and Ohta, H., "Discriminatory and Nondiscriminatory Spatial Prices and Outputs Under Varying Market Conditions", *Weltwirtschaftliches Archiv.*, **111**, 2 (June 1975), pp. 310–31.
[27] Greenhut, M. L. and Ohta, H., "Output Effects of Spatial Price Discrimination Under Conditions of Monopoly and Competition", *Southern Economic Journal*, **46**, 1 (July 1979), pp. 71–84.
[28] Greenhut, M. L., Hwang, M. and Ohta, H., "Observations on the Shape and Relevance of the Spatial Demand Function", *Econometrica*, **43**, 4 (July 1975), pp. 669–82.

[29] Gripsrud, G., "A Note on the Theory of Oligopoly: Comments to a Model Presented by Greenhut", *Weltwirtschaftliches Archiv.*, **110**, 3 (September 1974), pp. 509–17.

[30] Hay, D. A., "Sequential Entry and Entry-Deterring Strategies in Spatial Competition", *Oxford Economic Papers*, **28**, 2 (July 1976), pp. 240–57.

[31] Holahan, W. L., "The Welfare Effects of Spatial Price Discrimination", *American Economic Review*, **65**, 3 (June 1975), pp. 498–503.

[32] Holahan, W. L., "Spatial Monopolistic Competition Versus Spatial Monopoly", *Journal of Economic Theory*, **18**, (April 1978), pp. 156–70.

[33] Hoover, E. M., "Spatial Price Discrimination", *Review of Economic Studies*, **4**, 3 (June 1937), pp. 182–91.

[34] Lancaster, K. J., *Consumer Demand: A New Approach*, (Columbia University Press, New York, 1971).

[35] Lösch, A., *The Economics of Location*, (Yale University Press, New Haven, 1954).

[36] Norman, G., "Spatial Competition and Spatial Price Discrimination", *Review of Economic Studies*, **48**, 1 (January 1981), pp. 97–111.

[37] Norman, G., "Uniform Pricing as an Optimal Spatial Pricing Policy", *Economica*, **48**, 189 (February 1981), pp. 87–91.

[38] Ohta, H., "On Efficiency of Production Under Conditions of Imperfect Competition", *Southern Economic Journal*, **43**, 2 (October 1976), pp. 1124–35.

[39] Ohta, H., "Spatial Competition, Concentration, and Welfare", *Regional Science and Urban Economics*, **10**, 1 (March 1980), pp. 3–16.

[40] Ohta, H., "The Price Effects of Spatial Competition", *Review of Economic Studies*, **48**, 2 (April 1981), pp. 317–25.

[41] Phlips, L., "Spatial Pricing and Competition", *Studies of the Commission of the European Communities, Competition-Approximation of Legislation Series*, **29**, (Brussels, 1976).

[42] Phlips, L., "Intertemporal Price Discrimination and Sticky Prices", *Quarterly Journal of Economics*, **94**, 3 (May 1980), pp. 525–42.

[43] Price Commission, "UG Glass Containers—Price of Glass Containers", *Price Commission Report No. 5*, House of Commons 170, (H.M.S.O., London, 1978).

[44] Price Commission, "Metal Box Ltd.—Open Top Food and Beverage and Aerosol Cans", *Price Commission Report No. 3*, House of Commons 135, (H.M.S.O., London, 1978).

[45] Price Commission, "Tate and Lyle Refineries Ltd.—Sugar and Syrup Products", *Price Commission Report No. 6*, House of Commons 224, (H.M.S.O., London, 1978).

[46] Scherer, F. M., "The Welfare Economics of Product Variety: An Application to the Ready-to-Eat Cereals Industry", *Journal of Industrial Economics*, **28**, 2 (December 1979), pp. 113–34.

[47] Singer, H. W., "A Note on Spatial Price Discrimination", *Review of Economic Studies*, **5**, 1 (October 1937), pp. 75–77.

[48] Starr, R., "Quasi-Equilibrium in Markets with Non-Convex Preferences", *Econometrica*, **37**, 1 (January 1969), pp. 25–38.

[49] Stylos-Labini, P., *Oligopoly and Technical Progress*, (Harvard University Press, Cambridge, Mass., 1962).

THE JOURNAL OF INDUSTRIAL ECONOMICS
Volume XXXI September/December 1982 Nos. 1/2

DYNAMIC MARKET STRATEGY UNDER THREAT OF COMPETITIVE ENTRY: AN ANALYSIS OF THE PRICING AND PRODUCTION POLICIES OPEN TO THE MULTINATIONAL COMPANY*

GEORGE NORMAN AND NANCY K. NICHOLS

I. INTRODUCTION

THERE is extensive evidence indicating that firms price discriminatorily over their market areas, where price discrimination is defined to exist when the pattern of delivered prices departs from that which would be generated by f.o.b. pricing: see Greenhut, Greenhut and Li [8], Hwang [10], Phlips [16]. Underlying this evidence is an equally extensive body of theory which attempts to explain why such discriminatory pricing rules should be adopted, both in competitive and monopolistic markets: see Capozza and van Order [3], Greenhut and Greenhut [7], Norman [15].

One limitation of this theory is that it is essentially static. Even when competitive reactions and interdependencies are introduced there is no truly dynamic analysis. Rather, the theory concentrates on comparing long-run equilibria with, perhaps, some limited comment on how those equilibria might be achieved.

The analysis of price changes over time has received some attention, notably by Gaskins [6], Jacquemin and Thisse [11], and Phlips [17]. In these cases, however, analysis is spaceless. While some analogies are drawn between intertemporal and spatial price discrimination, these analogies are inevitably weak.

The major objective of this paper is to treat the spatial and temporal problems simultaneously. We ask whether the pricing rules and market choice of a firm operating over a spatially extensive market area will vary when it is placed in a dynamic setting. In particular, we investigate the pricing behaviour of a firm, to which we shall refer as "the leading firm", when it is subject to the threat of competitive entry in certain of its markets. Our model owes much to the analysis by Gaskins [6] but we show that Gaskins' analysis applies to only part of the spatial market area once we allow for the costs of distance. In particular, we show that if the firm enjoys a substantial long-run cost advantage in particular markets[1] it will adopt a pricing rule identical to that derived in the static, monopolistic case. This can be expected to be a very

* We are grateful to Mark Casson for extensive discussion. Remaining errors are, of course, the authors' responsibility.

[1] We shall consider in section IV why such an advantage might accrue to the firm.

special case, however, and we go on to investigate the firm's pricing policy as its cost advantage is eroded—if only by transport costs to distant markets. What we then find is that, if the firm's cost advantage in particular markets is "large" but not "substantial",[2] it will set its price to exclude entry. If this price, the limit price (Scherer [18]) is invariant across space, it follows that the firm will charge a uniform price in such markets.

As the leading firm's long-run cost advantage is weakened, the firm may be willing to accept some competitive entry—it is in such markets that the Gaskins analysis is applicable—but will in the long run tend towards a limit pricing strategy, although it will no longer be the sole supplier. Finally, we consider markets in which the firm enjoys no long-run cost advantage. Serving such markets by exports from a home production base is not a feasible long-run strategy—the firm will eventually be eliminated by competitive entry.

Our analysis carries implications for the choice between a single plant/export supply mode, and a multi-plant or multinational supply mode. We comment on the conditions which will determine the choice between these two modes, and show that the conditions so derived are consistent with much of the recent theoretical and empirical analysis of multinational production.

II. THE MODEL

We assume that the firm chooses that pricing policy which will maximize the present value of its profits, given by:

$$\Pi = \int_R \int_0^T q(p(t, r), t)(p(t, r) - (m + \tau r))D(r)e^{-\delta t} \, dt \, dr - F \tag{2.1}$$

where $q(p(t, r), t)$ = demand at time t and price $p(t, r)$ by consumers at location r,

$p(t, r)$ = price charged at time t to consumers at location r,

$D(r)$ = density of consumers at location r,

m = marginal production costs, assumed to be constant,

F = fixed production costs,

τ = transport cost per unit per unit distance,

δ = discount rate,

T = period over which the firm chooses to serve particular markets,[3]

R = market area supplied by the firm.

[2] These terms will be made more precise below.

[3] T should, perhaps, be written $T(r)$.

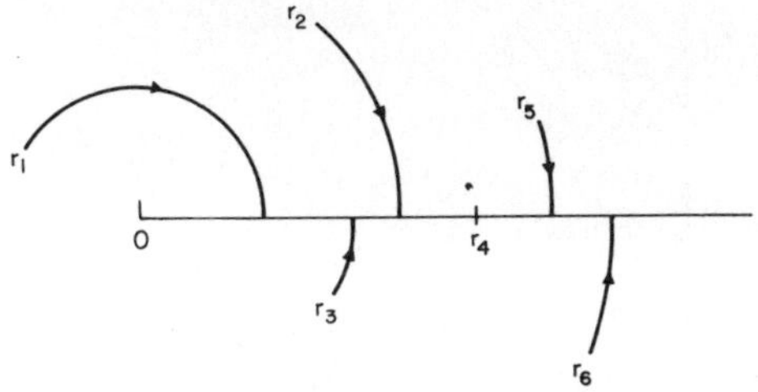

FIGURE 1
Market Mapping

The assumption of constant marginal production costs allows us to treat each local market separately. The objective of the firm, therefore, reduces to:

$$\max_{p(t,r),\,T} \Pi(r) = \int_0^T q(p(t, r), t)(p(t, r) - (m + \tau r))D(r)e^{-\delta t}\, dt \tag{2.2}$$

for each location r. It should also be noted that an assumption implicit in (2.1) and (2.2) is that transport costs from the leading firm to location r are τr and so that there is a one-to-one correspondence between "location r" and "the market distance r from the leading firm". Effectively, this implies that when all firms are mapped onto a straight line as in Figure 1 no two markets will map onto the same point. This assumption is made purely for notational simplicity and does not affect the analysis: we could instead have indexed each market, e.g. r_i^s would refer to the sth. market distance r_i from the leading firm.

Consumers are assumed to have identical linear demand curves, given by:

$$q(p(t, r), t) = a - bp(t, r) - x(t, r) \qquad (a, b > 0) \tag{2.3}$$

where: $x(t, r)$ = sales by competitors at time t at location r.

All firms are assumed to charge the same price in a particular market and the effect on the leading firm's demand of competitors' sales in market r is illustrated in Figure 2.

It has been suggested (Mansfield [14]) that the entry of rival firms to a particular market will be related to the expected profits to be made in that market. Following Gaskins [6] we assume that potential entrants perceive current product price as a proxy for future price. The rate of entry of rival firms ($\dot{x}(t, r)$) to market r will, therefore, be a monotonically nondecreasing function of current product price in market r. We assume this function to be linear:

$$\dot{x}(t, r) = k(r)(p(t, r) - \bar{p}(r)); \qquad x(0) = 0, \bar{p}(r) \geq m \tag{2.4}$$

where: $k(r)$ = entry response coefficient $\geq 0, \bar{p}(r)$ = limit price at location r.[4]

[4] Both $\bar{p}(r)$ and $k(r)$ can be expected to vary from market to market. Reasons for such variations will be discussed below.

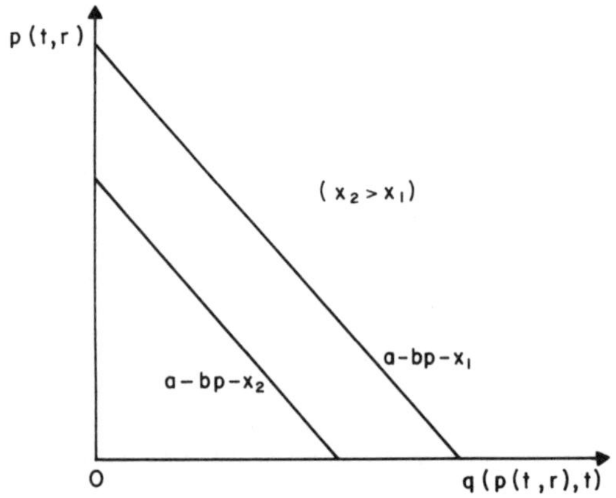

FIGURE 2
Effect on Demand of Competitors' Sales

The determination of the limit price $\bar{p}(r)$ and the entry coefficient $k(r)$ will be considered in some detail below, but we should, perhaps, say something about them at this stage. Essentially, $\bar{p}(r)$ should be viewed as that price which, if charged in market r by the leading firm will lead to no new competitive firms entering the market. Additionally, the structure of equation (2.4) is such that, if the leading firm charges less than the limit price existing competitive firms will be driven out of the market.[5] In this sense, the difference between $\bar{p}(r)$ and $(m + \tau r)$ is a measure of the long-run cost advantage enjoyed by the leading firm in market r: if all potential competitors in r are indigenous to r, one possible measure of $\bar{p}(r)$ will be long-run average costs of production of such indigenous firms in r.

The entry coefficient $k(r)$, on the other hand, can be viewed as a diffusion rate of the technology employed by the leading firm. It will be smaller the more easily the leading firm can keep its specialist knowledge private from its potential rivals in market r.

The model as specified is a problem in optimal control theory, in which the leading firm wishes to choose a control variable $p(t, r)$ to maximize (2.2), given (2.3) and subject to (2.4) where $x(t, r)$ is the state variable. We shall write the optimal values of $p(t, r)$ and $x(t, r)$ as $p^*(t, r)$ and $x^*(t, r)$.

III. ANALYSIS

In solving the model specified in section II we partition the leading firm's potential markets into a number of non-overlapping sets.

[5] We depart from Gaskins in assuming $x(0, r) = 0$, i.e. in assuming that there is no initial competitive fringe.

III.1. *Market Set* R_1

Market set R_1 is defined by the relation:

$$R_1 \equiv \{r: p^*(t, r) < \bar{p}(r)\} \tag{3.1}$$

For markets in R_1 the long-run cost advantage of the leading firm over its potential rivals is sufficiently great as to impose no effective constraint upon its pricing policy. The optimal policy in R_1 is, therefore, the familiar discriminatory price schedule under our linear demand assumption:

$$p^*(t, r) = a/2b + (m + \tau r)/2 \qquad (r \in R_1; \text{ all } t) \tag{3.2}$$

Equation (3.2) will be optimal in all markets r which are such that:

$$(m + \tau r) \leq p^*(t, r) < \bar{p}(r) \tag{3.3}$$

It can be shown that the right-hand constraint always binds before the left-hand constraint. It follows, therefore, that market set R_1, which is characterized by pricing policy (3.2), can be defined as that set of markets which satisfy the condition:

$$R_1 \equiv \{r: a/2b + (m + \tau r)/2 < \bar{p}(r)\} \tag{3.4}$$

In Figure 3 we illustrate a case in which market r_i is in R_1 but market r_j is not, because of the lower limit price applying in r_j, even though r_j is more proximate to the leading firm than is r_i.

As can be seen from (3.4) and Figure 3, a market r will belong to market set R_1 if and only if the long-run cost advantage $(\bar{p}(r) - (m + \tau r))$ enjoyed by the leading firm in market r is such that:

$$\bar{p}(r) - (m + \tau r) > \tfrac{1}{2}(a/b - (m + \tau r)) \tag{3.5}$$

where a/b is the maximum price consumers are willing to pay for the product (see equation (2.3)). If market r_j is not in R_1, and even if there is no entry threat, the leading firm can supply market r_j by exporting only if r_j is less than

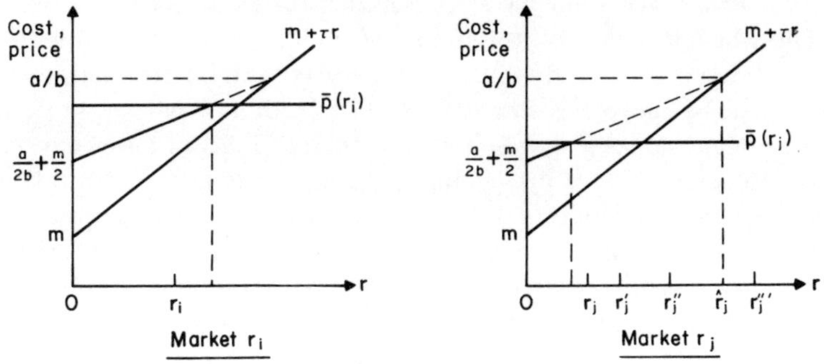

FIGURE 3
Market Set R_1

$\hat{r}_j$, where $\hat{r}_j$ is that distance at which marginal costs of production and transport just equals the maximum price the firm can charge. Thus if r_j is at distance r_j''' from the leading firm market r_j will not form part of the market area R.

For markets which are not in R_1 but which the leading firm can feasibly supply, e.g. r_j' or r_j'' in Figure 3, if $p^*(t, r)$ follows (3.2) price will exceed the limit price, rival firms will enter the market and, in the absence of any change in $p^*(t, r)$, the leading firm will eventually be driven out of the market. It may be preferable, therefore, for the leading firm to sacrifice short-run profits in order to ensure a higher level of long-run profits. Formally we now have the optimal control problem:

Choose the optimal value $(p^*(t, r))$ of the control variable $p(t, r)$ to maximize (2.2) subject to:

(i) $$\dot{x}(t, r) = k(r)(p(t, r) - \bar{p}(r))$$

(ii) $$x(t, r) \geq 0$$

Constraint (ii) is intended to ensure that the sales of rival firms are always non-negative. It might also be felt that there should be a constraint to ensure that sales of the leading firm are non-negative. Such a constraint was introduced but was found to be effective only at the boundary T. It has, therefore, been omitted from the analysis.

The Hamiltonian of the optimal control problem is:

$$H = F + \lambda_1(t, r)f = ((a - bp(t, r) - x(t, r))(p(t, r) - (m + \tau r))e^{-\delta t}D(r) + \lambda_1(t, r)k(r)(p(t, r) - \bar{p}(r)) \tag{3.6}$$

where $\lambda_1(t, r)$ is an adjoint variable, similar in many respects to the Lagrange multipliers which occur in the Kuhn-Tucker conditions.

Two technical difficulties arise in our formulation. First, the non-negativity constraint (ii) is a constraint on the state variable but does not involve the control variable.[6] We shall have to consider the possibility of a boundary solution in which this constraint is binding for some or all t. Secondly, the time period is left open at the right end: the time T is to be determined within the model. It can be shown, as might be expected, that T will be finite for all markets r which are such that $\bar{p}(r) \leq m + \tau r$, e.g. T is finite for market r_j'' in Figure 3. In such markets the leading firm has no long-run cost advantage over its rivals and, no matter its pricing policy, so long as it prices above marginal cost competitive entry will eventually drive the firm from these markets, at least as an exporter to them. On the other hand, for all markets r for which $\bar{p}(r) > m + \tau r$, e.g. market r_j' in Figure 3, $T = \infty$, i.e. the leading firm can ensure its long-run survival by appropriate choice of pricing policy.

[6] See Takayama [19, p. 665 fn. 1].

III.2. *Market Set* R_2

We consider first the set of markets in which long-run survival is possible: the set R_2. This set is defined by the relation:

$$R_2 \equiv \{r: \bar{p}(r) > m + \tau r \quad and \quad r \notin R_1\} \tag{3.7}$$

Two possibilities must be considered in this set. First, the firm may choose to price always at the limit price, so pre-empting all entry by potential competitors. Alternatively, the firm may choose initially to price above the limit price, but then to lower its price as competitors appear in order to ensure its long-run survival.[7]

It is to be expected that the choice between these two alternatives will be affected by the balance between

(i) the loss of short-run profits incurred by deviating from pricing policy (3.2), and
(ii) loss of long-run profits as a result of competitive entry if price rises above the limit price.

Technically, we must consider the possibility of a boundary solution to the optimal control problem, in which the constraint $x(t, r) \geq 0$ is always binding. Following Hadley and Kemp [9, Theorem 5.13.1, p. 317], we define:

$$T_1(t, x) \equiv -x(t, r) \leq 0 \tag{3.8}$$

$$Q_1(t, x, p) = \partial T_1/\partial t + \partial T_1/\partial x\, f(t, x, p) \tag{3.9}$$

where $f(t, x, p) = k(r)(p(t, r) - \bar{p}(r))$.

The necessary conditions for a boundary solution, that is, a solution in which $x(t, r) = 0$, are that continuous functions $\lambda_1(t, r)$, $\gamma_1(t, r)$ exist such that:

$$\dot{x}(t, r) = k(r)(p(t, r) - \bar{p}(r));\ x(0, r) = 0 \tag{A.1}$$

$$\dot{\lambda}_1(t, r) = -\partial H/\partial x - \gamma_1(t, r)\, \partial Q_1/\partial x \tag{A.2}$$

$$\partial H/\partial p + \gamma_1(t, r)\, \partial Q_1/\partial p = 0 \tag{A.3}$$

$$\text{If} \quad M(t, x, \lambda) = \sup H(t, x, p, \lambda) \quad \text{then} \quad H(t, x, p^*, \lambda) = M(t, x, \lambda) \tag{A.4}$$

$$\lim_{t \to \infty} H = \lim_{t \to \infty} \lambda_1 = 0 \tag{A.5}$$

are satisfied with $x(t, r) \equiv 0$.

[7] It can be shown that a pricing policy which involves pricing initially above $\bar{p}(r)$ and subsequently below $\bar{p}(r)$ to eliminate entrants is not optimal.

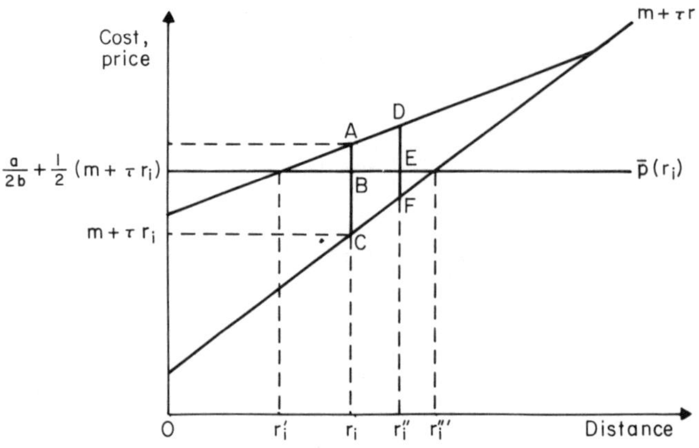

FIGURE 4

Solving the system (A.1)–(A.3), given $x(t, r) = 0$, gives:

(3.10) $\quad p^*(t, r) = \bar{p}(r);\ x^*(t, r) = 0;\ \lambda_1(t, r),\ \gamma_1(t, r)$ continuous

Condition (A.5) is satisfied, and (A.4) will be satisfied, that is (3.10) will maximize the Hamiltonian, so long as:

$$(3.11) \qquad \frac{a/2b + (m + \tau r)/2 - \bar{p}(r)}{\bar{p}(r) - (m + \tau r)} \leq \frac{k(r)}{2b\delta}$$

To interpret (3.11) we note that for a market r_i the numerator of the L.H.S. is the difference between the short run profit maximizing price and the limit price (see equation (3.2)), while the denominator measures the long-run profit per unit which the leading firm will make in r_i on each unit sold at the limit price. This is illustrated as the ratio AB/BC in Figure 4. Note that AB/BC is zero if $r_i = r_i'$, infinity if $r_i = r_i'''$ and will be greater the closer r_i is to r_i'''.

We define the market set R_{2A} by the relation:

$$(3.12) \qquad R_{2A} \equiv \left\{ r\colon \frac{a/2b + (m + \tau r)/2 - \bar{p}(r)}{\bar{p}(r) - (m + \tau r)} \leq \frac{k(r)}{2b\delta} \quad and \quad r \notin R_1 \right\}$$

Market r_i in Figure 4 will be in market set R_{2A} if $k(r_i)/2b\delta \geq AB/BC$ (r_i is not in R_1 since $r_i > r_i'$), e.g. if $k(r_i)/2b\delta = DE/EF$.

The necessary conditions (A.1)–(A.5) for a maximum with $x^*(t, r) = 0$ are satisfied in the market set R_{2A}, and optimal pricing policy for all markets in R_{2A} is given by equation (3.10). The leading firm will maintain exclusive control over all markets in R_{2A} by never charging more than the limit price in such markets. This policy clearly involves spatial price discrimination. If there are no competitors in any of the markets in R_{2A} at time zero, and if the same limit price $\bar{p}$ say, holds in all markets in R_{2A}, pricing policy (3.10) is such that the firm will always charge a uniform price $\bar{p}$ throughout R_{2A}.

In section IV we shall consider in more detail the factors which determine the bounds of the set R_{2A}. We now turn, however, to the case in which (3.11) is not satisfied and define the market set:

$$(3.13)\qquad R_{2B} \equiv \left\{ r: \frac{a/2b + (m + \tau r)/2 - \bar{p}(r)}{\bar{p}(r) - (m + \tau r)} > \frac{k(r)}{2b\delta} \quad \textit{and} \quad \bar{p}(r) > m + \tau r \right\}$$

Note that $R_2 = R_{2A} \cup R_{2B}$.

For all markets r in R_{2B} we have an interior solution to the optimal control problem, and the necessary conditions are now (Hadley and Kemp ([9], Theorem 5.4.1, p. 291):

$$(B.1)\qquad \dot{x}^*(t, r) = k(r)(p^*(t, r) - \bar{p}(r)); \; x(0, r) = 0$$

$$(B.2)\qquad \dot{\lambda}(t, r) = -\partial H/\partial x$$

$$(B.3)\qquad \partial H/\partial p = 0$$

$$(B.4)\qquad \lim_{t \to \infty} \lambda(t, r) = 0$$

The conditions (B.1)–(B.3) generate two differential equations which can be solved to give:[8]

$$(3.14)\qquad p^*(t, r) = \frac{C_1 \rho_1}{k(r)} e^{\rho_1 t} + \frac{C_2 \rho_2}{k(r)} e^{\rho_2 t} + \bar{p}(r) \qquad (r \in R_{2B})$$

$$(3.15)\qquad x^*(t, r) = C_1 e^{\rho_1 t} + C_2 e^{\rho_2 t} + A(r) \qquad (r \in R_{2B})$$

where $A(r) = (a - b\bar{p}(r)) - (k(r)/\delta + b)(\bar{p}(r) - (m + \tau r)) > 0$ for r in R_{2B};

C_1, C_2 are constants to be determined;

$\rho_1 = \delta/2 + \sqrt{((\delta/2)^2 + \delta k(r)/2b)} > 0;$

$\rho_2 = \delta/2 - \sqrt{((\delta/2)^2 + \delta k(r)/2b)} < 0.$

Since $\rho_1 > 0$, condition (B.4) can be satisfied only if $C_1 = 0$. Further, since we assume $x(0, r) = 0$, we find:

$$(3.16)\qquad C_2 = -A(r) < 0 \qquad (r \in R_{2B})$$

(recall our discussion of (3.11)). Equations (3.14) and (3.15) are now:

$$(3.14')\qquad p^*(t, r) = -\frac{A(r)}{k(r)} \rho_2 e^{\rho_2 t} + \bar{p}(r) \qquad (r \in R_{2B})$$

$$(3.15')\qquad x^*(t, r) = -A(r) e^{\rho_2 t} + A(r) \qquad (r \in R_{2B})$$

Typical paths for $p^*(t, r)$, $q(p^*(t, r), t)$, and $x^*(t, r)$ are illustrated in Figure 5 for a market r in R_{2B}.

[8] See Gaskins [6]. It should be noted that Gaskins does not consider the possibility of a boundary solution. His analysis applies, therefore, solely to markets in market set R_{2B}.

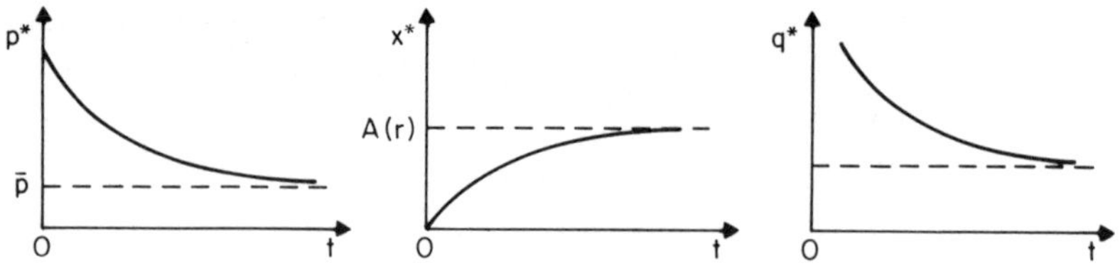

FIGURE 5
Time Variation of Price, Quantity and Competitors' Sales: Market Set R_{2B}

Since price declines over time in each market in the set R_{2B} there is evidence of intertemporal price discrimination. In addition, since each market in R_{2B} may have a different limit price or diffusion rate, prices at any given time are unlikely to follow an f.o.b. scheme. Even in the absence of variations in $\bar{p}(r)$ and $k(r)$, however, we can show that the leading firm will adopt a discriminatory spatial pricing policy in R_{2B}.

Assume:

(B.5) $\quad \bar{p}(r) = \bar{p};\ k(r) = k \quad$ all r in R_{2B}

Then the slope of the delivered price schedule[9] in R_{2B} is

(3.17) $\quad S_{2r}(p^*(t, r)) = -\rho_2(1/\delta + b/k)e^{\rho_2 t} \qquad (r \in R_{2B})$

Clearly, $S_{2r} \to 0$ as $t \to \infty$. In other words, over time spatial prices will tend to become more discriminatory and, given (B.5), in the limit a uniform pricing policy will be adopted in R_{2B}. We can also show that there will be spatial price discrimination at time $t = 0$. Equation (3.17) and the value of ρ_2 (see (3.14) and (3.15)) are such that:

$$\text{(3.18)} \quad \left.\begin{array}{l} S_{2r}(p^*(0, r)) \geq \tfrac{1}{2} \\ S_{2r}(p^*(0, r)) = 1 \quad \text{if and only if} \quad k/\delta = (1 + \sqrt{2})b \end{array}\right\} \qquad (r \in R_{2B})$$

Thus, for markets in R_{2B} characterized by (B.5) the leading firm will adopt a spatial pricing policy which is less discriminatory than that which would apply if there were no threat of entry (in which case (3.2) would hold and $S_{2r} = \frac{1}{2}$), but which is unlikely to be an f.o.b. scheme ($S_{2r} = 1$). It can further be shown that spatial price discrimination will increase as the ratio $k/b\delta$ decreases, i.e. as k decreases or b and δ increase.

Despite the lower degree of spatial price discrimination exhibited by (3.17), comparison of (3.2) and (3.14′) indicates that the leading firm always charges

[9] Note that we do not need to assume that the markets in R_{2B} form a continuous set when mapped onto a straight line. The slope of the DPS merely indicates that, for two markets r_f and r_g in R_{2B} such that, in terms of distance from the leading firm, $r_g > r_f$, delivered price in r_g exceeds delivered price in r_f by an amount $S_{2r}(p^*(t, r)) \cdot (\tau r_g - \tau r_f)$.

less than the "no entry threat" price. Indeed, whether or not (B.5) holds, prices in R_{2B} will always be less than the prices given by (3.2). For all markets in R_{2B} the leading firm is willing to sacrifice short-run profits in order to control the entry of potential competitors and so secure its long-run profits. At the same time, it should be noted that the long-run profits to be obtained by total exclusion of potential rivals are not sufficient in R_{2B} to offset the short-run profits lost by the limit pricing policy necessary to effect the exclusion.

III.3. *Market Set R_3*

Market set R_3 is defined by the relation:

$$R_3 \equiv \{r: \bar{p}(r) \leq m + \tau r \leq a/b\} \tag{3.19}$$

As we noted in section III.1, the leading firm has no long-run cost advantage in markets in R_3 since the limit prices $\bar{p}(r)$ in such markets are less than marginal costs of production and transport. The only advantage available to the leading firm is the advantage of being first. Its sales to markets in R_3 will eventually be driven to zero by competitive entry, and all the firm can hope to do is control the speed of such entry to at least some extent by its choice of pricing policy. The nearer it charges to marginal cost in any market r in R_3 the longer it can supply r, while the nearer it prices to the "no entry threat" price (3.2) the more quickly it will be driven out of the market.[10]

The problem facing the firm is again an optimal control problem, the necessary conditions for which are (B.1)–(B.3) above plus the transversality conditions:

$$\text{(B.4')} \quad \begin{cases} H = 0 \quad \text{at} \quad t = T \\ \lambda(T, r) = 0 \end{cases}$$

Solving (B.1)–(B.3) and (B.4') we obtain:

$$p^*(t, r) = \frac{C_1 \rho_1}{k(r)} e^{\rho_1 t} + \frac{C_2 \rho_2}{k(r)} e^{\rho_2 t} + \bar{p}(r) \qquad (r \in R_3) \tag{3.20}$$

$$x^*(t, r) = C_1 e^{\rho_1 t} + C_2 e^{\rho_2 t} + A(r) \qquad (r \in R_3) \tag{3.21}$$

where $A(r)$, ρ_1 and ρ_2 are as above,

$$C_1 = \frac{k(r)}{(\rho_1 - \rho_2)e^{\rho_1 T}} \left(1 + \frac{\rho_2}{\delta} + \frac{2\rho_2 b}{k(r)}\right)((m + \tau r) - \bar{p}(r)) \leq 0 \tag{3.22}$$

and

$$C_2 = -A(r) - C_1 \leq 0 \tag{3.23}$$

[10] We confine ourselves at this stage to the case in which the leading firm considers only the export mode for serving markets in R_3. Alternative strategies, e.g. local production in a branch plant, may, of course, be feasible, and we shall comment on these in section V.

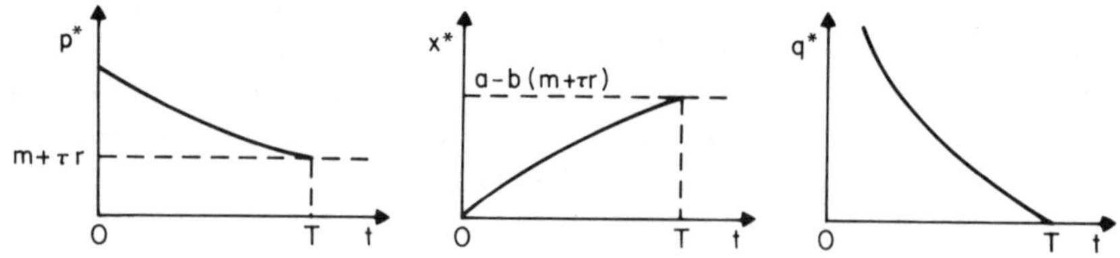

FIGURE 6
Time Variation of Price, Quantity and Competitors' Sales: Market Set R_3

The time horizon T can be found from the end point conditions (B.4′), which reduce to:[11]

$$(3.24)\qquad \begin{cases} p^*(T, r) = m + \tau r \\ a - bp^*(T, r) - x^*(T, r) = 0 \end{cases}$$

Equations (3.20)–(3.24) give rise to typical time paths for $p^*(t, r)$, $q(p^*(t, r), t)$ and $x^*(t, r)$ as illustrated in Figure 6. The leading firm chooses that temporal trajectory for its pricing policy which is such that price falls to marginal cost just as sales are driven to zero by competitive entry.

If we assume that (B.5) holds for markets in R_3, i.e. that limit prices and diffusion rates are invariant over all markets in R_3, the slope of the delivered price schedule in R_3 at time zero is:

$$(3.25)\qquad S_{3r}(p^*(0, r)) = -\rho_2\left(\frac{1}{\delta} + \frac{b}{k}\right) + \frac{1}{e^{\rho_1 T}}\left(1 + \frac{\rho_2}{\delta} + \frac{2\rho_2 b}{k}\right) \qquad (r \in R_3)$$

It can be shown that the second term of (3.25) is negative and that S_{3r} exceeds $\frac{1}{2}$. Comparison with (3.17) indicates:

$$(3.26)\qquad \tfrac{1}{2} \leq S_{3r}(p^*(0, r)) \leq S_{2r}(p^*(0, r))$$

Prices in R_3 are unlikely to follow an f.o.b. scheme, and while there will, at least initially, be a smaller degree of spatial price discrimination than characterises the "no entry threat" pricing policy, delivered prices will be more discriminatory than over markets in R_{2B}. It should also be noted that, since $\partial S_{3r}(p^*(t, r))/\partial t < 0$ delivered prices in R_3 become more discriminatory over time.

IV. DETERMINATION OF MARKET SEGMENTATION

The four market sets identified in section III are defined by the equations (3.4), (3.12), (3.13) and (3.19). Given knowledge of demand, cost, and entry parameters for a particular market r_i we can use these definitions to identify bounds on a particular market set within which the distance r_i must lie if the market r_i is to be allocated to that set. This is illustrated in Figure 7 (note that

[11] Explicit solution of (3.24) should be attempted only by the brave or foolhardy!

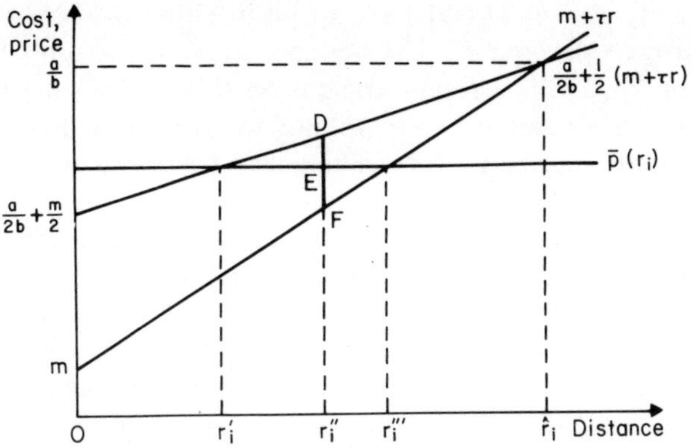

FIGURE 7
Bounds on Market Sets

r_i'' is such that $k(r_i)/2b\delta = DE/EF$). If $0 \leq r_i \leq r_i'$, r_i is in R_1, if $r_i' \leq r_i \leq r_i''$, r_i is in R_{2A} and so on.

We summarise in Table I the ways in which the various parameter values will affect the bounds on the various market sets and so the market set to which the leading firm will allocate market r_i.

Perhaps of most interest are the ways in which the parameter values will influence whether r_i will be in a market set to which the leading firm can ensure its long run survival as an exporter: market sets R_1, R_{2A} and R_{2B}. The bound r_i''' is determined solely by cost conditions and the limit price. *Ceteris paribus*, the lower are costs of production and transport or the higher is the limit price below which there is no threat of entry the more likely is it that the firm will be able to survive in the long run as an exporter to r_i.

Whether the firm will aim for exclusive control over market r_i, however, is affected by all the parameters in the model. Exclusive control is exercised over

TABLE I
EFFECTS OF DIFFERENCES IN PARAMETER VALUES IN MARKET r_i ON MARKET SET BOUNDS FOR MARKET r_i

Effect of a Higher Value for	*Effect on* r_i'	r_i''	r_i'''	$\hat{r}_i$
(1) Demand Parameters				
a	−	−	0	+
b	+	+	0	−
(2) Cost Parameters				
τ	−	−	−	−
m	−	−	−	−
δ	0	−	0	0
(3) Entry Parameters				
$\bar{p}(r_i)$	+	+	+	0
$k(r_i)$	0	+	0	0

all markets in R_1 and R_{2A}, and for r_i to be in either of these two sets it is necessary that r_i be less than r_i''. The bound r_i'', and so the probability that r_i will be in R_1 or R_{2A}, will be greater the greater the limit price with respect to the maximum price consumers are willing to pay, or with respect to the leading firm's marginal costs of production and transport, the lower the discount rate and the greater the diffusion rate.

Thus, the greater the monopolistic advantage of the leading firm over potential competitors in r_i, as measured by the relationship between the limit price and demand or cost conditions in r_i the more likely is it that the leading firm will be able profitably to exclude potential competitors from r_i. A lower discount rate, on the other hand, changes the relationship between short run and long run profits. We saw in our discussion of equation (3.11) that whether r_i is in R_{2A} is determined by the balance between long run profits obtained from precluding rivals from r_i and the attendant short run profits foregone by departing from the pricing rule (3.2). A lower discount rate enhances the value of long run profits and so will encourage the leading firm to price to exclude entry over a greater number of its markets.

Similar comments apply to the interpretation of the effects of differences in the entry coefficient, or diffusion rate, $k(r)$. The greater is $k(r_i)$, *ceteris paribus*, the more quickly will profits in r_i be eroded by competitive entry. Again, therefore, the more likely is it that the leading firm will aim for exclusive control of r_i.

Since the way in which the leading firm segments its potential market area is strongly affected by variations in both the limit prices $\bar{p}(r)$ and diffusion rates $k(r)$ over markets in this area, we should consider in rather more detail how $\bar{p}(r)$ and $k(r)$ should be interpreted and the factors which determine them and cause them to vary between markets.

The limit price $\bar{p}(r)$ has been defined as the minimum price at which potential competitors will be willing to enter the market r. We noted in section II that $\bar{p}(r)$ can be expected to be related to long run average costs (LRAC) of production in market r. The precise relationship between $\bar{p}(r)$ and LRAC will be affected, however, by a number of factors.

First, the product in question may have a well defined image, or rely upon a specialist technology. In terms of image, what we are suggesting is that the product being marketed consists of a set of physical characteristics plus a set of intangible characteristics associated with a brand name. New entrants are faced, not only with the problem of competing on price with the leading firm, but also with the task of defining a new image which will compete with that of the leading firm. If the product relies upon a specialist technology, on the other hand, new entrants may have to replicate that technology and comply with patent restrictions.

The definition of a new brand image and the replication (and differentiation) of a specialist technology impose initial set-up costs on potential entrants which will be greater the stronger the existing brand image (e.g.

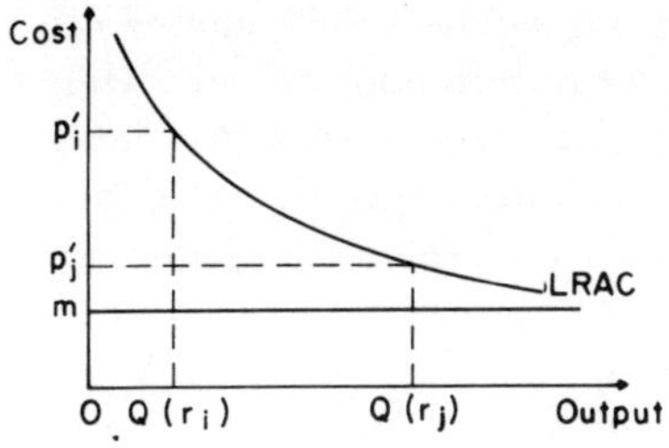

FIGURE 8
Effect of Consumer Density on Limit Price

initial advertising expenditures, market research etc.), the more complicated the technology, and the more is either image or technology derivative of, or integrated with other products and technologies developed by the leading firm.

The second major factor which will determine the appropriate limit price in a particular market is the quantity sold in that market, $Q(r)$—which in our model will be related to consumer density $D(r)$. Consider first the situation in which potential competitors are purely local in scope; if they export they do so only within narrow boundaries. For such competitors to be able to enter market r price must be sufficiently high to cover LRAC in r. Given the cost structure we have assumed (equation (2.1)) LRAC will be as in Figure 8. Entry to market r_i will be possible for an indigenous firm only if price exceeds p'_i, while in market r_j entry will be possible if price exceeds p'_j. The leading firm will be able to control entry to market r_i if marginal costs of production and transport $(m + \tau r_i)$ are less than p'_i, but will find it rather more difficult to control entry to market r_j.

Note the connection between this analysis and our discussion of Figure 3 above. It is perfectly conceivable that the leading firm be a long run exporter to market r_i but not to market r_j even if r_j is the geographically more proximate market.

Now consider the situation in which potential competitors are themselves exporters to several markets. A similar analysis to that of Figure 8 applies, but the leading firm will find it more difficult to maintain a long-run market presence as an exporter since potential competitors will be affected more by marginal costs than by LRAC in deciding whether to serve these markets. In addition, this type of competitor is likely to be rather more sophisticated than purely indigenous competitors, and so better able to overcome the image and technology barriers to entry discussed above. Control by the leading firm may still be possible, of course, particularly if the leading firm controls certain specialised inputs, whether raw materials, intermediate products, or specialised labour skills, but is rather less likely.

We should consider not just the size of a market, but also the extent to which it is sophisticated and developed. The more developed is a particular market the more difficult it will be for the leading firm to define and maintain an exclusive brand image or technology. Thus, while the firm may be able to use exports as a long-run supply strategy to less developed markets, it will find it much more difficult to maintain this strategy in developed markets.

A third factor which will determine the appropriate limit price in particular markets is the extent to which the leading firm can influence, or is influenced by, government policy within those markets. Anti-dumping regulations, for example, will inhibit the extent to which the leading firm can use selective price cutting to inhibit competition in large, but distant markets. The effects of tariff barriers should also be considered. When imposed on the leading firm, tariffs may well move a market from satisfying the conditions for it to be in R_1 or R_{2A}, say, to satisfying the conditions for it to be in R_{2B} or R_3. In either case, local production will be encouraged. Alternatively, if potential competitors are themselves exporters to the market in question, the leading firm may be able to inhibit competition by influencing tariff and other trade policies within that market. Clearly, this will be more likely for markets within the same national jurisdiction as the leading firm, e.g. Japanese firms influencing trading conditions facing firms attempting to export to Japan. But it is also likely to occur in external markets where the leading firm "has the ear" of government.

Turning to the entry coefficient $k(r)$, we have already interpreted this as a measure of the diffusion rate of the technology being exploited by the leading firm, and noted that it will be lower in a particular market the more easily can the leading firm keep the technology private from its potential competitors in that market. In this sense, $k(r)$ is a measure of appropriability (Magee [12], [13]), in other words a measure of the power the leading firm has to appropriate the returns from investment in new technology and information.

The diffusion rate can be expected to be lower the more complicated the technology. It can also be expected to vary between markets; it will be greater in a particular market the greater the degree to which potential competition comes from other exporting firms, and the more sophisticated and developed are the individuals and institutions within that market. Finally, the diffusion rate will be affected by judicial arrangements. It will be lower, for example, in those markets in which the leading firm can more easily define and enforce patent restrictions on its specialist ideas.

It can be seen that there is some commonality in those factors which influence the limit price $\bar{p}(r)$ and the diffusion rate $k(r)$. Markets can be expected to have high limit prices and low diffusion rates, and so to be in R_1 or R_2, the smaller and less developed they are. Similarly, limit prices can be expected to be low and diffusion rates high in large, developed markets containing sophisticated potential competitors. In the latter markets, while the high diffusion rate may make the leading firm wish to price to exclude entry and protect its technology—put the market in R_{2A}—the low limit price may well prevent this from being a feasible strategy, and, indeed, may put the market in R_3.

V. ALTERNATIVE SUPPLY MODES

Our discussion in sections II–IV assumes that the export mode is the sole method of supply considered by the leading firm. We found that for markets in R_3 (and, of course, for markets not in R) this is not a feasible long run supply mode, while for markets in R_2 the export mode is feasible only if the leading firm modifies its pricing strategy to control the entry of potential competitors.

Other supply modes are, however, available to the firm. In particular, the firm may consider multi-plant or, where markets are located in several different countries, multinational production through foreign direct investment (FDI). It is outside the scope of this paper to consider such options in any formal detail, but some brief statements should be made at this stage about the factors which will lead to an alternative supply mode being chosen. We confine ourselves to commenting on the choice between exporting and FDI, although the connections with multi-plant operation should also be clear.

The optimal pricing policies identified in section III are such that the net present value (NPV) of the profit stream which the leading firm will obtain from exports to market r_i will, for given values of the limit price and diffusion rate in r_i, be lower the more distant is r_i from the firm, and, for a given distance between r_i and the firm, be lower the lower the limit price or the higher the diffusion rate in r_i : this is illustrated in Figure 9.

For FDI to be a feasible supply mode in market r_i it is necessary that the leading firm can exploit a competitive advantage over its potential competitors in r_i—see Buckley and Casson [1], Dunning [4]. Such a competitive advantage will derive from just those factors discussed in section IV—possession of a well defined brand image, specialist technology, or control over specialised resources.

The NPV of profits from FDI in market r_i can be expected to be lower the more distant is r_i from the leading firm's home location. Initial set-up costs will include some elements which are not directly distance related, e.g. installation of plant and distribution facilities in the host country. They will also, however, include distance related items, e.g. costs of initial familiarisation with the foreign market. Similarly, operating costs will include distance related elements: information transmission and validation, the cost of exercising managerial control over the foreign affiliate, and the general recurrent costs of operating in a foreign environment.

It is to be expected, however, that NPV of profit from FDI will decline less quickly with distance than will NPV of profit from exporting, since we would expect distance related costs to have a weaker effect on profit from FDI than on profit from exporting. This leads to the possibility, as illustrated in Figure 9, that the two profit curves will intersect. Given the situation depicted in Figure 9, if r_i lies to the right (left) of $\tilde{r}_i$ FDI (exporting) is the preferred supply mode for market r_i.

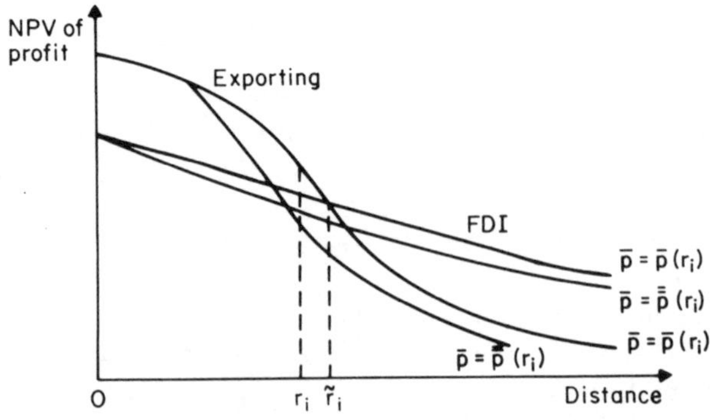

FIGURE 9

Alternative Supply Modes

The NPV of profits from FDI in market r_i will also be lower the lower the limit price and the higher the diffusion rate in r_i. Again, however, we would expect the impact of a lower limit price or a higher diffusion rate to be less on profits from FDI than on profits from exporting. First, we have noted that the lower is the limit price the more likely is it that r_i will be in R_3, and so the shorter the time period over which exporting to r_i is feasible. In contrast, so long as the cost advantage available to the leading firm (where costs now *exclude* transport costs) as a result of its competitive advantage over potential competitors in r_i is sufficiently great as to offset the distance related costs of FDI in r_i, FDI is a feasible long run strategy.

Secondly, a number of the factors which might be expected to lead to lower limit prices and higher diffusion rates will also reduce the costs of foreign operations, and so offset at least part of the profit loss noted above. We have seen that limit prices will be lower and diffusion rates higher in large, developed economies with a sophisticated consumer, producer and political environment. But this type of environment will also work to the advantage of the potential multinational company (Dunning and Norman [5]). Information generation, analysis and transmission will be easier and more effective, communications, whether telecommunications or personal travel, will be faster and more efficient, initial set-up costs, whether in training labour, commissioning and constructing production facilities, or developing distribution networks, will be lower.

In the example illustrated in Figure 9, if the limit price in market r_i is $\bar{p}(r_i)$ exporting will be the preferred supply mode. If, alternatively, the limit price is $\bar{\bar{p}}(r_i)$ FDI will be preferred.[12]

Similar considerations can be applied to the analysis of a mixed strategy in which, for example, the firm initially exports to r_i and subsequently switches

[12] There are many other advantages of FDI not included in this analysis. For example, FDI will allow the firm to jump tariff barriers, satisfy anti-dumping regulations, and benefit from transfer pricing.

to FDI in r_i. It is to be expected—see Buckley and Casson [2]—that exporting might precede FDI but not vice versa. We would then expect for any market r_i that the switch from exporting to FDI will be earlier[13]

(i) the more distant is r_i from the firm's home base,
(ii) the lower is the limit price and the higher the diffusion rate in r_i as compared with other markets, and so
(iii) the larger and more developed is r_i and
(iv) the lower the distance and other costs of operating in the initially foreign environment of r_i.

The connections between this analysis and the received theory of the multinational enterprise—see Buckley and Casson [1], Dunning [4], Vernon [20]—are clear. Our analysis explains why FDI by U.S. based firms could be expected to be directed initially at the developed economies of Western Europe, and concentrated on R&D intensive, consumer based (rather than intermediate) products. It is in just those industries that U.S. firms are felt to have held the strongest competitive advantages. Exploitation of these advantages by exporting may have been feasible, and, indeed, preferable as an initial strategy. In the longer run, however, the difficulties involved in controlling the diffusion of technology and the loss of export markets, and the profit penalty of pricing policies necessary to exercise such control, might be expected to be such as to force U.S. firms to respond by locating production facilities abroad.

Our discussion also indicates that, as experience is gained of operating abroad, and as other markets grow and develop, FDI can be expected to be channeled to smaller, less developed economies. This extension of FDI is additionally to be expected as competition in particular markets comes increasingly from other, third-country, e.g. Japanese, producers.

VI. CONCLUSIONS

We have seen that the way in which a firm prices in particular spatial markets, and the way in which its pricing policy changes over time are crucially dependent upon the conditions under which potential rivals can enter these markets.

Four market sets have been defined and the optimal pricing policy for markets in each of these sets identified. In two of the sets the firm is able, and wishes, to price to maintain exclusive control. Exclusive control is also possible in markets in the third set, but will impose a greater profit penalty than that consequent upon pricing to allow some competitive entry. In the fourth set, in contrast, the firm is unable profitably to exercise long run control. It will be forced out of markets in this set in some finite period.

[13] It must be remembered that FDI is feasible in the first instance only if the firm possesses and can exploit a competitive advantage of the type discussed above.

A market will be allocated to one or other of these sets depending upon the relationship between:

(i) marginal costs of production and transport incurred by the leading firm in supplying that market,
(ii) the limit price in the market—the minimum price at which potential competitors are willing to enter the market,
(iii) the technology diffusion rate in the market—which will be lower the more easily the leading firm can keep its specialist knowledge private from its potential competitors in the market.

Pricing to exercise either complete or partial control of competitive entry will be easier the higher the limit price and the lower are marginal costs. Given that control is feasible, a pricing policy which secures exclusive control will be preferred the lower is the discount rate—the greater the present value of future profits—and the greater the technology diffusion rate—the more quickly potential rivals can enter and erode the leading firm's market share.

If potential competition in a market r comes solely from indigenous producers in r we can take long run average costs of production in r as a measure of the limit price $\bar{p}(r)$. The limit price will be higher the stronger the brand image of the product, the more complicated the technology on which it is based, and the smaller and less developed is the market r. In contrast, if potential competitors supply several markets the limit price will be more closely related to marginal costs of production and transport from these competitors to market r, and so can be expected to be lower than that which would apply with purely indigenous competition.

The technology diffusion rate in a particular market can be expected to be lower the more complicated the technology, the less developed the market, and the less sophisticated are potential competitors in the market.

Finally, limit prices and diffusion rates. will be affected by government policy in different markets, that is, by policy on tariffs, anti-dumping regulation, and the willingness to grant enforcible patents.

Since limit prices and diffusion rates are affected by both product and market specific characteristics, it is to be expected that they will vary between markets in a manner which will not be directly distance related. It follows, therefore, that the factors which determine the market set to which a market is allocated (factors (i)–(iii) above) are only partially related to distance between the market and the leading firm's production base. As a result, it is perfectly conceivable that the firm will be a long run exporter to certain distant markets while being forced to accept partial or total erosion of its exports to other, more proximate markets.

With such variety of limit prices and diffusion rates across markets, it is highly unlikely that spatial prices will follow an f.o.b. scheme. We have shown, in addition, that even where limit prices and diffusion rates are constant in every market, spatial price discrimination is to be expected and will increase over time.

Finally, we considered briefly those factors which might lead to the firm changing its mode of market supply. We found, in particular, that FDI will be more likely to be preferred to exporting to a market the lower the limit price and the higher the technology diffusion rate in the market. Our analysis is shown to be consistent with other empirical and theoretical investigations of multinational production.

GEORGE NORMAN AND NANCY K. NICHOLS,
Respectively Departments of Economics and Mathematics,
University of Reading,
Whiteknights,
Reading, RG6 2AA, England

REFERENCES

[1] Buckley, P. J. and Casson, M. C., *The Future of the Multinational Enterprise*, (London, Macmillan, 1976).

[2] ——, "The Optimal Timing of a Foreign Direct Investment", *Economic Journal*, vol. 91, 1 (March 1981), pp. 75–87.

[3] Capozza, D. R. and Van Order, R., "A Generalised Model of Spatial Competition", *American Economic Review*, vol. 68, 4 (December 1978), pp. 896–908.

[4] Dunning, J. H., "Trade, Location of Economic Activity, and the Multinational Enterprise: A Search for an Eclectic Approach", in Ohlin, B., Hesselborn, P. O. and Wiskman, P. J. (ed.) *The International Allocation of Economic Activity*, (London, Macmillan, 1977).

[5] —— and Norman, G., *Factors Influencing the Location of Offices of Multinational Enterprises*, Location of Offices Bureau, Research Paper no. 8, (London, 1979).

[6] Gaskins, D. W., "Dynamic Limit Pricing: Optimal Pricing under Threat of Entry", *Journal of Economic Theory*, vol. 3, 3 (December 1971), pp. 306–22.

[7] Greenhut, J. G. and Greenhut, M. L., "Spatial Price Discrimination, Competition and Location Effects", *Economica*, vol. 42, 168 (November 1975), pp. 401–19.

[8] —— and Li, S.-Y., "Spatial Pricing Patterns in the United States", *Quarterly Journal of Economics*, vol. XCIV, 1 (March 1980), pp. 329–50.

[9] Hadley, G. and Kemp, M. C., *Variational Methods in Economics*, (London, North-Holland, 1971).

[10] Hwang, M. J., "A Model of Spatial Price Discrimination for the Price Schedule of Coal", *Journal of Regional Science*, vol. 19, 2 (May 1979), pp. 231–44.

[11] Jaquemin, A. P. and Thisse, J., "Strategy of the firm and market structure: an application of optimal control theory", in Cowling, K. (ed.) *Market Structure and Corporate Behaviour: Theory and Empirical Analysis of the Firm*, (London, Gray-Mills, 1972).

[12] Magee, S. P., "Technology and the appropriability theory of the multinational corporation", in Bhagwati, J. (ed.) *The New International Economic Order: the north–south debate*, (Cambridge, Mass., M.I.T. Press, 1977).

[13] ——, "The Appropriability Theory of Multinational Corporation Behaviour", *University of Reading Papers in International Investment and Business Studies*, no. 51, (Autumn 1981).

[14] MANSFIELD, E., "Entry, Gibrat's Law, innovation and growth of firms", *American Economic Review*, vol. LII, 4 (December 1962), pp. 1023–30.

[15] NORMAN, G., "Spatial Competition and Spatial Price Discrimination", *Review of Economic Studies*, vol. XLVII, 1 (January 1981), pp. 97–111.

[16] PHLIPS, L., "Spatial Pricing and Competition", Studies of the Commission of the European Communities, *Competition—Approximation of Legislation Series*, no. 29. (Brussels, 1976).

[17] ——, "Intertemporal Price Discrimination and Sticky Prices", *Quarterly Journal of Economics*, vol. XCIV, 2 (May 1980), pp. 525–42.

[18] SCHERER, F. M., *Industrial Market Structure and Economic Performance*, (2nd. ed.) (Chicago, Rand McNally Publishing, 1980).

[19] TAKAYAMA, A., *Mathematical Economics*, (Hinsdale, Dryden Press, 1974).

[20] VERNON, R., "The Product Cycle in a New International Environment", *Oxford Bulletin of Economics and Statistics*, vol. 41, 3 (August 1979), pp. 255–67.

THE JOURNAL OF INDUSTRIAL ECONOMICS
Volume XXXI September/December 1982 Nos. 1/2

SPATIAL PRICE DUOPOLY UNDER UNIFORM DELIVERED PRICING*

RICHARD E. SCHULER AND BENJAMIN F. HOBBS

I. INTRODUCTION

Previous analyses of spatial oligopoly, starting with Hotelling's classic one-dimensional model [7] and continuing through the work of Beckmann [1] and Eaton and Lipsey [3], have been limited to the case of mill-pricing, where customers bear the full transportation costs, or of spatial discriminatory pricing, as in the analysis by Greenhut and Greenhut [4], where customers pay some portion of the transportation cost. However, many producers absorb all of the transportation costs, particularly if these costs are small, and they post a single uniform price for all of their customers, regardless of where they are located. The choice of uniform-delivered-pricing (UDP) may be predicated on administrative and marketing convenience, but it is also a special form of price discrimination which subsidizes consumers located more distant from the production facility. Many governmental regulatory agencies in the United States encourage UDP, even if transportation costs are significant, possibly because of simplicity and equity considerations or out of the mistaken belief that the uniform pricing paradigm of a spaceless, perfectly competitive world is applicable. One example is in the electric utility industry, a regulated monopoly, where uniform prices are charged to all customers of similar commercial characteristics throughout the utility's widespread service territory.

Thus, it is interesting to analyze the competitive pricing behavior under UDP of spatial-oligopolistic firms, and it is curious that little attention has been devoted to this topic. The exception is a game-theoretic investigation by Beckmann [2], which is restricted to the simple case of constant demand, depending on whether price is above or below the reservation level. Other papers dealing with UDP identify the conjectural presumptions of the competitors, but then focus their attention on the zero-profit equilibrium conditions resulting from free entry, as in the recent paper by Gronberg and Meyer [5]. However, the short-run, dynamic pricing behavior of spatial duopolists under UDP has been neglected; indeed, as will be shown in this paper, neither price undercutting nor the setting of a collusive price may lead to profit maximization under certain initial price and inter-firm spacing conditions.

* This research was supported by a grant from the National Science Foundation, PRA-7913072.

One explanation of the previous analytic emphasis on mill-pricing (MP) is that the competitive analyses of price competition are neater, the results converge to equilibria, and the swings of service territory between one producer and another are small. The MP solutions are analogous to Cournot's results for a spaceless world where each competitor makes a zero-conjectural-variation (ZCV) assumption that other firms will not alter their level of production. Spatial competition under UDP, however, suggests the indeterminate oscillation of prices, initially proposed by Edgeworth for a spaceless world, in which duopolists alternatively engage in price wars and then concede and resort to monopolistic practices.

This analysis in fact extends Edgeworth's results to a spatial economy, but it shows that these price cycles may be rather tight and well confined. Furthermore, the conjectural assumptions are detailed, and anticipated profits are computed for the competitor under all possible combinations of price by and distance to the nearer firms. The analysis begins by laying out the economic, technological and behavioral assumption in Section II. Profit surfaces for alternative behavioral assumptions are worked out in Section III, and reaction curves are developed in Section IV. Finally, the results are summarized in the concluding Section V.

II. ECONOMIC, TECHNOLOGICAL AND BEHAVIORAL ASSUMPTIONS

For mathematical simplicity, a one-dimensional economy is assumed where customers, each having identical linear demand functions, are uniformly distributed along a line segment. The location of producers, whose cost functions are identical and consist of both a fixed and uniform variable cost component, is fixed in this short-run competitive analysis, so the effect of entry or relocation is not considered. Rather, the intent of the analysis is to gauge the degree of competition that might ensue prior to entry.

Producers are presumed to maintain zero-conjectural-variations with respect to their neighbors' prices (ZPCV) throughout, and the profitability of two alternative pricing policies, 1) undercutting the neighbor's price, and 2) changing price to a monopoly level are computed under this assumption. Which of these alternatives is most profitable hinges on the price initially charged by the neighbor and his cost characteristics, because the area served will usually change as the competitor alters price. As an example, under ZPCV, when a competitor undercuts his neighbor's price, the service territory of the neighbor will decrease and of the competitor will increase. In fact, the competitor will be willing to serve territory up to the point where the sum of marginal production and transportation charges just equals price. That is why a zero-quantity-conjectural-variation assumption is unrealistic under UDP. If the competitor assumes his neighbor will not change his output in response to the competitor's price decrease, it means that the neighbor must hold the same price *and service area* following the competitor's lowering of price. Such an

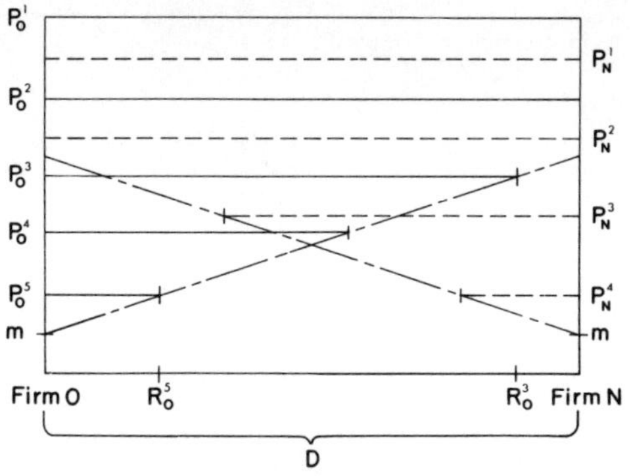

FIGURE 1
Undercutting Price Behavior

assumption by the competitor is inconsistent with his price strategy since the whole point of undercutting the neighbor's price is to *reduce* the neighbor's service territory. By comparison, assuming that the neighbor will hold his price constant in response to the competitor's undercut is at least consistent, if myopic, since the neighbor will then lose service territory and sales, as anticipated by the competitor. As will be developed later on in the paper, there are circumstances where a zero-conjectural-variation assumption about the neighbor's output is identical to an assumption about a fixed neighbor's service area, and where both are consistent with ZPCV.

The undercut scenario is illustrated in Figure 1. For purposes of analytic simplicity, the assumption is made in this paper that each producer is located at opposite ends of a line segment with customers lying only in the portion of the line between them. Thus, the problem of dealing with customers lying in the hinterlands where there is no adjacent producer is eliminated. (Note that the results derived under these assumptions are equivalent to those that would be obtained in the limit by assuming many equidistant producers arrayed along an infinite line coupled with a strategic behavioral assumption similar to the one made by Eaton and Lipsey in their MP analysis: that a competitive firm will not choose to serve customers at or beyond a neighbor's production location.) This conjecture recognizes the neighbor's zero transportation cost at his production site and the existence of a second competitor beyond it. In Figure 1, starting at high prices, each successive undercut will steal the entire service territory away from the neighbor. As competitor and neighbor continue to undercut each other's prices, one will reach a price where he will be unwilling to serve the entire territory, like price P_0^3, and the service area is restricted to R_0^3, where price just equals the sum of marginal production and transportation costs. Nevertheless, the undercut process may continue, if profitable, until a price like P_N^4 is reached. At this point further undercuts are not profitable since additional service territory is not gained; in fact lowering price merely reduces the sales territory of the price undercutter.

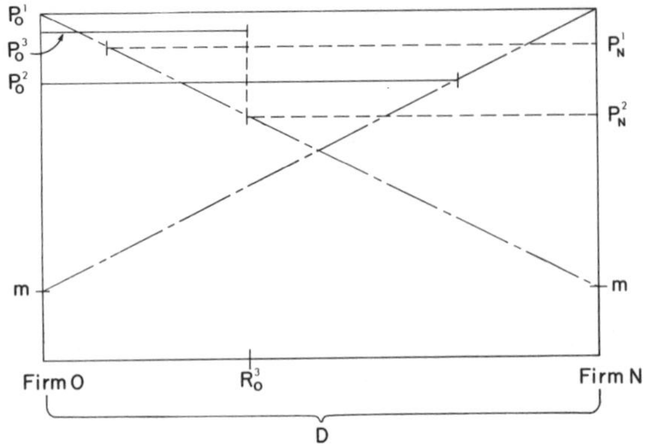

FIGURE 2
Transition from Undercut to Monopoly (Concede) Price Behavior

It is the recognition of a lower limit to the price that the neighbor is willing to charge, and the service boundary limits associated with each price, that leads to the second price-policy, setting a monopoly price, as a more profitable alternative to undercutting. Still assuming ZPCV, the competitors note that at prices below P_0^3, further price decreases impose increasing constraints on the service area each is willing to serve. So, further price decreases reduce the amount of contested service territory, and it is rational for the profit-maximizing firm to compare the added profit he may anticipate from an additional price undercut with the profit he might gain by merely granting the neighbor the maximum service territory he is willing to serve at his current price, and imposing a monopolistic price over the remaining area. This sequence of events is illustrated in Figure 2 where the normal price undercutting takes place until the neighbor is charging P_N^2 and serving a territory $D - R_0^3$. At this point, Firm *O* compares the profits of further price undercuts, but he concludes it is more profitable to "concede" the maximum service territory, $D - R_0^3$, the neighbor is willing to serve and to set an optimal monopoly price, P_0^3, over the remaining service territory R_0^3. Of course the customers between Firm *O* and point R_0^3 would prefer to buy from Firm *N* at his lower price, but firm *N* is unwilling to sell beyond $D - R_0^3$.

If production costs are identical, what is best for Firm *O* is also best for Firm *N*, both will increase their prices, both will be willing to sell in each other's territories, and the undercutting process may start all over again. This dynamic behavior will be analyzed in a subsequent section, but several other factors affecting the individual firm's pricing decision under ZPCV need to be noted.

First, if the firms are sufficiently close and transportation costs are small, successive price undercuts may continue to steal the entire service territory away from each other until price is close to marginal cost, *m*. Under these circumstances, the concession strategy will become more profitable than undercutting the neighbor's price only at very low price levels, since such large chunks of territory are gained with each undercut.

Second, under a very large spacing between existing producers, if the neighboring firm is charging an inordinately high price, above the one an isolated spatial monopolist might charge, the competitor may undercut directly to the spatial monopoly price if the distance between producers is larger than the optimal service boundaries for a spatial monopolist. Conversely, if under the same large interfirm distance, the neighbor is charging a price so low that a monopolist's service territory is available to the competitor, a concession strategy which raises price directly to the optimal spatial monopoly level is most profitable. These two, admittedly pathological, types of initial pricing behavior by the neighbor must be analyzed to map out the responses to all feasible initial price-interfirm distance combinations.

Finally, for comparison purposes, the potential profitability of collusion is computed for each interfirm distance. While the collusion result is inconsistent with ZPCV, since the additional assumptions must be made that both neighbors agree to jump to the same price and split their service territories, it is interesting to compare the anticipated profit gain from collusion with that from following either the concession or undercut strategy, starting at any initial neighbor's price. It is also interesting to see if the dynamic price cycles under undercut or concession strategies pass through the collusive points.

III. OPTIMAL STRATEGIES UNDER ZERO PRICE CONJECTURAL VARIATION (ZPCV)

A. *Undercut Strategy*

The firm's profit expression, given the neighbor's initial price is:

$$\max_{P_0} \pi_0^{Un} = \phi \int_0^{R_0 = \min[P_0 - m/T;\, D]} (P_0 - m - Tr)(a - bP_0)\, dr - F \tag{1}$$

where P_0 = the firm's undercut price
= $P_N - \varepsilon$, ε is small
P_N = the neighbor's price
R_0 = the firm's service boundary
D = interfirm distance
m = marginal production cost
F = fixed cost
T = unit transportation cost
ϕ = customer density
r = distance from firm to customer
a, b = demand parameters

This expression can be normalized as follows:

$$\text{(1a)} \qquad \underset{p_0}{\text{Max}}\ \pi_0^{Un} = (\phi b) \int_0^{R_0 = \min[p_0/T;\, D]} (p_0 - Tr)(p_m - p_0)\, dr - F$$

where $p_0 = P_0 - m =$ firm's price, net of marginal production cost
$p_m = (a/b) - m =$ customer's reservation price, net of marginal production cost
$p_N = P_N - m =$ neighbor's price, net of marginal production cost

The optimal price and profit-levels under the undercut strategy are:

$$\text{(2)} \qquad p_0^{Un} = p_N - \varepsilon;\ \pi_0^{Un}$$

$$= \begin{cases} \left(\dfrac{\phi b}{2T}\right) p_N^2 (p_m - p_N) - F; & p_N < TD \\ \left(\dfrac{\phi b}{2T}\right) (TD)(p_m - p_N)(2p_N - TD) - F; & p_N > TD \end{cases}$$

Note, in equation (2) that where $p_N > TD$, any undercutting of the neighbor's price will allow the competitor to serve the entire interfirm distance. This is because the maximum area each firm is willing to serve, $R_0 = p/T$, is larger than the actual interfirm distance.

B. *Concession Strategy*

The firm's profit expression is:

$$\text{(3)} \qquad \underset{p_0}{\text{Max}}\ \pi_0^{Con} = (\phi b) \int_0^{R_0 = [D - p_N/T]} (p_0 - Tr)(p_m - p_0)\, dr - F$$

where the service territory "conceded" to the competitor at the neighbor's price, p_N, is $D - (p_N/T)$. The competitor's profit level and optimal price are:

$$\text{(4)} \qquad p_0^{Con} = \frac{1}{2}\left[p_m + \frac{1}{2}(TD - p_N)\right];$$

$$\pi_0^{Con} = \left(\frac{\phi b}{4T}\right)(TD - p_0)\left[p_m - \frac{(TD - p_0)}{2}\right]^2 - F$$

C. *Spatial Monopolist:*

$$\text{(5)} \qquad \text{Max}\ \pi_0^{Mon} = (\phi b) \int_0^{R = \min[R_0^{Mon},\, D]} (p_0 - Tr)(p_m - p_0)\, dr - F$$

Here the firm chooses the optimal price and service territory, as long as the interfirm spacing is large enough; otherwise, the interfirm distance is accepted as the service territory. In order for the competitor to charge a monopolist's price, either the neighbor's price is so high that the optimal monopolist's price is lower (an undercut situation) or the neighbor's price is so low that the remaining service territory is larger than a monopolist would care to serve (a concede situation). Mathematically, either:

(6) $$p_0^{Mon} < p_N \text{ or } R_0^{Mon} < D - \frac{p_N}{T}$$

The optimal price, service area and profit level for the monopolist is:

(7a) $$p_0^{Mon} = (\tfrac{2}{3})p_m\ ;\ R_0^{Mon} = \left(\frac{2}{3}\right)\left(\frac{p_m}{T}\right);\ \pi_0^{Mon} = \left(\frac{2}{27}\right)\left(\frac{\phi b}{T}\right)p_m^3 - F$$

where $D \geq (\tfrac{2}{3})(p_m/T)$ or:

(7b) $$p_0^{Mon} = \frac{1}{2}\left[p_m + \frac{TD}{2}\right];\ R_0^{Mon} = D;$$
$$\pi_0^{Mon} = \left(\frac{1}{4}\right)\left(\frac{\phi b}{T}\right)\left[p_m - \frac{TD}{2}\right]^2 (TD) - F$$

where $D < (\tfrac{2}{3})(p_m/T)$.

D. *Collusion*

In this case, an equal division of service territory is presumed for firms with identical costs, and the profit expression is:

(8) $$\underset{p_0}{\text{Max}}\ \pi_0^{Coll} = (\phi b)\int_0^{D/2} (p_0 - Tr)(p_m - p_0)\, dr - F$$

The optimal price and profit level are:

(9) $$p_0^{Coll} = \frac{1}{2}\left[p_m + \frac{TD}{4}\right];\ \pi_0^{Coll} = \frac{1}{8}\left(\frac{\phi b}{T}\right)(TD)\left(p_m - \frac{TD^2}{4}\right) - F$$

E. *Profit Maximizing Strategies*

The mapping of these profit areas over a range of interfirm distances and initial neighbor prices is illustrated in Figure 3. The boundaries are set by comparing firm profits under alternative pricing strategies. As an example, the concession strategy dominates undercut pricing where $\pi_0^{Con} \geq \pi_0^{Un}$. Comparing equations (2) and (4) this yields:

(10) $$p_N \geq 2p_m - TD \text{ or}$$

(11) $$p_N \leq \frac{2TD - p_m + [p_m^2 + 10(TD)p_m - 3(TD)^2]^{1/2}}{7}$$

where $p_N \leq TD$

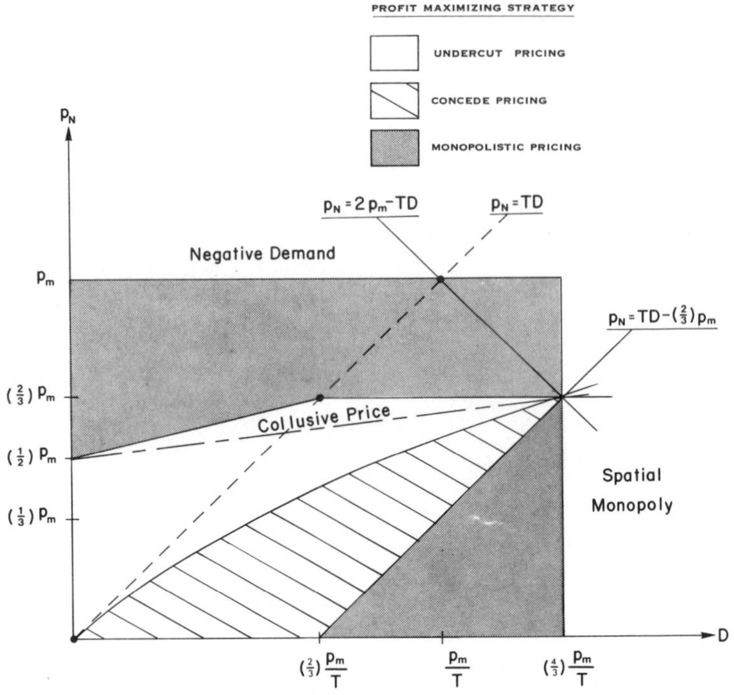

FIGURE 3
Locus of Profit-Maximizing Price Strategies Under ZPCV.

In the case where $p_N > TD$, it can be shown that undercut pricing always dominates the concession strategy since conceding offers the neighbor the entire interfirm area, D, at the neighbor's existing price, p_N.

In translating these regions onto Figure 3, note that the neighbor's price will never exceed p_m since demand is negative in that range. Furthermore, for interfirm distances greater than $(4/3)(p_m/T)$, there is ample room for each producer to satisfy their ultimate desire of pricing and reaping the profits of a spatial monopolist as outlined in equation (7a). Thus the analysis of spatial price competition can be restricted to the rectangle bounded by the price p_m and distance $(4/3)(p_m/T)$. The upper and lower bounds for which undercut pricing dominates the concession strategy, expressed in equations (10) and (11), are represented by a solid straight line and a solid concave function, respectively, in Figure 3. They intersect at the spatial monopolist's price where $D = (4/3)(p_m/T)$.

However, it is useful to plot the optimal price locus for a spatial monopolist, shown in equation (7a) where $D \geq (2/3)(p_m/T)$ and in equation (7b) where $D < (2/3)(p_m/T)$ and the monopolist's service territory is constrained by the interfirm distance, D. For neighbor prices in excess of this locus, it may be desirable for the competitor to consider moving directly to a monopoly price. This is certainly a feasible strategy under ZPCV since by undercutting the neighbor, the competitor can serve any service territory he chooses, including the monopolist's area. The only distinction between this monopolistic undercutting and the previously analyzed incremental undercutting is the magnitude of price cut; both are feasible. It remains to be shown which is more profitable, as revealed by exploring the inequality: $\pi_0^{Mon} \geq \pi_0^{Un}$. For $D \geq (2/3)(p_m/T)$, equation (7a) can be compared with the undercut profit level from equation (2) where $p_N < TD$. This reduces to the inequality in equation (12) which holds for all $p_N \geq 0$. By examining the profit expression from equation (2),

(12) $$(p_N - \tfrac{2}{3}p_m)^2(p_N + \tfrac{1}{3}p_m) \geq 0$$

where $P_N > TD$, it can be shown that undercut profit falls as P_N rises if $D > (2/3)(p_m/T)$. Since monopoly profits do not vary in this region because the optimal monopoly price and service radius are attainable, then undercutting directly to the monopoly price is more profitable than an incremental undercutting strategy. Finally, for $D < (2/3)(p_m/T)$ the inequality $\pi_0^{Mon} \geq \pi_0^{Un}$ must be explored using the constrained monopoly profit equation (7b) and the constrained undercut profit expression from equation (2). The resulting inequality is reduced to equation (13), which is always true and shows that the monopoly undercut price is always more profitable.

(13) $$\left[\left(p_m + \frac{TD}{2}\right) - 2p_N\right]^2 \geq 0$$

What remains to be shown in this upper region is that the undercut-to-monopoly price strategy dominates the concede strategy. A comparison of $\pi_0^{Mon} > \pi_0^{Con}$ using equations (7a) and (4) yields equation (14), and its

(14) $$\left[\frac{p_N - TD}{2} + \frac{4p_m}{3}\right]\left[\frac{(TD - p_N)}{2} - \frac{p_m}{3}\right]^2 \geq 0$$

validity is determined by the left bracket which reduces to $p_N \geq TD - (8/3)p_m$. The most stringent test occurs where $TD = (4/3)p_m$, but the inequality is still true, so the monopolistic price is the most successful price strategy throughout the upper shaded region of Figure 3.

Similarly, for $p_N < TD - (2/3)p_m$ the most profitable concede strategy is to move directly to the monopolistic conditions shown in equation (7b). Here this pricing strategy is feasible under ZPCV because at the neighbor's low initial price, adequate service territory is conceded to allow for a monopolist's optimum area. In summary, the monopolist's price and radius, if feasible, dominates the undercut and concession strategies because both of these impose a constraint on the optimizing solution, and, therefore, they result in smaller profits. The incremental price undercut strategy constrains price; the concession strategy constrains the radius served.

What remains is a comparison of these ZPCV pricing strategy profits with those that might be anticipated from collusion. First, note that the optimal collusive price from equation (9) lies entirely within the undercut range of Figure 3. Thus even if the competitors are colluding, a myopic profit increase can always be gained, under ZPCV, by undercutting the neighbor's price. But, suppose an asymmetric assumption is made and ZPCV is discarded, solely for the calculation of collusive profits, and this is compared with ZPCV-based undercut profits using equations (2) and (9). For the case where $p_N < TD$, and using the collusive price from equation (9), $\pi_0^{Un} \geq \pi_0^{Coll}$ results in equation (15) which is always true.

$$(15) \qquad \left[p_m - \left(\frac{3}{4}\right) TD\right]^2 \geq 0$$

Where $p_N \geq TD$, the inequality in (16) must be satisfied. This is always true where $D \leq (p_m/T)$,

$$(16) \qquad p_m - (\tfrac{5}{6}) TD \geq 0$$

which is the maximum interfirm distance where $p_N \geq TD$. So, any competitor comparing the profits from continued collusion and the myopic profits anticipated from undercutting would choose to lower price.

IV. REACTION CURVES AND DYNAMIC BEHAVIOR

The reaction curves resulting from following the optimal pricing strategies suggested in Figure 3 can be characterized in two cases: where $D <$ and

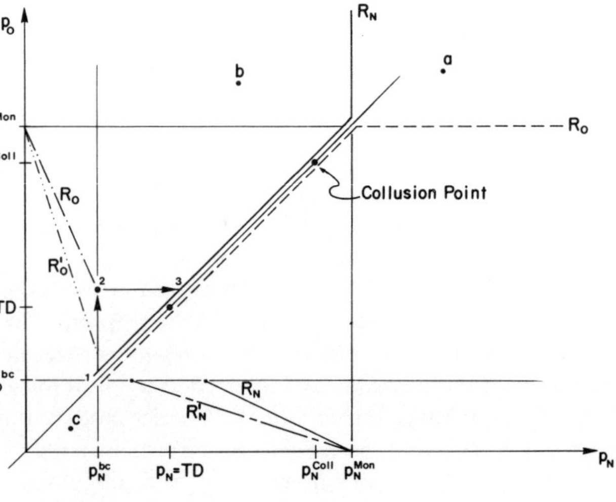

FIGURE 4
Reaction Curves and Dynamic Paths for $D < (\frac{2}{3})(p_m/T)$.

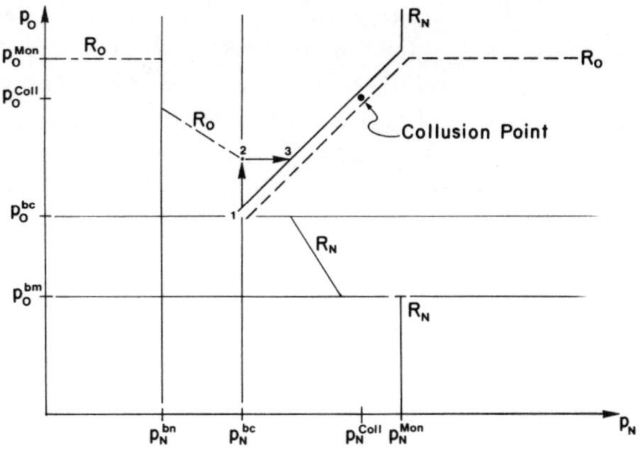

FIGURE 5
Reaction Curves and Dynamic Paths for $D \geq (\frac{2}{3})(p_m/T)$.

$D > (2/3)(p_m/T)$. Qualitatively, the only difference is that in the second case, the lower monopoly area appears as a viable strategy. The resulting reaction curves are summarized in Figures 4 and 5.

The loci of the reaction curves can all be spotted by use of the equations in Section III. The only indeterminacy is where each competitor's concede price function, from equation (4), cuts his neighbor's concede price boundary (p_0^{bc} and p_N^{bc}), from equation (11). As will be shown, this point governs the amplitude of the price cycle.

In Figure 4, starting from an initial point where both firms charge more than the monopolist's price, like "a", one firm will quickly undercut to the monopolistic price, followed by the other, and they will both slide down the 45 degree lines following their respective reaction curves R_0 and R_N. They continue to undercut each other, passing through the collusive point and on through the point where further undercuts no longer result in their stealing each other's entire service area ($p_0 = p_N = TD$). The undercutting finally stops when the first firm reaches point 1, concedes and raises its price to point 2. At this point, it pays the other firm to raise its price to the concession level at point 3, but from there the undercut cycle begins all over again. Note that starting from point "b", the firms may either move over to p_N^{Mon} or down to the 45 degree line, depending upon which firm makes the initial move, but the ultimate result is being caught in the undercut cycle between points 1, 2 and 3. The same end result is true for initial point "c" or any other combination of initial prices.

The only impact of the initial price is that only if both are above the collusive level is there any certainty that their dynamic behavior will pass through the collusive point. *Under this interfirm spacing, it can be shown that the final price cycle, 1-2-3, will never encompass the collusive point; it can't be found by accident.* Furthermore, depending on the slope of the firm's concede price reaction curve, the final cycle may not even include points where the competitors are willing to contest each other's entire service territory (curves R'_0 and R'_N). This result is obtained beyond some minimal firm spacing, so only for very close interfirm distances will some analogy be obtained for the competitive paradigm where the firm charging the lowest price will obtain all of the business.

Figure 5 illustrates the dynamic paths for interfirm spacings in excess of $(2/3)(p_m/T)$. Here, the general shape of the reaction curves are the same, with the exception that an additional lower boundary exists, p_0^{bm} and p_N^{bm}, where the concede price reverts to a monopoly level. Again, starting at any initial price combinations, the parties will ultimately find themselves trapped in the tight price cycle, 1-2-3, under ZPCV. Only if both initial prices are above the collusive level is there a certainty that the prices will pass through the collusive level; the ultimate price cycle does not encompass the collusive point.

V. SUMMARY AND CONCLUSIONS

This analysis shows that *spatial price competition between duopolists charging uniform delivered prices does ultimately lead to the constant oscillation of prices suggested by Edgeworth* under the assumption of zero price conjectural variation. However, *the bounds on this price oscillation lie above marginal cost,* $p_0 = p_N = 0$, *and below the collusive price level. This ultimate dynamic cycle is achieved regardless of the initial prices charged, and the dynamic paths pass through the collusive price point only if both initial prices are above the collusive level.* Otherwise, the collusive point can never be found by accident. Some different conjectural variation is required.

These results are extended and illustrated in a paper by Hobbs and Schuler [6] which estimates the range of prices that would result if the distribution of electricity were de-regulated but neighboring firms were required to charge a uniform delivered price. In that case, a two-dimensional model was developed and calibrated, but the results are similar and price bounds are established which are above marginal cost in the undercut case but below the collusive price for the concession strategy.

Finally, note that the alternative conjectural variation of assuming the neighbor will always maintain the same service boundary is analogous to the concede strategy. The competitor merely accepts those boundaries and sets a monopolistic price. In response, the neighbor maintains his boundaries and sets a monopolistic price. Here the final consequences are predetermined by the initial boundary claims. This could be a realistic short-run result if substantial fixed costs are associated with a firm's establishing a product distribution network, but in the long run, under uniform delivered price, competition for customers means invasion of territory and changing price. Thus only conjectural variations regarding price make sense for long run analyses. This analysis indentifies the likely long run bounds to those oligopolistic prices.

RICHARD E. SCHULER,
State of New York Public Service Commission,
3, *Rockefeller Plaza,*
Albany, N.Y.,
U.S.A.
(On leave from Cornell University)
and
BENJAMIN F. HOBBS,
Oak Ridge National Laboratory,
Oak Ridge,
Tennessee,
U.S.A.

REFERENCES

[1] BECKMANN, M. J. "Spatial Oligopoly Revisited: An Examination of Some Strategies in Mill Pricing in One and Two-Dimensional Markets", *Papers and Proceedings of the Regional Science Association, 17,* (1972).
[2] BECKMANN, M. J., "Spatial Oligopoly as a Noncooperative Game", *International Journal of Game Theory, 2,* (1973), pp. 263–68.
[3] EATON, B. C. and LIPSEY, R. G., "Freedom of Entry and the Existence of Pure Profit", *The Economic Journal, 88,* (September 1978), pp. 455–69.
[4] GREENHUT, J. and GREENHUT, M. L., "Spatial Price Discrimination, Competition, and Locational Effects", *Economica, 42,* (1975), pp. 401–19.
[5] GRONBERG, T. J. and MEYER, J., "Competitive Equilibria in Uniform Delivered Pricing Models", *American Economic Review, 71,* (1981), pp. 758–63.
[6] HOBBS, B. F. and SCHULER, R. E., "Estimating the Economic Consequences of Competition in the Distribution of Electricity—An Application of Location Theory", paper presented at the 28th Annual North American Regional Science Association Meetings, Montreal, (November 14, 1981).
[7] HOTELLING, H., "Stability in Competition", *Economic Journal, 39,* (1929), pp. 41–57.

THE JOURNAL OF INDUSTRIAL ECONOMICS
Volume XXXI September/December 1982 Nos. 1/2

PRICING POLICIES UNDER CONDITIONS OF SPATIAL COMPETITION*

MENAHEM SPIEGEL

INTRODUCTION

WHEN monopolistic competition exists, and especially in the case of spatial competition, a seller can choose from several alternative pricing policies. In this case, the pricing policy becomes "a variable" over which a seller has to "optimize", i.e., to choose the pricing policy which yields the highest profit. Aspects of this problem of optimization, and some of its implications for spatial competition are considered in the literature. On the one hand, Beckman [1] discusses and compares different pricing policies under conditions of a monopoly operating in an isolated market where the market size is predetermined. On the other hand, market equilibrium under conditions of monopolistic competition is considered by Cappoza and Order [2]. Their discussion, although covering several possible types of individual sellers' reaction functions, is limited to one type of pricing policy, as they concentrate on the f.o.b. mill pricing policy. The purpose of this note is to compare the profit performance of different pricing policies under conditions of monopolistic competition.

Three alternative pricing policies are considered:

1. Uniform f.o.b. price.
2. Uniform delivered price.
3. "Meet the competition" pricing policy (a generalized basing point system).

A comparison among the three is done from two points of view.

a: From the single sellers' point of view: what is the preferred pricing policy?
b: From a market equilibrium point of view: are all the three pricing policies compatible with a Nash type market equilibrium?

It will be shown here that the individual seller is not indifferent between the alternative pricing policies. Therefore, it follows that some price policies are inconsistent with a Nash type market equilibrium with free entry.

* This paper draws upon the work on Spatial Economics done while I was a Visiting Research Fellow at the Universite Catholique De Louvain, Belgium. Helpful comments and suggestions received from L. Phlips, D. Eldor, D. D. Haddock and J.-F. Thisse are gratefully acknowledged.

THE MODEL

The discussion here is based on the following standard assumptions:

A.1.: All consumers are identical (except for location), each consumer consumes (at his location) exactly one unit of the product, irrespective of its price.[1]

A.2.: The consumers are evenly distributed along the circular road of a given size, (i.e., market). The density of consumers is one, per unit of distance. (Thus each location, consumer, could be considered as a separate single unit trade sub-market with one buyer and few potential sellers).

A.3.: All producers are identical (except for location, each operates a single plant and produces the homogeneous product.

A.4.: Producer's total cost of production is characterized by a constant marginal cost (m) and a fixed cost (F).

A.5.: Transportation costs are constant (c) per unit of output and per unit of distance.

At first we will compare the f.o.b. pricing policy with uniform delivered price policy. By the f.o.b. pricing policy, the product is sold only at the production point to all consumers for the same mill price. The cost of the delivered product to a specific consumer (location) is the sum of the f.o.b. price plus the transportation cost which is a linear function of distance. This is, also, the cost to the consumer.

A uniform delivered price is a pricing policy under which the same single price is charged by a seller to all his customers, for each unit of product sold and delivered to the consumers' location. This single price includes all transportation costs. Thus the cost to the consumer of the delivered product is independent of the consumers' location.

Using Figure 1, we will compare the profit performance of a representative seller[2] under the alternative pricing policies. The representative producer is located, on the circular road, at point A. This location is halfway between its neighboring competitors located at points B and C on the road.[3] Let $P_f = \overline{AH}$ denote the f.o.b. mill price charged by all producers. The cost of the delivered product to consumers from the representative firm, is described by the ray HED and HGI. The cost of the delivered product of the neighboring competitors located at C and B are described by the corresponding ray passed through UET and through VGT.

[1] Introducing reservation prices and/or outside goods would burden the exposition without adding insight into the problem considered.

[2] Given the similarity of all sellers and the assumption of the circular road, it is sufficient to consider a representative firm and its two nearest competitors. All decisions taken by the representative firm will be repeated n times where n is the total numbers of firms operating in the market.

[3] Competitors which are beyond points B and C will not affect the representative firm's choice of the optimal price policy and therefore will not be discussed here. The total number of firms n, given the market size, does affect the profitability of the representative firm and thus the market equilibrium.

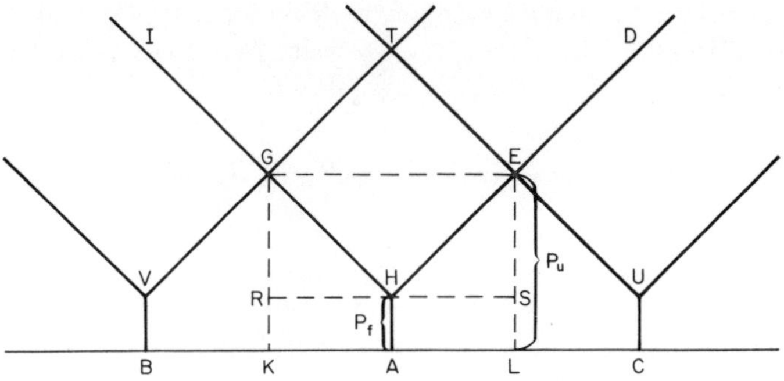

FIGURE 1
Prices, market area, and revenue of the representative firm located at point A (and its competitors located at B and C).

Consumers will buy their product from the producer with the least delivered cost, therefore the market area of the representative firm, given the f.o.b. price P_f, is described by the line segment $\overline{KL}$.

Proposition 1: Given the market area corresponding to the f.o.b. price P_f (charged by all producers), the representative firm can charge a uniform delivered price P_u which will increase its profit while not affecting other firms' market area and profit.

Explanation: Given the f.o.b. price $P_f = \overline{AH}$, the firm's total revenue net of transportation costs could be measured by the area of the rectangle $KRSL$. If the representative firm will charge a uniform delivered price $P_u = \overline{KG} = \overline{LE}$, its market area and its output will remain unchanged. The firm's gross revenue will increase by the amount represented by the area $GRSE$ which includes the transportation costs. Transportation costs are represented by the area $GRH + ESH$. The increase in revenues net of transportation cost is GHE. Since output and costs of production remain unchanged, this increase in revenues is equal to the increase in profits resulting from a change in the pricing policy from a uniform f.o.b. price, P_f, to a uniform delivered price, P_u.

Proposition 1 holds for any price P_f which yields non-negative profits to the representative firm. In particular it holds in the case where profits of all firms operating in the market are zero. Therefore:

Proposition 2: When given the option of uniform delivered price policy a free entry, zero profit f.o.b. price, is incompatible with a Nash type market equilibrium.

Explanation: Assume that P_f (of proposition 1) is also the long run free entry market price when all producers are using the f.o.b. pricing policy. As a long run equilibrium price, it implies zero profits for all producers. By reasoning analogous to that in proposition 1 we know that the representative firm can increase its profits by charging a uniform delivered price P_u (and thus it will earn *positive* profits). Therefore, the f.o.b. price P_f cannot be an equilibrium price under a Nash free entry market equilibrium.

"MEET THE COMPETITION" PRICING POLICY

In the framework of spatial economics the assumption of perfect information implies that each consumer (representing a sub-market) with a known location and each producer, with a known location, knows the cost function and the delivered marginal cost of all other producers to each of the sub-markets. If all sellers use the information, "meeting the competition" pricing policy will require that

(R.I): A seller will not make a transaction in a given sub-market unless his delivered marginal cost is the lowest (i.e.: the cheapest producer).

(R.II): A seller who makes the transaction will charge a price which is equal to the marginal cost of supplying that sub-market from an alternative source.

Therefore, requirement (R.I.) implies that the seller with the lowest delivered marginal cost of supplying a sub-market will be that producer whose location is the closest to that specified sub-market. The marginal cost of the delivered product is the sum of the marginal production cost plus the cost of delivery. Due to the similarity of all producers, the marginal cost of production is the same constant (m) for all producers for all units produced. The delivery cost is c times the distance, and is lowest for the producer closest to the consumer.

Requirement II will imply that each unit sold in a sub-market (i.e. to a consumer) receives a price which is equal to the consumer's alternative cost. This price is the maximum price the "cheapest" seller can charge and still maintain his market area.

Referring to Figure 1 assume that $BV = AH = CU$ is equal to m, the constant marginal cost of production. The marginal delivered cost of a representative producer is described by the rays HGI and HED. The marginal delivered costs of producer C and B are described by the rays UET and VGT. The representative producer, located at A, will be the "cheapest seller" for the market area $\overline{KL}$. By practicing "meet the competition" pricing policy the representative firm could charge its customers a price which is equal to the marginal cost of the alternative cheapest source. Therefore, the price of the delivered product which will be charged by the representative firm is given along segments GT and ET.[4]

[4] It is important to note that the customers have no interest to engage themselves in a resale policy as the difference in prices under "meet the competition" pricing policy is just equal to the transportation cost. Thus one can view this pricing policy as a generalized basing point system.

Proposition 3: Given the market area corresponding to the uniform delivered price P_u (charged by all producers) total revenue and profits of the representative firm will be higher under "meet the competition" pricing policy without changing other firms' market area and profit.

Explanation: The uniform delivered price $P_u = KG = LE$ (Figure 1) will determine that the representative firm's market area is the segment $\overline{KL}$ and total revenue can be described by the area $KGEL$ and net profit by the triangle GEH. Under a "meet the competition" pricing policy, by (R.I.), the output of the area served by the representative firm is the same ($\overline{KL}$). The gross revenue under this pricing policy is represented by the area $KGTEL$. Since the change in the pricing policy does not involve a change in the cost, the change in gross revenues is equal to the change in profits which can be measured by the triangle GTE.

Proposition 4: Given the option of "meet the competition" pricing policy, a free entry, zero profit uniform delivered price is inconsistent with a Nash type market equilibrium.

Explanation: The reasoning here is analogous to that of proposition 2. Assume that the uniform delivered price P_u is also the long run free entry market equilibrium (with zero profit). Using proposition 3 implies that: for the given uniform delivered price P_u, "meet the competition" pricing policy will increase the firm's profits. Thus, the existence of a "meet the competition" pricing policy will create an incentive for the representative firm to charge the prices dictated by this pricing policy which will guarantee positive profits. Therefore a zero profit uniform delivered price cannot survive.

CONCLUDING REMARKS

In this note it was demonstrated that the frequent use of f.o.b. pricing in standard spatial monopolistic competition models is unwarranted and cannot be justified unless some accompanying restricting assumptions concerning the completeness of information, and/or profit maximization, and/or regulation, are assumed.

In a perfect information framework "Nash-behavior" is characterized by a representative producer optimizing over pricing policies, given that other producers' output will not be changed. Therefore spatial competition, under the standard assumptions specified above, must be characterized by a "meet the competition" pricing policy.

Using the propositions (1) to (4) discussed above, we conclude that given the assumptions (A.1) to (A.5) the individual seller would rank the different pricing policies in the following order of preferences.

I. "Meet the competition" pricing policy.
II. Uniform delivered price.
III. Uniform mill price.

MENAHEM SPIEGEL,
Department of Economics,
University of Haifa,
Mount Carmel,
Haifa 31999, Israel

REFERENCES

[1] BECKMAN, M. J., "Spatial Price Policies Revisited," *Bell Journal of Economics*, Vol. 7, 2 (Autumn, 1976), pp. 619–30.

[2] CAPPOZA, D. R. and VAN ORDER, R., "A Generalized Model of Spatial Competition," *American Economic Review*, Vol. 68, 4, (December 1978), pp. 896–908.

[3] PHLIPS, L., "*Spatial Pricing and Competition*," Studies of the Commission of the European Communities, Competition-Approximation of Legislation Series, No. 29, (Brussels 1976).

[4] SCHERER, F. M., *Industrial Market Structure and Economic Performance*. (Rand McNally College Publishing Company, Chicago, 1980).

THE JOURNAL OF INDUSTRIAL ECONOMICS
Volume XXXI September/December 1982 Nos. 1/2

PUBLICATIONS RECEIVED

Achieving Financial Solvency in Social Security, by Mickey D. Levy. Published by American Enterprise Institute Special Analyses, 1981.

The American Steel Industry: Problems, Challenges, Perspectives, by Luc Kiers. Published by Westview Press, 1980, $27.50.

Analytical Input-Output Tables of the Greek Economy, Year 1970, by N. A. Mylonas. Published by the Centre of Planning and Economic Research, Athens, 1981. This gives an analysis of 128 production sectors, and includes an analysis of imports and investments according to sectors of origin and destination.

Business Cycle Analysis, Papers presented at the 14th GRET Conference Proceedings, Lisbon 1979, edited by Werner H. Strigel. Published by Gower, 1980, £17.50.

Business Fluctuations—Forecasting Techniques and Applications, by Dale G. Bails and Larry C. Peppers. Published by Prentice-Hall, 1982, £18.70.

Business Research Centre (Research Reports 2, 3, 5, 6), by J. R. G. Butler. Published by North Brisbane College of Advanced Education, 1979.

Business Taxation, Finance and Firm Behaviour, The Industrial Institute for Economic and Social Research, Stockholm.

Capital Investment Decision Analysis for Management and Engineering, by John R. Canada and John A. White Jr. Published by Prentice-Hall International, 1980, £17.50.

Conference in Applied Economic Research, by Reserve Bank of Australia, 1979, $A4.00.

The Congressional Budget Process after Five Years, edited by Rudolph G. Penner. Published by American Enterprise Institute for Public Policy Research, 1981.

The Consumer Price Index, Issues and Alternatives, by Phillip Cagan and Geoffrey H. Moore. Published by A.E.I.S.I.E.P., 1981, $4.25.

Contemporary Economic Problems, by William Fellner. Published by American Enterprise Institute for Public Policy Research, 1980, $9.25.

A Conversation with Alfred E. Kahn, by American Enterprise Institute Studies in Government Regulations. Published by A.E.I.S.G.R., 1981.

Corporate Management and Financial Planning, by D. J. Harris and D. G. Williams. Published by Granada Publishing, 1980, £12.00.

Demand for Electricity, by Nirmala Banerjee. Published by K. P. Bagchi and Company, Calcutta, 1979, Rs35.00.

The Development of Japanese Business, by J. Hirschmeier and Y. Yui. Published by George Allen and Unwin, 1981, £7.95.

Discrimination in Mortgage Lending: A Study of Three Cities, by New York University, 1981, $12.00

Dynamic Stock Option Trading, by Joseph T. Stewart Jr. Published by John Wiley & Sons Ltd., 1981, £20.40.

Economic Behaviour: An Introduction, by Colin Harbury. Published by George Allen and Unwin, 1980, £12.00 (hardback), £4.95 (paperback).

The Economics of Energy, by Michael G. Webb and Martin J. Ricketts. Published by Macmillan, 1980, £12.00 (hardback), £5.95 (paperback).

The Economics of Environmental Management, by J. Lowe and D. Lewis. Published by Philip Allan Publishers Ltd., 1980, £13.00 (hardback), £6.50 (paperback).

The Economics of Legal Minimum Wages, edited by Simon Rottenberg. Published by American Enterprise Institute for Public Policy Research, 1981.

The Economics of Women and Work, edited by Alice H. Amsden. Published by Penguin Books Ltd., 1980, £2.95.

Employment Hazards: An Investigation of Market Performance, by W. Kip Viscusi. Published by Harvard University Press, 1980, £13.50.

Employment Hazards, by W. Kip Viscusi. Published by Princeton University Press, 1980, £10.90.

Essays in Contemporary Economic Problems: Demand, Productivity and Population, by William Fellner, Project Director. Published by American Enterprise Institute, 1981.

Evaluating Technological Innovations, by Bela Gold, Gerhard Rosegger, and Myles G. Boylan Jr. Published by Lexington Books, 1981, £17.50. The central part of this valuable book consists of case studies of major technological innovations in steel making and blast furnaces. It is preceded by a critique of past research, pointing out short-comings of earlier analysis, and followed by a constructive discussion in the light of the studies for revising our evaluations of technological innovations.

Experiences with Stopping Inflation, by Leland B. Yeager and Associates. Published by American Enterprise Institute Studies in Economic Policy, 1982, $6.25.

The Federal Income Tax Burden on Households, the Effect of Tax Law Changes, by Attiat F. Ott and Ludwig O. Dittrich. Published by American Enterprises Institute Studies in Tax Policy, 1981.

The Financing of Foreign Direct Investment, by Martin Gilman. Published by Frances Pinter (Publishers) Ltd., London, 1981, £13.50.

The Firms in the Market Economy, IUI 40 years 1939–1979. Published by Industrial Institute for Economic and Social Research, Stockholm, 1981.

Flexible Exchange Rates and International Business, by John M. Blis, Stuart I. Greenbaum and Donald P. Jacobs. Published by British-North American Research Association, 1982, £3.00.

Forecasting Sectoral Final Demand by a Dynamic Generalized Linear Expenditure System, by Th. Gamaletsos. Published by Centre of Planning and Economic Research, Athens, 1981.

The Future of Oil, A Simulation Study of the Inter-relationships of Resources, Reserves and Use, 1980–2080; by Peter R. Odel and Kenneth E. Rosery. Published by Kogan Page, 1981, £20.00.

Getting Organized, by Alan Campbell and John McIlroy. Published by Pan Books Ltd., £1.75.

Government, Regulation, and the Economy, by Bernard H. Siegan. Published by Lexington Books, 1981, £11.00.

Health and Air Quality: Evaluating the Effects of Policy, by Philip E. Graves and Ronald J. Krumm. Published by American Enterprise Institute, 1981.

High Technology Industry and Industrial Location, by R. P. Oakey. Published by Gower, 1981, £12.50.

How to Measure Managerial Performance, by Richard S. Sloma. Published by MacMillan, 1980, £6.95.

Human Resources in Japanese Industrial Development, by Solomon B. Levine and Hisashi Kawada. Published by Princeton University Press, 1980, £11.00.

The Impact of the Minimum Wage on Regional Labor Markets, by Ronald J. Krumm. Published by American Enterprise Institute Studies in Economic Policy, 1981, $4.25.

Industrial Activity and Economic Geography, by R. C. Estall and R. O. Buchanan. Published by Hutchinson University Library, 1980, £8.95 (hardback), £4.25 (paperback).

The Industrial Geography of Japan, Edited by Kiyoki Murata. Published by Bell and Hyman, 1980, £10.50.

Industrial Innovation in the United Kingdom, Canada and the USA, by Kerry Schott. Published by British-North American Committee, 1981, £2.25.

Industrial Organization, Competition, Growth and Structural Change, Third Edition, by Kenneth D. George and Caroline Joll. Published by George Allen and Unwin, 1981, £15.00 (hardback), £6.95 (paperback).

Industrial Organization and Prices, by James V. Koch. Published by Prentice-Hall Incorporated, 1980.

Industrial Policies in Europe (A study of policies pursued in European countries and the EEC and their implications for the UK). Published by National Economic Development Office, London, 1981.

Industrial Trends and Prospects, by National Economic Development Council. Published by National Economic Development Office, London.

Input-Output Tables of the Greek Economy 1958–1977, by Th. A. Skountzos and G. S. Mattheos in collaboration with F. V. Panaretou, 1980.

International Production and the Multinational Enterprise, by John H. Dunning. Published by George Allen and Unwin, 1981, £20.00 (hardback), £8.95 (paperback).

International Technology Licensing, by Farok J. Contractor. Published by Lexington Books, 1982, £22.50.

The Investor's Quotient, by Jacob Bernstein. Published by John Wiley and Sons Limited, 1980, £9.00.

Issues in Public-Utility Pricing and Regulation, by Michael A. Crew. Published by Lexington Books, 1981, £14.00.

The Law of the Economy in the European Communities, by D. Lasok. Published by Butterworths, 1980.

Living with Technology, by Lotte Bailyn. Published by The MIT Press, 1981, £9.30.

Macroeconomics for Management, by Mary Louise Hatten. Published by Prentice-Hall International, 1981, £12.95.

Marketing Today, by Gordon Oliver. Published by Prentice-Hall International, 1980, £7.95.

Mergers and Economic Performance, by Keith Cowling, Paul Stoneman, John Cubbin, John Cable, Graham Hall, Simon Domberger, and Patricia Dutton. Published by Cambridge University Press, 1980, £19.50. The main theme of this book is the disentangling of the impact of merger activity of various types (horizontal, vertical and conglomerate) upon economic efficiency and monopoly power. After setting up a framework within which possible efficiency and market power effects can be analysed, the book proceeds with a series of case studies of significant mergers and investigations of specific industries which have been fundamentally restructured by mergers. The book also examines the effect of mergers on technological progress, product quality and variety, employment and the rate of price adjustment.

The Microeconomics of the Timber Industry, by David H. Jackson. Published by Westview Press, 1980, $18.50.

Micro Simulation-Models, Methods and Applications, Proceedings of A Symposium in Stockholm, September 19–22, 1977, Edited by B. Bergmann, G. Eliasson and G. Orcutt. Published by The Industrial Institute for Economic and Social Research, Stockholm.

Minimum Wages and On-the-Job Training, by Masanori Hashimoto. Published by American Enterprise Institute Studies in Economic Policy, 1981, $4.25.

Minimum Wages, Fringe Benefits and Working Conditions, by Walter J. Wessels. Publisheu by American Enterprise Institute Studies in Economic Policy, 1981. $4.25.

Minimum Wages: Measures and Industry Effects, by John M. Peterson. Published by American Enterprise Institute Studies in Economic Policy, 1981, $5.25 (paperback), $12.25 (hardback).

Minimum Wage Regulation in Retail Trade, by Belton M. Fleisher. Published by American Enterprise Institute Studies in Economic Policy, 1982, $5.25.

Modern Economics, by J. Pen. Published by Penguin Books Ltd., 1980, £1.95.

Mondragon: An Economic Analysis, by Henk Thomas and Chris Logan. Published by George Allen and Unwin, 1982, £12.00.

Monetary Policy in the Open Economy of Greece, by George D. Demopoulos. Published by Centre of Planning and Economic Research, 1981.

Multinationals Beyond the Market, Edited by Robin Murray. Published by Harvester Press, 1981, £22.50.

National Consumer Council, Consumers and Credit, by NCC. Published by NCC, 1980.

National Health Insurance. What Now, What Later, What Never? Edited by Mark V. Pauly. Published by the American Enterprise Institute for Public Policy Research, 1980, $8.25.

National Oil Companies, by L. E. Grayson. Published by John Wiley & Sons Ltd., 1981, £15.90.

Performance Measurement of the Petroleum Industry, by Alan R. Beckenstein, Leslie E. Grayson, Susan H. Overholt, and Timothy F. Sutherland. Published by Lexington Books, 1979, £12.75.

Performing Regulation, by Timothy B. Clark, Marian H. Kosters, and James C. Miller III. Published by American Enterprise for Public Policy Research Washington and London, 1981, $7.25.

The Political Economy of British Capitalism, A Marxist Analysis, by Sam Aaronvitch and Ron Smith with Jean Gardner and Roger Moore. Published by McGraw-Hill, 1981, £7.95.

Poverty and the Minimum Wage, by Donald O. Parsons. Published by American Enterprise Institute Studies in Economic Policy, 1980, $4.25.

Problems of Ship Finance for Developing Countries, by EL. A. Georgandopoulos. Published by Pireaus, 1980.

Productivity Measurement, Edited by David Bailey and Tony Hubert. Published by Gower, 1981, £15.00.

The Progress of Government Economic Policy Memorandum, by the Director General. Published by National Economic Development Office, London.

Project Cost Control Using Networks, by C. Staffurth. Published by William Heinemann Ltd., 1980, £5.50.

Proposals for a Subminimum Wage for Youth, by American Enterprise Institute for Public Policy Research. Published by A.E.I.F.P.P., 1981.

Proposals to Modify the Taxation of U.S. Citizens Working Abroad, by American Enterprise Institute Legislative Analyses, 1981.

Proposals to Regulate State and Local Taxation of Multijurisdictional Corporations, by American Enterprise Institute, 1981.

Proposed Revisions of the Foreign Corrupt Practices Act, by American Enterprise Institute for Public Policy Research, 1981.

Prospects for the Dry Bulk Shipping in the Eighties, by EL. A. Georgandopoulos. Published by Piraeus, 1980.

Psychological Attributes of Mergers, by Nicholas A. H. Stacey. Published by Scottish Academic Press, 1980, £1.25.

Public and Private Investments: Socioeconomic Analysis, by Henry Malcolm Steiner. Published by John Wiley & Sons Ltd., 1980, £16.30.

Reasoning about Discrimination, by Richard A. Lester. Published by Princeton University Press, 1980, £9.70.

Recent Proposals to Restrict Conglomerate Mergers, by American Enterprise Institute Legislative Analyses. Published by American Enterprise Institute for Public Policy Research, 1981.

Reforming the Income Tax System, by William E. Simon. Published by American Enterprise Institute Studies in Tax Policy, 1981, \$4.25.

Regularities of Sectoral Changes in Economic Activity, by Matti Leppo. Published by Akateeminen Kirjakauppa, 1980.

The Regulation of Foreign Banks: Policy Formation In Countries Outside the United States, by Adrian E. Tschoegl. Published by Solomon Brothers Center for the Study of Financial Institutions, New York University, 1981.

The Social Costs of Air Pollution in the Greater Athens Region, by D. Plessas, The Center of Planning and Economic Research, 1980.

Strategies for Declining Businesses, by Kathryn Rudie Harrigan. Published by Lexington Books, 1981, £18.50.

Structural Changes in the Greek Economy: Intertemporal Analysis in an Input-Output Framework, by Th. Skountzos. Published by Centre of Planning and Economic Research, 1980.

The Structure of British Industry, by P. S. Johnson. Published by Granada, 1975, £20.00

Studies in Shipping Economics, by Einar Hope. Published by Bedrifsøkonomens Forlag A/S, Oslo, 1982.

Taxation of Mineral Resources, by Robert F. Conrad and R. Bryce Hool. Published by Lexington Books, 1981, £10.00.

Techniques of Scenario Planning, by John Chandler and Paul Cockle. Published by McGraw-Hill, 1982, £13.95.

10 × Economics—A Simple Guide to the Economics of the Early Eighties, by Peter Donaldson. Published by Penguin Books Ltd., 1982, £1.50.

Testing Monetarism, by Meghnad Desai. Published by Frances Pinter (Publishers) Ltd., 1981, £15.00.

Theory and Practice of Money, by Jennie Hawthorne. Published by William Heinemann Ltd., 1981, £6.95.

The U.K. Life Assurance Industry, by P. J. Franklin and C. Woodhead. Published by Croom Helm Ltd., 1980, £30.00.

Value Added Taxation, The Experience of the UK, by A. R. Prest. Published by American Enterprise Institute Studies in Tax Policy, 1981.

Wealth of Nations in Crisis, by Ronald C. Nairn. Published by Bayland Publishing, Houston, Texas, 1979, \$12.95.

The World of Goods, Towards an Anthropology of Consumption, by Mary Douglas and Baron Isherwood. Published by Penguin, 1980, £2.50.

The Zero-Sum Society: Distribution and the Possibilities for Economic Change, by Lester C. Thurrow. Published by Penguin Books, 1981, £2.50.

We are grateful to the following, in addition to our Associate Editors, for acting as referees over the past year:

Ataman Aksoy,
Boston College, Chestnut Hill
Dan Algar,
Federal Trade Commission
James Anderson,
Boston College, Chestnut Hill
A. Bailetti,
Carleton University, Ottawa
Randall Bartlett,
Smith College, Northampton
Kenneth Baseman,
Owen, Cornell, Greenhalgh and Myslinski
J. J. Bernstein,
Carleton University, Ottawa
M. A. Bowe,
Carleton University, Ottawa
Marcel Boyer,
Université de Montréal
Ralph M. Bradburd,
Williams College, Williamstown
Timothy F. Bresnahan,
Stanford University
Laurits R. Christensen,
University of Wisconsin
John H. Ciccolo,
Boston College, Chestnut Hill
R. Clarke,
University of Sheffield
M. S. Common,
University of Stirling
Michael Conte,
University of New Hampshire
Bruce Curry,
University College, Cardiff
E. G. Davis,
Carleton University, Ottawa
Stacy S. Dick,
Harvard Business School
V. A. Dickson,
University of New Brunswick
J. S. Ferris,
Carleton University, Ottawa
Felix Fitzroy,
International Institute of Management, Berlin
Anne Friedlaender,
Massachusetts Institute of Technology
Judy Gelman,
Federal Trade Commission
Frank M. Gollop,
Boston College, Chestnut Hill
Richard O. Goss,
U.W.I.S.T., Cardiff
Douglas Greer,
San Jose State University
Keith Hartley,
University of York
John Hilke,
Federal Trade Commission
Ignatius Horstmann,
University of Western Ontario
Sharan Jagpal,
Rutgers University
E. Kantzenbach,
University of Hamburg
Mark Klock,
Boston College, Chestnut Hill
John Kwoka,
The George Washington University
S. J. Liebowitz,
University of Western Ontario
C. J. Maule,
Carleton University, Ottawa
J. Huston McCulloch,
Ohio State University
John McGowan (deceased),
Charles River Associates
James Meehan,
Colby College, Waterville
Philippe Michel,
Université de Paris I
Herbert Hohring,
University of Minnesota
Philip Nelson,
Federal Trade Commission
Roger Noll,
California Institute of Technology
David W. Pearce,
University of Aberdeen
Martin Perry,
Bell Laboratories
Harold Peterson,
Boston College, Chestnut Hill
Michael Porter,
Harvard Business School
Thomas Pugel,
New York University
David Qualls,
University of Tennessee

David Ravenscraft,
Federal Trade Commission
Mark Roberts,
Pennsylvania State University
Colin Robinson,
University of Surrey
Arthur J. Rolnick,
Federal Reserve Bank of Minneapolis
Robert Rothschild,
University of Lancaster
T. K. Rymes,
Carleton University, Ottawa
Stephen Sacks,
University of Connecticut
John Scott,
Dartmouth College, Hanover
I. Prakash Sharma,
Carleton University, Ottawa
R. W. Shaw,
University of Stirling
P. J. Sloane,
Paisley College of Technology
James L. Smith,
University of Illinois at Urbana-Champaign
Richard L. Smith,
Arizona State University
Barbara Spencer,
Boston College, Chestnut Hill
Jerome Stein,
Brown University, Providence
Robert Stillman,
Lexecon Inc.
Thomas J. Teisberg,
Natomas Company
Jacques Thisse,
S.P.U.R., Louvain-la-Neuve
William Tye,
Putnam, Hayes & Bartlett
R. Van Order,
Department of Housing and Urban Development, Washington
Lawrence White,
Department of Justice, Washington
Ronald P. Wilder,
University of South Carolina

THE JOURNAL OF INDUSTRIAL ECONOMICS

Published first in October 1952, this Journal was founded to develop the analysis of the problems facing modern industry. It is concerned with the individual business and its relation to the economy—e.g. with outputs and prices and their behaviour in the market, and with the business decisions which affect these. It therefore aims to contribute both to economic theory and to practical public and private policies in the industrial field. The journal is naturally meant to interest business men as well as economists.

The Editors welcome contributions covering the fundamental categories in economics (such as prices, costs, investment, finance, location, wages and productivity) as well as the broader 'background' circumstances (such as the changing structure of industry, management policy and public monopoly policy). Preference is given to MSS bearing on these subjects from the standpoint of individual firms or industries. Theoretical discussion is welcome. Abstract theory is not barred, but authors in this case should provide an introduction and conclusion, so that non-specialist readers may see what the article is about. Alongside articles of more normal length, the Editors are willing to publish shorter notes, especially when these give interim results of important research studies. Books are not reviewed, although books received will be listed, sometimes with a short note; but substantial review articles will be considered. No payment is made to authors, but 25 free offprints are provided. Contributors are asked to send an Abstract, not exceeding 100 words, with their article.

Editorial Offices:

Manuscripts from North America should be sent to Professor H. Michael Mann, Department of Economics, Boston College, Chestnut Hill, Massachusetts, 02167, U.S.A.; manuscripts from all other countries to the General Editor, c/o Department of Economics, University of Lancaster, Gillow House, Lancaster, LA1 4YX England, from whom detailed Information for Contributors is available.

Subscriptions, advertising, reprint enquiries, etc.

The journal is published by Basil Blackwell Publisher Ltd., 108 Cowley Road, Oxford OX4 1JF, England. US Mailing Agent, Expediters of the Printed Word Ltd., 527 Madison Avenue, Suite 1217, New York, NY 10022, U.S.A. Second Class postage paid at New York.

The journal is published four times a year in September, December, March and June. The subscription prices are as shown below.

All correspondence other than that dealing with contributions should be addressed to the publisher.

Price for this special issue: £7.50 (UK), £9.00 (overseas), $15.00 (USA), $20.00 (Canada)
Annual Subscription for Institutions: £21.50 (UK), £26.50 (overseas), $54.60 (USA), $67.00 (Canada)
Annual Subscription for Individuals: £13.75 (UK), £16.75 (overseas), $35.00 (USA), $43.25 (Canada)

Set by Santype International Ltd.,
Salisbury, Wilts. Printed and bound by
Whitstable Litho Ltd., Whitstable, Kent

CONTRIBUTORS TO THIS NUMBER

LOUIS PHLIPS: Professor, C.O.R.E., Universite Catholique de Louvain, and Editor of this *Journal*.

JACQUES-FRANÇOIS THISSE: Associate Professor, S.P.U.R., Université Catholique de Louvain.

DOMINIQUE GRAITSON: F.N.R.S. Assistant, Université de Liège.

DENNIS R. CAPOZZA: Professor, Faculty of Commerce and Business Administration, University of British Columbia.

ROBERT VAN ORDER: Department of Housing and Urban Development, Washington, D.C.

KELVIN LANCASTER: John Bates Clark Professor, Department of Economics, Columbia University in the City of New York.

R. ROTHSCHILD: Lecturer, Department of Economics, University of Lancaster.

R. W. SHAW: Lecturer, Department of Economics, University of Stirling.

AVNER SHAKED: Lecturer, London School of Economics.

KONRAD STAHL: Professor, University of Dortmund.

J. JASKOLD GABSZEWICZ: Professor, C.O.R.E., Université Catholique de Louvain.

NEIL DORWARD: Lecturer, Department of Accounting and Administrative Studies, The Polytechnic of North London.

GEORGE NORMAN: Lecturer, Department of Economics, University of Reading.

NANCY K. NICHOLS: Lecturer, Department of Mathematics, University of Reading.

RICHARD E. SCHULER: Commissioner and Deputy Chairman, New York State Public Service Commission. (on leave from Cornell University)

BENJAMIN F. HOBBS: Oak Ridge National Laboratory.

MENAHEM SPIEGEL: Assistant Professor, Department of Economics, University of Haifa.

The Contents of Volume XXX, No. 4, June 1982, were:

The Development of First-Class Cricket in England: An Economic Analysis, by J. A. Schofield, Associate Professor, Department of Economics, University of Victoria.

Excessive Advertising: An Empirical Analysis, by Jeffry M. Netter, Visiting Assistant Professor, The University of North Carolina at Chapel Hill.

Intangible Capital Aspects of Advertising and R&D Expenditure, by Mark Hirschey, Assistant Professor, University of Wisconsin–Madison.

Capacity-Neutral Investments and Capacity Measurement in Manufacturing, by Ronald F. Rost, Economist for the Board of Governors of the Federal Reserve System.

Monopoly Power and the Recycling of Raw Materials, by Robert E. Martin, Assistant Professor of Economics, Louisiana State University.

Diffusion of the Basic Oxygen Furnace in the U.S. Steel Industry, by James B. Sumrall, Jr., Lecturer, University of Massachusetts, Harbor Campus, Boston; Principal, JBS Economics, Boston; Manager of Economic Planning, Ratheon Company, Lexington.

The Demand for Alcohol in the UK: A Comment, by Brendan M. Walsh, Professor of National Economics, University College, Dublin.

The Demand for Alcohol in the UK: Reply, by Tony McGuinness, Lecturer in Economics, The University of Sheffield.

THE JOURNAL OF INDUSTRIAL ECONOMICS

Volume XXXI MARCH 1983 No. 3

B. CURRY and K. D. GEORGE
Industrial Concentration: A Survey 203

KATSUHIKO IKEDA and NORIYUKI DOI
The Performance of Merging Firms in Japanese Manufacturing Industry: 1964–75 257

J. F. PICKERING
The Causes and Consequences of Abandoned Mergers 267

NORMAN J. IRELAND
A Note on Conglomerate Merger and Behavioural Response to Risk 283

WILLIAM J. MERRILEES
Anatomy of a Price Leadership Challenge: An Evaluation of Pricing Strategies in the Australian Newspaper Industry 291

JOHN P. BONIN
Innovation in a Labor-Managed Firm: A Membership Perspective 313

ISSN 0022-1821
BASIL BLACKWELL OXFORD ENGLAND

THE JOURNAL OF INDUSTRIAL ECONOMICS
Volume XXXI March 1983 No. 3

INDUSTRIAL CONCENTRATION: A SURVEY*

B. CURRY AND K. D. GEORGE

I. INTRODUCTION

SELLER concentration refers to the size distribution of firms that sell a particular product or collection of products. It is usually regarded as a significant dimension of market structure because it is thought to play an important part in determining market power and thence business behaviour and performance. Some economists who have been interested in market power have sought to measure this power by using indices based upon familiar theoretical ideas. For example, Lerner (1934) suggested that the difference between price and marginal cost divided by price could serve as a direct measure of departures from the competitive ideal. Despite its intuitive appeal, however, this is essentially an *ex-post* measure of allocative inefficiency. It may be influenced by factors other than monopoly power, and to seek to measure market power in terms of its *effects* makes it impossible to test exactly what those effects are, since, as pointed out by Feinberg (1980), the relationship between observed effects and the existence of monopoly power has become a tautology. In addition, the required cost information will not be readily available and difficulties would arise in aggregating across firms. Kaldor (1935) suggested the use of cross-elasticities of demand, and Rothschild (1942) proposed a measure based upon the angle between the segments of a kinked demand curve. Again, although such indices have a certain amount of appeal, they are plagued by practical and theoretical difficulties. Both indices would be difficult to calculate, requiring the estimation of a complex system of demand equations. Furthermore there is the problem of deciding what level of cross-elasticity of demand, or what size of angle between the segments of a kinked demand curve, is associated with a given degree of market power.

An alternative to these theoretical measures is to use the characteristics of the size distribution of firms. The resulting indices of 'concentration' are reasonably easy to compute and relate naturally to the idea of the structure of an industry or other segment of an economy. In the next section we look at the

* For a long time past there has been considerable controversy in the industrial organisation literature over certain issues relating to industrial concentration. Over the last year or so this controversy has flared up in relation, in particular, to the role of mergers in explaining increases in concentration and to the most appropriate methodology to be employed in estimating the merger effect. It was suggested to the authors that a review of this debate would serve a useful purpose. As so often happens, however, 'one thing led to another' and what has emerged is a more general survey than was originally intended, on the measurement and determinants of concentration. We are grateful to Elizabeth Brunner, Peter Hart, Michael Mann, Aubrey Silberston and Geoffrey Whittington for many helpul comments. Needless to say all errors of judgement and of fact are the sole responsibility of the authors.

attempts that have been made to devise workable measures of concentration; section III deals with concentration in particular industries, i.e. the extent to which particular industries are dominated by a small number of sellers; section IV deals with aggregate concentration, i.e. the extent to which the economy as a whole, or a large sector of it such as manufacturing, is dominated by a small number of large firms; and section V with the contribution of mergers to the increase in concentration. As far as empirical work is concerned we should emphasise an important limitation of this survey, which is that it is confined in the main to the manufacturing sectors of the US and UK.

II. THE MEASUREMENT OF CONCENTRATION

No satisfactory explanation of the size–distribution of firms has yet been derived from economic theory. However, although it is clear that no ideal concentration index can be presumed to exist, it is possible to make some progress by specifying an *ad hoc* collection of desirable properties and considering the range of indices which might satisfy them.

II.1 *Desirable properties for concentration measures*

A list of six properties, or axioms, is suggested by Hall and Tideman (1967):

(i) A concentration index should be a one-dimensional measure.
(ii) Concentration in an industry should be independent of the size of that industry.
(iii) Concentration should increase if the share of any firm is increased at the expense of a smaller firm, i.e. 'the principle of transfers' should hold.
(iv) If all firms are divided into K equal parts then the concentration index should be reduced by a proportion $1/K$.
(v) If there are N firms of equal size, concentration should be a decreasing function of N.
(vi) A concentration measure should be between zero and one.

For the sake of simplicity of use, and of interpretation, the first axiom is obviously a sensible requirement. Most of the indices which have been suggested would conform to it, although one exception is the Fellner (1955) index which has four dimensions. The second axiom carries the implication that each firm's relative importance is indicated by its *share* of an industry or economy. Axiom (iii) would then follow as a natural corollary. Of the remaining axioms, the fourth represents one way of ensuring that a cardinal index is employed, and axiom (v) follows naturally from intuitive notions of market power. Axiom (vi) would seem to be unnecessarily restrictive.

A more comprehensive set of seven axioms is given by Hannah and Kay (1977):

(i) An increase in the cumulative share of the *ith* firm, for all i, ranking firms 1, 2, . . . i . . . N in descending order of size, implies an increase in concentration.
(ii) The principle of transfers should hold.
(iii) The entry of new firms below some arbitrary significant size should reduce concentration.
(iv) Mergers should increase concentration.
(v) Random brand-switching by consumers should reduce concentration.
(vi) If s_j is the share of a new firm, then as s_j becomes progressively smaller so should its effect on a concentration index.
(vii) Random factors in the growth of firms should increase concentration.

The axioms are again based on the use of firms' shares as a measure of their relative importance. If this idea is accepted the first four follow directly. Furthermore, Hannah and Kay argue that axioms (i), (ii), (v) and (vi) are equivalent statements. The fourth axiom, which is a necessary consequence of axioms (ii) and (iii), has, however, been the subject of some disagreement. For instance, Ijiri and Simon (1977) and Hart (1979) suggest that in some cases mergers would not be expected to influence concentration at all. To illustrate this point, Hart has argued that if a union is formed between two countries in which the size distribution of firms are identical and then firms of corresponding size are merged, the new distribution of firms' shares will be exactly the same as the two original, separate distributions, and so any chosen measure of concentration should not be affected. This illustration is, however, somewhat misleading since it incorporates two distinct and separate events, the union and the mergers. If the union takes place without the mergers the share of each firm will be halved. If the mergers then take place the shares of the merged firms will be twice what they would otherwise have been.

More generally, Stigler (1950) and Hart (1975) have argued that mergers between firms of intermediate size may lead to increased competition for the larger existing firms. This is certainly a possible outcome—though not the only one. Mergers between firms of intermediate size could also lead to a more cohesive oligopoly group and thus to more effective collusive behaviour. The outcome will be determined by numerous factors, including the actual number and size distribution of firms following the mergers, the type of product produced, the structure of costs and the state of trade. No concentration measure will succeed in capturing every conceivable aspect of business behaviour. The best that can be done is to devise sensible measures of concentration and to exercise caution in using them. From this point of view it would appear that the principle of transfers, extended to include the effects of mergers, would appear to be a useful *general* property. Given that no concentration measure can be expected to reflect every aspect of firms' behaviour, some exceptions and anomalies have to be tolerated.

Axiom (vi) highlights the difference between measures of concentration and measures of inequality, sometimes referred to as 'absolute' and 'relative' concentration. It requires that a measure of the influence of firms over their commercial environment should not be unduly affected by very small firms, whose market shares in total account for a small proportion of industry sales; these would merely respond passively to market forces and would have no significant impact on an industry's or sector's performance. In contrast, inequality measures compare the number and market shares of such small firms with those of the larger firms. Measures of concentration should not, therefore, necessarily be much influenced by the total number of firms, but more by the number of firms of 'significant' size.

As for axioms (v) and (vii) it is often argued that trends in concentration can be characterised wholly or partly as a random process. This argument is examined more fully in section III, but at this stage we simply note that it is desirable that an index should be sensitive to such random forces. A related argument, the main proponent of which is Hart (1971 and 1975), is that concentration measures should have a firm basis in statistical distribution theory, in the sense that they should be closely related to the parameters or moments of size distributions. The advantages of using a well-established and rigorous body of theory are obvious but should not be exaggerated, since the statistical approach relies on the existence of a theoretical curve capable of describing observed size distributions. There are two main contenders for this position, the Log–Normal and Pareto distributions. The Log–Normal distribution follows from the assumption that the logarithms of firm size are Normally distributed: its properties are set out by Aitchison and Brown (1957).

The Pareto distribution has the property that $P(x)$, the number of firms of size x or greater, can be expressed as:

$$P(x) = (x_0/x)^\alpha \text{ for } x \text{ greater than some minimum size } x_0;$$

where α is a constant. Transforming to logarithms gives:

$$\log P(x) = \alpha \log x_0 - \alpha \log x$$

so that on a double logarithmic scale the distribution is described as a downward-sloping straight line with α as its slope.

Both of these curves possess the high degree of skewness found in empirical studies, but neither is demonstrably superior to the other, as shown for instance by Steindl (1965), Quandt (1966), Silberman (1967 and 1968) and Engwall (1973). In any case, using a particular theoretical distribution does not guarantee that the Hall–Tideman and Hannah–Kay axioms will hold. Also the data used in research work are not generated by random sampling but constitute a truncated population of firms, so that conventional sampling theory is often inappropriate. In practice, therefore, statistical theory comes to have very much the same status in this field as economic theory. Concentration indices have some properties which can be examined from a statistical viewpoint, but they are best judged in terms of the axioms we have just discussed.

II.2 *Suggested indices*

The oldest and most commonly used of all indices is the K-firm concentration ratio, defined as the cumulative share of the K*th* firm. More formally, using s_i to denote the share of the *ith* firm, we may define

$$\text{CRK} = \sum_{i=1}^{K} s_i$$

It is extremely simple to calculate, but the choice of K is somewhat arbitrary (for studies of aggregate concentration K is frequently taken to be 100; for market concentration values between 3 and 8 are usually employed). The index is simply one point on the cumulative concentration curve and so it may neglect important information. Recognising this weakness, Miller (1967) introduces the concept of the marginal concentration ratio—the combined market shares of the fifth to eighth largest firms—which he includes alongside $CR4$ as an important element of market structure. However, Collins and Preston (1969) argue that little is gained by doing this because the two concentration measures are closely related. An inappropriate choice of K means that the above sets of axioms may not be satisfied. This is particularly true of the principle of transfers since the concentration ratio is not affected by changes outside the largest K firms, nor will it be influenced by transfers within the largest K firms if no firm disappears in the process. Such difficulties may be avoided by using a range of values for K, but interpretation of results becomes difficult if conflicting results emerge. Support for the concentration ratio can be found in the work of Saving (1970), who shows that if K dominant firms collude to fix a price for the remaining firms, the value of the Lerner index is directly related to their combined market share.

Another popular index, especially in recent work, is the so-called Herfindahl, or H index, defined as the sum of the squared values of firms' shares. The 'paternity' of the index is disputed. Although used in this form by Herfindahl (1950) the square root of H was used by Hirschman (1945): it is sometimes referred to as the Hirschman–Herfindahl index. It satisfies all of the Hall–Tideman and Hannah–Kay axioms, and, unlike the concentration ratio, depends on the share of each firm. The squaring of shares means that smaller firms contribute less than proportionately to the value of the index. Theoretical support for H as an index of market concentration is provided by Cowling and Waterson (1976). In their model, extended by Lyons (1979) to allow for foreign trade, all firms produce a homogeneous product at constant marginal cost and do not engage in collusive behaviour. Under such conditions they show that H is directly related to price–cost margins. Similar results emerge from the work of Hannah and Kay (1977) and Hause (1977). In addition, Stigler (1964) shows that the probability of continued operation of a cartel is directly related to H.

Hannah and Kay (1977) have shown that their seven axioms are satisfied by any index which is a strictly convex and symmetric function of firms' shares. Accordingly, their suggestion is that some simple convex function should be employed and they choose the sum of the values of firms' shares raised to the power θ. Their index is therefore a natural generalisation of the H index. An additional refinement is to follow the suggestion of Adelman (1969) that an increase in concentration should be described as being equivalent to a fall from, say, p equal sized firms to, say, q equal sized firms. The index is then given by

$$\mathrm{HK}(\theta) = \left(\sum_{i=1}^{N} s_i^{\theta} \right)^{1/(1-\theta)}$$

Unfortunately, there are no criteria on which to base the choice of θ, which measures the extent to which the index is influenced by larger firms, and so a range of values needs to be used. Although in its numbers–equivalent form the index is intended to provide a cardinal measure of concentration, the value of such a measure is obviously limited by the indeterminacy of θ.

Concentration indices can also be based upon the concept of entropy. This has various scientific interpretations, but to a statistician it measures the information that is implied by the shape of a probability, or frequency, distribution. If, for example, the probabilities for the whole range of possible values of a variable are all equal, the implication is that little or no specific information is available. Entropy can also be regarded as a measure of the uncertainty of firms about their market shares. In its simplest, first order form, it is measured by

$$E = -\sum_{i}^{N} s_i \log s_i$$

which for a given number of firms, N, takes its maximum value of log N where firms' shares are equal. At the other extreme E is zero if there is only one firm. The higher the value of E, therefore, the lower the level of concentration, and vice versa. An advantage of the entropy measure is that if there are distinct sub-groups of firms, it can be decomposed into within-group and between-group entropies. Thus in examining the level of industrial concentration within the European Economic Community, for example, Jacquemin and Kumps (1971) consider entropy both within and between two sub-groups comprised respectively of British firms and firms in the rest of the EEC.

If E is divided by its maximum value an index of relative entropy is produced which is constrained to lie between zero and 1. This measure was proposed by Horowitz and Horowitz (1968). A weakness of this index is that it might not register an increase in concentration when mergers take place, because although mergers reduce the value of E, implying that concentration has increased, there may be a proportionately greater fall in log N, so that relative entropy increases, thus implying a fall in concentration. The properties of entropy measures are fully discussed by Theil (1967) and Hart (1971).

The most controversial index is σ^2, the variance of logarithms of firms' sizes, used originally by Hart and Prais (1956) and strongly advocated by Hart (1971, 1975 and 1979). Many writers, e.g. Atkinson (1970) refer to σ^2, along with other measures such as the variance, the coefficient of variation, the relative mean deviation, and the Gini coefficient, as a measure of inequality, although Hart prefers to describe σ^2 as a measure of relative inequality rather than inequality *per se*. Here we are concerned with the properties of σ^2. One advantage of the measure is that it possesses a useful decomposition property similar to that of the entropy index. Its main disadvantage is that it will, for example, be close to zero if all firms are of similar size, regardless of the number of firms. Vastly different industry structures could therefore yield the same value of the index, violating the fifth axiom of Hall and Tideman. As Hannah and Kay (1977) demonstrate, violations of the principle of transfers are also possible. The σ^2 index is thus not a suitable measure of concentration at the industry level.

Hart maintains, however, that σ^2 can be used to measure aggregate concentration, especially if the size distribution of firms is close to the Log–Normal. His argument has two main strands. First of all he shows (1975) that σ^2 does not violate the principle of transfers in the Log–Normal distribution. Secondly he demonstrates (1979) that various concentration indices can be calculated very simply from σ^2. For example:

$$\mathrm{HK}(\theta) = N \exp \frac{-\theta\sigma^2}{2}$$

These arguments, however, require careful examination. The first applies only to partial transfers, i.e. where the number of firms, N, is constant and where one firm can only gain *some* business at the expense of another. Where N is fixed it is clear that a decrease in HK(θ) increases σ^2 and vice versa.

However, where mergers occur, so that N decreases, σ^2 suffers from serious defects. One way to see this is to rewrite the above equation as

$$\sigma^2 = \frac{-2}{\theta} \log_e \frac{\mathrm{HK}(\theta)}{N}$$

By Hannah and Kay's axiom (iv) mergers will lower HK(θ), i.e. HK(θ) will register a rise in concentration. However, the effect on σ^2 also depends on N, and it is possible, as in the case of relative entropy, that N could fall by an amount large enough to offset the fall in HK(θ), so that σ^2 falls, thus registering an apparent fall in concentration. Even if the fall in N is not substantial enough to produce a reduction in σ^2, the observed increase in σ^2 may be small and have the effect of underestimating the actual increase in the levels of concentration. An illustration of this problem is given on p. 211.

Thus, an apparently simple relation between σ^2 and HK(θ) is not sufficient, even in the Log–Normal case. It is merger activity which is the source of the problem. Strictly speaking it is not possible to deal with mergers at all in a Log–Normal model because, as we indicate in section IV, the theoretical reasoning behind the Log–Normal distribution requires a constant population of firms. However, if we ignore the theoretical foundation of the Log–Normal, and treat it just as a good approximation to observed size distributions, the conclusion is that σ^2 may still respond incorrectly to mergers.

If the Log–Normal approximation is not valid, violations of the principle of transfers are clearly possible when using σ^2, even for partial transfers. Creedy (1977) shows that violations are more likely: (a) the smaller the transfer as a proportion of the transferor's (i.e. the losing firm's) size; (b) the larger the ratio of the transferor's size to the geometric mean size; (c) the larger the initial relative difference between the two firms' sizes.

Sawyer (1979) argues that these conditions are likely to hold for populations of firms that are typically studied, so that researchers should be wary of using σ^2. Of course as Stigler and Hart have argued, there are circumstances where violation of the principle of transfers does not impair our understanding of the relationship between market structure and business performance. However, there is not guarantee that it is only in such circumstances that σ^2 will cause violations of the principle. Even in the analysis of aggregate concentration the appropriateness of using σ^2 is in doubt. At the industry level, where the number of firms is typically quite small, it is generally agreed that the measure is inadequate and often misleading.

Space limitations prohibit detailed discussion of the other concentration indices which have been put forward. We have confined our attention to those in most frequent use and we deal briefly with the remainder in the Appendix.

II.3 *Some comments on concentration measurement*

(i) *Relationships between indices*

The first point to note is that the Herfindahl index and the entropy index are effectively special cases of the Hannah–Kay index: H is in fact the reciprocal of HK(2), and E is the limit of HK(θ) as θ approaches 1. The Hannah–Kay index in its turn has been shown by Hart (1975) to be closely related to the more general entropy measure devised by Renyi (1970). Hart has also shown that most of the concentration measures which have been suggested in the literature are simple functions of the parameters of the first moment distribution, i.e. the distribution of firms' shares. His results are especially valuable if the form of the size distribution of firms is known. In the Log–Normal case, for example, we have already noted that HK(θ) is closely related to σ^2 and the number of firms.

The statistical relationships between various indices have been investigated by a number of authors. Rosenbluth (1955), Nelson (1963). Kilpatrick (1967), Bailey and Boyle (1971), Aaronovitch and Sawyer (1975a) and Schmalensee (1976), Hause (1977) and Kwoka (1981) report relationships between a number of sets of indices, but the strength of their correlations varies. This suggests that empirical work cannot be used as a substitute for theoretical analysis of the properties of the relevant measures. In particular, inequality measures such as σ^2 often give results which conflict with true measures of concentration, as shown, for instance, in Aaronovitch and Sawyer (1971), George and Ward (1975), Jacquemin and de Jong (1977). It is, however, mildly reassuring to know that if one's chosen ideal measure cannot be computed because of data limitations the use of simpler measures such as concentration ratios may well yield similar results.

(11) *Some examples*

To illustrate some of the relevant properties of the more widely used concentration indices, we compare the values the indices would take for four simple size distributions. The size of the market (or relevant aggregate) is assumed to be 100. In practice we would hardly require summary measures to deal with cases in which so few firms are involved, since the major characteristics of the distribution are readily apparent. However, the pattern of results shown in the Table I could emerge with larger numbers where summary measures would be needed. The number of firms in the example has been kept small for purposes of simplification and to encourage the student reader in particular to perform the calculations of the various indices.

A comparison of distributions *A* and *B* provides an illustration of the distinction between measures of concentration and measures of inequality. If market power is our primary concern there would seem to be little difference between the distributions. A concentration index should therefore show little or no change with any change reflecting a very slight tendency for concentration to fall. However, the addition of the five small firms in *B* does make the distribution markedly more unequal and one would expect measures of inequality to reflect this. These expectations are confirmed. The two concentration ratios, the Herfindahl and Entropy indices and the Hannah and Kay index (for values of θ from 1.5 to 2.5) all register a slight decline in concentration. In contrast, the two measures of inequality i.e. relative entropy and the variance of logarithms register a substantial *increase* in inequality. It is interesting to note, however, that although HK(0.5) registers a change in concentration in the right direction it would, in relation to the changes in market shares, appear to exaggerate the loss of market power of the leading

TABLE I
A COMPARISON OF POPULAR CONCENTRATION INDICES

Distribution	*A*	*B*	*C*	*D*
% Shares of firms	40 30 15 10 5	39 29 14 9 4 5 firms each with 1% share of market	45 30 15 10	40 30 25 5
Concentration Index				
3-firm *CR*	85	82	90	95
4-firm *CR*	95	91	100	100
Herfindahl	0.285	0.285	0.365	0.315
†Entropy*	1.352	1.577	1.235	1.224
†Relative Entropy*	0.84	0.685	0.891	0.817
Variance of Logarithms*	0.562	2.091	0.343	0.654
†HK(0.5)	4.441	6.437	3.694	3.590
†HK(1.5)	3.724	4.128	3.236	3.264
†HK(2)	3.509	3.759	3.077	3.175
†HK(2.5)	3.351	3.536	2.954	3.110

* calculated using natural logarithms.

† For these measures an increase in the index signifies a fall in concentration and vice versa.

firms. This is precisely because of the low weight which is given in this case to the leading firms.

Distribution *A* becomes distribution *C* when the largest firm in *A* takes over the smallest, which should mean that an increase in concentration is recorded. All of the indices except relative entropy and σ^2 do in fact register such increases, so that yet again these two indices appear to possess undesirable properties. The final comparison, between distributions *A* and *D* is intended to relate to the argument raised by Stigler and Hart against adoption of the principle of transfers. It may be argued that a merger between the third and fourth largest firms in distribution *A* might increase rather than decrease competition, but without exception the indices all record an increase in concentration: the Stigler–Hart argument cannot therefore be used to justify σ^2 at the expense of the others.

The above example shows clearly that relative entropy and σ^2 are not suitable measures of concentration where the number of firms is small. Although the most loyal supporters of σ^2 do not suggest that this measure should be used for industry studies it has in fact been used for such purposes, as for instance in Utton (1971).

(iii) *Static and dynamic measures*

One criticism of conventional indices is that they are 'static', in the sense that they simply record the characteristics of a size-distribution at some particular instant. If, however, the identity of the dominant firms were to change over time then even persistently high levels of concentration would not imply the absence of competitive forces. A possible way out of this difficulty is to examine correlations over time between firms' shares or rank positions as is done by Collins and Preston (1961), Gort (1963), Mermelstein (1969), Boyle and Sorenson (1971) and Shepherd (1975). Since, on the whole, the estimated correlations turn out to be fairly high, there is no need to reject static indices out of hand, but there is still some scope for modifications. The same conclusion emerges from the work of Grossack (1965), who measures the mobility of firms by the slope coefficient in a regression of market share at different dates. He shows that this slope is related both theoretically and statistically to the Herfindahl index, but argues that static measures are not in themselves adequate measures of monopoly power. In a later paper (1972) the same author claims some progress in the search for a true dynamic index. His suggestion is the concept of 'permanent' concentration, analogous to 'permanent' income, but he admits that his work has merely 'scratched the surface of the problem'.

(iv) *Definitional problems*

Although concentration measures are intended to describe the properties of size distributions of firms, size, itself can be measured in a number of ways—by value-added, sales, employment, and assets. The correct technical measure of the importance of a firm's activities is usually its net output or value-added, which amounts to sales revenue less the cost of inputs. If size is measured by sales alone there will be bias towards firms engaged in distribution as opposed to manufacture and towards firms which assemble a collection of costly components. However, for analysis of firms within the same market or for averages of concentration levels across markets, a sales measure would be preferable since value-added will also depend on the degree of vertical integration. To use employment as a size variable would understate the importance of capital-intensive firms. The assets of a firm provide a natural measure of economic influence but valuation of assets depends on accounting conventions. Value-added data are not readily available but fortunately, as shown for example in Blair (1972), the various size measures are often closely correlated. However, Smyth *et al.* (1975) and Shalit and Sankar (1977) point out that stricter conditions than correlation are necessary for size measures to be interchangeable. The latter report that employment appears to be a poor substitute for other size measures for prediction purposes, and that employment and sales are not good substitutes for each other for estimation purposes.

A second problem concerns the definition of industries and markets. A common approach to this problem is to use the two interchangeably, and to define an industry or market as a group of firms producing goods or services that are regarded as close substitutes by buyers and sellers. For instance, if a demand side approach is adopted a market will be defined as a group of firms producing similar, but not necessarily identical, products for which the cross elasticities of demand are 'significant'. But, as we have already noted, it is difficult to construct concentration measures from cross elasticities and even if estimation of cross elasticities is possible, which is unlikely, there is no simple criterion by which to judge whether or not products are sufficiently close in the chain of substitution to form part of the same market. This approach then goes on to emphasise that industries and markets will often be defined differently according to whether the demand-side or the supply-side approach is adopted.

For census purposes it is establishments and not firms that are grouped together and the main emphasis in allocating establishments is on supply side characteristics. Industries are defined in terms of establishments primarily engaged in producing a product or group of products that are related by technical process or by the raw material used. This is a sensible way of defining an industry insofar as firms using the same raw materials or technical processes are able to switch resources to producing each other's products and thus influence each other's behaviour and performance. Supply side groupings may, however, lead to industry classifications which do not correspond to the demand side definition of an industry as a group of products which are close substitutes to consumers. For instance, there are many metal products and plastic products which are close substitutes in consumption but which are classified to different industries because they are made from different raw materials and by different processes. A further problem arises where establishments produce more than one product. In these cases an establishment is normally allocated to an industry on the basis of its major activity only. The result is that the number of establishments producing a particular product may be underestimated and the total output of the product may be underestimated or overestimated.

Difficulties of this kind lead Brunner (1975) and Nightingale (1978) to advocate an alternative approach to the definition of industries and markets. Developing the ideas of Andrews (1951) Brunner argues that a clear conceptual distinction should be maintained between industries and markets; that the former should be defined in terms of supply side characteristics and the latter in terms of demand side characteristics. This approach does not get around the practical difficulties of measurement already alluded to, but it is useful in that it serves as a powerful reminder of the dangers of using 'industry' data to reach 'market' conclusions. In this connection one other important aspect needs to be emphasised, and that is the question of the geographical extent of the market. To define the size of a market for a group of products as the total domestic sales of domestic establishments will result in an overestimation of its size where regional markets are important and to an underestimate of its size where imports are substantial.

To summarise, therefore, concentration indices are based on industry data drawn from national censuses, with industry boundaries defined predominantly by supply side characteristics. Apart from supply side classification problems this procedure may neglect important demand side characteristics. The use of unadjusted concentration indices may therefore give completely misleading results if 'industry' and 'market' are substantially different. Adjustments to census classifications will frequently have to be made to ensure that establishment groupings are suited to the purpose at hand.

(v) *Concluding comments*

The literature which considers the mathematical properties of concentration measures has not resolved the question of which is the best measure to use. Consideration of the economic issues however suggests that this is hardly surprising. As we pointed out in the Introduction, market concentration is important in so far as it influences business behaviour, so that the most appropriate measure of concentration is the one that is most closely related to behaviour. Mention has been made of the theoretical claims made for the Herfindahl index. However, the complexity of business life is such that in practice it is unlikely that there is one concentration measure which will clearly be superior in all circumstances. For instance, if industry behaviour is dominated by the five leading firms who have regard for each other's competitive responses but ignore smaller insignificant competitors, then the five firm concentration ratio will be closer approximation to the reality of business behaviour than say the Herfindahl index which gives some weight to all the firms in an industry. On the other hand, if small firms have an important influence on general industry behaviour this influence will not be captured by the concentration ratio. Similarly, although the HK(θ) index has attractive properties the choice of θ, which determines the weight given to firms of different sizes, is indeterminate. Again what is required is a weighting system that reflects reality, and in practice this suggests the wisdom of using a range of values of θ.

There is general agreement, however, that at the level of the industry, and also of the industrial sector, where the number of firms is often quite small, σ^2 is not an appropriate measure of concentration. Its use will frequently give results which are 'perverse' as compared to those given by other measures. At the aggregate level (all manufacturing) this is less likely since the number of firms is much larger and their size distribution will approximate more closely to Log–Normality. Whether it be a study at the aggregate or the industry level, however, it is sensible to use more than one measure of concentration, although what is possible in this regard will depend on the availability of data.

III. CONCENTRATION AT THE INDUSTRY LEVEL

III.1 *Trends and levels*

An important issue in the analysis of industry structure is whether there is a strong tendency for the production of individual products to become increasingly concentrated in the hands of a small number of firms.

For the UK the evidence suggests that on average the level of concentration increased over the period 1935 to 1968. There are several studies covering various sub-periods, for instance Evely and Little (1960), Armstrong and Silberston (1965), George (1972 and 1975), Aaronovitch and Sawyer (1975a), and Hart and Clarke (1980). All of them show both an increase in the average level of the simple concentration ratio in manufacturing industry, and also a much larger number of industries showing an increase than a decrease in concentration. For the earlier periods it must be remembered that researchers were able to cover only a relatively small number of industries. For instance, for comparisons between 1935 and 1951 Evely and Little were able to examine only 41 out of 200 trades, although Hart and Clarke were able to extend this comparison to 98 trades. However, there is no seriously disputing the general upward trend up to the late 1960s.

From the late 1960s to the mid 1970s, however, the evidence for the UK suggests little change in average concentration levels. An accurate assessment is made difficult by changes in the method of collecting the data which are used for calculating market concentration. In particular a greater effort was made in the 1975 Census of Production to cover small firms, and estimates were also made of the output and employment of non-respondents. Both factors are likely to have increased the measured activity of small firms and thus would have had the effect of reducing the measured level of concentration. Allowing for this, the evidence, see HMSO (1978), and Hart and Clarke (1980), still suggests that there was little increase in average concentration from 1968 to 1975, and that the number of industries showing increases and decreases in concentration was about the same. For the UK then, the evidence points to a substantial increase in concentration up to the late 1960s and a marked levelling off since then.

In the US there has also been some tendency for the average level of concentration to increase, but the increase has been a very modest one. Mueller and Hamm (1974) report that the average 4-firm concentration ratio rose by a mere 1.8 percentage points, from 40.9 per cent to 42.7 per cent, over the period 1947–70. Weighting industries according to the size of shipments in each relevant year gives an overall rise of 3.9 percentage points. They also report that average concentration seems to have fallen in producer goods industries but increased substantially in the consumer goods sector. Caves and Porter (1980) present similar results. Tracing a sample of 166 4-digit manufacturing industries over the period 1954–72 they calculate that the unweighted four-firm concentration ratio rose by 2.3 percentage points over the whole period. For consumer goods industries only, the increase was much larger—5.9 points—whereas for producer goods there was virtually no change. These two studies together also show that the increase in concentration in the US is not the outcome of an uninterrupted upward trend. Increases in the average level of concentration occurred during the periods 1947–54, 1958–63 and 1967–72, but there were small declines during the periods 1954–58 and 1963–67.

There is little doubt then that the average level of concentration has increased over the past thirty or forty years. This is not to say, of course, that an increase in concentration is inevitable as a result, say, of technological forces. Indeed in a minority of cases concentration has decreased.

As far as levels of concentration are concerned there is, as one might expect a great variation in the level of concentration across industries. For instance, the UK Census of Production for 1975 lists 118 industries for which 5-firm net output concentration ratios are given. The average unweighted concentration ratio for these industries was 50.6 per cent. At the top end of the scale 8 industries had a concentration ratio of over 90 per cent and for 26 it was over 70 per cent. At the low end of the scale 3 industries had a concentration ratio of less than 10 per cent and for 40 it was less than 40 per cent. A further point of interest is that the ranking of industries by level of concentration is similar in a number of countries, i.e. the high concentration industries in one country tend to be the high concentration industries in another.

We turn now to the attempts made at explaining patterns of concentration. Why do some industries have higher levels of concentration than others? Why has concentration in some industries increased more quickly than in others while in some it has actually declined? We turn first to the explanation of levels of concentration and second to changes in concentration.

III.2 *Determinants of the level of concentration*

Although concentration, in its role as a measure of market power, constitutes an important part of the structure of an industry, it cannot be regarded as fundamental or exogenous. It is perfectly legitimate to discuss the potential effects of market power, but equally important is the question of why market power exists in the first place: the size distribution of firms at any instant must to some extent reflect the past behaviour of firms. Economic theory yields few, if any, firm predictions but on heuristic grounds it is generally hypothesised that inter-industry variations in concentration can be explained by a combination of explanatory variables such as scale economies, barriers to entry and the size of the market. If, as argued for example by Pashigian (1968), there is a unique optimum firm size then this optimum size, together with the size of the industry, determines the optimum number of firms which in turn determines concentration: the K-firm concentration ratio is then given by K divided by the optimum number of firms.

Several attempts have been made to explain variations in the level of industry concentration, mostly by means of regression analysis. The various researchers have all used the simple concentration ratio as their dependent variable but have used a variety of explanatory variables, not always convincingly justified, to explain these variations. Table II summarises some of the main findings. A tick shows that a particular explanatory variable was included in the analysis. The table also shows the signs of the regression coefficients, and an asterisk denotes statistical significance at the 5 per cent level.

TABLE II
DETERMINANTS OF THE LEVELS OF INDUSTRY CONCENTRATION

Researcher	*Plant Scale Economies*	*Average Firm size*	*Plants per firm*	*Industry Size*	*Initial Capital Requirements*	*Advertising Sales Ratio (A/S)*	*Indust. Growth*	*Best* R^2
Saving 1961	✓ * +		✓ * +					0.55
Comanor & Wilson 1967	✓ * +				✓ * +			0.81
Pashigian 1969	✓ * +			✓ * –				0.64 0.74
Greer 1971	✓ * +				✓ +	✓ * +	✓ –	0.91
Guth 1971	✓ * +				✓ * +	✓ – for 1958 + for 1963		0.71
Sawyer 1971	✓ * +		✓ * +					0.72
Ornstein *et al* 1973		✓ * +				✓ * +	Signs ✓ vary	0.65
Porter 1974	✓ * +				✓ * +		✓ –	0.85
Strickland & Weiss 1976	✓ * +					✓ * +		0.49
Lyons 1980	✓ * +		✓ * +					0.47
Hart & Clarke 1980	✓ * +		✓ * +	✓ * –				0.85

Notes 1. ✓ denotes a variable included in the analysis.
2. * denotes significance at the 5% level.

All the studies suggest the importance of plant economies of scale as a determinant of concentration. This is reassuring since one would certainly expect relative concentration levels to be influenced by technological differences between industries and these differences would be expected to show themselves at the plant level. Technological factors are also important in explaining the observed similarity across countries in the ranking of industries by concentration level.

The strength of the economies of scale variable does not however vary substantially across the various studies, which is perhaps not surprising in view of differences in such factors as the sample of industries examined, and the statistical measures used to estimate the importance of technical economies of scale. A number of studies, Weiss (1963), Strickland and Weiss (1976) and Hart and Clarke (1980) follow the suggestion of Florence (1933) that a reasonable estimate of the minimum efficient size of plant (MES) is given by the mid point of the first moment distribution of plant sizes, often referred to as the Florence median. The Florence median is a hypothetical plant of a size such that half of an industry's output or employment (depending on the size measure that is used) comes from larger plants and half from smaller ones. The basic argument for using it is that the observed size distribution of plant sizes will be clustered in some way around the optimum size, so that some measure of central tendency will provide a reasonable approximation to MES. Comanor and Wilson (1967), however, use as a measure of MES, the average size of plants producing more than the Florence median. They argue that this measure is more closely related to Bain's engineering estimates of MES. It is also insensitive to entry of single plant firms below optimal scale, and because the largest plants are operated by multiplant firms who are less likely to operate suboptimal sized plants the measure is less likely to underestimate MES. Other researchers who use the same measure are Greer (1971), Guth (1971) and Porter (1974). Other proxy measures of MES that have been used are average plant size measured by the survivor technique (Saving, 1961) and the Herfindahl index of plant sizes (Sawyer, 1971).

It might at first be thought that considerable success has been achieved in using these proxies to measure the importance of technical economies of scale. For example, Comanor and Wilson (1967) find that their proxy measure makes a substantial contribution to the explanation of variations in the level of concentration, contributing in fact the great bulk of the explained variance. Similarly, Strickland and Weiss (1976) and Hart and Clarke (1980) find that the Florence median performs well in their equations. However, these results need to be treated with a good deal of caution. At best the statistical MES proxies are a crude measure of optimal plant size, but the whole idea of using *ad hoc* measures based on the size-distribution of plants has been criticised by Wright (1978) and Davies (1980a). Their argument is that the distribution of plant sizes will *automatically* be related to the size-distribution of firms and hence to measures of firm concentration. Davies shows that the Florence median and Comanor and Wilson proxies can in fact be regarded as measures of plant concentration. For instance, assuming the size distribution of plants to be Log-Normal, the logarithm of the Florence median divided by industry size is the same as the entropy measure of plant concentration. The high level of 'explanation' achieved in the Comanor–Wilson equation is therefore not altogether surprising. Davies also goes on to argue that both the above proxies will tend to overstate the true optimal plant size. If, as frequently estimated in the US, less than 50 per cent of industry output is in fact typically produced in sub-optimal plants then the Florence median and *a fortiori* the Comanor–Wilson proxies will overstate optimal plant size. Such an overstatement however is not inevitable. In the UK for instance engineering estimates of minimum plant size made by Pratten (1971) reveal that in several industries optimal plant size is substantially greater than the Florence median.

Lyons (1980), aware of these weaknesses, suggests an alternative measure based on the decision of firms to operate a second plant. Relying on a number of simplifying assumptions, he argues that the expected number of plants per firm at an output level S*, defined as twice MES, will be 1.5. His suggestion is that S*, and hence MES, can be identified by finding the output level at which firms operate on average 1.5 plants and he finds this measure to be a significant determinant of concentration levels. Rather than relying on an arbitrary measure of central tendency Lyons' approach seeks to explain the distribution of plants around the MES and to use this as a means of estimating MES. Whether or not it succeeds in deriving more accurate estimates of optimal size is, however, debatable.

Another use of the plant/firm ratio is as a proxy for economies of multi-plant operation. Saving (1961), Sawyer (1971) and Hart and Clarke (1980) incorporate this variable in their analysis and find it to be significant. However, the plant/firm ratio is unlikely to be a good proxy. Multi-plant operation may be due to factors other than economies of size, and there is again some danger of circularity due to the fact that firm concentration is related to size of plant and multi-plant operation through a simple identity. The whole issue of multi-plant operation is analysed in detail by Scherer *et al* (1975).

Given the factors determining optimum firm size the firm concentration ratio will be influenced by the size of the industry, the ratio being lower, *ceteris paribus*, the larger the industry size. Pashigian (1969) and Hart and Clarke (1980) find evidence of a relationship of this kind. Some general tendency for the level of concentration to be inversely related to the size of the market is also found in international comparisons of concentration levels. This is most clearly apparent where there are very big differences in the size of countries, for instance when the comparison involves countries as large as the US on the one hand and as small as Sweden or the Netherlands on the other. But there is not much evidence of an inverse relationship over a more restricted size range. For instance, though the US market is considerably larger than that of the UK there is some dispute as to which is on average the most concentrated. Rosenbluth (1955), Pashigian (1968) and Sawyer (1971) suggest that UK industries are more concentrated. However, Shepherd (1972) estimated that when allowance is made for the greater importance of regional markets in the US and the greater importance of trade in the UK the average level of concentration might in fact be higher in the US.

Again, George and Ward (1975) compared concentration in the UK, West Germany, France and Italy in the 1960s and found that the UK was the most concentrated of the four even though it had a market which was only slightly smaller than Germany's and bigger than that in France or Italy. This finding may be partly explained by differences between countries in the definition of enterprises but definitional problems are unlikely to offer the whole explanation. In any case the absence of a strong negative correlation between concentration and market size draws attention to the fact that market size is only one determinant of concentration and also that the latter is only one dimension of industry structure. For instance, one reason why the level of concentration is higher in the UK than in France and Germany might be the greater sympathy shown towards cartels in the latter two countries. Another reason might be the differences in the finance of industry. The banking system in Germany, for instance, has traditionally played a more significant role in providing finance for industry than is the case in the UK. Such a system, especially where there are only a small number of large banks, can represent a means of ensuring that the joint interests of superficially independent companies are pursued, as well as providing a meeting ground for the exchange of information. The fact that the post-war growth of the UK market has been much slower than in Germany and France may also have contributed towards a higher level of concentration, partly by encouraging a higher level of merger activity and partly by reducing the opportunities for new entry.

The other major determinant of levels of concentration that is incorporated in a number of articles is some measure of barriers to entry. Scale economies themselves may, of course, constitute a barrier to entry, since potential entrants to an industry must either incur substantial capital expenditure or suffer some cost disadvantage by operating at a sub-optimal size. Estimates of the quantitative importance of this cost disadvantage are found in Pratten (1971) and Silberston (1972). Aside from MES proxies entry barriers have been measured by dummy variables constructed subjectively, for example by Bain (1956). Other measures of entry barriers include advertising, usually measured as a percentage of sales, e.g. Greer (1971), Guth (1971) and Ornstein *et al* (1973); initial capital requirements, e.g. Comanor and Wilson (1967), Greer (1971), Guth (1971) and Porter (1974); and industry growth e.g. Greer (1971), Ornstein *et al* (1973) and Porter (1974). Advertising is regarded as a barrier because of the buyer loyalty it generates and/or because of the sheer expense involved. Initial capital requirements (calculated for entry at MES) as an entry barrier is self-explanatory, but it may well be correlated with MES proxies and advertising intensity. Industry growth is sometimes included on the grounds that entry barriers are liable to be lower in fast growing industries than in slow growing ones.

Most of the studies so far referred to make use of ordinary least squares (OLS) estimation. A general criticism that has been made is the use of this methodology in what is essentially one equation in a simultaneous system. Greer (1971) employed a three-equation model with concentration, advertising expenditure, and growth as endogenous variables. Concentration was taken to be a function of MES, initial capital requirements, advertising intensity and growth, and the equation was estimated by both OLS and 2-stage least squares (2SLS). In both cases advertising intensity emerged as the most important influence on concentration. Strickland and Weiss (1976) also took concentration to be one of three endogenous variables in a simultaneous equation system, the other two being price-cost margins and advertising intensity. Both OLS and 2SLS suggested that concentration depends on MES and advertising intensity. Pagoulatos and Sorenson (1981) employ 3-stage least squares in a similar model. They find industry size, advertising intensity and initial capital requirements to be significant, but not industry growth.

In spite of the shortcomings of much of the statistical analysis there can be little doubt that technical factors, as reflected in optimal plant sizes, do play an important part in explaining inter-industry differences in the level of concentration. The broad similarity across countries in the ranking of industries according to the level of concentration is also commonly ascribed to the role played by technology. However, it is generally agreed that plant scale economies do not, except in a minority of cases, explain high levels of concentration. In the US, Blair (1972) points out that in highly concentrated industries (i.e. those in which CR4 is 50 per cent or higher), 55 per cent of output comes from industries in which the divergence between firm CR8 and plant CR8 is 40 percentage points or more. Multi-plant operation is also a feature of leading firms in highly concentrated UK markets although, because of the smaller domestic market, economies of scale may contribute more towards an explanation of the high levels of concentration.

In his pioneering work, Bain's (1956) estimates of multi-plant economies strongly suggest that they are modest, and this has remained the general consensus. This being so it will frequently be impossible to justify high industrial concentration on the basis of scale economies.

III.3 *Determinants of changes in concentration*

Several attempts have been made to explain changes in industry concentration by means of cross section studies, generally using multiple regression analysis. As in the case of the analysis of concentration levels a great variety of explanatory variables has been used.

An important constraint in the analysis of concentration changes is that each industry included in the analysis must be comparable over time; i.e. each industry must be the same, or broadly the same, in terms of product mix at the beginning and end of the period being studied. This leads immediately to the problem that the experience of the industries being studied may not be similar to those that have to be excluded. For the excluded industries are liable to be those that are, for instance, the most technologically progressive and where, therefore, the products produced may have changed substantially over time. Bearing in mind also that the number of comparable industries is often a relatively small proportion of the total number of manufacturing industries, the results of cross-section analysis must clearly be treated with considerable caution. A summary of the results of a number of studies is shown in Table III. As in the previous table a tick indicates that the variable is included in the

DETERMINANTS OF CHANGES IN CONCENTRATION

Researcher	Industry Growth	Changes in optimal plant size	Product Differentiation (Direct measures)	Advertising/ Sales Ratio	Initial level of CR	Industry Size	Change in Number of firms	Best R^2
Evely & Little (1960)	✓ * –	✓ * +						Not calculated
Nelson (1960)	✓ * –							Not calculated
Weiss (1963)		✓ * +	✓ * +					Not calculated
Shepherd (1964)	✓ * –				✓ * –		✓ * –	Not calculated
Shepherd (1966)	✓ +							Not calculated
George (1967)	✓ * –							Not calculated
Kamerschen (1968)	✓ –						✓ * –	0.23
Sawyer (1971)	✓ * –				✓ * +		✓ * –	0.32
Shepherd (1972)	✓ –				✓ * –			0.1
Duchesneau (1974)	✓ +				✓ –			0.48
Mueller & Hamm (1974)	✓ * –		✓ * +		✓ * –	✓ –	✓ * –	0.36
Aaronovitch & Sawyer (1975)					✓ * –			0.12
Gratton & Kemp (1977)	✓ –			✓ –	✓ * – above 43%	✓ –		0.34
Wright (1978)	✓ –		✓ * +		✓ * –	✓ –		0.44
Mueller & Hamm (1980)	✓ –		✓ * +	✓ * +	✓ * –	✓ –		0.36
Hart & Clarke (1980)	✓ * –	✓ * +		✓ +	✓ * –			0.40
Caves & Porter (1980)	✓ –	✓					– ✓ *	0.15

Notes 1. 1. ✓ denotes a variable included in the analysis. 2. * denotes significance at the 5% level.

analysis; the signs of the regression coefficients are shown, and an asterisk indicates statistical significance at the five per cent level.

Taken as a whole the studies suggest that the most important explanatory variable is the initial level of concentration, which is included in most of the studies listed in Table III, and is significant in all but one of them. It appears that the higher the initial level the smaller the likelihood that concentration will increase further and the greater the chances of a decline. One would expect some such relationship to be observed from a purely statistical point of view. Since the limiting values of the concentration ratio are zero and 100 per cent, an industry with an initial five-firm concentration ratio of 95 per cent can at the very most only increase concentration by a further 5 percentage points whereas the 'opportunities' for decline are much greater. Conversely, if the initial concentration is 10 per cent, the maximum possible decline in concentration is less than 10 percentage points. This means that the regression residuals will be dependent on the inital concentration ratio. One solution to the problem is to use a non-linear functional form as in Pashigian (1969), and Wright (1978). The use of the initial concentration ratio could also be justified in economic terms. As an industry becomes more highly concentrated it becomes more difficult for one firm to gain additional market share at the expense of the others. The ossification of an industry's structure may induce leading firms to diversify, and if they move into industries where the level of concentration is low, these low levels will tend to increase as a result. Furthermore, if high concentration means substantial market power, the leading firms may, in exploiting this power, adopt pricing policies that encourage the expansion of the market share of their smaller competitors.

Another variable which is generally included in cross section studies is industry growth. The *a priori* expectation is that here too there is a negative relationship, with a general tendency for slow growing industries to exhibit bigger concentration increases than faster growing ones, and for the fastest growing industries to show a decline in concentration. An economic basis for such an expectation is that in faster growing industries large established firms will find it more difficult to take advantage of all the opportunities for expansion and the opportunities for small firms will be greater. In addition, fast growth will attract new entrants and where this takes the form of an increase in the number of relatively small firms concentration will fall as these firms establish themselves in the industry. The statistical evidence, however, is not conclusive. Some studies such as those of Evely and Little (1960), Nelson (1960), Shepherd (1964), George (1967), Sawyer (1971), Hart and Clarke (1980) and Caves and Porter (1980) find a significant inverse relationship. In other studies, e.g. Shepherd (1966), Kamerschen (1968), Duchesneau (1974) and Gratton and Kemp (1977) this result is not repeated. Wright (1978) finds that growth is significant in a simple linear equation, but not when concentration change is expressed in proportionate terms.

Just as economies of scale help to explain differences in the level of contration so it may be thought that changes in concentration may in part be due to changes in the importance of economies of scale over time. This may occur both in respect of technical economies at the plant level and of multi-plant economies. As far as changes in plant-scale economies are concerned one difficulty in capturing its effect in regression studies is that the periods covered are often quite short, frequently of the order of 5–10 years, and substantial changes in the importance of scale economies may well take a much longer period fully to manifest themselves. In the case of changes in multi-plant economies the proxy variable usually used to try to capture this effect is changes in the average plant-firm ratio. However, a change in the ratio of plants to firms may occur for reasons unconnected with economies of scale. It may, for instance, be the result of an attempt to monopolise an industry through mergers. The effect of changes in technology is more adequately captured by means of case studies. In some industries as in certain areas of the chemical, metals, and vehicle sectors, technological developments have increased the optimum size of plant. However, Blair (1972) gives several examples, e.g. fabrication of finished and semi-finished plastic products, and electronics, to show that the march of technology does not always or even typically demand larger scale.

Style changes, product differentiation and advertising expenditure (sometimes used as a proxy measure of product differentiation) are three inter-related variables sometimes used to explain concentration changes. For instance Weiss (1963) examined the possibility that concentration is most likely to increase in industries where the prevailing form of competition is through style changes or product differentiation, and after classifying industries according to the durability and differentiation of their products he found some support for the hypothesis. Further support for the effect of product differentiation is found in Mueller and Hamm (1974) and Wright (1978). Product differentiation in itself, however, may have a concentration-reducing effect in so far as it may be easier to enter a market with a differentiated product than a homogeneous one, because differentiation may leave a niche in a market which a new entrant may fill. A possible reason for the product differentiation effect is that industries where product differentiation is important also tend to be those where advertising and other marketing expenditures are important–areas where large firms have a big advantage over smaller competitors. Product differentiation allied with heavy sales promotion may enable a firm to increase its market share and also prevent the erosion of the market shares of large firms.

As far as the effect of advertising is concerned the evidence contained in the various regression studies is not conclusive. In part this may be due to the fact that in certain circumstances advertising may be pro-competitive and thus hinder rather than facilitate the emergence of more concentrated industries. The data available on advertising are, however, often woefully inadequate. In Hart and Clarke (1980), for instance, advertising data are available for one year only and at a level of aggregation which is higher than that to which the concentration data refer. What is really needed is information on the absolute level of advertising and the advertising-sales ratio over a run of years and at a level of disaggregation that matches the concentration data.

Other studies, however, have stressed the importance of advertising. For instance, Blair (1972) examined changes in concentration in 33 US industries over the period 1947–63, a period when for US manufacturing as a whole increases in concentration were roughly matched by decreases. All 33 industries advertised extensively on television. In 25 cases concentration increased and in 17 of them by more than 10 percentage points.

Style changes and advertising may act as barriers to entry and thus affect the course of concentration. Other barriers to entry proxy variables that have been used in statistical work include the increase in the number of firms (an *ex post* measure of the effectiveness of entry barriers), industry size, and the "coverage ratio"—defined as the percentage of products primary to an industry which are shipped by plants in the same industry.

The concern which was expressed earlier, when discussing the determinants of the level of concentration, over the use of "explanatory" variables which can be linked to concentration in identities or near identities also applies to the analysis of changes in concentration. Caves and Porter (1980) suggest that a possible solution to the problem is to fit regression equations using lagged values of the independent variables. The explanatory power of their equations, embodying lagged values of the independent variables turns out to be very weak, the highest value of R^2 in nine equations being as low as 0.15. This suggests that earlier, more positive, results might have been due in large part to the identity problem.

The level of 'explanation' of concentration changes, as shown by the value of R^2, is in fact typically rather low, as can be seen from Table III. Part of the reason for the relatively poor results is that, even if the systematic factors that determine concentration changes could be properly specified and measured, this would not tell the whole story because of the contribution of non-systematic or stochastic forces. The latter are dealt with in detail in section IV. In addition there are, as we have seen, problems in specifying and measuring several of the systematic forces that one might expect to be important determinants of changes in concentration. The data on such factors as minimum efficient scale, advertising and other entry barriers, and mergers, are either very unsatisfactory or simply not available, so that a variable is often measured by using rather crude dummy variables or omitted altogether. Mergers, for instance, which one might expect to be one of the most important proximate causes of change in concentration is included as an explanatory variable in only two of the studies listed in Table III. This is surprising in view of the way in which some merger waves have transformed industrial structure. For instance in the US Markham (1955) estimated that between 1890 and 1904 approximately 71, or one in five large mergers, transformed oligopolistic or nearly competitive industries into near monopolies. In the UK the merger wave of the 1950s and 1960s resulted in very large structural changes in several industries in such sectors as textiles, vehicles, electrical engineering, and food, drink and tobacco. The UK merger wave of the early 1970s, however, does not appear to have had much impact on average concentration levels.

Our understanding of the determinants of changes in concentration has not been greatly enhanced by cross section analysis of a large number of industries using published data. Improvement in the data base would obviously improve the results, but it would be optimistic to expect more than a modest development in this area. More fruitful approaches are the study of individual industries, and the detailed analysis of individual causes of change, such as the analysis of mergers using the counter-factual approach — a topic which is reviewed in section V.

IV. AGGREGATE CONCENTRATION

IV. *General trends*

There is a general consensus that aggregate concentration in both the UK and the US has risen significantly since the turn of the century. For example, Prais (1976) presents the following estimates of the share of the 100 largest firms in manufacturing net output (denoted by CR 100).

	UK	*1909*	*1924*	*1935*	*1949*	*1953*	*1958*	*1963*	*1968*	*1970*
CR 100	100	16	22	34	22	27	32	37	41	41
	US	*1919*	*1929*	*1939*	*1947*	*1954*	*1958*	*1963*	*1967*	*1980*
CR 100	100	22	25	26	23	30	30	33	33	33

Hannah (1976) presents similar estimates for the same period in the UK, again using net output as a measure of size. Estimates of the share of the 100 largest companies in manufacturing assets give similar results. For instance, in the US the estimates of Means (1964), Blair (1972), and Scherer (1970) confirm the general picture, as do Hart and Prais (1956), Aaronovitch and Sawyer (1975a) and Hannah and Kay (1977) for the UK. There are two dissenting voices in the US. Nutter (1951) argued that concentration fell over the period 1901 to 1937, and Adelman (1964) argued that the 117-firm asset concentration ratio declined between 1933 and 1962. Both these studies, however, have been heavily criticised.

Apart from the broad agreement on the long term increase in concentration four other points of detail may be noted. First, the general trend of UK concentration is steeper than that of the US, having started at the turn of the century at a lower initial level and ending up in the 1970s at a distinctly higher level. The higher initial level of concentration in the US is probably due to the stronger merger wave that was experienced there at the end of the nineteenth century and the early years of the twentieth. The strong upward movement in concentration in the UK between 1953 and 1970, and the much weaker upward movement in the US over this period, (see White (1981)) also probably owes much to the stronger post-war merger wave in the UK. (The contribution of mergers to increasing concentration is examined in section V).

Second, according to most researchers, concentration in both the UK and the US fell during the 1930s and 1940s. This period included World War II which probably favoured small firms. Quotas of production, restrictions on capital investment etc., may have hindered the growth of large firms and kept alive some small firms, which had been given a quota, when otherwise they might have died. It is also possible that small firms were able to adapt more quickly than large ones to the major shifts in market circumstances during this period. The view that a number of large enterprises were experiencing sizeable diseconomies of scale and were thus losing ground to smaller firms has been advanced by Hannah, (1974). Another possible explanation is that despite the high unemployment of the 1930s the decade also saw considerable progress in the birth and development of new products and industries. This progress continued into the 1940s but eventually as the new industries matured the upward trend in concentration was re-established. A further line of argument, pursued by Hannah (1976) and Hannah and Kay (1977) is that the decline in the UK was the result of a low level of merger activity.

Hannah and Kay also explore in some detail the question of whether indeed concentration did fall during the period. As far as their population of firms is concerned a decline in concentration is registered for four different concentration ratios and for their own index. However, suspecting that their population may not fully reflect the lower half of the true size distribution for the period, they added a number of hypothetical medium and small-sized firms to their 1930 and 1948 distributions. Although for most values of the elasticity parameter, θ, a decline in concentration is still recorded, small values around 0.6 to 0.8 suggest an increase. Their tentative conclusion is that during the period the largest firms were losing ground while at the same time a number of small firms were eliminated. Whatever the true explanation of the course of events in the 1930s and 1940s the period does seem to have been a break in the general upward trend.

Third, the evidence of a general rise in concentration over a period of 60 years does not depend on the use of a particular concentration index. Although most researchers have used the simple 100-firm concentration ratio, Hannah and Kay used a variety of concentration ratios plus their own index for a range of values of θ. They find that despite its deficiencies, the variance of logarithms measure did not produce conflicting results. However, Aaronovitch and Sawyer (1975a) and Sawyer (1979) report that, for the periods 1958–63 and 1958–68 respectively, σ^2 would have registered a fall in concentration, in contrast to the results produced by other measures, but Hart (1980) and Prais (1980) claim that Sawyer's calculations of σ^2 are faulty.

Fourth, the rise in aggregate firm-concentration has not been accompanied by a rise in aggregate plant-concentration. For the UK Prais (1976) estimates that in 1968, as in 1930, the 100 largest plants account for approximately 11 per cent of manufacturing net output. In the US, over the same period, the share of the 100 largest plants in manufacturing employment was approximately constant at about 9 per cent. In both countries, therefore, it would seem that the 'explanation' for the increase in aggregate concentration is an increase in the number of plants operated by large firms rather than a greater than proportional increase in the size of large plants. There is clear evidence of the growing importance of the multi-plant operations of large firms. From 1958 to 1972 the average number of plants operated by the 100 largest UK manufacturing companies increased from 27 to 72. In the US the same process has been at work and Blair (1972) concludes that "for all but a minor segment of the industrial economy the explanation for concentration is clearly to be found in multiplant operations, not in the requirement of technology to achieve economies of scale".

IV.2 *Economic explanations of the rise in aggregate concentration*

There are three possible components of an increase in aggregate concentration—an increase in concentration within individual industries, an increase in the proportion of manufacturing output accounted for by industries in which concentration is above average, and an increase in the level of diversification of large firms. Aggregate concentration can obviously increase over time for any of the reasons discussed in the previous section in relation to market concentration. However, it may also increase when market concentration on average shows no change or is even declining, as a result for instance of conglomerate mergers. In addition to explanations of changes in market concentration some 'general' theories have been advanced to explain the growing proportion of activity accounted for by giant firms.

Marx (1887) aimed to "lay bare the economic law of motion of modern society", and regarded the capitalist system simply as one stage in its development. Although this historical approach has been severely criticised, especially by Popper (1961), there are a number of elements of the Marxist analysis which are relevant to the study of industrial concentration. In particular Marx's prediction and explanation of the general rise in concentration is worthy of critical attention. Marx's own phrase for what is now described as the process of increasing concentration was the "centralisation of capital". A major factor in the centralisation of capital is technological change which results in the increasing importance of large scale production, and the lower prices made possible by mass production drive out smaller, higher cost, competitors. An essential instrument in this process was the emergence of the joint stock company, and of a reliable market in corporate securities which allowed large amounts of capital to be concentrated in one enterprise, thus making possible scales of production that would have been beyond the reach of individual capitalists. As centralisation proceeds, however, the price competition between surviving firms becomes increasingly intense and this encourages the formation of cartels and of mergers. Although Marx himself did not include merger movements in his analysis they are perfectly consistent with his general line of argument, which was extended by Engels (1887), Hilferding (1910) and Sweezy (1942). Another element in Marxist theory is the role of the banks and other financial institutions. They aid the process of centralisation because of the profits they earn in the formation of companies and in promoting mergers. Increasing concentration is, therefore, seen as the inevitable outcome of a combination of technological and financial factors and the increasingly severe crises associated with competition.

Downie (1958) subjects the Marxist analysis to a more detailed examination, using two concepts which he takes to be essential mechanisms of the competitive process: the "transfer mechanism" and the "innovation mechanism". The transfer mechanism describes that process whereby efficient firms expand their market shares at the expense of the inefficient, the efficiency differences being due to past differences in innovative performance and the fact that new knowledge is diffused slowly. As the most inefficient firms are eliminated efficiency differences are reduced so that the transfer mechanism is weakened, a tendency which will be reinforced if the move towards more concentrated oligopolistic structures is accompanied by an increase in collusive behaviour. So the transfer mechanism pushes an industry at first quickly and then more slowly towards higher levels of concentration. However, the threat to the existence of inefficient firms embodied in the transfer mechanism is itself the stimulant to the innovation mechanism. At the same time the firms that are currently most efficient will feel less threatened by the transfer mechanism and may thus be less inclined to be diligent in their search for new technical advances. As a result there should be a tendency for technological leadership to change hands and for part of the work of the transfer mechanism to be undone. However, the likely balance of forces will be in favour of the transfer mechanism. Once a dominant group of firms has emerged they will reap all the benefits of size, and smaller innovative firms will find difficulty in dislodging them, possibly being taken over in the attempt. Another element in Downie's analysis is that the growth motive will lead firms in concentrated industries, where there is little room for further expansion because of a weakening of both the transfer mechanism and the innovation mechanism, to diversify into industries with low concentration, a process that will speed up the operation of the transfer mechanism. Overall, therefore, the theory predicts a general tendency for concentration to rise, and for large firms to hold positions of market power in more than one industry.

Technological change and its twin companion, organisation, is at the heart of the Galbraithian view of the economy. According to Galbraith (1967 and 1974) the development of modern technology has resulted in a longer gestation period for investment, increasing capital requirements, and more inflexible methods of production. It also requires more organisation, since little use can be made of technology from the knowledge available to any one person. Where these developments occur, and they occur mainly in the industrial and financial sector, it becomes necessary for the firm to control its environment—the prices it charges, the demand for its products, and the costs and availability of inputs. In seeking to achieve all this the firm will expand well beyond the technically optimum size. In turn the organisation is rewarded in terms of pay, promotion, prestige etc., all of which are associated with size.

The role of management in increasing concentration is developed in the work of Penrose (1959) and Williamson (1970). In Penrose's analysis a firm with appropriate managerial services will be able to expand without limit. There is no limit on absolute size, only on the growth rate per unit of time, but this does not mean that large firms will necessarily absorb ever larger proportions of the economy's resources. A firm's attainable growth rate will be determined by the ratio between the managerial services available for expansion and the managerial services required per unit of expansion. With increased size there may be a tendency for the proportion of managerial services required for current operations to increase, thus leaving a smaller proportion available for planning expansion. However, the administrative task need not grow proportionately with the size of the firm. New management methods, the use of labour-saving devices in management, and the use of more capital intensive methods in production may contribute to making the management task relatively easier. The factor most likely to increase the proportion of managerial services required for current operations is competition with other large firms. The managerial services required per unit of expansion depends on the character of the expansion and particularly on such factors as the variety of products that are produced, the number of separate plants, and, again, the intensity of competition.

The implications of this analysis for concentration are not very strong. Concentration increases if the growth potential of large firms exceeds that of the whole economy, so that large firms grow at the expense of others. Penrose herself expected overall concentration to stabilise and even fall as it becomes more difficult for large firms as a group to take advantage of the same percentage of total opportunities. There is nothing in the analysis, however, that tells us at what level of concentration this is likely to happen. It should also be added that the outcome will depend rather heavily on the rate of expansion of the economy as a whole, which in turn will determine the number of opportunities for productive investment.

Williamson has argued that managerial innovations, and in particular the development of the multi-divisional form of organisation, have eased the problems of managing large companies and have allowed companies to reach very large sizes without loss of efficiency. Apart from benefits to internal efficiency he suggests that there are important resource allocation advantages associated with the multi-divisional form of organisation. The large diversified firm can act like a mini-capital market, channelling funds from low to high profit areas more quickly than would occur in an economic system characterised by several specialised unitary-form organisations.

The view that technological developments inevitably lead to higher levels of concentration has been challenged by many economists. In the US, for example, Blair (1972) argues that technological change in the post-war years has on balance reduced the importance of economies of scale. In the UK, Bannock (1973) argues that large firms in general are not justified by the needs of technology, and that there are substantial diseconomies of scale, notably as a result of the lack of flexibility, in the problems of internal communication and morale, and hence in effective control and co-ordination. The overall contribution of technology and organisation towards the explanation of increased levels of concentration is difficult to judge. There is certainly no consensus of opinion amongst economists that either of these factors can 'explain' or 'justify' the high overall level of concentration.

There is more of a consensus on the importance of the financial and marketing power of big companies, which allows them to increase or to maintain their market shares. Meade (1968) suggests that one factor favouring the growth of large companies in the UK has been the favourable tax treatment of retained earnings, and he advocates a tax that encourages the distribution of profits as one measure for reducing the power of big business. Prais (1976) and Kay and King (1978) have also emphasised the role of financial factors. They argue that because of the tax advantages afforded in the UK towards investment in owner-occupied houses, pension funds and life insurance, capital has been channelled away from entrepreneurial ventures. Furthermore, the financial intermediaries hold a high proportion of the shares of industrial and commercial companies, but since they deal mainly in large blocks of shares they invest in the main in large companies. The latter, therefore, have favourable access to finance which gives them a substantial advantage over smaller competitors in product markets.

One final point worth emphasising is that the increasing dominance of large firms over the last 30 years has to be seen within the context of substantial changes in the industrial environment. In the UK, for instance, the changes since the 1950s have included an attack upon restrictive practices following the 1956 Restrictive Trade Practices Act, an increase in competition following upon membership of the European Economic Community, and an increase in the intensity of competition on a world wide scale in many industries. Andrews (1964) in the course of a critique of the neo-classical concept of equilibrium concluded that "we can still retain ideas of a firm in balance, a sort of equilibrium, but this would be a balance with its environment, the industrial environment". It follows that if there is a major change in the industrial environment there will be a response from firms as they attempt to restore what they regard as an acceptable balance between competition and market power. The attempt made by firms to adjust to a changing environment is likely to be an important part of the explanation for the merger wave of the 1950s and 1960s and the associated increase in the level of concentration. It should also be stressed that in the UK the attempts by firms to alter market structure has been facilitated by a permissive government policy towards mergers. This is in contrast to the US where, since 1950, mergers, particularly of the horizontal and vertical kind, have been more tightly controlled.

IV.3 *Mechanical explanations*

Economic theories such as that of Downie predict an increase in concentration due to mechanisms inherent in the market economy. Stochastic models take an entirely different approach to the explanation of concentration. These models stem from the idea that the growth of a firm is a purely random process. In other words the size distribution of firms is not the outcome of systematic forces but rather the result of a large number of random influences affecting all firms. The implication is that within a given population of firms there will be an increase in concentration. The reason for this is that although each firm faces the same distribution of growth possibilities in proportionate terms regardless of past history and initial size, actual growth rates will nevertheless differ over any particular period simply because some firms will have more luck than others. Consequently, starting from a situation where there are many firms of equal size, at the end of some arbitrary but short period, some firms will have jumped ahead of the pack. In the next period each firm from the largest to the smallest will again have the same chance of growing by a given proportionate amount. As a result some of the leading firms at the end of the first period will jump even further ahead, again because of chance factors. In this way a small number of firms will attain positions of dominance. Stochastic models, therefore, can explain why highly skewed distributions of firm size will tend to emerge. Indeed these stochastic models generate size distributions very similar to those found in the real world.

In its simplest and strictest form the principle that the growth of firms is an independent random variable is known as Gibrat's Law or the Law of Proportionate Effect (L.P.E.). There are three formulations of this law.

(i) The first, described in Hart and Prais (1956) takes the proportionate growth of a firm to be an independent random variable,

$$U_t = \frac{x_{i,t}}{x_{i,t-1}}$$

where $x_{i,t}$ denotes the size of firm i at time t. Growth is represented as a stochastic process in continuous space and discrete time. Dropping the subscript i the equation can also be written as

$$X_t = X_{t-1} + e_t = \sum_{j=0}^{\infty} e_{t-j}$$

where X_t denotes log size at time t and $e_t = \log U_t$. It can then be seen that the model is a so-called "random walk" in log size, and that the value of the process at time t is the sum of an infinite series of independent random shocks. It then follows from the Central Limit Theorem that X_t will be Normally distributed when t is large, and hence that the size distribution of firms will have the Log-Normal distribution. The speed at which concentration increases is positively related to the variation of growth rates—i.e. to the variance of the random variable e_t. It is necessary in this model to have a so-called 'absorbing barrier' at some point on the size scale since the random walk would cease when one firm had acquired the whole market or economy. However, there is no need for a 'barrier' at the bottom end of the size scale to prevent firms from disappearing. This is because the model deals with disproportionate changes in size so that zero size can only be approached asymptotically.

(ii) A second, less common, formulation of the LPE using the theory of Markov processes, was suggested by Champernowne (1953). Size is measured over a set of discrete size classes defined logarithmically. A movement along a logarithmic scale is equivalent to a proportionate change, and so Gibrat's Law is expressed as the assumption that the probability of a transition between two size classes r and s depends only on the distance between them, i.e. $|r - s|$. Champernowne obtains the Pareto curve as the equilibrium distribution of the process, subject to a stability condition that the mathematical expectation of growth should be negative. Put more simply this requires that there should be a general long-run tendency for existing firms to shrink, and without such a constraint the model would have no equilibrium distribution. Steindl (1965) suggests that the stability condition is equivalent to assuming that the birth of new firms causes continuous erosion of existing market structures. It is interesting, however, to note that the random walk model in (i) above requires no such restraints. A random walk is also a type of Markov process but the more specific formulation of the growth process as a random walk gives enough information to solve the model.

(iii) Simon and Bonini (1958), drawing on the work of Simon (1955), take the Gibrat assumption to mean that percentage growth is independent of size, in which case the expectation of absolute growth is proportional to size. All firms, regardless of size, are assumed to have the same probability of disappearing, and to deal with the birth of new firms it is assumed that the size of the market or relevant aggregate increases regularly by one "size unit", with a given probability that the additional size unit constitutes a new firm as opposed to an increase in the size of an existing firm. Where firms disappear their size units are re-allocated in the same way. These assumptions lead to the Yule distribution, the upper tail of which can be approximated by the Pareto curve.

All three formulations lead either to the Log Normal or Pareto distribution. They differ in the way growth is defined, but the reason why (ii) and (iii) lead to the Pareto curve and not the Log Normal is the stability condition in (ii) and the introduction of births and deaths in (iii). If, for example, growth is expressed in percentage terms as in (iii) but the Gibrat assumption is applied to a constant population of firms, the Log-Normal distribution will emerge as long as suitably small intervals of time are considered. Thus a number of variants of the LPE lead to the type of highly skewed distribution found in practice.

However, although the LPE is sufficient to generate these distributions it is not a necessary condition. In fact a wide range of growth models give similar results. For example, Kalecki (1945) and Hart and Prais (1956) make use of a slightly more general version of the random walk model in (i):

$$\hat{X}_t = \beta \hat{X}_{t-1} + e_t$$

where $\hat{X}_t$ denotes deviations of X_t from its mean.

The simple LPE holds when β is unity. The case where $\beta < 1$ is termed by Hart and Prais, "Galtonian Regression". Although the stochastic component e_t will generate an increase in concentration, small firms will grow proportionately less than larger firms, and if β is sufficiently less than unity concentration will fall. It is easy to show that X_t is again a sum of random variables and provided that e_t is Normally distributed, the size distribution will again be Log-Normal. If $\beta > 1$, there can be no equilibrium distribution.

It is also clear that more general p-period auto-regressive growth models, with suitable constraints on the parameters, can give similar results. If we write:

$$\hat{X}_t = \sum_{j=1}^{p} \beta_j \hat{X}_{t-j} + e_t$$

then X_t can again be expressed as a weighted sum of a sequence of random variables e_t. Alternatively, $\hat{X}_t$ could be expressed directly as a weighted sum of random shocks, a so-called "moving-average" model:

$$\hat{X}_t = \sum_{j=1}^{q} \theta_j e_{t-j}$$

It should also be noted that a finite order auto-regressive model can be expressed as an infinite order moving-average model and vice versa.

Finite-order autoregressive and moving average representations can be combined to give an autoregressive-moving average (ARMA) model, as in Box and Jenkins (1971). Since ARMA models are intended to provide a general class of functions capable of describing most types of time series behaviour it is not particularly surprising that skew distributions of the Log-Normal type appear to be very common.

Although ARMA models provide a convenient generalisation of the Galtonian Regression model it is much more difficult to generalise the models which generate Pareto distributions. Ijiri and Simon (1964 and 1967) assume serial correlation of growth rates by allowing the expected growth rates of firms to be proportional to weights, where the weights are the time-discounted sum of previous increments in size. They show, by simulation methods, that their model generates equilibrium distributions very similar to the Yule and Pareto distributions. Ijiri and Simon (1971 and 1974) consider the effects of mergers and acquisitions on the slope of the size distribution. They conclude from the data used in their first paper that the probability of a firm disappearing is independent of its size, and that the pooled assets of disappearing firms are allocated in such a way that growth is independent of size, in which case the size distribution will still be described by the Pareto curve. In their second paper however they no longer find these assumptions to hold, but rather that a slightly adjusted form of the Pareto curve provides a reasonable approximation.

IV.4 *Testing the models*

Since it is difficult to choose between the Log-Normal and Pareto curves as descriptions of observed size distributions, direct tests are required. One possible approach is to allow a particular growth model to start from the distribution of firms in some base year and thence to derive a hypothetical size-distribution for later years, comparing these with the actual distributions. The Gibrat model has been tested in this way by Prais (1976) who estimates the variance of the distribution of firms' growth rates. Assuming this to be the variance of the random variable affecting growth, Prais extrapolates forwards and backwards from his base year 1963. Calculating the 100-firm concentration ratio for his hypothetical distributions he obtains a hypothetical upward trend in concentration which, broadly speaking, is similar to his estimates of the actual trend. However, his hypothetical trend fails to fit the observed decline in concentration during the 1930s and 1940s so he resorts to the Hart–Prais explanation of that period in terms of Galtonian Regression.

A difficulty with this approach is that measures of firm growth relate both to internal and external components of growth, whereas the various statistical models relate more naturally to internal growth. Hannah and Kay (1977) test Gibrat's Law for internal growth alone by estimating the probability distribution of growth rates from the growth of firms not involved in merger activity. Their conclusion is that the Gibrat effect alone can only account for a small proportion of the observed increase in concentration, although Prais (1981) suggests that their results are biassed downwards because of the exclusion of certain firms that experienced rapid growth.

A second type of approach to the testing of growth models is to test the growth equation using cross sections of firms observed at two or more time points. A number of authors e.g. Hart and Prais (1956) for the period before 1930, Hymer and Pashigian (1962), Hart (1962), Archer and Maguire (1965), Simon and Bonini (1958) and Ijiri and Simon (1971), have arrived at the conclusion that there is no correlation between the size and growth of firms. However, Hart and Prais (1956) find that when their Regression model is applied to the period 1930–50, β is significantly less than unity. The same model was tested by Samuels (1965) and Utton (1971) for the post-war years and both found values of β that were greater than unity, implying a positive relationship between size and growth. Singh and Whittington (1975), probably the major UK study owing to the comprehensive coverage of their data, test the Regression model for a number of industries over the period 1947–70. The estimated values of β exceed unity for most industries, although the coefficient is not always significant. The same authors also found direct evidence of a mild tendency for larger firms to experience faster growth, a revision of their earlier (1968) conclusion which had been based upon a much narrower sample of firms and industries.

Singh and Whittington proceed to test for persistence of growth rates using the equation:

$$g_t = a + bg_{t-1} + e_t$$

where g_t is the proportionate change in size. Estimates of the slope term are found to be significant and positive for most industries, which raises the possibility that a single growth-size equation would suffer from the omission of an important variable, namely past growth. This would cause an upward bias in the estimated coefficient so that an apparent growth-size relationship may simply be due to serial correlation of growth rates. Testing the proposition by fitting an equation in which growth is dependent on both size and past growth shows that both are significant but that size is much less important than in simple growth-size equations.

A further point of interest is that Gibrat's Law requires that the probability distribution of growth rates should be the same for all firms and so the variance of growth rates should not be related to size. Hart and Prais (1956) and Ijiri and Simon (1964) find no evidence of growth rate variability being positively or negatively related to size. However, most researchers, e.g. Hymer and Pashigian (1962), Samuels (1965), Samuels and Chesher (1972), Scherer (1970) and Singh and Whittington (1968 and 1975) find evidence that the variability of growth declines with firm size. If this is so then it is not appropriate to test either the Gibrat model or the Regression model by using ordinary least squares (OLS) techniques. Owing to the heteroscedastic disturbance term OLS would yield inefficient, although still unbiassed estimates. However, as pointed out by Hart (1980), a heteroscedastic error term may still be consistent with Log-Normality of the size distribution of firms.

Chesher (1979) suggests that another argument against the use of OLS techniques concerns potential time dependence in the error term even with cross-section data. Allowing for this possibility he concludes that in the regression model β is close to unity, but he also finds evidence that the error term follows a first order autoregressive process. The first finding is consistent with Gibrat's law but the second is not. The cross-section approach is also subject to the difficulty mentioned above, namely that it combines the effects of internal and external growth. Finally it is only the simple growth models, such as the simple LPE and the Galtonian regression model, which have so far been tested. It would obviously be desirable to test more general auto-regressive models but data limitations have prevented this: cross-sections of firms observed at a number of time points are not readily available.

It is clear that some progress has been made in explaining trends in aggregate concentration in terms of random forces, although it seems unlikely that random forces alone can provide a sufficiently general explanation. Systematic factors relating growth to size and past growth need to be taken into account, but further research, both theoretical and empirical, is needed into the exact nature of these relationships. However, even if a full understanding of the growth process is eventually possible, the mechanical approach can be criticised precisely because it is mechanical. Stochastic models contain little of direct interest to the economist. Two studies, Hymer and Pashigian (1962) and Ijiri and Simon (1971) have tentatively suggested that the nature of the stochastic growth process depends on cost conditions, but their arguments are not based on formal theoretical models. They make no attempt to consider decisions made by firms, nor do they have much to say about market structure.

Nevertheless, the fact that the various stochastic models have not formed part of the mainstream of economic thought does not mean that the stochastic approach has no value. At the very least it has focussed attention on the dispersion of growth rates as a major factor in increasing concentration. Also, if we may, perhaps optimistically, anticipate the development of a more general dynamic theory of the firm under conditions of uncertainty, any such theory would need to be consistent with known size distributions and mechanical growth models.

V. MERGERS AND CONCENTRATION

The case for using concentration measures which register an increase in concentration when mergers take place has already been noted in section II. However, there is still a certain amount of dispute in the literature on the question of how important in quantitative terms merger activity has been in explaining the upward trend in concentration. It may seem a little surprising that such a dispute should arise especially in view of the effects of the waves of mergers that have been experienced in both the UK and the US. The very large and obvious effects these merger waves had on industrial structure have been pointed out by, for instance, Markham (1955), Nelson (1959) and Hannah (1976). The great majority of the major corporations which dominate the economies of both countries have expanded by merger at some time in their history.

Broadly speaking, it is possible to identify four main techniques by which the various authors have arrived at their conclusions: (1) Detailed case studies; (2) tests for correlation between measures of merger activity and changes in concentration; (3) attempts to explain changes in the size distribution of firms, and hence concentration, by models of internal growth; (4) the construction of artificial size distributions of firms intended to reflect what would have happened in the absence of mergers.

V.1 *Case studies*

The earliest work in the US was carried out by Moody (1904) who found that during the 1887/1904 merger wave, mergers tended to produce substantial increases in market control. For the same period Livermore (1935) found that just under half of his list of mergers resulted in the creation of firms with enough power 'markedly to influence the market'. Markham (1955) surveys the evidence on this and subsequent merger waves and concludes that although the later mergers contributed to increases in aggregate concentration their influence on industry concentration was much less pronounced.

Evely and Little (1960) adopt a similar approach for the UK except that they pose the slightly different question of whether in high concentration trades mergers have been responsible for market dominance. They identify 36 trades for which in 1951 the three-firm (or in one case four-firm) concentration ratio exceeds 67% and find that in most cases, mergers were responsible for high concentration. Hart, Utton and Walshe (1973) survey a random sample of thirty products over the period 1958–63. The concentration changes for the thirty products varied widely. For one product there was no change, for eight products concentration declined, for ten it increased primarily because of merger activity, and for the remaining eleven it increased without significant merger activity. Hart *et al* conclude that internal and external growth had approximately equal effects on concentration. An alternative interpretation of these results is that for the ten products where mergers were important, there was a substantial increase in the average unweighted level of concentration of 7.9 percentage points. However, for the twenty products where internal growth was the main cause of change, eleven showed an average increase in concentration of 5.7 percentage points and nine showed a decrease of 5.0 points, so that the overall picture for these twenty industries was one of a very slight increase in the unweighted concentration level.

Walshe (1974) surveys a sample of 32 products for which in 1958 the five-firm concentration ratio exceeded 90%, but concludes that only in eleven of these products did monopoly power arise as a result of merger activity. Mergers were, however, an important weapon used to prevent the subsequent erosion of this power. Walshe's sample is similar to that of Evely and Little in many respects but it includes many more new-technology products. This could account for his slightly different conclusion since one would expect that such firms would have had less need to resort to mergers to obtain a strong market position. Hart and Clarke (1980) extend the results of Hart *et al* (1973) to 1968, and conclude that mergers were responsible for half of the increase in average product concentration.

V.2 *Correlation methods*

Hannah (1976) constructs three indices of merger activity for the UK—the number of firms that disappear, the value of these firms, and the proportion of total investment expenditure of manufacturing firms accounted for by expenditure on acquisitions and mergers. None of the three indices can be regarded as ideal but they all show a broad correlation with changes in concentration. In particular the share of the hundred largest firms increased rapidly in the 1920s and 1960s, which were both periods of intense merger activity, and the fall in concentration during the 1930s and 1940s coincided with a period of low merger activity. George (1972) argues that mergers had a substantial effect on concentration in the UK over the period 1958/68. He shows that those industrial sectors which experienced the sharpest increases in concentration also tended to display big reductions in the number of companies with assets of over half a million pounds—disappearances that were predominantly due to mergers and acquisitions. In a second article (1975) it was found that industrial sectors which experienced substantial merger activity also tended to have the most striking increases in the five-firm concentration ratio.

The other applications of the correlation approach examine the impact of mergers at the industry level. Gratton and Kemp (1977) set out to explain changes in concentration at the four-digit industry level. Although their study is not intended to examine the impact of mergers as such, they include in their explanatory variables dummy variables to indicate industries with high, medium, and low merger activity. For their sample as a whole they find only the high merger activity variable to be statistically significant. The same conclusion emerges when the regression model is tested for producer goods alone, but for the consumer goods industries mergers do not appear to have been a significant influence. For all three equations the R^2 values are rather low. One point which should be stressed is that the importance of the merger variable in the regression equations is not indicated by the size of the estimated regression coefficient alone but depends also on the variation of the merger measure over the sample. Ideally, it would be best to proceed by decomposing the explained variation of the regression, or the overall value of R^2, into the separate contributions of the individual explanatory variables. Unfortunately, however, no suitable decomposition of this nature can be carried out (see Theil, 1971), but it is possible to consider the incremental contribution of the merger variables, *given* the other explanatory variables used. On this basis, Gratton and Kemp's results imply that over their sample as a whole the merger variable increases the explained variation by only about 2.5%. For producer goods alone the figure rises to around 4.5%.

Hart and Clarke (1980) also include merger activity in their list of variables chosen to explain concentration changes in 76 industries over the period 1958–68. The merger variable turns out to be significant, with a *t*-statistic of 2.6. However, the contribution of the merger variable to the overall explanation of the variation in concentration change is small, accounting for only 4.6% of the total variation, and the authors emphasise "the small part individually played by each of the independent variables". The importance of the merger variable is, however, likely to be understated, and for a number of reasons, as the authors clearly recognise. Their study deals with concentration at the 3-digit level, but in the absence of merger data at this level they were forced, as were Gratton and Kemp, to use 2-digit data instead. This has two effects. First, it increases the magnitude of the merger variable since the two-digit data includes mergers between firms in different three-digit industries and so the regression coefficient will be reduced. Secondly, since the merger variable takes on the same value for each three-digit industry within a particular two-digit grouping its variance will be kept artificially low. Hence the regression coefficient will be biassed downwards and the contribution of mergers to concentration change will be understated.

V.3 *Fitting models of internal growth*

This subject has been dealt with in some detail in the previous section, but it also has some relevance here, so it may be worth repeating briefly some of the salient points. If it could be demonstrated that a particular model of internal growth generates size distributions similar to those observed in practice then one would necessarily begin to doubt the importance of mergers as a major factor leading to higher levels of concentration. However, our earlier discussion indicates that there are a number of plausible models, from which it is difficult to make a choice. The difficulty is compounded by a certain amount of confusion between internal and external growth. The various theoretical models are presumed to relate to internal growth alone, but as far as statistical tests are concerned the data almost invariably include both the internal *and* external elements of growth. A model of the internal growth of firms may only appear plausible because it has been tested using data on overall growth. Thus, even though Prais (1976) shows that a simple Gibrat model is broadly consistent with the upward trend in concentration over this century, this can hardly be used to deny the importance of mergers.

V.4 *The counter-factual approach*

It is true by definition that the impact of any phenomenon can be described by comparing what actually happened with what would have happened without it. Thus to examine the effects of mergers we require "counter-factual" assumptions about what would have happened to aquired firms if they had remained independent. It is obvious that choosing the most appropriate assumption poses some difficulty.

A simple example of the approach is found in Lintner and Butters (1950). They show that for the period 1940–47 in the US the value of assets acquired by merger was small compared to the increase in the hundred firm asset concentration ratio for manufacturing industry. Also in the US, Weston (1953) examined a population of 74 firms over the period 1905–48 and concluded that the value of assets acquired amounted to only one third of overall growth.

An important defect in these studies, however, as Weston recognises, is that the potential internal expansion of the acquired companies is absorbed into the actual internal expansion of the acquiring company. In effect it is assumed that in the absence of the merger the acquired firm would have remained the same size as it was at the date of takeover. An alternative, and in general more realistic counter-factual assumption is that the growth rate of the two separate parties to a merger would have been the same as that of the merged firm. To illustrate what difference these alternative assumptions can make consider the following simple example.

	Firm A's Sales (Acquirer)	*Firm B's Sales (Acquired)*	*Industry Sales*
1970	400	200	1000
1980	1100		2000

Firms A and B are assumed to operate in the same industry and A acquires B in 1970. The first approach to estimating the effect of the merger reasons as follows. In 1980 A's share of industry sales without the acquired firm would have been 1100 – 200, or 45%. Its actual share was 55%. Thus the acquisition has increased A's share by 10 percentage points, from 45% to 55%, whereas internal growth is responsible for the remaining increase in market share of 5 percentage points. The second approach argues that in 1970 the acquisition of B increased A's share of industry sales by 20 percentage points to 60%. Since A's share in 1980 is 55% it would be concluded that the acquisition had caused an increase of 20 percentage points in A's share, whereas internal growth alone would have caused A's share to fall by 5 percentage points.

There are bound to be many cases where the actual outcome in the absence of merger would have been different from the counter-factual assumption adopted. For instance, if a merger resulted in managerial problems the independent firms might have grown faster than the merged company. Internal growth will therefore have been underestimated and the contribution of the merger overestimated. However, short of individual case studies (which would still not give a conclusive answer) a general statement of the most likely alternative position has to be made and the assumption that in general the relative sizes of the acquiring and acquired firms would have remained unchanged would seem to be a reasonable one.

More formally the counter-factual procedure can be described as follows. Denote the sizes of the firms in operation at the beginning of the study period by $x_1, x_2, \ldots, x_n$, and sizes at the end of the period by $y_1, y_2, \ldots, y_m$. Suppose that firms of size x_1 and x_2 are merged during the period to form a new firm of size y_1. The method is then to construct a vector $\mathbf{x}^*$ for the beginning of the period forming a new value x_1^* by adding x_1 and x_2. The estimate of the change in concentration due to internal growth is then the difference between $C(\mathbf{x}^*)$ and $C(\mathbf{y})$ where C denotes the chosen measure of concentration: the effect of mergers is estimated by the difference between $C(\mathbf{x})$ and $C(\mathbf{x}^*)$. It is also possible to demerge the size-distribution at the end of the period, forming a vector $\mathbf{y}^*$, then comparing $C(\mathbf{x})$ and $C(\mathbf{y}^*)$ to estimate internal growth.

This procedure was adopted by Hart and Prais (1956) in their study of concentration in UK manufacturing industry. They separate their population of firms into two groups, one denoted by subscript 1, involved in merger activity, the other denoted by subscript 2, not involved in merger activity. Their chosen measure of concentration is the variance of logarithms which for all its disadvantages has the advantage that it permits a simple decomposition of the total variance of log sizes in terms of the means and variances of the two groups:

$$\sigma^2 = w_1\sigma_1^2 + w_2\sigma_2^2 + w_1w_2(\bar{X}_1 - \bar{X}_2)^2$$

where w_1 and w_2 are the respective proportions of firms in the two groups, and $\bar{X}_1$, $\bar{X}_2$, σ_1^2 and σ_2^2 are the means and variances of log sizes for the two groups. This decomposition simplifies the construction of the hypothetical concentration value $C(\mathbf{x}^*)$. It is a simple matter to identify the sub-group of firms involved in amalgamations and then to calculate new values of σ_1^2 and $\bar{X}_1$ on the assumption that all mergers take place at the beginning of the period. The value of w_1 will fall, since after the amalgamations the surviving firms will be smaller in number. Comparing the resulting hypothetical distributions with the actual, Hart and Prais conclude that over the period 1896–1950 only a small proportion of any increases in concentration could be attributed to mergers. As shown in the table below, they find very little difference between the observed variance of logarithms at the beginning of each period, and the hypothesised variance.

	1896–1907	*1907–24*	*1924–39*	*1939–50*
Total variance at beginning of period	3.89	3.79	5.61	6.01
Total variance after amalgamation	3.85	3.86	5.69	6.13

Source: Hart & Prais (1956), Table 10.

In contrast Utton (1971), using the same concentration measure for the period 1954–65, concludes that the influence of mergers was substantial. He uses the slightly different counter-factual assumption that without mergers firms would have grown at the same rate as the industries in which they operated. Mergers appeared to account for almost half of the measured increase in concentration for manufacturing industry as a whole, and were the dominant factor in several industrial groups. Nevertheless it may still be the case that the use of σ^2 has understated the importance of mergers.

Aaronovitch and Sawyer (1975a and 1975b) examine the period 1958–68 using the simple concentration ratio and find that external growth was more important than internal growth as a determinant of increased concentration.

Hannah and Kay (1977) use their own concentration index to consider four periods, 1919–30, 1930–48, 1957–69, and 1969–73. For the first period, using a range of concentration ratios and values of their elasticity parameter together with the same counter-factual assumption as Hart and Prais they conclude, in strong contrast to Hart and Prais' findings for this period, that mergers accounted for more than half of the increase in concentration. Moreover they argue that their estimate is a lower bound since, when firms in their population acquire other firms, the transaction is treated as internal growth. Their result is obtained by de-merging the 1919 size distribution, but a similar result emerges if the end of period distribution is used instead.

Between 1930 and 1948 merger activity was much lower and concentration declined in the population of firms studied. For the third period mergers accounted for over 100% of the observed increase in concentration for all values of θ. In other words internal growth alone would have resulted in a decline in concentration. For example, they calculate that the share of the 100 largest firms rose by 14.8 percentage points from 60.1% to 74.9% over the period: mergers were responsible for an increase of 15.2 percentage points, whereas internal growth alone caused a small reduction of 0.4 percentage points. Similar results emerge if $HK(\theta)$ is used. Hannah and Kay also break down the internal growth into two components. One component is the differential growth effect, i.e. the difference in the average growth rates of large and small firms. If large firms on average grow more slowly than small ones this will reduce concentration. The other component is the stochastic element which exists even if firms of all sizes have the same expectation of growth. This effect will of course lead to an increase in concentration, but for the period 1957–69 it is outweighed by the negative contribution of the differential growth effect so that the net contribution of internal growth is negative. Similar conclusions are arrived at for the period 1969–73.

The main disagreement over the question of the importance of mergers in explaining increases in concentration is between Hart and Prais and Hannah and Kay. For the period 1919 to 1930 for instance Hannah and Kay conclude that mergers contributed between one half and three quarters of the increase in the market share of the top 100 manufacturing firms. Hart and Prais, however, concluded that mergers had a negligible effect on the level of concentration over this period. Hart (1979) also argues that Hannah and Kay have grossly exaggerated the contribution of mergers to increased concentration in the UK in the period 1957–73. There are two basic points at issue, one relating to the choice of concentration measure, the other to the data.

Hart and Prais have been criticised for their use of the variance of logs as their concentration measure. Without the assumption of Log-Normality there is certainly a danger that σ^2 will not respond correctly to mergers. But even in the Log-Normal case the firms involved in amalgamations are usually relatively small in number so the difficulties outlined on page 210 become important. There, in discussing the Log-Normal model, it was pointed out that where the number of firms N is fixed, so that only partial transfers can occur, σ^2 increases if large firms gain market share at the expense of smaller ones. However, in the case of mergers (i.e. complete transfers) N falls. This fall in N affects the value of σ^2 and may in fact be large enough to conceal the concentration-increasing effect of mergers. The table below is taken from table 9 of Hart and Prais (1956). It is apparent that for all periods the

FIRMS INVOLVED IN AMALGAMATIONS
Units = Log_2

	1896–1907		*1907–24*		*1924–39*		*1939–50*	
	Before	*After*	*Before*	*After*	*Before*	*After*	*Before*	*After*
Number	11	5	40	13	58	25	109	50
Mean	1.18	2.2	1.15	3.54	1.59	3.24	1.93	4.0
Variance	5.47	6.56	5.18	3.01	6.30	5.06	6.93	4.52

Source: Hart and Prais (1956).

proportionate reduction in N is always significant, and that for all periods after 1907 the variance for firms involved in amalgamations falls: it rises only slightly in the period 1896–1907. The use of σ^2 therefore seems to convey an incorrect impression of the impact of mergers on this subset of firms. In terms of the decomposition equation on page 243, amalgamations reduce σ_1^2 from 1907 onwards, and the weight w_1 also falls. The third term in the equation rises in each case, but merely serves to *balance* the perverse effect of mergers on σ_1^2, leaving the overall variance, in the table on p. 243, little changed. With a more suitable measure of concentration both of these effects (on σ_1^2 and on the difference between the geometric mean size) should work in the same direction. It would seem, therefore, that the Hart–Prais results may have been distorted by their use of σ^2 regardless of whether the size distribution can be assumed to be Log-Normal. However, Hannah and Kay (1977 and 1981) argue that in spite of its deficiencies the application of σ^2 to their own data appeared to register a similar overall trend in concentration to that shown by their index, and that it probably did not lead Hart and Prais to underestimate the impact of mergers. They conclude therefore that the differences in the results arrived at by the two pairs of protagonists must in the main be due to differences in the data base.

Hart and Prais (1956) confined their analysis to firms quoted on the London stock exchange whose shares were actively traded. Hannah and Kay (1977 and 1981) argue that Hart and Prais failed to identify a large number of mergers between quoted companies and also omitted altogether acquisitions involving unquoted companies, and consequently that this large uncovered area of acquisition activity would have been classified wrongly as internal growth. In order to minimise the danger of attributing growth through merger to internal growth Hannah and Kay include in their 1919 population firms which were known to have been subsequently acquired by other firms in the population, as well as some firms which were not involved in mergers. Their procedure meant that a small company was more likely to be included in their population if it were subsequently acquired than if it were not. Hart (1979) and (1981) argues that this overstates the merger rate and so imparts a serious upward bias to the Hannah–Kay estimates of the impact of mergers. Hannah and Kay concede that an upward bias may have resulted because their population probably increased its share of the manufacturing section *and* because internal growth probably contributed more to this element of concentration increase than it did to the concentration increase within their population. However, their attempts to allow for the likely quantitative importance of this bias suggests that at the very most the contribution of mergers to the increased market share of the 100 largest firms in the UK over the period 1919 to 1930 might fall from their original estimate of 77% to about one-half.

In the US the issue lay dormant for some time following the controversy of the early 1950s. However, Ijiri and Simon (1971) argue that mergers have not led to increased concentration. They begin by quoting the conclusion of Adelman (1964) that the concentration ratio averaged over industries showed no increase between 1931 and 1960. They then derive necessary and sufficient conditions under which their chosen concentration measure, the Pareto coefficient, will remain unaffected by mergers. These conditions, (that both the probability of disappearance of a firm and the percentage growth of surviving firms should be independent of size), appeared to hold for a selection of firms. However, as shown by Boyle (1973), averaging concentration over industries makes no allowance for the effects of diversification and Adelman's estimates of concentration trends are at variance with many other authors. Also, as pointed out in Section I the Pareto coefficient is a dubious concentration index measuring, as it does, inequality rather than concentration. Indeed one could almost use the conclusion of Ijiri and Simon as further evidence of its deficiencies. It is interesting to note that the same authors reach a different conclusion in a later study (1974). Using improved data for the period 1948–69 they constructed a de-merged distribution for 1969 and found that mergers had served to increase the Pareto slope by 7%, from 1.015 to 1.089.

V.5 *Concluding comments*

There are obvious difficulties involved in choosing appropriate counterfactual assumptions. If, for example, all mergers in the UK had been prohibited by law this would have changed the 'rules of the game' and firms would have behaved differently. A proportion of firms that were in fact acquired would have gone to the wall; the others would have been forced to realise their growth plans entirely by internal expansion. This would undoubtedly have made life more difficult for all concerned but particularly so perhaps for those firms that were in fact acquired. Indeed it is possible, in theory at least, that in the absence of mergers internal growth would have completely replaced external growth, in the sense that all of the taken-over firms would in any case have disappeared, in which case mergers simply lead to the same size distribution as would have occurred through internal expansion. Such speculation, however, will never succeed in getting at the truth. We are on firmer ground when we compare the post-war experiences of the UK and the US. In the US since 1950 there has been tough anti-merger legislation, particularly against horizontal and vertical mergers. As was seen in Section IV, there has been only a modest increase in concentration. In the UK, on the other hand, merger legislation has in general been permissive and concentration has increased very substantially. When all the facts and arguments have been assembled it is difficult to escape the conclusion that mergers have been the dominant factor in increasing concentration.

B. Curry and K. D. George
Department of Economics,
University College,
P.O. Box 78,
Cardiff, CF1 1XL

ACCEPTED DECEMBER 1981

APPENDIX: OTHER MEASURES OF CONCENTRATION

(a) The mean of the so-called 'first moment distribution' of firms' sizes, suggested by Niehans (1958). This is given by

$$\bar{X}_1 = \sum \frac{x_i^2}{x_i} = \sum x_i H$$

where x_i are firms' sizes and H denotes the Herfindahl index.

As pointed out by Hannah and Kay (1977) this amounts to applying the Herfindahl index to absolute sizes as opposed to firms' shares, giving what *they* call an 'absolute concentration' index. For an exposition of the use of moment distributions see Hart (1975).

(b) The Rosenbluth (1961) index, also advocated by Hall and Tideman (1967). This is defined as

$$R = \frac{1}{2\sum is_i - 1}$$

i.e. firms' shares are weighted by their rank positions. The index measures the area above the concentration curve and satisfies all of the Hall-Tideman axioms, but not Hannah and Kay's fourth axiom concerning the effects of mergers.

(c) The 'comprehensive concentration index' suggested by Horvath (1970). This is defined as

$$\text{CCI} = s_1 + \sum_{i=2}^{N} s_i^2(2 - s_i)$$

where s_1 is the share of the largest firm.

The index is similar to twice the Herfindahl index minus the sum of the cubes of firms' shares, except that greater weight is assigned to the share of the largest firm. It is intended to reflect both the relative size of the largest firm and the dispersion by size of all firms in the distribution, but as pointed out by Horowitz (1972) it may not satisfy the principle of transfers.

(d) The Pareto slope, advocated by Ijiri and Simon (1971). If the Pareto distribution is plotted on double logarithmic scales, the distribution function is linear, and its slope can be calculated if it is fitted to an observed size-distribution. The main motivation for using such a measure is that it has firm foundations in statistical theory, but it fails to satisfy the principle of transfers.

(e) The Linda index (1976), defined by

$$L = \frac{1}{N(N-1)} \sum_{i=1}^{N-1} Q_i$$

where Q_i is the ratio between the average share of the first i firms and the average share of the remaining $N - i$ firms.

This index is designed to measure the degree of inequality between values of the size variable accounted for by various sub-samples of firms. It is also intended to define the boundary between the oligopolists within an industry and other firms. Although used by the European Community, its designation as a measure of inequality suggests its disadvantages.

(f) The U Index, suggested by Davies (1980b). This has the general form

$$U = I^{*a} N^{-1}$$

where I^* is an accepted measure of inequality (in practice the coefficient of variation is suggested)
a is a constant
N is the number of firms.

Davies (1979) noting the relationship between the Hannah–Kay index, the number of firms and the variance of logarithms in the Log-Normal case, suggests that a concentration index should in general depend on both N and the inequality of firms' shares. His suggested index takes a simple multiplicative form with the parameter 'a' left to be estimated rather than being chosen *a priori*. This would apparently give the U index an advantage over $HK(\theta)$ since the elasticity parameter θ cannot be determined from the seven axioms. However, the properties of U need to be explored in more detail, and it should be noted that θ could in principle also be estimated, although the estimation procedure would be more complex.

REFERENCES

AARONOVITCH, S. and SAWYER, M. C., *Big Business; Theoretical and Empirical Aspects of Concentration and Mergers in the U.K.* (Macmillan, London) (Referred to as 1975(a)).

AARONOVITCH, S. and SAWYER, M. C., 'Mergers, Growth and Concentration', *Oxford Economic Papers*, 27, **1** (March 1975) pp. 136–55. (Referred to as 1975(b)).

ADELMAN, M. A., US Senate, Committee on the Judiciary, Sub-committee on Anti-trust and Monopoly Hearings "Economic Concentration" (1964).

ADELMAN, M. A., 'Comment on the "H" Concentration Measure as a Numbers Equivalent', *Review of Economics and Statistics* (February 1969), pp. 99–101.

AITCHISON, J. and BROWN, J. A. C., *The Lognormal Distribution*, (Cambridge University Press, Cambridge, 1957).

ANDREWS, P. W. S., 'Industrial Analysis in Economics with Special Reference to Marshall', in T. Wilson and P. W. S. Andrews (ed.) *Oxford Studies in the Price Mechanism*, (Clarendon Press, Oxford, 1951).

ANDREWS, P. W. S., *On Competition in Economic Theory*, (Macmillan, London, 1964).

ANDREWS, P. W. S. and BRUNNER, E., *Studies in Pricing*, (Macmillan, London, 1975).

ARCHER, S. H. and MAGUIRE, J., 'Firm Size and Probabilities of Growth', *Western Economic Journal*, **3** (Summer 1965), pp. 233–46.

ARMSTRONG, A. and SILBERSTON, A., 'Size of Plant, Size of Enterprise, and Concentration in British Manufacturing Industry 1935–58', *Journal of the Royal Statistical Society*, series A, 128, **3** (1965), pp. 395–420.

ATKINSON, A. B., 'On the Measurement of Inequality', *Journal of Economic Theory*, 2, **3** (Sept. 1970), pp. 244–63.

BAIN, J. S., *Barriers to New Competition*, (Harvard University Press, Cambridge, Mass. 1956).

BAILEY, D. and BOYLE, S. E., 'The Optimal Measure of Concentration', *Journal of the American Statistical Association*, **66**, No. 336 (1971), pp. 702–6.

BANNOCK, G., *The Juggernauts, The Age of the Big Corporation*, (Penguin Books Ltd., Harmondsworth, 1973).

BLAIR, J. M., *Economic Concentration: Structure, Behaviour and Policy*, (Harcourt Brace Jovanovitch, New York, 1972).

BOX, G. E. P. and JENKINS, G. M., *Time Series Analysis: Forecasting and Control*, (Holden–Day, San Francisco, 1971).

Boyle, S. E., 'The Average Concentration Ratio: An Inappropriate Measure of Industry Structure', *Journal of Political Economy*, 81, **1** (1973), pp. 414–26.

Boyle, S. E. and Sorenson, R. L., 'Concentration and Mobility: Alternative Measures of Industry Structure', *Journal of Industrial Economics*, XIX, **2** (April 1971), pp. 118–32.

Brunner, E., 'Industrial Analysis Revisited', in P. W. S. Andrews and Elizabeth Brunner, *Studies in Pricing*, (Macmillan, London, 1975).

Caves, R. E. and Porter, M. E., 'The Dynamics of Changing Seller Concentration', *Journal of Industrial Economics*, XXIX, (September 1980), pp. 1–15.

Central Statistical Office, *Standard Industrial Classification*, 3rd edition, (London, 1968).

Champernowne, D. G., 'A Model of Income Distribution', *Economic Journal*, **63** (June 1953), pp. 318–51.

Chesher, A., 'Testing the Law of Proportional Effect', *Journal of Industrial Economics*, XXVII, **4** (June 1979), pp. 403–411.

Collins, N. R. and Preston, L. E., 'The Size Structure of the Largest Industrial Firms 1909–1958', *American Economic Review*, **51** (Dec. 1961), pp. 986–1011.

Collins, N. R. and Preston, L. E., 'Price-Cost Margins and Industry Structure', *Review of Economics and Statistics*, **51** (August 1969), pp. 271–86.

Comanor, W. J. and Wilson, T. A., 'Advertising, Market Structure and Performance', *Review of Economics and Statistics*, **49** (November 1967), pp. 423–44.

Cowling, K. and Waterson, M., 'Price-Cost Margins and Market Structure', *Economic*, **43** (1976), pp. 767–74.

Creedy, J., 'The Principle of Transfers and the Variance of Logarithms', *Oxford Bulletin of Economics and Statistics*, **39** (1977), pp. 152–8.

Davies, S., 'Choosing Between Concentration Indices: the Iso-Concentration Curve', *Economica*, **46** (February 1979), pp. 67–75.

Davies, S., 'Minimum Efficient Size and Seller Concentration: An Empirical Problem', *Journal of Industrial Economics*, XXVIII, **3** (March 1980), pp. 287–301. (Referred to as 1980(a)).

Davies, S., 'Measuring Industrial Concentration: an Alternative Approach', *Review of Economics and Statistics*, LXII, **2** (May 1980), pp. 306–9. (Referred to as 1980(b)).

Downie, J., *The Competitive Process*, (Duckworth, London, 1958).

Duchesneau, T. D., 'Barriers to Entry and the Stability of Market Shares: A Note', *Journal of Industrial Economics*, XXII, **4** (June 1974), pp. 315–20.

Engels, F., Note inserted into Volume 3 of Marx's *Capital*, (1887). See Marx (1887).

Engwall, L., *Models of Industrial Structure*, (Lexington Books, Lexington, Massachusetts, 1973).

Evely, R. & Little, I. M. D., *Concentration in British Industry*, (Cambridge University Press, Cambridge, Massachusetts, 1960).

Feinberg, R. M., 'The Lerner Index, Concentration and the Measurement of Market Power' *Southern Economic Journal*, 46, **4** (April 1980), pp. 1180–86.

Fellner, L., "Comment" in "Business Concentration and Price Policy", National Bureau of Economic Research, (Princeton University Press, Princeton, 1955).

Florence, P. S., *The Logic of Industrial Organization*, (Routledge & Kegan Paul, London, 1933).

Galbraith, J. K., *The New Industrial State*, (André Deutsch, London, 1967).

Galbraith, J. K., *Economics and the Public Purpose*, (André Deutsch, London, 1974).

George, K. D., 'Changes in British Industrial Concentration 1951–58', *Journal of Industrial Economics*, XV, **3** (Nov. 1967), pp. 200–11.

George, K. D., 'The Changing Structure of Competitive Industry', *Economic Journal*, **82** (March 1972 Supplement), pp. 353–68.

GEORGE, K. D., 'A Note on Changes in Industrial Concentration in the U.K.', *Economic Journal*, **85**, No. 337 (March 1975), pp. 124–28.

GEORGE, K. D. and WARD, T., *The Structure of Industry in the EEC*, (Cambridge University Press, Cambridge, 1975).

GORT, M., 'Analysis of Stability and Change in Market Shares', *Journal of Political Economy*, **71** (February 1963), pp. 51–63.

GRATTON, C. and KEMP, J. R., 'Some New Evidence on Changes in U.K. Industrial Market Concentration', *Scottish Journal of Political Economy*, 24, **2** (June 1977), pp. 177–81.

GREER, D. F., 'Advertising and Market Concentration', *Southern Economic Journal*, **38** (July 1971), pp. 18–32.

GROSSACK, I. M., 'Towards an Integration of Static and Dynamic Measures of Industry Concentration', *Review of Economics and Statistics*, XXXVII (August 1975), pp. 301–8.

GROSSACK, I. M., 'The Concept and Measurement of Permanent Industrial Concentration', *Journal of Political Economy*, **80** (1972), pp. 745–60.

GUTH, L. S., 'Advertising and Market Structure Revisited', *Journal of Industrial Economics*, **19** (April 1971), pp. 179–98.

H.M.S.O., 'A Review of Monopolies and Merger Policy' CMND.7198, (London, 1978).

HALL, M. and TIDEMAN, N., 'Measures of Concentration', *Journal of the American Statistical Association*, **62** (March 1967), pp. 162–68.

HANNAH, L., 'Managerial Innovation and the Rise of the Large Scale Company in Interwar Britain', *Economic History Review* (Second Series), **27** (May 1974), pp. 252–70.

HANNAH, L., *The Rise of the Corporate Economy*, (Methuen, London, 1976).

HANNAH, L. and KAY, J. A., *Concentration in Modern Industry: Theory, Measurement and the U.K. Experience*, (Macmillan, London, 1977).

HANNAH, L. and KAY, J. A., 'The Contribution of Mergers to Concentration Growth: A Reply to Professor Hart', *Journal of Industrial Economics*, XXIX (3), (1981), pp. 305–13.

HART, P. E., 'The Size and Growth of Firms', *Economica*, **29** (Feb. 1962), pp. 29–39.

HART, P. E., 'Entropy and other Measures of Concentration' *Journal of the Royal Statistical Society*, Series A, 134, **1** (1971), pp. 73–85.

HART, P. E., 'Moment Distributions in Economics: An Exposition', *Journal of the Royal Statistical Society*, Series A, **138** (Part 3) (1975), pp. 423–34.

HART, P. E., 'On Bias and Concentration', *Journal of Industrial Economics*, XXVII (3), (1979), pp. 211–16.

HART, P. E., 'Lognormality and the Principle of Transfers' *Oxford Bulletin of Economics and Statistics*, 42, **3** (August 1980), pp. 263–67.

HART, P. E., 'The Effects of Mergers on Industrial Concentration' *Journal of Industrial Economics*, XXIX, **3** (March 1981), pp. 315–20.

HART, P. E. and CLARKE, R., *Concentration in British Industry 1935–75*, (N.I.E.S.R. Cambridge, 1980).

HART, P. E. and PRAIS, S. J., 'The Analysis of Business Concentration: a Statistical Approach', *Journal of the Royal Statistical Society*, Series A, **119** (1956), pp. 150–91.

HART, P. E., UTTON, M. A. and WALSHE, G., *Mergers and Concentration in British Industry*, (Cambridge University Press, Cambridge, 1973).

HAUSE, J. C., 'The Measurement of Concentrated Industrial Structure and the Size Distribution of Firms', *Annals of Economic and Social Measurement*, 6, **1** (1977).

HERFINDAHL, O. C., 'Concentration in the U.S. Steel Industry' (Unpublished thesis, Columbia Univerisity, New York, 1950).

HILFERDING, R., *Finance Capital*, (1910). A recent English language edition is published by Routledge and Kegan Paul, London, 1981.

HIRSCHMAN, A. O., *National Power and the Structure of Foreign Trade*, (University of California Bureau of Business & Economic Research, Berkeley, 1945).

HOROWITZ; A. R. and HOROWITZ, I., 'Entropy, Markov Processes and Competition in the Brewing Industry,' *Journal of Industrial Economics*, **16** (July 1968), pp. 196–211.

HOROWITZ, A: R., 'A Suggestion for a Comprehensive Measure of Concentration: a Comment', *Southern Economic Journal*, XXXVIII, **4** (April 1972), p. 602.

HORVATH, J., 'A Suggestion for a Comprehensive Measure of Concentration', *Southern Economic Journal*, XXXVI, **4** (April 1970), pp. 446–52.

IJIRI, Y. and SIMON, H. A., 'Business Firm Growth and Size', *American Economic Review*, **54** (March 1964), pp. 77–89. (Reprinted in Ijiri and Simon (1977)).

IJIRI, Y. and SIMON, H. A., 'Effects of Mergers and Acquisitions on Business Firm Concentration', *Journal of Political Economy*, **79** (March/April 1971), pp. 314–22. (Reprinted in Ijiri and Simon (1977)).

IJIRI, Y. and SIMON, H. A., 'Interpretations of Departures from the Pareto Curve Firm-Size Distributions', *Journal of Political Economy*, **82** (1974), pp. 315–31. (Reprinted in Ijiri and Simon (1977)).

IJIRI, Y. and SIMON, H. A., *Skew Distributions and the Size of Business Firms*, (North Holland, Amsterdam, 1977).

JACQUEMIN, A. P. and DE JONG, H. L., *European Industrial Organisation* (Macmillan, London, 1977).

JACQUEMIN, A. P. and KUMPS, A.-M., 'Changes in the Size-Structure of the Largest European Firms: an Entropy Measure', *Journal of Industrial Economics*, XX, **1** (November 1971), pp. 59–70.

KALDOR, N., 'Market Imperfections and Excess Capacity', *Economica*, **2** (February 1935), pp. 33–50.

KALECKI, M., 'On the Gibrat Distribution', *Econometrica*, **13** (January 1945), pp. 161–70.

KWOKA, J. E., 'Does the Choice of Concentration Measure Really Matter?', *Journal of Industrial Economics*, XXIX, **4** (June 1981) pp. 445–453.

KAMERSCHEN, D. R., 'Market Growth and Industry Concentration', *Journal of the American Statistical Association*, (March 1968), pp. 228–41.

KAY, J. A. and KING, M., *The British Tax System*, (Oxford University Press, Oxford, 1978).

KILPATRICK, R. W., 'The Choice among Alternative Measures of Industrial Concentration', *Review of Economics and Statistics*, XLIX, **2** (May 1967), pp. 258–60.

LERNER, A. P., 'The Concept of Monopoly and the Measurement of Monopoly Power', *Review of Economic Studies*, 1, **3** (1934), pp. 157–75.

LINDA, R., 'Methodology of Concentration Analysis Applied to the Study of Industries and Markets', Commission of E.E.C. (Brussels, 1976).

LINTNER, J. A. and BUTTERS, J. K., 'Effects of Mergers on Industrial Concentration 1940–47' *Review of Economics and Statistics*, XXXII, **1** (Feb. 1950), pp. 30–48.

LIVERMORE, S., 'The Success of Industrial Mergers' *Quarterly Journal of Economics*, 50, **1** (November 1935), pp. 68–96.

LYONS, B. R., 'Price-Cost Margins, Market Structure and International Trade'. Paper presented to the A.U.T.E. Conference, Exeter, (1979).

LYONS, B. R., 'A New Measure of Minimum Efficient Plant Size in U.K. Manufacturing Industry', *Economica*, **47** (February 1980), pp. 19–34.

MARKHAM, J. W., 'Survey of the Evidence of Findings on Mergers' in *Business Concentration and Price Policy*, National Bureau of Economic Research, (Princeton University Press, Princeton, 1955).

MARX, K., *Capital* (1887). (For a more recent edition see e.g. Lawrence and Wishart, London 1972–74).

MEADE, J. E., 'Is the New Industrial State Inevitable?', *Economic Journal*, 78, **2** (June 1968), pp. 372–92.

MEANS, G., US Senate, Committee on the Judiciary, Sub-committee on Antitrust and Monopoly, Hearings, "Economic Concentration". (1964).

MERMELSTEIN, D., 'Large Industrial Corporations and Asset Shares', *American Economic Review*, **59** (September 1969), pp. 531–41.

MILLER, R. A., 'Marginal Concentration Ratios and Industrial Profit Rates: Some Empirical Results', *Southern Economic Journal*, XXXIV (October 1967), pp. 259–67.

MILLER, R. A., 'Marginal Concentration Ratios as Market Structure Variables', *Review of Economics and Statistics*, LIII, **3** (August 1971), pp. 289–93.

MOODY, J., *The Truth about the Trusts*, (Moody Publishing Co., 1904).

MUELLER, W. F. and HAMM, L. G., 'Trends in Industrial Concentration', *Review of Economics and Statistics*, 56, **4** (November 1974) pp. 511–20.

MUELLER, W. F. and ROGERS, R. T., 'The Role of Advertising in Changing Concentration of Manufacturing Industries', *Review of Economics and Statistics*, 62, **1** (February 1980), pp. 89–96.

NEEDHAM, D., *The Economics of Industrial Structure, Conduct and Performance*, (Holt, Rinehart and Wilson, Eastbourne, Sussex, 1978).

NELSON, R. L., *Merger Movements in American Industry 1895–1956*, (Princeton University Press, Princeton, 1959).

NELSON, R. L., 'Market Growth, Company Diversification, and Product Concentration 1947–54', *Journal of the American Statistical Association*, **55**, No. 292 (December 1960), pp. 640–49.

NELSON, R. L., *Concentration in the Manufacturing Industries of the United States: A Mid-Century Report*, (Yale University Press, Newhaven, 1963).

NIEHANS, J., 'An Index of the Size of Industrial Establishments', *International Economic Papers*, **8** (1958), pp. 122–32.

NIGHTINGALE, J., 'On the Definition of "Industry" and "Market"', *Journal of Industrial Economics*, XXVII, **1** (September 1978), pp. 1–12.

NUTTER, G. L., *The Extent of Enterprise Monopoly in the United States*, (Chicago University Press, Chicago, 1951).

ORNSTEIN, S. E., WESTON, J. F., INTRILLIGATOR, M. A. and SHRIEVES, R. E., 'Determinants of Market Structure', *Southern Economic Journal*, XXXIX (April 1973), pp. 612–25.

PAGOULATOS, E. and SORENSON, R., 'A Simultaneous Equation Analysis of Advertising, Concentration and Profitability', *Southern Economic Journal*, 47, **3** (January 1968), pp. 728–41.

PASHIGIAN, B. P., 'Market Concentration in the United States and Great Britain', *Journal of Law and Economics*, **11** (October 1968), pp. 299–319.

PASHIGIAN, B. P., 'The Effect of Market Size on Concentration', *International Economic Review*, **10** (October 1969), pp. 291–314.

PENROSE, E. T., *The Theory of the Growth of the Firm*, (Blackwell, Oxford, 1959).

POPPER, K. R., *The Poverty of Historicism*, (Routledge and Kegan Paul, London, 1961).

PORTER, M. E., 'Consumer Behaviour, Retailer Power and Market Performance in Consumer Goods Industries', *Review of Economics and Statistics*, 56, **4** (November 1974), pp. 419–436.

PRAIS, S. J., *The Evolution of Giant Firms in Britain*, (Cambridge University Press, Cambridge, 1976).

PRAIS, S. J., 'Industrial Concentration: the Role of Statistical Theory', *Oxford Bulletin of Economics and Statistics*, 42, **3** (August 1980), pp. 269–72. (Referred to as 1980(a)).

PRAIS, S. J., 'On Mr. Sawyer's Reply', *Oxford Bulletin of Economics and Statistics*, 42, **3** (August 1980), pp. 279–80. (Referred to as 1980(b)).

PRAIS, S. J., 'The Contribution of Mergers to Industrial Concentration: What do we know?', *Journal of Industrial Economics*, XXIX, **3** (March 1981), pp. 321–29.

PRATTEN, C. F., *Economies of Scale in Manufacturing Industry*, (Department of Applied Economics, Occasional Paper No. 28, Cambridge, 1971).

QUANDT, R. E., 'On the Size Distribution of Firms', *American Economic Review*, **56** (June 1961), pp. 416–32.

RÉNYI, A., *Probability Theory*, (North Holland, Amsterdam, 1970).

ROSENBLUTH, G., 'Measures of Concentration', in N.B.E.R. 'Conference on Business Concentration and Price Policy', (Princeton University Press, Princeton, 1955).

ROSENBLUTH, G., Gesprach über Messung der Industriellen Konzentration", in *Die Konzentration in der Wirtschaft*, (Arndt ed.), (Berlin (1961)).

ROTHSCHILD, K. W., 'The Degree of Monopoly', *Economica*, IX (Feb. 1942), pp. 24–39.

SAMUELS, J. M., 'Size and the Growth of Firms', *Review of Economic Studies*, **32** (April 1965), pp. 105–12.

SAMUELS, J. M. and CHESHER, A. D., 'Growth, Survival and the Size of Companies, 1960–9', in K. Cowling (ed.), *Market Structure and Corporate Behaviour*, (Gray-Mills, London 1972).

SAVING, T. R., 'Estimation of Optimum Size of Plant by the Survivor Technique', *Quarterly Journal of Economics*, LXXV, 4 (November 1961), pp. 569–607.

SAVING, T. R., 'Concentration Ratios and the Degree of Monopoly', *International Economic Review*, 11, **1** (February 1970), pp. 139–46.

SAWYER, M. C., 'Concentration in British Manufacturing Industry', *Oxford Economic Papers*, **23** (November 1971), pp. 352–83.

SAWYER, M. C., 'The Variance of Logarithms and Industrial Concentration', *Oxford Bulletin of Economics and Statistics*, 41, **2** (May 1979), pp. 165–81.

SAWYER, M. C., 'The Variance of Logarithms and Industrial Concentration: A Reply', *Oxford Bulletin of Economics and Statistics*, 42, **3** (August 1980), pp. 273–78.

SCHERER, F. M., *Industrial Market Structure and Economic Performance*, (Rand McNally, Chicago, 1970).

SCHERER, F. M., *et al.*, *The Economics of Multiplant Operation*, (Harvard University Press, Cambridge, Mass., 1975).

SCHMALENSEE, R., 'Using the H-Index of Concentration: with Published Data', *Review of Economics and Statistics*, LIX, **2** (May 1977), pp. 186–93.

SHALIT, S. S. and SANKAR, U., 'The Measurement of Firm Size', *Review of Economics and Statistics*, LIX, **3** (August 1977), pp. 290–98.

SHEPHERD, W. G., 'Trends of Concentration in American Manufacturing Industries', *Review of Economics and Statistics*, XLVI, **2** (May 1964), pp. 200–12.

SHEPHERD, W. G., 'Changes in British Industrial Concentration 1951–8', *Oxford Economic Papers*, 18, **1** (March 1966), pp. 126–32.

SHEPHERD, W. G., 'Structure and Behaviour in British Industries, with U.S. Comparisons', *Journal of Industrial Economics*, XXI, **1** (November 1972), pp. 35–54.

SHEPHERD, W. G., *The Treatment of Market Power: Antitrust, Regulation, Public Enterprise*, (Columbia University Press, New York, 1975).

SILBERMAN, I. H., 'On Lognormality as a Summary Measure of Concentration', *American Economic Review*, **57** (Sept. 1967), pp. 807–31.

SILBERMAN, I. H., 'Lognormality and Concentration: Reply', *American Economic Review*, **58** (December 1968), pp. 1370–71.

SILBERSTON, Z. A., 'Economies of Scale in Theory and Practice', *Economic Journal*, **82** (March 1972 Supplement), pp. 369–91.

SIMON, H. A., 'On a Class of Skew Distribution Functions', *Biometrika*, **42** (Dec. 1955), pp. 425–40. (Reprinted in Ijiri and Simon, 1977).

SIMON, H. A. and BONINI, C. P., 'The Size Distribution of Business Firms', *American Economic Review*, **48** (Sept. 1958), pp. 607–17. (Reprinted in Ijiri and Simon (1977)).

SINGH, A. and WHITTINGTON, G., *Growth, Profitability and Valuation*, (Cambridge University Press, London, 1968).

SINGH, A. and WHITTINGTON, G., 'The Size and Growth of Firms', *Review of Economic Studies*, XLII, **1** (1975), pp. 15–26.

SMYTH, D. J., BOYES, W. J. and PESSAN, D. E., 'The Measurement of Firm Size: Theory and Evidence for the United States and the United Kingdom', *Review of Economics and Statistics*, XLII (Feb. 1975), pp. 111–13.

STEINDL, J., *Random Processes and the Growth of Firms*, (Hafner, New York, 1965).

STIGLER, G. J., 'Monopoly and Oligopoly by Merger', *American Economic Review*, XL, **2** (May 1950), pp. 23–24.

STIGLER, G. J., 'A Theory of Oligopoly', *Journal of Political Economy*, LXXII, **1** (February 1964), pp. 44–61.

STRICKLAND, A. D. and WEISS, L. W., 'Advertising, Competition, and Price-Cost Margins', *Journal of Political Economy*, 84, **5** (Dec. 1976), pp. 1109–21.

SWEEZY, P. M., *The Theory of Capitalist Development*, (Monthly Review Press, New York, 1942).

THEIL, H., *Economics and Information Theory*, (North Holland, Amsterdam, 1967).

THEIL, H., *Principles of Econometrics*, (North Holland, Amsterdam, 1971).

UNITED STATES BUREAU OF THE BUDGET, *Standard Industrial Classification Manual*, (Washington, D.C., 1967).

UTTON, M. A., 'The Effects of Mergers on Concentration: UK Manufacturing Industry 1954–65', *Journal of Industrial Economics*, XX, **1** (1971), pp. 42–58.

WALSHE, G., *Recent Trends in Monopoly in Great Britain*, N.I.E.S.R., (Cambridge University Press, Cambridge, 1974).

WEISS, L. W., 'Factors in Changing Concentration', *Review of Economics and Statistics*, **45** (Feb. 1963), pp. 70–7.

WESTON, J. F., *The Role of Mergers in the Growth of Large Firms*, (University of California Press, California, 1953).

WHITE, L. J., 'What has been Happening to Aggregate Concentration in the U.S.?', *Journal of Industrial Economics*, XXIX, **3** (March 1981), pp. 223–30.

WILLIAMSON, O. E., *Corporate Control and Business Behaviour*, (Prentice Hall, Englewood Cliffs, N.J., 1970).

WRIGHT, N. R., 'Product Differentiation, Concentration and Changing Concentration', *Review of Economic and Statistics*, LX, **4** (Nov. 1978), pp. 628–31.

THE JOURNAL OF INDUSTRIAL ECONOMICS
Volume XXXI March 1983 No. 3

THE PERFORMANCES OF MERGING FIRMS IN JAPANESE MANUFACTURING INDUSTRY: 1964–75

KATSUHIKO IKEDA AND NORIYUKI DOI*

I. INTRODUCTION

IN postwar years, firm mergers have tended to be worldwide. The merger trends are interesting for two reasons. First, they reflect the patterns of firm behavior in each country. Secondly, they suggest intercountry differences of public policies toward business. But both the public policies and economic analysis of mergers are still in a transitional stage. Thus, the understanding of merger problems leaves room for serious controversy.

In Japan, large mergers began to appear around the mid-1960s. The peak of the merger movement was the Yahata Steel–Fuji Steel merger (the new name is Nippon Steel) in 1970, which gave rise to the largest firm in Japan, and the world's second steel producer. Since the proposal, there has been a substantial amount of controversial discussion regarding the effects of mergers, especially large mergers. However, the empirical evidence of their effects is still scanty.[1]

The effects of mergers can be operationally classified into two aspects; the first is concerned with the performances of merging firms; the second is concerned with the possible effects of mergers on competition and overall concentration. The aim of the present study is to bring forward the additional evidence of the microeconomic effects of mergers, that is, the financial performances of merging firms in Japanese manufacturing industry.[2] The performances tested are: (1) profitability; (2) efficiency; (3) firm growth; (4) research and development.

* We wish to express our thanks to Professors F. M. Scherer, D. C. Mueller, C. K. Rowley, G. E. Buscom, and an anonymous referee of this Journal for their insightful suggestions and comments on an earlier version of this paper. We are, of course, responsible for any remaining errors and shortcomings.

[1] A few comprehensive studies have been made in Japan. Baba [1], Economic Planning Agency [4], Hoshino [7], and MITI [13, 14] show different results. But each of these studies has some of the following problems: (1) sample size is small; (2) smaller and insignificant mergers are included; (3) the mergers which occurred during the period marked by the "feverish larger mergers" are not included; (4) the paired firms which are not direct competitors are included; (5) the relative evaluation of merger performance in comparison with other rival firms is not used. Also, case studies may be found in Miwa [15], Shinohara [20] and Takayanagi [23].

[2] For the effects of mergers on industrial and overall concentration in Japan, see Ikeda and Doi [8].

II. MOTIVES FOR MERGERS

Firm mergers include three types: horizontal, vertical and conglomerate mergers, of which each may have different motives. However, among the more usual motives are the following: (1) increasing market share or market power; (2) increasing efficiency, especially realization of scale economies; (3) increase of research and development (hereafter denoted as R & D); (4) investment adjustment or avoidance of overlapping investment; (5) promotion of fund-raising capacity; (6) firm growth; (7) reducing risk of business, etc. These motives are not mutually exclusive. Then, the above motives are reduced to (1) increasing market share or market power; (2) increasing efficiency; (3) firm growth, and (4) increase of R & D.

If the motives of the mergers are recognized, then the results can be found in terms of the corresponding measures. We shall explain *a priori* the relationship of the main motives and the alleged results.

First, increasing market share or market power of merging firms may lead to increased profitability through higher prices of their products. Then, the performance may be a reflection of the "independent market power" of the merging firms, and/or of the reinforcement of "oligopolistic coordination," since mergers may increase the market share of the merging firms and the concentration of the industry concerned. The likelihood of anticompetitive effect, and concomitantly higher profitability, increases with the degree of industrial concentration or market share of dominant firms.

But the relationship may be disturbed by *X*-inefficiency, since increasing market power may induce "quiet life" and thereby lead to higher cost.

Secondly, increasing efficiency or cost saving effect will appear at various levels, such as innovation and scale economies in production and distribution, which ultimately leads to increased profitability. It is the motive which most merging firms always emphasize, particularly in large mergers. But, the cost savings effect also may be decreased or cancelled out by *X*-inefficiency ascribable to increasing market power and/or expansion of firm size.

Thirdly, firms may desire external growth because of various reasons: personal utility of management, an alternative to expansion investment, etc. Firm growth is reflected in rate of growth of sales, or assets, or employees, etc.

Finally, increase of R & D is frequently one of the main motives. The rationale is the "Schumpeter hypothesis," which considers firm size or market power as a factor favorable to technological progress. The alleged results are increased R & D expenses, and the appearances of new products or processes.

The market power and efficiency motives are, among them, of a particular significance. However, in fact, the effects of mergers on market power and efficiency remain now open problems. There have been many discussions regarding the relative importance of the two effects, and also these discussions raise the practical problem of disentangling one effect from the other. Then one of the most important analyses for the clarification of those problems is to make the *a posteriori* evaluation of financial performances of merging firms.

III. STATISTICAL CONSIDERATION

Forty-nine merging firms which were subject to merger performance tests, were selected from the firms which engaged in mergers during 1964–75. They were listed in Tokyo, Osaka, and Nagoya Stock Exchange. Most of them were also equivalent to the "main mergers" included in *The Annual Report of the Fair Trade Commission* (Ministry of Finance, Printing Bureau, each year). The analytical period of the merger performances was extended from 1959 to 1977, since five years before and after mergers were taken in principle.

1. *Measures of merger performance*

The measures of merger performance and the rationale for their inclusion are described below.

(1) Profitability (RE and RA). It is used as the overall measure of merger performance, of which the measures are often stock price or profit rate.[3] In this test, profit rate was used, since stock prices do not always reflect profitability because of an imperfect stock market in Japan. The used measures of profit rate are the average current profit before tax as a percentage of end-of-year equity (rate of return on equity; denoted as RE), and the average current profit before tax plus interest as a percentage of end-of-year total assets (rate of return on total assets; denoted as RA).

However, the profit rates used here may include the underestimate and/or overestimate of post-merger performance; RE may have upward distortion due to change in equity-total assets ratio; both RE and RA may have upward bias due to accounting convention used in period of merger when mergers do not occur at the beginning of the financial period, but may have downward bias because acquirers value acquired firms' assets at more than book value ("watered assets" problem). These problems are emphasized by Meeks and Meeks [12].

In this study, RE and RA are used, and are based on end-of-year equity and assets respectively. And, while merger performance is computed by including the performance in the period of merger when merger occurred at the beginning of the acquirer's financial period, it is computed by excluding the performance in the period of merger when merger

[3] In Japan's studies, the market valuation of merging firms was used only in Miwa [15]. Other studies used profit rate.

occurred at the end and in the middle of the financial period.[4] This approach takes into consideration the above problems. Even though the "watered assets" problem remains open, it will not distort our conclusion, as seen later, since that problem is likely to lead to an underestimate of post-merger performance.

(2) Selling, general and administrative expenses/sales (SG). It is included to examine the effects of mergers on efficiency in the selling and administrative sections of merging firms.

(3) Sales/total assets (SA). Sales as a percentage of end-of-year total assets is the measure which tests the effect of mergers on sales activity or equipment utilization. It is of course one of the efficiency measures.

(4) Sales/employee (SE). Sales/end-of-year employee is included as a proxy for productivity.

(5) Rate of firm growth (GR). It is the average of the year-to-year percentage change of sales, which is a measure for growth motive.

(6) R & D expenses (RD1) and its ratio to sales (RD2). They are the expenses for R & D included in income statements of firms, and R & D expenses/sales. They are included to test the alleged firm size–R & D activity relationship.

All measures defined above were computed from *Yuka Shoken Hokokusho* (*The Annual Report Under Securities and Exchange Act*), and Mitsubishi Research Institute, *Kigyo Keiei No Bunseki* (*Analysis of Firm Management*).

2. *Estimation methods of merger performance*

This study estimates merger performances through two tests: absolute test and relative test.

The first test, entitled the absolute test, is to compare post-merger performance of merging firms with their pre-merger performance. Then the

[4] In this study, when mergers occurred at the beginning of the financial period, for example, profitability of the first post-merger year can be shown by:

$$(\Pi_t + \Pi_{t+1})/K_{t+1} \qquad \text{(Half-Yearly Closing Account System)}$$

and

$$\Pi_t/K_t \qquad \text{(Yearly Closing Account System)}$$

where Π is profit (RE) or profit plus interest (RA), K equity (RE) or total assets (RA), and t period of merger. On the other hand, when mergers occurred at the end and in the middle of the financial period, it is:

$$(\Pi_{t+1} + \Pi_{t+2})/K_{t+2}$$

and

$$\Pi_{t+1}/K_{t+1}, \text{ respectively.}$$

Also, pre-merger profitability and then the other performance measures of acquiring firms can be calculated in the same way. Thus, this approach suggests that one year used here is not always corresponding to one financial year.

measure is the average performance in the given period after merger/the corresponding one in the same period before merger. The pre-merger performance is, in principle, that of acquiring firms. But, in case of merger between two big firms with almost equal size, we used a weighted average of their performances. The test is represented by:

$$(1) \qquad \dot{Am} = \overset{+}{Am}/\overline{Am}$$

where $\overset{+}{Am}$ = post-merger performance of measure A in merging firm M, $\overline{Am}$ = its pre-merger performance. $\dot{Am} > 1$ means the improvement effect of merger, $\dot{Am} < 1$ indicates the adverse effect, and $\dot{Am} = 1$ suggests constant performance.

The second test, entitled the relative test, is to examine the performances of the merging firms, compared with those of other rival firms in the industry to which the merging firms belong. This approach can exclude influences of the business cycle which may affect the results in the absolute test. But at the same time, it may exclude influences of the changed market structure consequent upon a merger, because all firms in the industry may enjoy them.

The performance paired for this test is the pooled one of main rival firms in the industry concerned, not the whole industry or one firm with no merger. Then, the industry is, in principle, based on the four-digit classification. And the main rival firms may engage in mergers during the analytical period of performances of merging firms. The performances of merging firms should be, we think, evaluated in comparison with the main rival firms, whether the latter may engage in mergers or not.[5] The second test is represented by:[6]

$$(2) \qquad \dot{Am}/\dot{Ao} = (\overset{+}{Am}/\overline{Am})/(\overset{+}{Ao}/\overline{Ao}) = (\overset{+}{Am}/\overset{+}{Ao})/(\overline{Am}/\overline{Ao})$$

where $\overset{+}{Ao}$ = pooled performance of main rival firms in the corresponding period after the merger of firm M, $\overline{Ao}$ = their performance in the corresponding period before the merger, and other notations are as defined earlier. $\overset{+}{Am}/\overset{+}{Ao}$ or $\overline{Am}/\overline{Ao}$ is called as relative performance, such as relative profit rates. If $\dot{Am}/\dot{Ao} > 1$, this is an indication that performance measure A of a merging firm M is improved in comparison with that of its main rivals, and *vice versa* if $\dot{Am}/\dot{Ao} < 1$. $\dot{Am}/\dot{Ao} = 1$ means constant relative performance.

IV. EMPIRICAL RESULTS

1. *Results of the absolute test*

Table I gives the distribution of improvement and deterioration, according to $\overset{+}{Am}/\overline{Am} \lesseqgtr 1$, as defined in equation (1). Then, the sample size was 49 cases in

[5] Professor D. C. Mueller suggested that including other merging firms in the control group sample made it difficult to evaluate the merger's effects. This problem may be important in some industries.

[6] This approach is different from those used by the previous studies, but is also applied in U.S., FTC [5].

TABLE I
DISTRIBUTION OF NUMBER OF MERGING FIRMS, BY MERGER PERFORMANCE: ABSOLUTE TEST

Performance Measure	Three-Year Test			Five-Year Test		
	increase	*decrease*	*total No. of firms*	*increase*	*decrease*	*total No. of firms*
Analysis 1						
RE	29	20	49	28	20	48
RA	24	25	49	28	20	48
SG	20	29	49	21	27	48
SA	25	24	49	27	21	48
SE	48	1	49	48	0	48
GR	27	22	49	28	20	48
RD_1	24	3	27	19	3	22
RD_2	15	12	27	11	11	22
Analysis 2						
RE	13	5	18	13	5	18
RA	11	7	18	12	6	18
SG	8	10	18	8	10	18
SA	10	8	18	10	8	18
SE	17	1	18	18	0	18
GR	9	9	18	10	8	18
RD_1	10	0	10	10	0	10
RD_2	6	4	10	6	4	10

Notes: (1) Notation: RE = rate of return on equity, RA = rate of return on total assets, SG = selling, general, and administrative expenses/sales, SA = sales/total assets, SE = sales/employee, GR = firm growth rate, RD1 = R & D expenses, RD2 = R & D expenses/sales; (2) Analysis 2 is concerned with "big mergers"; (3) For RE, RA, SA, SE, GR, RD1, RD2, improvement = increase, deterioration = decrease, and for SG, improvement = decrease, deterioration = increase.

the three-year test, but one case was excluded from them because of no availability of its financial data in the five-year test. There were some cases in which the change in profit rates was meaningless because of negative equity or negative profit rates. But we classified each case as improved or deteriorated, according to the attached signs or their changes.

R. & D expenses of 27 cases (three-year test) and 22 cases (five-year test) were available in the published data.

In the three-year test, rate of return on equity increased in more than half the cases, but rate of return on total assets was improved in about half the cases. But, both profit rates showed improvement in more than half the cases in five-year test. These findings suggest that firm performances after mergers began to be improved along with the internal adjustment of the merging firms. In other words, there was a necessary gestation period during which merging firms learn how to manage their new organizations.

Selling, general and administrative expenses/sales, sales/total assets, sales/employee, and firm growth rate showed improvement in more than half the cases of both the tests. While R & D expense increased in most of the available cases, its ratio to sales increased in a little more than or just half the cases.

On the other hand, if the analysis was confined to the "big mergers"[7] (18 cases), profit rates indicated improvement in more cases, while in the other measures, except sales/employee, there were not necessarily many cases with improvement.

However, the gained results should be interpreted prudently, since the covered periods of each merger case were different, ranging from 1959 to 1977. The "absolute" merger performances may depend largely on the business cycle. Therefore, these results are subject to the reservations.

2. *Results of the relative test*

Table II shows the distribution of improvement and deterioration, according to the relative merger performance index, as defined in equation (2). Also, for the problem of negative signs, we took the same step as in the absolute test. In this test, some cases were excluded because the "main rival firms" in the industries concerned were not able to be identified exactly. Then, the sample size was 44 cases in the three-year test, and 43 cases in the five-year test.

But, R & D performance test was not included here, since R & D data of the paired firms were not sufficiently available.

TABLE II
DISTRIBUTION OF NUMBER OF MERGING FIRMS, BY MERGER PERFORMANCE: RELATIVE TEST

	Three-Year Test			*Five-Year Test*		
Performance Measure	*increase*	*decrease*	*total No. of firms*	*increase*	*decrease*	*total No. of firms*
Analysis 1						
$\overline{RE}$	19	25	44	25	18	43
$\overline{RA}$	22	22	44	29	14	43
$\overline{SG}$	20	24	44	17	26	43
$\overline{SA}$	21	23	44	21	22	43
$\overline{SE}$	21	23	44	18	25	43
$\overline{GR}$	22	22	44	25	18	43
Analysis 2						
$\overline{RE}$	12	6	18	12	6	18
$\overline{RA}$	13	5	18	13	5	18
$\overline{SG}$	5	13	18	5	13	18
$\overline{SA}$	10	8	18	10	8	18
$\overline{SE}$	7	11	18	6	12	18
$\overline{GR}$	8	10	18	9	9	18

Notes: (1) Notation: $\overline{RE}$ = relative rate of return on equity, $\overline{RA}$ = relative rate of return on total assets, $\overline{SG}$ = relative, selling, general and administrative expenses/sales, $\overline{SA}$ = relative sales/total assets, $\overline{SE}$ = relative sales/employee, $\overline{GR}$ = relative firm growth rate; (2) Analysis 2 is concerned with "big mergers"; (3) For $\overline{RE}$, $\overline{RA}$, $\overline{SA}$, $\overline{SE}$, $\overline{GR}$, improvement = increase, deterioration = decrease, and for $\overline{SG}$, improvement = decrease, deterioration = increase.

[7] The "big mergers" were selected in terms of absolute size of merging firms, and/or their market position in the industries concerned. But the selection may be arbitrary.

The conclusion gained in the absolute test still holds. In the three-year test, only about half the cases showed improvement in any performance measures. But, in the five-year test, the relative performances of profit rates, selling, general and administrative expenses/sales, and firm growth rate were improved in more cases, while there are more decreases than increases in relative sales/total assets and relative sales/employee.

Especially, the relationship of change in relative profitability to change in absolute profitability was analyzed. The result in the five-year test is summarized in Table III. The absolute improvement in profitability often induced the relative improvement.

TABLE III
THE RELATION OF RELATIVE TEST TO ABSOLUTE TEST: FIVE-YEAR TEST

	Merger Performance		*Profitability*	
Group	*Absolute*	*Relative*	*RE*	*RA*
A	+	+	18	20
B	+	−	8	4
C	−	+	7	9
D	−	−	10	10
Total			43	43

Notes: (1) Notation: RE = rate of return on equity, RA = rate of return on total assets, + = increase, − = decrease; (2) Total number of firms is corresponding to the sampled cases in the relative test.

On the other hand, profit rates were relatively improved in more cases of the "big mergers," but the other performance measures had even the opposite tendency. Particularly, the growth-profitability trade-off relationship is very interesting. In this subgroup, mergers improved profitability, but did not so much contribute to firm growth. The findings seem to be different from those indicated by Baba [1] and Reid [18].

Furthermore, the cases which do not show improved performance, as exemplified by profit rates, are mergers among failing firms or mergers in depressed industries. Among the group are for example, Unitica, Mitsui–Toatsu Chemicals, Mitsui Sugar, and Snow Brand–Andes Foods. This result is also confirmed by the absolute test.

V. CONCLUDING REMARKS

The main results of the present study can be summarized as follows:

(1) There were more than half the cases in which mergers had allegedly improvement effects on the managerial performances of the firms concerned in five-year test, while the merger performances in the three-year

test were inferior to those in the five-year test. This fact may reflect the intra-firm adjustment after mergers.

(2) In the "big mergers" group, there were so many cases with improved profitability. And, the growth-profitability trade-off relationship was found, which was opposite to the findings indicated by earlier works.

(3) The mergers between failing firms did not show improvement in managerial performance.

However, the results are subject to two shortcomings, which are shared by virtually all studies of merger performance. First, this type of study cannot evaluate the post-merger performance of merging firms exactly, because we cannot consider the possible performance gained if they do not engage in merger. Secondly, it is difficult to derive the net effect of mergers, since the basic conditions of the economy often change.

Our findings are suggestive, although tentative in nature. Mergers typically resulted in improvement in profit performance in Japanese manufacturing industry.[8] This result is likely to be in contrast to the findings in the U.S. and the U.K., but is not inconsistent with the result of West Germany.[9]

Katsuhiko Ikeda and Noriyuki Doi,
Kwansei Gakuin University,
Uegahara,
Nishinomiya,
Hyogo,
662 Japan.

ACCEPTED DECEMBER 1981

REFERENCES

[1] BABA, M., *Economics of Anti-Monopoly* (In Japanese, Tokyo: Chikuma Shobo, 1974).

[2] CHIPLIN, B. and LEES, D., *Acquisition and Mergers, Government Policy in Europe* (London: The Financial Times, 1976).

[3] COWLING, K., STONEMAN, P. *et al.*, *Mergers and Economic Performance* (Cambridge: Cambridge University Press, 1980).

[4] ECONOMIC PLANNING AGENCY, *Economic White Paper: 1968* (In Japanese, Tokyo: Ministry of Finance, Printing Bureau, 1968).

[5] FEDERAL TRADE COMMISSION, *Economic Report on Conglomerate Merger Performance, An Empirical Analysis of Nine Corporations* (Washington, D.C.: United States Government Printing Office, November 1972).

[8] Our conclusion does not necessarily hold true in another sector. In fact, performances of firm mergers in the tertiary sector were not so improved as those of the "manufacturing" mergers. The managerial performance of those firms may include higher weight of human element and thereby cannot be so easily improved by integration of some organizations.

[9] Studies of other countries may be found in Cowling, Stoneman, *et al.*, [3], Hogaty [6], Kumps [9], Lev and Mandelker [10], Meeks [11], Mueller [17], Reid [18], Ryden [19], Singh [21], and Weston and Manshingka [24].

And the survey of merger performance may be found in Chiplin and Lees [2], Mueller [16], Reid [18] and Steiner [22].

[6] HOGARTY, T. F., "The Profitability of Corporate Mergers", *Journal of Business*, 43, No. 3. (July 1970), pp. 317–27.

[7] HOSHINO, Y., "An Analysis of the Effects of Mergers", (In Japanese). *Keiei Ronshu* (Toyo University), **8**. (December 1977), pp. 67–160.

[8] IKEDA, K. and DOI, N., "Mergers and Firm Concentration in Japanese Manufacturing Industry", *Industrial Organization Review*, **8** (1980), pp. 1–26.

[9] KUMPS, A.-M., *Le Conglomerat, Nouvelle Forme de Concentration: Le Cas Anglais* (Paris: La Renaissance du Libre, 1974).

[10] LEV, B. and MANDELKER, G., "The Microeconomic Consequences of Corporate Mergers," *Journal of Business*, 45, No. 1. (January 1972), pp. 85–104.

[11] MEEKS, G., *Disappointing Marriage: A Study of the Gains from Merger* (Cambridge: Cambridge University Press, 1977).

[12] MEEKS, G. and MEEKS, J. G., "Profitability Measures as Indicators of Post-Merger Efficiency," *Journal of Industrial Economics*, XXIX, No. 4. (June 1981), pp. 335–44.

[13] MINISTRY OF INTERNATIONAL TRADE AND INDUSTRY, *Effects and Problems in Firm Mergers* (In Japanese, Tokyo: Ministry of Finance, Printing Bureau, 1963).

[14] MINISTRY OF INTERNATIONAL TRADE AND INDUSTRY, *Firm Mergers: The Realities From Firm Management* (In Japanese, Tokyo: Ministry of Finance, Printing Bureau, 1970).

[15] MIWA, Y., "Effects of Big Mergers: Nippon Steel and the Dai-Ichi Kangyo Bank" (In Japanese). *Keizai Hyoron*, 27, No. 5. (May 1978), pp. 95–105.

[16] MUELLER, D. C., "The Effects of Conglomerate Mergers: A Survey of the Empirical Evidence", *Journal of Banking and Finance*, 1, No. 4. (December 1977), pp. 315–47.

[17] ——, (ed.), *The Determinants and Effects of Mergers: An International Comparison* (Cambridge: Oelgeschlager, Gunn and Hain, 1980).

[18] REID, S. R., *Mergers, Managers and the Economy* (New York: McGraw-Hill, 1968).

[19] RYDEN, B., *Mergers in Swedish Industry, An Empirical Analysis of Corporate Mergers in Swedish Industry, 1946–69* (Stockholm: Almqvist and Wiksell, 1972).

[20] SHINOHARA, M., *Industrial Structure*, 2nd ed. (In Japanese, Tokyo: Chikuma Shobo, 1976).

[21] SINGH, A., *Take-Overs* (Cambridge: Cambridge University Press, 1971).

[22] STEINER, P. O., *Mergers, Motives, Effects, Policies* (Ann Arbor: University of Michigan Press, 1975).

[23] TAKAYANAGI, S., "Managerial Merits and Demerits in Firm Concentration." In Chuo University, Institute of Economic Research (ed.), *Firm Concentration and Industrial Reorganization.* (In Japanese, Tokyo: Toyo Keizai Shinposha, 1971).

[24] WESTON, J. F. and MANSHINGHKA, S. K., "Tests of the Efficiency Performance of Conglomerate Firms", *Journal of Finance*, XXVI, No. 4. (September 1971), pp. 919–36.

THE JOURNAL OF INDUSTRIAL ECONOMICS
Volume XXXI March 1983 No. 3

THE CAUSES AND CONSEQUENCES OF ABANDONED MERGERS*

J. F. PICKERING

I. INTRODUCTION

MUCH attention has been paid in recent years to various aspects of the merger process and its implications for different groups in society. On balance, the evidence tends to suggest: that mergers have contributed to concentration increase; that the selection process tends to penalise smaller firms rather than less profitable companies; and that, on the basis of both quantitative and qualitative evidence, the effects of mergers tend, on balance, to be unfavourable in terms of the effects on efficiency and profitability.[1]

One of the critical methodological issues in attempting to study the effects of mergers is the need to establish what was likely to have happened had the merger not proceeded. In order to handle this, some studies have compared merging companies with control groups, others have compared merger-intensive companies with infrequent acquirers, while others have solely concentrated on the experiences of acquiring companies. For British evidence see Cowling *et al.* [1], Liesner [2], Meeks [3].

There is, however, one aspect of this that has not been extensively studied and which may help in various ways to shed light upon the possible alternative position had a merger not proceeded. This is the phenomenon of those proposed mergers that were abandoned after the possibility of merger had been made public (abandoned mergers). Previous investigation tends to suggest that this phenomenon occurs quite frequently. About one in seven of all the proposed mergers that qualified for investigation by the Monopolies and Mergers Commission (MMC) 1965–75 were abandoned (Pickering [5]). The experiences of such cases that nearly, but not quite, resulted in a merger might be particularly relevant both to the study of the merger process and to clarification of possible alternative outcomes had the merger not proceeded.

This paper is therefore concerned with reporting the results of an essentially qualitative study of such instances of abandoned mergers. The evidence was compiled from extensive desk research and literature reviews relating to such cases that occurred 1965–75; a postal questionnaire was used to follow up as

* The research reported in this paper was assisted by a grant from the Social Science Research Council and research assistance funded by the University of Manchester Institute of Science and Technology. Miss B. A. Lawson acted as research assistant in this investigation. A longer version of this paper was presented at the EARIE Conference in 1979 and is available as UMIST Department of Management Sciences Occasional Paper No. 7906.

[1] Much of the evidence is reviewed in Liesner [2]. It is surprising that evidence on the selection process involved in mergers (e.g. Singh [7]) is not reviewed there.

many cases as possible. In addition, 20 cases were studied in depth, involving also interviews in the companies concerned, merchant banks, government departments etc.[2] This methodology means that it is not practicable to attempt to quantify much of the information collected. However, the conclusions point to certain hypotheses and implications which would now be amenable to quantitative testing.

II. THE CHARACTERISTICS OF ABANDONED MERGERS

In our earlier analysis of the incidence of abandoned mergers (Pickering [5]) we showed that abandonments tended to be more likely in those cases where the size of the assets to be acquired was greater and where the target companies (i.e. those being bid for) were large relative to the bidders. Apart from this and also the possibility that the stock market was less likely to have anticipated the bid in the case of proposed mergers that were later abandoned (Smail [8]) it does not seem that the characteristics of abandoned mergers were very different from those that proceeded.

A broad spectrum of companies became involved in abandoned mergers. There were examples of strong and weak companies among both bidders and targets. Among the bidders there were certainly some that were fast growing and had a high stock market rating. A number had, however, already been in difficulties and sought to make an acquisition in order to overcome a particular problem or weakness such as: the slow growth in principal product areas; widely fluctuating earnings because of the trade cycle; the need to add products to spread overheads; the desire to increase size to reduce their own sense of vulnerability.

The target companies also represented a wide cross-section. Some were, by general agreement, successful companies whose very qualities in terms of management and growth made them particularly attractive takeover targets. However, many of the targets were, at the time, vulnerable and were recognised (including by the management concerned) as vulnerable to a takeover bid. Frequently it seems this was the case with a company that, though inherently sound and well managed, had suffered a short-term loss or downturn in performance. This may have been due to: a crippling strike in a plant; the effects of difficult trading conditions; the adverse consequences of fixed price contracts when the rate of inflation began to increase rapidly; the effects of recent heavy expenditures in marketing or increasing the workforce which, while important to the long term prospects of the company, in the short term adversely affected the Profit and Loss account. Thus a fall in the relative stock market rating of an inherently strong and attractive company seems likely to have prompted a takeover bid. However, in the inherent strengths of such

[2] It is interesting to note that whereas in studies of actual mergers it is often worthwhile talking also to trade associations, competitors and customers, in this study because the proposed mergers had not taken place such potential sources of information were much less useful.

companies lay, perhaps, the seeds of their own ability to escape an unwanted takeover.

However, not all the target companies involved in abandoned mergers could be categorised in this way. Others were vulnerable because of high liquidity or the presence of undervalued assets which offered the prospect of asset stripping. Others faced managerial problems, had an excessive dependence on a slow growing and unprofitable sector of the market or were weakened by the effects of a large minority shareholding in the company.

In other respects too, abandoned mergers appeared to have similar characteristics to those mergers studied by others (e.g. Newbould [4]) that did proceed. Thus, the logic advanced in the cases of abandoned mergers tended to emphasise such considerations as: the scope for synergy and cost reductions; benefits of faster growth and greater size; managerial gains either by using the bidder's management to raise the performance of the target or by using the target's management to raise the performance of the bidder; financial benefits through a more even flow of profits; the opportunity to use either the bidder's or the target's liquidity; the strengthening of the bidder's balance sheet.

The origins of the bids also varied as they do in the case of mergers that proceed. Even some cases that started off as agreed bids or that originated in a 'death wish' by the target ended up as abandoned mergers. It has been observed in other studies that the degree of prior planning and consultation before a proposed merger is announced is often extremely limited. There was no strong evidence that abandonments tended to occur where the parties to a proposed merger had engaged in detailed planning and consultation and had then come jointly to the conclusion that the merger would not work.

So far as management style and structures are concerned, it is clear that in some cases, especially with horizontal mergers, the companies often knew each other well and, quite frequently, were conscious of differences between them in such matters as the personalities of the chief executives or chairmen of the two companies; attitudes to the use of non-executive directors; the nature of organisation (e.g. whether divisionalised etc); the degree of autonomy allowed to local management etc. While it seems likely that such differences between partners exist in many merger cases, not just abandoned mergers, it may be that awareness of differences in management styles and organisational considerations influenced the resolve of some target companies to resist a takeover bid or caused bidders to have second thoughts about their wish to proceed with the acquisition.

III. THE CAUSES OF ABANDONED MERGERS

In this section we shall review the apparent reasons for the abandonment of those proposed mergers which have formed the basis for this study. While four main explanations are identified, it will be apparent that they are closely interrelated.

(a) *Abandonments arising from a change of mind*

A change of heart on the part of either the bidder or the target was a major contributor to some abandonments. In some cases the bidder realised the target was not as attractive as it had at first appeared. This was especially so where unanticipated financial problems were discovered or where assurances regarding the target's recent performance or present circumstances could not be given. Some bidders found that their own financial position had deteriorated so making the acquisition more difficult to complete or that deteriorating general economic conditions reduced the attractions of the acquisition. In other cases, the bidder was shaken by the strength of the initial opposition to the bid and decided not to press on with the bid in what could have been a hostile atmosphere. Such weakening of resolve was encouraged in some cases by the knowledge that not all the bidder's senior management were in favour of the bid in any case.

Even where the merger proposal had the initial agreement of the board of the target company some abandonments still occurred when the target decided it could no longer support the proposals. These changes of heart were caused by unexpected difficulties over the financial terms for the merger; personality clashes; problems concerning the deployment of particular individuals in the merged company; and concerns over possible incompatibilities in management styles. Whereas, if both companies agree the merger would be unworkable then, subject to the Takeover Code, the merger may be called off. If, however, the bidder still wishes to proceed the target has no alternative but to mount a spirited defence against the bid.

(b) *Lack of market support for the bid*

A failure to obtain sufficient acceptances in the market at the price which the bidder finally chooses to offer is perhaps the most obvious cause of an abandoned merger. However, while this is the ultimate cause of the outcome, the reasons and events leading up to this are complex and are best considered in terms of respective bidding and defence strategies.

(i) *Bidding problems*

Bidding problems seem to have both price and non-price aspects. Some companies had problems in arriving at a realistic valuation for their target, especially where the target had not recently revalued its assets and where there was uncertainty on the part of the bidder as to the quality of the assets e.g. whether they were leasehold or freehold. Where an initial offer was resisted, some bidders found difficulties in making a revised offer. In some cases this was because of their own financial weakness or because of the effects of adverse share price movements in the meantime raising the target's stock market valuation relative to that of the bidder. Some bidders were constrained over the size of any increased offer because of the risk of a dilution of the earnings of their own shareholders. In some cases a higher offer based on the issue of new shares would have involved a reverse takeover since the target shareholders would then own the majority of the bidding company's equity.

These explanations do not necessarily indicate a failure on the part of the bidding company. Indeed, some companies felt they had gained in standing, both for their initial identification of a company that was undervalued in the market *and* for their strength of mind in not being prepared to bid up the price beyond that which it would be realistic to pay. In his study of mergers Newbould showed that in many cases the compound rate of growth of post-acquisition earnings that many companies would need to achieve was way beyond what was realistic (Newbould [4]). It certainly seems that some of the bidders in abandoned mergers realised and avoided this danger.

There were, however, also a number of instances where companies acknowledged that they had made errors in bidding strategy which led to the abandonment. Strategic errors were made in relation to the timing of the bid. Some companies felt that a leak or upward movement in the target's share price forced them into a public announcement too early, before they had carried out all necessary appraisals and consultations. Others felt they had perhaps delayed too long in making their formal offer and this had allowed the target's share price to edge up, and/or had given the target's board more time to prepare its defence. The level of the initial offer was also a key strategic issue. While company views vary about the virtues of a high 'foreclosing' offer compared to a lower 'sighting shot', it is apparent that some companies felt, with the benefit of hindsight, that their initial offers had been too low. This therefore made it easier for the target's board to claim justification for resisting the bid, encouraged the market to re-evaluate the target's share price and encouraged other bidders to contemplate a counter offer. A related issue is the question whether bidding companies are well advised to buy shares in their target while a bid is in progress. Clearly, to do so makes the task of obtaining sufficient acceptances less difficult. However, some bidders chose not to buy in the market and, while some claimed this meant they did not have the subsequent problem of what to do with a minority stake, it does seem this was a tactical error.

Wider public relations issues are also important in a takeover bid. Often it seems that lack of attention to such matters contributed to the failure of a bid. The first aspect of this relates to the way in which the target company's board, senior management and employees are approached. It is apparent that in some instances an unduly aggressive initial approach to the target heightened the resolve to defend against the bid and so lessened the bidder's chances of success. With the growing concentration of share ownership in the hands of major institutions together with the influence in some companies of a few key family shareholdings, the need to gain the support of such shareholders is paramount. Some unsuccessful bidders clearly did not handle this aspect effectively and in consequence they also did not gain a favourable response in the City or the financial press. Lack of conviction in the offer documents on the general logic for the merger and on the benefits to the target's shareholders was another contributory factor.

(ii) *Effective defence*

When a target board receives an offer, its duty is to consider and advise on the best interests of all the shareholders. This is, of course, a nebulous concept and in practice there is quite considerable discretion to a board to decide whether it wishes to recommend acceptance of the offer or to resist in the hope of either a higher offer or of remaining independent. In the cases studied, it is apparent that effective defence was an important reason for many abandonments.

The reasons for initially deciding to oppose an offer were numerous including the effect of personality clashes; hostility engendered by the manner of the initial approach; doubts on the logic of the proposed merger; concerns among the board members about their own futures; a preference for remaining independent; a feeling that the offer placed too low a value on the company; a genuine belief that the company would do better on its own.

Whatever the reason, to resist successfully an unwanted takeover bid requires a particularly spirited defence. An important element was the nature of the defence documents issued. They normally contained the grounds for the view that the target was inherently strong and well able to survive on its own. Where the target had suffered a setback it attempted to reassure shareholders that its reorganisation was complete and recovery was well underway. Details of a revised profit forecast, revaluation of assets, the length of order books and assessments of the growth prospects for the markets in which it was operating were normally offered. All this supported the case that the offer clearly undervalued the target.

On the precept that 'attack is a good form of defence', successful defences against a takeover bid often contained an attack on the bidding company, drawing attention to its weaknesses, the lack of industrial logic for the merger and fears of asset stripping. It was often claimed that the bidder would not be able to offer any skills or resources to the benefit of the target.

Some target companies made major efforts to convince the financial press, institutional shareholders and others of the merits of their defence. Indeed, some recognised that previously their public relations had been deficient and that the effect of the takeover battle was to raise substantially the quality of their overall communications with shareholders and the City generally. Some were helped by having major institutions announce that they were not accepting the bidder's offer in respect of shares they held in the target. On occasions a friendly institution or merchant bank bought shares in the market in order to keep up the share price and reduce the proportion of shares committed to accepting the offer.

The publicising of management and/or union opposition to the takeover was also used in the defence in some cases. This may be seen simply as an attempt to discourage the bidder from proceeding for fear of hostility within the company and a loss of key personnel. It may however also be viewed as part of a wider strategy to influence public opinion against the merger and raise the possibility that the merger might be considered to raise questions concerning the wider public interest. This aspect is considered below.

(c) *The operation of competition policy*

Since the Monopolies and Mergers Act 1965 there has been the possibility that the operation of competition policy towards mergers could cause the abandonment of a particular proposed merger (see Pickering [6] for a discussion of the approach taken by the MMC). While the decision to refer is that of the Secretary of State, it is apparent that some companies have pressed for a reference as part of their defence strategy.

The operation of merger policy can cause abandonments at three different points. First, before making a public announcement of the possibility of a merger some companies seek confidential guidance from the Office of Fair Trading as to whether such a merger would be likely to be referred to the MMC. Although precise information is not available on such cases, it seems that between 1965 and 1975 some 50 major proposed mergers were abandoned following receipt of confidential guidance and no doubt a number of these were abandoned because of the possibility of reference to the MMC (Pickering [5]).

Secondly, some abandonments occur at the time a reference is made to the MMC. In fact, about one third of all merger proposals referred to the MMC have been abandoned on reference. Companies that withdrew following a reference have tended to explain that a full MMC enquiry would be costly in management time and would cause several months uncertainty for both the companies concerned. Other observers, however, suggest that some withdrawals have indicated a recognition that the case for the merger was not strong or a concern that information might be published that would be damaging to the bidder.

The third respect in which competition policy is significant is where the MMC reports that a merger would be contrary to the public interest. It is almost inevitable that the merger will not then proceed. However, it is interesting that there have been some instances where the MMC has reported that the merger would not be contrary to the public interest and yet the merger has still not proceeded. It seems that in such cases the MMC investigation may have prompted a reconsideration of the advantages of the merger on the part of the bidder; or relative share price movements in the meantime have made the merger financially more difficult to complete; or, although the MMC has not opposed the merger, the target company has been able to fight off the renewed bid following the report. In this case the additional time (and information) gained as a result of the MMC investigation has allowed a company greater opportunity to mount its defence.

(d) *Other acquisitions*

Just because one takeover bid occurs it does not mean that other activities involving the two companies concerned stand still. There have been instances where other merger activity has prevented the particular merger being completed.

In at least one case the bidding company was acquired while trying to make an acquisition on its own account. Some target companies also made acquisitions thereby becoming larger, more costly to purchase and more difficult to assimilate. In so doing they also possibly changed the nature and emphasis of their organisation so that they were no longer as attractive to the original bidder. Finally, and more frequently, once one bid for the target had been made, other companies also came in with bids. Sometimes these were simply companies whose attention to the possibilities of an acquisition had been alerted by the initial bid. Often, however, it appears that the target would find, or be offered, another more preferred bidder to bid for the target and drive off the unwelcome suitor. In some such cases the target was acquired by the preferred suitor. In other instances it seems the preferred partner was merely waiting in the wings; it did not bid if the target was successfully defending itself and could remain independent. Where the target was having difficulty in resisting the intial bid the second company would produce its counter offer and proceed to acquire.

IV. THE CONSEQUENCES OF ABANDONED MERGERS

In the literature there is considerable material regarding the rather disappointing overall effects of mergers that did go through. But what of those that do not proceed? Many mergers that did proceed might have been prevented, either by stronger resistance by investors, by stronger resistance by the target or through competition policy on mergers. Conversely, a small shift the other way in one or other of these influences could have turned an abandoned merger into a completed merger. So it may be that information on the outcomes of abandoned mergers might help corporate, financial and government policy makers to have a better appreciation of what the alternative outcomes might have been had they resisted other mergers.

(a) *Reactions to the abandonment*

The reactions of unsuccessful bidders tended to polarise. There were those who strongly regretted the abandonment. The reasons for such a view were:

that there had been industrial logic in the proposed merger that would have been of general public benefit; they would have derived an advantage for their own company through increased size, access to new markets or products, or the financial opportunities that the target presented; that they had not handled the proposed merger well and their general strategy in seeking to make the acquisition had been inadequate. Such unsuccessful bidders generally took the view that the failure to acquire had been a traumatic and demoralising experience.

Another group of unsuccessful bidders however had a much lower level of regret at the abandonment and, indeed, in some cases a sense of relief at the outcome. Such reactions were associated with the recognition that the integration of the two companies would have taken more time and effort and would have created more problems than had been originally recognised. Other reasons included the realisation that the bidder's managerial resources would have been very seriously stretched had the merger taken place and relief that particular problems with the target had become apparent before the bidder had been irrevocably committed.

Target companies, naturally, tended to feel a sense of relief and pleasure at the abandonment. They were pleased to have retained their independence, especially as they often claimed the merger would not have worked. The support from shareholders in the takeover battle was treated as an indication of approval and encouragement to the existing senior management and a general increase in morale was often considered to be a benefit of the outcome. On the other hand, there was also evidence of a sense of resentment that so much management time had been deflected from the real business of making and selling their products.

(b) *Action taken as a consequence*

While some companies, mainly unsuccessful bidders, claimed that they had not taken any subsequent action as a result of the abandonment of the particular merger proposals, the vast majority of companies, bidders and targets alike, did attribute a number of subsequent actions directly to the abandoned merger. Indeed, as some bidders pointed out, after a well publicised failure to make an acquisition there is a need to take some other positive action in order to sustain staff morale. In the case of target companies, the problems that a number had faced immediately prior to the merger, together with the sense of crisis at the receipt of an unwanted takeover bid, had created a favourable opportunity for internal changes to strengthen the company.

Three different types of subsequent action could be identified in the case of unsuccessful bidders. First, a number of them made, or attempted to make, an alternative acquisition or to establish links with another company. Some of them feel that they moved into another merger rather on the rebound and had cause to regret this action. Secondly, internal changes were made. The failure to acquire caused a reappraisal of the product or market areas in which they were operating and withdrawal from those where they had been particularly seeking help from the target. Changes in senior management and in the methods of production used occurred in some cases and there were at least two instances where, as a result of the discussions over the proposed merger, the bidders had learned from the target about various techniques which they then introduced into their own activities. The third type of action most frequently reported was the pursuit of internal growth—'growth the hard way' as one company put it. In some cases this involved a greater export effort. In others it meant keener competition with the target they had earlier failed to acquire. These also did not always produce the beneficial results that had been hoped for.

In the case of target companies, the most important response to the abandonment was to seek internal reorganisation and improvement. Given the weakness and vulnerability of a number of the targets at the time of the bid, this is not surprising, but the bid provided a further spur to reorganisation. Board room and senior management changes tended to be reported and rationalisation involving plant closures or sale of subsidaries also occurred. Other actions included the introduction of new organisational structures, moves into new products or markets, investments in new equipment and technology. Some companies realised that they were weak in their public relations and became more purposeful in their release of information. Target companies also paid greater attention to expansion and growth possibilities. Major overseas investments were made and new market opportunities were sought. In some cases, this 'dash for growth' was seen by observers, and confirmed by some of the companies, as entailing a high degree of risk. Mergers also entered the policy of the target companies. Some made acquisitions on their own account on the view that increased size would help reduce the risk of subsequent takeover bid. A few target companies however seemed to conclude that although one proposed merger had been abandoned they were still vulnerable and so arranged to be acquired by a preferred bidder.

Thus, it is apparent that both bidders and targets in abandoned mergers took consequential action. This action had common elements to both groups of companies in that it involved internal reorganisation, the pursuit of internal growth and alternative mergers and acquisitions. The importance attached to these alternatives seems to vary between the two groups and there clearly is cause for concern that some companies rather rushed into an alternative policy without a careful assessment of the likely implications.

(c) *Subsequent experience*

The subsequent experience of the companies involved in abandoned mergers suggests that as many bidders were later in difficulties and/or acquired as were target companies. While a full financial analysis is required fully to demonstrate this, it does appear that in a sizable number of cases target companies did improve and show a strong performance in the years following the abandoned merger. Many bidders appeared to do less well, due in some cases to general economic conditions, though also it seems to the inherent weakness of some of the companies.

For the 20 in-depth case studies an attempt has been made to assess the effects of the abandonment and to try to conclude whether the abandonment is likely to have been in the public interest or not. A view on each case has been reached taking into account the evidence of the subsequent performance of the companies concerned, together with the views of the companies and other observers. On this basis, there are 14 cases where it is considered that it is as well that the merger did not proceed, one case where it seems clearly unfavourable that the merger did not take place and 5 where the matter appears to be finely balanced with some grounds for taking either of the opposing views. As explained earlier, for reasons of confidentiality it is not possible to identify the individual cases but Table I indicates the assessment in respect of each case and, briefly, the circumstances surrounding the companies concerned. From this it will be observed that a number of bidders were subsequently in difficulties and that a number of the target companies did

TABLE I
ASSESSMENT OF THE PUBLIC INTEREST IMPLICATIONS OF 20 ABANDONED MERGERS

Case	*Assessment*	*Comments*
A	1	B reasonable performance, T later acquired, no strong regrets at abandonment
B	1	B and T have both done well, no strong regrets at abandonment
C	1	B subsequently in difficulties, T made strong improvement
D	2	B and T both in difficulties later
E	2	B and T both showed good performance, T slightly stronger
F	1	B subsequently in difficulties, T later acquired
G	1	B subsequently in difficulties, T improved but then declined
H	1	T stronger performance initially, B also healthy
I	1	T good performance but then some decline, B fairly healthy
J	1	B subsequently acquired, T made strong improvement
K	2	B and T both had some difficulties
L	1	B and T did well, B perhaps more so
M	1	B and T both quite strong, no major benefits lost
N	1	B and T both strong, T showed strong improvement
O	1	B subsequently in difficulty, T later acquired
P	1	B subsequently in some difficulties, T strong performance
Q	2	B and T both progressing well
R	3	B and T both in difficulties later
S	2	B subsequently faced problems, T recovered strongly
T	1	B and T both strong, T recovered well

Keys to Table: Assessment: 1 as well that the merger did not proceed, 2 neutral assessment on abandonment, seem to be relevant arguments either way, 3 unfortunate that the merger did not proceed.

B = bidding company.

T = target company.

achieve a strong improvement. However, it will be appreciated that the overall assessment takes into account other considerations, including in most cases, the assessment of the parties concerned.

In general, the view was more likely to be taken that it was as well there was no merger where: the bidder subsequently proved to be weak; there was a recognition on the part of both companies or of the bidder that the merger would have not worked or was unlikely to have added much to overall performance; the target company subsequently achieved a strong turnaround; there was reasonable ground for accepting the view of the target that there would have been difficulties of integration. On the wider aspects of the effect on the competitive performance of the industry, an abandonment was judged to have been in the public interest where the consequence appears to have been a greater degree of competition, an avoidance of a risk of further mergers or a stronger performance in the market by one or both of the companies concerned.

Uncertainty as to whether it was as well the merger had not proceeded was greatest where there did appear to be some strong industrial logic for the merger, where both companies appear subsequently to have been successful, where it did seem one company could have made a significant contribution to the other's needs without the risk of a major loss of performance and where the actual circumstances surrounding the abandonment had caused particular difficulties, not entirely of their own making, for either or both of the companies.

V. CONCLUSIONS AND COMMENTS

It is hoped that the study on which this paper is based has helped to draw attention to the practical significance of the phenomenon of abandoned mergers and the implications that follow from it. While a quantitative analysis of the causes and effects would now be appropriate, the qualitative approach used here does help to draw attention to aspects that would not readily be picked up in any other way. In particular, it does serve to draw attention to the importance of individual management action in determining the outcomes. This is an aspect that can be all too readily overlooked in research in industrial economics.

Our conclusions are that the reasons for abandoned mergers are complex and often involve issues of corporate bidding and defence strategy as well as the operation of competition policy. The effects of such abandonments do not generally appear to be harmful. Indeed, while there are no doubt exceptions, in general it appears that the consequences of abandonments were to raise performance in the target companies, avoid a loss of efficiency in bidding companies, sustain and even increase competition. If this is a valid generalisation and if it is reasonable to conclude that in many material respects the characteristics of abandoned mergers are similar to those of mergers that actually took place, the question arises as to whether there might not have been greater economic benefits had some mergers that actually took place also been abandoned.

If mergers are, all too often, unsuccessful and if the breakdown of merger proposals does not lead to adverse consequences and may, indeed, be beneficial, certain pointers may be drawn from this study to guide decision makers in the future. We can look at this from the point of view of company policy makers, those operating in financial markets and government policy makers.

Bidding companies would be well advised to adopt a greater sense of realism about the likely outcomes of any merger they have in mind and to carry out a more careful and thorough appraisal of the possibility first. There is much to be said for extensive and careful joint planning with the proposed target company and a need to be willing to admit the merger would not work and so to withdraw if necessary. The Takeover Code ought not to prevent companies withdrawing from a proposed merger even at a late stage if the merger appears unworkable. Companies should recognise that there may be other ways of achieving a particular corporate objective than by merger. If they do decide to seek to acquire another company, the tactics in the initial approach, in pricing the bid and proceeding with the offer, need careful attention. If a takeover bid is made and is unsuccessful, bidders should beware of taking precipitate and perhaps very risky action on the rebound.

Prospective target companies in a takeover bid should recognise that short term weaknesses in what is essentially a strong company can make them very vulnerable. If such situations do arise immediate action to turn the company round is important. It is quite apparent that a company committed to retaining its independence has a fair chance of success in this if its approach to its defence strategy is appropriate. It is worrying that some companies seem to believe that a takeover is inevitable and are concerned only to find the most attractive partner. There are, however, recognised to be questions facing a target company's board over the extent to which it is legitimate in the interests of its shareholders to proceed in resisting a takeover bid. If a company does succeed in fighting off a takeover bid, this is likely to represent a watershed in its history and to create a base from which improved performance can be achieved in the future.

The position of the financial institutions and others involved in the operation of financial markets needs careful attention. It is argued that the 'market for corporate control' is an important feature of the search for increased efficiency, yet as Singh [7] has shown acquisitions are more easily explained in terms of the size than profitability of the target companies. While the threat and indeed reality of selling off a shareholding is an important sanction for shareholders, the overall health of the corporate sector would be helped if major shareholders placed more emphasis on the long term nature of their shareholding and paid greater attention to their capacity to bring pressure on management for internal reorganisation and improvement.

Where an unsuccessful bidder has built up a share stake in the target company, after the abandonment of the merger issues arise as to the future of that stake. It is clear that this can be a source of considerable uncertainty for both the target company and the financial markets since it will not be apparent what action the bidder proposes regarding the stake. It may be used as a basis for a future bid by the same company. If sold in one block it may provide a basis for a future bid by whoever acquires the stake. Indeed if the stake represents more than 30% of the equity of the target the Takeover Code requires a bid. Until the intentions of the bidder are known, the uncertainty will be likely to depress the value of the remaining shares thus making a further takeover raid easier. There would seem to be a need for consideration of the general position of minority shareholdings built up by an unsuccessful bidder, with particular reference to the extent to which they may be used in a disruptive manner to the general detriment of the target company.

Governments may help influence the general climate of opinion by seeking ways to increase the rewards for internal growth relative to those for growth through merger. They should recognise that the effects of a merger not proceeding may be favourable and beneficial. The role of competition policy towards mergers is clearly important. The willingness of companies to abandon takeover proposals merely because of the need for a few months delay for investigation of the likely effects on the public interest seems to raise grave doubts about the logic for the merger at all. Perhaps greater use of MMC investigations of proposed mergers would remove some of the less logical mergers altogether and hence raise the proportion of mergers that do turn out to be successful and worthwhile. There would seem to be a case for a more structuralist approach to the decision-making process on references in order that major companies will know in advance where they stand on the need for an investigation. In the light of all the evidence on the effects of actual and abandoned mergers, the case for a reversal of the 'onus of proof' in the case of major mergers, to require the MMC to be satisfied that the merger was actually *in* the public interest, would have much to commend it. The competition policy authorities ought to recognise the extent to which pressure for a reference to the MMC is part of the defence strategy of many target companies. While this is clearly a legitimate tactic, references arising partly from this type of consideration ought not to be allowed to preclude the investigation of other mergers where perhaps both parties agree to the merger but where there may be monopoly power or other aspects that need to be considered as well.

J. F. Pickering,
Department of Management Sciences,
University of Manchester Institute of Science and Technology,
PO Box 88, Manchester M60 1QD.

ACCEPTED DECEMBER 1981

REFERENCES

[1] Cowling, K. *et al.*, *Mergers and Economic Performance* (Cambridge, Cambridge University Press, 1980).
[2] Liesner Committee, *A Review of Monopolies and Mergers Policy* Cmnd 7198 (London, HMSO, 1978).
[3] Meeks, G., *Disappointing Marriage* (Cambridge University Press, 1977)
[4] Newbould, G. D., *Management and Merger Activity* (Liverpool, Guthstead, 1970).
[5] Pickering, J. F., 'The Abandonment of Major Mergers in the UK 1965–1975', *Journal of Industrial Economics*, 27 No. 2. (December 1978) pp. 123–31.
[6] Pickering, J. F., 'The Implementation of British Competition Policy on Mergers', *European Competition Law Review*, 1 No. 2 (1980) pp. 177–98.
[7] Singh, A., *Takeovers* (Cambridge, Cambridge University Press, 1971).
[8] Smail, C. J., *A Study of the Financial Characteristics of Companies Involved in Unsuccessful Mergers* UMIST, Department of Management Sciences, Undergraduate Dissertation (1978).

THE JOURNAL OF INDUSTRIAL ECONOMICS
Volume XXXI March 1983 No. 3

A NOTE ON CONGLOMERATE MERGER AND BEHAVIOURAL RESPONSE TO RISK*

NORMAN J. IRELAND

I. INTRODUCTION

THE diversification incentive for, and behavioural consequences of, pure conglomerate merger in the absence of market power depend crucially on any necessary portfolio adjustments. Bradburd [1] and [2] implicitly assume that funds are provided by the owners of the acquiring firm to buy out the firm to be acquired and that this provision is from liquidating or forgoing assets the returns on which are independent of the return from the acquiring firm. Then, if the firm to be acquired has profits negatively (positively) correlated with those of the acquiring firm there is a gain (loss) in risk-reduction from the portfolio as a whole and behavioural responses correspond. If a risk-averse acquiring firm sets quantities in anticipation of uncertain prices, the firm will move toward (away from) the certainty profit-maximising output level by increasing (decreasing) output (see Bradburd [2]). If the firm is a price-setter, it will move towards (away from) the certainty profit-maximising price level by increasing (decreasing) price (see Bradburd [1]).

Bradburd's position is fundamentally opposed to that taken by at least one standard text. Hay and Morris [4, pp. 487–91] imply that there will be a reduction in risk from conglomerate merger, provided the profits from the firms are not *perfectly* positively correlated. This presumably would be the position if the merger could be completed without changes in portfolios of outside assets, as for instance when merger is accomplished by an exchange of shares which results in shareholders of both the "acquiring" and "acquired" firms becoming shareholders in the merged firm. Then shares in one firm are transformed into shares in the merged firm which has a diversified product set and thus a less risky profits profile (provided pre-merger profits were not perfectly positively correlated. Specifically we will propose the following type of capital market imperfection for inciting share exchange conglomerate mergers.

Suppose that the acquiring firm is controlled by a subset of shareholders who gain utility from remaining in control. The cost of such control is, however, that they are locked into having a large proportion of their wealth in that particular firm's shares. Although a board of directors may control the company while owning only as little as five or ten per cent of equity, this may

* An earlier version of this paper was presented at the Industrial Economics Workshop of the University of Warwick. The author is grateful to participants of this Workshop and an anonymous referee of this Journal for suggestions and comments.

represent the bulk of at least some directors' wealth, particularly in the case of former private companies still controlled by their founders. Such controlling shareholders would find it very difficult to diversify their asset portfolios; they may lose control and thus utility or they may ruin confidence in the firm and spoil the market by selling just some of their shareholdings. A solution to their problem is to acquire other firms on a share exchange basis and thus turn their shares into diversified stock.[1]

In Section II below, we consider the behavioural effects of conglomerate merger, by share exchange, of quantity-setting firms where price is then determined to equate supply and demand *ex post*. We contrast the situation where the acquiring firm controls both firms post-merger with that where each firm continues to be controlled by the pre-merger board. In Section III we present conclusions. Formal proofs are given in an Appendix.

II. QUANTITY SETTING

In this section we will look at the firms' behaviour pre- and post-merger when they set output levels *ex ante* of the realisations of uncertain prices. We will make the following assumptions.

(i) The coefficients of absolute risk aversion (A_i, $i = 1, 2$) of the controllers of firm i both pre-merger and post-merger are constants. We will assume universal risk aversion, i.e. $A_i > 0, i = 1, 2$.

(ii) Pre-merger, firm i is controlled by a subset of shareholders who own a proportion $\alpha_i \leq 1$ of the total number of shares (n_i) of firm i, and receive income equal to the same proportion of profit, Π_i.

(iii) The maximand of each firm pre-merger is given by

$$Z_i = E(\alpha_i \Pi_i) - \tfrac{1}{2}A_i \text{ variance } (\alpha_i \Pi_i) \qquad i = 1, 2$$

$$(1) \quad Z_i = \alpha_i E(\Pi_i) - \tfrac{1}{2}A_i \alpha_i^2 \text{ variance } (\Pi_i) \qquad i = 1, 2$$

(iv) Z_i is maximised pre-merger by choice of output level q_i. The ith firm's profit, Π_i, is a function of q_i and can be written as

$$(2) \quad \Pi_i = [p_i(q_i) + \varepsilon_i]q_i - c_i(q_i)$$

where ε_i is a random variable with zero mean and variance σ_i^2. Thus $E(\Pi_i) = \Pi_i^e = p_i(q_i)q_i - c_i(q_i)$ and variance $(\Pi_i) = \sigma_i^2 q_i^2$. $p_i(q_i)$ and $c_i(q_i)$ are expected average revenue and cost functions respectively and are such that Z_i is strictly concave in q_i.

[1] In a recent empirical analysis of (not necessarily conglomerate) mergers, Langetiez, Hanger and Wickern [5] "restrict attention to a subsample of mergers involving exchange of only common stock and presumably no leverage effect". This is exactly the kind of merger mechanism that we consider here.

Under the above assumptions, q_i satisfies, in the pre-merger situation, the first-order condition:

$$\frac{d\Pi_i^e}{dq_i} - A_i \alpha_i \sigma_i^2 q_i = 0 \qquad i = 1, 2 \tag{3}$$

The merger is accomplished by a share exchange such that $(1-s)n_1/n_2$ shares of the acquiring firm are given for each share of the firm to be acquired. $(1-s)n_1/n_2$ has the interpretation of the "exchange ratio" of Conn (3). The number of shares left in the hands of the acquiring firm after merger is sn_1, of which the controlling subset of shareholders own $\alpha_1 sn_1$. $(1-s)n_1$ shares are held by previous shareholders of firm 2. The parameter s is determined by a bargaining process.

Firm 1's controlling shareholders have income from the conglomerate firm of $s\alpha_1(\Pi_1 + \Pi_2)$ and maximise

$$Z_c = s\alpha_1 E(\Pi_1 + \Pi_2) - \tfrac{1}{2}A_1 \alpha_1^2 s^2 \text{ variance } (\Pi_1 + \Pi_2) \tag{4}$$

If the covariance of ε_1 and ε_2 is ω then variance $(\Pi_1 + \Pi_2) = q_1^2\sigma_1^2 + q_2^2\sigma_2^2 + 2q_1 q_2 \omega$ and first-order conditions for (4) to be maximised with respect to q_1 and q_2 are

$$\frac{d\Pi_1^e}{dq_1} - A_1 \alpha_1 s(q_1 \sigma_1^2 + q_2 \omega) = 0 \tag{5}$$

$$\frac{d\Pi_2^e}{dq_2} - A_2 \alpha_1 s(q_1 \omega + q_2 \sigma_2^2) = 0 \tag{6}$$

We can rewrite (5) and (6), using (1) and (3), as

$$\frac{1}{\alpha_1}\frac{dZ_1}{dq_1} = A_1 \alpha_1[sq_2 \omega - (1-s)q_1 \sigma_1^2] \tag{7}$$

$$\frac{1}{\alpha_2}\frac{dZ_2}{dq_2} = A_1 \alpha_1\left[sq_1 \omega - \left(\frac{\alpha_2 A_2}{\alpha_1 A_1} - s\right)q_2 \sigma_2^2\right] \tag{8}$$

If q_1^0, q_2^0 maximise pre-merger utilities Z_1, Z_2 and if q_1^*, q_2^* maximise post merger utility Z_c, then from (7) and (8) and concavity of Z_1, Z_2:

$$q_1^* \gtreqless q_1^0 \text{ iff } (1-s)q_1^* \sigma_1^2 \gtreqless sq_2^* \omega \tag{9}$$

$$q_2^* \gtreqless q_2^0 \text{ iff } \left(\frac{\alpha_2 A_2}{\alpha_1 A_1} - s\right)q_2^* \sigma_2^2 \gtreqless sq_1^* \omega \tag{10}$$

We can analyse these conditions in a number of stages. First consider that $\omega = 0$; that is the uncertainties in the two markets are independent. From (9) we have that as $0 < s < 1$, $q_1^* > q_1^0$. So that output of the acquiring firm is increased because of the increased spread of risks. Note however, that if the *acquired* firm was controlled pre-merger by owners of a very small proportion of shares, weighted by the coefficient of absolute risk aversion compared with the acquiring firm the merged firm may have a more cautious production policy with respect to the original firm 2's products than the original management and

$$q_2^* \geq q_2^0 \quad \text{as} \quad \frac{\alpha_2 A_2}{\alpha_1 A_1} \lesseqgtr s.$$

For $\omega < 0$, $q_1^* > q_1^0$ *a fortiori* and it becomes more likely that the acquired firm will increase output with merger.

Now assume $\alpha_1 = \alpha_2$, and $A_2 = A_1$ i.e. the asymmetries in risk aversion and shareholdings of pre-merger controlling subsets is assumed away. We can then demonstrate the following proposition.

Proposition 1 If assumptions i–iv hold and $\alpha_1 = \alpha_2$, $A_1 = A_2$ then at least one output level is greater post-merger than pre-merger, for any ω provided the merger increases the sum of the utilities of the pre-merger controlling subsets and the acquiring firm controls both output levels post-merger.

For proof see Appendix.

So far we have assumed that the acquiring firm would control firm 2's output decision post-merger. Now let us consider the behavioural effects of leaving firm 2's directorate in existence. After all, they may have bargained for this in the merger negotiations and/or may have special expertise. Then (4) is maximised by firm 1 only with respect to q_1. Firm 2's directorate chooses q_2 to maximise their expected utility, given their claim to a $(1 - s)\alpha_2$ share of the conglomerate's profits, i.e. they maximise Z_c' where

$$(11) \qquad Z_c' = (1 - s)\alpha_2 E(\Pi_1 + \Pi_2) - \tfrac{1}{2}A_2 \alpha_2^2(1 - s)^2 \text{ variance } (\Pi_1 + \Pi_2)$$

As the q_1, q_2 decisions are made independently, we will define a Cournot-Nash equilibrium where (7) holds but (8) is replaced by

$$(12) \qquad \frac{1}{\alpha_2}\frac{dZ_2}{dq_2} = A_2 \alpha_2[(1 - s)q_1 \omega - sq_2 \sigma_2^2]$$

We now have (9) and (13) where

$$(13) \qquad q_2^* \gtreqless q_2^0 \text{ iff } sq_2^* \sigma_2^2 \gtreqless (1 - s)q_1^* \omega$$

For this situation we can prove the following proposition.

Proposition 2 If assumptions i–iv hold then at least one output will increase as a result of a conglomerate merger, provided the pre-merger controlling shareholder subsets remain in control and provided there is less than perfect positive correlation between ε_1 and ε_2.

For proof see Appendix.

III. CONCLUSION

We have attempted to link the decision to form a conglomerate and behavioural effects arising from it to a desired portfolio adjustment of a controlling subset of shareholders in the presence of a particular kind of capital market imperfection. For brevity we have confined our attention to quantity-fixing firms. Parallel analysis and propositions are however possible for price-setting firms. Other models with different basic assumptions are likely to yield different results, as for instance did those of Bradburd [1] and [2].

An important feature of our analysis has been the distinction between the acquired firm remaining under the same control and where the output decisions of the acquired firm are taken over by the acquiring firm. In the former case each firm will regress towards the certainty situation provided the correlation of profits is non-positive. If correlation of profits is positive but not perfect then at least one firm will regress towards the certainty situation. When decisions are taken over by the acquiring firm, the same result holds providing there is some benefit in total risk reduction (sum of utilities are increased) and provided the acquiring firm's coefficient of absolute risk aversion and controllers' pre-merger proportion of shares are the same as those of the acquired firm pre-merger. The latter conditions are only sufficient not necessary. Nevertheless, we can conceive of parameter values (for α_1, α_2, A_1, A_2) including sets where $A_1 = A_2$, such that even for a negative correlation of profits, firm 1 imposes a more, not less, risk averse policy on firm 2, even though risk has been reduced overall by diversification.

These results are in direct opposition to those of Bradburd [2] (repeated for price-setting in Bradburd [1]), as he states that a division of a conglomerate will be more (less) risk-averse in its output decision as ω is positive (negative). We have found exceptions in both directions which are sufficient to suggest that conglomerate merger has much more complex effects than may be first thought. The reason for the differences in results lies in the assumption as to how conglomeration takes place. In this note it has been assumed that the financial transaction involved consists of an exchange of assets and is motivated by a desire for diversification: clearly any conglomerate merger then satisfies this objective to some extent. In contrast, Bradburd's fundamental assumption is that the financial transaction involved consists of adding assets to the current bundle held by the acquiring firm's shareholders, so that an extended financial commitment is involved. However no explicit account is taken of the portfolio effects of this. Presumably, if the finance for acquisition came from liquidating an asset with a return more (less) positively correlated, with the remaining portfolio, than the acquired stock, then, ceteris paribus, risk will be reduced (increased). The approach that we have taken in this paper has stressed a particular portfolio adjustment (exchange of shares), which appears empirically important. The conglomerate merger is thus placed in a specific framework with consistent and well-defined motivation and behavioural effects.

Although we have concentrated on a merger financed through a share exchange, a merger financed by a new or rights share issue would be covered by the same analysis provided the acquiring firm's controllers did not acquire any further shares, yet stayed in control of the conglomerate, and made decisions for both firms.

Norman J. Ireland,
Department of Economics, University of Warwick,
Coventry, CV4 7AL

ACCEPTED OCTOBER 1981

APPENDIX

Proof of Proposition 1

If $\omega \leq 0$, the Proposition follows directly from (9) and (10). If $\omega > 0$, then suppose the Proposition does not hold. From (9) and (10) we have

(A1) $(1-s)q_1^* \sigma_1^2 \leq s q_2^* \omega$

(A2) $(1-s)q_2^* \sigma_2^2 \leq s q_1^* \omega$

Multiply (A1) by q_1^* and (A2) by q_2^*, then

(A3) $(1-s)$ variance $^*\Pi_1 \leq s$ covariance $^*(\Pi_1, \Pi_2)$

(A4) $(1-s)$ variance $^*\Pi_2 \leq s$ covariance $^*(\Pi_1, \Pi_2)$

as covariance $^*(\Pi_1, \Pi_2) = q_1^* q_2^* \omega$

Adding (A3) and (A4) yields

(A5) variance $^*\Pi_1$ + variance $^*\Pi_2 \leq \dfrac{s}{1-s}$ covariance $^*(\Pi_1, \Pi_2)$

where the asterisk * continues to imply evaluation at q_1^*, q_2^*.

Now for $\alpha_1 = \alpha_2 = \alpha$ and $A_1 = A_2 = A$, the sum of utilities of the two controlling shareholder subsets will increase as a result of merger if

(A6) $\alpha(\Pi_1^{e*} + \Pi_2^{e*}) - \frac{1}{2}A\alpha^2[s^2 + (1-s)^2]$ variance $^*(\Pi_1 + \Pi_2)$

$> \alpha(\Pi_1^{e0} + \Pi_2^{e0}) - \frac{1}{2}A\alpha^2$ variance $^0(\Pi_1) - \frac{1}{2}A\alpha^2$ variance $^0(\Pi_2)$

where ^{0} superscript denotes evaluation at q_1^0, q_2^0.

Now from pre-merger optimisation:

(A7) $\alpha(\Pi_1^{e0} + \Pi_2^{e0}) - \frac{1}{2}A\alpha^2$ variance $^0(\Pi_1) - \frac{1}{2}A\alpha^2$ variance $^0(\Pi_2)$

$\geq \alpha(\Pi_1^{e*} + \Pi_2^{e*}) - \frac{1}{2}A\alpha^2$ variance $^*(\Pi_1) - \frac{1}{2}A\alpha^2$ variance $^*(\Pi_2)$

Combining A6 and A7 and simplifying yields

variance $^*(\Pi_1)$ + variance $^*(\Pi_2) - [s^2 + (1-s)^2]$ variance $^*(\Pi_1 + \Pi_2) > 0$

(A8) $\text{variance }^*(\Pi_1) + \text{variance }^*(\Pi_2)$

$$> \frac{2[s^2 + (1-s)^2]}{1 - [s^2 + (1-s)^2]} \text{ covariance }^*(\Pi_1, \Pi_2)$$

Now $$\frac{2[s^2 + (1-s)^2]}{1 - [s^2 + (1-s)^2]} = \frac{1}{s(1-s)} - 2$$

and is greater than $\frac{s}{1-s}$ for all $s < 1$.

Thus (A5) cannot hold while (A8) holds and the Proposition is proved.

Proof of Proposition 2

(A3) above still holds if $q_1^* \leq q_1^0$. For $q_2^* \leq q_2^0$ we have, multiplying 13 by q_2^*

(A9) $s \text{ variance }^*(\Pi_2) \leq (1-s) \text{ covariance }^*(\Pi_1, \Pi_2)$

Neither (A3) nor (A9) can hold if $\omega \leq 0$. If $\omega > 0$ then covariance $^*(\Pi_1, \Pi_2) > 0$ and multiplying right-hand sides and left-hand sides of (A3) and (A9) together yields, after cancelling $s(1-s)$:

(A10) $\text{variance }^*(\Pi_1) \text{ variance }^*(\Pi_2)$

$$\leq [\text{covariance }^*(\Pi_1, \Pi_2)]^2$$

i.e. $r^2 \geq 1$ where r is the correlation coefficient.

As $r < 1$, the contradiction is shown and the Proposition is proved.

REFERENCES

[1] Bradburd, Ralph M., "A Model of the Effect of Conglomeration and Risk Aversion on Pricing", *Journal of Industrial Economics*, XXVIII (June 1980), pp. 369–86.

[2] ——, "Conglomerate Power without Market Power: the effect of Conglomeration on a Risk Averse Quantity Adjusting Firm", *American Economic Review*, **70** (June 1980), pp. 483–88.

[3] Conn, Robert L., "Merger Pricing Policies by Owner-controlled versus Manager-controlled Firms", *Journal of Industrial Economics*, XXVIII (June 1980), pp. 427–38.

[4] Hay, Donald A. and Morris, Derek J., "*Industrial Economics*", Oxford University Press, 1979.

[5] Langetiez, T. C., Hanger, R. A. and Wickern, D. W., "Mergers and Shareholder Risk", *Journal of Financial and Quantitative Analysis* (September 1980), pp. 689–718.

THE JOURNAL OF INDUSTRIAL ECONOMICS
Volume XXXI March 1983 No. 3

ANATOMY OF A PRICE LEADERSHIP CHALLENGE: AN EVALUATION OF PRICING STRATEGIES IN THE AUSTRALIAN NEWSPAPER INDUSTRY

WILLIAM J. MERRILEES*

THREE companies (John Fairfax and Sons, Herald and Weekly Times and News Limited) completely dominate the daily Australian newspaper industry, with takeovers having played a spectacular part in the pursuit of dominance. Product differentiation has also been an important competitive weapon. However, here we wish to concentrate on another strategic weapon, namely price. Historically price competition has not played a vital role in inter-firm rivalry in the newspaper industry. This position changed dramatically in the 1975–80 period in one of the key sectors of the industry—the Sydney market—where rivalry between News Limited and John Fairfax and Sons intensified.

In this study we aim to explore the causes of this intensified price competition and evaluate the relative merits of the marketing strategies employed by the two companies involved. Despite an obsession with price as a key decision variable in most economics and management textbooks, very little is known about pricing tactics in real world oligopolistic industries. For a few overseas exceptions see Stigler [20], Nichols [13] and Fog [4].

The analysis proceeds in terms of informal models of strategic thinking. However, existing formal models of strategic thinking, such as game theory, have little to say about prolonged periods of disequilibrium associated with mistakes by management. Price wars and related phenomena can be analysed with game theory models, but this assumes rational, reasonably informed decisions by managers. Consequently we use more discoursive models of strategic thinking to analyse the pricing tactics used by each firm. Part of this analysis draws upon the concept of cross elasticity of demand.

The effect of time in particular segments the morning and evening markets. This adds an interesting dimension to our study because the competitive tactics used by News Limited and John Fairfax and Sons Limited differ between the two markets. Although we will be concentrating on the evening market, it is useful to make cross references to the morning market. Our emphasis is on cover prices, but corresponding data are also available on

* I would like to thank the two Sydney based newspaper firms for their cooperation and especially Mr Jim McPherson, General Manager of Mirror Newspapers (interviewed 18/8/76) and Mr Noel Hodges, Chief Circulation Manager of the Sun (interviewed 22/4/80). The sales figures were kindly supplied by the non-government body, Audit Bureau of Circulation. Useful comments on the paper were made by a colleague John Stuckey. An anonymous referee greatly contributed to the final shape of the article, providing invaluable ideas in relation to advertising rates and promotional outlays in particular.

advertising rates. The evolution of (cover) pricing policies can be broken up into chronological epochs and it is more meaningful and interesting if presented as such.

THE RELATIONSHIP BETWEEN ADVERTISING REVENUE AND CIRCULATION REVENUE

Our analysis of price competition refers explicitly to cover price competition. This is where most public attention is focused. However, circulation revenue (cover price times circulation) is only about a third of total revenue, with two-thirds coming from advertising revenue (advertising rate times volume of advertising). Therefore, it would be misleading to ignore advertising rate setting prices in our discussion of this industry. Fortunately we do have fairly good data on advertising rates by company (though for nominal rather than for transaction prices—discounts are not known) over time, with more fragmented data on advertising volume and revenue.

Despite the size of the media industries, very little work has been carried out on the determinants of media prices in Australia. At this stage, it is difficult to say whether newspaper advertising rates and other media rates are market-determined (with readership mix, circulation and media competition being important) or monopolistically-determined (a small number of dominant, large firms are conglomerates across several media types).

A superficial impression from studying the media industries for several years is that the market model rather than the monopoly model better describes inter-media price setting. The print media generally (mainly newspapers and magazines) are very conscious of competition from television. For example, in response to the arrival of colour television in 1976, they have brought out colour supplements and advertisements (in newspapers) and glossier paper (in magazines). This competitive response occurred despite considerable overlap in the ownership of print and television media firms.

Within the newspaper media group, we can assume that other media influences affect each firm equally. Therefore, in comparing inter-firm advertising rate differentials within the newspaper industry, we can effectively ignore other media competition. We have already noted readership-mix and circulation as possible determinants of inter-firm advertising rates. In the first instance, we might associate affluence as the key readership characteristic enhancing advertising rates. This is consistent with the Sydney morning newspaper market, where the advertising rate for News Limited's *Daily Telegraph* is only marginally ahead of Fairfax's *Sydney Morning Herald,* despite a substantial lead in circulation. It is widely believed that the *Herald* readers are more discerning and more affluent. However, this is not consistent with the Sydney evening newspaper market, where News Limited's *Daily Mirror* has persistently achieved a higher advertising rate over Fairfax's *Sun,* even when the circulations have been equal. The *Sun*'s readers come mainly from the more affluent Northern and Eastern suburbs, so affluence *per se* is not the dominant characteristic of reader enabling higher advertising rates. Thus advertisements in the *Mirror* may be more effective (from the advertiser's point of view) because *Mirror* readers are more gullible or alternatively more price conscious. Retail advertising could be an area where the *Mirror* has an advantage. In general, newspapers attempt to specialize in particular areas (retail, national, classifieds and components thereof) which, if successful, enables a lift in advertising rate for a given level of circulation.[1]

As an initial approximation, we assume that the *comparative* effectiveness of advertising between the *Sun* and the *Mirror* is unchanged during the time period under review. This would then leave changes in relative circulation as the main determinant of changes in relative advertising prices between the *Sun* and the *Mirror*. This is consistent with the data. Prior to mid-1975, the *Mirror*'s advertising rate was a few percent above the *Sun*'s reflecting an historical advantage in advertising effectiveness. During 1975–76, the *Mirror*'s relative circulation rose 7 percent. Also during 1975–76, the *Mirror*'s advertising rate rose by 15 percent and the *Sun*'s by 8 percent; i.e. by 7 percent in relative terms. This makes commercial sense: 7 percent more messages commands 7 percent more price. This wider circulation differential persisted over the 1975–78 period, as did the higher than usual relative advertising price of the *Mirror*. When circulations swung back towards equality in 1978–80, the relative advertising price of the *Mirror* also moved back to historical levels; in November 1980 the premium was 3 percent.

There is therefore a very close relationship between changes in relative circulation and changes in relative advertising rates over the 1974–80 period in the evening newspaper market. To double-check this phenomenon, there was no tendency, for instance, for the companies' own promotional campaigns to raise their relative advertising prices.

Analytically we can formulate the relationship between advertising revenue and circulation revenue as:

(1) $$\Pi = PQ + RA - C$$

(2) with $$R = f(Q)$$

(3) in addition to $$P = g(Q) \text{ and } C = h(Q)$$

where Π is profit, P is cover price, Q is circulation, R is the advertising rate, A is advertising volume and C is total cost.

Equation (2) has several important implications. For one, it may *justify* profit-maximizing monopolists (duopolists) rationally setting a price level corresponding to an inelastic part of their demand curve. In the absence of equation (2), this would have entailed negative marginal revenue and would

[1] It would seem that in the Sydney morning market the *Herald* has had more success in specializing (notably in classifieds), while in the evening market, the *Mirror* has been more successful.

have been irrational. Secondly, we now see why newspaper cover prices are often relatively low, perhaps below marginal costs. There are offsetting benefits in terms of advertising revenue. Indeed equation (2) is imperative for an understanding of the cover price decisions of the *Mirror* in the analysis below.

STAGE 1. 1941–73: AN ERA OF PRICE COLLUSION?

Prior to 1941, the market was monopolised by Associated Newspaper's *Sun*. Mirror Newspapers entered with the *Mirror* in May 1941 and simply adopted the same price as the *Sun*. In 1953 John Fairfax and Sons, well established in the morning market with their *Sydney Morning Herald*, took over Associated Newspapers and the *Sun* with it. In 1959 the *Mirror* was taken over for a brief period by a company friendly to John Fairfax and Sons, but was sold in 1960 to News Limited.[2] No further ownership changes have occurred since. None of these ownership changes seemed to make any difference to the infrequent pattern of price changes, as can be seen in Table I. Nor did the ownership changes alter the salient fact that between 1941 and 1973 the prices of the *Sun* and the *Mirror* were identical to the day.

Identical prices over time are consistent with either an overt, collusive agreement or with advance signalling tacit price coordination. From the consumer's perspective it probably does not matter which price system is causing identical prices. From a behavioral perspective the difference is noteworthy, while from a legal perspective the difference is controversial. Currently collusive agreements are illegal while the legality of 'non-collusive' parallel pricing is obscure. Just as identical prices do not prove collusion, nor do unequal prices disprove collusion. Fog [4, p. 156] gives an example of three Danish firms whose collusive oral agreement stipulates that agreed price increases were not to be made simultaneously so that it would look as if there were no mutual agreement.

Price agreements were very common in Australia in the 1950s and 1960s and were legal in most cases. There is some evidence[3] that newspapers was one of the many industries where collusive agreement flourished. Further to substantiate this view, I checked the announcement dates of price increases for the *Sun* and *Mirror* over the 1964–74 period. Both papers gave *simultaneous* notice of two, five and four days for the 1964, 1970 and 1974 price increases. This can only be construed as joint announcements of mutual agreements.

Instead of price competition, the emphasis had been on non-price policies.

[2] This is an interesting phase in the history of the *Mirror*. As of 1959 *Mirror Newspapers* was in danger of bankruptcy and the eventual takeover by News Limited was seen as a means of revitalising the company. Fairfax's brief control of the *Mirror* via O'Connell Pty Ltd's purchase in January 1959 was to ensure that the *Mirror* did not fall into the hands of the Melbourne-based *Herald* and *Weekly Times*. It is ironic that Fairfax saw the Melbourne Herald group as a greater threat than News Limited. Twenty years later, Fairfax and the Melbourne Herald group are allied, while News Limited is the common adversary. For information on the 1959 takeover, see *Jobson's Investment Digest*, [8, May 26, 1960, p. 28].

[3] See Hunter [7] and Sheridan [18, p. 14].

TABLE I
COVER PRICES IN THE SYDNEY EVENING NEWSPAPER INDUSTRY, 1930–81

Date of Change	*Price of the Sun (Cents)*	*Price of the Mirror (Cents)*
1930, Aug. 4	1.3	—
1940, Feb. 5	1.7	—
1941, May 12		1.7 (entry)
1949, Sept. 12	2.5	2.5
1951, Mar. 12	3.3	3.3
1956, Oct. 8	4.2	4.2
1964, Sept. 14	5.0	5.0
1970, Mar. 31	7.0	7.0
1974, Jan. 21	8.0	8.0
1974, Sept. 30	9.0	—
1974, Oct. 1	—	9.0
1974, Nov. 25	10.0	—
1974, Dec. 10	—	10.0
1975, July 7	12.0	
1979, Jan. 15	10.0	
1979, Nov. 1	15.0	15.0*
1980, July 7	20.0*	20.0
1981, Sept. 21	25.0	25.0*

Note: * Denotes price leader in terms of the first firm to announce a price rise, effective on the same date for both firms.

Sources: John Fairfax and Sons, Mirror Newspapers, and Mitchell Library, Sydney.

Each evening paper has come out with all sorts of innovations and style changes (using sporting celebrities, competitions, racing form liftout guides, etc.) and the other has usually been quick to imitate.

STAGE 2. 1974–75: FROM PRICE COLLUSION TO PRICE LEADERSHIP

While the notion of 'collusive agreement' is likely to be construed in terms of a clear, predictable and watertight system of industry price control, there are well known reasons why cartel-type agreements break down. Conflict between members of a co-operative agreement occurs for all sorts of reasons: different cost structures, different objectives, power struggles, etc.

Although a bargaining process underlies collective agreements, it seems likely that one firm plays a dominant firm in the newspaper price agreement. As of the mid-1960s it was probably John Fairfax and Sons. Fairfax dominated the Sunday market, had an equal share of the evening market and was well represented in the morning market. No other firm was in all three markets. The *S.M.H.* (Fairfax) led the *Telegraph* (Packer) in the 1964 market price change.

The arrival of the *Australian* in 1964 and News Limited's 1972 takeover of the *Telegraph* radically changed the status quo. There are clear signs that

Rupert Murdoch (News Limited) had become the dominant member of the price alliance in the 1973–74 period; as revealed in the morning and Sunday markets.

Although News Limited seemed to be the dominant member of the price alliance, it was nevertheless Fairfax which made the first application to the Prices Justification Tribunal in July 1974 for price increases in the *Sun* and *S.M.H.* This does not necessarily indicate conflict within the alliance. It is likely that it was in the interests of News Limited to allow John Fairfax and Sons to make the first application to the P.J.T. since the newsprint cost increase was known to be greater for Fairfax and therefore would provide a stronger justification for a price rise (based on the increase in unit production costs). The cause of the greater newsprint cost increase is discussed below. The need to provide a strong case for a price rise reflected the need to deal with a more experienced and assertive P.J.T. compared to an earlier (December 1973) application. In retrospect, the expectations of the two newspaper firms proved correct. In contrast to the uncomplicated granting of the December

TABLE II
PRICE ROUNDS IN THE SYDNEY MORNING NEWSPAPER MARKET, 1970–81

Price Level	*Price Leader*	*Price Follower*	*Lag (weeks)*
7 cents	Telegraph May 11, 1970	S.M.H., June, 1970	4
8 cents	Telegraph April 23, 1973	S.M.H., June 25, 1973	8
9 cents	S.M.H.* Sept. 30, 1974	Telegraph Sept. 30, 1974	0
10 cents	S.M.H. Jan. 13, 1975	Telegraph Feb. 17, 1975	5
12 cents	S.M.H. June 2, 1975	Telegraph July 28, 1975	7
13 cents	Telegraph Dec. 20, 1976	S.M.H. July 11, 1977	29
14 cents	Telegraph Mar. 21, 1977	S.M.H. Feb. 27, 1978	49
15 cents	Telegraph Oct. 3, 1977	S.M.H. Sept. 25, 1978	51
20 cents	Telegraph* Feb. 8, 1980	S.M.H. Feb. 8, 1980	0
25 cents	Telegraph* Oct. 12, 1981	S.M.H. Oct. 12, 1981	0

Notes: * Prices effective the same date, but earlier announcement. The *Australian* newspaper represents about 6% of the Sydney market. If included it led the price rises to 10 cents (9/12/74), 15 cents (11/9/76) and 20 cents (July 1977).

Sources: As in Table I.

1973 price application, the July 1974 price application was subjected to a prolonged public inquiry. Ironically, the P.J.T. Report on this inquiry indicates that the additional newsprint cost increase for Fairfax was unusual and potentially unjustifiable, but was allowed in the end for extraneous reasons (its support of the local newsprint industry).

More or less simultaneously with the price round associated with the P.J.T. newspaper public inquiry, there emerged the tougher 1974 Trade Practices Act which made price agreements illegal. By default, this left price leadership as the only effective means of price coordination. As can be seen in Tables I and II, Fairfax was the price leader in both the morning and evening markets from mid-1974 to mid-1975.

STAGE 3. MID-1975: THE FIRST SHOTS OF A PRICE WAR

On July 7, 1975, after 34 harmonious years, price coordination collapsed in the evening market. The *Sun* increased its price from 10 to 12 cents, but the *Mirror* did not follow. What sparked off this price war?

Discovering the cause of the price war is complicated by the difficulty of assigning the initiating role to a particular firm. Ostensibly the *Sun* made the first move by raising its price to 12 cents. Yet by not following this rise, the *Mirror* was effectively cutting price. At least this is true in an inflationary milieu when inaction amounts to a price cut in real terms. Our difficulty in identifying an initiator to the price war is echoed in my interviews with managers of the two newspapers. The *Mirror* manager saw their role as purely passive, with the *Sun* initiating the price differential, while the *Sun* manager saw the *Mirror* as the aggressor.

Although the *Sun* did create the initial price differential, it is clear that it did so in a non-threatening way. Indeed, few if any price increases are threatening in the way price cuts can be. Moreover, the ultimate price retreat by the *Sun* suggests that it originally believed the *Mirror* would follow the rise to 12 cents. The *Sun*'s expectations in this regard were confirmed in my interview; the whole industry (including the *Sun,* newsagents, etc.) expected the *Mirror* would quickly follow to 12 cents. Thus we need to seek out the *Mirror*'s motivation in initiating price competition. The fact that the *Mirror* manager denied initiating the price war made it difficult to pursue this line of thought directly with the *Mirror.* We are therefore forced to proceed indirectly, with four hypotheses checked for plausibility. The first hypothesis is the least plausible, the next two hypotheses acted as catalysts in the price war while the fourth hypothesis is seen as fundamental.

(a) It has been argued (Wiltshire and Stokes, [22]) that the editorial quality of a newspaper tends to be higher, the greater the relative contribution from circulation revenue to total revenue. Given the tendency of the *Sun* to play up its image as a quality paper relative to the *Mirror,* it is possible that the *Sun* is more concerned with a higher cover price to raise circulation revenue (given inelastic demand). This hypothesis is rejected outright. In its July 1974 P.J.T. submission, John Fairfax requested a higher percentage rise in advertising rates compared to cover price. Additionally, in the interview, the *Sun* manager did not rank the issue of any importance.

(b) The introduction of the 1974 Trade Practices Act provided a fillip to price experimentation. Several quick and punitive Trade Practice decisions made it clear to all firms that the rules of the game had changed. No doubt many firms reframed their attitude to competition.

(c) The failure of the *Mirror* to match the July 1975 price rise could reflect the uniqueness of the *Sun*'s production cost changes, or at least the magnitude of such. Newsprint is a major component of the cost of newspapers. In Australia A.N.M. (Australian Newsprint Mills) has a monopoly of newsprint production, though with low rates of duty, imports are important. Most major newspaper publishers, including Fairfax, were vertically integrated backwards into A.N.M. as of 1972–73. However, from 1972, News Limited did not have a holding in A.N.M.

In June 1966 A.N.M. began ten-year contracts with its customers, which provided for small annual increments in prices. With the acceleration of inflation in the early 1970s, these long-term contracts placed A.N.M. in a desperate financial situation. In 1972–73 A.N.M.'s customers voluntarily agreed to pay more for their newsprint, to ensure the survival of A.N.M. and hence the continuity of future supplies. The fact that most customers were also owners no doubt further prompted this gesture. News Limited, as a non-owner customer, did not join in with a voluntary price rise to A.N.M. to the displeasure of the rest of the industry. Apart from pecuniary motive, Murdoch's non-altruistic behaviour was no doubt influenced by a long standing rift between the *Mirror* and A.N.M.

Thus the costs of newsprint for the *Sun* (and other Fairfax papers) rose much faster than those of the *Mirror* (and other News Limited papers) over the 1973–76 period. The saving to News Limited over this period amounted to about $6 million, spread over all papers including the *Mirror*.[4] The windfall cost differential between the *Sun* and the *Mirror* provided useful leverage for Murdoch to conduct his pricing strategy.

(d) In our previous section (Stage 2), the discussion suggested that, as of mid-1974, News Limited was the dominant member of a collusive price agreement in the Sydney newspaper markets. In the evening market, the *Mirror* had a marginal edge over the *Sun*. In the morning market, News Limited's *Telegraph* had a substantial lead over Fairfax's *S.M.H.*, with another paper (the *Australian*) in support. In the Sunday market, the combined sales of the *Sunday Telegraph* and *Sunday Mirror* greatly exceeded those of the *Sun Herald*. Yet from mid-1974 to mid-1975, John Fairfax and Sons had been elevated to price leader.

[4] For further discussion, see Davidson and Stewardson [3, especially pp. 142–46].

There is little doubt that News Limited was unhappy about being forced into a followship role, especially given the all embracing marketing aspirations of Rupert Murdoch. We have argued that News Limited acquiesed in the July 1974 price leadership initiative by Fairfax. Presumably News Limited intended to assert their inter-firm bargaining power in the next round of price increases. However, Fairfax moved unexpectedly fast in initiating further price increases in both the evening and morning markets. One sign that News Limited was unhappy with such action came in November 1974. The *Mirror* delayed over two weeks before increasing its price in line with the *Sun*, which was a long delay in light of previous experience. It could be regarded as a warning of the impending price war which began seven months later. Similar, though less clear, "warnings" were also made in the morning market.

It is instructive at this stage to consider reasons why firms seek price leadership. If both (all) firms charge the same price, then it could be argued that it does not matter who is the price leader. In terms of profit this may be true, but in terms of the utility of owner-managers, it may not be. When, say, two firms are evenly balanced in economic strength and carrying out similar routine operations day after day, a large weight may attach to being in control of infrequent strategic decisions including price policies. Certainly Murdoch would attach value to strategic control and Fairfax may do likewise as a reflection of its "historic rights" in this area. This suggests that both firms would be prepared to sacrifice profits in order to retain or retrieve price leadership.

Apart from kudos or utility effects, it is possible that possession of price leadership could benefit profits and related objectives for the holder. If the two firms have different price objectives, then clearly the price leader is in a position to edge price changes closer to its target. Of course, if the price objectives are wide apart and the price leader moves too far from a centre position, then a leadership challenge is possible. In our context there is the possibility that News Limited was uneasy about the frequency and magnitude of price rises initiated by Fairfax during 1974–75. Perhaps News Limited felt that newspapers needed to moderate price increases in order to compete against other media sectors. This hypothesis is dismissed as unlikely because of the very low own-price elasticity of newspapers, opposite actions by News Limited in the morning market during 1976–81, and opposite actions by News Limited in the evening market during 1979–81.[5]

We therefore emphasize the utility-augmenting effects of price leadership. Given Rupert Murdoch's desire to regain the price leadership title, it is certain that he carefully considered the questions of *when*, *how*, and *where* the challenge should take place. The question of 'when' to challenge was presumably 'as soon as possible'.

[5] For discussion of a price leadership challenge based on conflict in pricing objectives, see Merrilees [12].

'How' to challenge a price leader involves three pricing options: initiating a price rise, initiating a price cut or by not following the established price leader. The first option could backfire if the 'price leader' (Fairfax as of mid-1975) did not match the move, forcing a retreat by the rebellious 'follower'. The second option is limited by potential resistance from newsagents in the retail market. With newsagents' gross margin proportional (usually 25%) to the cover price, they could have hampered distribution of the *Mirror* if its price were too low. At least one low price paper (the *Melbourne Daily Morning Post,* 1925–27) had been killed off by a newsagents' boycott. This leaves the third option as the preferred tactic and is the one chosen by Murdoch; when the price of the *Sun* went up in July 1975, he did not follow.

'Where' to strike was essentially a choice between the morning and evening markets. The evening market was preferable for two reasons. First, it seemed likely that the cross elasticity of demand was greater in the evening market because of a higher casual/contract sales ratio and because product differentiation seemed less than in the morning newspapers. As of mid-1975 this was an untested hypothesis because the absence of a price differential in the previous 34 years prevented empirical measurement of cross demand elasticities. Secondly, traditionally there had been a minimal (if any) lag between changes in the prices of the *Sun* and *Mirror*, whereas in the morning market a lag of two or three months had been common. Therefore, a policy of not following a Fairfax price lead would have had the quickest impact in the evening market. Within a few weeks after the *Sun*'s price rise on July 7, 1975 it was clear that News Limited was not following, whereas it would have taken months after the *Herald*'s price rise on June 2, 1975 to get the same message across. The time, means and place had been successfully plotted for a leadership challenge.

In summary, an attempt to regain the price leadership position from Fairfax seems to have been the overriding motivation behind the 1975 price war. However, News Limited's move received encouragement from the 1974 Trade Practices Act and a temporary windfall in the cost of newsprint.

STAGE 4. 1975–79: THE BATTLE; ITS EFFECT ON MARKET SHARES

The price war lasted more than $3\frac{1}{2}$ years, from July 1975 to January 1979. The *Mirror*'s price of 10 cents lasted five years, from November 1974 to November 1979. Both of these figures are quite amazing when one considers that inflation averaged 10% p.a.

Like most oligopolistic price wars, it was not a case of price changing continuously. Rather there was one discrete change which was then maintained. This pattern is similar to recent price wars in the margarine industry, with prices taking one or two downward moves, reaching a zero or negative profit situation very quickly. Notwithstanding, in the *Sun-Mirror* case, the prolonged nature of the conflict could lead one to interpret the price cutting process as continuous for *both* the *Mirror* and *Sun*; at least in real terms.

TABLE III
SALES AND MARKET SHARES IN THE SYDNEY EVENING NEWSPAPER INDUSTRY, 1973–81

Six-monthly Period Ending:	*Average Sales of Mirror*	*Average Sales of Sun*	*Mirror's Market Share* (%)
March 1973	349,522	347,437	50.2
September 1973	361,549	352,709	50.6
March 1974	304,317	301,017	50.3
September 1974	369,153	364,288	50.3
March 1975	358,836	356,994	50.1
September 1975	379,081	340,434	52.7(a)
March 1976	371,944	326,990	53.2
September 1976	389,078	341,754	53.2
March 1977	375,107	318,370	54.1
September 1977	377,508	328,731	53.5
March 1978	361,615	318,558	53.2
September 1978	391,393	331,530	54.1
March 1979	387,173	338,511	53.4(b)
September 1979	399,450	374,726	51.6
March 1980	361,520	342,284	51.4
September 1980	358,907	348,715	50.7
March 1981	345,917	342,244	50.3
September 1981	387,868	358,825	51.9

Notes: (a) Half of this six month period involved a newly established price differential; (b) The last two months of this six month period involved the elimination of the price differential.
Source: Sales figures from *Audit Bureau of Circulation* [1].

In analysing the economic effects of the price war, most interest focuses on changes in market shares. In this regard we are fortunate to have reliable (audited) data by firm on a continuous (six-monthly) basis. Table III records the changes in firm sales and market shares over the 1973–80 period.

Prior to the July 1975 price changes, the sales of the two evening newspapers moved in a near parallel fashion, with market shares virtually constant. Minor fluctuations in market shares can be attributed to publishing problems (industrial relation problems), distributional problems (petrol or transport strikes), random distributions in front page stories between the two papers and inter-firm variations in promotion.

In fact, given the virtual constancy of market shares prior to July 1975, one is tempted to attribute most of the post-July 1975 market share variations to the emergence of a price differential. Thus, as a first approximation, the price differential appears to have increased the *Mirror*'s market share from 50.1% in the period ending March 1975 to 54.1% in the six months period ending March 1977; about four percentage points. While this method is crude, it seems reasonable in light of prior market share behaviour in the industry. Moreover the method is indistinguishable from the 'experimental approach' underlying Reekie's [16] U.K. results.

Adding to the plausibility of the crude method is the apparent symmetry between the creation and removal of the price differential. Thus nine months after the establishment of the price differential, the *Mirror*'s market share increased by 3.1 percentage points. Eight months after the price differential was removed, the *Mirror*'s market share decreased by 2.5 percentage points.

These estimates can be checked using more refined empirical tests. The availability of price and market share time series data enables us to use regression analysis. With a relatively small sample there is no guarantee that the more sophisticated regression technique is more reliable than our crude method. However, our hypothesis that recent variations in market shares are dominated by one systemmatic influence (relative product prices) and many random influences, makes regression analysis a particularly attractive tool.

Apart from price, an attempt was made to include more salient aspects of promotional and innovational activity. Minor stylistic changes (such as the use of sporting celebrities to write columns) were not included as these changes were quickly imitated by the other firm. This imitative behaviour is explicable in terms of either Hotelling's [6] spatial variety model or simply in terms of game theory (either constant or non-constant sum models). Quite often, as with the bingo competition promotion initiated in July 1981, the rival's response came within a couple of days. However, as detailed below, the bingo example eventually involved differential strategies and so we have included it in the regression analysis. It therefore is an exception to the rule of imitation.

Data on general promotional (advertising) expenditure are not available on a time series basis by firm. We do have knowledge of peak promotional spending, which is included as a simple dummy variable for each firm. Thus the *Sun*'s advertising expenditures peaked in the six months ending September 1976, while the *Mirror*'s expenditures peaked in the following six months. There is a tendency to "cannibalize" (*cf.* Scherer, [17]) the other firm's advertising expenditure by matching them in amount. Assuming equal effectiveness of the advertisements, this "cannibalizing" policy prevents any firm elevating its market share via advertising expenditure. Given a short response lag, much of the *Mirror*'s response to the *Sun*'s peak outlay occurred in the same period as the *Sun*'s peak; that is, cannibalization was partly operative. It is therefore virtually impossible to identify a period where promotional outlays differed much by firm. We are therefore not hopeful that our peak outlay variables will be significant.

A variety of price lag structures were tried, but the best results were obtained by adding one lagged term to the current price term. Thus we get for 1971-I to 1981-II (with standard errors in brackets):

$$\begin{aligned} MS_{Mt} = {} & \underset{(0.068)}{-0.32} + \underset{(0.026)}{0.129} \log(P_S/P_M)_t + \underset{(0.026)}{0.051} \log(P_S/P_M)_{t-1} \\ & \underset{(0.005)}{-0.006}\ \text{ADS} + \underset{(0.005)}{0.003}\ \text{ADM} + \underset{(0.005)}{0.014}\ \text{Bingo} \qquad (4) \\ & \bar{R}^2 = 0.902 \qquad \text{D.W.} = 1.75 \qquad n = 20 \end{aligned}$$

where MS_{Mt} is the *Mirror*'s market share, P_S/P_M is the relative cover price of the *Sun* to the *Mirror*, ADS is the *Sun*'s peak advertising outlay (which takes on a value of one for 1976-II and zero otherwise), ADM is the *Mirror*'s peak advertising outlay (which takes on a value of one for 1977-I and zero otherwise) and bingo is a product variety variable emphasized more by the *Mirror* than the *Sun* (and it takes on value of one for 1981-II and zero otherwise).

From a statistical viewpoint the results are quite good, with more than 90 percent of the 1971–81 variations in market shares in the evening newspaper market explained. This high explanatory power together with the satisfactory Durbin-Watson statistic suggest that omitted influences are minor and fairly random. Relative prices is the key explanatory variable.

The sum of the price coefficients is 0.18, which means that a doubling of relative prices would add 18 percentage points to the *Mirror*'s market share (*ceteris paribus*).

Thus a 20 percent increase in the *Sun*'s relative price would raise the *Mirror*'s market share by $3\frac{1}{2}$ percentage points, not greatly different from our "eyeball" estimate. Nearly three-quarters of the market adjustment occurs within the first six months of a relative price change, with effectively all of the adjustment completed within a twelve-month period.

The bingo competition emphasized by the *Mirror* appears to have raised its market share by 1.4 percentage points in 1981-II. Future observations, especially the next release of market share data, will help confirm this phenomenon. The bingo term is highly significant—at the one percent level.

Neither of the peak advertising outlay coefficients (relating to ADS and ADM) are particularly large and neither is significant at the 5 percent level. At least the signs are as expected. The *Sun*'s advertising outlays seem to be slightly more effective, but the difference is not significant. We are unable to say whether the lack of significance of these outlay terms is due to cannibalization by the other firm or simply because advertising has little impact on consumer preferences in this sector.

A similar market share analysis has been carried out for the morning market. No lagged effect is evident here and relative prices explain very little of the 1971–81 variations in market shares. The price coefficient is at best marginally significant from zero and only a tenth of the size of the corresponding coefficient in the evening market. Clearly the two morning newspapers are segmented from each other, while the two evening newspapers are reasonably close substitutes with each other.

In summary, the relatively lower price of the *Mirror* over the 1975–79 period apparently raised its market share by about $3\frac{1}{2}$ percentage points (i.e. 7 percent). In the morning market the relatively lower price of the *S.M.H.* apparently raised its market share by about half a percentage point (i.e. one percent) over the 1976–78 period.

STAGE 4. 1975–79: THE BATTLE; ITS EFFECT ON PROFITABILITY

We will concentrate on the effects of the price war on relative profitability for the year 1975–76. Profits of the two companies altered greatly in 1975–76 compared to the preceding year, while the 1976–77, 1977–78 and 1978–79 profit picture was very similar to 1975–76.

With some trepidation I have attempted to construct the change and composition of profits for the two companies in Table IV. Profit data always have to be treated with caution. In our case a full account of the *Sun*'s operations is not available separate from Fairfax's other newspapers, with fewer problems in the case of measuring the *Mirror*'s profits.

Table IV is quite revealing. If we exclude the special effects of higher newsprint prices paid by Fairfax and additional promotional expenses, then profits fell by $1.3 million in 1975–76. In contrast, News Limited's profits rose by $1.6 million. Thus the profit effects of events in 1975–76 were close to a zero sum game, with News Limited winning what Fairfax lost.

The compositional breakdown of these changes is interesting. It is clear that

TABLE IV
INCREMENTS IN COMPANY PROFITS 1974–75 TO 1975–76
($ MILLION)

	Mirror	*Sun*
Increment to Revenue		
Circulation Revenue	+0.4[1]	+0.8[1]
Advertising Revenue	+4.4[2]	+0.3[2]
Total	+4.8	+1.1
Increment to Costs		
Mirror's Cost	+3.2[4]	+3.2[5]
Higher Newsprint Prices for Sun		+0.3
Higher Promotional Costs for Sun		+0.1
Lower Production Costs for Sun		−0.8[6]
Total	+3.2	+2.8
Increment to Gross Profit	+1.6[2]	−1.7[4]

Notes: [1] Based on wholesale *net* prices and circulation data from Tables I (adjusted from gross price) and III.

[2] Company annual report.

[3] *Mirror* source. Checked in part by *Thompson Publication* [21] Australian Advertising Rate and Data Service Newspaper Edition. This confirms advertising price component.

[4] Residual.

[5] The *Mirror*'s increment in costs are taken as a numeraire and adjusted for differential factors.

[6] The lower production costs for the *Sun* arise because of a reduced production volume, while the *Mirror*'s production volume rose. Each aspect amounts to $0.4 million given that marginal production costs are about equal to marginal circulation revenue. The latter information came from my interview with the *Mirror* management and is consistent with data in the 1974 P.J.T. report on John Fairfax and Sons.

Fairfax outperformed News Limited in terms of circulation revenue. With demand price inelastic the increased price of the *Sun* increased circulation revenue. With a constant price and increased circulation, the *Mirror* also increased its circulation revenue, but not as much. Reinforcing these gains is the effect on operating costs. The *Mirror*'s operating costs *rose* $0.4 million because of increased production volume (marginal costs about equal to marginal circulation revenue), while the *Sun*'s operating costs *fell* by a corresponding $0.4 million because of decreased production volume. The sum of these production cost changes and cover price changes puts the *Sun* ahead by $1.2 million. However, we now have to bring equation (2) into effect. About half of the *Mirror*'s increased advertising revenue shown in Table IV is attributable to the equation (2) effect, that is, to greater circulation increasing its relative advertising rate. Greater advertising volume explains the remainder of the increased advertising revenue. No doubt some of the increased advertising volume can be attributed to increased circulation, though this component is more fickle; year to year changes reflect changes in the mix of advertising, economic activity, etc. *Excluding* advertising volume changes, the increase in the *Mirror*'s relative circulation via equation (2) added $1.7 million to its *relative* profit, which exceeds the *Sun*'s gains, noted above, by $0.5 million. This can be taken as the *minimum* annual volume of the price war game to News Limited, somewhat larger if advertising volume effects were also related to circulation. Over a four year period, the price war netted News Limited about $2 million and cost Fairfax the same.

STAGE 4 CONTINUED. 1975–79: TACTICS DURING THE BATTLE

The *Mirror*'s tactics over the 1975–79 period concentrated on price competition in the evening market, backed up by discontinuous bursts of advertising which emphasized price. As we saw above, this pricing strategy added about seven percent to the *Mirror*'s sales in relatively quick time. We have also shown that this pricing strategy was very profitable, adding at least $0.5 million annually to News Limited's gross profits.

The advantage of delineating the Sydney newspaper market becomes clear when we discover that News Limited simultaneously employed the opposite strategy in the morning and Sunday markets. In these markets, from late 1976 (see Table II), News Limited led John Fairfax in increasing prices. Several factors underlie this opposite strategy. First, as of mid-1976, the *Australian* newspaper had been operating at heavy losses ($3 million p.a.) which required special attention, namely hefty cover price increases. Secondly, the strategy fits the objective of News Limited to regain the overall price leadership.

With prices deadlocked in the evening market, News Limited had an open hand to initiate changes in the morning market. Thirdly, the opportunity cost to News Limited from pushing price in the morning market was minimal in light of the likely small own and cross price elasticity of demand. Fourthly, another factor stems from the uncertainty in which the evening newspaper price was couched. News Limited lacked experience in price experimentation, so the morning market provided a useful hedge in case events did not go to plan.

The *Sun*'s tactics were altogether different. Its early competitive response to the *Mirror*'s attack was not the orthodox price matching move, but rather an intensified advertising campaign. Presumably Fairfax was not in a hurry to relinquish its price leadership role and therefore resisted surrendering to Murdoch's challenge. This proved to be a costly mistake, with heavy declines in circulation, advertising volume and advertising revenue, which were only partially offset by the gain in circulation revenue (a 20% increase in price and a 7% loss in sales volume). The *Sun* lost at least $0.5 million in profit annually because of its higher relative price. Other factors compounded this loss.

In a subtle way, the *Sun*'s advertising response can be interpreted as a pricing strategy. Many oligopolistic firms employ product segmenting techniques whereby brands are differentiated on the basis of real or imagined quality. Frequently the brand price structure reflects or even identifies the segmented range of brands. Given that the *Sun*'s advertising extolled its quality, we have some basis for interpreting this as part of a product-price segmentation tactic. As we have shown in the previous section, the *Sun*'s promotional campaign was not particularly successful. The lack of success by the *Sun* in this area was caused partly by cannibalization and perhaps partly by the general ineffectiveness of advertising in the newspaper industry. For the former the Hotelling or game theoretic models provide an explanatory framework.

Although the *Sun*'s emphasis on advertising rather than price in the evening market was a strategic error, so too was its emphasis on price in the morning and Sunday markets. As can be seen in Table II, the *Telegraph* led the *S.M.H.* in price rises to 13, 14, 15 and 20 cents. For the first three of these, the lag in Fairfax's response was 7, 11 and 12 months respectively. This is most puzzling. What was Fairfax trying to do? It would seem that Fairfax was playing the Murdoch game with a slightly different slant; by following the *Telegraph* with an increasingly long lag, the *Herald* offered the threat that one day it might not follow at all. It certainly seems a cumbersome, though intriguing alternative to what Murdoch did with the *Mirror* after July 1975. Unfortunately, as we have now confirmed, the morning and evening markets are quite different. The lower *S.M.H.* price over the 1976–78 period cost the *Telegraph* less than one percent of its sales volume and equally little advertising volume or revenue.

STAGE 5. 1979–80: THE END OF THE BATTLE BUT NOT THE WAR

On January 15, 1979, backed by a large $500,000 advertising campaign the *Sun* retreated to 10 cents. This signalled a tactical victory to Murdoch. Until the *Mirror* had been appeased, the *Sun* was unable to increase its price beyond

12 cents. Thus Fairfax's price move to 12 cents proved abortive and indeed the next round of price increases to 15 cents in November 1979 were led by News Limited.

In the previous section we have criticised Fairfax's tactics. Three and a half years was a long time to retreat on price. The emphasis on advertising was criticised as being ineffective in raising market share and also for inappropriately deploying funds which could have been used to finance a price war. In recent margarine price wars, by contrast, most firms severely trimmed their advertising budgets during the peak of the war.

In retrospect one might have anticipated that the price war would have ended much earlier, say in late 1976 or early 1977. By that time there was apparently sufficient evidence of the cross elasticity of demand with respect to price and of the effect of increased promotional expenditures upon circulation.

One suspects that an important element in the long delay by Fairfax relates to the conglomerate media interests of Fairfax in Sydney: in television (Channel 7), radio (2GB), magazines and other specialised papers (including the *Financial Review* and *National Times*). These other media outlets provided a means of cross-subsidizing the *Sun*. There is also the possibility of internal transfer pricing manipulation, whereby the *Sun* could have paid a price below the market rate to Fairfax's other media outlets. Such manipulation is usually discussed in an international context, where differences in company tax rates between countries could make such schemes profitable on an after-tax basis. Within Australia fully owned subsidiaries are treated as separate tax paying units, so there is some scope for internal transfer pricing arrangements. But would they be profitable if both the parent and the subsidiary pay the same company tax rate? The answer is yes because modified transfer prices can *defer* tax payments, which in present-value terms is a benefit in the same way as accelerated depreciation allowances are. Having said all this, there are *limits* on the ability of companies to manipulate internal transfer prices for taxation purposes under the Companies Tax Act. To the extent that the *Sun* did take advantage of lower media charges by other Fairfax media organizations, then its true loss would be even greater than shown in Table IV!

If instead the *Sun* paid *market* rates for its use of other Fairfax media services, it could be argued that the opportunity cost was below the price charged for similar advertising time to outside organizations. Under what conditions would this be true? Last minute cancellations of advertising time on 2GB or Channel 7 would create vacant time slots in which advertisements for the *Sun* could be run. This suggests a novel advantage of diversified firms, which may be unique to media industries. However this practice may not be *flexible* enough to accommodate a planned large increment of advertising by the *Sun* in desired times of the year or day, especially when there is high demand for television time, as in the mid-1970s.

In summary, the ability of the *Sun* to operate within a conglomerate media network and either pay less than market price for other media services, or market prices, but at reduced opportunity cost, goes a long way in explaining the slow response by Fairfax in ending the price war. However, cheaper prices for other media services simply makes Fairfax's tactics less irrational; it does not make them rational. Even if the cost of other media services were zero it still cost Fairfax half a million dollars in profits in having higher relative cover prices. Similarly, Fairfax was earning less than maximum profits in the morning newspaper market because its prices were too low!

There is no escaping the conclusion that Fairfax was determined to retain its price leadership in the evening newspaper market and was prepared to sacrifice profits in the process. Perhaps Fairfax thought that the *Mirror*'s price freeze would be short-lived, ending, say, in June 1976 when News Limited's windfall newsprint cost advantage ended.[6] In turn, Fairfax may have underestimated the importance of price leadership to Murdoch. The Trade Practices Act must be partly credited for engendering confusion on the price setting front, with price leadership proving to be an imperfect substitute for collusion in the formative years of establishing leadership.

Although the 1975–79 price battle was won by News Limited, who demonstrated their newly won price leadership in initiating the November 1979 price increase, events in 1980 made it clear that the struggle was not over. On June 30, 1980 John Fairfax gave a week's notice that the price of the *Sun* was to rise to 20 cents. The *Mirror*'s counterpart announcement followed two days later. With the convenience of 'one coin shopping' and ground lost to inflation since 1974, there was perhaps little doubt about whether the *Mirror* would match the move to 20 cents. As things stand, Fairfax cleverly sneaked back in as price leader in the evening market. Moreover, the *Sun* cemented its newly found dominant position by leading the November 1980 advertising rate increases. Similarly in the Sunday newspaper market, Fairfax led the May 1981 round of cover price increases.

STAGE 6. 1981–82: A NEW NON-PRICE BATTLE

With both firms vying for power, it would be surprising if Fairfax's initiatives in 1980 ushered in a new era of stability. In fact, an unusually aggressive bout of non-price competition began in July 1981 and continues as of mid-1982. The *Mirror* initiated the bingo competition ploy, but was quickly matched by the *Sun* with a slightly different version of the competition. The Australian fever in the area trails England's Fleet Street events by about a month. In the

[6] Over the longer term, Fairfax could have been hoping for a newsagent's boycott in light of the temporal decline in the real value of the *Mirror*. Money illusion may have partly avoided such action. Moreover the case noted in our Stage 3 discussion, the Melbourne *Daily Morning Post*, was 50 percent cheaper than its rivals (compared with 20 percent in the case of the *Mirror*); there was more choice of newspapers in the 1925–27 case (three rivals, not one) and the *Morning Post* did not have News Limited's overall bargaining power in the publishing industry. For these reasons, a boycott would have required a much greater cover price differential than the actual figure of 20 percent.

U.K. the cost of running bingo games in newspapers is expected to be £15 million for prizes alone in 1981–82 (Garcia [5]). Distribution costs are additional. Circulation, especially for Express Newspapers' *Daily Star* and Murdoch's *Sun* are up dramatically, but so are costs, so there has been little change in profitability. This pattern on a smaller scale is repeated in the Sydney evening newspaper market.

In the U.K., with the exception of the "quality" nationals, the move into bingo competition has been across the board. The same was true in the initial phases in the Sydney evening market. Again these imitative strategies are explicable in terms of Hotelling or game theoretic models. Initially the Sydney *Sun* accelerated the pace of the bingo promotion by raising the prize money compared to what the *Mirror* offered initially. However, shortly after, the *Sun* scaled down its involvement and has since withdrawn altogether from bingo competition while the *Mirror* continues. This is a calculated risk for the *Sun*. To refrain from a popular promotional strategy when a rival is aggressively implementing such a strategy, spells doom in a game theoretic framework. At least in terms of market share, there are clear short-term gains for the *Mirror* (*cf.* Table III and also equation (4)). The *Sun*'s management (Garcia, [5]) believes that these gains may be temporary—which may include the prospect of the bingo novelty wearing out. As well, there is a presumption that circulations increased by bingo competitions will not be attractive to advertisers because such additional sales may be by people who do not read the rest of the paper. Readership and circulation volumes would diverge.

The *Sun* is hoping that the *Mirror* will haemorrhage from a cost squeeze, at which time it can assert its power aspirations. Similarly the *Mirror* is trying to move into a position of strength. In the current intermediate phase, neither company is as yet ready to take a firm resolve for leadership. As a result, initiatives on price setting in recent years have oscillated from one company to the other, as shown in Table I. This may continue until one company feels it is in a favoured position. As with New York and London, only one evening newspaper might survive such an encounter.

CONCLUSIONS

The emergence of a competitive price struggle in this industry is particularly interesting because it is preceded by three decades of identical prices. Government policy designed to facilitate competition in the economy can learn much from cases such as this one. While more cases will enrich our understanding of the competitive process, one point already seems especially clear. Even in what appear to be very stable oligopolies, there is always a latent power struggle between the major firms. The theory of games emphasizes the inherent conflict between firms which can only artificially and temporarily be resolved by collusive price leadership or similar practices. It is up to government agencies to exploit this latent conflict.

One by-product of this research is the idea that theories of cartel behaviour need to be modified to incorporate the possibility of a dominant firm. The role of Saudi Arabia in the OPEC Cartel is a case in point. As such the role is very similar to that of a price leader, except most of the assertion of power is behind closed doors. In the Australian newspaper case the dominant firm switched in the early 1970s from Fairfax to News Limited. We know very little about this switchover. Why was it so smooth? Why didn't Fairfax resist and spark off a price war?

The other theme looked at in this paper is the quality of management in forming appropriate marketing strategies. We have generally praised News Limited's tactics in both the morning and evening markets, which effectively exploited the differing cross elasticities of demand and correctly judged other aspects of the challenge to Fairfax's price leadership. There is no doubt that Fairfax used inappropriate strategies in both the evening and morning markets; advertising was an ineffective instrument in the evening market and price an ineffective instrument in the morning market. Perhaps the desperate struggle for leadership induced these irrational actions by John Fairfax and Sons. None the less, better use of economic theory and practice could have averted the worst of these management mistakes and conserved resources for a more informed counter-attack on the Murdoch empire at a later date.

William J. Merrilees
Department of Economics,
The University of Sydney,
New South Wales 2006,
Australia.

ACCEPTED MAY 1982

REFERENCES

[1] AUDIT BUREAU OF CIRCULATION, 'Six Monthly Circulation Data', available on request and published in *Australian Financial Review, passim.*

[2] COMANOR, W., 'Market Structure, Product Differentiation and Industrial Research', *Quarterly Journal of Economics,* 81, **1** (November 1967), pp. 639–57.

[3] DAVIDSON, F. and STEWARDSON, B., *Economics and Australian Industry* (Longman, Melbourne, 1979).

[4] FOG, B., *Industrial Pricing Policies* (North Holland, Amsterdam, 1960).

[5] GARCIA, L., 'Who are the Winners in the Bingo War,' Article in the *Sydney Morning Herald,* December 12, 1981.

[6] HOTELLING, H., 'Stability in Competition', *Economic Journal,* 39, **153** (March 1929), pp. 41–57.

[7] HUNTER, A., 'Restrictive Practices and Monopolies in Australia,' *Economic Record,* 37, **77** (March 1961), pp. 25–52.

[8] JOBSON'S INVESTMENT DIGEST, 'Spotlight on Mirror Newspaper Ltd.', 41, **10** (May 26, 1960), p. 290.

[9] JONES, R., 'The Sydney Newspaper Industry', in C. Terry (ed.) *Australian Microeconomics* (Prentice Hall, Sydney, 1980).

[10] LIPSEY, R., *Positive Economics* (Wiedenfeld and Nicolson, London, 1979).

[11] MAYER, H., *The Press in Australia* (Lansdowne Press, Melbourne, 1964).
[12] MERRILEES, W., 'Price Competition in the Magazine Industry', in K. Heys and B. Langworthy (eds.) *ECTA Readings in Economics* Volume 3 (Economic Commercial Teachers' Association of N.S.W., Sydney, 1982), pp. 143–50.
[13] NICHOLLS, W., *Price Policies in the Cigarette Industry* (Vanderbilt Press, Nashville, 1951).
[14] PORTER, M., 'Consumer Behaviour, Retailer Power and Market Performance in Consumer Goods Industries', *Review of Economics and Statistics,* 56, **4** (November 1974), pp. 419–36.
[15] PRICES JUSTIFICATION TRIBUNAL, 'Report on John Fairfax and Sons Limited', September 13, 1974.
[16] REEKIE, W., 'The Price Elasticity of the Demand for Evening Newspapers', *Applied Economics,* 8, **1** (March 1976), pp. 69–79.
[17] SCHERER, F., 'The Welfare Economics of Product Variety: An Application to the Ready-to-Eat Cereals Industry', *Journal of Industrial Economics,* 28, **2** (December 1979), pp. 113–34.
[18] SHERIDAN, K., *The Firm in Australia,* (Thomas Nelson, Melbourne, 1974).
[19] STEINER, P., 'Monopoly and Television in Television: Some Policy Issues', *Manchester School of Economics and Social Sciences,* 29, **2** (May 1961) pp. 107–31.
[20] STIGLER, G., 'The Kinky Oligopoly Demand Curve and Rigid Prices', *Journal of Political Economy,* **55** (October 1947), pp. 432–49.
[21] THOMSON PUBLICATIONS, 'Australian Advertising Rate and Data Service: Newspaper Edition', *passim.*
[22] WILTSHIRE, K. and STOKES, C., *Government Regulation in the Printed Media Industry* (Committee for Economic Development of Australia, Melbourne 1977).

THE JOURNAL OF INDUSTRIAL ECONOMICS
Volume XXXI March 1983 No. 3

INNOVATION IN A LABOR-MANAGED FIRM: A MEMBERSHIP PERSPECTIVE*

JOHN P. BONIN

I. INTRODUCTION: INNOVATION IN A LABOR-MANAGED FIRM

IN his treatise on on the general theory of the labor-managed economy, Vanek [10] argues that the organizational principle of labor-management has an advantage over other forms in promoting minor innovation. Minor innovation can be distinguished from major innovation according to capital-financing characteristics. Major innovation corresponds to research and development ventures which require long-term financing. Minor innovation involves using the Hayekian time and place specific information of the worker to improve productivity. Implementation occurs in a learning-by-doing atmosphere and externalities among workers are likely, but no long-term financing is required.

Vanek argues that a labor-managed organization provides a conflict-free environment within which Hayek's man-on-the-spot is willing to share his information with fellow workers to improve overall performance. Vanek states that a natural channel of communication exists between those who have the information and innovative ideas and those who choose production techniques to implement this choice because of the participatory decision-making structure in the labor-managed firm. Furthermore, he claims that goal congruence exists between those with the information and those who incorporate the fruits of innovation into the distribution scheme of the firm because of each member's property right to residual earnings in the labor-managed firm. Vanek concludes that the labor-managed firm is better able to elicit the information necessary to undertake the minor technical innovation and to accommodate and adjust to any negative effects of implementing such innovation by cushioning adverse employment effects.

Vanek considers explicitly the reaction of the labor-managed firm to only one type of technical innovation, Hicks' neutral technological change. He argues that the dividend-maximizing firm faces countervailing employment reactions to such innovation. The scale effects tend to increase employment while a capital-cost sharing effect, familiar to the dividend-maximizing firm

* This research was undertaken while I was a NATO Postdoctoral Fellow at Birkbeck College, University of London, on sabbatical-leave from Wesleyan University. I would like to thank NATO and Wesleyan for financial-support and Birkbeck for an environment conducive to research. The ideas in this paper were presented to the Social Science Research Council's Industrial Economics Study Group at Warwick University. I would like to thank the members of the workshop, in particular Norman Ireland and Peter Law, for helpful comments. Of course, all errors and omissions are my own responsibility.

from the early work of Ward [11] tends to decrease employment. To study minor innovation more generally, we distinguish the labor-managed firm from the dividend-maximizer in the short run by explicitly considering membership rights to income shares and the participatory voting rights. Treating minor innovation as a shift parameter in the short run production function, we separate the distribution and employment effects of technical change. A solidarity result emerges to lend some support for Vanek's claim that the labor-managed firm will cushion any adverse employment effects resulting from dividend-maximization at least in the short run. However, a profit-maximizing firm would employ even more labor in the same situation. Of course, the distribution of the short term rents to innovation differ between the labor-managed firm and the profit-maximizing one. Consequently, in the absence of the appropriate bonus transfers to workers in the profit-maximizing firm, Vanek's claim that the Hayekian man-on-the-spot with the information is more willing to share it in the labor-managed firm has a distributional support. We conclude our discussion of short run minor innovation with a consideration of the incentives, both for individuals and groups, to share information in three different organizational forms; the labor-managed firm, the dividend-maximizer, and the profit-maximizer.

To analyze the long run effects of minor innovation, we assume that the labor-managed firm behaves as a dividend-maximizer in the long run. Using various familiar specifications for technical change, we demonstrate that the labor-managed firm prefers more labor-saving technical innovation than its competitive profit-rate maximizing counterpart. We show that Hicks' neutral technical change induces the dividend-maximizer to choose a more capital-intensive production technique. Consequently, minor innovation is likely to generate pressures for long run adverse employment effects in the labor-managed firm. To some extent, natural attrition may render the required reduction in the work force consistent with the property rights structure. In our analysis, we assume a linear homogeneous production function so that our results can be used as a basis for empirical work studying the effects of technical innovation on productivity across industries in Yugoslavia.

Finally, we do not consider major innovations for the labor-managed firm. Earlier work comparing the dividend-maximizer to the profit-maximizer is relevant here if we take long term financing as the distinguishing characteristic. Atkinson [1] compares the two organizational forms in an environment in which there is no choice of techniques but exogenous labor-augmenting technical change is occurring. He concludes that the labor-managed firm grows more slowly than its competitive counterpart even when capital accumulation can be financed externally. Atkinson's result indicates that labor-managed firms may undertake less research and development activity than profit maximizers even when such investment can be financed externally. Ireland and Law [5] have compared advertising expenditures for the two organizational forms assuming that advertising shifts the demand curve, and hence the earnings potential, of both firms. Advertising expenditures are subtracted from earnings so that the situation is similar to firms financing internally the entire cost of major innovation (R & D) due to a lack of access to external financing. Ireland and Law show that the dividend-maximizer chooses a different, more capital-intensive, input mix from the profit-maximizing one in this situation. Therefore, their results are consistent with the tendencies we discover in the long run for minor innovation.

Consequently, Vanek's claims for superiority of the labor-managed form in promoting innovation would seem to receive strongest support from distributional differences in the short run. This result is not insignificant since analytical models usually do not suggest situations in which the labor-managed firm outperforms its capitalist counterpart. An exception to this general statement is found in Ireland [6] where work environment is considered to be a choice variable. Using a proxy variable of efficiency labor units, Ireland derives a necessary and sufficient condition for the choice to be different in the two types of firms. Consequently, he characterizes situations in which the labor-managed principle is preferable to profit-maximization due to the introduction of a decision about work environment. We abstract from these considerations by assuming a fixed relationship between members and the labor input and, therefore, allow no individual choice of efficiency units. Nonetheless, by introducing the property rights of the membership to the theory of the labor-managed firm, we are able to provide some partial analytical support for Vanek's intuition about team spirit and goal congruence within the labor-managed firm.

II. SOLIDARITY AND DISTRIBUTION: INNOVATION IN THE SHORT RUN

The labor-managed firm under consideration might be called more appropriately an egalitarian cooperative to distinguish it from the inegalitarian cooperative discussed by Meade [7]. There is no internal labor-ladder in the firm so distribution of residual income involves each member receiving an equal share of net earnings. Labor-leisure considerations are suppressed by assuming that all members work the same number of effective hours, consequently the distribution principle is equitable. Our analysis assumes an initial situation of equilibrium in which the dividend earned within the firm, i.e., net earnings per member, equals the next best earnings alternative, denoted y_0. In the short run, the initial membership, L_0, is assumed to have incurred a fixed debt obligation, $\bar{C}$, in return for the use of a production technology, $Q(L, \alpha)$ where the stock of capital is implicitly embedded in the production function and α is a shift parameter used to describe technical innovation during the period. For simplicity, product price is assumed to be fixed equal to one.

Membership in the cooperative entitles one to a share in net earnings during the period and a vote in making any policy decision during the period. The second membership right may be related to the participatory decision-making structure of the labor-managed firm. However, as we shall see, it is similar in form to the rules for permissible membership change in any labor-cooperative laid down by Meade [17, p. 420]. By explicitly considering the membership rights of the initial group comprising the firm, we demonstrate how the labor-managed firm behaves differently from a Ward-type of dividend-maximizer with respect to short run innovation.

Given our discussion above, we can define dividend in the short run as

$$(1)\qquad y(L, \alpha) = \frac{Q(L, \alpha) - \bar{C}}{L}$$

Denote as $y^*(\alpha)$, the solution to

$$(2)\qquad \max_{L} y(L, \alpha) = y^*(\alpha)$$

which has as a necessary condition

$$(3)\qquad L^* \text{ such that } Q_L = \frac{Q - \bar{C}}{L} = y$$

The initial internal equilibrium with L_0 members can be described as

$$(4)\qquad y^*(\alpha) = y(L_0, \alpha) = y_0$$

Assuming that the earnings alternative is available for any members who leave the cooperative during the period, the income of the initial membership can be written as:

$$(5)\qquad Y(L_0, L, \alpha) = Ly(L, \alpha) + (L_0 - L)y_0 \text{ for } L \leq L_0$$

To analyze the incentives for innovation in the short run, consider initially two values for α where

$$(\text{A-1})\qquad \alpha_2 > \alpha_1 \rightarrow \frac{Q(L, \alpha_2)}{L} > \frac{Q(L, \alpha_1)}{L} \quad \text{but} \quad Q_L(L, \alpha_2) = Q_L(L, \alpha_1).$$

In other words, innovation increases average product but leaves marginal product unchanged for all levels of labor. This case will illustrate distributional differences between three forms of organization; the profit maximizing firm, the dividend-maximizing firm, and our egalitarian cooperative. Let y_0 be the parametric wage paid by a profit-maximizing firm. Then L_0 is the profit-maximizing labor force for both α_2 and α_1 from (3) and (4). However, $\pi(L_0, \alpha_2) > \pi(L_0, \alpha_1)$ and $Q(L_0, \alpha_2) > Q(L_0, \alpha_1)$ so that the entire benefit of the short-run innovation accrues to the owner(s) of the firm. In contrast, consider a dividend-maximizing firm. In Figure 1, we diagram the optimal solution for the dividend maximizer, i.e.,

$$L_1 < L_0 \text{ and } y^*(\alpha_2) > y_0 .$$

The effect of this type of short run innovation is to reduce membership,

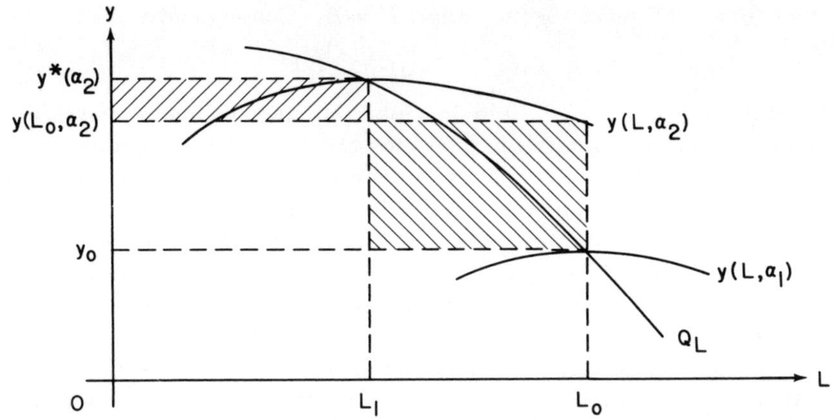

FIGURE 1
Solidarity, the Distributional Effect.

increase the dividend to the remaining members and have an ambiguous effect on output. The benefits accrue to the remaining members only.

For Vanek's notion of team spirit and cohesion to apply, it would seem necessary that no one with information pertinent to technical innovation be dismissed involuntarily. Since the nature of Hayekian information suggests that the sources of information for minor innovation are not readily identifiable *ex ante*, any involuntary dismissal of members should be ruled out. Referring again to Figure 1, we see that, since $y(L_0, \alpha_2) > y_0$, no one will voluntarily leave for the earnings alternative y_0. Furthermore, an arrangement by which the members would agree to reduce labor to L_1, thus generating the higher dividend $y^*(\alpha_2) > y(L_0, \alpha_2)$, and share total income, consisting both of income earned within the cooperative [i.e. $y^*(\alpha_2)L_1$] and income earned from the alternative source [i.e., $y_0(L_0 - L_1)$] among all L_0 members turns out to yield less income per member than the solidarity response of everyone remaining in productive employment within the cooperative. We demonstrate this in the following proposition and interpret the formal similarity between participatory voting rights and transfers necessary to induce voluntary withdrawals from the cooperative in the remarks that follow the proof.

Proposition: If $y^*(\alpha_1) = y(L_0, \alpha_1) = y_0$, then $Y(L_0, L_0, \alpha_2) > Y(L_0, L_1, \alpha_2)$ for $\alpha_2 > \alpha_1$ where $L_0 > L_1 = \max_L : y(L, \alpha_2)$.

Proof: Define L' to be $\max_L \; Y(L_0, L, \alpha_2)$ for all L and notice that L' solves

$$(6) \qquad 0 = Y_L(L_0, L, \alpha_2) \leftrightarrow Q_L(L', \alpha_2) = y_0$$

Also, $Y_{LL}(L_0, L, \alpha_2) = Q_{LL}(L, \alpha_2) < 0$ by assumption so that L' is unique and Y is strictly concave in L. Now (A-1) implies $Q_L(L, \alpha_2) = Q_L(L, \alpha_1)$ for any L and therefore, from (3) and (4)

$$(7) \qquad y_0 = Q_L(L_0, \alpha_1) = Q_L(L_0, \alpha_2)$$

Now (6) and (7) taken together imply $L' = L_0$. Consequently,

$$Y(L_0, L_0, \alpha_2) > Y(L_0, L_1, \alpha_2). \quad \text{Q.E.D.}$$

From the perspective of the initial membership, the maximum total income available for sharing occurs when all members remain in a productive capacity within the firm after the technical innovation. Therefore, the basic membership right has important policy implications. Suppose an arrangement was made to pay transfers to individuals just sufficient to make them willing to leave the firm and take employment at the earnings alternative y_0. The maximum dividend earnable $y^*(\alpha_2)$ would require compensating $(L_0 - L_1)$ members. The necessary compensation per member would be $y(L_0, \alpha_2) - y_0$, i.e., the difference between the dividend earned if all remain and the alternative. Total compensation paid by the L_1 remaining members would equal

$$(L_0 - L_1)[y(L_0, \alpha_2) - y_0]$$

so that total earnings net of this compensation which would be available to divide among the L_1 members is given by

$$y^*(\alpha_2)L_1 - (L_0 - L_1)[y(L_0, \alpha_2) - y_0].$$

If, on the other hand, all members remain in a productive capacity within the firm, the dividend is $y(L_0, \alpha_2)$ and total income shared by these same L_1 members is $y(L_0, \alpha_2)L_1$. Now, the proposition insures that

$$y(L_0, \alpha_2)L_1 > y(\alpha_2)L_1 - (L_0 - L_1)[y(L_0, \alpha_2) - y_0] \tag{8}$$

since rearranging terms in (8) yields $Y(L_0, L_0, \alpha_2) > Y(L_0, L_1, \alpha_2)$. Consequently, the income left for distribution among the L_1 remaining members after the necessary compensation is paid to the $(L_0 - L_1)$ members to induce them to leave voluntarily yields a smaller dividend than the solidarity dividend earned when all members remain in a productive capacity within the firm. Therefore, transfers cannot be made to encourage workers to leave the firm voluntarily and allow the workers remaining in the firm to be better off than they would have been if no workers were dismissed.

Notice that the analysis to this point has assumed that any individual is interested in maximizing only his own income. The solidarity result does not depend on group consciousness but rather on a right to the enhanced earnings of the firm due to short run innovation by virtue of initial membership in the cooperative. The formal similarity between such transfers and the participatory decision-making structure of a labor-managed firm is apparent in the following scenario due to Steinherr and Thisse [9]. Suppose individual members are asked to vote on two proposals:

Proposal one: solidary with a dividend of $y(L_0, \alpha_2)$ or

Proposal two: a reduction in membership to L_1 with dividend $y^*(\alpha_2)$.

Suppose further that any reduction in membership would be undertaken by random dismissals so that any individual member considers the probability of his dismissal to be

$$\pi = \frac{L_0 - L_1}{L_0}.$$

Although other rules which establish a pecking order for dismissals (e.g., seniority) are possible, they would violate the spirit of our egalitarian cooperative in which all members are to be treated equally. A dismissed worker earns the alternative y_0. Denoting by $(1 - \pi)$ the probability that any individual will retain membership and thus earn $y^*(\alpha_2)$, each individual's expected income if the second proposal involving membership reduction prevails can be written as

$$\pi y_0 + (1 - \pi)y^*(\alpha_2) = \left[\frac{L_0 - L_1}{L_0}\right]y_0 + \frac{L_1}{L_0}y^*(\alpha_2) \tag{9}$$

On the other hand, if the first proposal of membership solidarity is accepted, each member's income is simply $y(L_0, \alpha_2)$. Algebraic manipulation and the use of (8) and (9) will demonstrate that

$$y(L_0, \alpha_2) > \pi y_0 + (1 - \pi)y^*(\alpha_2).$$

Consequently, only a risk-preferring individual would vote for the second proposal. Unless more than half of the initial members of the cooperative are risk-preferring, the solidarity proposal will be passed by a voting procedure satisfying majority rule.

For this simple formulation of short run technical innovation, our egalitarian cooperative behaves like a profit maximizing firm by keeping membership constant and producing $Q(L_0, \alpha_2)$. The only difference is distributive; the worker-members share the increased net earnings equally in the cooperative whereas workers continue to receive a wage equal to y_0 in the profit-maximizing firm and the owner(s) of the firm receives the increased earnings in increased profits. On the other hand, the dividend-maximizing solution is different in an allocative sense as well since labor is reduced to achieve still higher shares for the remaining members. However, the membership rights in the labor-managed firm suggest a preference for the egalitarian cooperative model over the dividend-maximizing one. That the egalitarian cooperative and the profit-maximizer respond in the same allocative way is sensitive to our specification of short run technical innovation as we demonstrate in the next section.

III. SHORT RUN ALLOCATIVE EFFECTS AND INCENTIVES

By considering a somewhat more general condition on the innovative shift parameter, allocative differences between the egalitarian cooperative and the profit maximizer can occur. As we have argued in [2], a necessary and sufficient condition for the two organizational forms to act in an allocatively-equivalent way in the short run is that the cooperative be allowed to hire temporary workers at the opportunity cost y_0. Yugoslavian institutional changes seem to encourage this arrangement due either to a pool of temporary workers or to transfer agreements which allow subcontracting for services from other firms. However, we assume here that any addition to the labor input in our cooperative requires original members to accept a new member with full membership rights.

In our environment, consider a technical innovation which shifts the production function in the following way.

Suppose, for

$$\text{(A-2)} \qquad \alpha_2 > \alpha_1, \; Q_L(L, \alpha_2) > Q_L(L, \alpha_1)$$

and

$$\frac{\partial(Q/L)}{\partial\alpha} > \frac{\partial Q_L}{\partial\alpha} > 0 \text{ for any } L.$$

In other words, both average and marginal products increase with α but the marginal product of labor increases less than the average product. This is a sufficient condition for the dividend-maximizing firm to respond in a directionally-different way from the profit-maximizing firm. To see this, totally differentiate (3) and solve for $dL^*/d\alpha$. Rewriting (3),

$$Q_L(L^*, \alpha) = \frac{Q(L^*, \alpha) - C}{L^*}$$

Now, totally differentiating with respect to α yields:

$$Q_{LL}\frac{dL^*}{d\alpha} + \frac{\partial Q_L}{\partial\alpha} = \frac{\left[Q_L - \left(\frac{Q-C}{L}\right)\right]}{L}\frac{dL^*}{d\alpha} + \frac{\partial(Q/L)}{\partial\alpha}$$

However, the first term on the right-hand side of the above equation is zero at L^* from (3) so that

$$\frac{dL^*}{d\alpha} = \frac{\dfrac{\partial(Q/L)}{\partial\alpha} - \dfrac{\partial Q_L}{\partial\alpha}}{Q_{LL}}$$

Now $dL^*/d\alpha < 0$ from (A-2) since $Q_{LL} < 0$ by assumption. Denote $\partial Q_L/\partial\alpha$ as $Q_{L\alpha}$ and notice that $Q_{L\alpha} > 0$ means that the profit maximizing firm will hire more workers at the wage of y_0. The situation is diagrammed in Figure 2 where L_1 is the dividend-maximizing labor force and L' is the profit-maximizing one.

The egalitarian cooperative no longer responds in an equivalent allocative

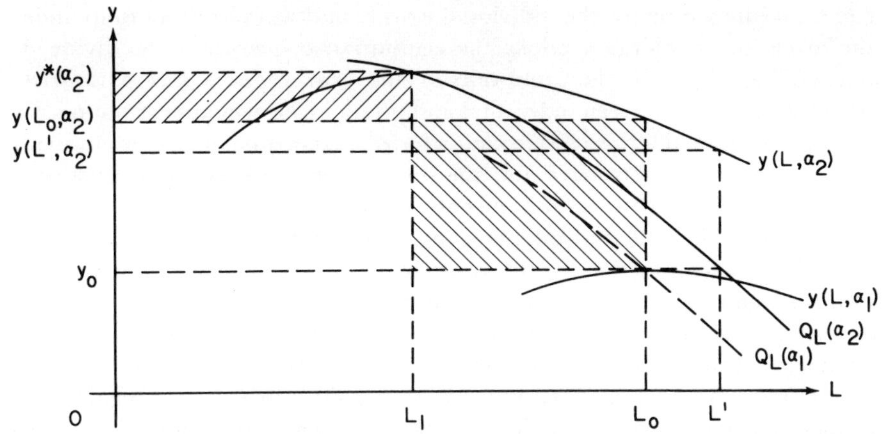

FIGURE 2
Solidarity and Employment.

way to short run innovation as the profit-maximizer. In fact, the propostion in the previous section can be demonstrated by noticing that when $Q_{L\alpha} > 0$ equations (6) and (7) can be combined as follows:

$$(10) \qquad Q_L(L', \alpha_2) = y_0 = Q_L(L_0, \alpha_1) < Q_L(L_0, \alpha_2)$$

when $\alpha_2 > \alpha_1$. The extremes of (10) along with $Q_{LL} < 0$ indicate that $L' > L_0$ where L' maximizes the total income of the initial membership if any increases in labor could be achieved by hiring new workers temporarily at an alternative wage y_0. However, if any new workers must be given full membership rights, an increase in labor above L_0 will lower the income share received by each original member. This follows from noticing that $y(L, \alpha_2)$ is decreasing in L for $L > L_1$ (cf. Figure 2). Consequently, L_0 maximizes the income share of an initial member and the egalitarian cooperative again produces $Q(L_0, \alpha_2)$. Now the membership right in the labor-managed firm induces both allocative and distributive effects different from profit-maximizing behavior.

With the above framework, we can assess the incentives for workers to pass on the information necessary to implement a short run technical improvement. We combine assumptions (A-1) and (A-2) into $0 \leq Q_{L\alpha} < \partial(Q/L)/\partial\alpha$ and consider the situation where $\alpha_2 > \alpha_1$. Table I records the benefits of

TABLE I
FINANCIAL BENEFITS TO SHORT RUN TECHNICAL INNOVATION

	Individual Worker	*Workers as a Group*
Egalitarian Cooperative	$y(L_0, \alpha_2) - y_0$	$Y(L_0, L_0, \alpha_2) - y_0 L_0$
Dividend-Maximizer:		
Remaining Worker(s)	$y^*(\alpha_2) - y_0$	$Y(L_0, L_1, \alpha_2) - y_0 L_0$
Profit-Maximizer	—	$y_0 L' - y_0 L_0$

technical innovation for the individual worker and workers as a group under the three forms of organization; the egalitarian cooperative, the dividend-maximizing firm, and the profit-maximizing firm when all face parametric prices. A tradeoff between individual and group incentives appears across the two organizational forms used to characterize a labor-managed firm. Individual incentives are stronger for the remaining workers in a dividend-maximizing firm while group incentives are stronger in the egalitarian cooperative. This follows from the comparison of dividend differences with differences in total income for the group of original members. Comparing the profit-maximizing firm to the two labor-managed forms of organization will depend on its internal structure of incentives. Suppose $L' = L_0$, and the revenues generated by the technical improvement were distributed to the workers as a group. Group incentives would be the same for the egalitarian cooperative and the profit-maximizer although profits would not increase. On the other hand, the profit-maximizer could pay a bonus to an individual worker (or subset of workers) in order to provide more individual incentive than either of the other two forms and still increase profits. For this strategy to work, some supervisory organ must be able to identify the individuals responsible for the technical improvement and separate them from the rest of the work force. The suggestion box coupled with a price competition might be such an arrangement. Nonetheless, the information requirements and the implications for division in the work force seem clear.

Of course, if the profit-maximizer hires workers in response to technical innovation, i.e., $L' > L_0$, additional differences result. Then, the original work force L_0 could be compensated with the same group incentives as in the egalitarian cooperative and profits could be increased at the expense of newly-hired workers. To the extent that the cooperative can make similar arrangements by temporarily hiring additional workers at the prevailing market wage, the difference disappears. However, the profit-maximizer always maximizes the total return to technical innovation, i.e.,

$$\Upsilon(L_0, L', \alpha_2) \geq \Upsilon(L_0, L_0, \alpha_2) > \Upsilon(L_0, L_1, \alpha_2).$$

By sharing this return with the work force, the potential for eliciting the required information exists.

The issue of individual vs. group incentives seems to depend crucially on the separability of the work force into a group with the required information and/or a group which will wholly bear any costs of innovation. To maintain simplicity, we have not yet introduced the cost of innovation to the worker's decision whether or not to pass on information. To the extent that such a cost is individual, perhaps due to disruption of a single individual's work routine, group incentives are less useful. By bearing the full individual cost but receiving in return only a share of the incremental benefits through an increased dividend paid to all members, the individual worker will not find it in his own self-interest to pass on information about potentially useful innovation. In other words, an inefficient Nash equilibrium will result in the labor-managed firm from individuals maximizing self-interest. Even when the costs of the innovation denoted $C(\alpha)$ are borne by the entire group and not individually-separable (e.g., everyone must adjust to new techniques) the financial group incentives may not be sufficiently strong in the cooperative to induce some Pareto-improving types of technical innovation. When allocative differences are present between the cooperative and the profit-maximizer, a shift parameter α' such that

$$Y(L_0, L', \alpha') > C(\alpha') > Y(L_0, L_0, \alpha')$$

could be found. In this case, a short-run technical innovation which is Pareto-improving, and consequently undertaken by a profit-maximizing firm, would not be undertaken by the cooperative due to its inability to hire labor. The general case for incentive superiority in short run innovation for the labor-managed firm must depend on more than financial considerations if allocative effects are present.

SECTION IV. CHOICE OF TECHNIQUE: INNOVATION IN THE LONG RUN

In the long run view, membership rights may not have as significant an impact on the behavior of the labor-managed firm. In particular, natural attrition may permit the labor force to be reduced as departing members are not replaced. Then, the increased dividend would be shared by the remaining original members. Consequently, it seems appropriate to assume that the labor-managed firm would behave like a dividend-maximizer for purposes of long-run equilibrium comparisons. Therefore, we derive the response of a dividend-maximizer's optimal choice of technique to technological change in the long run when output price and the capital-rental rate are parametric. Our benchmark for comparison will be the choice of technique for a profit-rate maximizer facing the same output price and a parametric wage equal to the initial dividend in the labor-managed firm. The usual Hicks and Harrod notions of technological change will be considered.

When studying long run equilibria, economists often assume that production functions are linear homogeneous both for analytical simplicity and empirical convenience. Meade [8] considers long run behavior of a dividend-maximizer for such a technology concluding that an optimal choice of technique only is determined. Elsewhere [4], we argue that the long run optimal scale of the labor-managed firm is indeterminate with a linear homogeneous technology and parametric prices. Intuitively, this indeterminacy is similar to the indeterminate size of a profit-maximizing firm under conditions of constant returns to scale. With a linear homogeneous technology and constant prices, profits are homogeneous of degree one and dividends are homogeneous of degree zero. To address this issue, costs of adjustment have been introduced to reconcile profit maximization and long run industry equilibrium in the neoclassical theory of the competitive firm. For the labor-managed dividend-maximizing firm, we have included costs of adjustment in a dynamic programming model in order to avoid the size indeterminacy problem in [3]. There we concentrate on short-run adjustment phenomena while here we compare long run equilibria ignoring the costs of adjustment.

Let both capital and labor be freely variable and assume that the production function $Q = Q(K, L)$ is linear homogeneous. Then, as is well-known,

$$q \equiv \frac{Q}{L} = f(k) \quad \text{where} \quad k = K/L \quad \text{and } f(\cdot) \text{ is strictly concave.} \tag{11}$$

With output price set equal to one and the unit cost of capital equal to ρ, dividend can be written as,

$$y = q - \rho k \tag{12}$$

Consequently, dividend-maximization yields an optimal choice of technique k^* which solves

$$f'(k^*) = \rho \tag{13}$$

This is a formalization of Meade's result where each worker's share, the dividend, is given by $q^* - \rho k^*$.

We introduce an innovation shift parameter to the per-capita production function so that now technology is expressed as $f(k, \alpha_1)$, and the optimal choice of technique is given by $k^*(\alpha_1)$ with dividend calculated as

$$q^*(\alpha_1) - \rho k^*(\alpha_1) = y^*(\alpha_1).$$

Referring to Figure 3, the distance between the origin and the "y" intercept of the straight line with slope ρ is the dividend, i.e., $y^*(\alpha_1)$. To continue our

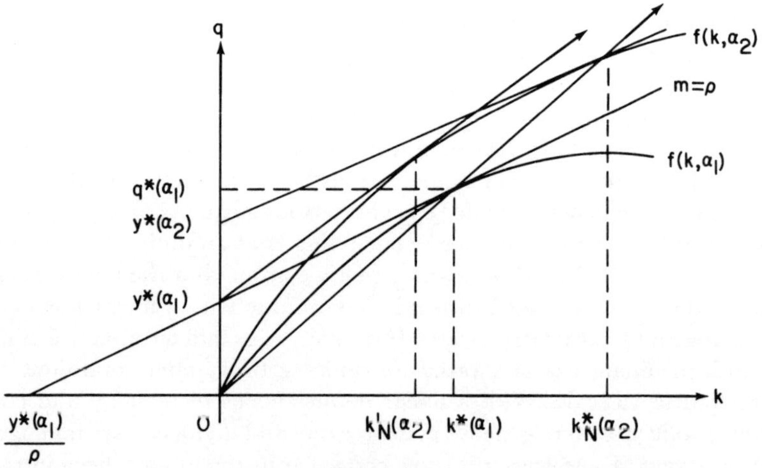

FIGURE 3
Harrod-Neutral Technical Innovation.

comparison of the dividend-maximizer with the neoclassical capitalist firm, we analyze the benchmark firm which maximizes the profit rate, ρ, given a parametric wage rate equal to $y^*(\alpha_1)$. Such an objective is consistent with the usual rentier notion in neo-classical growth theory.

In the initial equilibrium, both the dividend-maximizer and the profit-rate maximizer choose the same technique. The rentier's share is given by

$$\rho k^* = q - y^*(\alpha_1) = q^* - w.$$

In Figure 3, we diagram a technical innovation which is "Harrod-neutral", i.e., the output-capital ratio is constant for a given ρ. Therefore, the new dividend-maximizing technique which solves (13) is given by $k_N^*(\alpha_2)$. Harrod-neutral technical innovation leads a dividend-maximizer to choose a more capital-intensive technique. The profit-rate maximizer, on the other hand, considers $y^*(\alpha_1)$ to be the constant wage rate and maximizes the angle of a feasible ray from the displaced origin on the "y" axis. Clearly, concavity of $f(k, \alpha_2)$ means that the optimal choice of technique for the profit-rate maximizer $k_N'(\alpha_2)$ is less capital-intensive than $k_N^*(\alpha_2)$. It is also possible to show that Harrod "labor-saving" innovation yields a choice of technique for the dividend-maximizer, denoted $k_L^*(\alpha_2)$, which is greater than $k_N^*(\alpha_2)$. In Figure 3, the slope of the new production function would equal ρ at a more capital-intensive technique than with Harrod-neutral innovation. Similarly, Harrod capital-saving innovation yields a tangency at a more labor-intensive choice of technique. Consequently, Harrod "capital-saving" innovation induces a dividend-maximizing choice of technique $k_K^*(\alpha_2) < k_N^*(\alpha_2)$. However, in all cases, the choice of technique by the dividend-maximizer is still more capital-intensive than that of the profit-rate maximizer.

Suppose we consider a scenario in which both types of firm face a variety of possible technical innovations and relate the choice of innovation to organizational form. In Figure 4, we diagram a situation in which the profit-rate maximizer is indifferent between three possible innovations, α_2, α_3 and α_4 which yield the same ρ^*. However, the dividend-maximizer will prefer the more labor-saving innovation. In Figure 4, this is illustrated by observing that

$$y^*(\alpha_4) > y^*(\alpha_2) > y^*(\alpha_3).$$

Now α_4 represents Harrod labor-saving innovation while α_2 and α_3 represent Harrod neutral and capital-saving innovation respectively. It is also easy to construct a diagram to show that various types of technical innovation which leave the dividend-maximizer indifferent among the alternatives will induce the profit-rate maximizer to choose the more capital-saving one. This illustrates the tendency of a dividend-maximizing firm to prefer technical innovation which is more labor-saving than that chosen by a profit-rate maximizer. Consequently, innovation possibilities would reinforce any tendency for the labor-managed firm to choose a production technique which is more capital-intensive than its capitalist counterpart in the long run.

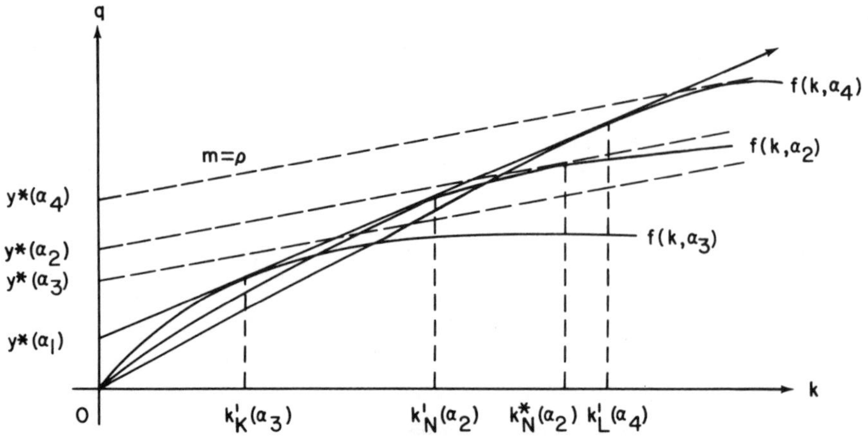

FIGURE 4
Profit Rate vs. Dividend Maximization.

Returning to Figure 3, it is easy to demonstrate that Hicks' neutral technical change will lead the dividend-maximizer to choose a more capital-intensive input mix than the initial one. Consider the "x" intercept of the initial line with slope ρ tangent to $f(k, \alpha_1)$ at $k^*(\alpha_1)$. The distance between this intercept and the origin corresponds to the factor price ratio $y^*(\alpha_1)/\rho = w/\rho$. Hicks' neutral technical change occurs when a ray from the "x" intercept is tangent to the new production function at the initial choice of technique $k^*(\alpha_1)$. Therefore, our graphing of $f(k, \alpha_2)$ could represent Hicks' neutral technical change. This would require that the original production function $Q(K, L)$ be Cobb-Douglas, i.e., have an elasticity of substitution equal to one. Clearly, any ray representing Hicks' neutral technical change would be steeper than ρ and, therefore, the choice of technique satisfying (13) would be more capital-intensive. The dividend-maximizer again chooses a more capital-intensive technique than the initial mix in response to Hicks' neutral technical change. Other types of Hicks' technical change can be considered using Figure 3 since these variants differ from Harrod-neutral change only according to the elasticity of substitution of the original production function. We leave such an exercise to the interested reader.

Finally, we note that Vanek's comments about Hicks' neutral technological change require careful interpretation due to their comparative-static nature. As we have discussed, long run optimal scale for a dividend-maximizing firm facing parametric prices is indeterminate with the linear-homogeneous production function. Suppose we consider instead a variable-returns-to-scale technology like the simple one discussed in Vanek where returns to scale depend on the level of output only. Then, Hicks' neutral technological change is equivalent to increasing the magnitude of the output index on each and every isoquant without altering the original mapping. For this technology, a unique optimal long run scale for the dividend maximizing firm occurs at the single level of output where the returns to scale measure switches from increasing to decreasing.

Since the mapping is unaltered by Hicks' neutral technological change, the isoquant along which optimal long run scale is achieved will not change. However, the output index is now higher and, therefore, so is the dividend earned by using the original amounts of all inputs given constant prices. From our analysis of dividend-maximizing behavior in the long run, we conclude that the dividend-maximizer will choose a more capital-intensive technique than the original choice in the presence of Hicks' neutral technological change. Therefore, the only employment effect for this simple variable-returns-to-scale technology is a decrease in the labor input due to a substitution effect along the uniquely-determined isoquant representing the optimal long run scale. There is no proper scale effect since the increase in output is attributable to technological change not to an increase in inputs. Consequently, a Hicks' neutral technological change is likely to decrease employment in a dividend-maximizing firm since it leads to a substitution effect only with no countervailing scale effect.

IV. CONCLUSION: IS THE LABOR-MANAGED ENVIRONMENT CONDUCIVE TO INNOVATION?

The financial advantage of labor-managed firms over their profit-maximizing counterparts in inducing minor technical innovation depends on distributional differences. In the short run, the original members of the labor-managed firm benefit as a group since each member receives a share in the higher earnings generated by technical innovation. Compared with a profit maximizing firm in which the owner(s) receives all the benefits, worker-members earn more income than the workers who are paid their value marginal product wage by the profit-maximizer. However, the profit-maximizing firm will always generate the maximum financial return on any innovation by hiring additional workers at the going wage while the labor-managed firm will not increase membership if new entrants must be granted full membership rights. Therefore, whether or not the profit-maximizing firm can actually provide the financial incentive to elicit the information from the work force required to undertake minor technical improvements will depend on its ability to identify the sources of innovative information and to share profits appropriately with the innovating workers. Nonetheless, by comparing the simple benchmark models of the egalitarian cooperative and the profit maximizing firm without sharing schemes, we find support for Vanek's position. Based on distributional grounds, the labor-managed environment is more conducive to minor technical innovation and any adverse employment effects, which follow from dividend-maximizing behavior, are mitigated by membership rights in the short run.

Our basic short-run analysis could be extended to consider a two-period framework in which the cost of minor innovation is considered more realistically. Suppose period one is a tooling-up period in which workers incur the costs of work disruption and learning new techniques. Quite possibly, production is less efficient in an engineering sense during this tooling-up period so that the present dividend share is reduced at the same time workers are incurring higher costs of disutility in their work environment. Clearly, workers would not willingly incur these costs without some expectation of future return. For simplicity, consider period two to be an application period where minor innovation leads to increased productive efficiency and higher dividend potential. Our results here indicate that basic membership rights will promote membership solidarity during the application period. Therefore, workers who incur the tooling-up costs are assured of a share in the future benefits. This property right to a share in the present and future earnings of the organization differentiates the labor-managed firm from the profit-maximizing one.

In future work, we will model the labor-managed firm in this two period framework where the choice of technical innovation will depend on maximizing discountered net earnings minus disutility costs of work disruption per member. Whether or not the labor-managed firm has an inherent advantage over its profit-maximizing counterpart in such a situation will depend on a comparison with a firm in which tooling-up costs are shared; the workers bearing the disutility cost of work disruption while the owner(s) bears the cost of reduced earnings, but the future benefits are reaped by the owner(s) only. Intuition suggests Vanek's conjectures about the potential for the labor-managed organization to elicit the Hayekian information necessary for minor innovation will be even more apparent in the two-period framework.

On the other hand, our results here do indicate that long-run employment distortions are likely due to the tendency of the labor-managed firm to behave like a dividend-maximizer. As we demonstrate, labor-saving innovations will be preferred to capital-saving ones. For all types of technical innovation, the dividend-maximizer chooses a more capital-intensive technique than the one chosen by the profit rate maximizer. As long as access to capital-financing is not difficult, we expect labor-managed firms experiencing technical innovation to choose a more capital-intensive growth path than their capitalist counterparts. Consequently, Vanek's claim that a labor-managed organization will adjust to mitigate any adverse employment effects due to innovation seems valid only in the short run and only then if membership rights are introduced properly to the maximizing behaviour of the labor-managed firm. The example that Vanek uses to argue for countervailing employment effects under Hicks' neutral technological change is incorrect.

Although the long-run results do not include the membership rights of the initial group in the same way in which we incorporate these in our work which compares incentives to innovate across organizational forms in the short run, they are nonetheless important. Any empirical work which attempts to address questions of innovation and productivity using Yugoslavian data must include some assumptions on the structure of production technology. If cross-industry studies are done for Yugoslavia using production functions with the neutral technological change assumptions which are quite common in such studies of Western economies, biased results would occur. In industries where technological change is rapid, labor-managed firms are likely to choose labor-saving methods. Hence, explaining differences in productivity and earnings across industries should take into account biases in the choice of technological innovation due to the different organizational principle of labor management. Otherwise, high productivity levels may be attributed to inappropriate explanatory variables.

John P. Bonin,
Department of Economics, Wesleyan University,
Middletown, Ct. 06457.

ACCEPTED OCTOBER 1981

REFERENCES

[1] ATKINSON, ANTHONY, "Worker Management and the Modern Industrial Enterprise", *Quarterly Journal of Economics*, LXXXVII, **3** (August 1973), pp. 375–92.

[2] BONIN, JOHN P., "The Theory of the Labor-Managed Firm from the Membership's Perspective with Implications for Marshallian Industry Supply", *Journal of Comparative Economics*, 5, **4** (December 1981), pp. 337–51.

[3] BONIN, JOHN P., "Optimal Employment Policies for a Multiperiod Labor Managed Socialist Cooperative forthcoming in *Jahrbuch der Wirtschaft Osteuropas*.

[4] BONIN, JOHN P., "Long Run Optimal Scale and Adjustment Processes: Are Labor-Managers Perverse in the Long Run?", *Economic Letters*, 7, **1**, 1981, pp. 47–50.

[5] IRELAND, NORMAN and LAW, PETER J., "Advertising and the Labor-Managed Firm", *Journal of Industrial Economics*, 25, **3** (March 1977), pp. 231–37.

[6] IRELAND, NORMAN J., "The Behaviour of the Labor-Managed Firm and Disutility from Supplying Factor Services", *Economic Analysis and Workers' Management*, XV, **1**, 1981, pp. 21–43.

[7] MEADE, JAMES E., "The Theory of Labour-Managed Firms and of Profit Sharing", *Economic Journal*, 82, **1** (March Supplement, 1972), pp. 402–28.

[8] MEADE, JAMES E., "The Adjustment Processes of Labour Co-operatives with Constant Returns to Scale and Perfect Competition", *Economic Journal*, 89, **356** (December 1979), pp. 781–88.

[9] STEINHERR, ALFRED and THISSE, J-F., "Are Labor-Managers Really Perverse?", *Economic Letters*, 2, **2**, 1979, pp. 137–42.

[10] VANEK, JAROSLAV, *The General Theory of Labor-Managed Market Economies* (Cornell University Press: Ithaca and London, 1970).

[11] WARD, BENJAMIN, "The Firm in Illyria: Market Syndicalism", *American Economic Review*, 48, **4** (September 1958), pp. 566–89.

THE JOURNAL OF INDUSTRIAL ECONOMICS

Published first in October 1952, this Journal was founded to develop the nalysis of the problems facing modern industry. It is concerned with the ıdividual business and its relation to the economy—e.g. with outputs and rices and their behaviour in the market, and with the business decisions which ffect these. It therefore aims to contribute both to economic theory and to ractical public and private policies in the industrial field. The journal is aturally meant to interest business men as well as economists.

The Editors welcome contributions covering the fundamental categories in conomics (such as prices, costs, investment, finance, location, wages and roductivity) as well as the broader 'background' circumstances (such as the hanging structure of industry, management policy and public monopoly olicy). Preference is given to MSS bearing on these subjects from the andpoint of individual firms or industries. Theoretical discussion is welcome. bstract theory is not barred, but authors in this case should provide an ıtroduction and conclusion, so that non-specialist readers may see what the rticle is about. Alongside articles of more normal length, the Editors are illing to publish shorter notes, especially when these give interim results of nportant research studies. Books are not reviewed, although books received ill be listed, sometimes with a short note; but substantial review articles will e considered. No payment is made to authors, but 25 free offprints are rovided. Contributors are asked to send an Abstract, not exceeding 100 ords, with their article.

litorial Offices:

Manuscripts from North America should be sent to Professor H. Michael ann, Department of Economics, Boston College, Chestnut Hill, assachusetts, 02167, U.S.A.; manuscripts from all other countries to the eneral Editor, c/o Department of Economics, University of Lancaster, illow House, Lancaster, LA1 4YX England, from whom detailed Information r Contributors is available.

ıbscriptions, advertising, reprint enquiries, etc.

The journal is published by Basil Blackwell Publisher Ltd., 108 Cowley oad, Oxford OX4 1JF, England. US Mailing Agent, Expediters of the Printed ord Ltd., 527 Madison Avenue, Suite 1217, New York, NY 10022, U.S.A. econd Class postage paid at New York.

The journal is published four times a year in September, December, March ıd June. The subscription prices are as shown below.

All correspondence other than that dealing with contributions should be ldressed to the publisher.

rice

nnual subscription for institutions: £21.50 (UK), £26.50 (overseas), $54.60 (USA), $67.00 (Canada)

nnual subscription for individuals: £13.75 (UK), £16.75 (overseas), $35.00 (USA), $43.25 (Canada)

ingle issue price for institutions: £5.75 (UK), £6.95 (overseas), $14.50 (USA), $17.50 (Canada)

ingle issue price for individuals: £4.25 (UK), £5.25 (overseas), $11.00 (USA), $13.50 (Canada)

Set by Santype International Ltd.,
Salisbury, Wilts. Printed and bound by
Whitstable Litho Ltd., Whitstable, Kent

CONTRIBUTORS TO THIS NUMBER

B. CURRY: Lecturer in Economics, University College, Cardiff.

K. D. GEORGE: Professor of Economics, University College, Cardiff, and Editor of this Journal.

KATSUHIKO IKEDA: Professor of Economics, Department of Business Administration, Kwansei Gakuin University.

NORIYUKI DOI: Assistant Professor of Economics, Department of Economics, Kwansei Gakuin University.

J. F. PICKERING: Professor of Industrial Economics, UMIST, and Associate Editor of this Journal.

NORMAN J. IRELAND: Senior Lecturer in Economics, University of Warwick.

WILLIAM J. MERRILEES: Lecturer, Department of Economics, University of Sydney.

JOHN P. BONIN: Associate Professor of Economics, Wesleyan University, Middletown, Connecticut.

Contents of Volume XXXI, Nos. 1 and 2, September and December 1982, were:

Spatial Competition and the Theory of Differentiated Markets: An Introduction, by Louis Phlips and Jacques-François Thisse, respectively Professor C.O.R.E., Université Catholique de Louvain and Editor of this *Journal*, and Associate Professor, S.P.U.R., Université Catholique de Louvain.

Spatial Competition à la Hotelling: A Selective Survey, by Dominique Graitson, F.N.R.S. Assistant, Université de Liège.

Product Differentiation and the Consistency of Monopolistic Competition: A Spatial Perspective, by Dennis R. Capozza and Robert Van Order, respectively Professor, Faculty of Commerce and Business Administration, University of British Columbia, and Department of Housing and Urban Development, Washington, D.C.

Innovative Entry: Profit Hidden Beneath the Zero, by Kelvin Lancaster, John Bates Clark Professor, Department of Economics, Columbia University in the City of New York.

Competitive Behaviour in Chain-Linked Markets, by R. Rothschild, Lecturer, Department of Economics, University of Lancaster.

Product Proliferation in Characteristics Space: The UK Fertiliser Industry, by R. W. Shaw, Lecturer, Department of Economics, University of Stirling.

Existence and Computation of Mixed Strategy Nash Equilibrium for 3-Firms Location Problem, by A. Shaked, Lecturer, London School of Economics.

Differentiated Products, Consumer Search, and Locational Oligopoly, by Konard Stahl, Professor, University of Dortmund.

Product Differentiation with Income Disparities: An Illustrative Model, by J. Jaskold Gabszewicz and J. Thisse, respectively Professor, C.O.R.E., Université Catholique de Louvain, and Associate Professor, S.P.U.R., Université Catholique de Louvain.

Recent Developments in the Analysis of Spatial Competition and Their Implications for Industrial Economics, by Neil Dorward, Lecturer, Department of Accounting and Administrative Studies, The Polytechnic of North London.

Dynamic Market Strategy under Threat of Competitive Entry: An Analysis of the Pricing and Production Policies Open to the Multinational Company, by George Norman and Nancy K. Nichols, respectively Lecturer, Department of Economics, and Department of Mathematics, University of Reading.

Spatial Price Duopoly Under Uniform Delivered Pricing, by Richard E. Schuler and Benjamin F. Hobbs, respectively Commissioner and Deputy Chairman, New York State Public Service Commission, and Oak Ridge National Laboratory.

Pricing Policies Under Conditions of Spatial Competition, by Menahem Spiegel, Assistant Professor, Department of Economics, University of Haifa.

THE JOURNAL OF INDUSTRIAL ECONOMICS

Volume XXXI JUNE 1983 No. 4

MALCOLM R. BURNS
An Empirical Analysis of Stockholder Injury Under §2 of the Sherman Act 333

BJÖRN WAHLROOS
Regulation of 'Administered' Prices: An Empirical Analysis of the Microeconomics of Price Movement in Finland 1972–77 363

J. A. ZERBY and R. M. CONLON
Joint Costs and Intra-Tariff Cross-Subsidies: The Case of Liner Shipping 383

BERNARD GARDNER and PETER MARLOW
An International Comparison of the Fiscal Treatment of Shipping 397

J. E. DAVIES
An Analysis of Cost and Supply Conditions in the Liner Shipping Industry 417

P. MARITI and R. H. SMILEY
Co-operative Agreements and the Organization of Industry 437

ALAN ROCKWOOD
The Impact of Joint Ventures on the Market for OCS Oil and Gas Leases 453

REX L. COTTLE and MYLES S. WALLACE
Economic Effects of Non-Binding Constraints 469

ISSN 0022-1821
BASIL BLACKWELL OXFORD ENGLAND

CHANGE OF GENERAL EDITOR

As from 1st July, 1983, Elizabeth Brunner will be retiring as General Editor. She will be succeeded by Donald A. Hay, Fellow of Jesus College in the University of Oxford.

Manuscripts arising from all countries other than North America should in future therefore be sent to Donald A. Hay, General Editor, *The Journal of Industrial Economics*, The Institute of Economics and Statistics, The University of Oxford, St. Cross Building, Manor Road, Oxford, OX1 3UL.

Mrs. Doris A. Loft will continue as Editorial Assistant and Secretary to the Board, and will deal with proofs and the business side generally, once manuscripts have been accepted.

Manuscripts from North America should, as formerly, be sent in the first instance to Professor H. Michael Mann, Department of Economics, Boston College, Chestnut Hill, Mass. 02167, U.S.A.

THE JOURNAL OF INDUSTRIAL ECONOMICS
Volume XXXI June 1983 No. 4

AN EMPIRICAL ANALYSIS OF STOCKHOLDER INJURY UNDER § 2 OF THE SHERMAN ACT

MALCOLM R. BURNS*

I. INTRODUCTION

WITHOUT some type of protection, capital losses for the owners of a monopolistic corporation are an inevitable consequence of a competitive dissolution decree imposed under § 2 of the Sherman Act. *Ceteris paribus*, these losses result from the lesser value of the securities issued by the successor companies, relative to the pre-litigation prices of the superceded trust certificates, once the capital markets discount the reduced earnings and/or greater operating risks brought on by genuine rivalry between the new firms. Dewey [14] argues, in an important but largely overlooked article,[1] that the solicitude of the federal courts for the property interests of shareholders has been the principal barrier to a more widespread use of structural relief in monopolization cases. As discussed in Section II, it arises from a judicial perception that some owners of a condemned trust cannot be held responsible for proven § 2 misconduct and should not be unfairly subjected to capital losses. Accordingly, the usual remedy has been mild conduct restraints or minor divestitures which failed to restore vigorous competition in the affected industries.[2] This reluctance of the courts to punish "innocent" investors by ordering substantial dissolution will be referred to below as the problem of stockholder injury.

Under these circumstances, advocates of more extensive trust-busting should attempt to quantify the harm inflicted upon different certificate classes by a Sherman Act prosecution and pursue administrative safeguards that will overcome the judiciary's bias toward established property rights in monopoly. Both tasks are undertaken here in an empirical analysis of the investment

* I am indebted to Ali Sharzehi, who performed much of the preliminary statistical work, and to Maurice Joy, Richard J. Pierce, Sidney A. Shapiro and De-Min Wu for their comments. The entire analysis has been improved significantly by the criticisms of an anonymous referee. I am responsible for any remaining errors.

This paper was awarded the P.W.S. Andrews Memorial Prize for 1981.

[1] A revised version is contained in Dewey's treatise [15, pp. 246–56]. There is no consideration of his analysis in such leading discussions of antitrust policy as Bork [5], McGee [33] and Posner [41], although it is accepted by Elzinga and Breit [18, pp. 48–50].

[2] See Adams [3] and O'Connor [39]. Leading § 2 cases where conduct restraints or the divestiture of marginal assets was substituted for dissolution include: United States v. Eastman Kodak Co., 225 F. 62 (W.D.N.Y. 1915); United States v. Corn Products Refining Co., 234 F. 964 (S.D.N.Y. 1916), *appeal withdrawn*, 249 U.S. 621 (1919); United States v. International Harvester Co., 274 U.S. 693 (1927); United States v. Aluminum Co. of America, 148 F.2d 416 (2d Cir. 1945); United States v. National Lead Co., 332 U.S. 319 (1947); and Timken Roller Bearing Co. v. United States, 341 U.S. 593 (1951). The negligible effects of the remedies imposed in *Kodak, Corn Products, International Harvester* and *Alcoa* are reviewed by Kottke [29, pp. 58–69, 77–81].

performance of the debt and equity securities issued by the old American Snuff and American Tobacco companies and their respective successors. These trusts were dissolved on December 1, 1911.[3] The results demonstrate that the prices of preferred stocks and bonds, as well as the values of common stocks, are generally sensitive to new developments in a § 2 suit which foreshadow dissolution. The susceptibility of senior securities to such price changes is not obvious theoretically as they have prior (but fixed) claims to corporate earnings. Hence a reorganization that is expected to create viable, albeit less profitable, successor companies need not invariably jeopardize the income accruing to bonds and preferred stocks. Since previous research (Ellert [17] and Garbade *et al.* [25]) on the stock price effects of antitrust enforcement has focused exclusively on equities, the analysis supplies a factual basis for the courts' sympathy to pleas of shareholder injury because owners of non-voting senior securities typically lack § 2 culpability. Heretofore this basis has been entirely impressionistic.

More importantly, a detailed examination of the security exchanges in the snuff–tobacco decree reveals two simple techniques for coping with the problem of stockholder injury. It is of course impossible to substitute competing firms for a full-fledged monopoly without inflicting capital losses on someone. But it is both administratively feasible and evidently lawful for a court to transfer income to an "innocent" class of owners, at the expense of other shareholders, in the process of dividing up trust assets and financing new enterprises to operate them. Precedent exists in *American Tobacco* for use of the following transfer devices: *refunding*—the replacement of a favored class of trust bonds or preferred stock with certificates of the successor companies bearing higher coupon rates; and *redemption*—the cash-out of a favored trust security at fair market value. Refunding protects owners of senior securities by awarding them additional income from interest payments or preferred dividends to offset the expected increase in the risk of their holdings in the new firms. Redemption completely insulates deserving owners by allowing them costlessly to withdraw their investment from the industry. Properly applied separately or in combination, each device could fully compensate "innocent" investors for the capital losses anticipated from dissolution, thus making their financial experience independent of the decree's competitive effects.[4]

[3] U.S. v. American Tobacco [48]. The Standard Oil dissolution was excluded for two reasons. First, as discussed in the text below, the really interesting questions of stockholder injury arise when the decree attempts to protect "innocent" owners of senior trust securities by transferring income to them at the expense of the common shareholders. Standard Oil issued only one class of stock so no direct compensation was feasible. Second, a transfer scheme is precluded in a reorganization effected solely by the divestiture of subsidiary corporations, as occurred in the *Standard Oil* case. See Standard Oil Co. of N.J. v. United States, 221 U.S. 1 (1911), and U.S. Courts [50, pp. 129–44]. The analysis also omits the explosives dissolution resulting from United States v. E.I. du Pont de Nemours & Co., 188 F. 127 (D. Del. 1911), due to inadequate stock price data.

[4] Government compensation of "innocent" shareholders has been suggested by Shepherd [45, p. 199] and analysed by Adams [1] [2]. Refunding and redemption have a substantial comparative advantage over government payments in not requiring new legislation to authorize the expenditure of public funds.

Finally, the study highlights some of the limitations inherent in any transfer scheme intended to further the use of dissolution as a remedy for anticompetitive market structures. One difficulty is identifying the classes of "innocent" shareholders who merit judicial protection, and it is discussed in Section II. A potentially more serious problem arises from the inability to determine *ex ante* the degree of rivalry that will develop between the successor companies and the magnitude of its impact on security prices. Hence there is a danger that the compensation of some owners will be inadequate or, worse yet, too generous. Excessive awards are especially likely when the decree transfers income among shareholders in a reorganization with no competitive effects *ex post* due to the establishment of new firms who either collude successfully or enjoy regional monopolies. Then the favored owners will experience net capital gains from dissolution! Some evidence supporting this outcome for the preferred stock- and bondholders of American Tobacco is presented in Sections III & VI. Such windfalls (or unintended losses) are probably unavoidable when the effects of any dissolution plan cannot be forecast with complete accuracy.

The remaining discussion is organized as follows. Section III summarizes the dissolution of American Snuff and American Tobacco with an emphasis on the rearrangement of their outstanding securities and the accompanying income transfers between certificate classes. The data and mechanics of share accumulation are described in Section IV while Section V develops the statistical tests of injury and gain. Then the empirical results are presented in Section VI, and the discussion concludes in Section VII with some comments on the propriety of the judicial bias toward "innocent" investors.

II. WHO ARE "INNOCENT" SHAREHOLDERS?

The cases and commentaries have identified two categories of investors who might suffer unfairly from dissolution and therefore may qualify for judicial protection.[5] In the first group are recent buyers of trust common stock whose purchase prices included the discounted value of the benefits of output restriction. They can expect only normal returns because the capital gains generated by achieving a monopoly will have been realized by its organizers in a prior sale of shares. The colorable innocence of these Johnny-come-lately investors results from the fact that most (if not all) of the § 2 misconduct occurred before their acquisition of trust securities, so they could not have authorized it. The second category contains owners of non-voting shares, typically bonds and preferred stock. Their inability to influence the operating policies of the trust precludes culpability for the Sherman Act violations.

Because no effective dissolution decree can insulate all shareowners from loss, the courts may have to choose in future § 2 cases between late-arriving

[5] Compare United States v. International Harvester Co., 214 F. 987, 1010 (D.Minn. 1914); U.S. v. American Tobacco [48, p. 185]; and Dewey [14, p. 98].

common stockholders and non-voting owners as candidates for protection. However it appears that substantial administrative difficulties would attend any effort to compensate the owners of common stock. A refunding arrangement is uninviting as equities do not carry fixed dividend rates. Likewise a redemption of the trust's common stock would be feasible only if other investors could be induced to purchase equivalent securities at such prices and in sufficient quantities as to adequately finance the successor companies. When only recent buyers are to be cashed out, there is the further problem noted by Adams [2, p. 61] of determining an appropriate cut-off date reflecting the full capitalization of monopolistic rewards in observed share prices. Since market dominance is usually achieved, and higher stock prices are presumably generated, through the gradual elimination of competitors, specifying a date after which only subsequent equity purchasers are entitled to fair value would be arbitrary and thus a source of more litigation. In contrast, extending judicial protection solely to non-voting owners would create a rule of law that could be administered with relative ease. Refunding or redeeming bonds and preferred stocks also does not jeopardize the financing of the successor companies because the common shareholders remain available to absorb the compensation paid for these securities.

This last point requires more explanation. Any protective arrangement which transfers additional income from the trust or its successors to owners of senior securities will aggravate the capital losses imposed on the common stockholders by reducing the net earnings that would otherwise be available to them. Along with the decrease in equity values caused by the competitive effects of dissolution, further price reductions should result from: a redemption of bonds or preferred shares which depletes the liquid assets of the trust by more than the market value of the liabilities discharged; and/or a refunding of senior securities that forces the successor companies to divert greater fractions of combined earnings to interest payments and preferred dividends. Judges who feel compelled to single out the common stockholders to bear the capital losses arising both from competition and compensation may have to assert that these harsh consequences were essential to an effective remedy or resort to such doctrines as "the fruits of monopolization" and assumption of the risk.[6]

III. THE SNUFF–TOBACCO DECREE[7]

Between 1900 and 1910, the American Tobacco and American Snuff companies dominated every branch of the tobacco industry, except the manufacture of cigars, with market shares generally above 70 per cent. American Snuff

[6] Compare United States v. E. I. du Pont de Nemours & Co., 366 U.S. 316, 327 (1961), and United States v. Crescent Amusement Co., 323 U.S. 173, 189 (1944). With considerably less authority, the assumption of the risk justification has been proposed by Nader *et al.* [35, p. 230] and Shepherd [45, p. 194].

[7] The discussion in this section is taken from *Poor's Manual* [40, (1912), pp. 1643–4, 1657–60], U.S. Bureau of Corporations [49] and U.S. Courts [50, pp. 165–91].

is properly viewed as a subsidiary of American Tobacco which controlled 43 per cent of its voting stock. Both corporations were extremely profitable, and, although the evidence is not conclusive, they seemed to have performed as textbook monopolies prior to dissolution.

The § 2 suit was filed in July 1907 and the U.S. Supreme Court decided the case on May 29, 1911. Speaking for the majority, Justice White held that the trust violated the Sherman Act and ordered it dissolved. But he cautioned the trial court to maintain

> . . . a proper regard for the vast interests of private property which may have become vested in many persons as a result of the acquisition . . . of . . . the stock or securities of the combination without any guilty knowledge or intent to become actors or participants in the wrongs which . . . inspired and dominated the combination . . . (U.S. v. American Tobacco [48, p. 185]).

A disintegration plan was approved by the U.S. Circuit Court (S.D.N.Y.) the following October, and the successor companies began operation after an exchange of shares on December 1, 1911.

The dissolution is summarized in Table I. Some 14 successor companies emerged from the tobacco trust. The old American Snuff Company was split into three new firms—George W. Helme, Weyman-Bruton and a reorganized American Snuff. There were four successors in general manufacturing, namely

TABLE I
THE DISSOLUTION OF THE TOBACCO TRUST
DECEMBER 1, 1911

Defendant	*Successor Companies*	*Principal Operations*	*Method of Separation*
American Snuff	American Snuff	Snuff	Partition
	George W. Helme	Snuff	Partition
	Weyman-Bruton	Snuff	Partition
American Tobacco	American Tobacco	General manufacturing[a]	Partition
	Liggett & Myers	General manufacturing	Partition
	P. Lorillard	General manufacturing	Partition
	R. J. Reynolds	General manufacturing	Divestiture
	British-American Tobacco	Foreign	Divestiture
	Conley Foil	Tin foil	Divestiture
	Johnston Tin Foil & Metal	Tin foil	Divestiture
	MacAndrews & Forbes	Licorice paste	Divestiture
	Porto Rican-American Tobacco	Foreign	Divestiture
	United Cigar Stores	Retailing	Divestiture
	J. S. Young	Licorice paste	Divestiture

[a] Primarily chewing tobacco, cigarettes, fine-cut, little cigars and smoking tobacco.
Source: U.S. Courts [50, pp. 165–91].

Liggett & Myers, P. Lorillard, R. J. Reynolds and a new American Tobacco. The remaining firms were typically small input suppliers or foreign producers. Among the major successors, only Reynolds was separated by divestiture. The others were created *de novo* to operate factories partitioned from trust control. It was the financing of these enterprises that provided the court with an opportunity for transferring income to owners of bonds and preferred stocks.

This process is most clearly visible in the refunding arrangement of the snuff dissolution. The old American Snuff Company was capitalized with 110,000 shares of common stock and 120,000 shares of 6% preferred stock. In payment for the properties awarded them by the decree, the Helme and Weyman-Bruton companies distributed their securities—40,000 shares of common and preferred stock for each firm—to the owners of American Snuff. Every 11 common shares received 4 shares each of the Helme and Weyman-Bruton equities and, subsequently, fractional amounts of other securities. In the exchange of preferred stocks, every 3 old shares received 1 certificate each of the new American, Helme and Weyman-Bruton preferred stock. What makes this exchange so interesting is that, while an American Snuff preferred share continued to pay $6 annually, dividends on the Helme and Weyman-Bruton shares were fixed at $7 per year. The result was a diversion of snuff income to preferred stockholders. Prior to dissolution, every three preferred shares was paid $18 annually; thereafter the amount was $20. This 11 per cent increase in fixed charges cost the common stockholders of the snuff successors $80,000 a year, or about 2.2 per cent of the net snuff earnings available for equity distribution in 1911.

The more complex exchanges of the tobacco dissolution illustrate both refunding and redemption. American Tobacco had four classes of securities outstanding: common stock, 6% preferred stock, 4% bonds and 6% bonds; the stocks had par values of $100 while the bonds were issued in units of $1000. The entire capitalization of Liggett & Myers and Lorillard was paid to American Tobacco for the assets awarded them, and these securities were redistributed in the following manner. The court issued subscription rights to the common shareholders of American Tobacco for the Liggett & Myers and Lorillard equities. They could purchase the shares at par in amounts pro rata to their current holdings, and both issues were fully subscribed. American Tobacco was then ordered to redeem all of its debentures. Every old 6% bond was paid $600 cash and fractional shares of 0.29325 and 0.20675, respectively, in new Liggett & Myers and Lorillard 7% bonds. Each old 4% bond was exchanged for the same fractions of Liggett & Myers and Lorillard 5% bonds along with $480 in cash. The organization of the new firms was completed by a refunding of preferred stocks. Every 3 old 6% shares received 2 new 6% American Tobacco certificates as well as fractional shares of 0.5865 and 0.4135, respectively, of Liggett & Myers and Lorillard 7% preferred stock. Finally, American Tobacco was forced to distribute the securities of American Snuff, R. J. Reynolds and the other subsidiaries in Table I among its common stockholders.

The exchange of tobacco preferred stocks diverted income from the common shareholders in the same manner as the snuff dissolution. But the decree redeemed so much debt that annual interest payments fell by almost $2.1 million, or 5.8 per cent of the net income reported by American Tobacco in 1911. Its common stockholders paid for this reduction in interest charges with their subscriptions to the Liggett & Myers and Lorillard equities. However these expenditures, which were necessary to maintain a proportionate residual claim in the post-decree industry, financed only part of the cash awards to bondholders. The remainder was paid from the retained earnings of American Tobacco. Hence excessive premiums for the bonds would have injured the common stockholders not by transferring future income to other owners but by shrinking the assets of the trust more than the reduction in its indebtedness.

Tables II–III summarize the foregoing exchanges of securities. With one exception, they list all of the receipts which accrued to each trust certificate (beyond cash dividends and interest payments) between December 1, 1911 and August 31, 1916. Snuff securities were deleted from the receipts of American Tobacco common stockholders in Table II because the empirical analysis treats the snuff and tobacco dissolutions as separate events by adjusting the pre-1912 prices of American Tobacco equity for its ownership of American

TABLE II
EXCHANGE OF COMMON STOCKS

Common Stock	*Basis of Exchange*	*Date*		*Receipts*[a]
American Snuff	11 shares	December 1, 1911	11	American Snuff
			4	Helme
			4	Weyman-Bruton
		June 30, 1913	0.5	American Cigar 6% preferred
			1.1	American Tobacco 6% preferred
		September 30, 1914	0.344	Liggett & Myers 7% preferred
			0.2425	Lorillard 7% preferred
American Tobacco	1 share	December 1, 1911	1	American Tobacco
			$37.95	Liggett & Myers subscription right
			$29.80	Lorillard subscription right
			5.6742	British-American Tobacco
			0.0123	Conley Foil
			0.0045	Johnston Tin Foil & Metal
			0.0526	MacAndrews & Forbes
			0.0329	Porto Rican-American Tobacco
			0.1244	R. J. Reynolds
			0.1493	United Cigar Stores
			0.0175	J. S. Young
		April 20, 1914	0.0299	American Machine & Foundry
			0.8977	Imperial Tobacco deferred

[a] Common stocks unless otherwise noted.

Sources: U.S. Courts [50, pp. 165–91], *CFC* [11: (June 7, 1913), p. 1631 col. 2; (September 15, 1914), p. 676 col. 1], and *Poor's Manual* [40 (1915), p. 115].

TABLE III
EXCHANGE OF SENIOR SECURITIES

Trust Security	Price Range 1904–1910	Basis of Exchange	Type of Exchange	Receipts	
American Snuff 6% Preferred	$90 to $105	3 shares	Refunding	1	American Snuff 6% preferred
				1	Helme 7% preferred
				1	Weyman-Bruton 7% preferred
American Tobacco 6% preferred	95 to 105	3 shares	Refunding	2	American Tobacco 6% preferred
				0.5865	Liggett & Myers 7% preferred
				0.4135	Lorillard 7% preferred
American Tobacco 4% bonds	750 to 850	1 share	Redemption and refunding	$480	Cash
				0.29325	Liggett & Myers 5% bonds
				0.20675	Lorillard 5% bonds
American Tobacco 6% bonds	1050 to 1150	1 share	Redemption and refunding	$600	Cash
				0.29325	Liggett & Myers 7% bonds
				0.20675	Lorillard 7%bonds

Source: U.S. Courts[50, pp. 165–91].

Snuff. Otherwise any interpretation of the results for the tobacco common stocks would be clouded by the refunding of the snuff preferred stocks. An identical adjustment is not feasible for American Snuff's pre-dissolution holding of miscellaneous trust securities. Consequently, these shares and derivative receipts are included in Table II and in the analysis of the snuff equities.

The summary of the awards to senior trust securities in Table III suggests a deliberate attempt to treat their owners rather generously in the decree. However some certificates fared considerably better than others. Relative benefits can be evaluated by computing the potential capital gain available on each class of securities as follows. If the decree had no competitive effects, then every new share would be as risky as its parent certificate. Hence their cash yields should equalize according to

$$(1) \qquad \frac{r_0}{P_0} = \frac{r_1}{P_1} = \frac{r_2}{P_2} = \frac{r_3}{P_3}$$

where r_i denotes the applicable coupon rate, P_i is the corresponding price per share, and the subscript $i = 0$ identifies a trust certificate while $i = 1,2,3$ refers to the derivative shares of the successor companies. The values of P_0 and the r_i's are known, so (1) can be solved for P_1, P_2, and P_3. The final step is to assemble the cash and/or securities received for each holding of old shares and calculate the difference in their market values. The results are presented in

TABLE IV
POTENTIAL CAPITAL GAINS ON THE EXCHANGE OF SENIOR TRUST SECURITIES

Exchange	*Implied Price Range of New Shares*	*Potential Capital Gain*	*Per Cent*
Snuff 6% preferred	\$105.00 to \$122.50	\$30.00 to \$35.00	11.11
Tobacco 6% preferred	110.83 to 122.50	15.83 to 17.50	5.55
Tobacco 4% bonds	937.50 to 1062.50	161.25 to 198.75	18.97 to 26.50
Tobacco 6% bonds	1225.00 to 1341.70	120.83 to 162.50	10.51 to 15.48

Source: Table III and equation (1).

Table IV. They indicate that the prospective gains from the compensation arrangements were greatest for the 4% and 6% bonds. Conversely, only marginal benefits were likely for owners of American Tobacco preferred stock.

IV. THE DATA SAMPLE AND PORTFOLIO ACCUMULATION

The financial history of the tobacco trust and its successors is well-documented. Market prices of the securities in Tables II–III were published in the *Commercial & Financial Chronicle* [11], hereafter *CFC*, and its *Bank & Quotation Supplement* from March 1904 through August 1916. This interval spans the last eight years of trust exploitation along with the first four years of the reorganized industry. The time-series of prices is complete except for the months of December 1911–February 1912 and August–December 1914.[8] A full record of cash distributions is likewise available in *Moody's* [34] and *Poor's* [40] industrial manuals. These data will measure the investment performance of individual trust and successor securities from the market values of portfolios which bracket the 1911 dissolution and reflect expectations of its competitive effects along with the income transfers between certificate classes.

The analysis assumes that a hypothetical stockholder followed a buy-and-hold strategy, with reinvestment, for every security in Tables II–III. Cash receipts and market prices are denoted by C_{ijt} and P_{ijt}, respectively.[9] The first subscript refers to the issuing corporation where $i = 0$ for American Snuff or American Tobacco and $i = 1,2, \ldots$ for the corresponding new firms in Table I. The subscript j identifies the class of shares as

(2) $j =$
1: Snuff preferred stock
2: Tobacco preferred stock and 4–5% bonds
3: Tobacco 6–7% bonds
4: Snuff common stock
5: Tobacco common stock,

and t refers to monthly observations where

0: March 1904
1: April 1904
⋮
$t = t^*$: December 1911–February 1912
⋮
T: August 1916.

For securities traded on the New York Stock Exchange (NYSE), the market price was taken as the average of the highest and lowest sale prices during the month.[10] The prices of shares listed only on the New York Curb Exchange (NYCE) were computed as the average of the bid/ask quotations in the first and fourth weeks of each month. All prices were adjusted for cash dividends when necessary.

[8] A full set of price data is not available for December 1911–February 1912 due to the exchange of successor company securities. The New York Stock Exchange was closed between the months of August and December 1914.

[9] A cash receipt is normally a dividend or an interest payment. Since most declarations were made quarterly or semi-annually, many C_{ijt}'s = 0 during a calendar year for all i and j.

[10] Cowles [12, p. 17] assembled observed prices in the same manner. The Cowles Index of All Common Stocks (Table C-1, pp. 168–9) is the market index used in Section VI, and the mechanics of portfolio accumulation reported here duplicate the Cowles procedures (described on pp. 17–25) wherever possible.

With reinvestment of dividends or interest payments in fractional shares, the holding of each trust security accumulates over time via

$$(3) \qquad S_{0jt} = S_{0j,t-1}\left[1 + \frac{C_{0jt}}{P_{0jt}}\right] \qquad \begin{array}{l} j = 1,2,\ldots,5 \\ t = 1,2,\ldots,t^* - 1 \end{array}$$

where $S_{0jt} = 1.0$ in March 1904. When dissolution occurs, the various exchanges give the investor new shares in amounts equal to

$$(4) \qquad S_{ijt*} = S_{0j,t*-1}\left[w_{ij} + \frac{C_{ijt*}}{P_{ij,t*+1}}\right] \qquad \begin{array}{l} i = 1,2,\ldots \\ j = 1,2,\ldots,5. \end{array}$$

The w_{ij}'s in (4) are the certificate receipts per trust share calculated from Tables II–III, and the C_{ijt*}'s identify any corresponding cash awards. These holdings of successor securities typically increase with reinvestment in the same manner as the trust shares:

$$(5) \qquad S_{ijt} = S_{ij,t-1}\left[1 + \frac{C_{ijt}}{P_{ijt}}\right] \qquad \begin{array}{l} i = 1,2,\ldots \\ j = 1,2,\ldots,5 \\ t = t^* + 1, t^* + 2,\ldots,T. \end{array}$$

The market values of the pre- and post-dissolution portfolios are given by

$$(6) \qquad A_{jt} = \begin{cases} S_{0jt}P_{0jt}: & \text{Trust securities} \quad t = 0,1,\ldots,t^* - 1 \\ \sum_i S_{ijt}P_{ijt}: & \text{Successor securities} \quad t = t^* + 1, t^* + 2,\ldots,T. \end{cases} \qquad j = 1,2,\ldots,5$$

Finally, the empirical analysis is based on rates of return computed as

$$(7) \qquad R_{jt} = 100 \ln \frac{A_{jt}}{A_{j,t-1}} \qquad \begin{array}{l} j = 1,2,\ldots,5 \\ t = 1,2,\ldots,T. \end{array}$$

Equation (7) measures the approximate percentage gain or loss in month t on the jth portfolio of trust/successor securities resulting from price changes and cash distributions.[11]

Note that (2) combines the tobacco preferred stocks and 4–5% bonds into a single portfolio. This consolidation is unfortunate but unavoidable. As described in *Moody's Manual* [34 (1905), pp. 1586–7], these securities replaced a single issue when American Tobacco was re-capitalized in October 1904, so separate portfolios of its preferred stock and 4% bonds cannot be assembled without shrinking the already limited data for the regression models below.

[11] Equation (7) closely approximates the percentage transformation of portfolio values when they differ by less than 15 per cent, as is usually the case with monthly data. It has the advantage of generating symmetric returns for positive and negative changes of the same magnitude. See Blattberg and Gonedes [4, pp. 252–3].

Since Table IV indicates that the potential gains from dissolution were substantial for the 4% bonds but quite small for the preferred shares, combining them into one portfolio reduces the likelihood that these benefits will be discernable empirically. However there is no feasible alternative to consolidation that both preserves degrees of freedom in estimation and accurately replicates the investment experience of trust shareowners.

V. STATISTICAL TESTS OF CAPITALIZATION AND SHAREHOLDER INJURY OR GAIN

The objectives of the empirical analysis are to test the hypothesis that the benefits of a monopoly are capitalized in the prices of all its securities and to examine the consequences of refunding and redemption as methods for protecting "innocent" investors. Of particular interest is the prospect that some of them experienced capital gains or losses solely from the compensation arrangements of the snuff–tobacco decree. Three statistical tests are developed below from the capital asset pricing model (CAPM)[12] and the efficient markets hypothesis (EMH).[13] The first two involve residual analysis where the significance of observed trust–successor values is assessed against equivalent distributions compiled from the securities of contemporary manufacturing corporations. The third test evaluates changes in the risk of each portfolio in (2) after 1911 that would have affected the realization of capital gains for preferred stock- and bondholders.

The CAPM and the EMH

In the CAPM, the expected return on any security is equal to a risk-free rate plus a premium dependent on its systematic, or non-diversifiable, risk:

$$E(R_j) = R_f + \beta_j[E(R_m) - R_f] \tag{8}$$

where $E(R_j)$ = the expected return on the jth security

R_f = the return on a riskless security

$E(R_m)$ = the expected return on a value-weighted portfolio of all assets in the capital market

$$\beta_j = \frac{\operatorname{cov}(R_j, R_m)}{\sigma^2(R_m)}$$

= the systematic risk of the jth security or its contribution to the variance of the market return.

[12] The CAPM was developed by Lintner [31] and Sharpe [44]. It is discussed at length in Fama and Miller [24, pp. 215–320].

[13] The literature on the EMH is reviewed in Fama [21], and the leading empirical study is currently Fama and MacBeth [23]. A relatively non-technical discussion of the EMH is presented in Lorie and Hamilton [32, pp. 70–97].

The market price per unit of risk $[E(R_m) - R_f] > 0$ is identical for all securities in the CAPM. However these assets will have varying degrees of risk as measured by β_j, so greater expected returns are necessary to induce investors to hold comparatively risky shares. With some additional assumptions, Fama [20, p. 39] and Jensen [27, pp. 178–82] demonstrate that (8) is consistent with the popular[14] "market model"

$$R_{jt} = \alpha_j + \beta_j R_{mt} + \varepsilon_{jt} \tag{9}$$

where

$$\alpha_j = (1 - \beta_j) R_f \tag{10}$$

and $\varepsilon_{jt} \sim \mathcal{N}(0, \sigma_\varepsilon^2)$ denotes random error. Equation (9) asserts that the time-series of returns on any security exhibits a linear and risk-adjusted relationship with the corresponding average return for all assets in the capital market.

The EMH explains values of R_{jt} which depart from $(\alpha_j + \beta_j R_{mt})$ in various months because $\varepsilon_{jt} \neq 0$.[15] An efficient capital market revises security prices promptly and accurately on the basis of whatever new information becomes available about a particular company or its industry. These disclosures arrive in the market randomly and generate once-and-for-all price changes—upward if the news signifies increased future earnings or reduced operating risks and downward otherwise. Current owners of affected securities experience capital gains or losses, but, once these facts are fully reflected in observed prices, their returns tend to resume the relationship in (8) with the market average. This analysis underlies the following statistical tests.

Major Developments in the Litigation and the Reorganized Industry

Prior to any threat of dissolution, the returns on American Tobacco and American Snuff securities are described by least-squares estimates of (9):

$$R_{jt} = \hat{\alpha}_j^{(I)} + \hat{\beta}_j^{(I)} R_{mt} + u_{jt} \qquad \begin{matrix} j = 1,2, \ldots, 5 \\ t = 1,2, \ldots, t_1 - 1. \end{matrix} \tag{11}$$

Equation (11) is unaffected by the *American Tobacco* litigation because the estimating interval ends one month before the filing of the § 2 complaint in t_1 = July 1907.[16] The superscript (I) denotes estimates from the pre-complaint period. Hence $\hat{\alpha}_j^{(I)}$ and $\hat{\beta}_j^{(I)}$ measure the unrestricted exploitation of a monopoly by the tobacco trust as reflected in the risk-return configurations of its stocks and bonds.

[14] Previous uses of (9) in industrial organization and finance include Burns [9], Dodd [16], Fama *et al.* [22], Garbade *et al.* [25], Lev and Mandelker [30], and Smith [46].

[15] This discussion is based on Fama [21, pp. 384–96] and Lorie and Hamilton [32, pp. 79–82].

[16] There is no evidence of leakage from the developing prosecution of the tobacco trust. The weekly "Intelligence Reports" of the *CFC* do not reveal any information between January 1904 and June 1907 suggesting that such litigation was imminent.

The proposition that monopolistic performance is capitalized in all security prices can be evaluated from the price revisions that accompany major developments in the § 2 prosecution and its aftermath. Four events are known to reveal important information: the beginning of the antitrust suit (month t_1), the Supreme Court decision (t_2 = June 1911), the announcement of the dissolution plan (t_3 = September–October 1911), and the initial declaration of interest payments and dividends by the successor companies (t_4 = March–June 1912).[17] If the capitalization hypothesis is accurate, the complaint and decision should be followed immediately by capital losses for every trust security because these events threaten to terminate output restriction through a possibly drastic restructuring of the industry. Given the absence of competitive effects reported in previous studies of the snuff–tobacco decree[18] along with the income transfers to preferred stock- and bondholders, the disclosure of the dissolution plan and the initial announcement of successor distributions should generate capital gains for the majority of owners.

An appropriate testing procedure requires the evaluation of

$$\hat{u}_{jt_i} = R_{jt_i} - [(1 - \hat{\beta}_j^{(I)})R_{ft_i} + \hat{\beta}_j^{(I)}R_{mt_i}] \qquad j = 1, 2, \ldots, 5 \quad t_i = t_1, t_2, t_3, t_4. \tag{12}$$

The $\hat{u}_{jt_i}$'s are estimated residuals which measure the approximate percentage price change of each portfolio, adjusted for risk and market trends, brought on by the new information disclosed in the corresponding month.[19] The model in (12) is linked to the CAPM by including the risk-free rate R_{ft_i} via (10) as a predictor of observed returns.[20] The following outcomes are admissible *a priori*:

Complaint and Decision

$$E(\hat{u}_{jt_1}),\ E(\hat{u}_{jt_2}) \begin{cases} < 0: & \text{Capital losses on all securities} \quad j = 1, 2, \ldots, 5 \\ = 0: & \text{No capitalization of monopoly performance in security prices} \end{cases} \tag{13}$$

[17] See Burns [9, pp. 730–2], Ellert [17, pp. 80–3, 85, 89–93, 99–101, 112–4], and Garbade *et al.* [25, pp. 7–9].

[18] Compare Burns [9, pp. 718–9, 734], Cox [13, pp. 217–8], Nicholls [38, p. 409], Tennant [47, p. 342] and U.S. Bureau of Corporations [49 (part III), pp. 13–4, 328, 332–3].

[19] The risk-free return in (12) and (20) below is the yield to maturity from a U.S. government bond traded on the NYSE between 1907 and 1912.

[20] Smith [46] presents an interesting application of (12) to study the hypothesis of collusion among automobile manufacturers. It is also recommended by Schwert [43, pp. 125–30] over

$$\hat{u}_{jt_i} = R_{jt_i} - [\hat{\alpha}_j^{(I)} + \hat{\beta}_j^{(I)}R_{mt_i}] \qquad j = 1, 2, \ldots, 5 \quad t_i = t_1, t_2, t_3, t_4, \tag{12'}$$

in the present context, because typically $\hat{\alpha}_j \neq (1 - \hat{\beta}_j)R_f$ contrary to (10). Although (12′) could therefore generate erroneous residual estimates, it has been used extensively to measure market-adjusted price changes—as illustrated in the work of Burns [9], Dodd [16], Fama *et al.* [22] and Garbade *et al.* [25]—without apparent difficulty. Based on a large sample of estimated residuals from equations analogous to (12) and (12′), Brenner [6, p. 928] reports enough discrepancies in the results to warrant the simultaneous use of both models, and that practice was followed here. The corresponding values of $\hat{u}_{jt_i}$ are very similar in terms of statistical significance, since R_f was essentially constant during the brief interval $t_2 - t_4$ and thus performs in (12) much like $\hat{\alpha}_j^{(I)}$ does in (12′). However the estimates from (12) support conclusions which are slightly more conservative than those dependent on (12′), and the former are presented in Section VI.

Dissolution Plan and Initial Cash Distributions

$$(14)\qquad E(\hat{u}_{jt_3}),\ E(\hat{u}_{jt_4})\ \begin{cases} = 0: & \text{No capitalization of monopoly performance in security prices} \\ > 0: & \text{Capital gains on all securities.} \end{cases}\qquad j = 1,2,\ldots,5$$

Non-zero residuals in (13)–(14) indicate that the capital market is efficient with regard to the excess profits and/or reduced operating risks from output restriction. Conversely, if these benefits are not capitalized in trust and successor market values, then dissolution-related events would have no particular significance for any investor, and they should not be accompanied by systematic price variations.

The tests of (13)–(14) generally cannot be reinterpreted as evidence of shareholder injury or gain because positive residuals normally reflect a mixing of income transfers along with the negligible competitive effects of the snuff–tobacco decree. Once the dissolution plan and successor company distributions convinced investors that prior forecasts were unduly pessimistic, market-adjusted price increases would tend to offset any reductions that followed the § 2 complaint and the Supreme Court decision. The sources of capital gains are additive for bonds and preferred stocks because the expected lack of competition increases the probability that the new firms could pay the higher coupon rates set by the decree. Revised forecasts of minimal rivalry also tend to counterbalance the income diversions from the common stockowners. Thus the inability to disentangle compensation payments from the broader implications of the snuff–tobacco decree makes it impossible to infer injury and gain from the behavior of individual residuals.

An alternate procedure will in principle test net injury or gain directly. It assumes that news of the complaint, decision, dissolution plan, and initial cash distributions exhausts the information from a § 2 suit which cause market-adjusted price changes on trust and successor securities. Then the gains and losses on each portfolio that reflect differing forecasts of competitive effects will cancel out one another when all four events are considered jointly. That is, as investors became convinced that the snuff and tobacco dissolutions were essentially cosmetic, the $E(\hat{u}_{jt_1}),\ E(\hat{u}_{jt_2}) < 0$ should be offset by $E(\hat{u}_{jt_3}),\ E(\hat{u}_{jt_4}) > 0$ because, *ceteris paribus*, the latter tend to re-establish security prices consistent with undisturbed output restriction. And any excess or deficiency of the residuals before and after the summer of 1911 signifies a net gain or injury, respectively, that reflects only the compensation arrangements of the decree. Therefore the effects of those transfers should be discernable from

$$(15)\qquad E(\hat{u}_{jt_1} + \hat{u}_{jt_2} + \hat{u}_{jt_3} + \hat{u}_{jt_4})\ \begin{cases} < 0: & \text{Shareholder Injury— net capital losses from dissolution} \\ > 0: & \text{Shareholder Gain— net capital gains from dissolution.} \end{cases}\qquad j = 1,2,\ldots,5$$

Positive values of the residual sums in (15) would be expected for portfolios of senior securities ($j = 1,2,3$) while negative values are likely for the common stocks ($j = 4,5$).

Changes in Risk

The final test derived from the CAPM measures changes in the risks of snuff and tobacco securities following the dissolution decree.[21] It relates directly to the hypothesis of shareholder gain because market-adjusted price increases for the new senior securities are predicated on their being no more risky than the parent shares of the trust. Otherwise the higher coupon rates would merely tend to compensate preferred stock- and bondholders for a greater investment risk in the reorganized industry. The $\hat{\beta}_j^{(I)}$'s in (11) measure the risks of trust securities. Corresponding estimates for the successor portfolios are generated by

$$(16) \qquad R_{jt} = \hat{\alpha}_j^{(II)} + \hat{\beta}_j^{(II)} R_{mt} + u_{jt} \qquad \begin{array}{l} j = 1,2, \ldots, 5 \\ t = t_4 + n_j, t_4 + n_j + 1, \ldots, T \end{array}$$

where n_j satisfies $[T - (t_4 + n_j)] = (t_1 - 2)$ for all j so that (16) is estimated over the same number of months as (11) in the immediate post-decree period. The corresponding estimates are denoted by the superscript (II).

The risk-change measure is $[\hat{\beta}_j^{(II)} - \hat{\beta}_j^{(I)}]$, and it has the following interpretation:

$$(17) \qquad [\hat{\beta}_j^{(II)} - \hat{\beta}_j^{(I)}] \quad \begin{array}{l} < 0\text{: Successor shares less risky than the parent trust certificates} \\ \qquad j = 1,2, \ldots, 5 \\ > 0\text{: Successor shares more risky than the parent trust certificates} \end{array}$$

where the corresponding t-statistics are given by

$$(18) \qquad t_{[\hat{\beta}_j^{(II)} - \hat{\beta}_j^{(I)}]} = \frac{\hat{\beta}_j^{(II)} - \hat{\beta}_j^{(I)}}{\sqrt{[\text{var } \hat{\beta}_j^{(I)} + \text{var } \hat{\beta}_j^{(II)}]}}, j = 1,2, \ldots, 5.$$

The snuff and tobacco successors fully paid their preferred dividend and interest obligations after 1911, so negative or insignificantly positive values in (17) for $j = 1,2,3$ will support a presumption of capital gains for owners of senior securities.

The Control Group

Proper evaluation of (13)–(15) requires evidence of the ordinary experience of contemporary manufacturing corporations. Otherwise there is no assurance that the snuff and tobacco residuals do not reflect major developments in the

[21] The initial use of this test in industrial organization was by Lev and Mandelker [30, pp. 95–7].

TABLE V
THE CONTROL GROUP

Company	*Primary Outputs*
American Agricultural Chemical	Fertilizer, glue and gelatine
American Beet Sugar	Sugar
American Car & Foundry	Freight and passenger cars
American Cotton Oil	Cotton seed products
American Hide & Leather	Meat and leather
American Linseed	Linseed oil and varnish
American Locomotive	Locomotives
American Malting	Beer
American Smelting & Refining	Metal products
American Type Founders	Printing machinery and type
American Woolen	Wool products
American Writing Paper	Stationery and envelopes
Borden's Condensed Milk	Evaporated milk and candy
Crucible Steel	Steel products
Distillers Securities	Liquor
General Chemical	Chemicals
International Paper	Lumber, wood pulp, and newsprint
National Biscuit	Biscuits and crackers
National Enameling & Stamping	Metal products
National Lead	Lead products and vegetable oils
Otis Elevator	Elevators and lifts
Pressed Steel Car	Freight cars
Railway Steel Spring	Steel springs and related products
Republic Iron & Steel	Steel products
Union Bag & Paper	Pulp, paper and paper bags
U.S. Cast Iron Pipe & Foundry	Iron pipe and steel products
U.S. Rubber	Rubber products
Virginia-Carolina Chemical	Chemicals and fertilizer

economy which affected the security prices of all manufacturing corporations in a similar manner. The impact of extraneous events is substantially limited by restricting the analysis to months that coincide with the disclosure of important information from the *American Tobacco* litigation and the reorganized industry. But interpretive difficulties remain due to the incompleteness of the market model in (9), which underlies all of the empirical tests, and the generally noisy character of stock price data noted by Fama [19] and King [28]. To further reduce the likelihood of erroneous inferences, the results in (13)–(15) are evaluated against equivalent distributions compiled from the equity and debt securities of the 28 firms listed in Table V. It contains every manufacturing corporation with at least two classes of outstanding securities that were quoted continuously on either the NYSE or the NYCE between March 1904 and August 1916.[22] Included in this control group are many of

[22] These data are listed in Burns [8] which is available upon request. All of the debt issued by the control group firms are preferred stocks except the 5% bonds of Distillers Securities. According to Navin and Sears [36, pp. 116–21], manufacturing corporations typically raised additional capital after 1890 through sales of preferred stock rather than bonds.

the largest industrial firms of the early 20th century along with several others which dominated their respective markets.[23]

Residual distributions are constructed by replicating the calculations of (3), (5)–(7) and (11)–(12) for each pair of securities issued by the corporations in Table V. The control group counterpart of (11) is

$$(19) \qquad R_{ckt} = \hat{\alpha}_{ck}^{(I)} + \hat{\beta}_{ck}^{(I)} R_{mt} + u_{ckt} \qquad \begin{array}{l} c = 1,2, \ldots, 28 \\ k = \begin{array}{l} 1: \text{debt securities} \\ 2: \text{equity securities} \end{array} \\ t = 1,2, \ldots, t_1 - 1, \end{array}$$

and

$$(20) \qquad \hat{u}_{ckt_i} = R_{ckt_i} - [(1 - \hat{\beta}_{ck}^{(I)}) R_{ft_i} + \hat{\beta}_{ck}^{(I)} R_{mt_i}] \quad \begin{array}{l} c = 1,2, \ldots, 28 \\ k = \begin{array}{l} 1: \text{debt securities} \\ 2: \text{equity securities} \end{array} \\ t_i = t_1, t_2, t_3, t_4 \end{array}$$

generates cross-section distributions of the estimated residuals underlying (13)–(15). The $\hat{u}_{ckt_i}$'s are independent of the specific risks of the 56 equity and debt portfolios because (19) assigns larger slope coefficients to more risky securities. The means and approximate standard deviations of the control group residual distributions are given by

$$(21) \qquad \bar{u}_{kt_i} = \sum_{c=1}^{28} \frac{\hat{u}_{ck_i}}{28} \qquad k = \begin{array}{l} 1: \text{debt securities} \\ 2: \text{equity securities} \end{array}$$

$$(22) \qquad \hat{\sigma}(\hat{u}_{ckt_i}) = \left[\sum_{c=1}^{28} \frac{(\hat{u}_{ckt_i} - \bar{u}_{kt_i})^2}{27} \right]^{1/2} \qquad t_i = t_1, t_2, t_3, t_4$$

respectively. They determine the statistical significance of the snuff and tobacco residuals according to

$$(23) \qquad t_{[\hat{u}_{jti}]} = \frac{\hat{u}_{jt_i} - \bar{u}_{kt_i}}{\hat{\sigma}(\hat{u}_{ckt_i})} \qquad t = t_1, t_2, t_3, t_4,$$

where $k = 1$ for $j = 1,2,3$ (bonds and preferred stocks) while $k = 2$ for $j = 3,4$ (common stocks).[24]

Two issues are raised by the use of a control group to assess the statistical significance of market-adjusted price changes on portfolios of snuff and to-

[23] Data on the absolute and relative sizes of these corporations are presented in Collins and Preston [10] and Scherer [42, pp. 55, 121].

[24] The use of $\hat{\sigma}(\hat{u}_{ckt_i})$ in (23) to evaluate the significance of trust-successor residuals assumes that the residual variance in (19) is identical for all 28 equity or debt portfolios as well as for the corresponding securities of American Snuff and American Tobacco. As a check on the validity of the latter assumption, the residual variances from (11) and (19) were compared for equity and debt securities. Each of the trust values was within one standard deviation of the mean of the corresponding residual variance distribution from the control group.

bacco securities. The first concerns the shape of the cross-section residual distributions assembled from (20). Normality appears likely due to the comprehensive selection of firms, and this possibility was examined with a Kolmogorov-Smirnov (KS) test for goodness of fit (described in Hays and Winkler [26, pp. 817–21]). The application of the KS test is not exact because the parameters of each distribution must be taken from (21)–(22). Even so, the results favor the normality hypothesis: of the 24 KS statistics computed, only two exceeded the critical value at a 95% confidence level. Thus despite the limitations of the KS test, there is little basis for rejecting the normal distribution as a reasonable characterization of the test statistics in (13)–(15).

A more serious difficulty is that control group residuals are not completely independent of one another. Rather they are positively correlated over time for selected pairs of corporations, presumably due to shared industry effects within Table V. Hence (22) will underestimate the true dispersion of each distribution so that all of the t tests are biased upward. Since it is impossible to adjust every $\hat{\sigma}(\hat{u}_{ckt_i})$ for all covariation in the returns on 28 equity or debt portfolios, the following procedure was adopted as a first-approximation. Substantial interfirm residual correlation is known to originate with Pressed Steel Car and either International Paper or Union Bag & Paper. These sources were eliminated by dropping the former along with one of the latter corporations from the control group and then re-computing the distribution summary statistics for a 26-firm sample. The result is usually larger estimated variances, as would be expected with a full correction for positive correlations between pairs of returns, but clearly not all of the covariance within the control group has been removed. This limitation qualifies inferences from the statistical significance of the snuff and tobacco residuals presented in Section VI. To keep them conservative, the analysis reports the summary statistics of the corresponding 26- or 28-firm distribution with the highest estimated variance.

VI. EMPIRICAL RESULTS

Least-squares estimates of (11) and (16) are presented in Table VI for the security portfolios of American Snuff, American Tobacco and their successors. Table VII summarizes the coefficients estimated from (19) for control group securities. In all cases the market rate of return R_{mt} is defined analogously to (7) from the Cowles [12] Index of All Common Stocks, the most comprehensive measure of market-wide activity available. The sample periods are April 1904–June 1907 for trust and control group securities and January 1913–August 1916 for the successor companies. Each interval contains 39 monthly observations.

In general, these estimates support the market model rather strongly, not only for common stocks but also for bonds and preferred stocks. There is no indication of heteroscedasticity or non-linearity in a sampling of scatter diagrams, and Tables VI–VII contain little evidence of serial correlation.[25] The vast majority (55/66) of the estimated slope coefficients are statistically significant at the 95% confidence level.[26] For purposes of interpreting the residual and risk-change tests, the only noteworthy exceptions involve portfolios of the snuff preferred stocks where the market model has little explanatory power. Another interesting feature of the results is that the $\hat{\beta}$'s are consistent with *a priori* notions of relative risks. For example, the American Tobacco 6% bonds had a smaller estimated risk than a portfolio of its preferred stock and 4% bonds which in turn was more secure than the common stock. Similar rankings are visible throughout Tables VI–VII. In short, these estimates reinforce the findings of Fama *et al.* [22] that market-wide price trends exert a systematic and statistically significant influence on the time-series of security returns.

The results of the risk-change test in (17) are readily apparent from Table VI. For each certificate class, the estimated systematic risk of the successor portfolio is less than that of the corresponding trust shares.[27] These reductions range in absolute value from -0.013 for the snuff preferred stocks to -0.546 for the snuff common stocks. Thus in view of the income transfers reported in Section III, the lower estimated risks of senior snuff and tobacco securities after 1912 favors the prospect of net capital gains for their owners. This conclusion is strongest for the tobacco bonds and preferred stocks where the post-dissolution risk changes are significantly negative at the 95% confidence level on a two-tailed application of (18).

Table VIII presents the estimated residuals from (13)–(15) for the securities of American Snuff, American Tobacco, and their successors along with the corresponding summary statistics of the control group residual distributions. Since the data are "mid-month" averages of sale prices, the impact of any dissolution-related event typically will spill over into the following month, and the residuals must be accumulated accordingly. In general, they show market-adjusted price declines accompanying the complaint the Supreme

[25] The critical values of the Durbin-Watson statistic are $d_L = 1.43$ and $d_U = 1.54$ at the 95% confidence level for 39 observations and 2 independent variables (including a constant). The mean values of d for the control group (Table VII) satisfy $d_U < d < 4 - d_U$, as do all of the trust values in Table VI, which indicates that the corresponding error terms for (11) and (19) are serially independent. Positive and negative serial correlation exists in the successor equations for the tobacco common stocks and the snuff preferred stocks, respectively, but it does not bias the estimates of systematic risk.

[26] Blattberg and Gonedes [4, pp. 248–9, 275–7] report that the Student t distribution accounts for the thick tails observed in the time-series of daily stock returns. Under these conditions, monthly return distributions will be approximately normal so the statistical significance of the coefficient estimates in Tables VI–VII can be evaluated in the conventional manner.

[27] An explanation for these results is not readily apparent because risk changes have not been studied previously in an antitrust context. One interesting possibility is that a benign dissolution reduces systematic risks by removing an antitrust cloud from the affected corporation(s). That is, American Snuff and American Tobacco were leading candidates for a §2 prosecution prior to July 1907, and the capital market may have increased the risks of their securities to reflect this threat of remedial action. However if no further litigation was foreseeable once the final decree was implemented, then these risk premiums would vanish. The difficulty with this interpretation is that the risk of a §2 prosecution may be specific to a few large and monopolistic corporations. Then it would be diversifiable and should not be compounded in the $\hat{\beta}_j^{(T)}$'s of (11).

TABLE VI

REGRESSION RESULTS: INDIVIDUAL TRUST AND SUCCESSOR PORTFOLIOS

TRUST SECURITIES

$$R_{jt} = \hat{\alpha}_j^{(I)} + \hat{\beta}_j^{(I)} R_{mt} + u_{jt}$$

Sample Period: April 1904–June 1907
Number of Observations: 39

Security Portfolio	$\hat{\alpha}_j^{(I)}$	$\hat{\beta}_j^{(I)}$	R^2	F	d
American Snuff					
Preferred Stock	0.745	0.137	0.050	1.94	2.25
	(0.340)	(0.099)			
Common Stock	1.373	0.860	0.178	7.99	2.44
	(1.05)	(0.304)			
American Tobacco					
6% bonds	0.560	0.302	0.378	22.50	1.72
	(0.220)	(0.064)			
Preferred Stock and 4% Bonds	0.916	0.520	0.384	23.05	1.74
	(0.374)	(0.108)			
Common Stock	0.399	0.778	0.119	5.01	1.74
	(1.21)	(0.347)			

SUCCESSOR SECURITIES

$$R_{jt} = \hat{\alpha}_j^{(II)} + \hat{\beta}_j^{(II)} R_{mt} + u_{jt}$$

Sample Period: January 1913–August 1916
Number of Observations: 39

Security Portfolio	$\hat{\alpha}_j^{(II)}$	$\hat{\beta}_j^{(II)}$	R^2	F	d
Snuff Successors					
Preferred Stock	0.578	0.124	0.026	0.97	2.93
	(0.344)	(0.125)			
Common Stock	0.293	0.314	0.121	5.08	2.21
	(0.381)	(0.140)			
Tobacco Successors					
6–7% Bonds	0.573	0.075	0.031	1.18	2.32
	(0.189)	(0.069)			
Preferred Stock and 4–5% Bonds	0.544	0.129	0.125	5.28	2.04
	(0.154)	(0.056)			
Common Stock	0.275	0.701	0.393	23.98	1.28
	(0.393)	(0.143)			

Note: The figures listed in parenthesis are standard errors.

Court decision followed by price increases associated with the disclosure of the dissolution plan and the successor cash distributions. Many of these price changes are statistically significant, but they are sufficiently offsetting so that none of the residual sums are distinguishable from zero.

The initiation of the § 2 suit in July 1907 inflicted capital losses on owners of all the outstanding securities of the tobacco trust. The range of market-adjusted price reductions was 5–30 per cent with the greatest losses falling on

TABLE VII

SUMMARY OF REGRESSION RESULTS: CONTROL GROUP DEBT AND EQUITY PORTFOLIOS

$$R_{ckt} = \hat{\alpha}_{ck}^{(I)} + \hat{\beta}_{ck}^{(I)} R_{mt} + u_{ckt}$$

Sample Period: April 1904–June 1907

Number of Observations: 39

Portfolio	*Statistic*	*Range* *Low*	*High*	*Mean*	*Median*	*Standard Deviation*	*Percentage Greater than the Critical Value at the 95% Confidence Level*
Debt	$\hat{\alpha}_c^{(I)}$	−2.049	1.830	0.492	0.569	0.859	50.0[a]
	$\hat{\beta}_c^{(I)}$	0.071	1.861	0.613	0.458	0.489	82.1[a]
	R^2	0.026	0.567	0.286	0.296	0.158	—
	F	1.00	48.41	17.51	15.61	12.98	82.1
	d	1.10	2.65	1.89	1.93	0.446	—
Equity	$\hat{\alpha}_c^{(I)}$	−3.978	2.723	0.119	0.299	1.630	19.2[a]
	$\hat{\beta}_c^{(I)}$	0.236	2.275	1.452	1.481	0.556	89.3[a]
	R^2	0.021	0.694	0.352	0.350	0.177	—
	F	0.81	83.92	24.95	19.95	19.53	92.9
	d	0.91	2.46	1.62	1.58	0.358	—

[a] Two-tailed test.

the American Tobacco common stock. Further declines of between 7 and 26 per cent on both equities and the snuff preferred stock followed the decision ordering dissolution. These estimated losses are significant at the 95% confidence level. The negative entries for the tobacco 6% bonds and preferred stock/4% bonds in June 1911 are not statistically different from zero. Otherwise the residuals show clearly that § 2 enforcement can be expected to cause market-adjusted losses on virtually every security of a defendant corporation, debt and equity alike.

Table VIII has a quite different appearance after August 1911. Disclosure of the dissolution plan occurred in two stages. Relatively accurate rumors of the reorganization of American Tobacco began circulating in September as alternative proposals were exchanged between the trust and the government.[28] Although there was evidently no leakage of information regarding the dissolution of American Snuff, the residuals of its securities also were evaluated for September because investors may have anticipated that the attractive refunding of senior tobacco securities would be ordered for the snuff preferred stocks as well. Then the official plan containing all of the features analysed in Section III was published during the third week of October 1911.[29] This new information produced a fairly sharp increase in the price of every trust security except the snuff preferred stock. The range of market-adjusted gains was approximately 5–18 per cent with the largest increase occurring on the tobacco common stock. At least one of the residual entries associated with the

[28] Compare *New York Times* [37 (September 8, 1911), p. 10 col. 1] and *CFC* [11 (September 30, 1911), p. 874 col. 1].

[29] See *CFC* [11 (October 21, 1911), pp. 1122–4].

TABLE VIII
ESTIMATED RESIDUALS: DEBT AND EQUITY PORTFOLIOS OF TRUSTS AND SUCCESSOR COMPANIES

Trust and Successors	Portfolio	Event	Month(s)	Residual(s)[a]	Control Group Residual Distribution: Mean	Control Group Residual Distribution: Standard Deviation
Snuff	Preferred Stock	Complaint	July 1907	−11.630[b]	−1.762	1.924
			July, August 1907	−18.937[b]	−2.550	4.811
		Decision	June 1911	−7.090[b]	−0.711	3.252
		Dissolution Plan	September 1911	−1.548	−1.031	3.908
			September, October 1911	3.496	−2.084	4.849
			September, October, November 1911	−1.072	−4.084	5.715
		Dividends	March 1912	5.037	2.016	6.616
			March, April 1912	4.298	2.499	8.271
		All	July, August 1907 June 1911 September, October, November 1911 March, April 1912	−22.801	−4.706	15.708
	Common Stock	Complaint	July 1907	−10.495[b]	1.123	5.944
			July, August 1907	−7.096	1.281	10.180
		Decision	June 1911	−26.262[b]	0.707	5.168
		Dissolution Plan	September 1911	−9.771[d]	0.912	6.945
			September, October 1911	−8.383	−0.023	10.341
			September, October, November 1911	2.126	−1.523	9.993
		Dividends	June 1912	10.464[d]	0.076	7.148
			June, July 1912	21.592[e]	1.222	12.272
		All	July, August 1907 June 1911 September, October, November 1911 June, July 1912	−9.640	1.836	25.956

TABLE VIII—(*continued*)

Trust and Successors	*Portfolio*	*Event*	*Month(s)*	*Residual(s)*[a]	*Control Group Residual Distribution* *Mean*	*Standard Deviation*
Tobacco	6–7% Bonds	Complaint	July 1907	−4.790[c]	−1.762	1.924
			July, August 1907	−8.357	−2.550	4.811
		Decision	June 1911	−3.933	−0.711	3.252
		Dissolution Plan	September 1911	3.993	−1.031	3.908
			September, October 1911	5.771[d]	−2.084	4.849
			September, October, November 1911	6.064[e]	−4.084	5.715
		Dividends	March 1912	1.034	2.016	6.616
			March, April 1912	0.137	2.499	8.271
		All	July, August 1907 June 1911 September, October, November 1911 March, April 1912	−6.089	−4.706	15.708
	Preferred Stock & 4–5% Bonds	Complaint	July 1907	−6.073[b]	−1.762	1.924
			July, August 1907	−10.353[c]	−2.550	4.811
		Decision	June 1911	−4.292	−0.711	3.252
		Dissolution Plan	September 1911	5.002[d]	−1.031	3.908
			September, October 1911	5.990[e]	−2.084	4.849
			September, October, November 1911	4.888[d]	−4.084	5.715
		Dividends	March 1912	4.351	2.016	6.616
		All	July, August 1907 June 1911 September, October, November 1911 March 1912	−5.406	−5.188	12.991

TABLE VIII—(*continued*)

Trust and Successors	*Portfolio*	*Event*	*Month(s)*	*Residual(s)*[a]	*Control Group Residual Distribution* *Mean*	*Standard Deviation*
	Common Stock	Complaint	July 1907	−8.482[c]	1.123	5.944
			July, August 1907	−29.657[b]	1.281	10.180
		Decision	June 1911	−13.141[b]	0.707	5.168
		Dissolution Plan	September 1911	11.080[d]	0.912	6.945
			September, October 1911	7.763	−0.023	10.341
			September, October, November 1911	17.850[e]	−1.523	9.993
		Dividends	May 1912	3.467	6.740	10.812
			May, June 1912	15.112	6.727	10.311
			May, June, July 1912	18.287	7.554	13.691
		All	July, August 1907 June 1911 September, October, November 1911 May, June, July 1912	−6.661	8.202	28.490

[a] The residuals are accumulated over successive months because the impact of a particular event on trust and successor security prices ordinarily is carried over into the following month. This effect results from the use of average monthly price data. Thus the residual entry for July, August 1907 is $(\hat{u}_{jt_1} + \hat{u}_{j,t_1+1})$, etc.

[b] Statistically significant at the 95% confidence level on a one-tailed test.

[c] Statistically significant at the 90% confidence level on a one-tailed test.

[d] Statistically significant at the 85% confidence level on a two-tailed test.

[e] Statistically significant at the 90% confidence level on a two-tailed test.

dissolution plan is significantly positive for three of the five portfolios in Table VIII.

Substantial advances in the common stock prices of the snuff successors also coincided with their initial declarations of cash dividends. Relatively large residuals in early 1912 are visible for some of the other securities too, but they are not statistically significant. The explanation for this result seems essentially mechanical. As to the bonds and preferred stocks, the synchronization of (12) and (20) at month t_4 required the deletion of control group data for December 1911–February 1912; this process creates an indirect accumulation of residuals in March 1912 which reflects extraneous events and increases the variance of that distribution. In addition, residual analysis does not always detect systematic price changes of small magnitude (Brown and Warner [7]), such as might be associated with the successor companies' announcement of cash distributions on senior securities. This event would have had little information content if these fixed and prior receipts were widely anticipated. Finally, the timing of the initial dividends on the new tobacco equities works against statistical significance because the distributions were made over an entire year, preventing the price effects from being fully captured in Table VIII. However no such problems arise with the common stocks of the snuff successors, and their 10.5 and 21.6 per cent price increases in June and July 1912 are significant at the 85% and 90% confidence levels, respectively.

Net injury or gain must be evaluated from the residual sums test of (15) that explicitly accounts for large residuals with opposite signs. None of these entries in Table VIII are statistically significant. Thus the only fully direct test of the investment experience of American Tobacco and American Snuff shareholders implies that dissolution left each group unaffected, neither punishing some owners nor awarding windfall gains to others. This outcome conformed to Justice White's mandate for reorganizing the tobacco trust, and it is consistent with a delightfully reassuring assessment by the editors of the *CFC* published just three weeks after the decree:

> The action of the . . . Court has made it incontrovertibly evident that however the anti-Trust law may be applied in any particular case, its enforcement does not mean the ruthless destruction of property or the sacrifice of material interests of any kind. The law is to be carried out, but with a minimum of harm and suffering to the multifarious interests involved in these industrial organizations, which have become an integral part of the every-day business activities of the country . . . (*CFC* [11 (November 11, 1911), p. 1282 col. 1]).

However there is at least a suggestion of injury for a pair of trust and successor securities in the large discrepancies between their residual sums and the control group means. Relative to an average manufacturing share, the snuff preferred stock and the tobacco common stock lost 18.1 [−22.8–(−4.7)] and 14.9 (−6.7–8.2) per cent in market value, respectively, as a consequence of all four events. The latter accords with the substantial transfers to tobacco preferred stock- and bondholders noted in Section III. That these apparent losses are not statistically significant—or that there is no corresponding evidence of net gains in Table VIII—may simply mean that the residual sums test is not especially powerful.

VII. SUMMARY AND CONCLUSIONS

The prices of individual securities issued by American Snuff, American Tobacco and their successors were generally quite sensitive to new information with antitrust implications disclosed between 1907 and 1912 in the Sherman Act litigation. This finding applies with almost equal force to the sample of bonds, preferred stocks and equities. The responsiveness of these prices to the threat of dissolution indicates that the excess profits and/or reduced operating risks of a monopoly tend to be fully capitalized in the market values of its outstanding securities, regardless of their priority to income. The data are also consistent with Dewey's contention that capital losses for all shareowners would normally result from effective trust-busting. Perhaps this evidence will ensure that the problem of stockholder injury receives explicit consideration in academic and judicial discussions of antitrust policy.

The snuff-tobacco decree contains a practical solution to the dilemma of balancing the consumer's interest in vigorous inter-firm rivalry with shareholder concern for the preservation of capital values in monopoly. Investments in senior securities can be safeguarded either by the creation of successor company debt carrying higher coupon rates or by forcing the defendant to redeem the certificates at a fair price. In principle, these measures can fully protect favored owners from renewed competition. Of course, neither arrangement is entirely free of disadvantages. Since refunding and redemption are essentially schemes for transferring income between certificate classes, they will exacerbate the losses imposed on common stockholders by the competitive effects of the decree. Old legal doctrines may have to be expanded, or new ones created, to rationalize such deliberate and selective punishment. There is also a danger that any attempt to protect the owners of senior securities will over-estimate competitive effects *ex ante* so that one or more of these issues experiences net capital gains from a dissolution which is unexpectedly benign *ex post*. Although the direct tests were inconclusive, the analysis has presented extensive circumstantial evidence of such gains for the preferred stock- and bondholders of American Tobacco. This outcome obviously should be avoided in future cases.

Notwithstanding the feasibility of the protective measures examined here, it is doubtful that there can be any proper scope for judicial solicitude toward "innocent" investors in dissolution proceedings. For if the courts' receptiveness to pleas of stockholder injury is not ended, there will remain a striking disparity between the fates of §§ 1–2 defendants that seems impossible to reconcile with the goal of a rational administration of antitrust remedies.

The Sherman Act is directed primarily toward eliminating monopolistic output restriction, whether by collusive agreements or single-firm aggrandizement. The private benefits of these practices are capitalized in the values of the defendants' securities, so market-adjusted price reductions will result from the Act's enforcement. Under § 2, this contingency is recognized in framing remedies for illegal monopolization. In § 1 cases, however, the *per se* rule gives no consideration to the prospect of capital losses for the shareholders of price-fixing conspirators after the collusion is terminated. Furthermore, few judges appear troubled by the injury subsequently inflicted on shareowners from multi-million dollar awards to aggrieved buyers under § 4 of the Clayton Act. Since actual damages are tripled, it is conceivable that some price-fixing judgments exceed the present value of the earnings reduction caused by a competitive dissolution decree. It follows that the current policy of the law may not be protecting those "innocent" owners with the most to lose from antitrust enforcement. The vitality of the stockholder injury doctrine in § 2 cases is therefore difficult to understand when the entrenched *per se* rule bars its application under § 1. Finally, abandoning the doctrine may not cause substantial hardship in the long run. After all, if structural relief was routinely imposed on condemned monopolists with the sole purpose of establishing vigorous rivalry in the affected industries, then the additional risk associated with this change in judicial policy should be compensated with greater expected returns in the capital markets.

Malcolm R. Burns,
Department of Economics,
The University of Kansas,
207 Summerfield, Lawrence, Kansas 66045

REFERENCES

[1] ADAMS, JEAN W., 'Reconsideration of the Equity Argument Against Structural Remedies', Staff Paper No. 59 (Department of Economics, Iowa State University, June 1977).

[2] ADAMS, JEAN W., 'Trustbusting and the "Innocent" Shareholder: "Compensation" if Stock Prices Fall?', *Antitrust Law & Economics Review,* X, **1** (1978), pp. 56–65.

[3] ADAMS, WALTER, 'Dissolution, Divorcement, Divestiture: The Pyrrhic Victories of Antitrust', *Indiana Law Journal,* XXVII, **1** (Fall 1951), pp. 1–37.

[4] BLATTBERG, ROBERT C., and GONEDES, NICHOLAS J., 'A Comparison of the Stable and Student Distributions as Statistical Models for Stock Prices', *Journal of Business,* XLVII, **2** (April 1974), pp. 244–80.

[5] BORK, ROBERT H., *The Antitrust Paradox* (Basic Books, New York, 1978).

[6] BRENNER, MENACHEM, 'The Sensitivity of the Efficient Market Hypothesis to Alternative Specifications of the Market Model', *Journal of Finance,* XXXIV, **4** (September 1979), pp. 915–29.

[7] BROWN, STEPHEN J., and WARNER, JEROLD B., 'Measuring Security Price Performance', *Journal of Financial Economics,* VIII, **3** (September 1980), pp. 205–58.

[8] BURNS, MALCOLM R., 'The Distribution of Manufacturing Stock Returns, 1904–1916', Research Paper No. 62 (Department of Economics, University of Kansas, December 1975).

[9] BURNS, MALCOLM R., 'The Competitive Effects of Trust-Busting: A Portfolio Analysis', *Journal of Political Economy,* LXXXV, **4** (August 1977), pp. 717–39.

[10] COLLINS, NORMAN R., and PRESTON, LEE E., 'The Size Structure of the Largest Industrial Firms, 1909–1958', *American Economic Review,* LI, **5** (December 1961), pp. 986–1011.

[11] *Commercial & Financial Chronicle,* selected issues (William B. Dana Co., New York, 1904–16).

[12] COWLES, ALFRED, *Common-Stock Indexes* (Principia Press, Bloomington, 1938).

[13] COX, REAVIS C., *Competition in the American Tobacco Industry* (Columbia University Press, New York, 1933).

[14] DEWEY, DONALD, 'Romance and Realism in Antitrust Policy', *Journal of Political Economy,* LXIII, **2** (April 1955), pp. 93–102.

[15] DEWEY, DONALD, *Monopoly in Economics and Law* (Rand McNally, Chicago, 1959).

[16] DODD, PETER, 'Merger Proposals, Management Discretion and Stockholder Wealth', *Journal of Financial Economics,* VIII, **2** (June 1980), pp. 105–37.

[17] ELLERT, JAMES C., 'Antitrust Enforcement and the Behaviour of Stock Prices', unpublished Ph.D. dissertation (University of Chicago, 1975).

[18] ELZINGA, KENNETH G., and BREIT, WILLIAM, *The Antitrust Penalties* (Yale University Press, New Haven, 1976).

[19] FAMA, EUGENE F., 'The Behavior of Stock Market Prices', *Journal of Business,* XXXVIII, **1** (January 1965), pp. 34–105.

[20] FAMA, EUGENE F., 'Risk, Return and Equilibrium: Some Clarifying Comments', *Journal of Finance,* XXIII, **1** (March 1968), pp. 29–40.

[21] FAMA, EUGENE F., 'Efficient Capital Markets: A Review of Theory and Empirical Work', *Journal of Finance,* XXV, **2** (May 1970), pp. 383–417.

[22] FAMA, EUGENE F., FISHER, LAWRENCE, JENSEN, MICHAEL C., AND ROLL, RICHARD, 'The Adjustment of Stock Prices to New Information', *International Economic Review,* X, **1** (February 1969), pp. 1–21.

[23] FAMA, EUGENE F., and MACBETH, JAMES D., 'Risk, Return, and Equilibrium: Empirical Tests', *Journal of Political Economy,* LXXXI, **3** (May/June 1973), pp. 607–36.

[24] FAMA, EUGENE F., and MILLER, MERTON H., *The Theory of Finance* (Holt, Rinehart & Winston, New York, 1972).

[25] GARBADE, KENNETH D., SILBER, WILLIAM L., and WHITE, LAWRENCE, 'Market Reaction to the Filing of Antitrust Suits: An Aggregate and Cross-Sectional Analysis', unpublished manuscript (Graduate School of Business, New York University, 1978).

[26] HAYS, WILLIAM L., and WINKLER, ROBERT, L., *Statistics: Probability, Inference, Decision* (Holt, Rinehart & Winston, New York, 1971).

[27] JENSEN, MICHAEL C., 'Risk, the Pricing of Capital Assets, and the Evaluation of Investment Portfolios', *Journal of Business,* XL, **2** (April 1969), pp. 167–247.

[28] KING, BENJAMIN F., 'Market and Industry Factors in Stock Price Behavior', *Journal of Business,* XXXIX, **1** (January 1966), pp. 139–90.

[29] KOTTKE, FRANK, *The Promotion of Price Competition Where Sellers Are Few* (D. C. Heath, Lexington, 1978).

[30] LEV, BARUCH, and MANDELKER, GERSHON, 'The Microeconomic Consequences of Corporate Mergers', *Journal of Business,* XLV, **1** (January 1972), pp. 85–104.

[31] LINTNER, JOHN, 'Security Prices, Risk, and Maximal Gains from Diversification', *Journal of Finance,* XX, **4** (December 1965), pp. 587–616.
[32] LORIE, JAMES H., and HAMILTON, MARY T., *The Stock Market: Theories and Evidence* (Richard D. Irwin, Homewood, 1971).
[33] MCGEE, JOHN S., *In Defense of Industrial Concentration* (Praeger, New York, 1971).
[34] *Moody's Manual of Industrials*, selected volumes (Moody Publishing Co., New York, 1905–09).
[35] NADER, RALPH, GREEN, MARK J., and SELIGMAN, JOEL, *Taming the Giant Corporation* (Norton, New York, 1976).
[36] NAVIN, THOMAS R., and SEARS, MARIAN V., 'The Rise of a Market for Industrial Securities, 1887–1902', *Business History Review,* XXIX, **2** (June 1955), pp. 105–38.
[37] *New York Times,* selected issues (New York Times Publishing Co., New York, 1911).
[38] NICHOLLS, WILLIAM H., *Price Policies in the Cigarette Industry* (Vanderbilt University Press, Nashville, 1951).
[39] O'CONNOR, KEVIN J., 'The Divestiture Remedy in Sherman Act § 2 Cases', *Harvard Journal on Legislation,* XIII, **4** (June 1976), pp. 687–775.
[40] *Poor's Manual of Industrials,* selected volumes (Poor's Manual Co., New York, 1910–17).
[41] POSNER, RICHARD A., *Antitrust Law: An Economic Perspective* (University of Chicago Press, Chicago, 1976).
[42] SCHERER, F. M., *Industrial Market Structure and Economic Performance,* second edition (Rand McNally, Chicago, 1980).
[43] SCHWERT, G. WILLIAM, 'Using Financial Data to Measure Effects of Regulation', *Journal of Law & Economics,* XXIV, **1** (April 1981), pp. 121–58.
[44] SHARPE, WILLIAM F., 'Capital Asset Prices: A Theory of Market Equilibrium under Conditions of Risk', *Journal of Finance,* XIX, **3** (September 1964), pp. 425–42.
[45] SHEPHERD, WILLIAM G., *The Treatment of Market Power* (Columbia University Press, New York, 1975).
[46] SMITH, RICHARD L., 'The 1958 Automobile Information Disclosure Act: A Study of the Impact of Regulation', *Journal of Industrial Economics,* XXVIII, **4** (June 1980), pp. 387–403.
[47] TENNANT, RICHARD B., *The American Cigarette Industry* (Yale University Press, New Haven, 1950).
[48] *United States v. American Tobacco Co.,* **221** U.S. 106 (1911).
[49] United States Bureau of Corporations, *Report on the Tobacco Industry,* three volumes (Government Printing Office, Washington, 1909–15).
[50] United States Courts, *Decrees and Judgments in Federal Antitrust Cases: July 2, 1890–January 1, 1918* (Government Printing Office, Washington, 1918).

THE JOURNAL OF INDUSTRIAL ECONOMICS
Volume XXXI June 1983 No. 4

REGULATION OF "ADMINISTERED" PRICES: AN EMPIRICAL ANALYSIS OF THE MICROECONOMICS OF PRICE MOVEMENT IN FINLAND 1972–77*

BJÖRN WAHLROOS

I. INTRODUCTION

CURIOUSLY enough, the concept of administered prices launched by Gardiner Means in his 1934 report to the U.S. Secretary of Agriculture,[1] still shows up in discussions on price policy and control today, almost fifty years since it was coined and three decades after the discussion[2] in which it should have been buried. Even more astonishing is the fact that its spin-off "administered inflation", a term introduced by the Kefauver committee in 1957,[3] is still a part of economic language in some instances.

In the basic formulation, that of Means in 1935, administered prices are not assumed to be explicitly linked with market power but simply prices "set by administrative action and held constant for a period of time" (Means, [12, p. 78]). Although the hypothesis in this form was based on no economic reasoning of acceptable clarity, it might still be accepted for the simple truism it is. Clearly some prices will change more seldom than others since, for one thing, costs of price changes will vary. As is intuitively clear and as shown by Sheshinski and Weiss [17, pp. 294–95] the optimal strategy of a firm in an inflationary environment will consist of longer intervals between successive price changes the higher the cost of such a change is. Under some very special assumptions, risk aversion may also serve as an explanation to a decrease in the number of price changes relative to the number of changes in cost, as indicated by the results of Schramm and Sherman [15].[4]

The administered inflation hypothesis as forwarded by Means in his 1957 testimony before the Kefauver committee (Means, [12, pp. 101–29]) and by

* This paper was written while working as a visiting professor at Brown University. I wish to thank my colleagues at Brown and especially Daniel F. Spulber for illuminating discussions. Financial support by the Neste Foundation, Finland, is gratefully acknowledged.

[1] This report was published in January 1935 as Senate Document 13, Fifth Congress, 1 Session under the title "Industrial Prices and Their Relative Inflexibility", and has subsequently been reprinted in Means [12, pp. 77–96]. The whole background story may be found in Stigler-Kindahl [19, ch. 2].

[2] The reference here is to the so-called "marginalist controversy" of the late forties. The central arguments and references may be found in Machlup [10].

[3] On July 9, 1957 hearings on Administered Prices were opened before the Senate Antitrust and Monopoly Subcommittee under the chairmanship of Senator Kefauver. By 1960 the subject was dropped without any suggestions for further action by the majority of the committee (see Stigler, [18, p. 1 and pp. 12–13]).

[4] The analysis of Schramm and Sherman [15] rests on an assumption of managerial risk aversion which of course is inappropriate in a CAPM setting. The results might, however, be reproduced under more correct assumptions of corporate diversification.

Galbraith [8] and Ackley [1], is much more difficult or virtually impossible to accept from a standpoint of economic theory since the hypothesis implies the existence of a positive dependence between market power and the rate of price increases. The inflationary process, to quote Ackley [1, pp. 428–29], "arises from a largely autonomous upward pressure on wage rates relative to the cost of living, interacting with administered-price markups applied to rising wage costs, compounded again through agricultural prices, raw materials, the cost of living, wage rates, and industrial prices in an endless chain." In the words of Means [12, p. 104] inflation simply "arises from the exercise of pricing power in concentrated industries such as steel or automobiles or from the wage pressure of strong unions".

The publication of such arguments produced two main effects. Both in the U.S. and (with a considerable lag) in other countries, bills to make government interference in price formation processes possible were introduced by eager legislators.[5] Secondly, a huge amount of empirical work where cross-sectional price increase data were regressed on concentration ratios and, at times, cost changes was published in many journals.[6] Mostly the results of the empirical papers were statistically insignificant and often contradictory. There is still, for obvious reasons, nothing like a consensus on the empirical issue.

There are two reasons why the present paper focuses on a topic that might be considered both theoretically completely uninteresting and perhaps also slightly out of date, although the debate on the issue has been persistent up until quite recently. Firstly, there is clearly a need for a clarification of some of the issues relating to price dynamics in an industrial organization setting. Secondly, in 1974 the Finnish parliament followed the example of the Kefauver committee and a number of legislatures by passing a law on regulation of administered or monopolistic prices.[7] This law makes it possible for the government to interfere in the price formation mechanism through a specially formed agency, the National Board for Trade and Consumer Interest. Basically, prices can either be totally frozen for a limited period of time, or subjected to confirmation or notification procedures. In the latter two cases the agency is supposed to supervise the prices of regulated products and, if needed, enforce a given price determined as a multiple of approved costs.

The purpose of this paper is to develop a testable model for price movement

[5] In the U.S. concern for the pricing of individual products took the form of the price notification bill proposed by Senator O'Mahoney and strongly supported by Galbraith and Means. For details, see Stigler [18, pp. 12–13].

[6] The first empirical paper by DePodwin and Selden [7] reached a negative result with respect to the hypothesis. With some improvements in methodology Weiss [25] was able to find support for it. Consequent work includes Phlips [14] and Sellekaerts-Lesage [16]. On the price stickiness side the central contributions to the discussion are Stigler-Kindahl [19], Means [13], Stigler-Kindahl [20], Weiss [26] and McRae-Tapon [11].

[7] The central legislation on this issue includes the law on price freeze (155/74) and the Permanent Act on Price Control (156/74) both passed by parliament on February 15, 1974. Provisions of this legislation were made explicit in a number of government ordinances most important among which is the Statute on Price Control (235/74). Further details on the legislation can be found in Wahlroos [21, pp. 19–23 and pp. 91–95].

in an industrial organization setting which makes testing for regulatory impact possible. Specifically we wish to examine what kinds of hypotheses concerning price dynamics may be put forward in this connection and whether these are the ones that have been tested in earlier papers. Accordingly we look for relationships between market structure, demand characteristics, cost development and prices. The model developed is tested on Finnish cross-sectional data on the four digit industrial level and on the product level. The paper is organized as follows: Section II includes derivation of the model together with brief discussions on related topics. In Section III the test methodology and data are outlined. Sections IV and V contain results from empirical tests: Section IV covers the central analysis both on the industrial and on the product level whereas Section V constitutes a short digression on cost development in regulated industries. Section VI concludes the paper.

II. A FRAMEWORK FOR ANALYSIS

Basics

The formal setting for the analysis is a market in equilibrium given by the demand and supply functions (1) and (2) for the *i*th industry

$$(1) \qquad q_{D_i} = \varepsilon_{o_i} p_i^{\varepsilon_{1,i}} Y^{\varepsilon_{2,i}}$$

$$(2) \qquad q_{S_i} = \alpha_{o_i} R_i^{\alpha_1} C_i^{\alpha_2} p_i^{\alpha_{3,i}}$$

where

q_{D_i} quantity of i output demanded
q_{S_i} quantity of i output supplied
p_i unit price of i output
Y income
R_i a measure of market power such as the concentration ratio
C_i marginal costs of production
ε_{1_i} price elasticity of demand for the i product
ε_{2_i} income elasticity of demand for the i product
α_{3_i} price elasticity of supply of i product
ε_{o_i}, α_{o_i} industrial coefficients
α_1, α_2 cross-industrial coefficients.

Taking first differences, natural logarithms and solving (1) for p we have the demand function

$$(3) \qquad \Delta \ln p_i = \frac{1}{\varepsilon_{1_i}} \Delta \ln q_i - \frac{\varepsilon_{2_i}}{\varepsilon_{1_i}} \Delta \ln Y$$

and similarly but without solving for p, the supply function

$$(4) \qquad \Delta \ln q_i = \alpha_1 \Delta \ln R_i + \alpha_2 \Delta \ln C_i + \alpha_{3_i} \Delta \ln p_i .$$

Substituting (4) into (3) produces

$$(5) \qquad (\varepsilon_{1_i} - \alpha_{3_i}) \Delta \ln p_i = \alpha_1 \Delta \ln R_i + \alpha_2 \Delta \ln C_i - \Delta \ln Y \varepsilon_{2_i} .$$

Note that as long as the coefficients of (3), i.e., the price and income elasticities of demand are known, this equation is not subject to the traditional identification problems.

Adminstered Inflation

As has been pointed out by the opponents of the administered inflation hypothesis and most forcibly by Stigler [18] there exists no economic theory which would predict a dependency between relative price changes and levels of concentration. Even though absolute price changes may, and mostly will, differ between two firms with different power over their markets in an inflationary environment, price increases will always be proportional to increases in marginal cost. To see this, let a monopoly maximize

$$\pi = pq(p) - c(q). \tag{6}$$

The first-order condition for a maximum is

$$\frac{d\pi}{dp} = q + p\frac{\partial q}{\partial p} - \frac{\partial c}{\partial q} \cdot \frac{\partial q}{\partial p} = 0 \tag{7}$$

which produces

$$p = \frac{C\varepsilon_1}{1 + \varepsilon_1} \quad \text{and} \quad \Delta p = \frac{\Delta C\varepsilon_1}{1 + \varepsilon_1} \quad \text{for a constant } \varepsilon_1 . \tag{8}$$

Since $\varepsilon_1/(1 + \varepsilon_1) = p/C$, $\Delta p/p = \Delta C/C$ holds for a monopoly as well as for a competitive firm in a constant elasticity environment. Dropping the assumption of constant elasticity and/or infinitesimal shifts in marginal costs, we do not arrive at the administered inflation hypothesis but rather at its opposite. That is, as the demand function approaches linearity the relative increase in monopolistic prices following given increases in marginal costs decrease. For linear demand the relative price change equals.

$$\frac{\Delta p}{p} = \frac{\Delta C}{C + a} \tag{9}$$

where a is the demand function intercept. In this framework at least, no support for the administered inflation hypothesis can be found. The fact that price responses to cost changes are dependent on the shape of the demand function may in part explain the widely varying results obtained by writers who have chosen to subject the Means-Galbraith proposition to the test of reality.

Regulation

The textbook prediction relating to price regulation is shortages. This does not, however, hold for regulatory systems where price is not fixed arbitrarily but proportionately to cost. The basic rationale of Finnish markup regulation is that prices for goods subjected to confirmation procedures are set as a given multiple of average cost. The price formula used may be stated as[8]

$$(10) \qquad p_R = \phi\left(C + \frac{F}{q_o}\right)$$

where ϕ is the markup factor, C is variable cost, F is fixed cost and q_o is "normal output", a magnitude subjected to the regulator's discretion. Assuming q_o constant the following picture evolves (Figure 1).

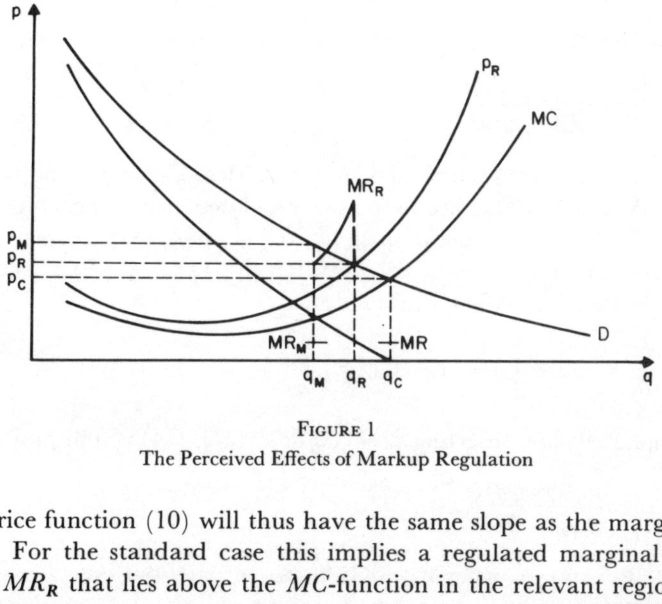

FIGURE 1
The Perceived Effects of Markup Regulation

The price function (10) will thus have the same slope as the marginal cost function. For the standard case this implies a regulated marginal revenue function MR_R that lies above the MC-function in the relevant region and is noncontinuous at q_R or the intersection of the price and demand functions. The optimal strategy of the regulated firm clearly consists of supplying the market demand at the regulated price.

If the above analysis holds, supply will no longer be determined by (4) but by the price function (10). Indicating the presence of regulatory intervention in industry i by assessing the value 1 to a dummy variable β_i we may generalize (5) and the logarithmic first difference version of (10) into (11):

$$(11) \qquad \Delta \ln p_i = (1 - \beta_i)\,\frac{\alpha_1 \Delta \ln R_i + \alpha_2 \Delta \ln C_i - \Delta \ln Y\varepsilon_{2_i}}{\varepsilon_{1_i} - \alpha_{3_i}} + \beta_i \ln\left[\phi\left(\Delta C_i + \frac{\Delta F_i}{q_{oi}}\right)\right].$$

[8] A more detailed specification, allowing for the differential in treatment of depreciation, promotional outlays, etc., can be found in Wahlroos (1978, pp. 93–94 and p. 99).

Two main counterarguments exist, however. Firstly, the rules and procedures associated with determining the regulated price are such as to imply reallocation of factors within the regulated firm[9] similar to those observed for the American regulation of public utilities.[10] Accordingly, cost functions will change due to regulation. Secondly, and more important for the case at hand, regulation produces an incentive effect which, in the presence of information costs and/or low demand elasticity, may produce gold plating. The argument is as follows:

Let a monopolistic firm maximize

$$\pi = p(C, F)q(p) - Cq(p) - F \tag{12}$$

subject to (10). First, study the case where F is changed:

$$\frac{d\pi}{dF} = \frac{\partial\pi}{\partial F} + \frac{\partial\pi}{\partial p}\frac{dp}{dF} \tag{13}$$

The unregulated firm experiences a profit decrease equalling -1 since $(\partial\pi/\partial p) = 0$, whereas the profits of the regulated firm, since regulation is effective only if $(\partial\pi/\partial p) > 0$ and since $(dp/dF) = (\phi/q_o) > 0$, decrease by some smaller amount. This implies an incentive loss. To see when gold-plating becomes profitable, rewrite (13) into

$$\frac{d\pi}{dF} = -1 + \left[q + (p - C)\frac{\partial q}{\partial p}\right]\frac{\phi}{q_o} \tag{14}$$

for the regulated case. Inserting $\varepsilon_1 = (\partial q/\partial p) \cdot (p/q)$ (14) will be positive if

$$\varepsilon_1 > \frac{p(q_o - \phi q)}{\phi q(p - C)}. \tag{15}$$

Note that $q_o < \phi q$ is necessary. Setting $\varepsilon_1 = -1$, inserting (10) for p and solving we get

$$Cq_o + F < Cq \tag{16}$$

which is sufficient for all cases of $(\partial\pi/\partial p) > 0$. Gold plating may be profitable even if demand is elastic given that $q_o < q$ which may be true in periods of expansion when the regulatory agency's output information is outdated.

The case with respect to variable costs is slightly different. The profit impact of a cost change is now given by

$$\frac{d\pi}{dC} = \frac{\partial\pi}{\partial C} + \frac{\partial\pi}{\partial p}\frac{\partial p}{\partial C} = -q + \left\{q + (p - C)\frac{\partial q}{\partial p}\right\}\phi. \tag{17}$$

[9] See Wahlroos [21, ch. 3] and Ylä-Liedenpohja [27].

[10] The reference here is to the voluminous discussion started by the Averch-Johnson [2] paper. An overview of the early discussion is found in Baumol-Klevorick [5] whereas most results to come out of it are surveyed in Bailey [4].

In this case an incentive loss is necessarily implied only for concave demand functions[11] whereas wasteful use of variable factors of production is profitable if $(d\pi/dC) > 0$, i.e., if

$$\varepsilon_1 > \frac{p(1-\phi)}{\phi(p-C)}. \tag{18}$$

Note that the RHS is always negative, i.e., gold-plating may become profitable in this case also. Condition (18) will, however, hold for $\varepsilon_1 < -1$ only if $p < \phi C$ which obviously contradicts (10). Accordingly excessive variable costs may add to regulated profits only under conditions of inelastic demand.

There is therefore reason to believe that the potentially beneficial effects of regulation on monopolistic prices do not necessarily materialize due to decreasing efficiency incentives or a reversed relationship between costs and profits on the margin. Simulation studies of regulated multiproduct firms facing highly elastic demand operating on the production frontier furthermore indicate that optimal reallocation of resources following regulation mostly is severe enough to imply almost the same prices as those quoted prior to regulation.[12] The *a priori* expected outcome of an empirical test of regulatory impact on prices, i.e., price decreases, might therefore prove incorrect.

III. EMPIRICAL TESTS: METHODOLOGY AND DATA

The starting point of the analysis is equation (11). Interpreting Y as a coefficient and inserting γ_1, $E(\gamma_1) = 1$ into the last term we may write the regression equation (19):

$$\Delta \ln p_i = \alpha_1 \frac{1-\beta_i}{\varepsilon_{1_i} - \alpha_{3_i}} \Delta \ln R_i + \alpha_2 \frac{1-\beta_i}{\varepsilon_{1_i} - \alpha_{3_i}} \Delta \ln C_i - \Delta \ln Y \frac{1-\beta_i}{\varepsilon_{1_i} - \alpha_{3_i}} \varepsilon_{2_i} + \gamma_1 \beta_i \ln\left[\phi\left(\Delta C_i + \frac{\Delta F_i}{q_{oi}}\right)\right]. \tag{19}$$

The expression now has four cross-industrial coefficients α_1, α_2, Y and γ_1. Data are available for all variables p_i, R_i, C_i, F_i and for the parameters ε_{1_i}, ε_{2_i}, and β_i. No data on α_{3_i} are, however, available or readily estimable from existing time-series data. An assumption of constancy must therefore be introduced. Estimation of α_3 can then be performed using an iterative technique. Only if a constant term is assumed included in the first-difference specification of the supply function (4), i.e., we have a time-trend in the level formulation,

[11] See Wahlroos [21, pp. 51–52].

[12] When unlimited costs of advertising were allowed to be included in the regulated price, this price could, in fact, exceed the monopoly price (Wahlroos [21, pp. 136–40 and pp. 156–57]).

will a constant term enter (19) also. The expected signs and magnitudes of the coefficients of (19) are the following:

Coefficient	Sign	Insignificantly different from
α_1	$-$	
α_2	$-$	
γ_1	$+$	1
$\Delta \ln Y$	$+$	0.786

The expected magnitude of $\Delta \ln Y$ equals the natural logarithm of the index of national income for Finland in 1977 with 1972 = 1.00 or 2.19. If regulation was effective we would expect to receive correct estimates for the elasticities α_1 and α_2 by estimating (19) for the correct value of α_3. The significance of coefficient γ_1 is, however, no test of regulatory impact since cost items highly correlated with $\phi(\Delta C_i + \Delta F_i/q_{o_i})$ enter the unregulated supply function also. Accordingly, we would expect γ_i to be in the neighbourhood of 1 even if (5) is the true model, only in that case (11) would not fit the data as well as (5).

Explicit testing for regulatory impact seems possible by introducing the dummy β_i directly into (5) to measure deviation from optimal unregulated behaviour in regulated industries. The regression equation then equals (20):

$$\Delta \ln p_i = \alpha_1 \frac{\Delta \ln R_i}{\varepsilon_{1_i} - \alpha_3} + \alpha_2 \frac{\Delta \ln C_i}{\varepsilon_{1_i} - \alpha_3} - \Delta \ln Y \frac{\varepsilon_{2_i}}{\varepsilon_{1_i} - \alpha_3} + \gamma_2 \beta_i \tag{20}$$

where a significantly negative value of γ_2 should be the outcome if regulation is effective. For the case where γ_2 receives an insignificant value, the estimates of α_1 and α_2 to come out of (20) for a correct value of α_3 should be superior to those estimated from (19).

The Data

All data are obtained from public sources in Finland. Estimations will be performed on two different sets of data. The main analysis is based on industry-level price and regulation data covering the 87 four-digit industries in Finland. The price data in this case consist of the industrial price indices derived from the Industrial Statistics of Finland (ISF) and reported on in Backström-Wahlroos [3]. The cost data also come out of the ISF. Market power is measured by the three-firm concentration ratio[13] calculated from distributions of value-added according to ISF. Values for ε_1 and ε_2, i.e., the price and income elasticities of demand, are obtained from Backström-Wahlroos [3]. The estimates used are those obtained for model 3 and the

[13] The reason for the use of the three-firm concentration ratio instead of the standard four-firm one is the size of the Finnish economy. Twenty-five percent of the four-digit industries already have three-firm concentration ratios exceeding 85 percent. Use of four-firm ratios would therefore clearly reduce the quality of the data. Use of one- or two-firm ratios is made impossible by the secrecy rules of the central statistical office.

period 1959–77. We chose to compare prices at two points of time with approximately the same cyclical and seasonal properties. December 1972 and December 1977[14] were chosen for the product level study whereas the price data on the industrial level are the annual averages of 1972 and 1977 respectively.

Values of β_i are, in both analyses, based on two government decisions: Nr 20/1975 of January 16, 1975 and Nr 129/1976 of February 12, 1976. In these decisions, products subjected to different forms of regulation varying from a price-freeze to notification, are enumerated. These two government decisions were far from the only ones dealing with regulation of commodity prices in the years covered by the present study and therefore the conclusion that regulation was instituted at the above dates should not be drawn. In fact, the products enumerated were mostly subject to regulation from its introduction in early 1974 throughout the period under study. The two decisions used for reference were chosen more or less at random. Values for β_i on the industry level were assessed based on whether a significant proportion (at least 50 percent) of the sales of a given industry went to regulated markets. Thirty-one of the 87 four-digit industries were thus classified as regulated. On the product level two different dummies were defined. δ_i (GD 20/75) indicates presence of price freeze at some time during the period studied whereas β_i indicates price confirmation procedures (GD 129/76). The use of these measures will shortly be discussed in connection with the product sample in Section IV.

The 158 products forming the base of the product-level analysis cover 41 of the 87 four-digit industries in Finland. They were selected from the more than 300 items included in the consumer price index. Eliminated were products that had undergone significant quality changes or that otherwise had been eliminated from the CPI in the seventies, together with non-industrial products, alcoholic beverages, heavily directly regulated products like sugar, butter, medicines, and tobacco, utilities, housing and products which could not be referred to a specific industry or represented an extremely small fraction of the total output of the industry. Price data for the remaining 158 products were obtained directly from the CPI.

The problem with the product level data is that, with the exception of the regulatory data, all other independent variables are measured on the industry level. For the concentration and the fixed cost variables use of industry-level values seems correct, whereas data on the product level would certainly be preferable where elasticities and marginal costs are concerned. Such data are, however, not available at present.

[14] All other data, save the data on changes in the concentration ratio, refer to the same time period. Changes in concentration are measured for the period 1970–77, i.e., a period two years longer than the corresponding one for the rest of the data. Concentration data are available only for 1970 and 1977 and since it was felt that elimination of potential cyclical bias in the data was of primary importance the possibility of a measurement error in the operationalization of changes in market power was accepted.

Proxies

Cost measurement will always include an element of approximation since data are generally too aggregated to make possible perfect assessment of, for instance, marginal cost. We shall be using two different cost concepts. The first, an index of costs of materials and energy in production is used to approximate marginal cost whereas the second, average costs of production equalling costs of materials, energy and wages, will be used to approximate average cost. Both indices are derived from the ISF.

In a small open economy market power is not necessarily well measured by a simple concentration ratio. It seems likely that changes in concentration do not imply the same change in market power if they occur in industries subjected to different amounts of import competition. To account for this, two different measures of change in market power will be tested, one equalling the simple change in the three-firm concentration ratio and the second-equalling this change multiplied by one minus the import ratio.

IV. A CROSS-SECTIONAL ANALYSIS OF 87 FOUR-DIGIT INDUSTRIES

We start out by estimating the coefficients of equations (19) and (20) from the complete sample of 87 industries using simple three-firm concentration ratios (R_1) on one hand and import-corrected ratios (R_2) on the other.

The general impression is one of support for our main hypotheses. All coefficient signs except that of γ_2 are as expected throughout, although, with the exception of the cost-related coefficients, not significantly different from zero on very high levels. The r^2's appear reasonable given the fact that we are dealing with first differences. Where F-tests could be performed it is clearly indicated that not all coefficients are equal to zero. Coefficient magnitudes for γ_1 and $\Delta \ln y$ appear correct where the intercept is not included—neither one is significantly different from its expected value in any of the cases studied. When the intercept is included, major changes in coefficient magnitudes take place, possibly calling for restrictions to be imposed upon the coefficients at a later stage of the analysis. The comparatively high estimate for α_3 reflects the traditional assumption of high price elasticity of supply in the longer run. In general, it appears that price formation in regulated industries does not significantly differ from that in unregulated ones since equation (20) explains the variation somewhat better than (19). However, the positive γ_2 calls for great caution in this respect since, if anything, it suggests that prices, corrected for changes in cost and market conditions, have increased more rapidly in regulated than in unregulated industries.

Most importantly, an examination of the residuals of the estimates presented in Table I shows strong heteroscedasticity with respect to industry size. This is not surprising—indeed it is a well-known (Comanor-Wilson, [6, pp. 127–28] and Wahlroos [22, pp. 65–67]) outcome due to differing degrees

TABLE I
COEFFICIENT ESTIMATES FOR EQUATIONS (19) AND (20) OVER 87 FOUR-DIGIT INDUSTRIES

Eq.	*R*	*Intrcpt*	α_3	α_1	α_2	$\Delta \ln y$	γ_1	γ_2	r^{2a}	SEE	*F*
19	R_1	—	9.75	−0.160	−8.77	0.786	0.954	—	0.550	0.154	—
				(−0.09)	(−16.4)	(2.67)	(28.2)				
19	R_2	—	8.00	−0.223	−7.28	0.643	0.954	—	0.550	0.154	—
				(−0.08)	(−16.5)	(2.65)	(28.1)				
19	R_1	0.248	8.00	−0.546	−5.23	0.238	0.661	—	0.557	0.138	25.8
		(4.65)		(−0.43)	(−8.80)	(1.00)	(9.47)				
19	R_2	0.246	8.00	−0.230	−5.26	0.226	0.663	—	0.556	0.138	25.7
		(4.62)		(−0.09)	(−8.94)	(0.96)	(9.51)				
20	R_1	—	14.00	−0.871	−12.8	0.707	—	0.062	0.576	0.150	—
				(−0.41)	(−21.0)	(2.18)		(1.84)			
20	R_2	—	13.00	−2.77	−12.0	0.649	—	0.058	0.577	0.150	—
				−0.78)	(−21.0)	(2.16)		(1.73)			
20	R_1	0.256	10.75	−0.738	−7.25	0.030	—	0.032	0.587	0.133	29.2
		(4.99)		(−0.51)	(−10.5)	(0.12)		(1.05)			
20	R_2	0.254	10.50	−1.35	−7.12	0.021	—	0.031	0.587	0.133	29.2
		(4.95)		(−0.52)	(−10.6)	(0.09)		(1.02)			

α_1 = concentration elasticity of supply, α_2 = cost elasticity of supply, and α_3 = price elasticity of supply, *t*-values in parentheses, R_1 = simple concentration ratio, R_2 = import-corrected concentration ratio.

[a] The r^2 given is not the coefficient of determination since the absence of an intercept makes its use and interpretation awkward, but the square of the correlation coefficient between observed and predicted values of $\Delta \ln p$.

of diversification in industries of different sizes. Since smaller industries typically are less diversified, both with respect to markets and productive technologies,[15] than are the big industries, their price indices will be more susceptible to changes in demand conditions temporary enough not to show up in long-run demand elasticities. This effect, since it is not included in the model, will of course, only show up in the residuals and will accordingly produce heteroscedasticity. This was corrected for by introducing the square root of sales in millions FMK as the weighting factor.

Just as in the unweighted estimates of Table I, equation (20) proved to fit the weighted data better than equation (19). This indicates that only insignificant differences between the pricing processes in regulated an unregulated industries exist. The fact that the level of significance of γ_2—the coefficient associated with the regulation dummy β_i—is decreased to a very low level further strengthens this argument. The results for the weighted regressions of (20) are given in Table II.

With the exception of the tremendous increase in explanatory power, nothing much seems to have happened to the estimates. The only thing to make a point of is that γ_2 is no longer positive but insignificantly negative.

The sample analyzed, all 87 four-digit industries in Finland, may be subjected to some criticism. It includes a number of industries which, for various

[15] Concerning the relationship between the size of the firm and the number of plants it will operate in a risky world see Wahlroos [23].

TABLE II
COEFFICIENT ESTIMATES OF WEIGHTED REGRESSIONS OF EQUATION (20) OVER 87 INDUSTRIES

R	*Intrcpt.*	α_3	α_1	α_2	$\Delta \ln t$	γ_2	r^2	SEE
R_1	—	16.50	−1.58	−14.3	1.06	−0.590	0.967	3.82
			(−0.83)	(−23.2)	(2.83)	(−0.42)		
R_2	—	13.00	−2.12	−11.3	0.862	−0.603	0.967	3.84
			(−0.84)	(−22.2)	(2.85)	(−0.42)		
R_1	0.203	9.00	−0.151	−6.52	0.094	−0.391	0.971	3.38
	(5.30)		(−0.16)	(−16.2)	(0.45)	(−0.31)		
R_2	0.203	9.00	−0.185	−6.51	0.095	−0.386	0.971	3.38
	(5.27)		(−0.12)	(−16.1)	(0.45)	(−0.31)		

t-values in parentheses.

reasons may be assumed to answer poorly to the structure laid out in Section II of this paper. Firstly, there are some industries which are heavily directly regulated by the government. These include the sugar refining, liquor and tobacco manufacturing industries. Secondly, all public utilities, municipally or coöperatively owned are included. Due to tax considerations, the price policies of these will certainly differ from those of private suppliers. Thirdly, two state-controlled industries which supply only state-owned firms or organizations, namely the railroad equipment and airplane industries, can also be found in the sample. Finally, the residual industry 3909, manufacturing products n.e.c., must be considered a poor operationalization of the theoretical concept of an industry since it includes all products which have not been classified as belonging to any industry in particular. Removing these ten[16] industries from the sample and rerunning the regressions of Table II we get the results set out in Table III. Since, as has been evident in previous runs, $\Delta \ln y$ tends to be significantly different from its expected value of 0.786 when an intercept is included, we restrict it to this value where necessary.

In terms of explanatory power, the results did not improve over those of Table II. To an extent, where the intercept is included, this is explained by the restriction on $\Delta \ln y$. The coefficient magnitudes now imply that whereas a percentage unit increase in costs on the average decreases supply by 12-15 percent, a percentage unit increase in the three-firm concentration ratio reduces supply by 2–5 percent. While costs and income elasticities of demand significantly affect price development, α_1—the concentration elasticity of supply—is at best significantly negative only on the 10 percent level using a one-tailed test. Price regulation seems to affect price increases negatively but the outcome in this respect is extremely uncertain due to extremely low *t*-values.

[16] The industries removed are the public utilities 4101, 4102, 4103, and 4200, the sugar (3118), distilling (3131), and tobacco (3140) industries, all heavily directly regulated by taxation and licensing, the state-owned rail-road equipment (3842) and airplane manufacture (3845) industries supplying only the state railroads, the state-owned airline and the airforce, and finally the residual industry 3909.

TABLE III
COEFFICIENT ESTIMATES OF WEIGHTED REGRESSIONS OF EQUATION (20) OVER 77 INDUSTRIES WITH $\Delta \ln y$ RESTRICTED TO 0.786 WHEN INTERCEPT IS INCLUDED

R	*Intrcpt.*	α_3	α_1	α_2	$\Delta \ln y$	γ_2	r^2	SEE
R_1	—	16.50	−2.12	−14.5	0.955	−0.825	0.962	3.94
			(−1.01)	(−20.8)	(2.32)	(−0.44)		
R_2	—	16.00	−5.16	−14.1	0.920	−0.708	0.963	3.92
			(−1.36)	(−20.8)	(2.32)	(−0.38)		
R_1	0.160	17.00	−1.27	−12.1	0.786	−0.268	0.966	3.52
	(4.32)		(−0.65)	(−15.3)		(−0.16)		
R_2	0.157	17.00	−2.86	−12.1	0.786	−0.213	0.966	3.51
	(4.22)		(−0.78)	(−15.4)		(−0.13)		

t-values in parentheses.

The last problem to be dealt with here is that arising from the fact that industrial price indices reflect not only domestic prices but export prices as well. Since the measure of market power adopted refers to domestic markets only, an error is produced. Below we try to account for this error in two ways. First, we assume that Finnish exporters have no market power in the international markets, i.e., that exports, given factor price equalization, are priced at marginal cost. Clearly, the concentration elasticity estimated from a sample of industries supplying only the export markets would then be zero. The model estimated in this paper would accordingly overpredict price levels in any industry proportionately to its export-to-sales ratios. Inserting the natural logarithm of the exports to sales ratio into equation (20) we would accordingly expect the associated coefficient γ_4 to receive a negative coefficient. Regression results are reported upon in Table IV using the import-corrected concentration ratios only since, as has been true throughout, these estimates are slightly superior to those where ordinary concentration ratios have been used.

γ_4 indeed receives a negative value when the intercept is not included. However, it receives a value equal to zero in the second run. In general, the results resemble those of Table III very closely. The reason for this may, of course, be that the assumption of deficient market power on the part of

TABLE IV
COEFFICIENT ESTIMATES FOR WEIGHTED REGRESSIONS OF EQUATION (20) EXPANDED BY THE NATURAL LOGARITHM OF THE EXPORT RATIO (γ_4) OVER 77 INDUSTRIES. $\Delta \ln y$ RESTRICTED TO 0.786 WHEN INTERCEPT IS INCLUDED

R	*Intrcpt.*	α_3	α_1	α_2	$\Delta \ln y$	γ_2	γ_4	r^2	SEE
R_2	—	16.50	−4.72	−14.0	1.02	−1.16	−0.12	0.963	3.91
			(−1.19)	(−17.5)	(2.45)	(−0.61)	(−1.22)		
R_2	0.159	17.00	−2.67	−12.1	0.786	−0.223	0.0003	0.967	3.54
	(4.02)		(−0.71)	(−15.2)		(−0.13)	(0.03)		

t-values in parentheses.

TABLE V
COEFFICIENT ESTIMATES OF WEIGHTED REGRESSIONS OF EQUATION (20) OVER 59 INDUSTRIES. $\Delta \ln y$ RESTRICTED TO 0.786 WHEN INTERCEPT IS INCLUDED

R	*Intrcpt.*	α_3	α_1	α_2	$\Delta \ln y$	γ_2	r^2	SEE
R_2	—	25.0	−10.4	−22.1	1.17	−0.294	0.945	4.24
			(−1.57)	(−16.0)	(1.50)	(−0.13)		
R_2	0.163	27.0	−6.30	−19.4	0.786	1.05	0.947	3.86
	(3.43)		(−0.95)	(−12.0)		(0.50)		

t-values in parentheses.

Finnish exporters is incorrect and that accordingly, what we should use is a measure of international concentration. Such a measure is, however, not available. Instead, to study the effect of the major exporters on the analysis we removed all industries with exports to sales ratios exceeding 50 percent—:a total of 18 industries[17]—from the sample and reran the regressions. The outcome is given in Table V.

In Table V the explanatory power is slightly down as compared to previous runs. This is mainly a reflection of the smaller contribution to the explanation obtained from the income elasticities. As could be expected, once industries where the domestic concentration ratio may be expected to measure market power very poorly were removed, the significance of α_1 increased somewhat although it is still not impressive. The only other thing to note is that in the second run γ_2, the coefficient for the regulation dummy, is once more positive but not significantly so. Note also that since optimal α_3 will now be in the 25–27 region, coefficient magnitudes will in general slightly exceed those estimated earlier.

The second set of data analyzed consists of 158 products included in the consumer price index between 1972 and 1977 selected in accordance with the principles set out in Section 3. Of the total of 158 products 71 have been subjected to price-freeze during at least six months. To account for this a dummy variable δ_i indicating price-freeze is inserted into equations (19) and (20). Its coefficient is denoted by γ_3.

The main problem with the analysis is that we lack product-level data for cost and concentration changes and elasticities. The fact that industry level data are used instead will certainly reduce the quality of the estimates. As was pointed out above, it is mainly the measures of marginal cost and demand elasticities that may be expected to perform badly.

Table VI gives the coefficient values for equations (19) and (20) expanded by the price-freeze dummy.

[17] These are 2909, other stone quarrying; 3213, knitting mills; 3232, fur dressing and dyeing; 3240, leather footwear; 3311, sawmills; 3411, pulp, paper and paperboard; 3419, pulp, paper and paperboard articles, n.e.c.; 3720, nonferrous metals; 3821, engines and turbines; 3823, metal and woodworking machinery; 3825, office, computing and accounting machinery; 3829, mac hinery and equipment n.e.c.; 3833, electrical appliances and housewares; 3841, shipbuilding; 3849, transport equipment n.e.c.; 3851, instruments; 3902, musical instruments; 3903, sporting and athletic goods.

TABLE VI
COEFFICIENT ESTIMATES FOR EQUATIONS (19) AND (20) OVER 158 PRODUCTS INCLUDED IN THE CPI

Eq.	*R*	*Intrecpt.*	α_3	α_1	α_2	$\Delta \ln y$	γ_1	γ_2	γ_3	r^2	SEE	*F*
19	R_2	—	5.75	−6.42	−5.08	0.634	0.833		0.111	0.160	0.186	—
				(−2.48)	(−11.6)	(2.83)	(16.9)		(2.56)			
19	R_2	0.441	5.50	−3.78	−2.30	0.010	0.337		0.031	0.176	0.156	6.48
		(8.19)		(−1.80)	(−4.88)	(0.05)	(4.60)		(0.83)			
20	R_2	—	5.50	−4.86	−5.04	0.387		−0.003	0.061	0.146	0.199	—
				(−2.34)	(−16.2)	(2.55)		(−0.06)	(1.24)			
20	R_2	0.515	5.25	−2.99	−1.97)	0.204		−0.027	0.023	0.206	0.153	7.87
		(10.3)		(−1.94)	(−5.47)	(1.63)		(−0.76)	(0.59)			

γ_2—coefficient associated with the price confirmation dummy β_i.
γ_3—coefficient associated with the price-freeze dummy δ_i.
t-values in parentheses.

As could be expected, the coefficients of determination are now significantly lower than in the industry-level analyses. This is, of course, a reflection of the shortcomings of the data. Nevertheless, in some respects these results seem more interesting than those previously obtained. α_1 is now mostly significantly negative on at least the five percent level and the remaining coefficients, save those for the dummies, have correct signs, mostly highly significant. However, where intercepts are included, and in equation (20) generally, the values of $\Delta \ln y$ and γ_1 differ significantly from the ones expected. Contrary to what one, based on an incentive-argument such as the one formulated in Section II, would have expected γ_3 receives a (at times highly significant) positive value while γ_1 is insignificantly negative throughout. The dogma among the profession appears to be that while short-term freezes through their effects on expectations may have a minor moderating effect on price increases, continuous regulation certainly will not. If anything, the results indicate the opposite, i.e., that price freezes rather than decreasing the rate of price increases tends to increase them in the intermediate run. Such an outcome, if indeed valid, can only be explained by the freeze causing a distortion in expectations, resulting in excessive price increases just before or immediately after its application.

V. A DIGRESSION ON COST DEVELOPMENT IN REGULATED INDUSTRIES

If regulation produces a decrease in efficiency incentives and/or a gold-plating effect we would expect this to show up in cost figures for the regulated industries. Indeed, "full cost" seems to have increased about five percent more in regulated industries than in unregulated ones during 1972–77. Note, however, that the analysis in Section II of this paper suggested not only that cost increases may be a profitable way to adapt to regulation but also that the profitability of waste and/or the likelihood of waste increases with (signed)

TABLE VII
COEFFICIENT ESTIMATES FOR EQUATION (21) EXPLAINING DIFFERENCES IN COST DEVELOPMENT IN 87 REGULATED AND UNREGULATED INDUSTRIES

Cost Item	∂_0	∂_1	∂_2	r^2	SEE	F
Wages	1.96	0.179	0.117	0.02	0.449	0.81
	(31.7)	(1.22)	(0.53)			
Materials	2.08	0.121	0.313	0.02	0.498	0.84
	(30.5)	(0.74)	(1.29)			
"Full Cost"	2.05	0.212	0.361	0.04	0.452	1.46
	(33.0)	(1.44)	(1.64)			

t-values in parentheses.

price elasticity of demand. Assuming linearity we should then be able to observe a relationship such as (21)

(21) $$\Delta C_{i_t} = \underset{(+)}{\partial_0} + \underset{(+)}{\partial_1} \beta_i + \underset{(+)}{\partial_2} \beta_i \varepsilon_1$$

where ∂_0 is the unregulated inflation rate for period t.

Equation (21) was estimated from data on wages, costs of materials and "full cost". The results are given in Table VII.

As could be expected, the explanation works best when applied to "full cost" since this is the "rate base" of the regulation. Although we get the correct signs throughout, coefficients are significantly different from zero only on low levels. For the "full cost" case, however, the F-statistic is significant on the modest 10 percent level. Accordingly, we find an indication, but not much more, that costs increase more rapidly under regulation than otherwise. The indication is quite in line with our theoretical argument.

VI. CONCLUSION

This paper proposes a new way to tackle the problem of measuring the impact of market power and price regulation on the level of industrial prices. At the outset the concept of "administered prices" is dismissed and instead a hypothesis that a measure of market power enters the supply function is put forward. The reduced version of the consequent two-equation system, identified through the introduction of the demand elasticities, is then estimated from two samples, one on the industry, the second on the product level.

The two main results to come out of the empirical study are (1) the concentration elasticity of supply is negative and most likely of the magnitude -2.5–-6.5, i.e., a percentage unit increase in the three-firm concentration ratio will, on the average, produce a 2.5 to 6.5 percent decrease in quantity supplied, and (2) neither price regulation nor freeze has had a significant negative influence on intermediate run price increases. There appeared to exist a weak positive relationship between cost increases and price regulation, however—an effect predicted by the theory set forward in Section II of this paper.

Since, indeed, concentration has increased in Finnish industry in the seventies—the average three-firm concentration ratio went from 60.9 percent in 1970 to 62.2 percent in 1977—the argument that the evils of inflation, at least to some extent, are due to imperfect competition (or rather increases in the imperfections), is not completely invalid. However, even if average concentration, weighted by the weights of the consumer price index, has increased by more than 1.3 percent, say by 3 percent, the consequent increase in the CPI assuming unit demand elasticity will have amounted to only 1.25–2.80 percent over a period of seven years, or 0.18 to 0.40 percent annually.[18] In an era when annual inflation figures approached 20 percent this effect seems negligible.

The fact that increases in concentration contributed very little to the explanation of inflation in the seventies does not of course mean that it was free of negative welfare effects. Since a measure of the concentration elasticity of supply which, at times, was significantly negative was obtained, estimations of welfare losses due to market concentration are possible. The data available—the coefficients of the industrial supply and demand functions—seem to make calculations which may exceed the precision of the classical Harberger [9] paper possible. Estimation of these welfare losses constitutes the subject matter of another paper.[19]

The fact that price regulation, whether in the form of confirmation procedures or freezes, had no significant negative effect on either the industrial price level or prices in the product sample is of course not surprising. A number of explanations to the insignificant coefficient signs can and have been offered above. What was slightly surprising was that in the product level sample, which was more detailed with respect to regulation, we at times obtained a significantly positive sign for the freeze dummy while the confirmation dummy received an insignificantly negative sign. If anything, due to the incentive properties of the two forms of regulation, one would have expected the opposite outcome. Since the two dummies are severely correlated and since several objections to data quality in the product-level sample can be made, one should avoid far-reaching conclusions. However, at the very least, it seems that the case for the use of price regulation is weak, not only from a theoretic but from an empirical point of view also.

Björn Wahlroos,
Swedish School of Economics and Business Administration,
Arkadiagatan 22,
00100 Helsinki 10.
Finland

ACCEPTED OCTOBER 1981

[18] Assuming unit price elasticity of demand and the elasticity pairs $\alpha_1 = -2.5$, $\alpha_3 = 5.0$ and $\alpha_1 = -6.5$, $\alpha_3 = 6.0$ which correspond fairly closely to the best results obtained in the above analysis, since $\partial \ln p/\partial \ln R = \alpha_1/(\varepsilon_1 - \alpha_3)$, Δp caused by the 3 percent increase in concentration over the years 1970–77 equals 1.25–2.80 percent.

[19] See Wahlroos [24].

REFERENCES

[1] ACKLEY, GARDNER, "Administered Prices and the Inflationary Process", *American Economic Review*, 49, **2** (May 1959), pp. 419–30.

[2] AVERCH, HARVEY and JOHNSON, LELAND L., "Behavior of the Firm under Regulatory Constraint", *American Economic Review*, 52, **5** (December 1962, pp. 1053–69.

[3] BACKSTRÖM, MAGNUS and WAHLROOS, BJÖRN, "Efterfrågan på industriprodukter i Finland 1959–77", *Swedish School of Economics and Business Administration* (Working Papers 50, 1980).

[4] BAILEY, ELISABETH E., *Economic Theory of Regulatory Constraint* (Lexington Books, Lexington, 1973).

[5] BAUMOL, WILLIAM J. and KLEVORICK, ALVIN K., "Input Choices and Rate-of-Return Regulation: An Overview of the Discussion", *Bell Journal of Economics*, 1, **2** (Autumn 1970), pp. 162–90.

[6] COMANOR, WILLIAM S. and WILSON, THOMAS A., *Advertising and Market Power* (Harvard University Press, Cambridge, Mass., 1974).

[7] DE PODWIN, HORACE and SELDEN, RICHARD T., "Business Pricing Policies and Inflation", *Journal of Political Economy*, **71** (April 1963), pp. 116–27.

[8] GALBRAITH, JOHN KENNETH, "Market Structure and Stabilization Policy", *Review of Economics and Statistics* (May 1957), pp. 124–33.

[9] HARBERGER, ARNOLD C., "Monopoly and Resource Allocation", *American Economic Review*, 44, **2** (May 1954), pp. 77–87.

[10] MACHLUP, FRITZ, "Marginal Analysis and Empirical Research", *American Economic Review*, **36** (September 1946), pp. 519–54.

[11] MCRAE, JAMES J. and TAPON, FRANCIS, "A New Test of the Administered Pricing Hypothesis with Canadian Data", *Journal of Business*, 52, **3** (1979), pp. 409–27.

[12] MEANS, GARDINER, C., *The Corporate Revolution in America* (Cromwell-Collier, New York, 1962).

[13] ——, "The Administered Price Thesis Reconfirmed", *American Economic Review*, 62, **3** (June 1972), pp. 292–306.

[14] PHLIPS, LOUIS, "Business Pricing Policies and Inflation—Some Evidence from EEC Countries", *Journal of Industrial Economics*, **18** (1969), pp. 1–14.

[15] SCHRAMM, RICHARD and SHERMAN, ROGER, "A Rationale for Administered Pricing", *Southern Economic Journal*, **44** (July 1977), pp. 125–35.

[16] SELLEKAERTS, WILLY and LESAGE, RICHARD, "A Reformulation and Empirical Verification of the Administered Prices Inflation Hypothesis: The Canadian Case", *Southern Economic Journal*, **39** (April 1973), pp. 345–60.

[17] SHESHINSKI, EYTAN and WEISS, YORAM, "Inflation and the Costs of Price Adjustment", *Review of Economic Studies*, **44** (June 1977), pp. 287–303.

[18] STIGLER, GEORGE J., "Administered Prices and Oligopolistic Inflation", *Journal of Business*, 35, **1** (January 1962), pp. 1–13.

[19] —— and KINDAHL, JAMES K., *The Behavior of Industrial Prices* (Columbia University Press, New York, 1970).

[20] —— and ——, "Industrial Prices as Administered by Dr. Means", *American Economic Review*, **63** (September 1973), pp. 717–21.

[21] WAHLROOS, BJÖRN, "Waste and Reallocation under Average Cost Price Regulation", *Publications of the Swedish School of Economics and Business Administration*, **28** (Helsinki 1978).

[22] ——, "The Economics of the Finnish Industrial Structure", *Swedish School of Economics and Business Administration; Research Reports*, **4** (1980).

[23] ——, "On the Economics of Multiplant Operation: Some Concepts and an Example", *Journal of Industrial Economics*, 29, **3** (March 1981), pp. 231–45.

[24] ——, "The Welfare Cost of Imperfect Industrial Competition in an Open Economy with an Application to Finland", *Scandinavian Journal of Economics*, 84, **3** (1982).

[25] WEISS, LEONARD, "Business Pricing Policies and Inflation Reconsidered", *Journal of Political Economy*, 74, **2** (March–April 1966), pp. 177–87.

[26] WEISS, LEONARD, "Stigler, Kindahl and Means on Administered Prices", *American Economic Review*, **67** (September 1977), pp. 610–19.

[27] YLÄ-LIEDENPOHJA, JOUKO, "A Static Microanalysis of the Finnish Price Regulation System", *The Helsinki Research Institute for Business Economics*, Reports No. 24 (Helsinki 1978).

THE JOURNAL OF INDUSTRIAL ECONOMICS
Volume XXXI June 1983 No. 4

JOINT COSTS AND INTRA-TARIFF CROSS-SUBSIDIES: THE CASE OF LINER SHIPPING

J. A. ZERBY AND R. M. CONLON

I. INTRODUCTION

THE problem of allocating joint costs arises in attempts to analyse the profit-maximising behaviour of multiple-product firms. If the production occurs in technically fixed proportions, so that an increase in the output of any one product always entails an increase in the output of all other products,[1] then it is invalid to attempt to separate costs in a manner which assumes away the indivisibilities.[2] In such circumstances it is therefore not possible to determine unambiguously the marginal cost of the separate products, and any attempt to use such estimates to represent "normative" prices, is untenable as an objective statement.[3]

The joint cost problem is less pressing in the perfectly competitive case as the long-run equilibrium requires that the marginal cost of producing the joint bundle is equal to the price at which the marginal unit of the joint bundle is sold, and the relative prices of the outputs contained in the bundle can be determined from the respective demand functions. If, however, the firm is not operating in a perfectly competitive environment, then the possibility of price discrimination between different buyers of any one product cannot be dismissed, and if it does exist, monopoly power cannot be measured in terms of the relationship between long-run marginal cost and prices when the firm's outputs are joint products. Similarly, a further segmentation of the market according to common products,[4] with the prices of some products in excess of their separable costs, will not necessarily reveal the extent of monopoly profit. If the firm charges different prices for different products[5] only to the point of allocating fully the joint costs, with gross revenue exactly equal to the minimum return required for sustained operation in the long run, then the firm's prices can be considered to be equivalent to the perfectly competitive

[1] The converse is also true, so that either the joint bundle is produced as a whole, or is not produced at all. See Kolsen [14, p. 75].

[2] The controversy began in 1913 with arguments by Taussig [23] and Pigou [18]. Recent comment is given by Walters [26], Ferguson [6] and Kolsen [14, Chap. 3].

[3] The tendency to give the problem a "normative" content nevertheless persists. See, for example, Jansson and Shneerson [13, p. 570].

[4] In this case the alternative to producing more of one output is more of another output, rather than treating the former as waste.

[5] In the case of price discrimination, differing demand elasticities are attributed to the different preferences of buyers; in the case of common products there may be no difference between buyers of any of the slightly different products. In practice, the distinction is sometimes difficult to establish, but is important theoretically since the former is generally associated with monopoly power while the latter is not.

case. In both instances, the matter depends upon whether the demand elasticities are exploited to a point in excess of joint-cost recovery.

Discussions of cross-subsidisation among products suffer similar problems. If a cross-subsidy is defined as a negative contribution to common costs, then proof of its existence requires a comprehensive allocation of costs in order to determine the appropriate level of common costs and the amount contributed by each product. Some researchers have avoided the necessity of such an allocation by relying on the firm's long run marginal cost to denote the minimum contribution of each product which is necessary in order to sustain the activity in the long run. Market prices below that level are then taken as evidence of long run cross-subsidisation. With joint production, however, since the minimum price for an individual output is the difference between the costs of treating it as a product and of treating it as a waste, the existence of prices or some products which are less than the long-run marginal cost of the bundle is consistent with the perfectly competitive model and does not constitute cross-subsidisation. It is necessary to obtain information about the marginal cost of each output in the joint bundle, rather than the marginal cost of the joint bundle, and failure to do so by assuming that costs per unit of output are homogeneous may result in a serious overstatement of the magnitude of cross-subsidisation.

In the case of liner shipping, the existence of cross-subsidisation is usually taken for granted and the discussion has been restricted to its relative merits.[6] Since both homogeneity of costs (among common products) and constant returns to scale are generally accepted, evidence of freight rates on certain commodities greatly in excess of the lowest rates, which are taken to be approximately equivalent to the shipowner's cost of accepting marginal cargo, suggests that some degree of redistribution occurs in the pricing system. As well, since current views, for example, maintain that shipowners do not earn excessive profits and that the levels of capacity utilisation are both relatively stable over time and uniform over major trade routes in the long run, the joint cost problem is largely dismissed. It nevertheless presents an impediment to a more complete public acceptance of the principle of "charging what the traffic will bear", and fails to satisfy fully the regulatory issues which are currently under discussion in many of the major maritime nations.[7]

[6] Deakin [4, Chapter 4] as well as Zerby and Conlon [28] give some estimates based upon liner data. Evans [5] and Laing [16] offer explanations to the practice and Heaver [10], Jansson [13], Shneerson [20] and Sturmey [22] express concern over the welfare consequences. A notable exception to the recognition of the existence of cross-subsidisation is found in the Grigor Report [1, p. 35], which argued that higher freight rates on the low-rated and low-valued items would result in a decline in traffic, thus inducing a shift to smaller vessels with higher average operating costs. If these economies of scale (in vessel size) and the decline in traffic are substantial, then a different pricing system which fails to maximise the total volume of traffic may result in rates for high-valued cargoes which are equal to, or greater than, the existing rates, and may thus offset completely any cross-subsidy. The matter is almost entirely an empirical one, and is examined in Section III below. For purposes here, the economies of scale considerations do not, in themselves, rule out the possibility of cross-subsidisation.

[7] See U.S. Department of Justice [24] and the criticism of it by the University of Wales Institute of Science and Technology [25] and Zerby [27].

II. JOINT COSTS AS A RESIDUAL

Defining separable costs as the components of total cost which can be specifically allocated to particular commodities, and treating all other costs as joint costs, it follows that

$$\text{TOTAL REVENUE} = \text{SEPARABLE COSTS} + \text{JOINT COSTS} + \text{PROFITS}$$

Denoting the price and quantity of the ith product as p_i and q_i respectively, the summation of price times quantity over n products yields total revenue, and separable costs can be found from the double summation over n products and k production activities:

$$(1) \qquad \sum_{i=1}^{n} p_i q_i = \sum_{i=1}^{n} \sum_{j=1}^{k} c_{ij} q_i + e$$

where c_{ij} is the unit cost of the ith product in the jth activity and e is the residual of joint costs plus profits.

In most cases c_{ij} in equation (1) is not available as cost data are generally not recorded on a disaggregated basis. As a consequence, two general approaches have been followed. The first relates to the allocation of fixed and variable costs among the products according to often arbitrary principles. For example, in apportioning certain fixed costs on the basis of the time devoted to each product, it is necessary to assume that productivity is constant for each interval of time. Similarly, the allocation of administrative costs (overheads) requires assumptions as to the proper measure of output for the respective products. While specific assumptions may be defended as "*a priori* reasonable",[8] there is no objective way of justifying them empirically.[9] Estimates of cross-subsidisation may therefore be biased against products which have been assessed more than their proper share of the fixed costs, and the estimates of joint costs will be overstated with an excessively large "inseparable" cost component.

The second approach is based upon hedonic price functions (product-characteristics equations) which were originally applied to the construction of price indices conveying qualitative change. Implicit prices are estimated by regressing product prices on the selected characteristics in order to obtain relative values for the utility bearing attributes of the product. Griliches [8], one of the first proponents of the method, emphasised the importance of selecting attributes which denote physical characteristics rather than those which are outcomes of market experiments. Even if such care is exercised, however, an identification problem remains, since the valuation of the utility

[8] See Jansson [12, pp. 300–301].

[9] An exception will occur if the various units of measure yield substantially the same result, an event which is most unlikely in liner shipping. The diversity of cargo is sufficient to ensure that measurement tons, weight tons or revenue tons will produce significantly different allocations.

bearing attributes is normally based upon equilibrium conditions. In more technical terms, since the hedonic price function is the reduced form of an equilibrium supply and demand model, it is generally impossible to obtain an unambiguous separation of cost and demand influences for the chosen attributes.

Recent applications of the hedonic hypothesis to transport costs have attempted to overcome the identification problem with variations of Rosen's [19] suggested method of employing exogenous shift variables in the demand and supply functions. It is essentially a two-stage procedure which resembles the conventional two-stage least squares estimation of simultaneous equation models.[10] Relative variations in the shift variables help to identify the endogenous relationship as either a compensated demand function (with real income held constant) or a supply function. Spady and Friedlaender's hedonic cost functions for the U.S. trucking industry [21] was based upon the argument that commodity characteristics such as average load, length of haul, shipment size and cargo composition are beyond the individual firm's control, and are therefore exogenous variables. The resulting one-step estimates were interpreted as hedonic coefficients in the cost function and were used as representations of technology. The Friedlaender, Ferguson and Sloss study of unit coal trains [7] concentrated on the structural changes in the rate structure and cost influences were deduced from the invariant nature of specific shift variables.[11]

Earlier studies of ocean liner rates by Bryan [2] [3], Heaver [9] [11] and Lipsey and Weiss [17], were also based upon an assumed exogeneity of commodity characteristics, but without explicit recognition of the hedonic hypothesis. Although such assumptions are less straightforward than is the case with the regulated trucking industry, the ability of the shipowner to control the mixture of cargo available for each voyage is greatly limited.[12] Additionally, value per tonne is regarded as having a negligible influence on operating costs and the ability of specific shippers to bargain for lower rates is related almost entirely to their demand for liner services. However, since some commodity and shipper characteristics are less easily classified, the method is exposed to problems of ambiguity which are similar to those described previously. The advantage accorded to the hedonic method relates primarily to the fact that recent experience has shown that failure to take account of output characteristics in nonhedonic formulations can create

[10] In the first stage, observed product prices are regressed on all characteristics (excluding the shift variables) with the resulting estimates of implicit marginal prices used as endogenous variables in the supply and demand functions (with the shift variables included).

[11] In this case the major shift variables were partial derivatives: the change in unit train marginal costs with respect to unit train output, and the change in the demand for unit train services with respect to rail rates.

[12] See Zerby and Conlon [28].

estimation errors which are more serious than those resulting from misclassification of a relatively small number of characteristics.[13]

III. HEDONIC MODEL FOR LINER SHIPPING

The underlying cost function should include data representing factor inputs, output levels and technological influences. Inputs which do not vary with the type of cargo handled were neglected since their impact on freight rates can be subsumed in the constant term. Cost influences included in the function are:

index for ease of loading,
index for port efficiency,[14]
dummy variable for special handling,[15]
dummy variable for hazardous cargo, and
dummy variable for refrigerated cargo.

Output levels for each commodity are measured by the stowage factor (cubic space occupied by a tonne of the cargo) and the percentage of the commodity shipped by containers is used as a measure of differing technological requirements. Data were immediately available only for stowage factors; all other variables were obtained through estimates.[16]

The demand functions should contain information concerning the elasticities of demand for the freighted goods and their elasticities of supply in the importing countries. Data limitations necessitated the use of value per tonne as a proxy. An index of the shippers' bargaining disadvantage was subjectively constructed on the basis of the size and activity of the respective shippers' organisations. Commodity characteristics which tend to exert an influence on conference rate-making (large quantities of nonseasonal cargo shipped in large consignments) were evaluated separately as an index of volume and availability. A fourth influence is called index of charter potential. In order to make the variable conform to the requirement of exogeneity, it was constructed primarily on the basis of the presumed ability to transport the commodity in shipload lots, with consideration given to an estimate of

[13] The recent experience is more valuable in the trucking industry study [21]. The same argument should apply to industries for which there is considerable diversity among products. The hedonic method also makes it easier to "hedge" the estimation by recalculating the implicit marginal rates using the alternative classification for the ambiguous characteristics.

[14] The index was constructed from information relating to average loading rates at each Australian ports and the percentage of the total exports of each commodity loaded at the port. Ports of discharge were neglected since their distribution is more uniform than is the case for cargo loaded near the source of supply.

[15] Estimates were based upon the need for special attention on the part of the shipowner. For example, bloodmeal and certain chemicals can easily contaminate cargo placed near it. Other commodities can themselves be easily contaminated. Large pieces of machinery require special storage to prevent damage; certain types of cargo may be considered fragile; and valuable or otherwise desirable items have a high potential for pillage.

[16] The estimates were largely subjective, though published information was used whenever possible. A discussion of the estimating procedure can be found in Zerby and Conlon [29].

the export growth rate, degree of homogeneity of the commodity and the degree of both buyer and seller concentration. For example, mineral sands in containers and grain in bags have a high charter potential, while food, instruments and glass have a low potential.

Distance is generally treated as a cost influence, but in order to compare the results of three of Australia's outward trades this influence was removed from the dependent freight rate variable prior to the estimation of the remaining coefficients.[17] The constant term of the regression equations was not specifically classified in the first part of the analysis. Since the three trade routes differ considerably in terms of inward load rates, it was hoped that inferences could be made from a comparison of the relative magnitudes of the constant term. The data relate to 1972–73 from Europe, Japan and Arabian Gulf trade and are derived from (seven-digit) exports classified by the Australian Export Commodity Classification.

A regression equation explaining the $n \times 1$ vector of observed prices, p, by an $n \times k$ matrix of exogeneous cost variables, X, and an $n \times p$ matrix of observations reflecting the exogenous non-cost variables, N, will yield ordinary least squares estimates of the coefficient vector β and γ, and the constant term α in

$$(2) \qquad p = \alpha + \beta X + \gamma N + u$$

where u is the $n \times 1$ vector of stochastic disturbances. The joint cost plus profits residual can be obtained from

$$(3) \qquad e = \sum_{i=1}^{n} \sum_{j=1}^{p} \gamma_j^* N_{ij} q_i$$

where γ_j^* is proportional to $\hat{\gamma}_j$, the estimated coefficient in equation (2). The proportionality stems from the fact that the quantity weights in (3) are likely to distort the least squares effect on the residual.[18] A suitable scale factor is one which maintains the same total revenue as is shown in (1). Therefore

$$(4) \qquad \sum_{i=1}^{n} p_i q_i = k_1 \left(\hat{\alpha} \sum_{i=1}^{n} q_i + \sum_{n=1}^{n} \sum_{i=1}^{k} \hat{\beta}_j X_{ij} q_i + \sum_{i=1}^{n} \sum_{j=1}^{k} \hat{\gamma}_j N_{ij} q_i \right)$$

and the scale factor k_i can then be applied to the non-cost factors to obtain an estimate of joint costs plus profits.

Intra-tariff cross-subsidy effects can be analysed in a similar manner by calculating the implicit marginal freight rates and evaluating them at the

[17] The effect of distance was estimated to be $D^{0.276}$, where D denotes the distance in nautical miles. The coefficient 0.276 was obtained in a log-linear regression using a combined set of data for all three outward trades, with a random sample of 100 observations from each. The t-value associated with the estimated coefficient was 6.40, and the value of R^2 for the equation was 0.86.

[18] The minimisation of the sum of squared errors results in a zero sum of (signed) errors only when no external set of weights is applied to the errors.

"amount" of each commodity's characteristics (numerical value of X_{ij}). For this purpose, the estimates of β_j are subject to a scale factor arising from the use of both cost and demand variables which are assumed to be exogeneous (and therefore independent and separable) in the estimated equation. The scale factor which preserves total revenue for the observed quantities of each commodity is

$$(5) \qquad k_2 = \sum_{i=1}^{n} p_i q_i \Big/ \sum_{i=1}^{n} \sum_{j=1}^{k} \hat{\beta}_j X_{ij} q_i$$

with an additive term in the denominator if the constant term is treated as a cost influence. The difference between the actual and the implicit freight rates gives an indicator of the degree of cross-subsidisation among different commodities.

Since k_1 and k_2 alter the units of measurement, relative to the regression equation, the usual tests of significance cannot be applied directly to either the estimate of e or the implicit freight rates. Reliance must therefore be placed upon the statistical significance of the unadjusted regression equation in order to assess the probable nature of the final estimates. [19] A more inhibiting feature of the method is the explicit assumption that the quantity weights remain unchanged with a new, artificially determined set of prices. Since the magnitudes of the hedonic variables in the underlying demand function are likely to be inversely related to the elasticity of demand for the respective products, a substantial increase in the prices for the low-rated products is almost certain to be associated with a significant fall in the quantity demanded. Even if the resulting reduction in output is exactly offset by an increase in the quantity demanded of products whose price is reduced,[20] the new set of quantity weights is likely to alter both scale factors, producing a new set of implicit freight rates.

The estimated rates are nevertheless useful in conveying summary descriptions of the particular pricing system. Since individual differences in cost and in elasticities of demand are taken into account, the artificial prices represent a considerable improvement over estimates of the long-run marginal cost (of the overall production process) as a basis for judging cross-subsidy effects. Second, the magnitude of the scale factor, k_2, reflects the relative importance of the hedonic variables for costs in the determination of price. Values close to unity would suggest that prices are, in fact, cost based. Third, the pattern of the signs associated with the disparities between the actual and the implicit prices conveys information concerning the range and variability of the cost variables, as well as the interaction between the cost and non-cost influences.

[19] Since the quantity weights are generally known with certainty, they will not decrease the level of significance associated with the relationship as a whole. The change in scale, however, prevents comparisons of different values for e and of individual implicit rates.

[20] This is possible only for common products.

TABLE I
RESULTS OF LOG-LINEAR REGRESSIONS FOR THREE AUSTRALIA-OUTWARD LINER TRADES
1972–73

Variables	*Europe*	*Japan*	*Arabian Gulf*
Hedonic Cost Variables			
Stowage factor	0.838	0.822	1.097
	[70.11]	[30.85]	[64.71]
Index for ease of loading	0.100	0.154	0.130
	[5.28]	[4.35]	[5.81]
Dummy variable for special handling	0.003	0.006	0.005
	[2.30]	[2.30]	[2.26]
Dummy variable for hazardous cargo	−0.003	0.008	0.018
	[−1.38]	[1.96]	[4.90]
Dummy variable for reefer cargo	0.030	0.042	0.039
	[18.83]	[11.91]	[19.97]
Index for port efficiency	0.080	−0.169	−0.910
	[0.66]	[−0.71]	[−5.20]
Percentage shipped by containers	−0.047	−0.001	n.a.
	[−3.58]	[−0.06]	
Constant term	0.769	1.628	3.077
	[3.09]	[3.22]	[8.50]
Hedonic Demand Variables			
Value per tonne	0.041	0.090	0.022
	[31.03]	[9.35]	[2.61]
Index of bargaining disadvantage	−0.055	−0.064	−0.057
	[−2.00]	[−1.10]	[−2.01]
Index of charter potential	−0.149	−0.043	−0.340
	[−6.24]	[−0.91]	[−5.03]
Index of volume and availability	−0.273	−0.284	−0.196
	[−9.06]	[−3.54]	[−2.77]
Sample size	3,611	747	1,126
R^2	0.79	0.74	0.86

Note: *t*-values are shown in brackets. The dependent variable is freight rate per tonne taken from Conference tariffs, or calculated with estimated stowage factor conversion for measurement based rates, with the distance influence "removed".

IV. ESTIMATES OF CROSS-SUBSIDY EFFECTS

The regression results are shown in Table I, and indicate that the coefficients associated with cost variables are remarkably similar for the three liner trades. Since a much larger percentage of the cargo on the Arabian Gulf trade was carried in break-bulk vessels,[21] it is not surprising that stowage factors and the index for Australian port efficiency had a slightly greater effect in that trade. The most substantial difference between the three trades occurs in the constant term. The Australia-to-Europe liner trade is reasonably well balanced in terms of quantities (by weight) of incoming and outgoing cargo, and the value of the constant term for that trade is the smallest. Trade with Japan is less balanced since a major part of Australia's

[21] i.e. Non-unitised.

TABLE II
SCALE FACTORS AND RELATED AGGREGATES FOR AUSTRALIA-TO-EUROPE TRADE
1972–1973
(Dollar values in millions of Australian dollars)

Actual revenue	\$110.472
Revenue contribution of hedonic cost variables	42.113
Revenue contribution of constant term	48.751
Revenue contribution of hedonic demand variables	2.915
k_1 (scale factor to adjust for aggregation error)	1.178
k_2 (scale factor with constant term as a cost factor)	1.216
e (joint-cost and profit residual, including constant term) = 1.178 (48.751 + 2.915)	\$60.863

exports to that country are large bulk cargoes. The Arabian Gulf trade is the least balanced with relatively little liner cargo carried on the inward Australian journey, and for that regression the value of the constant term was the largest. It appears, therefore, that the constant term captures a portion of the joint costs associated with unutilized space on the backhaul journey.[22] If this is the case, then joint costs are at least partly recovered by an across-the-board adjustment to prices. The weaker significance of the coefficients associated with value per tonne for the Japan and the Arabian Gulf trade tends to imply that discriminatory pricing has occurred and is less useful in recovering joint costs, compared with the Australia-to-Europe trade.

The scale factor calculations are shown in Table II, with $k_2 = 1.216$ used to calculate the implicit rates shown in Table III. In this example, the revenue contribution of the constant term is greater than that associated with the hedonic cost variables. However, it is the very small overall contribution of the non-cost variables (of which value per tonne is the most important) which stands out vividly. Since the constant term is not associated with individual commodities, it enters into the calculation of the implicit prices as an additional term in the multiplicative scale factor shown in equation (5). Despite the relatively low weight given to hedonic variables in the demand function, they remain important for over one-half of the commodity groups shown in Table III.[23] Grain shipments by containers compete with the bulk trade, and dried fruits, nuts, and seeds from Australia experience competition from Eastern Mediterranean countries. Low rates on these items therefore reflect competitive market conditions, as well as a relatively low value per tonne.[24]

[22] It is readily conceded by the carriers in the Arabian Gulf trade that Australian exports bear in a large portion of the round voyage costs. In the case of the trade with Japan, the joint costs are presumably shared between exports and imports, but it is not possible to state the relative proportions without a similar analysis of Japan's exports to Australia.

[23] Only five of the groups have implicit rates which differ from the actual rate by 20 percentage points or less.

[24] For example, during 1972–73 sultanas exported on the Australia-to-Europe trade which had an average value of \$340 per tonne were charged just over \$19 a tonne for shipment. Tannery products of roughly the same value paid approximately \$80 a tonne.

TABLE III
ACTUAL AND IMPLICIT FREIGHT RATES FOR AUSTRALIA'S EXPORTS TO EUROPE
1972–1973
(By commodity groups)

Commodity group	*Gross tonnes shipped*	*Actual rate $A*	*Implicit rate $A*	*Implicit rate as percent of actual rate %*	*Estimated LRAC*[a] *as percent of actual rate %*
Metal products and machinery	278,959	156.48	114.14	72.9	39.0
Meat and meat products	247,091	102.73	90.38	88.0	59.4
Dairy products	64,069	86.05	77.24	89.8	70.9
Fresh fruit	140,410	69.26	71.59	103.4	88.1
Wool[b]	321,939	68.00	77.22	113.6	89.7
Other crude materials	198,298	57.33	62.81	109.6	106.4
Other food products	26,094	46.27	60.97	131.8	131.8
Nuts and seeds	93,687	26.21	41.49	158.3	232.7
Dried fruit	191,668	21.31	37.24	174.8	286.3
Minerals, ores, and chemicals	171,872	18.09	23.56	130.2	337.2
Grain	151,160	11.96	45.84	383.3	510.0

Notes: [a] Long-run average costs were estimated by the authors in a separate study (see Zerby and Conlon [28], to be $61 per tonne.

[b] The vast majority of Australian wool to Europe is sent by through rates as part of the conference's "door-to-door" service. Estimates of the equivalent "shed-to-shed" rate were made in order to achieve comparability with other commodities.

Source: Estimated from Table II results.

The implicit rates display a considerably smaller disparity with the actual rates, compared with the estimated long-run average cost of the liner service (shown in percentage terms in the last two columns of Table III). Though a cross-subsidy effect may still exist in terms of implicit rates, it is much smaller than the alternative method suggests. If the last four commodity groups were eliminated entirely from the Australia-to-Europe trade, as a result of a pricing policy based upon implicit prices, there would be a decline in traffic of about 30 per cent. Without an accompanying decline in the frequency of service, the average costs would increase as a result of the utilisation of vessels which are 30 per cent smaller. Even if this were to cause a 100 per cent increase in average costs, which seems unreasonably high,[25] a limited amount of cross-subsidisation would probably continue to exist. But if additional withdrawals from the trade are assumed, say, a reduction of one-half or two-thirds of the traffic, then the highest rate may well be roughly equivalent to average costs.

A further qualification arises from the lack of information about costs and revenue of cargo moving from Europe to Australia. An accurate assessment of the magnitude of the joint-cost-plus-profits residual would require a regression equation containing commodities from both directions. The estimated residual reported here, therefore, gives only the contribution of the Australian-outward cargo to joint costs. There is no reason to believe, however, that the proportional allocation between separable and joint costs for that cargo will be altered. A more complete analysis will almost certainly change the scale factor, if an effort is made to preserve total, round-voyage revenue. This will have the effect of increasing or decreasing the estimated implicit rates by a specific proportion, and will thus influence the evaluation of potential changes in quantities if the implicit rates were to be applied. The possibility of a cross-subsidy effect between Australian-outward cargo will be greater if the Australian inward rates are more fully cost-based than those observed here, since the equilibrating scale factor would be lower and the presumed decline in the outward traffic would be less.

V. EVALUATION

The results of the analysis give additional support to the view that nonhedonic formulations of freight transport costs can create serious errors in their failure to adjust for the diversity of output characteristics. The hedonic hypothesis, on the other hand, asserts that each freighted item can be viewed as an aggregate of individual components or characteristics, so that the heterogeneity can be adequately described (it may be hoped) by a small number of characteristics. However, as with most attempts to analyse the

[25] A number of cost comparisons for differing ship speeds, sizes, and types are given by Laing [15]. Available evidence indicates that substantial changes are required in order to experience drastically different cost conditions.

cost structure of an industry, data limitations frequently necessitate the use of proxy variables and constructed indices. Such procedures may reduce the generality of the results and affect the accuracy of the estimated relationships. Moreover, since the valuation of the utility-bearing attributes is normally regarded as market determined, direct inferences of cost or technological influences may be viewed with suspicion. While rate setting procedures in freight transport depart considerably from the competitive model, it is generally not possible to eliminate all ambiguities in the classification of attributes. The hedonic method is therefore more "acceptable" for industries which are characterised by a continuum of qualities in the goods or services produced. In such cases, what is lost in the failure to specify the heterogeneity is generally greater than the errors imposed by imprecise specification of particular quality-attributes.

The liner shipping industry continues to be sensitive to the possible degree of intra-tariff cross-subsidisation and the extent to which conference rate-setting policies are cost-based. Relatively few observers argue that the two related issues are inconsequential. Rather, they are fundamental to regulatory decisions involving the structure of the industry and the role of conferences. Existing pricing policies have either been criticised as an obviously sub-optimal departure from competitive conditions or defended as an acceptable institutional device for achieving maximum efficiency under severe constraints. Both arguments tend to rely upon conjecture regarding the cost effects of changes in the frequency of service or density of traffic. That some shippers pay less than what could reasonably be considered a long-run marginal cost, while other shippers pay substantially more is generally agreed. The central point is whether the industry as a whole would be better off without such rate disparities.

While the likely effects of different pricing policies cannot be established through a careful analysis of existing practices, the hedonic method nevertheless gives a clearer indication of the extent to which the existing practices create distortions. This study indicates that, with an assumed classification of available hedonic variables, a large part of the Australia-to-Europe voyage revenue can be attributed to cost influences, and that cost-subsidy effects may be considered to be not "excessive". To the extent that the results run counter to previously held beliefs, it raises the question as to why conferences do not exploit more fully the differing elasticities of demand. It is generally recognised that they have the ability to "charge what the market will bear", so if they choose not to do so, they are apparently not operating in a rational fashion. The answer may lie partly in the fact that shippers generally have access to information about the scheduled rates associated with the various tariff classes, so that machinery exporters from Australia to Europe, for example, may know that their particular rate per tonne is normally about 13 times greater than that charged for grain. While the different characteristics of the two products could be offered as an explanation for the disparity, the elusive nature of the characteristics and their effect on costs create pressures to restrict the rate structure to more obviously justifiable limits.

Therefore, while conferences are frequently treated as monopolists, there is reason to believe that pressure from shippers, shipper's organisations and governments may have substantially altered their ability to operate fully in that manner.

J. A. ZERBY, AND R. M. CONLON,
Department of Econometrics
The University of New South Wales,
P.O. Box 1,
Kensington,
New South Wales, Australia 2033

ACCEPTED MAY 1982

REFERENCES

[1] AUSTRALIAN DEPARTMENT OF TRANSPORT, "Report on a Review of Overseas Cargo Shipping Legislation", October 1977 (Grigor Report).

[2] BRYAN, I. A., "Regression Analysis of Ocean Liner Rates on Some Canadian Export Routes", *Journal of Transport Economics and Policy*, 10, (May 1974) pp. 161–73.

[3] BRYAN, I. A., "The Effect of Ocean Transport Costs of the Demand for Some Canadian Exports", *Weltwirtschaftiches Archiv*, 110, (1974) pp. 642–62.

[4] DEAKIN, B. M., *Shipping Conferences: A Study of Their Origins, Development and Economic Practices* (Cambridge: Cambridge University Press, 1973).

[5] EVANS, J. J., "Liner Freight Rates, Discrimination and Cross-Subsidisation", *Maritime Policy and Management*, 4 (April 1977) pp. 227–33.

[6] FERGUSON, D. C., "Joint Products and Road Transport Rates in Transport Models", *Journal of Transport Economics and Policy*, 8 (January 1974) pp. 69–76.

[7] FRIEDLAENDER, A. F., FERGUSON, W. L. and SLOSS, J., "The Rate Structure of Unit Coal Trains in the 1970s", *Journal of Industrial Economics*, 28, (March 1980) pp. 269–86.

[8] GRILICHES, Z., ed., *Price Indexes and Quality Change*, (Harvard University Press, 1971), Chapter 1.

[9] HEAVER, T. D., "Trans-Pacific Trade, Liner Shipping and Conference Rates", *Transportation and Logistics Review*, 8, No. 2, (1972) pp. 3–28.

[10] HEAVER, T. D., "A Theory of Shipping Pricing Policies", *Maritime Studies and Management*, 1, (July 1973) pp. 17–33.

[11] HEAVER, T. D., "The Structure of Liner Conference Rates", *Journal of Industrial Economics*, 20, (July 1973) pp. 257–64.

[12] JANSSON, J. O., "Intra-Tariff Cross-Subsidisation in Liner Shipping", *Journal of Transport Economics and Policy*, 10 (September 1974) pp. 294–311.

[13] JANSSON, J. O. and D. SHNEERSON, "The Effective Protection Implicit in Liner Shipping Freight Rates", *Review of Economics and Statistics*, 60, (November 1978) pp. 569–73.

[14] KOLSEN, H. M., *The Economics and Control of Road-Rail Competition* (Sydney: Sydney University Press, 1968).

[15] LAING, E. T., "Containers and Their Competitors: The Economics of Deep Sea General Cargo Shipping in the 1970s", (Martime Transport Centre, University of Liverpool, January 1975).

[16] LAING, E. T., "The Rationality of Conference Pricing and Output Policies", *Maritime Studies and Management*, 2, (October 1975) pp. 103–11 (Part 1) and 3, (January 1976) pp. 141–51 (Part 2).

[17] LIPSEY, R. E. and M. Y. WEISS, "The Structure of Ocean Transport Charges", *Occasional Papers*, National Bureau of Economic Research, Summer 1974, pp. 162–93.

[18] PIGOU, A. C., "Railway Rates and Joint Costs", with "Rejoinder" by F. W. Taussig, *Quarterly Journal of Economics*, 27, (May 1913) pp. 536–38.

[19] ROSEN, S., "Hedonic Prices and Implicit Market: Product Differentiation in Pure Competition", *Journal of Political Economy*, 82 (January–February 1974) pp. 34–55.

[20] SHNEERSON, D., "The Rationality of Conference Pricing and Output Policies", *Maritime Studies and Management*, 3 (April 1976) pp. 245–48.

[21] SPADY, R. H. and FRIEDLAENDER, A. F., "Hedonic Cost Functions for the Regulated Trucking Industry", *Bell Journal of Economics*, 9, (April 1978) pp. 159–79.

[22] STURMEY, S. G., *British Shipping and World Competition* (London: Athlone Press, 1962).

[23] TAUSSIG, F. W., "Railway Rates and Joint Cost Once More", *Quarterly Journal of Economics*, 27, (February 1913) pp. 378–84.

[24] UNITED STATES DEPARTMENT OF JUSTICE, Antitrust Division, "The Regulated Ocean Shipping Industry", January 1977.

[25] UNIVERSITY OF WALES INSTITUTE OF SCIENCE AND TECHNOLOGY, Department of Maritime Studies, "Liner Shipping in the U.S. Trades", A UWIST Study for CENSA, April 1978.

[26] WALTERS, A. A., "The Allocation of Joint Costs", *American Economic Review*, 50, (June 1960) pp. 419–32.

[27] ZERBY, J. A., "Impact of New Maritime Legislative Proposals: Potential Change in the Structure of the Shipping Industry", Report to the Federal Maritime Commission, Bureau of Industry Economics, 1980.

[28] ZERBY, J. A. and CONLON, R. M., "Capacity Utilisation in Liner Shipping", *Journal of Transport Economics and Policy*, 12, (January 1978) pp. 27–46.

[29] ZERBY, J. A., CONLON, R. M. and KAYE-KUCHARZEWSKI, S. L., "Major Determinants of Ocean Freight Rates for Australia's Exports to Selected Areas", Report to the Bureau of Transport Economics, School of Economics, University of New South Wales, 1981.

THE JOURNAL OF INDUSTRIAL ECONOMICS
Volume XXXI June 1983 No. 4

AN INTERNATIONAL COMPARISON OF THE FISCAL TREATMENT OF SHIPPING*

BERNARD GARDNER AND PETER MARLOW

I. INTRODUCTION

ALMOST without exception the governments of nations possessing merchant fleets, whether state-owned or privately owned, offer some form of special assistance to their industries. In this paper we attempt to compare the subsidies and aids that are offered by different countries and which influence the incentive to invest in shipping within those countries. We are particularly concerned with the treatment of shipping industries in Belgium, Denmark, France, the Federal Republic of Germany, Greece, Ireland, Italy, Japan, Liberia, the Netherlands, Spain, the United Kingdom and the United States of America. To this end we have developed a general computer programme capable of examining the fiscal regimes in the various countries. The purpose of the programme is to provide a means by which the incentive to invest in shipping on the part of such nations may be compared objectively, as well as to measure the effect of changes in the fiscal regime on the incentive to invest in shipping within those countries.

II. THE MODEL

The development of the computer model stems from some earlier work in this field, by UK Government economists at the Department of Trade and Industry, which was reported by Gardner and Richardson in the Journal of Industrial Economics [1]. The origins of the work, however, are to be found in an article by Goss published in 1967 [2]. The methodology and terminology used is consistent with that of these earlier papers. The method is based on the present value criterion and in its more sophisticated form this criterion is capable of incorporating rates of inflation and shipbuilding loans. The basic form is

$$\text{NPV} = E\sum_{i=1}^{n} A_i(1+r)^{-i} + (1-E)$$

$$\times\left[\sum_{i=0}^{k}(A_i+P_i)(1+r)^{-i} + R(1+r)^{-k-1}\right] + G_n C_o(1+r)^{-L} - C_o$$

* We are grateful to the Commission of the European Communities for providing the funding for the research described in this paper and also for permission to publish the paper. We also wish to thank the referee of this paper for his helpful comments and advice. The views expressed and the conclusions drawn, however, are entirely our own, as is the responsibility for any errors or omissions.

where $R = (\beta + \gamma) - \sum_{i=0}^{k} (A_i + P_i)$,

β is the value of the tax allowance on the capital cost involved in the investment proposal,

γ is the value of accumulated tax allowances from other sources which can be set against the profits from the investment proposal,

P_i is gross profits from other sources,

G_n is the nominal rate of investment grant (if any),[1]

C_o is the initial (capital) cost of the investment proposal,

i is a year in the life of the investment proposal,

n is the economic life of the proposal,

k is the period before tax allowances are finally exhausted if $R \neq 0$ and the period in which tax allowances are exhausted if $R = 0$, $E = 1 - t(1 + r)^{-L}$,

t is the nominal rate of corporation tax,

L is the lag in the receipt of investment grant or payment of corporation tax,[2]

r is the rate of discount per year, and

A_i is the annual real net cash flow before payment of tax and excluding any investment grant received.

Where A_i and P_i are constant streams the formula can be written as:

$$\begin{aligned} \text{NPV} = {} & EA\left[\frac{1-(1+r)^{-n}}{r}\right] + (1-E) \\ & \times \left\{(A+P)\left[\frac{1-(1+r)^{-k}}{r}\right] + P + R(1+r)^{-k-1}\right\} \\ & + G_n C_o (1+r)^{-L} - C_o \end{aligned}$$

In plain language all this simply means is that the net present value of an investment is equal to the present value of the annual cash flows accruing to it (net of tax), plus the present value of any tax allowances used, plus the present value of any grant that may be received, minus its initial capital cost.

This formula explicitly defines the net present value of any investment proposal financed by retained earnings. Thus it defines the NPV of an investment proposal so financed to the shipping company in the general tax position; a shipping company's specific tax position being defined in terms of the number of years which it will take to write off its tax allowances. Three specific tax positions are worth considering, since together they encompass the full range of possibilities. These tax positions are:

[1, 2] In the more general version of the formula, G_n is redefined as the unlagged present value of any investment grant or net tax credit and L as the lag in receipt of such investment grant or tax credit or in payment of corporation tax.

1. *The Full Tax Position.* A company is in this tax position if it is earning sufficient profits from other sources to take full and immediate advantage of any tax allowances which may be available on the capital cost involved in the investment proposal.
2. *The No Tax Position.* A company will be in this position if it has accumulated tax allowances from earlier years to the extent that it is now in a position where it is unlikely to have any tax liability for the indefinite future.
3. *The New Entry Position.* A company is in this tax position if, given the tax allowances available on the capital cost involved in an investment proposal and the level of profit expected to be earned on it, it is neither earning sufficient profits from other sources nor has it accumulated tax allowances from earlier years for either of these factors to have any influence at all on the net present value of the investment proposal.

The importance of specifying different tax positions stems from the fact that although the nominal value of the allowances which are available will be the same for each company, the ability of the company to make use of those allowances, and hence the real value of those allowances to the company, will be different depending on which tax position the company is in.

Inflation can be taken into account by discounting all relevant monetary values by an appropriate factor. The formula then becomes

$$\mathrm{NPV} = E\sum_{i=1}^{n} A_i(1+r_r)^{-i} + (1-E)$$

$$\times \left\{ \sum_{i=0}^{k} (A_i + P_i)(1+r_r)^{-i} + R[(1+r_p)(1+r_r)]^{-k-1} \right\}$$

$$+ G_n C_o[(1+r_r)(1+r_p)]^{-L} - C_o$$

where r_p = rate of inflation,

r_r = real rate of discount,

$E = 1 - t[(1+r_r)(1+r_p)]^{-L}$, and

$R = (\beta + \gamma) - \sum_{i=0}^{k} (A_i + P_i)(1+r_p)^i$

The final step is to modify this equation to take account of financing by shipbuilding loan. Interest payments and any other costs associated with a loan reduce the amount of corporation tax which a company would otherwise have to pay in a given year.

Thus, letting T_i equal the present value of this reduction in corporation tax in year i, we may say that S, the present value of the sum of such reductions in corporation tax over a period of m years, equals $\sum_{i=1}^{m} T_i$ $(1 < m < \Upsilon)$. If we now define Y as the life of the loan, V as the present value of the loan if no corporation tax is payable during the term of the loan, $(W + S)$ as the present value of the loan if corporation tax is payable during part of the term of the loan, Z as the proportion of the loan sum paid in initial legal costs, j as the six-monthly rate of interest on the loan inclusive of management rate, b_i as the sum on which interest is payable in year i, F as the proportion of the capital cost (C_o) which is financed by equity issue or retained profits and the other terms, except R, in the same manner as before then, when an investment is to be financed wholly or partly by shipbuilding loan, the equation becomes

$$\begin{aligned}\text{NPV} = {} & E\sum_{i=1}^{n} A_i(1+r_r)^{-i} + (1-E) \\ & \times \left\{\sum_{i=0}^{k}(A_i+P_i)(1+r_r)^{-i} + R[(1+r_r)(1+r_p)]^{-k-1}\right\} \\ & + G_n C_o[(1+r_r)(1+r_p)]^{-L} \\ & - [FC_o + (1-F)(W+S)]\end{aligned}$$

$$\begin{aligned}\text{where } R = {} & (\beta+\gamma) + (1-F)C_o Z + j\sum_{i=1}^{k} b_i \\ & - \sum_{i=0}^{k}(A_i+P_i)(1+r_p)^i \text{ if } Y \geq k \quad \text{or} \\ & (\beta+\gamma) + (1-F)C_o Z + j\sum_{i=1}^{Y} b_i \\ & - \sum_{i=0}^{k}(A_i+P_i)(1+r_p)^i \text{ if } Y < k \quad \text{and}\end{aligned}$$

$(W + S)$ is defined so as to take account of inflation.

If A_i and P_i are constant streams this formula may be written as

$$\begin{aligned}\text{NPV} = {} & EA\left[\frac{1-(1+r_r)^{-n}}{r_r}\right] + (1-E) \\ & \times \left\{(A+P)\left[\frac{1-(1+r_r)^{-k}}{r_r}\right] + P + R[(1+r_r)(1+r_p)]^{-k-1}\right\} \\ & + G_n C_o[(1+r_r)(1+r_p)]^{-L} - [FC_o + (1-F)(W+S)]\end{aligned}$$

In order to take account of the scrap value of an investment proposal in the calculations the following formula was added:

$$\text{PV(scrap)} = \alpha C_o E(1+r_r)^{-n}$$

where $E = 1 - t_n[(1+r_r)(1+r_p)]^{-L}$,

α is the real scrap value as a percentage of capital cost (C_o), and
t_n is the expected tax rate in year n (defined so that where the company expects to be in the No Tax position $t_n = 0$).[3]

Several important assumptions have been made in constructing the present model which perhaps ought to be made explicit. These are:

1. It is assumed that the incidence of taxation on distributed profits falls solely on the shareholders.
2. It is assumed that capital payments to shipbuilders are not made in instalments during the construction period of a vessel as is normal practice but as a lump sum on delivery.
3. It is assumed that loans are repaid in equal six-monthly instalments and that tax liabilities may be offset against any interest on the outstanding balance provided all the allowances carried forward have been used up.
4. In cases where the rate of return on the investment exceeds the permitted depreciation allowances in a given year it is assumed that the order for using additional allowances is as follows:
   (a) unused allowances carried forward from the current investment are used first; then
   (b) accumulated tax allowances from past investments; and finally
   (c) any interest charges on loan repayments made in that year.

III. THE DATA

In order to compute the net present values on which the subsequent analysis is based, it has been necessary to assume that shipping companies are solely concerned with the profitability aspect of an investment and that their objective is to maximise their return. Consequently, their financing mix and their choice of depreciation method, where they have the latter choice, will reflect this objective. Moreover, certain assumptions concerning data values have also been made. The assumed values are clearly marked as such in Tables II and III.[4]

It is also worth mentioning that only companies in the "full tax" position are in a position to accumulate tax free reserves where the fiscal regime permits this. Moreover, any tax free reserves which are used in purchasing a vessel reduce its depreciable base and therefore are analytically equivalent to a first year allowance.

Table I contains a rough outline of the systems operating in each country and their application to the shipping industry.

[3] These formulas are the basis of the original computer programme as presented in [1]. In order to take account of the special features of the different regimes under consideration, modifications had to be made to this programme. For details contact the authors.

[4] Furthermore, since meaningful comparisons may only be made in one currency, it is an implicit assumption of this study that if the countries under consideration are expected to experience differential rates of inflation in the future, then the effects of this on the purchasing power of their currencies will be reflected in the exchange rates.

TABLE 1
AN OUTLINE OF THE FISCAL SYSTEMS

Country	*Type of Tax System*	*Corporation Tax Rates*	*Method of Depreciation*	*Rate of Depreciation*	*Other*	*Comments*
Belgium	Imputed	48%	Straight-line Declining balance	8 years*		* 20% in year 1 15% in years 2 & 3 10% in years 4, 5, 6, 7 & 8
Denmark	Imputed	40%	Pooled declining balance	Maximum of 30% in any year	Advance* depreciation, Investment Reserves	* No more than 15% of acquisition cost may be depreciated in any one year
France	Imputed	50%	Straight-line Declining balance	8 years min. 31.25%	Investment Grant*	* Size of grant depends on ship type
Germany	Imputed	56%	Straight-line Declining balance	12 years min. 20.833%	Special depreciation allowance of up to 40%* Investment grant Tax free reserves	* To be used only with straight-line depreciation
Greece	Shipping is subject to a special tax in lieu of corporate taxation (see comments)					For tax purposes ships under the Greek flag are classified into two groups. Tax on Group I is computed on the basis of grt and age of vessels
Ireland	Imputed	45%	Free	Shipowner free to choose		

Italy	Imputed	36.25%	Straight-line	10%	Accelerated* depreciation Tax free reserves	* Also possible to claim accelerated depreciation of up to 40% of the original cost spread over the 1st 3 years of the asset's life subject to a max. of 15% in any one year
Japan	Split rate	30% on distributed income, 40% on retained income	Straight-line Reducing balance*	15 years, 13 years 14.2% 16.2%	Special depreciation allowance of 20% Tax free reserves	* Most commonly used by shipping companies
Liberia	Shipping is subject to a special tax in lieu of corporate taxation (see comments)					Tax is computed on the basis of nrt of vessels
Netherlands	Classical	48%	Straight-line Reducing balance	15 years 15%	WIR premium of 15% (±7.5%) Tax free reserves	Also a special 5.5% premium in five equal annual instalments
Spain	Classical	33%	Straight-line Reducing balance	4% 8%	Tax credit Tax free reserves	
U.K.	Imputed	52%	Free	Shipowner free to choose		
U.S.A.	Classical	46%	Straight-line Reducing balance	14.5 years 13.79%	Tax free reserves (Capital Construction Funds) Investment credit	

TABLE II
DATA USED IN THE PROGRAMME

Data	*Belgium*	*Denmark*	*France*	*Germany*	*Ireland*	*Italy*	*Japan*	*Netherlands*	*Spain*	*U.K.*	*U.S.A.*
Rate of with-holding tax	0.20	0.30	0.50	0.25	0.00	0.10	0.30	n/a	n/a	0.30	n/a
Distribution level	0.20+	0.20+	0.20+	0.20+	0.20+	0.20+	0.20+	0.20+	0.20+	0.20	0.20+
Tax rate	0.48	0.40	0.50	0.56+	0.45	0.3625	0.40	0.48	0.33	0.52	0.46
Tax lag	0.00	0.00	0.25	0.00	1.00	0.50	0.1666	0.0833	0.50	1.75	0.00
Grant/Tax credit	0.00	0.00	0.05	0.125	0.00	0.00	0.00	0.011(× 5) 0.150	0.15	0.00	0.10
Grant lag	0.00	0.00	1.00+	1.00+	0.00	0.00	0.00	0.667*	1.50	0.00	0.00
Straight line rate	n/a	n/a	0.1250	0.0833	n/a	0.1000	0.0769	0.0667	0.0400	n/a	0.0689
Declining balance rate	n/a	0.3000	0.3125	0.2083	Free	n/a	0.1420 (0.1620)	0.1500	0.0800	Free	0.1379

Notes: (1) The values marked + have been assumed; (2) The value marked * for the Netherlands applies only to the lag in payment of the WIR premium; (3) No values have been included for Greece or Liberia since they may be treated as special cases of any regime without investment grants or tax credits such as Belgium.

Table II contains the values fed into the programme as data for each country. Those values which have been assumed are marked with the symbol +. While we have striven to be accurate with the information contained in these tables, we would stress that the absolute values of the variables are really of little consequence in formulating the general model. We have presented the most recent data we can find and even if these values are no longer operative it is unlikely that the fiscal regime will have altered.

Table III provides details of the loan arrangements which are available in each of the countries.

TABLE III
DOMESTIC CREDIT ARRANGEMENTS

Country	*Amount of Loan*	*Life of Loan*	*Rate of Interest*	*Length of Moratorium*
Belgium	80%	15 yrs	1%	
plus	10%	15 yrs	5%	
Denmark	80%	14 yrs	8%	4 yrs
France	80%	8.5 yrs	7.5%	
Germany	80%	8.5 yrs	7.5%	
Greece	80%	10 yrs	16.0%	1 yr
Ireland	80%	8.5 yrs	7.5%	
Italy	70%	15 yrs	7%	
Japan (a)	65%	11 yrs	3.65%	1 yr*
plus	20%	8 yrs	4.70%	
Japan (b)	65%	11 yrs	4.65%	1 yr*
plus	20%	8 yrs	5.70%	
Japan (c)	75%	11 yrs	3.65%	1 yr*
plus	25%	8 yrs	4.70%	
Japan (d)	75%	11 yrs	4·65%	1 yr*
plus	25%	8 yrs	5.70%	
Netherlands	80%	8.5 yrs	8%	
Spain	80%	12 yrs	8%	2 yrs
U.K.	80%	8.5 yrs	7.5%	
U.S.A.	75%	20 yrs	12.5%	

* An estimate, since the the 3 year moratorium includes the construction period.

IV. ANALYSIS OF RESULTS

Tax profiles for each country, with the exception of Greece and Liberia where tax positions do not apply, are shown in Figure 1. The profiles are drawn for rates of return,[5] inflation and discount of 10% respectively. The lowest point

[5] Assuming a constant stream of returns, it is possible to generate the annual cash flow equivalent to any given real pre-tax discounted cash flow (DCF) rate of return over a project's life using the formula

$$A = \frac{r_d}{1 - (1 + r_d)^{-n}};$$

where r_d = the DCF rate of return per unit of capital cost. For the analysis in this section such streams were generated assuming an economic life for a ship of 20 years and a capital cost of £10 million.

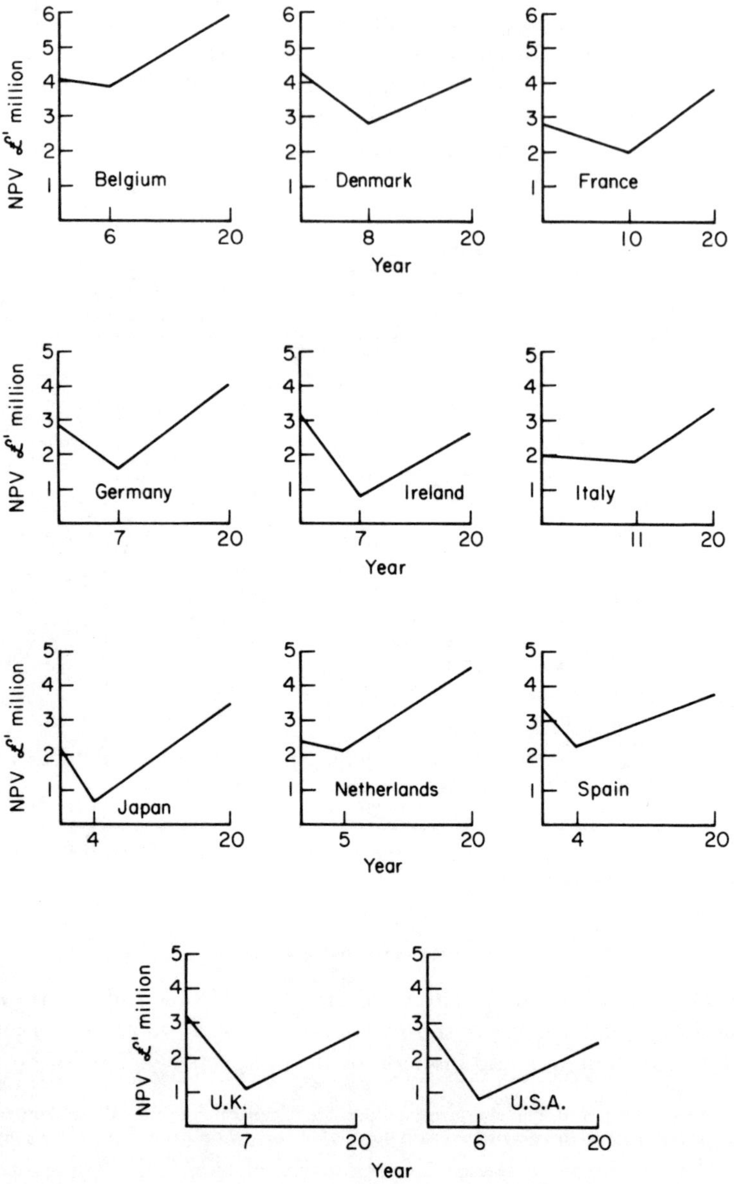

FIGURE 1
Investment £10 million: NPVs of various tax positions with loan

on each graph indicates the NPV of an investment of £10 million to a company in the "new entry" position, the point on the extreme left of each graph the NPV to a company in the "full tax" position, and the point on the extreme right of each graph the NPV to a company in the "no tax" position. The NPVs of such an investment to companies in the tax positions other than the key tax positions are assumed to lie on the lines joining the "new entry" positions to the other two key tax positions. Whilst this is not strictly true, it is approximately correct.

The purpose of drawing these tax profiles is to illustrate the discriminating nature of the respective regimes. All the regimes are discriminatory in the sense that they create barriers to entry for new firms. In general, the extent of these barriers is indicated by the difference between the NPV for a company in the "full tax" position and the NPV for one in the "new entry" position. This is because whilst it is theoretically possible for companies to be in the "no tax" position under any of the regimes, it is unlikely that any established company will consider itself to be in this tax position nowadays, with present rates of inflation and limits on the carry forward of trading losses (after depreciation) in most of the countries making it difficult to accumulate tax allowances. A higher NPV for a given rate of return (pre-tax) indicates that a lower rate of return will be required on marginal investments, that is, those on which the NPV is zero. Consequently, where there is price competition, new firms will require to earn higher rates of return pre-tax in order to earn the same post-tax of return as established companies on marginal investments.

The tax profiles show that the British, Irish and American regimes are the most discriminatory, whereas the Dutch, Italian and Belgian are the least discriminatory. This is hardly surprising, since in the UK and Ireland there is free depreciation and in the USA substantial tax credits are available which benefit companies in the "full tax" position the most. In the Netherlands the WIR premium is equally as beneficial to new companies as it is to established ones, and the degree of accelerated depreciation available there is limited, as it is in Italy and Belgium.

One of the objectives of this study was to enable a meaningful comparison to be made of the incentive to invest in shipping in the thirteen countries selected for investigation. In making such comparisons, we would argue, in general, that they should be made for the "full tax" position where the fiscal regimes in the countries under consideration create the possibility of different tax positions for companies. This is because fiscal incentives, such as accelerated depreciation allowances and tax credits, which are the principal cause of companies having different tax positions are designed to help companies in this tax position the most. Hence, assuming that incentive schemes are working correctly, then the "full tax" position is arguably the proper basis for international comparisons.

Figure 2 compares the incentive to invest in the different countries assuming rates of return, inflation and discount of 10% respectively. The comparison

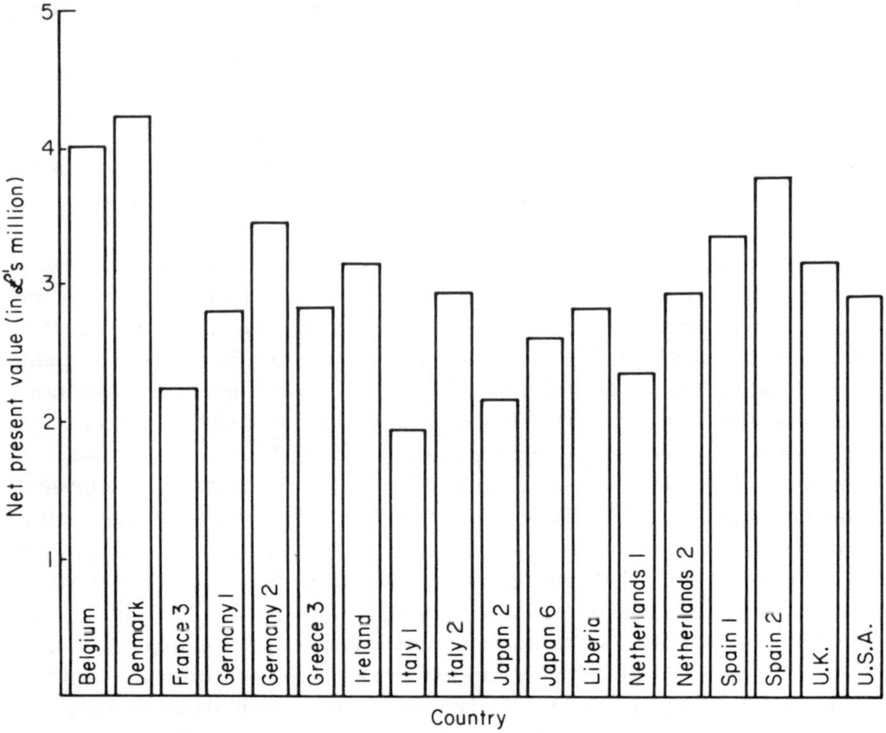

FIGURE 2
A comparison of the incentive to invest in an oil tanker of £10 million, based on 10% rates of discount, inflation and return

relates to an investment of £10 million in an oil tanker. If France, Japan, Greece and Liberia are excluded then the comparison relates to any type of vessel. The comparison is made for companies in the "full tax" position apart from Greece and Liberia where tax positions do not apply. As the German, Italian, Japanese, Dutch and Spanish regimes are more generous with respect to replacement investment than new investment, at least as far as companies in the "full tax" position are concerned, the results are presented for both types of investment. Given the assumed rates of return, inflation and discount it is clear that the incentive to invest is greatest under the Danish, Belgian and Spanish regimes and least under the French, Japanese and Italian regimes. The latter two cases being where new investment is involved.

Table IV takes the analysis a stage further by comparing the incentive to invest assuming the same rate of discount, namely 10%, but making comparisons on the basis of 5% and 15% rates of inflation for all three rates of return considered, namely 5%, 10% and 15%. The rankings of the regimes are not consistent across the six possibilities but we note that, in general, the fiscal

TABLE IV
A COMPARISON OF NET PRESENT VALUES:
CAPITAL COST OF VESSEL £10 MILLION, DISCOUNT RATE 10%

	Rate of Inflation 5%			*Rate of Inflation 15%*		
	Rate of Return			*Rate of Return*		
	5%	*10%*	*15%*	*5%*	*10%*	*15%*
Belgium	1.822(1)	3.596(1)	5.613(2)	2.500(2)	4.275(3)	6.292(6)
Denmark	1.248(3)	3.340(2)	5.716(1)	2.752(1)	4.843(1)	7.220(1)
France 3	−0.150(15)	1.760(16)	3.930(14)	0.770(15)	2.685(16)	4.862(14)
Germany 1	0.773(6)	2.325(10)	4.090(13)	1.632(9)	3.185(13)	4.950(13)
Germany 2	1.342(2)	2.894(4)	4.659(9)	2.351(3)	3.903(5)	5.668(10)
Greece 3	−1.276(18)	1.893(15)	5.494(4)	0.374(17)	3.543(9)	7.144(3)
Ireland	0.474(8)	2.408(9)	4.607(10)	1.733(5)	3.774(6)	6.095(8)
Italy 1	−0.694(16)	1.408(18)	3.797(17)	0.206(18)	2.319(18)	4.722(16)
Italy 2	0.315(13)	2.418(8)	4.807(7)	1.205(12)	3.318(11)	5.721(9)
Japan 2	0.088(14)	1.653(17)	3.431(18)	0.991(14)	2.568(17)	4.360(18)
Japan 6	0.460(9)	2.025(12)	3.803(16)	1.459(11)	3.036(14)	4.828(15)
Liberia	−1.239(17)	1.930(14)	5.431(5)	0.390(16)	3.559(8)	7.159(2)
Netherlands 1	0.358(12)	2.010(13)	3.888(15)	1.033(13)	2.688(15)	4.570(17)
Netherlands 2	0.843(4)	2.495(6)	4.373(11)	1.643(8)	3.298(12)	5.179(12)
Spain 1	0.408(10)	2.603(5)	5.099(6)	1.684(6)	3.923(4)	6.468(5)
Spain 2	0.815(5)	3.011(3)	5.506(3)	2.135(4)	4.374(2)	6.919(4)
U.K.	0.394(11)	2.430(7)	4.744(8)	1.571(10)	3.773(7)	6.277(7)
U.S.A.	0.529(7)	2.240(11)	4.185(12)	1.664(7)	3.375(10)	5.320(11)

Notes: (1) Companies in "full tax" position with the exception of those registering in Greece and Liberia where tax positions do not apply; (2) Figures in brackets denote ranking of regimes e.g. (1) indicates the regime which yields the highest NPV and hence the highest post-tax return; (3) The Greek, Liberian, French and Japanese regimes relate only to investment in tankers; (4) Germany 1, Italy 1, Japan 2, Netherlands 1, and Spain 1 relate to new investment. With the exception of Spain these regimes are usually low in the rankings which means that they do not compare favourably with the other regimes; (5) Germany 2, Italy 2, Japan 6, Netherlands 2, and Spain 2 relate to replacement investment which receives more favourable treatment than does new investment under the same regimes.

regimes of Denmark, Belgium and Span 2 offer the greatest incentive to invest in shipping while, in general, the fiscal regimes of France 3, Italy 1, Japan 2, and the Netherlands 1 offer the least incentive to invest in shipping.

Note that the rankings of both Greece and Liberia improve markedly as the rate of return increases from 5% to 15% for both rates of inflation. The rankings of Germany 2 and Netherlands 2 decrease as the rate of return increases. However, apart from these four exceptions, the other changes in ranking are not dramatic. This is not surprising since the incentive to invest in all countries, apart from Greece and Liberia, does not only depend on the return generated by the investment itself and on the loan arrangements pertaining to that investment, but also on the results of past investment decisions. Hence it is to be expected that the order of ranking for these regimes will not change markedly with changes in the values of the variables.

Although all the comparisons we have made so far have assumed the rates of return, inflation and discount to be similar in all countries, this assumption is somewhat heroic. Ideally comparisons should be made on the basis of what shipping companies in the respective countries consider acceptable in terms of their required post-tax rate of return (reflected by the chosen discount rate). They should also be based on their expectations about future rates of inflation and the likely magnitude of their future pre-tax returns. In this respect the immediate past might be considered, in the absence of further information, to be the best guide to the future. Moreover, in an international industry such as shipping, expectations about the future pre-tax rates of return are likely to be similar provided that companies, regardless of flag, are equally efficient and that country of registry affords no operating cost advantage or disadvantage.

TABLE V
ANTICIPATED ANNUAL RATES OF INFLATION

Country	*% Rate of Inflation*
Belgium	6
Denmark	10
France	10
Germany	4
Greece	15
Ireland	14
Italy	15
Japan	7
Netherlands	6
Spain	16
U.K.	14
U.S.A.	9

Note: These estimates of future inflation rates in the respective countries are based on evidence of past trends. Average rates of inflation for both five and ten year periods were derived from retail and wholesale price indices and these were compared with annual rates over the past four years and quarterly rates since mid-1979 in order to arrive at a judgement about future trends.

Source: OECD Main Economic Indicators and International Financial Statistics.

In our judgement it would be appropriate, when comparing the incentive to invest in shipping in the respective countries, to base the comparison on a rate of return of 5%, on a discount rate of 10% and on the rates of inflation shown in Table V. The outcome of this comparison is shown in Table VI and in Figure 3.

It will be noted that Table VI and Figure 3 enable a comparison to be made, if Greece and Liberia are excluded, for any type of vessel and for both new and replacement investment, since the various cases for France, Germany, Italy, Japan, Netherlands and Spain (see notes for Table VI) are all included.

TABLE VI

REPRESENTATIVE RESULTS FOR THE FULL TAX POSITION

Country	Rate of Discount	Rate of Return	Rate of Inflation	Net Present Value	Rank
Belgium	10%	5%	6%	1.926	3
Denmark	10%	5%	10%	2.159	2
France 1	10%	5%	10%	0.214	24
France 2	10%	5%	10%	0.297	23
France 3	10%	5%	10%	0.379	21
France 4	10%	5%	10%	0.710	17
France 5	10%	5%	10%	0.875	14
France 6	10%	5%	10%	1.289	7
Germany 1	10%	5%	4%	0.660	18
Germany 2	10%	5%	4%	1.207	8
Greece 1a	10%	5%	15%	−0.767	28
Greece 1b	10%	5%	15%	−0.768	29
Greece 2a	10%	5%	10%	−0.003	26
Greece 2b	10%	5%	10%	0.001	27
Greece 3a	10%	5%	7%	−0.865	32
Greece 3b	10%	5%	7%	−0.870	33
Ireland	10%	5%	14%	1.635	5
Italy 1	10%	5%	15%	0.206	25
Italy 2	10%	5%	15%	1.205	9
Japan 1	10%	5%	7%	0.405	20
Japan 2	10%	5%	7%	0.322	22
Japan 3	10%	5%	7%	1.124	10
Japan 4	10%	5%	7%	1.005	12
Japan 5	10%	5%	7%	0.826	15
Japan 6	10%	5%	7%	0.718	16
Liberia (a)	10%	5%	7%	−0.830	30
Liberia (b)	10%	5%	7%	−0.839	31
Netherlands 1	10%	5%	6%	0.442	19
Netherlands 2	10%	5%	6%	0.944	13
Spain 1	10%	5%	16%	1.771	4
Spain 2	10%	5%	16%	2.224	1
United Kingdom	10%	5%	14%	1.479	6
United States of America	10%	5%	9%	1.105	11

France 1 is a bulk carrier with a 2% investment grant; France 2 is a product carrier with a 3% investment grant; France 3 is a bulk carrier with a 4% investment grant; France 4 is a small bulk carrier with a 8% investment grant; France 5 is a conventional vessel with a 10% investment grant; France 6 is a container or ro-ro vessel with a 15% investment grant.

Germany 1 refers to new investment; Germany 2 refers to replacement investment.

Greece 1a is a bulk carrier built domestically, financed by drachma; Greece 1b is a tanker built domestically, financed by drachma; Greece 2a is a bulk carrier built domestically, financed by foreign currency; Greece 2b is a tanker built domestically, financed by foreign currency; Greece 3a is a bulk carrier built abroad, financed by foreign currency; Greece 3b is a tanker built abroad, financed by foreign currency.

Italy 1 refers to new investment; Italy 2 refers to replacement investment.

Japan 1, 2, 3, and 4 refer to new investment in a general carrier, a tanker, a container ship and LNG carrier; Japan 5 and 6 to replacement investment in the first two categories of ship.

Liberia (a) is a bulk carrier built abroad, financed by foreign currency; Liberia (b) is a tanker abroad, financed by foreign currency.

Netherlands 1 refers to new investment; Netherlands 2 refers to replacement investment.

Spain 1 refers to new investment; Spain 2 refers to replacement investment.

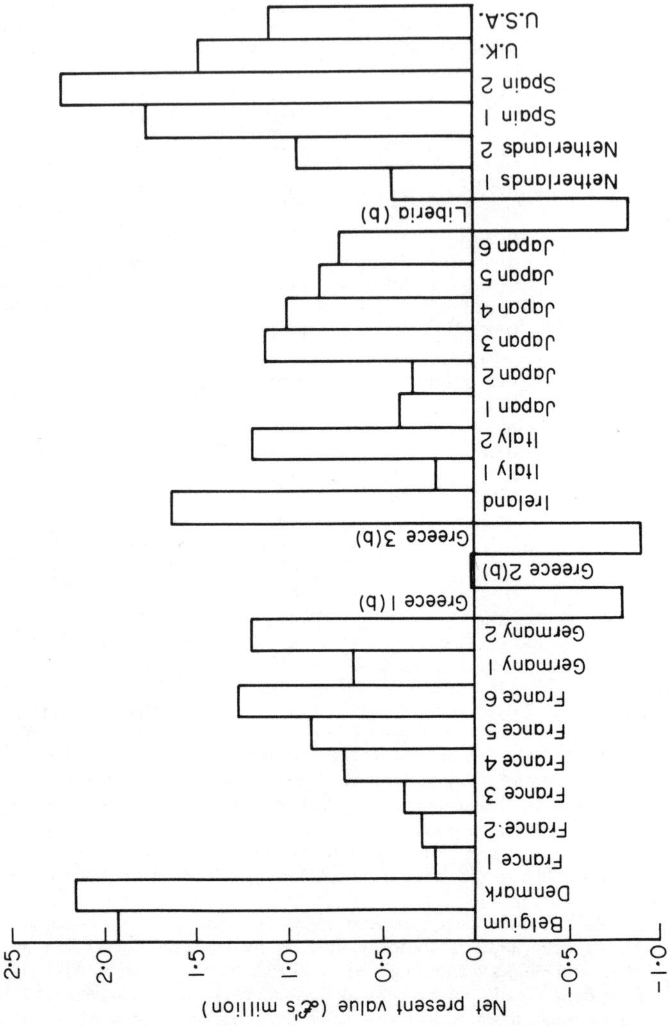

FIGURE 3
Representative results for the full tax position, based on an investment of £10 million.

A comparison which includes Greece or Liberia should only be made, strictly speaking, for tankers or bulk carriers. However as choice of ship type only marginally alters the results for Greece or Liberia, a comparison for any other vessel type may be made using either the Greek or Liberian NPV figure for an investment in a tanker, or the corresponding figure for an investment in a bulk carrier without fear of any significant error in the rankings.

It can be seen from these results that, within the EEC member states, Denmark (generous loan arrangements, favourable depreciation arrangements and investment reserves), Belgium (very generous loan arrangements), and Spain (tax credit, and generous loan arrangements) provide the most favourable treatment to their shipowners. These are followed by Ireland and the United Kingdom both of which offer free depreciation (not unique to shipping in these countries) as the major incentive. Next come Germany, the Netherlands, France and Italy to be followed, finally, by Greece (note that the position of Greece will improve as the rate of return in shipping increases).

Comparing the EEC countries as an entity with competition from Japan and the United States of America we can see, from Table VI, that shipping companies in most of the EEC countries (with the exception of Italy and Greece) receive more favourable treatment than their Japanese counterparts. The comparison for the USA is not quite so straightforward but, in general, shipping companies in Denmark, Belgium, Spain, Ireland and the United Kingdom receive more favourable treatment than their American counterparts. Shipping companies in Germany, the Netherlands, France, Italy and Greece may receive less favourable assistance than those in America.

V. GENERAL CONCLUSION

With the exception of Greece and Liberia, all the fiscal regimes we have considered are to some extent discriminatory. Under such regimes, the incentive to invest depends at least partially on the outcome of past investment decisions. This has two consequences. First, it gives rise to the possibility, because companies have different tax positions, that investment proposals which yield very low pre-tax rates of return may be undertaken, whereas other proposals which may have yielded much higher pre-tax rates of return are rejected on the grounds that their post-tax profitability is insufficient. This is, of course, very undesirable, since it promotes inefficiency and has a dampening effect on the rate of economic growth. Second, it tends to increase the amplitude of the business cycle because companies in the "full tax" position need to make less investment when pre-tax profits are low in order to stay in this tax position and avoid taxation than when such profits are high. Again this is very undesirable from an economic standpoint, since the effect is destabilizing, causing booms and recessions to be more severe than they otherwise would have been.

VI. IMPLICATIONS FOR AN EEC SHIPPING POLICY

Points to consider:

1. Assistance given to shipowners consists of the whole package of fiscal and financial aids, so it would be no good just harmonizing domestic credit terms if the objective of any policy is to put an end to any advantage enjoyed by shipowners in particular EEC countries as a consequence of flag of registry.
2. It is unlikely, however, that agreement on harmonizing fiscal incentives and taxation will be reached in the near future as this issue affects other industries besides shipping. Hence, perhaps the best way to proceed would be to allow domestic credit terms to compensate for any advantage bestowed by fiscal incentives. In other words, the objective of policy should be to harmonize the whole fiscal and financial package rather than the separate parts of the package.
3. A problem which bedevils the harmonization of the fiscal and financial package is differential rates of inflation in the respective EEC countries. This could be largely overcome if both repayments of credit and interest on such credit were made in real rather than money terms. Harmonization could, of course, be successfully achieved only if export credit terms also reflected domestic credit terms available to shipowners in their own countries.
4. Another problem which must be faced is what level of support should EEC shipowners receive and whether this should be the same as their major competitors in countries outside the EEC, given that the benefits of competitive subsidization accrue to the effective consumers of shipping services and that with Greece becoming a full member of the community, the EEC may become a net provider rather than a net purchaser of such services.[6] This is an issue which requires to be researched further.
5. Finally, there is the problem posed by the fact that the fiscal regimes of all member countries apart from Greece are to some extent discriminatory and that the incentive to invest under such regimes is partially related to the outcome of past investment decisions. A solution to this problem perhaps would be to adopt the Greek approach to the taxation of shipping if member countries can insulate their shipping industries from other sectors of their economies for tax purposes. This may not be possible, however, since many shipping companies are now part of large conglomerate firms.[7]

Bernard Gardner and Peter Marlow,
Department of Maritime Studies,
UWIST, King Edward VII Avenue,
Cardiff, CF1 3NU

ACCEPTED SEPTEMBER 1981

[6] For a discussion of the likely economic consequences of the competitive subsidization of shipping services see [3].

[7] It is worth noting that the nature of the regimes themselves has encouraged the growth of conglomerate firms, since the existence of unused tax allowances resulting from low pre-tax

REFERENCES

[1] GARDNER, B. M. and RICHARDSON, P. W., "The Fiscal Treatment of Shipping", *Journal of Industrial Economics*, XXII (2) (December 1973), pp. 95–117. Reprinted in *Advances in Maritime Economics*, Goss, R. O. (ed.) (Cambridge University Press, 1977).

[2] Goss, R. O., "The Economics of Automation in British Shipping", *Transactions of the Royal Institution of Naval Architects*, 109 (1967), p. 347. Reprinted in *Studies in Maritime Economics*, Goss, R. O. (Cambridge University Press, 1968).

[3] MARLOW, P. B. and GARDNER, B. M., "Some Thoughts on the Dry Bulk Shipping Sector", *Journal of Industrial Economics*, XXIX (1), (September 1980), pp. 71–84.

profitability of firms in particular industries has promoted cross-entry, that is, entry to an industry by firms already established outside the industry. Cross-entry may result from diversification, for example, shipping companies setting up new businesses in other industries where the level of pre-tax profitability is higher, or merger or takeover. Examples of the latter are the takeovers of Cunard by Trafalgar House and of Bovis by P & O.

THE JOURNAL OF INDUSTRIAL ECONOMICS
Volume XXXI June 1983 No. 4

AN ANALYSIS OF COST AND SUPPLY CONDITIONS IN THE LINER SHIPPING INDUSTRY

J. E. Davies

INTRODUCTION

The purpose of this paper is to examine the nature of the cost and supply conditions incurred by companies engaged in the provision of scheduled cargo liner services. It has been motivated both by what the author perceives as omissions in the theory developed and applied to the case of break-bulk shipping and by the major changes effected by the container revolution on the way in which shipping companies organise and cost their services. In particular, the paper will seek to examine the behaviour of costs with respect to the operation of both an individual vessel and a fleet of vessels and the implications of this in terms of how the industry should be organised if society is to be provided with scheduled shipping services at least cost. It is hoped that the paper may provide a methodology or insights that could be applicable to other scheduled transport services and, by virtue of addressing the conditions necessary for minimising costs, that it may also be of use in the debate over the formulation of national maritime policies.

I. COSTS IN THE SHORT RUN[1]

It is generally regarded that the most salient characteristic of the cost structure of providing scheduled liner services is the high proportion of costs that are fixed and which do not vary with changes in output. These high fixed costs arise both from the capital intensiveness of modern liner shipping and from the committed nature of scheduled transport services which renders many operating costs invariant in the short run.

Concerning capital intensiveness, it is evident that liner shipping demands a greater financial stake than virtually any other shipping sector. In terms of vessel costs, a containership costs in the order of three and a half times that of a similar sized bulk carrier; thus whereas in December, 1980 a standard 25,000 DWT bulk carrier cost £8,250,000, a standard 25,000 DWT (1,200 TEU) container ship had a purchase price of £29,200,000.[2] Moreover, whereas it is

[1] In liner shipping the short run may be defined as that period of time within which it is not possible to vary either the size of the fleet operated by a company or the frequency of service it endeavours to supply. As will be discussed in the text the precise length of the short run period varies considerably in response to the nature of the service changes contemplated and the size of the vessels involved.

[2] Figures from *Fairplay*, January 29, 1981.

TABLE I
THE CAPITAL INVESTMENT REQUIRED TO ENTER THE U.S.A./FAR EAST TRADE

Type of Equipment	*Cost $ U.S.**	*Amount of Equipment*	*Total Cost $ U.S.*
Containership (1240 Forty foot equivalents)	45,000,000	5	225,000
Containers (forty foot)	4,500	15,625	70,312,500
Container Chassis (forty foot)	4,500	12,500	56,250,000
Switching Tractor	30,000	60	1,800,000
Container Cranes	2,500,000	8	20,000,000
			$373,362,500

* 1978 Figures
Source: Ellsworth [8, p. 505].

possible to run a bulk or tramp service with a single ship, the provision of a scheduled liner service demands a *fleet* of ships together with an investment of 2–3,000 containers and 1,000–1,500 container chassis per vessel and a substantial shore based organisational and marketing infrastructure. An indication of the magnitude of the capital investments required of a liner operator is given in Table I which relates to the U.S.A./Far East trade where a minimum fleet size of five vessels is required to supply the demanded frequency of service. As can be seen, the size of the investment needed to enter the trade is quite immense, even ignoring shore based administrative infrastructure.

With respect to the committed nature of liner services, it is evident that once a schedule has been agreed upon, cost items such as fuel, crew wages, subsistence, maintenance and repair—costs which legitimately could be regarded as variable costs in other industries—now become fixed and constant costs which cannot be avoided within the short run planning horizon.

If we consider now variable costs which change directly with the magnitude of output (i.e. the amount of cargo carried) it becomes apparent that these are confined almost solely to commissions paid to agents for the soliciting of cargo and the actual costs associated with handling, loading and stowing cargo. However, if cargo volumes on a route are imbalanced, a full complement of containers may have to be carried whether full or not, for repositioning and therefore in such cases many cargo handling costs may also become fixed in nature.

Concerning the actual proportion of fixed to variable costs this will vary according to the degree of capacity utilisation achieved, though under normal trading conditions in break bulk trades it is generally regarded that around 70% of total short run costs are fixed.[3] This can be seen with reference to

[3] Marx [13, p. 19–22] puts the figure slightly higher at 75%.

TABLE II
STRUCTURE OF COSTS: CONVENTIONAL CARGO LINER

	%
Commissions	5.3
Cargo Handling	26.5
Fuel	5.4
Port dues, tug hire, custom fees, etc.	9.7
Crew wages	10.7
Crew provision	1.6
Stores	2.1
Repairs	8.9
Insurance	3.9
Administration	3.9
Sundries	0.8
Capital charges	21.2
TOTAL	100.0

Source: R. O. Goss, "The Turnround of Cargo Liners", *Journal of Transport Economics and Policy*, January 1967.

Table II which breaks down the structure of costs for a conventional cargo liner and shows that variable costs—commissions and cargo handling expenses—comprise just 31.8% of total costs leaving 68.2% fixed.

In the case of container trades, conventional wisdom accords fixed costs even greater significance with figures of 80%–90% + having been cited in the literature.[4] The author's own investigations, however, were unable to confirm these findings and for three different container companies consulted the proportion of reported fixed costs was of the surprisingly low order of 50–65%. This can be seen from Table III below. The accuracy of the split, however, is open to question as in each case the companies involved simply assumed that all cargo related costs were variable when in fact a not insubstantial part of such costs (13% in the case of Company 1 which was the only one specifically to isolate it) are incurred as a result of leasing containers[5] and therefore should be treated, over the duration of the lease period, as fixed costs. Consequently it seems reasonable to assume that the real magnitude of fixed costs, under normal trading conditions, is in the order of 65–70%.

This ratio, however, will vary if trading conditions change so as to produce corresponding changes in load factors. Generally, as load factors fall the proportion of fixed costs will rise since less cargo is being handled therefore fewer cargo related costs are being incurred. This situation of a rising proportion of

[4] Ellsworth [8] puts fixed costs at 80% of the total, whereas a figure of 94% was cited in a letter from J. N. Ingolia of the General Council of the U.S.A.'s Federal Maritime Commission to W. B. Alcorn, concerning the latter's testimony (on cost structure) to the Antitrust Commission October 23, 1978.

[5] Hall [10] shows that the practice of leasing containers is extremely widespread and that nearly half of the world's 2.6 million containers are owned by specialist container leasing companies.

TABLE III
THE COST STRUCTURE FOR 3 DIFFERENT CONTAINER COMPANIES
(ALL 1980 FIGURES)

Company 1		*Company 2*		*Company 3*	
Terminal costs	15%	Terminal Costs	21.5%	Cargo Related Costs	35%
Container Costs	13%	Transport Costs	9.6%		
Transport Costs*	9%	Commissions	16.0%		
Commissions	5%				
Port Charges	4%	Port Charges	4.8%	Capital Costs	23%
Bunkers	10%	Positioning	4.0%	Running Costs	16%
Vessel Costs	24%	Overheads & Promotion	4.8%	Bunkers	22%
Administration	10%	Vessel Costs	21.7%	Administration	4%
Other Fixed Costs	10%	Equipment	9.6%		
		Bunkers	8.0%		
42% variable		47.1% variable		35% variable	
58% fixed		52.9% fixed		65% fixed	

Company 1—small company operating primarily in trades from Europe to East Mediterranean, South Africa and Australia

Company 2—large company operating on North Atlanpic

Company 3—large company operating in Europe/Far East trade

* Transport Costs are the costs of moving containers from inland points to/from ports

(i) Figures based on normal budgeted load factor of 75%
(ii) Figures based on normal budgeted load factor of 75%
(iii) Figures based on normal budgeted load factor of 90%

Sources: Confidential.

fixed costs as load factors fall is illustrated in Figure 1 which is based on actual cost data supplied by Company 3 (see Table III) in respect of its services to the Far East. Notice also that the figure shows that *average* costs rise substantially as load factors fall, something which will be discussed much more fully below.

As a final comment on the nature of fixed costs, it is important to realise that, unlike in many other industries, the fixed costs incurred in supplying scheduled liner services cannot in the main be postponed in the short run. In the case of Company 2 (see Table III) for example, only 2.5% of its fixed costs do not directly give rise to cash payment.[6] This was because the bulk of its assets were chartered, leased or rented, with the small percentage not generating cash payments applying to those few assets which gave rise to depreciation charges. And even with companies which do not charter or lease on the

[6] The significance of fixed costs demanding continuous cash payments and which cannot therefore be postponed in the short run was first noted by Andrews [2]. He coined the term "paying out costs" to classify all costs which gave rise to continuous cash payments and showed that their magnitude gives a much better insight into a company's financial strength and competitive position than does the customary distinction between fixed and variable costs.

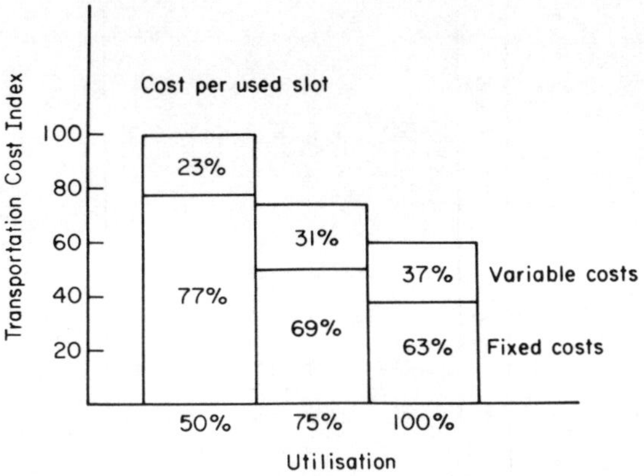

FIGURE 1
The relationship between fixed, variable and total costs as vessel utilisation changes
Source: Company 3 in Table III.

same scale the proportion of fixed costs which impose continuous cash payments is again likely to be very high because of the nature of some of the costs involved (fuel, wages, etc.) and because the favourable credit terms offered by shipyards have induced the majority of shipping companies to finance their vessel purchases with debt rather than equity (see Davies *et al.* [5, p. 259] and INSEAD [15, p. 5]).

Turning now to the shape of the average fixed cost and average variable cost curves, it is evident that the former, like all AFC curves, will fall continuously as output (capacity utilisation) increases up to full capacity. With respect to the AVC curve, it has been claimed in the literature that whereas it tends to be horizontal over low levels of capacity utilisation—reflecting constant average variable costs—once load factors exceed 85–90%, in respect of both break bulk and fully containerised ships, average variable costs will rise substantially (see Zerby and Conlon [21]).

The author's own discussions with ship operators, however, while they do confirm that in break-bulk shipping the AVC curve may rise at high utilisation levels (though probably not sufficiently to cause the ATC curve substantially to rise) in consequence of stevedoring becoming progressively more difficult and time consuming, manifestly do not confirm the same to be true in the case of fully containerised services. I could find no evidence to suggest that average variable costs associated with running container ships rose at high utilisation levels.[7] Moreover, it may be inferred from the empirical data on

[7] It is likely, however, that average variable costs would rise sharply if a container company were to endeavour to increase capacity through raising speed at sea due to the exponential relationship between fuel consumption and speed. The possibilities of this, however, are usually limited as container ships generally stick to very rigid sailing schedules, schedules which would be disrupted by significant changes in sailing speed.

TABLE IV
SYSTEM COSTS AND SLOT COSTS FOR 5 LINES ON A MAJOR DEEP SEA TRADE
(1980 COST LEVELS)

		Line 1		*Line 2*		*Line 3*		*Line 4*		*Line 5*	
	Capital ($M)	16,250		2,800		6,650		7,900		15,800	
	Running ($M)	28,050		17,300		11,000		10,700		11,050	
		44,300		20,100		17,650		18,600		26,850	
To provide full capacity	(TEUS pa)	210,000		83,500		120,000		155,000		175,800	
	Bunkers ($M)	36,700		16,250		14,350		18,700		20,600	
	Port Costs ($M)	3,000		3,250		3,500		3,250		6,500	
	System Cost ($M)	84,000	(100%)	39,600	(100%)	35,500	(100%)	40,550	(100%)	53,950	(100%)
Slot Costs	@ 100% ($/TEU)	$400		$486		$291		$262		$307	
	@ 75% ($/TEU)	$533		$648		$388		$349		$409	
	@ 50% ($/TEU)	$800		$972		$582		$524		$614	
	@ 25% ($/TEU)	$1600		$1944		$1164		$1048		$1228	

Source: Confidential.

average total costs presented in Table IV (and also Figure I) that the AVC curve is horizontal,[8] for average total costs appear to fall continuously as utilisation increases.

The average total cost curve encountered in running a containership in a scheduled service will be composed of the vertical summation of the continuously declining AFC curve and horizontal AVC curve, as shown in Figure 2. Like the AFC curve, it too will fall continuously until full capacity OQF is reached. Theoretical considerations of vessel operating costs, then, clearly predict rapidly decreasing unit costs with increasing utilisation, something supported by the empirical observations contained in Table IV (and Figure 1) which testify, thereby, to the soundness of the abstraction. Ellsworth [8] also reports the same.

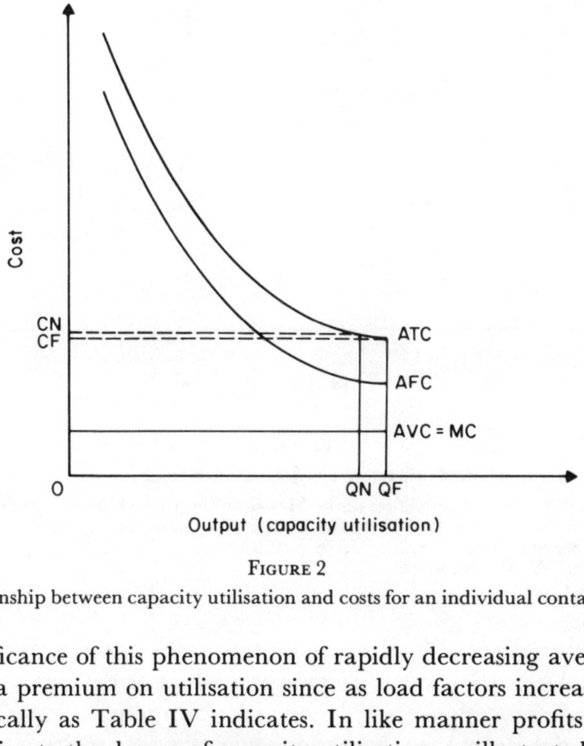

FIGURE 2

The relationship between capacity utilisation and costs for an individual container vessel

The significance of this phenomenon of rapidly decreasing average costs is that it puts a premium on utilisation since as load factors increase unit costs fall dramatically as Table IV indicates. In like manner profits too will be highly sensitive to the degree of capacity utilisation, as illustrated in Figure 3 which shows the relationship between voyage profits and capacity utilisation for three different types of vessels on the U.S. East Coast–Venezuela trade.

It should be noted, however, that the breakeven load factors indicated in Figure 3 may not be typical of liner shipping generally because of substantial

[8] There may, however, be opportunity costs which do not enter published accounts associated with very high levels of capacity utilisation; as will be discussed subsequently in the text.

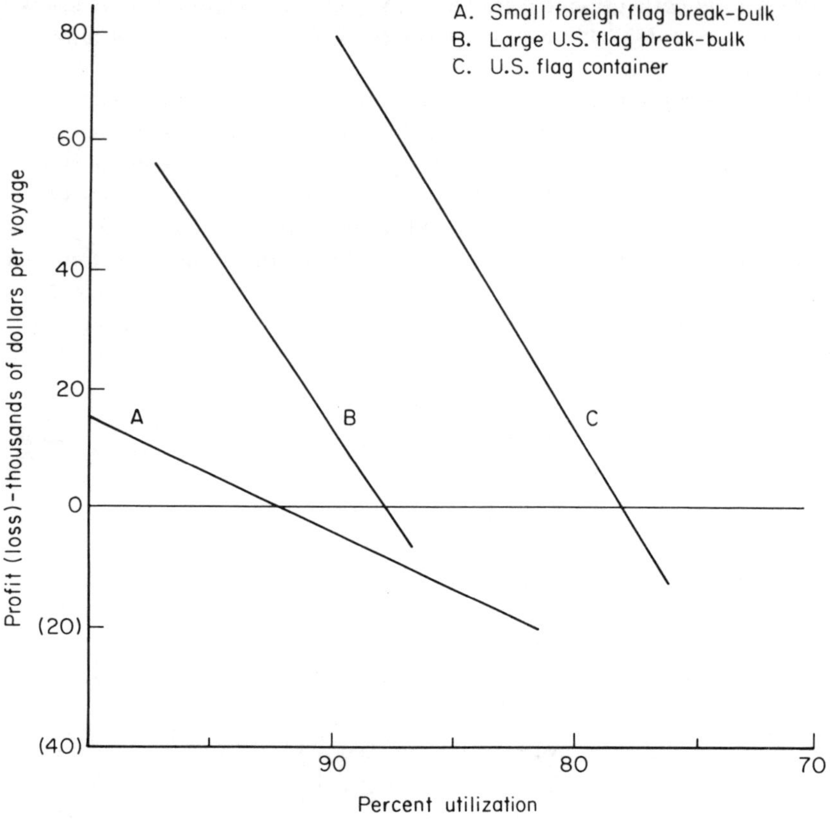

FIGURE 3

Voyage profits as a function of utilization for three different types of vessels on one trade route*

Source: David L. Gorman, "Innovation in the Maritime Industry: Landbridge Services." in *Case Studies in Maritime Innovation*, prepared for the Maritime Transportation Research Board, Washington, D.C.: Academy of Sciences, May 1978, p. 109.

* U.S. East Coast—Venezuela route.

government interference in that trade, especially in terms of rate setting.[9] Precisely what breakdown load factors are under normal commercial trading conditions is almost impossible to ascertain as shipping companies rarely divulge such information. An exception, however, is provided by Sea–Land Services Inc., which testified to the Federal Maritime Commission (of the U.S.A.) that its trans Pacific vessels must realise round trip utilisation levels of

[9] It was pointed out to the author by David L. Gorman—the original compiler of Figure 3—that the Venezuelan government has forced shipowners serving the trade to accept freight rates on certain commodities that are substantially below market rates. This in turn forces break even load factors to be higher than would otherwise be the case.

70–80% to break even (see Ellsworth [8]), though the validity of the claim is open to question.[10]

In practice, the break even level will vary according to the nature of the trade concerned—on the degree to which it is imbalanced and on the freight rates the commodities moving can bear—and to the type of vessels employed. Normally break even load factors will be lower the larger the vessel involved due to the lower unit costs large vessels can achieve through economies of scale. This point is in evidence in Figure 3. As a general observation, however, conversations with ship operators induce the author to believe that round voyage breakeven load factors can vary from 55–80% in response to the behaviour of the above described variables.

Given the cost and profit functions facing a ship operator, common sense suggests that it would be most advantageous if vessels could run at 100% utilisation as their profits would be maximised and unit costs minimised. However, given that on any route cargo volumes can vary quite substantially from week to week and given that ships are not elastic and cannot instantaneously adjust their capacity to meet such fluctuating demand, it is not in practice possible consistently to operate with 100% load factors. Moreover, it may also not be wise or feasible to operate for extended periods at utilisation levels very close to 100% as an opportunity cost, and one which would not be included in normal accounts, may be imposed on carriers in the form of damage to customer goodwill. This could arise because, when operating at very high load factors, the risks of not being able to lift all cargo awaiting shipment increases substantially and if cargo is left behind repeatedly over a protracted period, the shippers who suffer may be induced to look for alternative transport services. At the same time, the availability of cargo awaiting shipment provides an opportunity for new lines to get a foothold in the market. This in turn could jeopardise the original carrier's future market share and therefore its long term profit prospects.

To avoid this possibility, carriers which endeavour to offer a full across the board service (i.e. usually but by no means always those lines which are members of shipping conferences[11]) invariably incorporate into their services an element of reserve capacity. This reserve capacity—which should not be confused with excess capacity—ensures that space is regularly available to cope with all but the largest and most unexpected fluctuations in demand. It is thus part of the 'service' element in a shipping company's output and also provides the added benefit of facilitating loading, stowing and discharge operations when the cargo mix is complex. Exactly how much reserve capacity is

[10] A former chairman of the F.M.C., Dr. L. Kanuk, informed the author that Sealand's claim, as presented above, was based not on factual data but heresay.

[11] A shipping conference is a cartel organised on the basis of a voluntary unincorporated institutional agreement, reached between the separate lines which serve a particular trade, for the purpose of controlling their mutual competition through the covenated provision of regular and often rationalised sailing schedules and ports of call, and sometimes for the pooling of cargo and revenue. For a comprehensive description of their nature and character see Marx [13] *passim*.

warranted depends on the extent to which the carrier (or conference) expects the demand for its services to fluctuate, the possibility of speedily chartering in appropriate tonnage to meet peak demands, the relative costs of either chartering or the company itself providing the extra capacity and the risks involved in the alternative strategies.

Carriers offering complete services will then provide reserve capacity to avoid the intangible but nevertheless real cost of damage to customer goodwill but by so doing they will impose upon themselves, visible, tangible costs the nature of which can be illustrated by referring back to Figure 2. As shown, the provision of reserve capacity involves maintaining a normal (or average) capacity utilisation, OQN, which is less than full capacity, thus imposing higher costs, OCN, than the technical minimum, OCF. This, however, facilitates the management and competitive stability of the operator and his service and thus the costs involved in providing reserve capacity may be termed "management costs".[12]

It should not be supposed, however, that a conference or individual carrier will cease to take on cargo once its utilisation has reached or exceeded the normal level, for at any particular time it will obviously carry all the cargo it can, in view of the profit function as depicted in Figure 3. The existence of reserve capacity means only that services will be organised so that *on average* capacity will be used at its normal level. If, however, conditions change and it is found that load factors consistently exceed the normal level and that the growth in trade or market share that occasioned this is likely to be permanent, extra capacity will be provided to ensure again that a margin for reserve exists.

It is important, of course, that the margin of reserve capacity provided be kept as small as possible as this will allow lower unit costs of operation and the realisation of greater profits. This, in turn, will necessitate steps to minimise the volatility of the cargo offerings the trade generates, for if a conference or carrier is able to ensure that it is continuously supplied with a regular and dependable flow of cargo, it will be able to organise its services so as to minimise its requirement for reserve capacity. To achieve such demand regularity, conferences normally operate loyalty ties—such as dual rate contracts or the deferred rebate system—to encourage shippers exclusively to use their services. Economic theory would also suggest the use of some form of peak–load pricing policy to even out utilisation levels when demand is variable (see [17]). Conference freight tariffs, however, are noted not for their flexibility and responsiveness to demand conditions but for their rigidity (see Deakin and Seward [7, p. 111–17] and McLachlan [14]). The stability of conference freight rates, however, may often mask an implicit form of peak loading, for frequently when demand is high and capacity constrained, conference lines

[12] The term "management costs" was first coined by Andrews [2], who observed that many manufacturing companies provide reserve capacity to accommodate the vagaries of demand and production and he used the term to describe the costs associated with providing such capacity.

refuse to offer space for low rated cargo. But when demand is low and capacity freely available, they will gladly carry as much low rated cargo as they can. In this way the overall level of rates will rise when demand is high, and will fall when demand is low, even though the freight tariff itself may have remained unchanged.

II. FLEET PLANNING AND COSTS IN THE LONG RUN

So far, discussion has been confined to the behaviour of costs in the short run as the utilisation of the individual vessel changes. In the real world, however, it is not possible to operate a liner service with just a single vessel, for, in the words of one observer,

> "There is an irreducible minimum number of ships below which a single operator may not go and still remain competitive with sufficiently frequent sailings to meet the needs of regularity his customers demand" (Agman [1]).

Consequently, as the UNCTAD Secretariat has put it,

> "This means, in practice, that in liner shipping the minimum size of the productive unit cannot be regarded as a single ship but must be taken as a fleet of several ships" (UNCTAD [18]).

The precise minimum number of ships needed to service a particular trade will depend upon the length of the trade route and the magnitude of the cargo flow, the size of the vessels chosen, their speed of sailing and the time each vessel has to spend in port, and finally on the frequency of service demanded by shippers. On the North Atlantic, for example, shippers demand at least a weekly service and as a round voyage takes three weeks, this means that a minimum stake of three ships is required of shipowners (Gilman *et al.* [9, p. 100–101]).

Prior to the container revolution, this basic fleet dimension to shipping capacity was of little consequence for vessels could be added to or withdrawn from the fleet with relative ease, due to their small size and the more flexible scheduling arrangements which were then possible.[13] This was mirrored in the fact that the basic unit of cost accounting was taken as the performance of an individual voyage and not some unit measure of total service costs.

With containerisation, however, fleets became much smaller and the service provided more rigidly organised. Moreover, most of the expenses companies faced became functions of time rather than the sailing of individual voyages; thus charter hire is now normally expressed as a per day rate, overheads (salaries, rates, interest, etc.) are generally incurred by the month while certain types of rentals, leases and insurance are paid on a yearly basis. Together

[13] The flexibility of break bulk services and the rigidity of container services is discussed more fully subsequently in the text.

these developments forced many container companies to think and plan in terms of systems of ships and has required them to change the nature of their accounting procedures from the break bulk voyage accounting practice to a *system cost basis* predicated upon the total cost of supplying so much cargo capacity at a particular frequency over a given period of time.

In the long run, of course, the conditions of demand may substantially change so as to require corresponding changes in the service system provided. In this respect, adjustments to supply may be of two distinct types depending on whether an expansion or contraction of services is warranted.

Consider firstly contractions of supply. If recession sets in and trade decreases, carriers will find that their average vessel load factors will fall, their unit costs rise and that their profit dries up. A likely response from a manufacturing company faced with this kind of problem would be to reduce the burden of fixed costs by closing and selling off under utilised plant and equipment so that the installations that remain may be used more intensively and profitably. This kind of response, however, is not normally possible in liner shipping for if a carrier attempts to improve its average load factors by withdrawing an individual vessel, it may not be able to provide the requisite frequency of service with the fleet that remains, especially in containerised services where the minimum fleet size is small, and therefore its customers are liable to desert it thereby causing load factors to decline on the remaining vessels [12]. The only other alternative available for contracting capacity is reducing ship size (by replacing the existing fleet with a numerically similar fleet of smaller ships) but this, however, is not feasible as it is both time consuming to effect and moreover illogical in the face of economies of scale at the level of the individual ship. Thus it is no surprise to find that when carriers encounter even the severest of trading and financial problems they will not sell off vessels on an individual, piecemeal basis but will continue to operate until, as a last resort, they are forced to sell off their entire fleet and withdraw totally from the trade.[14]

When demand increases, however, the situation is rather different. If we consider initially break bulk shipping, it is comparatively easy to accommodate an increased demand through adding an individual vessel because break bulk services invariably require a large fleet of small vessels which, in turn, allows the sailing speeds of each to be juggled so as to absorb the newcomer without causing serious scheduling problems and without disrupting the frequency of service which produces most cargo. In the case of container shipping, however, the number of vessels needed to mount a scheduled service falls dramatically (normally a single containership replaces 4–6 break bulk vessels)

[14] As recent instances of this situation, Farrell Lines, operating on the North Atlantic, were beset by chronic operating, corporate and financial problems throughout 1980 and in October of that year sold their entire fleet of 5 vessels to MARAD (U.S. Maritime Administration). Likewise, Seatrain withdrew from the North Atlantic in September 1980, through selling off its complete fleet to T.F.L. (Trans Freight Lines) for $28.5 million.

and therefore the addition of a comparable extra vessel will both add massively to capacity and may make it more difficult to maintain the requisite frequency of service.[15] An alternative method, however, would be to sell off the existing fleet, or move them to other trades, to be replaced by a like sized fleet of larger vessels. This would allow the same service frequency to be maintained though again capacity would greatly be increased. In this case, however, the expansion of capacity would bring with it the advantages of economies of scale and in consequence it is normally the more desired approach.[16]

The implications of the above analysis are fourfold. Firstly, it is evident that the short run planning period in respect of decisions to reduce capacity is very long indeed, especially in the case of container services. As a result of economies of scale in ship size operators naturally seek to employ the largest vessels their market share allows though at the same time the need to control total system costs results in pressures to reduce the fleet size to the minimum possible commensurate with the requirements of service frequency and the conditions of the trade. These forces, in turn, make it extremely difficult to reduce capacity and therefore greatly extend the short run period operative in respect of decisions to reduce capacity.[17]

With respect to decisions to increase capacity, the short run period is not nearly so long, as ships can be chartered quite speedily[18] and, whereas it is extremely difficult (and self defeating) to reduce service frequencies below the level demanded by the trade, there are, apart from the possibility of diminishing returns, few problems surrounding frequency improvements. Nevertheless, because the running costs and carrying capacity of a modern container vessel are so great, the incremental impact of a single extra vessel is likewise considerable and therefore it warrants the most careful consideration and planning. This in turn means that the short run period in respect of decisions to

[15] Service frequencies can, of course, be increased quite readily and in certain circumstances this may give the company concerned an important marketing advantage. If, however, a company is already operating at an optimum frequency, increasing it may result in diminishing returns, with proportionately less cargo being offered with each successive frequency improvement.

[16] As an illustration, an increase in vessel size was the tactic used by CAST Line (the fastest growing company on the North Atlantic) to expand its capacity. It commenced its rise in September 1976 operating six 385 TEU vessels, it now has six 768 TEU ships and these in turn will ultimately be replaced by six 70,000 container/bulk carriers, each with a capacity of 1,450 TEU's.

[17] The existence of an active second hand market for cargo ships and the fact that vessels can be moved from trade to trade may temper this conclusion somewhat for they indicate that a variety of alternative uses are available for a carrier's ships. Such possibilities may therefore make it much easier to entertain capacity reductions through total withdrawal than would otherwise be the case. However, the fact that many companies have spent years, some decades, developing their connections with a trade means that they will not willingly withdraw, despite such possibilities, without a very protracted period of consideration.

[18] It was reported to the author by shipping companies that in early 1981 it was possible to obtain a chartered containership of greater than 1,100 TEU capacity in a period of 3–6 months, and smaller ships in a considerably shorter period of time.

increase capacity is likely to be considerably longer with container shipping than the period applicable in the case of break bulk services.[19]

Secondly, it appears that the long run average cost curves of supplying a scheduled liner service may be of two distinct types. If, as in break bulk trades it is not possible to increase the size of vessels due to constraints in port costs and cargo handling techniques, the LRAC curve may be L-shaped as shown in Figure 4, as in such cases capacity can be increased only by adding to the existing fleet vessels of similar dimensions and cost characteristics.

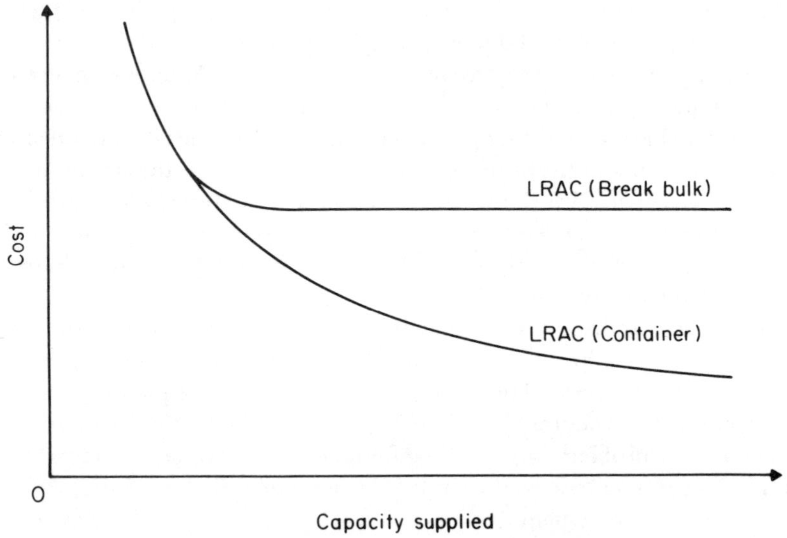

FIGURE 4
The long run average cost curves of running a liner shipping service

When it is possible technically to expand capacity by increasing vessel size, as it is the case in may containerised trades, the LRAC curve, far from being horizontal, may fall progressively due to the realisation of economies of scale. Eventually the curve may level out as further technical constraints or managerial diseconomies are encountered which may prevent further cost reduction through increases in scale, though nevertheless it will be falling over a prolonged range of output.[20]

This again is illustrated in Figure 4.

Thirdly, because of the indivisible nature of the capacity provided by a modern containership, it is evident that any attempt to satisfy an increase in

[19] Deakin and Seward, [7, p. 92] also point out that the length of the short run period is likely to vary directly with ship size.

[20] Examples of constantly declining LRAC curves, constructed from empirical evidence are contained in Gilman *et al.*, [9].

demand that is over and above the capability of the existing fleet will result, inevitably, in a massive increase in carrying capacity, much of which cannot immediately be utilised. For the existence of indivisible capacity increments means, as Joan Robinson put it, that,

> "It is therefore impossible for (such) an industry to equip itself to produce one unit of a commodity without immediately providing capacity or produce more than one unit" (Robinson [16]).

The significance of such indivisible capacity increments is that they indicate that great savings in systems costs may be realised if separate liner companies co-operate so as to rationalise the use of their combined capacity, for then what is indivisible to the individual becomes, in much larger measure, divisible to the group. For if lines were to co-ordinate their services, instead of acting atomistically, it would be possible for supply to be matched more closely to the requirements of the trade ensuring thereby a greater degree of capacity utilisation, something imperative given the declining (short run) cost situation which faces the firm at any point in time. In addition, if firms co-operate in this way, as they do under the conference system,[21] it is possible for them to service a trade with fewer and much larger ships, and therefore benefit from economies of scale to a much greater extent, than would be the case if each firm attempted individually to supply the regularity and frequency of service demanded by shippers. The importance of this is demonstrated clearly in the North Atlantic trades where, because of a regulatory system which decrees that firms must at all times compete, and which thereby prevents co-operation, it has not been possible to introduce optimally sized ships nor to rationalise services in the most economic manner (Gilman *et al.* [9, p. 101] and Hapag Lloyd [11]).

In contrast to the North Atlantic, an indication of the positive advantages of rationalisation has been provided by the trades between Europe and the Antipodes. Thus when rationalisation was initially undertaken by the Australian Tonnage Committee (i.e. the UK/Australia Conference) in 1966, the number of vessels in the conference fleet was reduced by between 25–30 and later in 1970 when containerisation was introduced, the number of ships was again reduced, this time by a factor of 4–5.[22] The benefits of rationalisation, of

[21] It should be pointed out that not all conferences do rationalise their services. The conference system provides only an opportunity and a vehicle for rationalisation, though in view of the economies of rationalisation under containerisation it is likely that eventually market forces will demand that conferences effectively rationalise their combined services.

The conference system, however, is not the only way of achieving rationalisation. It can also be effected through the formation of consortia (or more general increases in concentration). Such developments have already taken place both within an existing conference framework and outside it. As an illustration of the former, 95% of the total capacity offered by the Far East Freight Conference is supplied by the three consortia ACE, TRIO, and SCANDUTCH. Concerning the latter, Overseas Containers Ltd., (OCL), Associated Container Transport (ACT), Atlantic Container Line (ACL) and Dart Line are consortia which all formed on the North Atlantic where conference organisation, in terms of the ability to rationalise, effectively does not exist.

[22] Information supplied to the author by a member of the Australian Tonnage Committee.

course, will show up in the average utilisation levels achieved by conference ships and this respect, vessels operating on the Europe/New Zealand conference attained, over the decade 1970/80, average load factors of 95% despite the fact that the country's meat exports are subject to considerable seasonal variation.[23]

Fourthly, because the costs of providing rationalised services will always be lower than those incurred in sustaining unrationalised services,[24] *the liner industry will tend towards natural monopoly*, especially in the containerised trades where the cost savings from rationalisation are greatest. It is unlikely, however, that the industry could ever achieve this state in its fullest, strictest sense due to the pervasiveness of multi-scale and multi-modal competition [4], [6]. Nevertheless, in terms of providing ocean liner transport, elements of natural monopoly will, of necessity, be present, since an individual shipping line offering a full across the board service outside a closed conference will, other things being equal (subsidies especially), always incur higher costs than those of the conference in providing a similar quality of service, due to the inability of the single line, acting atomistically, to achieve the economies of scale and rationalisation which flow from collectively mounting joint services.[25] This also helps explain why independent concerns aim principally at cornering particular market segments rather than offering full services, where the cost advantages of conferences are most pronounced, for by doing so they can dispense with the need for providing the same degree of reserve capacity, can operate at load factors consistently approaching 100%—by throwing any variations in demand onto the conference to cope with, and can therefore compete effectively in that submarket even if they have to operate with smaller and therefore higher cost vessels.

CONCLUSIONS

Despite the great increase in the capital intensiveness of the liner shipping industry brought about by containerisation, it appears, contrary to the conventional wisdom, that this has not resulted in a substantial or even a signifi-

[23] The New Zealand figures are derived from an affidavit by Alan John Bott in connection with the case of Waitaki Refrigerating Ltd. v. New Zealand Meat Producers' Board, at the High Court of New Zealand, 1979–80.

[24] It was for just this reason that the Rochdale Committee [3, p. 132] in evaluating the desirability or otherwise of liner conference concluded that, "The closed conference, with fully rationalised sailings therefore appears to us most likely to serve the best interests of both shippers and shipowners."

These sentiments were also echoed by the Carter administration's chairman of the Federal Maritime Commission, R. J. Daschback, who publically supported the closed conference as a vehicle for improving the lot of the American shipping industry for, "By rationalising the trade, the amount of capital equipment required would be reduced, allowing higher utilisation rates, reduced per unit costs, and increased profit margins for the carriers". (American Shipper, March 1978, p.4.) See also Ellsworth [8], and Agman [1].

[25] An exception to this general rule, however, could occur if a non-conference line had grown to size comparable to an entire conference for in such a case the non-conference line, through appropriate internal organisation, could derive similar economies of rationalisation. See also note 21 *supra*.

cant increase in the proportion of fixed to variable costs. At about 65–70% of total costs they remain roughly the same as in break bulk shipping. The great majority of these fixed costs, moreover, are paying out costs which cannot be postponed in the short run. Consequently if open competition in the liner industry still produces destructive or cutthroat competition, as has often been claimed (Agman [1] and Ellsworth [8]), it appears that this cannot solely be due to the level of short run variable costs—the pricing floor of a rate war—as not only are they higher than traditionally thought but at the same time many of the residual fixed costs are not open to postponement.[26]

Something which may, however, help to explain the seeming ferocity of the rate wars the industry periodically appears to experience is the importance of service frequency in the short run. For the requirement to supply a desired and demanded frequency of service makes it extremely difficult to reduce capacity. Consequently, if a company's demand, and therefore vessel load factors were substantially to fall in consequence, say, of a trading depression or the entry of a large capacity newcomer, the company is unlikely to be able to reduce capacity to accommodate the new demand situation. To help absorb the high fixed cost of unused capacity it may be forced then to slash rates in the hope of increasing utilisation.

In the long run, when capacity and service frequencies can be adjusted, problems of a different nature arise. The need for economies of scale induces operators to run their services with the largest vessels their market share and trade conditions allow. This, in turn, renders the cargo carrying potential of capacity increments extremely great because of their indivisibility and in consequence makes it difficult for an individual firm optimally to utilise such capacity increments.

In sum, then, it appears that in liner trades we have a total situation where profits and unit costs are highly sensitive to the degree of capacity utilisation, where both fixed and paying out costs are relatively high, where capacity is extremely difficult to reduce and where capacity increments are subject to great indivisibilities. The net result of this assemblage of factors is that a premium has been put on rationalisation, as the combined market of a group of individual carriers acting and planning together allows larger and therefore lower cost vessels to be employed, it makes it easier to adjust capacity to match demand and therefore permits higher sustained utilisation levels than would otherwise be the case.

This rationalisation, in turn, can proceed along either of two fronts—concentration or co-operation. Which of these provides the best solution in terms of pure economics is a matter of conjecture. However, if the conference

[26] It should be pointed out, however, that since shipping companies usually operate in more than one trade and are often owned by parent conglomerates it appears that their high paying out costs may not always constitute a major limitation to the propensity to indulge in rate wars, as these could be financed from external sources.

system were to be dismantled[27] it is doubtful whether concentration would be acceptable on political grounds as it would result inevitably in the absorption, merger or extinction of many individual lines and therefore it may not be acceptable to the governments of the flag states of the carriers involved. Hence it appears that the liner conference system, despite now being over a century old, still has a valuable role to play in the servicing of world trade and a role that is likely to remain for many years to come.

J. E. Davies,
Department of Economics,
Acadia University, Wolfville,
Nova Scotia, Canada, BOP 1XO

ACCEPTED SEPTEMBER 1981

REFERENCES

[1] Agman, R. S., "Competition, Rationalisation and United States Shipping Policy", *Journal of Maritime Law and Commerce*, Volume 8, No. 1 (1976); pp. 1–50.
[2] Andrews, P. W. S., "*Manufacturing Business*" (Macmillan, London, 1949).
[3] "*Committee of Inquiry into Shipping*" (the "Rochdale Report"), (Cmnd. 4337, H.M.S.O., London, 1970).
[4] Davies, J. E., "The Competitive Environment of Liner Conferences", *Maritime Policy and Management*, Volume 5 (1978), pp. 97–106.
[5] ——, Evans, J. J., Gardner, B. M., and Lowe, A. V., "Liner Shipping in the U.S. Trades", *Maritime Policy and Management*, Volume 5, No. 3 (1978), pp. 141–266.
[6] ——, and Evans, J. J., "The Market Power and Competitive Environment of Conferences", contained in "*Liner Shipping in the Eighties*", ed. Beth, H.L., (Bremen, 1980), pp. 305–18.
[7] Deakin, B. M. and Seward, T., "*Shipping Conferences—a Study of their Origins, Development and Economic Practices*" (Cambridge U.P., London, 1973).
[8] Ellsworth, R. A., "Competition or Rationalisation in the Liner Industry", *Journal of Maritime Law and Commerce*, Volume 10, No. 4 (1979), pp. 497–517.
[9] Gilman, S., Maggs, R. P., and Ryder, S. C., "*Containers on the North Atlantic*" (Marine Transport Centre, University of Liverpool, 1977).
[10] Hall, W., "Sea Containers", *Financial Times* (February 13, 1981).
[11] Hapag Lloyd, A. G., "*The Organisation of Liner Shipping in the Container Age illustrated by the North Atlantic Trade*", (Hapag Lloyd A. G., Hamburg, 1978).
[12] Janson, J. O., "Intra Tariff Cross Subsidisation in Liner Shipping", *Journal of Transport Economics and Policy*, Volume 8, No. 3 (1974), pp. 294–311.
[13] Marx, D., "*International Shipping Cartels*" (Princeton U.P., Greenwood Press, New York, 1953).
[14] McLachlan, D. L., Index Number of Liner Freight Rates in United Kingdom Trades 1946–1957", *Yorkshire Bulletin of Economic and Social Research*, Volume 10, No. 1 (1958), pp. 50–62.
[15] "*The Regeneration of an Industry*" (anonymous) (INSEAD, 1976).
[16] Robinson, J., "*The Economics of Imperfect Competition*", (Macmillan, London, 1948).

[27] As advocated by the U.S.A.'s Department of Justice [20].

[17] "Symposium on Peak Load Pricing", containing articles by Joskow, P. L., Crew, M. A., Kleindorfer, P. R., Wendes, J. T., and Nguyen, D. T., *Bell Journal of Economics*, Volume 7, No. 1, (Spring 1976), pp. 197–248.
[18] UNCTAD, "*Establishment or Expansion of Merchant Marines in Developing Countries*", TD/26/Rev. 1 (New York, 1968).
[19] ——, "*The Liner Conference System*", TD/B/C.4/62 Rev. 1, (New York, 1970).
[20] U.S. Department of Justice, "*The Regulated Ocean Shipping Industry*", (U.S. Justice Department, January, 1977).
[21] Zerby, J. A. and Conlon, R. M., "An Analysis of Capacity Utilization in Liner Shipping", *Journal of Transport Economics and Policy*, Vol. 12, No. 1, (1978), pp. 27–46.

THE JOURNAL OF INDUSTRIAL ECONOMICS
Volume XXXI June 1983 No. 4

CO-OPERATIVE AGREEMENTS AND THE ORGANIZATION OF INDUSTRY*

P. MARITI AND R. H. SMILEY

I. INTRODUCTION

THE field of industrial organization involves, in major part, the study of how industry is organized and why. The organization of industry, including for example the size distribution of firms, depends in turn on how firms interact. In *Markets and Hierarchies*, Williamson [11] has identified two major types of interaction: the marketplace (either competition between firms or single transactions between buyers and sellers), and mergers. Earlier, Coase [6] identified the two methods for organizing economic activity as internal to the firm or external to the firm. This paper investigates an intermediate form of interrelationship between firms, which provides yet another way of organizing economic activity, the co-operative agreement.

It is important to state just what we mean by co-operative agreements, and to differentiate these type of agreements from other transactions. For our purposes, a co-operative agreement is any long term, explicit agreement amongst two or more firms. This agreement may or may not involve financial remuneration. There can be payment for some good or service: alternatively, the firms may agree to exchange information or other commodity or service: both are co-operative agreements. To meet our definition, the agreement must be long term: a one time purchase of goods and services is not a co-operative agreement, but an agreement to purchase all inputs from one supplier over the next ten years is a co-operative agreement. The agreement must be explicit: just because a majority of all purchases happen *ex-post* to have been from one supplier does not imply that a co-operative agreement was in force unless there was an explicit understanding before the fact that this would be so. Although the agreement must be explicit, there need not be a written contract for a co-operative agreement to exist. Co-operative agreements can be made verbally, although most agreements are indeed based on a written contract. Finally, a co-operative agreement can take various legal forms: two legal forms that are investigated in this paper are the joint venture and the bidding consortium (which itself may or may not be a joint venture). Since the objective of this paper is to study that transactional middle ground between single transactions in the marketplace and internal organization

* A preliminary draft of this paper was presented at the 8th Conference of the European Association for Research in Industrial Economics, September 16–18, 1981, in Basel, Switzerland. The Consiglio Nazionale delle Ricerche (CNR) provided funding for Professor Smiley while he was a visiting professor at the University of Pisa.

which often occurs through merger, acquisitions and mergers are not treated as co-operative agreements.

As the reader can see from the above definition, this paper undertakes a rather broad field of study. Since there have been virtually no previous attempts to study this field, most of this paper is purposely rather descriptive. Our objective is to draw the attention of the academic community to a broad range of interfirm transactions which have been previously ignored.

The organization of the paper is as follows. Section II discusses some earlier research in the field, and offers some preliminary comments on the study. Section III discusses data sources and concepts used to classify the information gathered, while Section IV presents some overall findings. Section V deals with the analysis of and factors affecting the various motivations for co-operative agreements; in Section VI there is a preliminary discussion of trends in the use of co-operative agreements and Section VII discusses public policy towards co-operative agreements. The paper ends with some final comments.

II. THE FIELD OF STUDY

The firm is most commonly viewed as an entity purchasing inputs from which it obtains marketable products according to its underlying production function. What the firm does—its range of activities—is treated as a datum of the problem. However as Stigler points out [10], to reach the stage of marketable products or services, firms engage in a whole series of distinct activities or functions which may or may not be technologically related: buying inputs; transforming them into semifinished products; designing products and doing research for product innovation; searching for financing; extending credit to buyers; searching for suppliers and new markets; etc.

For each such activity a firm has at least three alternatives:

(1) organizing it internally;
(2) making recourse to individual market transactions;
(3) developing a co-operative agreement with one or more firms (intermediate forms of organization).

Alternatives (1) and (2) can be illustrated by reference to the technological approach—based on economies and diseconomies of scale and Adam Smith's principle of division of labor—refined by Stigler [10] integrated with the transaction approach originally advocated by Coase [6], and elaborated on by Williamson [11] [12], amongst others [7].

Several authors have mentioned the existence of intermediate forms of organization of economic activity. As early as 1952, P. W. S. Andrews wrote:

> ". . . Industrial Economics has a lively interest in the relationship between individual businesses . . . One thinks at once of competitive relationships—of the ways in which many prices, for example, emerge out

of the competitive struggle between businesses. But in fact, even in very competitive industries it is important not to overlook the complementary relationships which exist as well" [1, p. 77].

K. Arrow has written:

> "The price system, for all its virtues, is only one conceivable form of arranging trade, even in a system of private property. Bargaining can assume extremely general forms" [2, p. 50].

Aside from these and several other papers (e.g. Richardson [9]), co-operative agreements have received almost no attention in the academic literature. This is a serious deficiency which this paper is intended to correct.

There are several reasons for studying co-operative agreements. Casual perusal of the financial press indicates that they are indeed an important component of interfirm relations. In addition, ignoring the existence of co-operative agreements can lead on to incorrect theoretical results and policy descriptions. For example, Baumol and Fischer argue [3] that one can deduce the optimal number of firms in an industry from the size of the market and knowledge of economies of scale in the production process. However, they ignore the possibility that is investigated in this paper: namely that through co-operative agreements, firms can take advantage of economies of scale in one or more of their production processes while remaining separate entities. The realization that the achievement of economies of scale is available (through co-operative agreements) to firms that are otherwise unrelated leads one to predict a greater number of firms than would be predicted by the Baumol and Fischer results.

III. DATA SOURCES AND CO-OPERATIVE AGREEMENT CLASSIFICATION

This study develops and makes use of two sources of data. First, we examined published reports of all co-operative agreements that were initiated in 1980 in the European financial press. Second, we interviewed a number of senior executives in European firms. These firms were chosen for interview because they had engaged in a large number of co-operative agreements. The firms interviewed were in the automobile, basic metals, computer, and electronic systems industries.

Due to the nature of the data gathering process, the sample is not a random one. The firms whose activities are reported in the financial press are generally quite large, and only important co-operative agreements between these firms are reported. Also, while the in depth interviews span a broad range of economic activity, the industries were not selected at random.

Seventy agreements were identified for the year 1980 in the financial press. Through a careful reading of the text of the article, each of the agreements was classified as to the major motivation of the partners. The motivations, which are discussed in detail below, are: technology transfer, technological complementarity, marketing agreement, risk sharing, and economies of scale (in production or other fields). We also noted whether the agreement took the legal form of a joint venture and/ or a bidding consortium.

Two of the motivations are knowledge or technology related. The first, *technology transfer*, refers to the transfer of technology from one firm to another, in exchange for some consideration such as money or the right to market certain products. A patent license is the most common form of technology transfer, although the examples cited in this study were of a more permanent or ongoing type of technology transfer than a single patent license would provide.

Technology transfer implies a one way flow of information, while the category *technological complementarity* is for long term transactions where technology is exchanged or shared between two parties. Each of the firms will possess some unique knowledge or patent, and the co-operative agreement provides for a sharing of the knowledge of the two firms, usually in developing new products or services.

Marketing agreements can vary from something as simple as a single product marketing and distribution contract to a long term multi-product agreement, usually between a manufacturer and a firm with wholesale or retail outlets (often in different parts of the world than its partner currently covers). The marketing agreements included in this study are of the latter type, where a long term relationship is initiated by the agreement. Several agreements are between retailing chains with strengths in different parts of the world, rather than an agreement between a manufacturer and a distributor.

Economies of scale agreements refer to both production and distribution efficiencies which come with larger size. These agreements often involve production rationalization where one firm will manufacture all of several components while the other will manufacture all of the remainder of the components. Such an arrangement allows longer production runs for each of the firms and the achievement of economies of scale and learning by doing.

The final motivation for co-operative agreements identified in this study is *risk sharing*. Agreements of this type generally provide for the management of the operation by one of the partners, while the others merely contribute capital and absorb some of the risk of failure. In order for an agreement to be classified as a risk sharing agreement in this study, it must possess none of the attributes of agreements listed above; i.e. it must not be an agreement to achieve economies of scale, it must not be a marketing agreement, etc. If we did not use this classification rule, all co-operative agreements would be classified as risk sharing since in every case risk is shared between the parties. However, we wanted to identify those agreements where risk sharing was the only motivation.

One motivation for co-operative agreements which is omitted from this study is *reduction in transactions costs*. Reading Coase [6] and Williamson [11 and 12], one would expect to find the avoidance of the cost of repeated transactions to be a primary motivation for undertaking co-operative agreements. It was because of this sort of expectation that we asked each of the senior executives we interviewed whether transactions cost were important in their decision making regarding co-operative agreements. We defined transactions costs as all costs of negotiating contracts including management's time, legal fees, and other identifiable costs. In all cases, they replied that avoiding transactions costs was not an issue in deciding to undertake co-operative agreements. The amount of money involved in the cost of making transactions was in all cases overwhelmed by other benefits and costs from co-operative agreements. For this reason, we have eliminated the transactions costs motivation from this paper. However, we should recognize that some would argue that we defined transactions costs too narrowly in discussing only the costs of normal transactions. If that is the case, then perhaps some of the motivations listed above could also be taken to read transactions costs motivations.

The co-operative agreements identified in this study take several legal forms. Two of the forms that are expressly identified are the *joint venture* and the *bidding consortium.* The joint venture is defined as an agreement in which two independent legal partners establish a third independent legal firm. A bidding consortium is a co-operative agreement that exists for a single project. The partners will each contribute some skill or portion of the task, and the project usually involves some sort of construction. A bidding consortium project can be a joint venture. Also, many of the technological complementarity or economies of scale co-operative agreements are joint ventures.

Firms taking part in the agreements were classified into industries at the two digit level according to the Italian standard industrial classification system, which is comparable to the classification schemes of the European Economic Community. Many agreements identified had more than one motivation, so there is some double counting in the tables below. Also, a motivation (such as economies of scale) was reported for every joint venture and bidding consortium.

IV. OVERALL FINDINGS

Table I presents the overall picture which emerges after classification of the seventy co-operative agreements identified. The most frequent motivation for co-operative agreements is technological complementarity, with forty-one percent of the total agreements. Since technology transfer is an additional twenty-nine percent of the total number of agreements, we see that seventy percent of the total number of agreements in 1980 involved a transfer or sharing of knowledge. (Note that unlike the other categories, technological transfer and technological complementarity are mutually exclusive. A knowledge related agreement is either one or the other.) Economies of scale, risk sharing, and marketing agreements make up much smaller proportions of the total number of co-operative agreements.

TABLE I
MOTIVATIONS IN THE SAMPLE OF 70 CO-OPERATIVE AGREEMENTS

Motivation and Legal Form	*Percentage*
Technology Transfer	29%
Technological Complementarity	41
Marketing Agreement	21
Economies of Scale	16
Risk Sharing	14
Joint Ventures	55
Bidding Consortium	29

Fifty-five percent of the co-operative agreements take the legal form of a joint venture. This does not imply that in forty-five percent of the cases there is no contract between the parties; in some cases an explicit contract is negotiated although no new firm is established, and therefore the agreement is not a joint venture. There are, however, some occasions in which a co-operative agreement is established with *no* legal contract.

The two-digit industry was identified for each of the parties to the seventy co-operative agreements, and this identification provides the basis for Table II. The figure 1 is indicated in the appropriate category in Table II for each case in which the firms are in the same two-digit industry; a zero is entered if the firms are in different two-digit industries. There will therefore be twice as many zeros entered in the table as there were co-operative agreements between firms.

Before turning to a discussion of motivation for co-operative agreements on the part of different industries, we can state some general findings from an inspection of Table II:

(a) The two-digit industries most active in establishing co-operative agreements are electrical and electronic appliances, chemicals, electronics (including equipment for data processing), automobiles, and oil refining.
(b) The legal form—joint venture—is chosen by these industries with roughly the same frequency.
(c) Bidding consortia predominate in the oil refining industry.
(d) For the industries which have a large number of co-operative agreements both inter- and intra-industry agreements are chosen, with the exception of oil refining where firms make agreements predominantly with firms in other industries.

V. THE MOTIVATION FOR CO-OPERATIVE AGREEMENTS

In this section we analyze firms' motivations for entering into co-operative agreements, utilizing both the sample of seventy co-operative agreements reached in 1980 and our personal interviews with senior executives in a number of European firms.

TABLE II
MOTIVATION OF AGREEMENTS BY INDUSTRY

Two-digit Industry	*Technology Transfer*	*Technological Complementarity*	*Marketing Agreement*	*Economies of Scale*	*Risk Sharing*	*Joint Venture*	*Bidding Consortium*
Electrical and Electronic Appliances, Telecommunications Equipment	1110	11111111000	11100	10	0	111111000	1
Electronics, Equipment for Data Processing	10	00	110	0	0	100	0
Chemicals	11	11000	1			11110	11
Automobiles	111	10	0	111110		11100	
Means of Transportation other than Automobiles		111		111			111
Mechanical Engineering	1	1000	0			100	0
Retailing of Food, Textiles, Pharmaceuticals	11	10	10			110	
Precision Machinery and Appliances		00	00			00	
Services to Firms	0	000			1	1	0
Oil Refining	00	00		0	100000	0000	1000000
Metal Production and Transformation	0	00			0	10	00
Food and Beverages	1		1			00	
Food Raw Materials	10		1		0	1	0
Pulp and Paper	1					1	1
Metal Mining						1	1
Banking			10		0	00	
Coal Mining					00	0	00
Utilities					0		0
Travel Agency, Transportation Intermediates			0			0	
Oil and Natural Gas Drilling	0				0		0
Non Ferrous Mining (Diamonds)	0						0
Agriculture	0						0
Air Transportation						0	
Wholesaling						0	
Retailing (Vehicles, Books, Gas)						0	
Building		1				1	

1 indicates intra-industry agreement and 0 inter-industry agreement

The most common type of co-operative agreement involves the exchange of information. Co-operative agreements of this type can take two forms: technology transfer and technological complementarity representing twenty-nine and forty-one percent respectively of the total number of co-operative agreements in our sample of seventy. From the point of view of the firm acquiring the information, a reason for entering into a technology transfer agreement is that it is often cheaper and less risky to purchase information than it is to produce it. Technology transfer agreements involve, in most cases, purchase of the information by a large firm with the necessary manufacturing scale and distribution outlets, and sale of the information by a smaller firm which does not have the necessary manufacturing and/or marketing scale.

One of the more interesting types of technology transfer co-operative agreements to emerge in recent years is between the automobile industry and the electronics instrumentation industry. Both Renault and Peugeot have recently signed long term research and development contracts for automobile instrumentation and control technology. The benefits of a longer term agreement for the purchase of technology include a reduction in search costs, a better working relationship, and a better understanding by the research group of the needs of the automobile company. Both firms feel that these benefits exceed the benefits of a shorter term contracting strategy (such as the opportunity to choose the best product available from a number of different producers).

Technological complementarity agreements, in which each firm contributes some basic technological expertise to a joint project, are even more frequent than technology transfer agreements. One would expect to find such co-operative agreements where markets are expanding rapidly and/or technology is changing quickly. These conditions are both met in the electrical and the electronics industries, which make up sixteen out of thirty-nine of the cases. They are also common in the mechanical engineering and means of transportation industries.

The introduction of new products is often accompanied by a different type of co-operative agreement, the marketing or distribution agreement. We would expect to find more marketing co-operative agreements in those industries with more rapidly changing technology, since more new products will be introduced in those industries. Fifteen of the seventy agreements studied indicated marketing as a major motivation, and eight of these fifteen were in the electronics industries (including electronic data processing, telecommunications equipment, and electrical and electronic appliances).

If production is characterized by economies of scale and learning by doing, firms may attempt to decrease costs by expanding output to achieve these benefits. Low product demand and the costs of firm growth may, however, limit this strategy. Horizontal mergers are another possible way to achieve the cost reducing benefits of larger output. But mergers involve the combination of whole firms with numerous uncertainties about the ability of the parts to function smoothly together, and the resulting difficulties of the merger may overwhelm the cost reducing benefits of larger volume in one or several individual products. Co-operative agreements, on the other hand, allow firms in the same industry to rationalize production, thus reducing costs through economies of scale and learning by doing, without the uncertainties and difficulties of full scale mergers.

Co-operative agreements for economies of scale or production rationalization are important in the automobile industry. Eleven of the seventy co-operative agreements studied indicated production economies of scale as a major motivation. Six of these eleven were in the automobile industry, and three others were in the non-automobile transportation industry (motorcycles and aircraft). As an example of one of these production rationalization co-operative agreements, Alfa Romeo and Nissan have just concluded an agreement whereby Alfa Romeo will produce the engine and Nissan will produce the body for a new automobile to be marketed throughout Europe. The benefits to each firm include the introduction of a new automobile at a substantially reduced investment cost, and the savings due to learning which will accompany a larger production run than either firm could have achieved separately.

Investment rationalization also appears to be important in the metals industry. For example, an Italian firm and the Italian subsidiary of a French non-ferrous metals company reached an agreement in the mid 1970s to avoid duplicating irreversible capacity investments in Italy, thereby rationalizing production capacity between them. Production economies of scale and learning can also be reached by such simple co-operative agreements as long term purchase contracts. The longer the term of the contract, the more extensive will be the learning induced cost reductions for the supplier. One of the automobile companies interviewed was making a special attempt to reduce its purchased parts cost through concentrating contracts on fewer suppliers, with longer production runs resulting.

Another motive for entering a co-operative agreement is *risk sharing*. In this type of agreement one of the partners is responsible for the project, while the others contribute only capital. Ten of the seventy agreements studied were risk sharing: six of these risk sharing projects were in the oil refining industry.

In our interviews with senior executives of European firms, a number of important points were made that do not lend themselves to the classification in Table II. These are essentially strategic aspects that managers consider when deciding whether or not to engage in a co-operative agreement, and in deciding on the form of the agreement. For example, large defense firms may not prefer to develop weapons systems through technological complementarity co-operative agreements with foreign firms, but strategic considerations dictate they do so since the purchaser (e.g. NATO) prefers it. One acknowledged side benefit is that there are then fewer competitors (they are part of the co-operative agreement) when the weapons system is marketed in other countries.

Strategic considerations also modify the speed or pace with which firms enter into agreements. If the industry is highly concentrated, there will be a limited number of potential partners for production rationalization agreements, and firms will reach agreements earlier than otherwise would be the case for fear of being left out in the future. Firms interviewed in the automobile industry indicated that this was an important factor. If, however, there are a large number of firms, such as in small computers or basic metals, this factor is much less important.

Firms are also careful in reaching agreements that the product of the agreement doesn't harm their own position: two examples will illustrate the point. When metals companies build plants in less developed countries, the new firm (even if partly owned by the original metals company) may export its low cost product back into the country that originated the plant, thereby harming its parents. Also when Renault agreed to allow Talbot (a Citroen–Peugeot subsidiary) to use its superior engine, the overall acceptance of the Talbot was considerably enhanced, thereby harming Renault. As might be expected, firms attempt to reduce these types of risks through restrictive clauses in the agreements and careful preagreement planning.

Other factors can also cause firms to seek out partners for co-operative agreements. For example, Nissan Motors agreed to co-operate with Alfa Romeo only after being thwarted by prohibitive quotas in its attempts to import automobiles into Italy. The only way that non-EEC firms can enter the Italian automobile market is through such agreements. Another factor is at work causing an increased use of co-operative agreements in the consumer electronics market, in that market worldwide competition is putting intense pressure on firms to reduce costs. These firms are attempting to reduce costs through the economies of scale benefits of large output and the learning by doing benefits of longer production runs. In order to sell the large volume of products required to reap these benefits, consumer electronics firms are making numerous marketing co-operative agreements.

VI. TRENDS IN THE USE OF CO-OPERATIVE AGREEMENTS

It is difficult to establish for certain whether there is a trend in the use of co-operative agreements among firms because no institution has collected data for a sufficient period of time. The discussion in this section should therefore be viewed as somewhat tentative, since it is not based on hard data but rather on interviews with senior managers in European firms.

Most managers felt that competition had increased markedly in their industry in the last ten years. In autos and basic metals this increase in competition is due to a drop in the annual real growth rate of demand in the industry from 5–6% to 2–3%. This decrease in the real growth rate makes substantial individual firm growth more difficult without an increase in the firm's market share. Managers in these industries felt that the pace of battles for market share had increased. In the automobile industry the form of competition has shifted (probably as a result of the Japanese influence) from styling and the number of different models toward price (and thus cost) competition. Finally, the improvement in worldwide communications has increased international competition. All these factors together have increased pressures on firms to minimize costs. In the past, cost minimization was necessary for profit maximization (as always), but not for survival. Now cost minimization is necessary for survival. Since co-operative agreements appear to allow a reduction in costs without the disadvantagous side effects of mergers, it is not surprising that the managers interviewed reported that their use has increased markedly in the last 15 years. As can be seen from Table II, the auto industry engages heavily in agreements motivated by economies of scale.

But if co-operative agreements do allow reductions in costs, why were they not in use as much 15 years ago as they are today? Is it possible that firms were indeed not minimizing costs in the past? (It does not appear that much in the technology of auto production has changed, so these agreements would probably have reduced costs 15 years ago just as they do now). At least two hypotheses are possible: firms were not minimizing costs in the past. It has taken the increased competition resulting from decreases in demand growth (and fears for survival) to push firms into a full cost minimization mode. Alternatively, when demand was growing rapidly, the best (most profitable) use of management's scarce time was in serving the growing market and expanding output, not in minimizing costs through co-operative agreements. Indeed, one auto industry manager said that reaching an agreement like those in effect now would have been impossible 15 years ago: there were no interested partners. Every firm was too busy building up its own capacity.

The reasons for the increasing trend in basic metals and computers are similar to autos, but have some aspects of their own. In metals, there were major investments made in the late 1940s which were due for replacement in the mid 1970s. As the firms considered replacing entire plants with essentially irreversible costly facilities, it occurred to them to limit industry excess capacity through co-operative agreements.

In computers the reasons for the increased use of co-operative agreements include the speed of technological development and the fact that many innovations come from firms with no marketing experience. It is marketing agreements to solve these problems that are providing the trend in computers and other high technology industries. (See Table II).

Finally, managers in the defense industry felt that there is no trend in that industry. Co-operative agreements have been used extensively for the past 15–20 years.

VII. PUBLIC POLICY TOWARDS CO-OPERATIVE AGREEMENTS

Public policy can affect the rate at which co-operative agreements are reached in several ways. Specific agreements can be prevented through anti-trust policy, while a general atmosphere toward agreements of all types can be provided by government through various means discussed below. While policy toward any particular agreement should only be developed through an analysis of the details of that agreement, some things can be said at a general level about all co-operative agreements, and some comments can be made about the desirability of different types of agreements.

By their nature as a relatively long term accord between firms, co-operative agreements usually exclude other firms from doing business with the parties to the agreement. If firm *A* agrees to work with firm *B* to develop new products in a particular industry, co-operation or individual transactions between other firms and firms *A* and *B* is precluded. If firm *C* agrees to purchase all future electronic instrumentation for its automobiles from firm *D*, other makers of instrumentation are precluded from supplying parts to firm *C*. As a result, competition is lessened. On the other hand, competition can be enhanced by co-operative agreements. Competition for partners for co-operative agreements is usually much more intense than is the usual competition in shorter term or individual transactions. So the effect of co-operative agreements on competition is mixed.

The one thing that is clear is that the increased use of co-operative agreements will change the process of competition. Competition for partners to a long term co-operative agreement involves more negotiation, more search, and more consideration of the internal versus external production (make vs. buy) type of decision than will individual transactions of the more traditional type.

Some comments can be made only about certain types of agreements: consider first horizontal production rationalization or economies of scale and learning agreements. If successful, these agreements will generally increase minimum efficient scale and will always reduce unit costs. Both factors will make future entry less likely since the new entrant will then be forced to enter at a larger scale (with higher capital costs) or enter only after reaching a co-operative agreement of its own. (Concluding co-operative agreements *before* entering an industry will be difficult, if not impossible.) It is difficult, however, seriously to challenge co-operative agreements because they reduce costs and increase minimum efficient scale: to do so and to be consistent we would need also to oppose nearly all technological progress.

Horizontal agreements to exploit scale economies may decrease the number of competitors if both firms cease production of their independently produced products. As a result, competition may be less intense. Again, however, the picture is not so simple. Co-operative agreements may be the only way that a firm can enter the market: e.g. Nissan was denied entry into the Italian auto market and could enter only through an agreement with Alfa Romeo. Or one or both firms may have failed if the co-operative agreement had not taken place, opening the possibility that an agreement may actually increase the number of firms and thus competition. Finally, two firms may co-operate to enter a new industry when, without the advantages yielded by this co-operation, they would not have entered for economic reasons. Again, competition can be enhanced by this type of co-operation.

All co-operative agreements require the establishment of interorganizational linkages; e.g. between the production departments. These linkages, as well as the cordial atmosphere that prevails between partners may preclude vigorous competition between the partners on other products or after the agreement has ended. Mead [8] found that oil firms which enter into joint venture bids for oil leases are less likely to compete for future leases. Collusion and cartellization are also facilitated by the communication taking place as a result of horizontal co-operative agreements.

Horizontal co-operative agreements should be especially suspect in concentrated industries for two reasons. The removal of competition through a horizontal agreement will be more damaging the fewer the number of competitors that remain. Also, firms in a more concentrated industry are more likely to be large, and thus able internally to take advantage of the benefits of economies of scale and learning that horizontal co-operative agreements offer.

Turning to co-operative agreements for the purpose of utilizing established marketing distribution networks for small firms which develop new products, we must be careful to specify the alternative to such an agreement. When a small firm makes a technological breakthrough, it faces three alternatives in bringing the new product to market. It can develop a distribution network itself, which can be costly or infeasible in well-developed markets characterized by intense rivalry. Alternatively, it can sell the patent (or the entire firm) to a larger firm which does possess the required distribution network. Finally, the firm with the new product can reach a co-operative agreement with a firm which has a well-developed marketing/distribution network. Although an analysis of the effect of each mode on competition is difficult without details of the specific situation, we would expect *a priori* that a co-operative agreement would be more pro competitive than the sale of the firm, at least to the extent that the smaller innovative firm continues to exist as a potential competitor.

Public policy recommendations for co-operative agreements which involve technological exchange are very complex: again, a major consideration is what institutional or competitive arrangement would exist in the absence of the co-operative agreement. One can always say that the existence of a co-operative agreement will reduce duplicative research and development expenditures which would otherwise be made by the partners. Technological transfer agreements increase the market for innovations, and thus increase the reward to the provision of information. Since information is a public good, increasing the rewards to the production of information through co-operative agreements has a beneficial social impact. When each of two or more firms contributes some knowledge or innovation as in a technological complementarity agreement, the resulting final product will generally be produced at lower cost and more quickly than in the absence of an agreement.

But the reduction in duplication of research and development expenditures may have negative side effects. One of the main benefits of a market system for producing innovation is that many different approaches are taken to the solution of important research and development problems: co-operative agreements for the exchange of information necessarily reduce the number of such duplicate approaches. Also, co-operative agreements for the purpose of knowledge exchange obviously foreclose firms who are not members of the agreement from some segment of the market for the period of the agreement. If the agreement is only for the purpose of a single project, such as the bidding consortiums reported in Table II, this foreclosure will almost never be a problem. However, several French automobile electronics producers do have reason to complain over the fact that they are now foreclosed from selling to the two leading French automobile manufacturers for a period of many years.

Finally, managers of small firms in the computer industry complain of a sort of predatory behaviour on the part of large computer firms. They stated that some time after they had signed long term licensing agreements, and ceased a portion of their own research and development activities as a result, the larger licensing firm (usually American) would bring out a superior product, and refuse to license this product to the smaller firm. In some cases the smaller firm can be forced out of business as a result of being denied access to the improved technology while at the same time being limited to inferior technology by the long term co-operative agreement.

VIII. SOME FINAL REMARKS

The field of study of co-operative agreements between firms seems a very promising one. It has been neglected in the literature of industrial organization in the past, with the possible exceptions of research on joint ventures (see Berg and Friedman [4] and vertical integration (see Blois [5]). One reason for such lack of attention may be traced to a tendency to look at industrial organization in terms of a sharp dichotomy between markets and individual transactions on one side, and conscious planning within the firm on the other; the great variety of forms co-operative agreements can take may also have discouraged research.

Co-operative agreements appear as an intermediate form for both resource allocation and firms' activities organization. As an alternative to the firm as a managed (co-ordinated) system, they seem to require an extension of the boundary of firms and a reconsideration of the firm as an integrating device. As an alternative to the market, they seem to serve to compensate for failure or limitation of markets, though each agreement is likely to involve transaction costs of its own.

The final impact of co-operative agreements on competition is somewhat mixed, especially if one thinks of competition as a short run, deterministic principle of social organization and not as a long run process. One could also argue that co-operative agreements reduce the importance of price in the bargaining mix, thereby changing the mode of competition. Many co-operative agreements resemble barter in that no funds change hands between the partners.

ACCEPTED DECEMBER 1981

P. Mariti,
University of Pisa,
Faculty of Political Science,
Via Serafini 3, 56100 Pisa.

R. H. Smiley,
Graduate School of Business and Public Administration,
Cornell University,
Malott Hall, Ithaca, New York, 14853.

REFERENCES

[1] Andrews, P. W., "Industrial Economics as a Specialist Subject," *Journal of Industrial Economics*, Vol. I, No. 1, (November 1952), pp. 72–79.
[2] Arrow, K. J., "The Organization of Economic Activity: Issues Pertinent to the Choice of Market versus Nonmarket Allocation," in *The Analysis and Evaluation of Public Expenditures: The PPB System*, Vol. 1, No. 1, pp. 47–64 (Joint Economic Committee, Washington, D.C., 1969).
[3] Baumol, W. J. and Fischer, D., "The Cost Minimizing Number of Firms and the Determination of Industry Structure," *Quarterly Journal of Economics*, Vol. XCII, No. 3, (Aug. 1978), pp. 439–68.
[4] Berg, S. V. and Friedman, P., "Technological Complementarities and Industrial Patterns of Joint Venture Activity, 1964–1975," *Industrial Organization Review*, Vol. 6, 1978, pp. 110–16.
[5] Blois, K. J., "Vertical Quasi-Integration," *Journal of Industrial Economics*, Vol. XX, No. 3, (July 1972), pp. 253–72.
[6] Coase, R., "The Nature of the Firm," *Economica*, Vol. IV, No. 16, (November 1937), pp. 386–405.
[7] Mariti, P., "Sui Rapporti tra Imprese in una Economia Industriale Moderna," *Franco Angeli*, Milano, 1980.
[8] Mead, W. J., "The Competitive Significance of Joint Ventures," Antitrust Bulletin, Vol. XII, (Fall, 1967), pp. 819–49.
[9] Richardson, G. B., "The Organisation of Industry," *Economic Journal*, Vol. 82, No. 327, (September 1972), pp. 883–96.
[10] Stigler, G. J., "The Division of Labour is Limited by the Extent of the Market," *Journal of Political Economy*, Vol. LIX, No. 3, (June 1951), pp. 185–93.
[11] Williamson, O. E., "*Market and Hierarchies: Analysis and Antitrust Implications*," (The Free Press, London, 1975).
[12] ——, "Transaction—Cost Economics: the Governance of Contractual Relations," *Journal of Law and Economics*, Vol. XXII, No. 2, (October 1979), pp. 233–61.

THE JOURNAL OF INDUSTRIAL ECONOMICS
Volume XXXI June 1983 No. 4

THE IMPACT OF JOINT VENTURES ON THE MARKET FOR OCS OIL AND GAS LEASES

ALAN ROCKWOOD*

I. INTRODUCTION

The OCS Lands Act Amendments of 1978 stipulated that the Secretary of the Interior offer at least 20 percent of the offshore oil and gas leases through alternative bidding systems to the cash-bonus method. The requirement was motivated by the belief that the alternative systems would enable more independent firms to participate in the OCS lease sales [12]. This belief is based on the assumption that capital markets are incapable of efficiently supplying funds for oil and gas exploration. Smaller firms which are more sensitive to the external capital market are deterred from entering the lease sales. Those that do successfully bid are drained of their financial resources and must delay exploration. Further, exploration firms require a higher rate of return on their investment, leading to lower cash bonuses.

Recently, a federal appeals court ruled in favor of a suit brought by the Energy Action Education Foundation to prohibit further leases sales until all bidding options set forth in the 1978 OCS Lands Act Amendment are available for use. The Energy Action Education Foundation had complained that the widespread use of the cash-bonus system had failed to yield the government a fair market value for the leases [2]. In addition, there has been recent political pressure to extend the ban on joint bidding to the sixteen largest U.S. oil and gas firms. However, the present administration's drive to accelerate the pace of OCS leasing could very well increase the industry's demand for joint ventures. Thus, a fresh look at the actual performance of past joint bidding practices seems particularly relevant at this time.

Concerns about small firm participation are, of course, not without foundation. The initial capital requirement for participating in the OCS market is very substantial and places a potential barrier. Average winning bids in the established areas of offshore Louisiana and Texas are in the range of $2000 to $10,000 per acre or $10 to $50 million per tract. In a recent Gulf of Mexico sale, a consortium of Superior Oil Company, Pennzoil

* This paper, taken from a Ph.D. dissertation at Washington University, was presented in an earlier form in the Center for the Study of American Business Regulatory Workshop. Financial assistance from the Center, the Earhart Foundation, and the U.S. Geological Survey is gratefully acknowledged, although the views expressed in this paper are those of the author. The author is grateful to Frederick R. Warren-Boulton, Edward Greenberg, and Murray L. Weidenbaum for helpful discussions and comments.

Company and Standard Oil of Ohic submitted a record bid of $52,457.81 per acre [1]. In addition, the average cost of a completed well in the Gulf of Mexico was in excess of four million dollars.[1] Joint ventures provide a vehicle for sharing the financial burden and risks of these investments. Joint bidding agreements thus represent an intermediate step between diversification by firms and diversification by investors, and probably involve lower transaction costs than diversification by investors.

Not all analysts of the industry have condoned the extensive use of joint ventures by exploration firms. They point to the potential abuse of the institution and the opportunities for collusion. Critics of joint ventures maintain that the typical firm in the offshore market is sufficiently large not to need further diversification, that the motives of these firms are anti-competitive, and that the creation of joint ventures reduces the number of independent agents to the point that collusion is sustainable. Collusion could be present in both the market for federal leases and the market for crude oil. In the market for oil and gas leases the incentive to create a monopsony (i.e., a single buyer) would be especially strong in an effort to capture a portion of the land rents. It is further argued that combines of competitors in the downstream markets will discourage independent actions and will provide the means for coordinating output restrictions. In an environment dominated by vertically integrated firms, joint ventures could enhance the position of these firms by further foreclosure of the raw feed stocks.

Contrary to popular opinion, the U.S. petroleum industry is not especially concentrated. However, the pervasive influence of interfirm associations could provide the means to maintain oligopolistic discipline. For example, Wilson [17] suggests that joint ventures, taken together with other interfirm associations such as interlocking directorates, provide the collusive fabric in the industry. The critics of the petroleum industry discount arguments based upon the traditional structural measures of market power, such as concentration ratios.

Specifically, criticisms of the use of joint ventures in acquiring oil and gas leases have followed two lines. First, it has been suggested that joint bidding has facilitated both monopsony and monopoly power: monopsony power by reducing the number of bidders in the sales and/or providing the opportunity for collusion; and monopoly power by joint ownership of leases. The second criticism has been that the process of forming the bidding combines gives a few firms strategic information on the bidding plans of other firms [5]. This information may have enabled them to obtain certain leases for less than their competitive values. The first of these hypotheses, monopsony power, will be discussed in this paper.[2]

[1] Joint Association Survey of the U.S. Oil and Gas Producing Industry 1981, Section I Drilling Costs, American Petroleum Institute, Independent Petroleum Association of America and Mid-Continental Oil and Gas Association. This figure is an average of all wells drilled. Exploratory wells tend to be much more costly because they are drilled by mobile rigs.

[2] For a discussion of the second criticism, see Rockwood [14].

The role of joint ventures in the petroleum industry has become a point of debate among industrial organization economists. The debate has prompted some authors to write: "Few practices in the oil industry have given rise to so much criticism, and so little research, as the widespread formation of joint ventures" [7]. While research on the topic is expanding, the conclusions drawn are often quite divergent, as exemplified by the following statement:

> These data are a very strong indication that offshore activity is undertaken in a very competitive economic environment [4].

> The empirical results of Wilson's [17] study lead overwhelmingly to the conclusion that the petroleum industry is not workably competitive [15].

One of the common problems of most of the previous studies has been their preoccupation with the structure of the market itself, rather than a focusing on formulating direct tests of the market's performance.

The analyst who has devoted the most effort to a study of the market for OCS oil and gas leases is Walter Mead. He has completed two studies of the subject separated by more than a decade [10] [11]. Mead's original study examined the bidding behavior of former joint venture partners and found evidence that led him to conclude that joint bidding could result in less direct competition by those firms. In Mead's later study with Sorenson [11], no evidence was found to support an anticompetitive hypothesis of joint bidding.

Markham [9] examined four hypotheses related to impact of joint bidding on the number of bidders, the size of distribution of bidders, revenues received by the government, and the industry's rate of return. Although Markham's empirical results consistently rejected anti-competitive hypothesis of joint ventures, his findings were not highly significant. Wilson [17] examined the incidence of joint bidding by firm size. Finding that the rate of submitting joint bids did not decline proportionately with increase in the size of the firm, Wilson concluded that firms have an anticompetitive motive in forming bidding groups. Erickson and Spann [4] investigated the distribution of successful bids by major firms (eight largest) and independent firms. They observed that almost half the winning bids, both joint and solo, came from the independent firms and that the share of non-major firms had been increasing in recent years. Erikson and Spann also noted that the rate of return on OCS properties are relatively low and thus concluded that the market is workably competitive.

II. MODELING PERFORMANCE

The approach taken in this investigation is to test the direct impact of joint bidding on the performance of the offshore segment of the industry. The hypothesis that extensive joint ventures for exploring and developing petroleum prospects increases the market power of the firms in the industry can be tested by estimating the expected cash bonuses bid for OCS tracts, while controlling for the concentration of joint bids. If joint ventures are anti-competitive, then cash bonuses should decrease as the concentration of joint bids increases. The data from federal OCS oil and gas lease sales provide an excellent sample for measuring the effects of joint bidding because there has been a wide variation of the use of this form of bidding over time and across different OCS areas.

Several analysts have worked on the questions of whether there is an optimal bidding strategy and what determines the strategy.[3] The foundation of the bidding strategy models has been either the maximization of the expected value (profit) of bidding or the expected utility of bidding. For an optimum bidding strategy to exist, it is necessary to assume that firms can ascribe a probability distribution to the highest competing bid and know the number of competitors for the tract. Much of the empirical work stemming from the optimal strategy literature has utilized simulation techniques. However, a simulation model cannot evaluate the impact of such structural characteristics as joint ventures. Thus a stochastic specification of the bid equation is developed below.

The bidding system employed by the Department of the Interior over the period studied is for an initial cash bonus after a fixed production royalty has been set. Under this system the cash bonus is supposed to capture the economic rent for the federal government. The highest bonus bid (B) is determined by three sets of factors: the gross value of the tract (V), the proportions of that value which are rents (k) and strategic or market factors (m).

$$B = V \cdot k \cdot m \tag{1}$$

In turn these factors are functions of observable variables. These relationships are defined in Equations (2) through (4).

$$V = f(P, Q) \tag{2}$$

$$k = g(D, W, t, Q) \tag{3}$$

$$m = h(N, JV, U) \tag{4}$$

In equation (2) the gross value of a tract is defined to be a function of the current price (P) and the quantity (Q). The rent factor is determined by the costs of operating in the area. The costs are a function of the depth of the formation (D) and the depth of the water at the prospect (W). Theory suggests that the proportion of output going to the "land" will not be constant over time, thus a time variable (t) is included. Time will capture expected changes in the net price of the resource. The market factor (4),

[3] The interested reader should see Reece [12] or Brown [3].

is a function of a number of variables including: the number of bidders (N), the concentration of joint venture bids (JV), and the uncertainty surrounding the information on the tract (U).

The observable cash bonus paid for a tract is then the product of the function $f(\cdot)$, $g(\cdot)$ and $h(\cdot)$ and an error term (e). Because we have assumed these factors to be multiplicative, the equation should be linear in the natural logarithm of its arguments. The resulting estimatable function is given in Equation (5).

$$\ln B = \ln[a + b + c] + \beta_1 \ln P + \beta_2 \ln Q + \beta_3 t + \beta_4 \ln D + \beta_5 \ln W + \beta_6 \ln N + \beta_7 JV + \beta_8 U + e \tag{5}$$

$$\beta_1 \beta_2 \beta_3 \beta_6 > 0$$

$$\beta_4 \beta_5 \beta_8 < 0$$

$$\beta_7 \lesseqgtr 0$$

In this case, the observational unit chosen can be critical to the power of the test for anticompetitive impacts of joint bidding. If joint ventures enhance the industry's ability collusively to set the bonuses paid for offshore prospects, then the relationship between the joint ventures and the bonus can be obscured by observing individual tracts. Suppose that by forming bidding combines the number of potential independent bidders is reduced to two solo firms and two combines, a sufficiently small number to enforce collusive bids. Then suppose three tracts are sold in an area, each receives two bids. Observing the individual tract the concentration of joint bids can vary from 0 to 100 percent. In each case the bid was reduced by collusion, but its relation to joint ventures is unobserved. The dummy variable for leases won by joint ventures would not identify the impact of joint bidding.

The more appropriate observational unit for measuring the influence of joint ventures is an OCS area. At this level of observation in the case above, 50 percent of the bids were from joint ventures. The concentration of joint ventures is a measure which can better capture changes in the incidence of joint bidding. Therefore, an OCS area seems to be the relevant market, since it is large enough to cover several reservoirs and small enough such that their expected outcomes may be related. The grouping of observation will induce heteroscedasticity. The regressions thus are fitted to the grouped data with the necessary statistical corrections for heteroscedasticity as suggested by Johnston [8].

As mentioned previously, the primary hypothesis to be tested is that the increased use of joint ventures has given market power to firms in the offshore industry, leading to an oligopsony (i.e., few buyers) in the market for new prospects. Support for this hypothesis would be evidenced in the model by a negative coefficient on measures of the joint venture concentration. The alternative hypothesis is that joint ventures aid firms in diversifying risks more efficiently than investors can in the capital market, and that they also provide each participant with direct information on the area while requiring only a partial financial obligation. These conditions would tend to increase the amounts bid for leases. Also, if the joint evaluation of the prospects gives the consortium participants greater confidence in their estimated value, then an increase in the bonuses bid would result. Thus the alternative hypothesis would be supported by a positive coefficient for the joint bidding variables.

The estimation of this model will provide other indications of the competitiveness of the market for OCS tracts. In the theoretical models of bidding strategies, the expected number of bidders is an important determinant of the bonus bid. If the bids are being determined by collusive agreements, then the number of bidders will have little or no correlation with the high bid. Thus an insignificant coefficient on the number of competing bids would be consistent with the anticompetitive hypothesis.

Description of the Data and Variables Constructed

The data on cash bonuses bid for leases, on bidding combines, and on the number of bidders came from the U.S. Geological Survey's records on the OCS lease sales. The observations included in the study came from offshore Louisiana, Texas and California.

Each observation is the mean winning bid in an OCS area on a given date. There are 166 observations with complete information. The number of observations per time period ranged between 2 and 58. The validity of pooling observations from Texas and Louisiana area was confirmed.[4] Tracts for which the bids were rejected by the Department of the Interior were not included in the data set.

The variables which measure the expected gross value of the tracts include the quantity of petroleum produced (Q) and the price of the output (P). Because it is impossible to observe the firm's pre-sale expectations of oil and gas deposits, it is necessary to develop an instrumental variable. To do this, all revenues, exclusive of the bonus received by the government from each tract, are summed and ranked for all tracts sold in a given year. The price variables are wellhead oil and gas prices prevailing in the state.[5]

To determine the proportion of the gross value accruing to land, it is necessary to control for the costs of drilling the developing the tracts. As previously mentioned, the physical factors which are most important in

[4] A "Chow" test was constructed for the Texas and Louisiana areas. The resulting F-statistic was 0.358, confirming the hypothesis that the model's coefficients are the same across those states. There were insufficient observations from the California areas to test the validity of pooling California and Gulf of Mexico data. Because California was comparable to Gulf sales in terms of the number and types of bidder's California was included.

[5] The source of the data is the U.S. Bureau of Mines (Minerals Yearbook Vol. 1 Metals, Minerals and Fuels).

determining costs are the water depth (*W*) and the depth of the formation (*D*).[6] Since the proportion of the gross value accruing to land rents may not be constant over time, a variable was included to account for the number of years (*YR*) since the original sale in 1954.

The variables which should influence a firm's bidding strategy include the number of expected competing bids (*BD*), the concentration of joint ventures, and measures of the certainty of the information on the tracts (*U*). The concentration of joint bids from the largest eight firms (*JV*8) is measured by the proportion of successful bids for all tracts in an OCS area that were joint ventures having at least one of the eight largest firms as a member of the combine. The overall joint venture concentration variable (*JV*) is the proportion of all bids submitted (whether successful or not) which came from a combine of two or more firms. The distribution of actual bids was assumed to describe the distribution of expected values. The variables used in the regressions are summarized in Table I.

Empirical Results

In the four specifications of the model shown in Table II, measures of the concentration of joint ventures display a consistent and highly significant positive relationship to the cash bonus for oil and gas leases. This is clear evidence in support of the efficiency hypothesis of joint ventures.

The results of the joint venture variables are strengthened by the overall performance of the model. For example, in equation (2) all of the coefficients have the expected sign and are statistically significant at the 1 percent level except for the coefficient of variation.[7]

Equations (1) and (2) in Table II are designed to show the influence of a time variable. Allowing the rent component to vary with time improves the predictive power of the model and alters certain coefficients in a predictable way. The price elasticity (*LNP* in Table II) is reduced from approximately 2 to 1. With the inclusion of the time variable, the price coefficient no longer includes expected future net price changes. A coefficient of one implies that a ten-percent increase in output prices will *ceteris paribus* result in a ten percent increase in rents.

In the specifications shown in Table II, the coefficient estimates are 0.070 and 0.077. In Table III the coefficient estimates on time are 0.068 and 0.081. Together these estimates from alternative specifications imply that the rents on petroleum lands were increasing at a rate of 6.8 to 8.1 percent

[6] The average water depth in fathoms of an OCS area is taken from U.S. Geological Survey Maps. The drilling depth is an average for offshore wells drilled in the state for the year following the lease sale taken from the *Joint Association Survey of Drilling Costs*.

[7] The insignificance of the dispersion variable may be due to several factors. First, our estimated coefficient may be a poor measure for the dispersion of the expected tract value. Second, multicolinearity with the number of bidders may reduce the *t*-statistic. The final explanation is that bidders are able to diversify risks to the point that they are risk-neutral.

TABLE I
SUMMARY OF INDEPENDENT VARIABLES[a]

Variable	*Symbol*	*Description*
Quantity	*Q*	Because the expected volume of petroleum deposits cannot be observed, a proxy variable was created. It is the rank of the tracts sold in a given year based on the revenues received, exclusive of bonus, by the government. Computed from U.S.G.S. LPR-10.
Price	*P*	Average of the wellhead value of natural gas and the well-head value of crude oil by state and by year. Source: U.S. Bureau of Mines.
Drilling Depth	*D*	Average well depth for dry holes drilled offshore by state, lagged one period from the lease data. Source: Joint Association Survey of Drilling Costs, 1955–75.
Water Depth	*W*	Average water depth in fathoms for each OCS area. Source: U.S. Geological Survey Bathometric Maps.
Time	*YR*	Computed as the year of lease sale less 1954.
Number of Bids	*BD*	Number of bids submitted for the tract. Source: U.S.G.S., LPR-5.
Skew of Bonus Bids	*SK*	Skewness of the distribution of bonus bids received on a tract. Source: computed from U.S.G.S., LPR-5.
Coefficient of Variance	*CV*	Coefficient of variation of the distribution of bonus bids received on a tract. Source: computed from U.S.G.S., LPR-5.
Bidder Size	*FX*	Value of a firm's oil and gas production divided by the value of the average output of firms ranked between 20 and 26. The index was summed for all firms in a joint bidding group. Firms smaller than the 26th largest firm were arbitrarily given a value of (0.5). Source: Mullholland and Webbink, U.S.FTC.
Joint Venture	*JV*	Proportion of all bids submitted in an OCS area on the sale data that were joint ventures. Source: computed from U.S.G.S., LPR-5.
Joint Venture with firm ranked in the top eight.	*JV*8	Proportion of successful bids submitted in an OCS area on the sale date by joint ventures with at least one of the eight largest firms. Source: computed from U.S.G.S., LPR-5.
Joint Venture without a firm ranked in the top eight	*JVI*	Proportion of successful bids submitted in an OCS area on the sale date by joint ventures without any of the eight largest firms. Source: computed from U.S.G.S., LPR-5.

[a] To capture the uncertainty associated with the bid values, the coefficient of variation of the bids was used to measure the dispersion of values (*CV*). The skewness of the distribution was included to test for sensitvity to potential asymmetry in the value (*SK*). To construct these variables for each tract, it was necessary to assume that at least three bidders seriously considered each tract. If fewer than three bids were actually made, then it was assumed one or two other firms bid zero.

TABLE II
REGRESSION RESULTS: ESTIMATED WINNING CASH BONUS DEPENDENT VARIABLE: LOG BONUS ($N = 166$)

	1	*2*	*3*
Intercept	39.884	33.581	33.36
LNQ	0.212	0.308	0.522
	(2.21)	(3.74)	(5.81)
LNP[a]	2.048	0.998	0.674
	(13.64)	(5.44)	(3.19)
LNW	0.016	−0.139	−0.144
	(0.23)	(2.30)	(2.04)
LND	−3.240	−2.577	−1.327
	(8.806)	(7.98)	(3.36)
YR		0.077	0.070
		(7.94)	(5.73)
LNBD	1.693	1.416	
	(10.95)	(10.45)	
SK			0.517
			(3.80)
LNCV	0.039	0.125	−2.28
	(0.11)	(0.43)	(7.71)
JV			1.572
			(5.42)
JV8	2.247	1.847	
	(5.01)	(4.82)	
R^2	0.846	0.890	0.851

(t-statistics are given in parentheses).

[a] The price variable used in these equations is the average of the crude oil and natural gas wellhead prices. Interpretation of the results was very difficult when each price was entered separately because of the colinearity between the prices. Constraining the bidding response to be equal for changes in either price does not appear unreasonable. The weights assigned each price were varied in alternative regressions until it was determined that the simple average of the two had slightly more explanatory power than other weights. The same composite price was used in all reported regressions.

per annum. This conforms with the theory of natural resource exhaustion. For the efficient allocation of exhaustible resources over time, the net price (output price less extraction costs) must rise at a rate equal to the rate of return on alternative investments of similar riskiness which could be made by the resource holder (Hotelling, 1931 [6]). To cite perhaps the closest alternative investment, over the 1965–70 period the rate of return on total assets by the 30 largest oil companies ranged from 6.2% average to 7.6% per annum. The coefficient estimates on time thus provide a unique confirmation of the Hotelling exhaustible resources model, as well as support for the efficient market hypothesis which is assumed by this model. Increasing

TABLE III
REGRESSION RESULTS: ESTIMATED WINNING CASH BONUS
DEPENDENT VARIABLE: LOG CASH BONUS

	1	*2*
Intercept	31.130	31.264
LNQ	0.358	0.274
	(4.44)	(3.59)
LNP	0.987	0.905
	(5.18)	(4.89)
LNW	−0.127	−0.127
	(2.10)	(2.25)
LND	−2.274	−2.239
	(6.86)	(6.68)
YR	0.081	0.068
	(8.13)	(6.80)
LNBD		1.210
		(12.11)
BD	0.671	
	(9.65)	
BSQ	−0.038	
	(6.10)	
FX		0.025
		(1.81)
JV	0.602	
	(5.01)	
JVI		0.761
		(2.70)
JV8		1.346
		(3.07)
D60		0.421
		(3.29)
R^2	0.889	0.907

(*t*-statistics are given in parentheses)

familiarity with the leasing procedure and experience in offshore operations could also be reflected in the time trend.

In Table III two other specifications are shown. Equation (1) estimates the relative magnitude of joint bids and solo bids. Even though joint venture concentration has a positive impact upon the bonuses received by the government, bonus revenues still could be increased by prohibiting certain joint ventures. If joint venture bids by some firms are purely substitutes for solo bids, then an increase in expected competition could alter the firms' strategies such that overall bids would increase. The number of actual bids is entered in arithmetic form (*BD*) and the square of the number of bidders (*BSQ*) is also included to measure nonlinear effects. The number of the largest eight firms bidding in combines is then entered (*JV*8). The coefficients on the number of bids and joint concentration variables are thus directly comparable.

The regression results indicate that the expected bonus paid would not be increased by banning the largest eight firms from entering bidding combines. Given the relative magnitude of the three coefficients *BD* (0.671), *BSQ* (−0.038) and *JV*8 (0.602) and the mean number of bidders (3.5), receiving one more bid would increase the cash bonus by 0.365 percent, yet this would be more than offset by the reduction in big eight joint ventures (0.6 percent).[8]

Another way of testing the effect of firms bidding through combines which might otherwise place solo bids is to separate the joint ventures measure into two groups. In this way the impact of joint bids from combines with a "big-eight" firm (*JV*8) can be estimated simultaneously with a measure of joint bids from smaller firms (*JVI*). Equation (2) in Table III shows the results. The coefficient on *JV*8 is larger than the coefficient on *JVI*, however the difference is not significant at a reasonable confidence level.[9] After controlling for all other factors, it appears that an increase in the use of joint ventures by either group of firms will increase the expected bid by the same amount.

Equation (2) in Table III also tests for the impact of firm size (*FX*), as measured by petroleum production, on the bonus bids. If firms engage in exploration in proportion to their current production, then a measure of the output would capture the firms' ability to diversify into several prospects.[10] The coefficient on the size variable is positive. This suggests that, because of their ability to bear risk, larger firms may bid more aggressively for tracts than do smaller firms. However, the coefficient is not statistically significantly different from zero.

The anticompetitive hypothesis of joint ventures could be supported by two other results, the insignificance of the number of bidders and a negative coefficient on the skewness variable. Reviewing all specifications in Tables II and III there is no evidence to support either position. If there is overt collusion among bidders, then the high bid will be determined by the amount of the anticipated reservation price for the tract. In this case the number of bids actually received will be incidental to the amount paid and will not be expected to have a great impact on the high bid.

[8] A dummy variable was introduced for the lease sale held in 1960 to capture the effect due to scarcity of prospects available. It had been five years since the last OCS offerings, and exploratory drilling in the U.S. was declining rapidly indicating an absence of acceptable prospects. Also, the earlier lease sales may have been a significant learning experience for the industry. As expected, *D*60 is positive and significant.

[9] The F-statistic for a test of the restriction that the two coefficients are equal is 1.66. With 1 and 155 degrees of freedom, there is a 20 percent probability that this difference could occur by chance alone.

[10] The index of the bidder's size (*FX*) was constructed by dividing a firm's production by the average output of firms ranked by production between 20 and 26. This group was selected as numeraire based upon the survivrship analysis. The index for a combine of two or more firms was the sum of the individual's firm's index value. Production volumes were available from the years 1950, 1960, 1965, and 1970 so that the index for intervening years was set equal to the value for the nearest available year.

TABLE IV
STANDARDIZED BETA VALUES FOR BONUS MODEL

Variable	*Std. B.*
LNBD	0.455
YR	0.327
LND	−0.236
LNP	0.203
JV	0.162
LNQ	0.105
FX	0.093
D60	0.088
LNW	−0.068

The estimated elasticity of the cash bonus with respect to the number of bids (*LNBD*) is consistently between 1.081 and 1.693 and its *t*-statistic ranges between 6.37 and 13.93 across all specifications. The importance of the number of bidders in determining the bonus paid for tracts is further demonstrated by the estimated standardized beta coefficients. These are shown in Table IV. The standardized beta coefficients show the relative importance of the independent variables in explaining the variation in the dependent variable. The variable *LNBD* is the most important determinant of the bonus, followed by the year, depth, and output prices. The strong showing of *LNBD* is contrary to the expected result if bonuses are being set collusively.

The test for collusion in the bidding process based upon the skewness variable applies to the particular situation where bidders seek to fix prices on the high value tracts. If this is the case, then the upper end of the distribution of bids would be constrained yielding a negative skew on tracts with a higher value. Where *SK* was entered, there is no evidence to support the hypothesis of collusion on high value tracts. In the specification which excluded the number of bidders. *SK* has a positive coefficient which is significantly different from zero (Equation (3) in Table II).

III. ENDOGENEITY OF JOINT BIDS

It is possible that the concentration of joint ventures in the equations estimated above is endogenous to the bidding process. Two arguments can be advanced as to why the expected level of the winning bonus would influence the concentration of joint ventures. (1) Tracts with large formations and potentially thick sedimentary strata may be easily identified. They attract bidding interest from a wide variety of firms, and thus increase the demand for joint ventures. (2) If bidders are risk averse, then, as the expected winning bid increases, the demand for joint ventures will increase. If either or both of these effects are present, then the explanatory variable (*JV*) is not independent of the error term, violating an assumption of the general linear model. This results in a bias in the coefficient on the joint venture variables.

To test for the potential effect of the bonus size on the level of joint bidding, a two equation model is estimated. One equation estimates the level of the bonus, and the other equation estimates the concentration of joint bids. As before, the bonus is determined by the expected net value of the lease, and the "structure" of the market for the leases. Specific arguments of the bonus equation are the concentration of joint bids in the OCS (*JV*), pre-sale estimated value by the U.S. Geological Survey in log form (*LPRVAL*), the number of competitors (*LNBID*), time elapsed since 1954 (*TR*) and the size of the tract (*LACRE*). The dependent variable, as above is the bonus per acre (*LNBONUS*). The level of joint bidding is determined by the bonus (*LNBONUS*); the amount of information on the area, which is measured by the number of times tracts have been leased in the area before (*TEN*); and the size of the firms bidding (*FSIZE*).[11]

$$(6) \qquad LNBONUS = \gamma_{12} JV + \beta_{10} + \beta_{11} LPRVAL + \beta_{12} LACRE + \beta_{13} YR$$

$$(7) \qquad JV = \gamma_{21} LNBONUS + \beta_{20} + \beta_{24} TEN + \beta_{25} FSIZE$$

The pre-sale value estimates replaced the revenue and cost data in the earlier regressions. The variable *LACRE* was added to test if companies will pay proportionally more for larger tracts, which would be expected if there are informational economies of scale. The new variable, tenure (*TEN*), has been included to measure the level of knowledge about the area (or lack of uncertainty). The supposition is that as the industry's familiarity with an area increases, the uncertainty decreases resulting in a decline in the demand for joint ventures.

The two stage least squares estimates of structural parameters for equations (6) and (7) are shown below. The most significant result of the simultaneous estimation with the bonus equation is the reduction in the size of the coefficient on the joint venture variable (*JV*) from previous OLS (ordinary least squares) estimates. However, from the standpoint of testing the collusion hypothesis of joint ventures, the important result is the direction of the impact.

In the two stage estimates, joint ventures continue to have a significant positive effect on the level of the bonuses received for the leases, which is consistent with the earlier results.

[11] Data used to estimate the simultaneous system of equations are from the U.S.G.S. LPR-10 data base, which is the merged version of LPR-5 and LPR-10. It has been supplemented with the pre-sale estimated tract values available since 1968 and production platform information.

$$LNBONUS = +0.094JV + 9.611 + 1.042LNBID$$
$$\quad\quad (2.11) \quad (7.70) \quad (5.22)$$
$$+ 0.090LPRIVAL$$
$$(4.42)$$
$$+ 0.208LACRE + 0.078YR$$
$$(1.46) \quad\quad (2.19)$$

$$JV = 0.053LNBONUS - 0.133 - 0.006TEN$$
$$(2.55) \quad\quad (0.408) \; (-1.58)$$
$$-0.00003FSIZE$$
$$(-6.02)$$

In addition, the time variable in the bonus equation is significantly different from zero, and the coefficient is of the expected magnitude. This would imply that the U.S. Geological Survey has not been changing the pre-sale value at a rate reflecting the expected net value of the resource. The variable *LACRE* is positive but not significantly different from zero. The coefficient on the pre-sale value is positive and significant; however, it is surprisingly low at 0.09.

In the joint venture equation, the cash bonus (*LHBID*) is positive as expected and significant at the 98 percent confidence level. The uncertainty measure (*TEN*) is not statistically significant, but it does enter the regression with the expected negative sign. The final variable is the asset size of the bidders (*FSIZE*), which has a negative relationship with the concentration of joint bids indicating that larger firms are less prone to bid in joint ventures.

IV. CONCLUSION

It has been shown in this study that the industry's organization is responsive to the peculiarities of the exploration process. Moreover, joint ventures in leasing and exploring oil and gas prospects can offset potential imperfections in the capital markets by substantially diversifying risks at the firm level. This study has further shown that joint ventures have had a significant positive impact on the level of cash-bonuses bid for OCS leases. Thus, joint ventures can offset the potential problems of an imperfect capital market without weakening the competitiveness of the market for leases.

Recently, there has been political pressure to extend the ban on joint bidding to the sixteen largest U.S. oil and gas firms. Based upon the results of this study, this action would seem unwarranted and unwise. While the current ban on joint ventures has likely had only a small effect on the operation of the industry, restricting joint venture formation by the second tier of firms could result in a substantial loss of revenue for the government. This study, taken together with other recent investigations of the OCS leasing march, would also indicate that the cash-bonus system has performed well. Finally, this evidence of good performance by the bidding system, due largely to the significant capabilities of joint ventures in reducing any capital constraint, bodes well for the prospects for accelerated leasing of federal lands.

ALAN D. ROCKWOOD,
Texas Energy and Natural Resources Advisory Council,
200 East 18th Street,
Austin,
Texas, 78701.

ACCEPTED FEBRUARY 1982

REFERENCES

[1] Anonymous, "Gulf Lease Sale Shatters Two Records", *Oil and Gas Journal*, 78 (40) (October 6, 1980), pp. 34–36.

[2] Anonymous, "Court Orders Use of More OCS Bid Systems", *Oil and Gas Journal*, 78 (45) (November 10, 1980), p. 162.

[3] Brown, K. C., "Sealed Bid Auction: A Look at the Whole Elephant." Paper No. 659. Krannert Graduate of Management, Purdue University, West Lafayette, Indiana. (1978).

[4] Erickson, E. W. and R. M. Spann, "The U.S. Petroleum Industry", *The Energy Question: An International Failure of Policy*, Vol. 2. ed. E. W. Erickson and L. Waverman (University of Toronto Press, Toronto, 1974).

[5] Gaskins, Darius W. and Vann Barry, "Joint Buying and the Seller's Return—The Case of OCS Lease Sales", Memo. University of Michigan. (May 1976).

[6] Hotelling, H., "The Economics of Exhaustible Resources", *Journal of Political Economy*, 39 (2), (1931) pp. 137–75.

[7] Johnson, W. A., R. E. Messick, S. Van Vactor and F. R. Wyant, *Competition in the Oil Industry*. Occasional Paper on Energy Policy, Vol. 1. Energy Policy Research Project. George Washington University: Washington, D.C. (1975).

[8] Johnston, J., *Econometric Methods*, 2nd Edition (McGraw-Hill Book Company, New York, 1972) pp. 228–38.

[9] Markham, Jesse W., "The Competitive Effects of Joint Bidding by Oil Companies for Offshore Oil Leases", *Industrial Organization and Economic Development: In Honor of E. S. Mason*. eds. J. W. Markham and G. F. Papanek (Houghton Mifflin, Boston, 1970).

[10] Mead, Walter J., "The Competitive Significance of Joint Ventures", *Antitrust Bulletin*, 12, (1968) pp. 819–49.

[11] Mead, W. J. and P. E. Sorensen, "Competition and Performance in OCS Oil and Gas Lease and Lease Development, 1954–1969." Final Report to U.S. Geological Survey. Reston, Virginia, Contract No. 14-08-0001-16552. (1980).

[12] Reece, D. K., "Competitive Bidding for Offshore Petroleum Leases", *Bell Journal of Economics*, 9 (2), (1978) pp. 369–84.

[13] Rockwood, A. D., J. M. Callaway, R. J. Nesse and S. A. Smith, "Determinants of Investment in the U.S. Petroleum Exploration Industry." Draft Final Report, Pacific Northwest Laboratory PNL-3423, Richland WA. (1981).

[14] Rockwood, A. D., Information Externalities and the Structure of the U.S. Petroleum Exploration Industry. Unpublished Ph.D. dissertation. Washington University, St. Louis, MO. (1980).

[15] Schwartz, D. S., Comments on "Market Structure and Interfirm Integration", *Journal of Economic Issues*, 9 (2), (1975), pp. 337–40.

[16] Sumpter, Randy, "Why Independent Aren't Rushing Offshore", *Oil and Gas Journal*, 77 (10), (March 5, 1979), pp. 67–70.

[17] Wilson, John W., "Market Structure and Interfirm Integration in the Petroleum Industry", *Journal of Economic Issues*, 9 (2), (1975) pp. 319–36.

THE JOURNAL OF INDUSTRIAL ECONOMICS
Volume XXXI June 1983 No. 4

ECONOMIC EFFECTS OF NON-BINDING PRICE CONSTRAINTS

Rex L. Cottle and Myles S. Wallace*

For decades, the conventional wisdom among economists has been that a "non-binding" price floor or price ceiling has no effect whatsoever on the market equilibrium and quantity.[1] This hypothesis rests on the shaky theoretical assumption that the competitive firm's perception of future market conditions is not altered when the government imposes a price control.

Recent experiments by Isaac and Plott [6] and Smith and Williams [18] cast doubt on this conventional wisdom, but they offer no theory to explain their findings. Similarly Working [19], Benedict [1], and Johnson [8] alluded that price supports set below the market equilibrium price would distort the supply response of farmers without explaining why. Only Lee [10] and Eeckhoudt and Hansen [4] have developed theories to explain why firms react this way. Lee used an intertemporal decision-making model to show that a price ceiling implemented above the current price would affect both price and output in the current period. However, Lee discussed only those cases where resources have a finite inventory (non-renewable resources), which once depleted cannot be produced again.

Following Sandmo [15], Ishii [7], and Coes [3], Eeckhoudt and Hansen analyzed the restraining effects of minimum and maximum prices on a competitive firm. Using a static equilibrium model, they explained the short run response of a utility maximizing firm to the imposition of price constraints. However, Eeckhoudt and Hansen were unable to sign the effect that a price ceiling has on the volume of industrial output. Furthermore, they ignored all long run adjustments.

Our model differs from the previous studies in that we assume firms maximize the market value of the firm. In so doing, we are able to determine both the short run and the long run effects that currently non-binding price restrictions have on a competitive industry.

Consider the conventional competitive market in which the long run equilibrium is achieved when all the firms in the industry have an expected net worth comparable to their next best alternative. For simplicity, assume a price floor, Pf, is inacted that is lower than the current market price and will remain constant for the forseeable future. Furthermore, assume the government agrees

* Names appear in alphabetical order. The authors wish to thank Hugh Macaulay, Richard McKenzie, Bruce Yandle, and an unidentified reviewer of this journal for their helpful comments on earlier drafts of this paper.

[1] A binding price ceiling refers to a maximum allowable price less than the current market price. Similarly, a binding price floor is a minimum price in excess of the current market price.

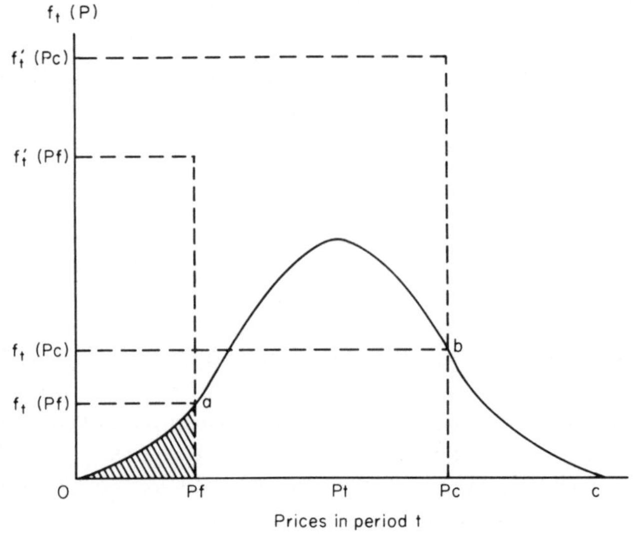

FIGURE 1
Probability Distribution of Prices in Period t

to purchase and destroy any residual output. These assumptions are made to eliminate the risk that firms might have about oversupplying the market at any known price in a future period. Let input prices be fixed over time for a given degree of risk so that each firm's supply curve is also its marginal cost curve. Assume firms maximize profit in each period and there is no production lag, e.g., once price is known for the current period, production takes place instantaneously. For future periods, assume that the typical competitive firm believes that prices will vary symmetrically around some mean price, *Pt*, with some known probability distribution similar to the one shown in Figure 1.

Following the standard textbook analysis, such a governmentally imposed price floor has no effect on market equilibrium and would not distort future production. However, such a policy action will, in and of itself, reduce the probability of future downside price fluctuations. The shaded area, *OaPf*, in Figure 1, $f'_t(Pf) = \sum_{P_t<P_f} f_t(P)$, is the cumulative probability that price in period t will be less than *Pf*. However after a price floor is imposed, the probability of all prices lower than *Pf* are mapped directly onto *Pf* causing $f_t(Pf)$ to increase to $f'_t(Pf)$.

The possibility of an upside movement in price still remains intact, but the extent of the downside price variation is reduced for period t. Since this holds for all periods in the future, investors recognize that the present value of the future expected profits is now higher as a result of the price floor raising expected prices. The stock prices of the firms in this industry will subsequently rise as investors respond to the new situation. Because the likelihood that firms will go out of business is now lower, factors of production may be willing to receive lower financial compensation in return for the lower transitory risk associated with the industry.[2]

Several long run effects take place as the industry responds to its new affluence brought about by higher expected prices and lower production costs. First, firms will be attracted into this industry increasing industrial production. Second, with entry of new firms, the probability distribution for each future period shifts to the left, denoting a higher probability that prices near the floor will occur in the future, causing a decline in expected prices and expected profits. This leftward shift of the entire probability distribution is comparable to an increase in supply causing price to decline along a nonstochastic demand curve. Third, as expected prices fall, the existing firm's market value declines, thus eliminating any rents originally created by the price floor.

All these long run adjustments will continue until the present value of the future expected profits returns to normal and entry ceases. With more firms in the industry, total output is higher than before the imposition of the price floor. Prices near the floor will increase in frequency to compensate for the lack of very low prices to offset the high prices which still might occur.[3]

Several general observations can be drawn from this model. First, increasing the price floor leads to higher expected profits in the short run, more firms in the industry, and more resources being utilized in production. Second, the imposition of the price floor causes low prices to occur more frequently in the future. Indeed, prices at the "non-binding" floor will occur more often in the future than prior to the imposition of the control. Third, any surplus resulting from a price floor will be larger than predicted by conventional theory. Imposing a guaranteed price enhances the attractiveness of entering the industry, expanding industrial production beyond what it would have been otherwise. Fourth, by acting as a free insurance policy, a guaranteed price floor causes over utilization of society's scarce resources in the production of the good in question, thus leading to economic inefficiency.

"Non-binding" price ceilings will also distort market equilibrium. Starting once again from long run competitive equilibrium, assume government imposes a price ceiling, Pc, set above the current market price that will remain constant for all future periods (see Figure 1).[4] The probability that Pc will occur in any future period t changes according to $f'_t(Pc) = \sum_{P>Pc} f_t(P)$. Because the possibility of high prices (and short-run profits) is reduced while the

[2] For example, if the cost of borrowing includes a risk premium based upon the probability of default, lending rates to the firms will now be lower. Similarly, risk averse workers fearing layoffs may be willing to work for lower wages now that the chance of being unemployed is lower. For an extensive treatment of risk in a firm's decision making see Sherman, [16], Knight, [9], and Sherman and Tollison, [17].

[3] For example, if the numbers 1, 2, 3 occur with equal frequency, then the mean is 2. However, to obtain a mean of 2 with the numbers 1.8, 2, 3, the number 1.8 must occur more frequently than the other numbers.

[4] The analysis of a ceiling does not need to include the assumptions of guaranteed government purchases at the ceiling price. Private market excess demand guarantees that what is produced will be sold.

chance for lower prices (and possible losses) remains unaffected, a firm's market value will decline. Investors will divest themselves of firms in this industry causing firms to exit. As firms emigrate from the industry, the probability distribution of prices shifts to the right increasing the likelihood that higher prices will occur. As industrial output falls, expected price moves towards *Pc*. The remaining firm's present value of expected profits returns to normal. Long run equilibrium will be restored with fewer firms, less industry output, and less resources being utilized in production than before *Pc* was legislated.

The following generalizations can be made about price ceilings: (1) lowering the price ceiling further reduces both the number of firms in the industry and total production; (2) the frequency of prices near the ceiling will be increased creating more shortages in the future; (3) any resulting shortage due to a binding price ceiling will be larger than conventionally predicted because the price ceiling reduces the number of firms in the industry; and (4) a mandated price ceiling causes the competitive industry to retract resources that would have normally been allocated to production, leading to under-allocation of society's resources and, subsequently, to economic inefficiency.

We have demonstrated that apparently "non-binding" price floors and ceilings generate changes in a competitive industry's output. The magnitude of these changes is based upon the extent of entry and exit of firms into the industry. For that matter, we have shown that the very presence of a "non-binding" control price will cause the control price to be observed more frequently in the future than would have otherwise been the case.

Imposing limits on future prices leads resource decision makers to evaluate alternative options available rather than maintaining the status quo. Past profits have nothing to do with financing future profitable investments. Just because a price constraint is presently non-binding, the chance that future market conditions might render it binding will be incorporated into a resource owner's calculus when deciding where to offer services. It is a constraint's potential impact that reallocates resources today.

Our findings have far-reaching implications for previous empirical investigations that have attempted to estimate the impact of government price control policies. Failure to take into account pricing policy distortions causes specification error in estimating industrial supply. Using supply forecasts based on data void of price control will consistently lead to underestimates of both shortages and surpluses after a control is inacted. By the same token, estimates of the impact of removing controls will be biased even currently "ineffective" ones.

For example, recent studies of the effects of usury laws on mortgage loans and housing construction by Ostas [12] and Robins [14] fail to consider that a lending rate maximum will have an impact in periods where it appears to be ineffective. To our knowledge, only McNutty [11] considers any potential impact on mortgage credit of ceiling rates slightly above the average mortgage rate. Noting that for a given mean rate, there is a distribution of contract rates around the mean (presumably based on considerations of risk and less than perfect arbitrage in a local markets), he finds that as lending rates approach the ceiling rate some lending is curtailed for marginal borrowers. However, McNutty does not consider the existence of other effects of ceilings (besides eliminating some current borrowers) such as long run decisions to relocate facilities. Indeed, as pointed out in two recent issues of the *Wall Street Journal*, financial institutions respond to differential restrictions by locational changes.[5] Our theory is but a first attempt to explain why non-binding price constraints affect the behavior of competitive firms.

REX L. COTTLE AND MYLES S. WALLACE
Department of Economics,
Clemson University,
Clemson,
South Carolina, 29631

ACCEPTED MAY 1982

REFERENCES

[1] BENEDICT, M. R., 'Attempts to Restrict Competition in Agriculture: The Government Program,' *American Economic Review*, XXXXIV, 2 (May 1954), pp. 90–106.
[2] CARLSON, E., 'Delware Grabs an Early Lead in Luring Out-of-State Banks,' *The Wall Street Journal*, CXCVIII, 117 (Dec. 15, 1981), p. 33.
[3] COES, D., 'Firm Output and Change in Uncertainty,' *American Economic Review*, LXI, 1 March 1971), pp. 65–73.
[4] EECKHOUDT, L. and P. HANSEN, 'Minimum and Maximum Prices, Uncertainty and the Theory of the Competitive Firm,' *American Economic Review*, LXX, 5 (December 1980), pp. 1064–68.
[5] FERGUSON, C. E. *Microeconomic Theory* (rev. ed.) (Richard C. Irwin, Inc. Homewood, IL, 1969).
[6] ISAAC, R. M. and C. R. PLOTT, 'Price Controls and the Behavior of Auction Markets: An Experimental Examination,' *American Economic Review*, LXXI, 3 (June 1981), pp. 448–59.
[7] ISHII, Y., 'On the Theory of the Competitive Firm Under Price Uncertainty: Note,' *American Economic Review*, LXVII, 1 (March 1977), pp. 249–51.
[8] JOHNSON, D., 'Competition in Agriculture: Fact or Fiction,' *American Economic Review*, XXXXIV, 2 (May 1954), pp. 107–15.
[9] KNIGHT, F. H., *Risk, Uncertainty and Profit* (Hart, Schaffner, and Marx, New York, 1921).
[10] LEE, D. R., 'Price Controls on Non-Renewable Resources: An Intertemporal Analysis,' *Southern Economic Journal*, 46, 1 (July 1979), pp. 179–88.
[11] McNUTTY, J., 'A Reexamination of the Problem of State Usury Ceilings: the Impact in the Mortgage Market,' *Quarterly Review of Economics and Business*, 20, 1 (Spring 1980), pp. 16–28.
[12] OSTAS, J., 'Effects of Usury Ceilings in the Mortgage Market,' *Journal of Finance*, XXXI, 2 (June 1976), pp. 821–34.
[13] POWELL, E. A., 'Move to Ban Usury Ceilings Starts Fight Over Federal Role Gouging,' *The Wall Street Journal*, CXCXIX, 1 (Jan. 4, 1982), p. 33.

[5] See Carlson [2] and Powell [13] for details pertaining to institutional relocation.

[14] ROBINS, P., 'The Effects of State Usury Ceilings on Single Family Homebuilding,' *Journal of Finance*, XXIX, 1 (March 1974), pp. 227–35.

[15] SANDMO, A., 'On the Theory of the Competitive Firm under Price Uncertainty,' *American Economic Review*, LXI, 1 (March 1971), pp. 65–73.

[16] SHERMAN, R., *The Economics of Industry*, (Little, Brown and Company, Boston, 1974).

[17] SHERMAN, R. and R. TOLLISON, 'Technology, Profit Risk and Assessments of Market Performance,' *Quarterly Journal of Economics*, LXXXVI, 3 (August 1972), pp. 448–62.

[18] SMITH, V. L. and A. W. WILLIAMS, 'On Nonbinding Price Controls in a Competitive Market,' *American Economic Review*, LXXXI, 3 (June 1981), pp. 467–74.

[19] WORKING, H., 'Price Supports and Effectiveness of Hedging,' *Journal of Farm Economics*, 35, 4 (Dec. 1953), pp. 811–18.

THE JOURNAL OF INDUSTRIAL ECONOMICS

Published first in October 1952, this Journal was founded to develop the analysis of the problems facing modern industry. It is concerned with the individual business and its relation to the economy—e.g. with outputs and prices and their behaviour in the market, and with the business decisions which affect these. It therefore aims to contribute both to economic theory and to practical public and private policies in the industrial field. The journal is naturally meant to interest business men as well as economists.

The Editors welcome contributions covering the fundamental categories in economics (such as prices, costs, investment, finance, location, wages and productivity) as well as the broader 'background' circumstances (such as the changing structure of industry, management policy and public monopoly policy). Preference is given to MSS bearing on these subjects from the standpoint of individual firms or industries. Theoretical discussion is welcome. Abstract theory is not barred, but authors in this case should provide an introduction and conclusion, so that non-specialist readers may see what the article is about. Alongside articles of more normal length, the Editors are willing to publish shorter notes, especially when these give interim results of important research studies. Books are not reviewed, although books received will be listed, sometimes with a short note; but substantial review articles will be considered. No payment is made to authors, but 25 free offprints are provided. Contributors are asked to send an Abstract, not exceeding 100 words, with their article.

Editorial Offices:

Manuscripts from North America should be sent to Professor H. Michael Mann, Department of Economics, Boston College, Chestnut Hill, Massachusetts, 02167, U.S.A.; manuscripts from all other countries to the General Editor, c/o Department of Economics, University of Lancaster, Gillow House, Lancaster, LA1 4YX England, from whom detailed Information for Contributors is available.

Subscriptions, advertising, reprint enquiries, etc.

The journal is published by Basil Blackwell Publisher Ltd., 108 Cowley Road, Oxford OX4 1JF, England. US Mailing Agent, Expediters of the Printed Word Ltd., 527 Madison Avenue, Suite 1217, New York, NY 10022, U.S.A. Second Class postage paid at New York.

The journal is published four times a year in September, December, March and June. The subscription prices are as shown below.

All correspondence other than that dealing with contributions should be addressed to the publisher.

Price

Annual subscription for institutions: £21.50 (UK), £26.50 (overseas), $54.60 (USA), $67.00 (Canada)

Annual subscription for individuals: £13.75 (UK), £16.75 (overseas), $35.00 (USA), $43.25 (Canada)

Single issue price for institutions: £5.75 (UK), £6.95 (overseas), $14.50 (USA), $17.50 (Canada)

Single issue price for individuals: £4.25 (UK), £5.25 (overseas), $11.00 (USA), $13.50 (Canada)

Set by Santype International Ltd.,
Salisbury, Wilts. Printed and bound by
Whitstable Litho Ltd., Whitstable, Kent

CONTRIBUTORS TO THIS NUMBER

MALCOLM R. BURNS: Assistant Professor, Department of Economics, University of Kansas.

BJÖRN WAHLROOS: Professor of Economics, Swedish School of Economics and Business Administration, Helsinki.

J. A. ZERBY: Senior Lecturer, Department of Econometrics, University of New South Wales.

R. M. CONLON: Senior Lecturer in Economics, University of New South Wales.

BERNARD GARDNER: Senior Lecturer in Shipping and Economics, UWIST.

PETER MARLOW: Lecturer in Transport and Economics, UWIST.

J. E. DAVIES: Assistant Professor of Economics, Acadia University, Nova Scotia.

P. MARITI: Associate Professor of Industrial Economics and Policy, University of Pisa.

R. H. SMILEY: Associate Dean for Academic Affairs, Graduate School of Business and Public Administration, Cornell University.

ALAN ROCKWOOD: Senior Economist, Texas Energy and Natural Resources Advisory Council.

REX L. COTTLE: Head of Department of Economics, Clemson University.

MYLES S. WALLACE: Associate Professor, Department of Economics, Clemson University.

Contents of Volume XXXI, No. 3, March 1983, were:

Industrial Concentration: A Survey, by B. Curry and K. D. George, respectively Lecturer in Economics and Professor of Economics, University College, Cardiff and Editor of this Journal.

The Performance of Merging Firms in Japanese Manufacturing Industry: 1964–75, by Katsuhiko Ikeda and Noriyuki Doi, respectively Professor of Economics, Department of Business Administration, and Assistant Professor of Economics, Department of Economics, Kwansei Gakuin University.

The Causes and Consequences of Abandoned Mergers, by J. F. Pickering, Professor of Industrial Economics, UMIST, and Associate Editor of this Journal.

A Note on Conglomerate Merger and Behavioural Response to Risk, by Norman J. Ireland, Senior Lecturer in Economics, University of Warwick.

Anatomy of a Price Leadership Challenge: An Evaluation of Pricing Strategies in the Australian Newspaper Industry, by William J. Merrilees, Lecturer, Department of Economics, University of Sydney.

Innovation in a Labor-Managed Firm: A Membership Perspective, by John P. Bonin, Associate Professor of Economics, Wesleyan University, Middletown, Connecticut.